2014 release

Adobe Illustrator
Photoshop & InDesign CC

Graphic Design Portfolio

AGAINST THE CLOCK
mastering graphic technology

Managing Editor: Ellenn Behoriam
Cover & Interior Design: Erika Kendra
Editor: Angelina Kendra
Copy Editor: Liz Bleau

The image on the cover shows the Frederick R. Weisman Art Museum at the University of Minnesota, designed by Canadian-American architect Frank Gehry.

10   9   8   7   6   5   4   3   2   1

Print ISBN: 978-1-936201-49-5
Ebook ISBN: 978-1-936201-50-1

4710 28th Street North, Saint Petersburg, FL 33714
800-256-4ATC • www.againsttheclock.com

Acknowledgements

ABOUT AGAINST THE CLOCK

Against The Clock, long recognized as one of the nation's leaders in courseware development, has been publishing high-quality educational materials for the graphic and computer arts industries since 1990. The company has developed a solid and widely-respected approach to teaching people how to effectively utilize graphics applications, while maintaining a disciplined approach to real-world problems.

Having developed the *Against The Clock* and the *Essentials for Design* series with Prentice Hall/Pearson Education, ATC drew from years of professional experience and instructor feedback to develop *The Professional Portfolio Series*, focusing on the Adobe Creative Suite. These books feature step-by-step explanations, detailed foundational information, and advice and tips from industry professionals that offer practical solutions to technical issues.

Against The Clock works closely with all major software developers to create learning solutions that fulfill both the requirements of instructors and the needs of students. Thousands of graphic arts professionals — designers, illustrators, imaging specialists, prepress experts, and production managers — began their educations with Against The Clock training books. These professionals studied at Baker College, Nossi College of Art, Virginia Tech, Appalachian State University, Keiser College, University of South Carolina, Gress Graphic Arts Institute, Hagerstown Community College, Kean University, Southern Polytechnic State University, and many other educational institutions.

ABOUT THE AUTHOR

Erika Kendra holds a BA in History and a BA in English Literature from the University of Pittsburgh. She began her career in the graphic communications industry as an editor at Graphic Arts Technical Foundation before moving to Los Angeles in 2000. Erika is the author or co-author of more than thirty books about Adobe graphic design software. She has also written several books about graphic design concepts such as color reproduction and preflighting, and dozens of articles for online and print journals in the graphics industry. Working with Against The Clock for more than thirteen years, Erika was a key partner in developing *The Professional Portfolio Series* of software training books.

CONTRIBUTING AUTHORS, ARTISTS, AND EDITORS

A big thank you to the people whose artwork, comments, and expertise contributed to the success of these books:

- **Chris Barnes,** Wilson Community College
- **Olwen Bruce,** Creative Backup LLC
- **Debbie Davidson,** Against The Clock, Inc.
- **Charlie Essers,** photographer, Lancaster, Calif.
- **Matthew Guanciale,** Fanboy Photo
- **Chana Messer,** Artist, Designer, Adobe Software Evangelist Adobe, ACE/ACI
- **Beth Rogers,** Nossi College Of Art
- **Richard Schrand,** Corporate Education Professional
- **Joseph A. Staudenbaur,** Dakota State University

Finally, thanks to **Angelina Kendra**, editor, and **Liz Bleau**, copy editor, for making sure that we all said what we meant to say.

Project Goals

Each project begins with a clear description of the overall concepts that are explained in the project; these goals closely match the different "stages" of the project workflow.

The Project Meeting

Each project includes the client's initial comments, which provide valuable information about the job. The Project Art Director, a vital part of any design workflow, also provides fundamental advice and production requirements.

Project Objectives

Each Project Meeting includes a summary of the specific skills required to complete the project.

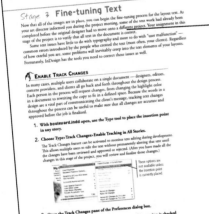

Real-World Workflow

Projects are broken into logical lessons or "stages" of the workflow. Brief introductions at the beginning of each stage provide vital foundational material required to complete the task.

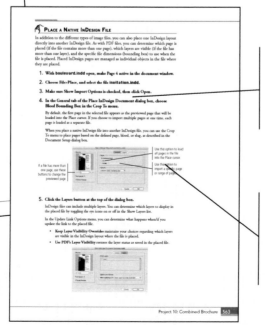

Step-By-Step Exercises

Every stage of the workflow is broken into multiple hands-on, step-by-step exercises.

Visual Explanations

Wherever possible, screen shots are annotated so that students can quickly identify important information.

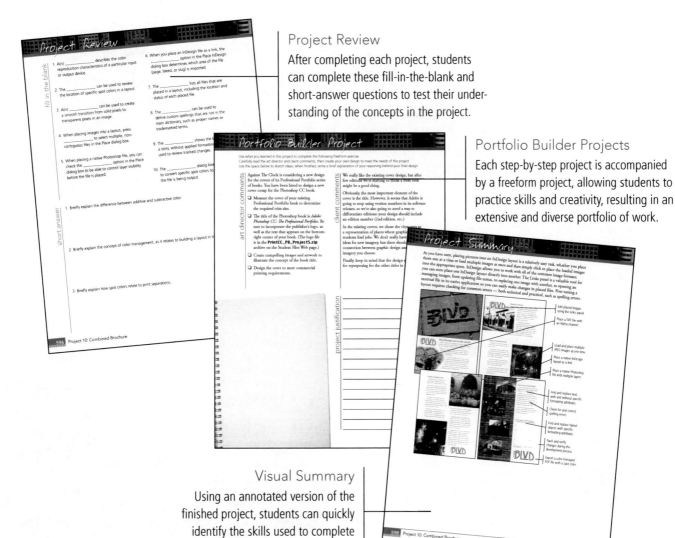

Design Foundations

Additional functionality, related tools, and underlying graphic design concepts are included throughout the book.

Advice and Warnings

Where appropriate, sidebars provide shortcuts, warnings, or tips about the topic at hand.

Project Review

After completing each project, students can complete these fill-in-the-blank and short-answer questions to test their understanding of the concepts in the project.

Portfolio Builder Projects

Each step-by-step project is accompanied by a freeform project, allowing students to practice skills and creativity, resulting in an extensive and diverse portfolio of work.

Visual Summary

Using an annotated version of the finished project, students can quickly identify the skills used to complete different aspects of the job.

Projects at a Glance

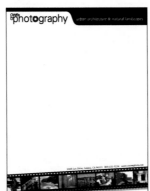

The Against The Clock *Portfolio Series* teaches graphic design software tools and techniques entirely within the framework of real-world projects; we introduce and explain skills where they would naturally fall into a real project workflow.

The project-based approach in *The Professional Portfolio Series* allows you to get in depth with the software beginning in Project 1 — you don't have to read several chapters of introductory material before you can start creating finished artwork.

Our approach also prevents "topic tedium" — in other words, we don't require you to read pages and pages of information about text (for example); instead, we explain text tools and options as part of a larger project.

Clear, easy-to-read, step-by-step instructions walk you through every phase of each job, from creating a new file to saving the finished piece. Wherever logical, we also offer practical advice and tips about underlying concepts and graphic design practices that will benefit you as you enter the job market.

The projects in this book reflect a range of different types of print design jobs using Adobe Illustrator, Photoshop, and InDesign. When you finish the ten projects in this book (and the accompanying Portfolio Builder exercises), you will have a solid foundational knowledge of the three most popular applications in the print design market — and have a substantial body of work that should impress any potential employer.

Contents

Project 5   VINTAGE CAR MONTAGE   259

Contents

Contents

PREREQUISITES

The Professional Portfolio Series is based on the assumption that you have a basic understanding of how to use your computer. You should know how to use your mouse to point and click, as well as how to drag items around the screen. You should be able to resize and arrange windows on your desktop to maximize your available space. You should know how to access drop-down menus, and understand how check boxes and radio buttons work. It also doesn't hurt to have a good understanding of how your operating system organizes files and folders, and how to navigate your way around them. If you're familiar with these fundamental skills, then you know all that's necessary to use the Portfolio Series.

RESOURCE FILES

All the files you need to complete the projects in this book — except, of course, the Adobe application files — are on the Student Files Web page at againsttheclock.com. See the inside back cover of this book for access information.

Each archive (ZIP) file is named according to the related project (e.g., **Symbols_Print14_RF.zip**). At the beginning of each project, you must download the archive file for that project and expand that archive to access the resource files that you need to complete the exercises. Detailed instructions for this process are included in the Interface chapter.

Files required for the related Portfolio Builder exercises at the end of each project are also available on the Student Files Web page; these archives are also named by project (e.g., **Airborne_Print14_PB.zip**).

ATC FONTS

You must download and install the ATC fonts from the Student Files Web page to ensure that your exercises and projects will work as described in the book. Specific instructions for installing fonts are provided in the documentation that came with your computer. You should replace older (pre-2013) ATC fonts with the ones on the Student Files Web page.

SYSTEM REQUIREMENTS

The Professional Portfolio Series was designed to work on both Macintosh or Windows computers; where differences exist from one platform to another, we include specific instructions relative to each platform. One issue that remains different from Macintosh to Windows is the use of different modifier keys (Control, Shift, etc.) to accomplish the same task. When we present key commands, we always follow the same Macintosh/Windows format — Macintosh keys are listed first, then a slash, followed by the Windows key commands.

SOFTWARE VERSIONS

This book was written and tested using the initial versions of the 2014 release of Adobe Creative Cloud (CC) software, as released in July 2014:

- Adobe InDesign 10.0
- Adobe Photoshop 2014.0
- Adobe Illustrator 18.0

(You can find the specific version number of your applications in the Splash Screen that appears while an application is launching.)

Because Adobe has announced periodic upgrades rather than releasing new full versions, some features and functionality might have changed since publication. Please check the Errata section of the Against The Clock Web site for any significant issues that might have arisen from these periodic upgrades.

EXPLORE THE INDESIGN INTERFACE

Adobe InDesign is a robust publishing application that allows you to integrate text and graphics, either prepared in the program or imported from other sources, to produce files that can be printed or published digitally.

The user interface (UI) is what you see when you launch the application. The specific elements that you see depend on what was done the last time the application was open. The first time you launch an application, you see the default workspace settings defined by Adobe. When you relaunch after you or another user has quit, the workspace defaults to the last-used settings.

1. **Create a new empty folder named WIP (Work In Progress) on any writable disk (where you plan to save your work in progress).**

2. **Download the Interface_Print14_RF.zip archive from the Student Files Web page.**

3. **Macintosh users: Place the ZIP archive in your WIP folder, then double-click the file icon to expand it.**

    This **InterfaceCC14** folder contains all the files you need to complete this introduction.

Double-click the archive file icon to expand it.

Windows users: Double-click the ZIP archive file to open it. Click the folder inside the archive and drag it into your primary WIP folder.

Open the archive file...

...then drag the InterfaceCC14 folder from the archive to your WIP folder.

Menus in Adobe Applications

ADOBE FOUNDATIONS

If a specific menu command can be accessed with a keyboard shortcut, those shortcuts are listed to the right of the related command.

Some menu commands are toggles, which means a feature can be turned on or off, or an option is either visible or hidden. A checkmark indicates that the command is currently active.

Some menu commands include the "Show" or "Hide" indicator at the beginning of the menu command. When visible, the command appears as "Hide [Option]"; when not already visible, the command appears as "Show [Option]".

Finally, if a specific menu command is grayed out (it can't be selected), that command does not apply in the current context (usually, depending on what is selected in the document).

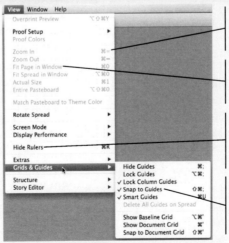

Keyboard shortcuts (if available) are listed on the right side of the menu.

If a menu command is grayed out, it is not available for the current selection.

Some commands appear as Hide [Option] when visible or Show [Option] when not visible.

Many menu commands are toggles; the checkmark indicates that an option is visible or toggled on.

The image here shows the View menu in the 2014 release of InDesign CC. The concepts identified here apply to menus in all Adobe applications.

4. **Macintosh users: While pressing Command-Option-Control-Shift, start InDesign. Click Yes when asked if you want to delete preference files.**

   Windows users: Launch InDesign, and then press Control-Alt-Shift. Click Yes when asked if you want to delete preference files.

   This step resets InDesign to the preference settings that are defined by Adobe as the application defaults. This helps to ensure that your application functions in the same way as what we show in our screen shots.

Note:

If you have a previous version of InDesign CC installed on your computer, you will see a message the first time you launch the 2014 release that presets and settings from previous CC versions will be migrated to the 2014 release of the software. This means your defined preferences and other custom settings will automatically be available in the current version.

If you do not see this message, you can also choose Edit>Migrate Previous Local Settings to manually import previous-version preferences into the 2014 release. In this case, you will see a message that the application must restart for the migration to take effect.

5. **Review the options in the What's New dialog box, then click Done.**

   This dialog box includes a series of videos that introduce features new to the 2014 release of InDesign CC. You can click any video link to get more information about a specific feature, or click Done to close the What's New dialog box.

   If you don't see the What's New screen, or if you have already closed it, you can choose Help>What's New to open this dialog box at any time.

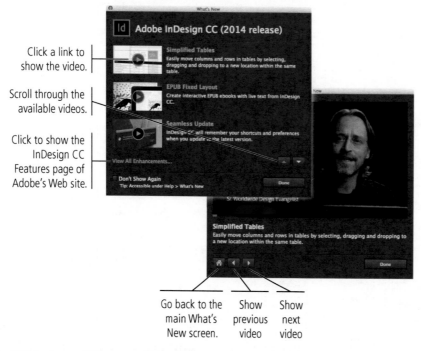

The 2014 release of Illustrator CC includes a multi-pane Welcome screen that includes a number of videos about new features, getting started using the application (for new users), and tips and tutorials. At the time of this writing, Photoshop CC does not include a Welcome screen or introductory videos.

6. **Macintosh users: Open the Window menu and choose Application Frame to toggle that option on.**

   Many menu commands and options in InDesign are **toggles**, which means they are either on or off; when an option is already checked, that option is toggled on (visible or active). You can toggle an active option off by choosing the checked menu command, or toggle an inactive option on by choosing the unchecked menu command.

Note:

On Windows, the Application Frame menu command is not available; you can't turn off the Application Frame on the Windows OS.

   This option should be checked.

   The default workspace includes the Tools panel on the left side of the screen, the Control panel at the top of the screen, and a set of panels attached to the right side of the screen. (The area where the panels are stored is called the **panel dock**.)

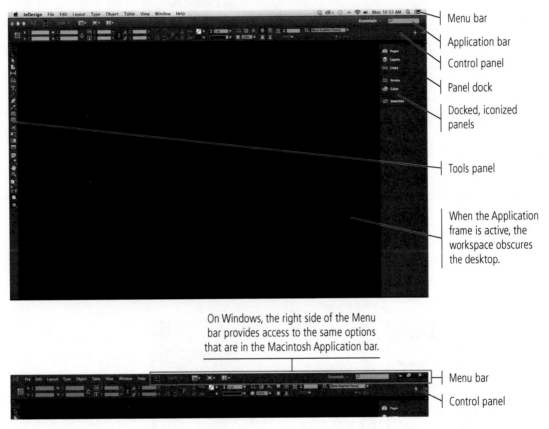

   Menu bar

   Application bar

   Control panel

   Panel dock

   Docked, iconized panels

   Tools panel

   When the Application frame is active, the workspace obscures the desktop.

   On Windows, the right side of the Menu bar provides access to the same options that are in the Macintosh Application bar.

   Menu bar

   Control panel

   The general Macintosh and Windows workspaces are virtually identical, with a few primary exceptions.

   - On Macintosh, the application's title bar appears below the Menu bar; the Close, Minimize, and Restore buttons appear on the left side of the title bar, and the menu bar is not part of the Application frame.

   - On Windows, the Close, Minimize, and Restore buttons appear at the right end of the Menu bar, which is part of the overall Application frame.

   - On Macintosh systems, the Application bar at the top of the workspace includes a number of buttons for accessing different view options. On Windows systems, those same options are available on the right side of the Menu bar.

   - Macintosh users also have two extra menus (consistent with the Macintosh operating system structure). The Apple menu provides access to system-specific commands. The InDesign menu follows the Macintosh system-standard format for all applications; this menu controls basic application operations such as About, Hide, Preferences, and Quit.

On Windows, each running application is contained within its own frame; all elements of the application — including the Menu bar, panels, tools, and open documents — are contained within the Application frame.

Adobe also offers the Application frame to Macintosh users as an option for controlling your workspace. When the Application frame is active, the entire workspace exists in a self-contained area that can be moved around the screen. All elements of the workspace (excluding the Menu bar) move when you move the Application frame.

In InDesign, Illustrator, and Photoshop, you can toggle the application frame on or off by choosing Window>Application Frame. If the menu option is checked, the Application frame is active; if the menu option is not checked, it is inactive.

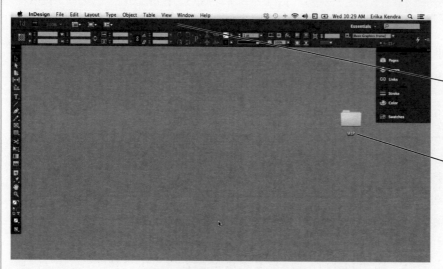

When the Application frame is not active, the Application bar appears below the Menu bar; in this case, the Application bar can be moved or turned off.

When the Application frame is not active, the desktop is visible behind the workspace elements.

7. **Macintosh users: Choose InDesign>Preferences>Interface.**

   Windows users: Choose Edit>Preferences>Interface.

   Remember that on Macintosh systems, the Preferences dialog box is accessed in the InDesign menu; Windows users access the Preferences dialog box in the Edit menu.

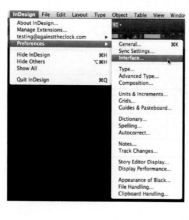

Macintosh

Windows

Preferences customize the way many of the program's tools and options function. When you open the Preferences dialog box, the active pane is the one you chose in the Preferences submenu. Once open, however, you can access any of the Preference categories by clicking a different option in the left pane; the right side of the dialog box displays options related to the active category.

8. **In the Appearance section, choose any option that you prefer.**

   You might have already noticed the rather dark appearance of the panels and interface background. InDesign uses the medium-dark "theme" as the default. (We used the Light option throughout this book because text in the interface elements is easier to read in printed screen captures.)

9. **In the Panels section, check the option to Auto-Collapse Icon Panels.**

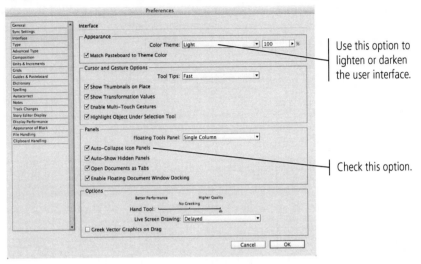

Use this option to lighten or darken the user interface.

Check this option.

Note:

As you work your way through the projects in this book, you'll learn not only what you can do with these different collections of preferences, but also why and when you might want to use them.

Note:

You can also activate the Auto-Collapse Icon Panels option in the panel dock title bar's contextual menu.

10. **Click OK to close the Preferences dialog box, then continue to the next exercise.**

Identifying InDesign Tools

INDESIGN FOUNDATIONS

The following image offers a quick reference of nested tools in InDesign, as well as the keyboard shortcut for each tool (if any). Nested tools are shown indented and in italics.

Selection tool (V)	Pencil tool (N)	Free Transform tool (E)
Direct Selection tool (A)	*Smooth tool*	*Rotate tool (R)*
Page tool (Shift-P)	*Erase tool*	*Scale tool (S)*
Gap tool (U)	Rectangle Frame tool (F)	*Shear tool (O)*
Content Collector tool	*Ellipse Frame tool*	Gradient Swatch tool (G)
Content Placer tool	*Polygon Frame tool*	Gradient Feather tool (Shift-G)
Type tool (T)	Rectangle tool (M)	Note tool
Type on a Path tool (Shift-T)	*Ellipse tool (L)*	Eyedropper tool (I)
Line tool (\)	*Polygon tool*	*Measure tool (K)*
Pen tool (P)	Scissors tool (C)	Hand tool (H)
Add Anchor Point tool (=)		Zoom tool (Z)
Delete Anchor Point tool (-)		
Convert Direction Point tool (Shift-C)		

Explore the Arrangement of Application Panels

As you gain experience and familiarity with Adobe Creative Cloud applications, you will develop personal artistic and working styles. You will also find that different types of jobs often require different but specific sets of tools. Adobe recognizes this wide range of needs and preferences among users; InDesign includes a number of options for arranging and managing the numerous panels, so you can customize and personalize the workspace to suit your specific needs.

We designed the following exercise to give you an opportunity to explore different ways of controlling InDesign panels. Keep in mind that all panels can be toggled on and off in the Window menu:

- If you choose a panel that's already open but iconized, the panel expands to the left of its icon.

- If you choose a panel that's already open in an expanded group but is not the active panel, that panel comes to the front of the group.

- If you choose a panel that's already open and active in an expanded group, that panel group is closed.

- If you choose a panel that isn't currently open, it opens in the same place as it was when it was last closed.

Because workspace preferences are largely a matter of personal taste, the projects in this book instruct you to use certain tools and panels, but where you place those elements is up to you. The same techniques apply in Photoshop and Illustrator, so we will not repeat these instructions for each of the applications. In general, all three applications have the same functionality; we do note where differences occur.

1. **Click the Color button in the panel dock to expand the panel.**

   By default, expanded panels remain open until you manually close them or expand another panel in the same dock column. When Auto-Collapse Iconic Panels is toggled on, the expanded panel collapses as soon as you click away from it.

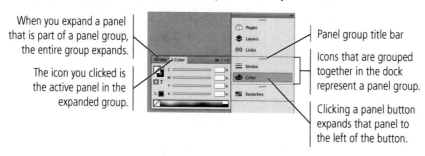

When you expand a panel that is part of a panel group, the entire group expands.

The icon you clicked is the active panel in the expanded group.

Panel group title bar

Icons that are grouped together in the dock represent a panel group.

Clicking a panel button expands that panel to the left of the button.

2. **Click away from the expanded panel to collapse it.**

3. **Click the left edge of the docked panels and drag right.**

   When panels are iconized, you can reduce the button size to show icons only. Doing so can be particularly useful once you are more familiar with the application and the icons used to symbolize the different panels.

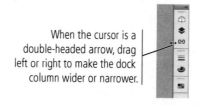

When the cursor is a double-headed arrow, drag left or right to make the dock column wider or narrower.

Note:

Most interface functions and behaviors are the same across all three applications that are discussed in this book (InDesign, Illustrator, and Photoshop). Any significant differences are noted throughout this chapter.

Note:

*Collapsed panels are referred to as **iconized** or **iconic**.*

4. Double-click the title bar above the column of docked panels.

Double-clicking the dock title bar expands a collapsed column or collapses an expanded column.

Each panel in the group is represented by a tab.

The area behind the panel tabs is called the **drop zone**.

Accessing Tools in Adobe Applications

ADOBE FOUNDATIONS

Adobe applications have no shortage of tools; you will learn how to use many of them as you complete the projects in this book. For now, you should simply take the opportunity to identify the tools, and understand how to access the nested variations.

Nested Tools

Any tool with an arrow in the bottom-right corner includes related tools below it. When you click a tool and hold down the mouse button, the **nested tools** appear in a pop-up menu. (In Photoshop and InDesign, you can also Control/right-click a tool to reveal the menu of nested tools.) When you choose one of the nested tools, that variation becomes the default choice in the Tools panel.

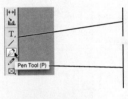

This arrow means the tool has other nested tools.

When you hover the mouse cursor over the tool, a tool tip shows the name of the tool.

Click and hold down the mouse button (or Control/right-click a tool) to show the nested tools.

Most default tools can be accessed with a keyboard shortcut. When you hover the mouse cursor over a tool, the pop-up **tool tip** shows the name of the tool and a shortcut letter in parentheses. If you don't see tool tips, check the Interface preferences (InDesign and Photoshop) or General preferences (Illustrator); the Show Tool Tips check box should be active.

Keyboard Shortcuts

If a tool has a defined shortcut, pressing that key activates the associated tool. In Photoshop, most nested tools have the same shortcut as the default tool. By default, you have to press Shift plus the shortcut key to access the nested variations. You can change this behavior in the General pane of the Preferences dialog box by unchecking the Use Shift Key for Tool Switch option. When this option is off, you can simply press the shortcut key multiple times to cycle through the variations.

Spring-Loaded Tool Shortcuts

In InDesign and Photoshop, if you press and hold a tool's keyboard shortcut, you can temporarily call the appropriate tool (called **spring-loaded keys**); after releasing the shortcut key, you return to the tool you were using previously. For example, you might use this technique to switch temporarily from the Brush tool to the Eraser tool while painting.

Tool Hints in InDesign

The Tool Hints panel (Window>Utilities>Tool Hints) provides useful tips about the active tool, including a brief description of the tool and an explanation of the tool's behavior if you press one or more modifier keys and the tool's keyboard shortcut.

Tear-Off Tools in Illustrator

If you drag the mouse cursor to the bar on the right of the nested-tool menu, the nested-tool options separate into their own floating toolboxes so that you can more easily access the nested variations. (The primary tool is not removed from the main Tools panel.)

While holding down the mouse button, drag to here, then release the mouse button...

...to tear off a separate panel with all the related tools.

5. **On the left side of the workspace, review the Tools panel. If you don't see all of the panel options, double-click the Tools panel title bar.**

The Tools panel can be displayed as either one or two columns; double-clicking the Tools panel title bar toggles between these two modes.

Some monitors — especially laptops — are too small to display the number of tools that are available in InDesign's Tools panel. If this is the case, you should use the two-column mode.

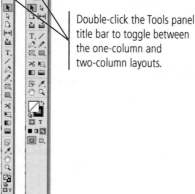

Double-click the Tools panel title bar to toggle between the one-column and two-column layouts.

The Tools panel can also be floated (moved out of the dock) by clicking its title bar and dragging away from the edge of the screen. To re-dock the floating Tools panel, simply click the panel's title bar and drag back to the left edge of the screen; when a blue line highlights the edge of the workspace, releasing the mouse button places the Tools panel back in the dock. If the Tools panel is floating, you can toggle through three different modes — one-column vertical, two-column vertical, and one-row horizontal.

6. **Click the drop zone behind the Color panel and drag the group out of the dock.**

Panels and panel groups can be **floated** by clicking a panel tab and dragging away from the dock.

Click the panel group drop zone and drag to move the panel group out of the panel dock.

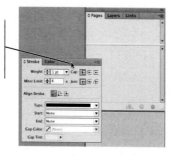

Floating panel group Close button

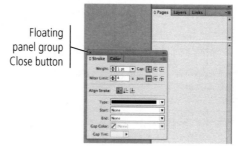

7. **Click the Close button on the panel group to close all panels in the group.**

You can also choose an open and active panel in the Window menu to toggle off (hide) that panel. If a panel is open but not active (in other words, it is not the visible panel in a particular group), choosing that panel in the Window menu makes it the active panel in the group.

In Illustrator and Photoshop, you can Control/right-click a panel tab and choose Close or Close Tab Group from the contextual menu. This option is not available in InDesign at the time of this writing.

8. **Click the Links panel tab and drag between the Pages and Swatches panels. When you see a blue line between the existing docked panels, release the mouse button.**

Panels and panel groups can be dragged to different locations (including into different groups) by dragging the panel's tab; the target location — where the panel will reside when you release the mouse button — is identified by the blue highlight.

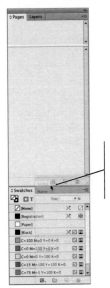

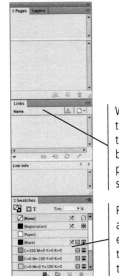

The blue highlight shows where the panel will be placed if you release the mouse button.

When you release the mouse button, the moved panel becomes a separate panel group in the same dock column.

Panels and groups already in the dock expand or contract to make room for the new panel.

Note:

You can click and drag a panel group's drop zone to float or move the entire group.

Note:

Each dock column, technically considered a separate dock, can be expanded or collapsed independently of other columns.

Note:

Each column of the dock can be made wider or narrower by dragging the left edge of the column.

Dragging the left edge of a dock column changes the width of all panels in that column.

9. **Click the Pages panel tab and drag left until the blue highlight shows a second column added to the dock.**

As we mentioned earlier, you can create multiple columns of panels in the dock. This can be very useful if you need easy access to a large number of panels and have a monitor with enough available screen space.

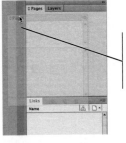

This pop-out "drawer" indicates that releasing the mouse button...

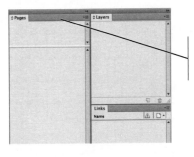

...creates a second column in the panel dock.

10. **Double-click the title bar of the left dock column to iconize that column.**

You can independently iconize or expand each column of docked panels and each floating panel (group).

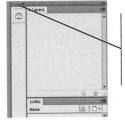

Double-click the title bar at the top of the dock column to collapse or expand it independently of other dock columns.

11. In the right dock column, double-click the Swatches panel tab two times to minimize the panel group.

The first time you double-click the Swatches panel tab, you reduce the panel to a minimum size; the second time you double-click, you collapse the panel to show only the panel tabs.

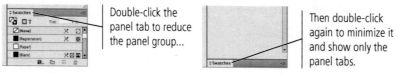

Double-click the panel tab to reduce the panel group...

Then double-click again to minimize it and show only the panel tabs.

You can click any tab in a collapsed panel group to expand the group and make the selected panel active.

12. In the right dock column, click the bottom edge of the Layers panel group and drag down until the Layers panel occupies approximately half of the vertical dock space.

When you drag the bottom edge of a docked group, other panels in the same column expand or contract to fit the available space.

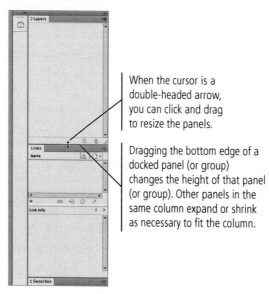

When the cursor is a double-headed arrow, you can click and drag to resize the panels.

Dragging the bottom edge of a docked panel (or group) changes the height of that panel (or group). Other panels in the same column expand or shrink as necessary to fit the column.

13. Continue to the next exercise.

Customizing Menus and Keyboard Shortcuts

People use Adobe design applications for many different reasons, sometimes using only a specific, limited set of tools to complete a certain project. Adobe CC applications have several sophisticated options for customizing the user interface, including the ability to define the available menu options and the keyboard shortcuts associated with various commands.

InDesign & Photoshop

In InDesign and Photoshop, you can choose Edit>Keyboard Shortcuts or Edit>Menus to customize those options. Once you have defined custom shortcuts or menus, you can save your choices as a set so you can access the same choices again without having to redo the work.

If you don't see a specific menu command, it's possible that someone has already modified the visibility of specific menu commands. (Some of the built-in workspaces include limited sets of tools — including menu commands.) When menu commands are hidden, you can choose Show All Menu Items at the bottom of an individual menu to show the hidden commands in that menu.

Illustrator

In Illustrator, you can add to or modify the keyboard shortcuts used for different functions in the application. Choosing Edit>Keyboard Shortcuts opens a dialog box where you can modify the shortcuts for menu commands and tools. If you assign a shortcut that isn't part of the default set, you have to save a custom set of shortcuts (Illustrator won't let you modify the default set of keyboard shortcuts). When more than one set of shortcuts exists (i.e., if you or someone else has added to or changed the default settings), you can switch between the different sets using the menu at the top of the dialog box.

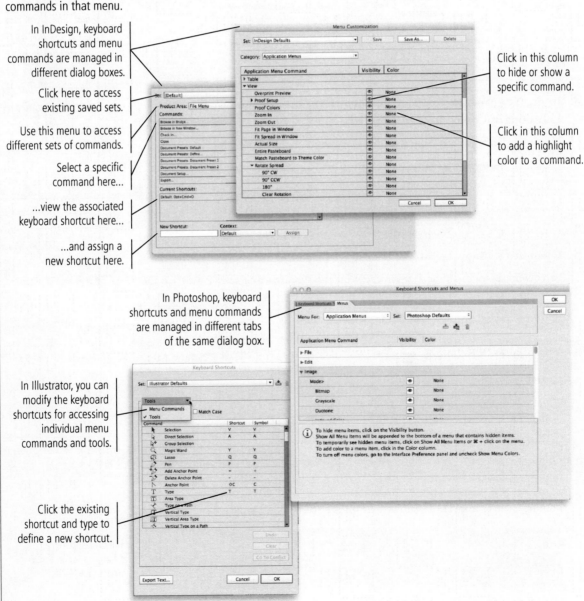

In InDesign, keyboard shortcuts and menu commands are managed in different dialog boxes.

Click here to access existing saved sets.

Use this menu to access different sets of commands.

Select a specific command here...

...view the associated keyboard shortcut here...

...and assign a new shortcut here.

Click in this column to hide or show a specific command.

Click in this column to add a highlight color to a command.

In Photoshop, keyboard shortcuts and menu commands are managed in different tabs of the same dialog box.

In Illustrator, you can modify the keyboard shortcuts for accessing individual menu commands and tools.

Click the existing shortcut and type to define a new shortcut.

CREATE A SAVED WORKSPACE

By now you should understand that you have extensive control over the appearance of your InDesign workspace — what panels are visible, where and how they appear, and even the size of individual panels or panel groups.

Over time you will develop personal preferences — for example, the Colors panel always appears at the top — based on your work habits and project needs. Rather than re-establishing every workspace element each time you return to InDesign, you can save your custom workspace settings so you can recall them with a single click.

1. **Click the Workspace switcher in the Application/Menu bar and choose New Workspace.**

   Again, keep in mind that we list differing commands in the Macintosh/Windows format. On Macintosh, the Workspace switcher is in the Application bar; on Windows, it's in the Menu bar.

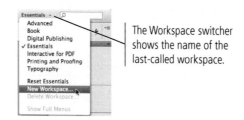

The Workspace switcher shows the name of the last-called workspace.

Note:

The Delete Workspace option opens a dialog box where you can choose a specific user-defined workspace to delete. You can't delete the default workspaces that come with the application.

2. **In the New Workspace dialog box, type `Portfolio`. Make sure the Panel Locations option is checked and click OK.**

   You didn't define custom menus, so that option is not relevant in this exercise.

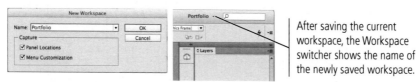

After saving the current workspace, the Workspace switcher shows the name of the newly saved workspace.

Note:

If you are using a shared computer, you might want to also include your own name in the workspace name.

3. **Open the Window menu and choose Workspace>Essentials.**

   Saved workspaces can be accessed in the Window>Workspace submenu as well as the Workspace switcher on the Application/Menu bar.

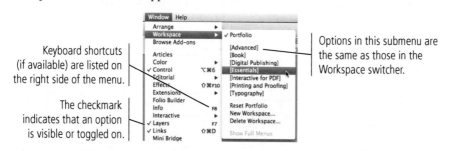

Keyboard shortcuts (if available) are listed on the right side of the menu.

The checkmark indicates that an option is visible or toggled on.

Options in this submenu are the same as those in the Workspace switcher.

Note:

If a menu option is grayed out, it is not available for the active selection.

Calling a saved workspace restores the last-used state of the workspace. You made a number of changes since you launched InDesign with the default Essentials workspace, so calling the Essentials workspace restores the last state of that workspace — in essence, nothing changes from the saved Portfolio workspace.

The only apparent difference is the active workspace name.

4. **Choose Window>Workspace>Reset Essentials (or click the Workspace switcher and choose Reset Essentials).**

Remember: calling a workspace again restores the panels exactly as they were the last time you used that workspace. For example, if you close a panel that is part of a saved workspace, the closed panel will not be reopened the next time you call the same workspace. To restore the saved state of the workspace, including opening closed panels or repositioning moved ones, you have to use the Reset option.

5. **Continue to the next exercise.**

 ## Explore the InDesign Document Views

There is far more to using InDesign than arranging panels around the workspace. What you do with those panels — and even which panels you need — depends on the type of work you are doing in a particular file. In this exercise, you open an InDesign file and explore the interface elements you'll use to create documents.

1. **In InDesign, choose File>Open. Navigate to your WIP>InterfaceCC14 folder and select sfaa1.indd in the list of available files.**

The Open dialog box is a system-standard navigation dialog box. This dialog box is one area of significant difference between Macintosh and Windows users.

Note:

Press Command/ Control-O to access the Open dialog box.

2. **Press Shift, and then click sfaa5.indd in the list of files.**

Pressing Shift allows you to select multiple contiguous (consecutive) files in the list.

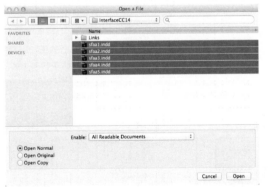 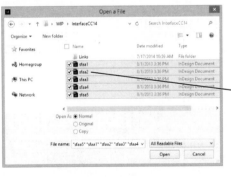

On Windows, the file extensions are not included in the file names in the Open dialog box.

You can also press Command/Control to select and open non-contiguous files. (Depending on how files are sorted in your operating system, folders might be listed before other files. If that's the case on your system, you can press Shift or Control to select all five files.)

One final reminder: we list differing commands in the Macintosh/Windows format. On Macintosh, you need to press the Command key; on Windows, press the Control key. (We will not repeat this explanation every time different commands are required for the different operating systems.)

3. **Click Open to open all five selected files. If you get any warnings about modified images, click the Update Links button.**

The concept of linked files will be explained in depth in later projects. For now, simply click the Update Links button.

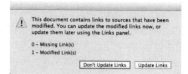

InDesign files appear in a **document window**.

Each open document is represented by a separate tab.

The **document tabs** show the file name and current view percentage.

The active file tab is lighter than the other tabs.

4. **Click the sfaa3.indd tab to make that document active.**

5. **Click the Zoom Level field in the Application/Menu bar and change the view percentage to 200.**

Different people prefer larger or smaller view percentages, depending on a number of factors (eyesight, monitor size, and so on). As you complete the projects in this book, you'll see our screen shots zoom in or out as necessary to show you the most relevant part of a particular file. In most cases we do not tell you what specific view percentage to use for a particular exercise unless it is specifically required for the work being done.

View Options

Zoom Level

Screen Mode

Go to Bridge

Arrange Documents

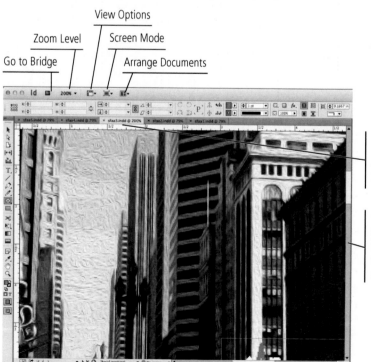

Click the tab to activate a specific file in the document window.

Changing the view percentage of the file does not affect the size of the document window.

6. Choose View>Fit Page in Window.

Fit Page in Window automatically calculates view percentage based on the size of the document window.

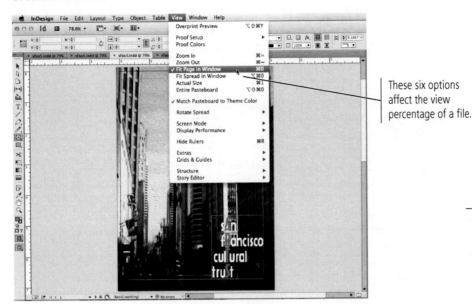

Note:

All open files are listed at the bottom of the Window menu.

These six options affect the view percentage of a file.

Note:

Fit Spread in Window relates to documents that have left- and right-facing pages, such as a book.

7. Click the Zoom tool in the Tools panel. Click in the document window and drag a marquee around the logo in the bottom-right corner.

Dragging a marquee with the Zoom tool enlarges the selected area to fill the document window.

Zoom tool cursor

The area of the marquee enlarges to fill the document window.

8. **With the Zoom tool selected, Option/Alt-click in the document window.**

One final reminder: When commands are different for the Macintosh and Windows operating systems, we include the different commands in the Macintosh/Windows format. In this case, Macintosh users should press the Option key while clicking; Windows users should press the Alt key.

Clicking with the Zoom tool enlarges the view percentage in specific, predefined steps. Pressing Option/Alt while clicking with the Zoom tool reduces the view percentage in the reverse sequence of the same percentages.

With the Zoom tool active, pressing Option/Alt changes the cursor to the Zoom Out icon.

Option/Alt-clicking with the Zoom tool reduces the view percentage in the predefined sequence of percentages.

9. **Click the Hand tool near the bottom of the Tools panel.**

10. **Click in the document, hold down the mouse button, and drag around.**

The Hand tool is a very easy and convenient option for changing the visible area of an image in the document window.

Hand tool cursor

Note:

Press the Z key to access the Zoom tool.

Press the H key to access the Hand tool.

Note:

If you click and hold down the mouse button when the Hand tool is active, the page zooms out and a red "view box" appears. You can drag the view box and release the mouse button to recenter the view on the area inside the view box.

11. Choose View>Display Performance>High Quality Display.

You might have noticed that the images in this file look very bad (they are badly bitmapped). This is even more evident when you zoom in to a high view percentage. By default, InDesign displays a low-resolution preview of placed images to save time when the screen redraws (i.e., every time you change something). Fortunately, however, you have the option to preview the full-resolution images placed in a file.

Using the High Quality Display, images do not show the bitmapping of the default low-resolution previews.

Controlling Display Performance

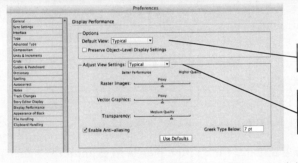

By default, files display in the document window using the Typical display performance settings. In the Display Performance pane of the Preferences dialog box, you can change the default view settings (Fast, Typical, or High Quality), as well as change

Choose Fast, Typical, or High Quality view as the default.

Use this menu to review and change the settings for Fast, Typical, and High Quality display.

the definition of these settings. In the Adjust View Settings section, individual sliders control the display of raster images, vector graphics, and objects with transparency.

In the layout, you can change the document display performance using the View>Display Performance menu. If **Allow Object-Level Display Settings** is checked in the View>Display Performance submenu, you can also change the preview for a specific image (in the Object>Display Performance submenu or using the object's contextual menu).

You can turn object-level display settings on and off using the Allow Object-Level Display Settings toggle. To remove object-level settings, choose **Clear Object-Level Display Settings**. (Object-level display settings are maintained only while the file remains open; if you want to save the file with specific object-level display settings, check the **Preserve Object-Level Display Settings** option in the Preferences dialog box.)

Fast displays gray boxes in place of graphics.

Typical shows the low-resolution proxy images.

High-quality shows the full resolution of placed files.

INDESIGN FOUNDATIONS

12. **Using the Selection tool, click the background image to select it. Control/ right-click the selected image and choose Display Performance>Typical Display from the contextual menu.**

Macintosh users who do not have right-click mouse capability can press the Control key and click to access the contextual menu. You do not have to press Control *and* right-click to access the menus.

Control/right-clicking an object on the page opens a contextual menu, where you can change the a number of aspects default panel behavior. Many elements in InDesign have contextual menus, which make it easy to access item-specific options.

In the View menu, the Allow Object-Level Display Settings option is active by default (see the image in the previous step); this means you can change the display of individual objects on the page.

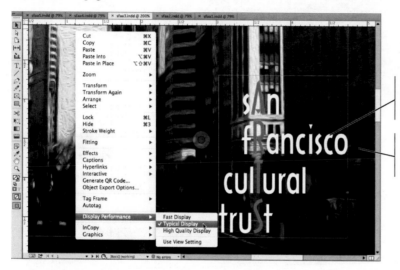

High-Quality Display is especially evident where sharp lines exist.

Typical Display uses a low-resolution preview of placed images.

13. **Choose View>Fit Page in Window to see the entire page.**

14. **Double-click the title bar above the docked panels to expand the panels.**

15. **In the Pages panel, double-click the Page 2 icon to show that page in the document window.**

The Pages panel is the easiest way to move from one page to another in a multi-page document. You will use this panel extensively as you complete the projects in this book.

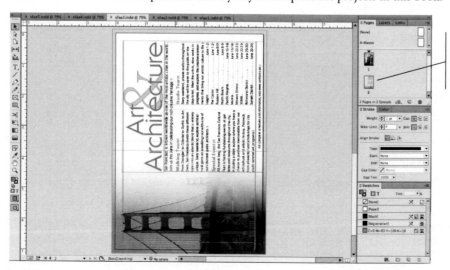

Double-click a page icon to display that page in the document window.

16. **Control/right-click the Page 2 icon in the Pages panel and choose Page Attributes>Rotate Spread View>90° CW from the contextual menu.**

Rotating the view only changes the display of the page; the actual page remains unchanged in the file. This option allows you to work more easily on objects or pages that are oriented differently than the overall document. In this example, the front side of the postcard has portrait orientation, but the mailer side has landscape orientation.

Note:

You can also rotate page views using the options in the View>Rotate Spread menu.

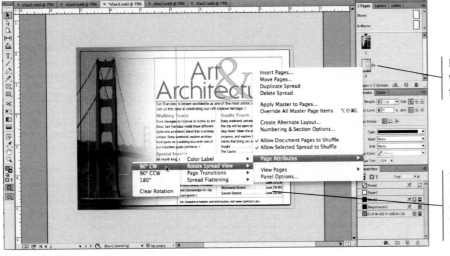

Pages with a rotated view are identified in the Pages panel.

The rotated display makes it easier to work on pages with orientations different from the document definition.

17. **Continue to the next exercise.**

Summing Up the InDesign View Options

INDESIGN FOUNDATIONS

Most InDesign projects require some amount of zooming in and out to various view percentages, as well as navigating around the document within its window. As we show you how to complete various stages of the workflow, we usually won't tell you when to change your view percentage because that's largely a matter of personal preference. But you should understand the different options for navigating an InDesign file so you can easily and efficiently get to what you want.

View Menu

The View menu provides options for changing the view percentage. You should also become familiar with the keyboard shortcuts for these commands:

Zoom In	Command/Control-equals (=)
Zoom Out	Command/Control-minus (-)
Fit Page in Window	Command/Control-0 (zero)
Fit Spread in Window	Command-Option-0/Control-Alt-0
Actual Size (100%)	Command/Control-1
Entire Pasteboard	Command-Option-Shift-0/ Control-Alt-Shift-0

Zoom Level Field/Menu

You can use the Zoom Level field in the Application/Menu bar to type a specific view percentage, or you can use the attached menu to choose from the predefined view percentage steps.

Zoom Tool

You can click with the **Zoom tool** to increase the view percentage in specific, predefined intervals (the same intervals you see in the View Percentage menu in the bottom-left corner of the document window). Pressing Option/Alt with the Zoom tool allows you to zoom out in the same predefined percentages. If you drag a marquee with the Zoom tool, you can zoom into a specific location; the area surrounded by the marquee fills the available space in the document window.

Hand Tool

Whatever your view percentage, you can use the **Hand tool** to drag the file around in the document window, including scrolling from one page to another. The Hand tool only changes what is visible in the window; it has no effect on the actual content of the file.

EXPLORE THE ARRANGEMENT OF MULTIPLE DOCUMENTS

In many cases, you will need to work with more than one layout at the same time. InDesign incorporates a number of options for arranging multiple documents. We designed the following simple exercise so you can explore these options.

1. **With sfaa3.indd active, choose Window>Arrange>Float in Window.**

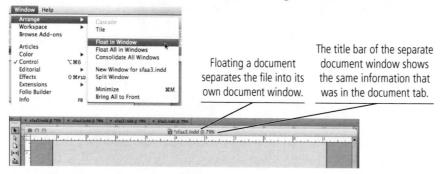

Floating a document separates the file into its own document window.

The title bar of the separate document window shows the same information that was in the document tab.

2. **In the Application/Menu bar, click the Arrange Documents button to open the panel of defined arrangements.**

3. **Click the 2 Up button in the Arrange Documents panel.**

   The defined arrangements provide a number of options for tiling multiple open files within the available workspace; these arrangements manage all open files, including those in floating windows.

   The Consolidate All button (top left) restores all floating documents into a single tabbed document window. The remaining buttons in the top row separate all open files into separate document windows and then arrange the different windows as indicated.

   The lower options use a specific number of floating documents (2-Up, 3-Up, etc.); if more files are open than an option indicates, the extra files are consolidated as tabs in the first document window.

Note:

When multiple document windows are open, two options in the Window>Arrange menu allow you to cascade or tile the document windows. You can separate all open files by choosing Window>Arrange>Float All in Windows.

Note:

If the Application Frame is not active on a Macintosh, the Application bar must be visible to access the Arrange Documents button.

The Arrange Documents panel includes a number of tiling options for arranging multiple open files in the workspace.

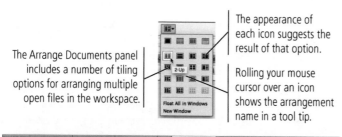

The appearance of each icon suggests the result of that option.

Rolling your mouse cursor over an icon shows the arrangement name in a tool tip.

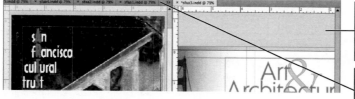

The 2-Up arrangement divides the document window in half, as indicated by the button icon.

Extra documents remain as tabs in the left document window.

4. **Click the sfaa3.indd document tab and drag left until a blue highlight appears around the document tabs in the other panel.**

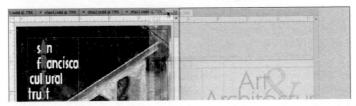

When you release the mouse button, all of the open files are again part of the same document window.

5. **Click the Screen Mode button in the Application/Menu bar and choose Preview.**

The files you explored in this project were saved in Normal screen mode. In Normal mode, you can see all non-printing elements including guides and frame edges (if those are toggled on). You can now also see the pasteboard surrounding the defined page area; your development work is not limited by the defined page size.

Preview screen mode surrounds the page with a neutral gray background. Page guides, frame edges, and other non-printing areas are not visible in the Preview mode.

Note:

By default, the pasteboard matches the color of that you defined for the user interface in the Interface pane of the Preferences dialog box. If you uncheck the Match Pasteboard to Theme Color option, the pasteboard is white.

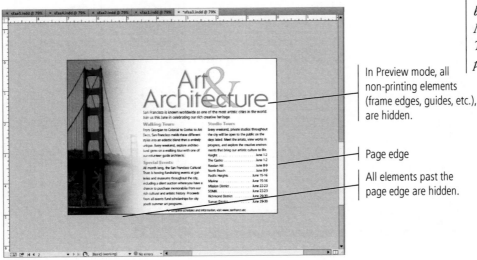

In Preview mode, all non-printing elements (frame edges, guides, etc.), are hidden.

Page edge

All elements past the page edge are hidden.

6. Click the Screen Mode button at the bottom of the Tools panel and choose Bleed from the pop-up menu.

This menu has the same options as the button in the Application/Menu bar. As you will learn throughout this book, there is almost always more than one way to accomplish a particular goal in InDesign.

The Bleed screen mode is an extension of the Preview mode; it shows an extra area (which was defined when the document was originally set up) around the page edge. This bleed area is a required part of print document design — objects that are supposed to print right up to the edge of the page must extend past the page edge, usually 1/8″ or more. (Bleed requirements and setup are explained in Project 7: Letterhead Design.)

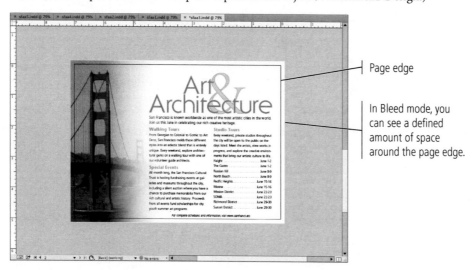

Page edge

In Bleed mode, you can see a defined amount of space around the page edge.

7. Using either Screen Mode button, choose the Presentation mode.

Presentation mode fills the entire screen with the active spread. By default, the area around the page is solid black; you can press W to change the surround to white or press G to change it to neutral gray. In Presentation mode, clicking anywhere on the screen shows the next spread; Shift-clicking shows the previous spread.

In Presentation mode, the page, surrounded by solid black, fills the entire screen.

8. Press ESC to exit Presentation mode.

9. Click the Close button on the active document tab.

9. **Click the Close button on the active document tab.**

When multiple files are open, clicking the close button on a document tab closes only that file.

An asterisk before the file name indicates that the file has been changed and not yet saved.

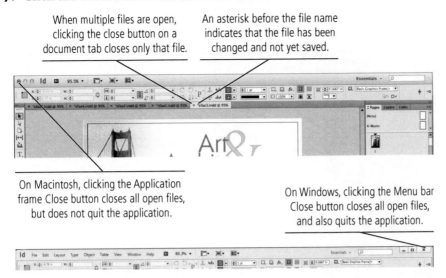

On Macintosh, clicking the Application frame Close button closes all open files, but does not quit the application.

On Windows, clicking the Menu bar Close button closes all open files, and also quits the application.

Closing the Macintosh Application frame closes all open files but does not quit the application. Clicking the Close button on the Windows Menu bar closes all open files and quits the application; to close open files without quitting, you have to manually close each open file.

10. **Click Don't Save when asked if you want to save changes to sfaa3.indd.**

By rotating the spread view on Page 2, the file has technically been changed. InDesign automatically asks if you want to save any file that has been changed before closing it.

11. **Close (without saving) all but the sfaa5.indd file.**

12. **Continue to the next exercise.**

 ## EXPLORE THE ILLUSTRATOR USER INTERFACE

Illustration is a very broad career path, with potential applications in virtually any industry. In other words, mastering the tools and techniques of Adobe Illustrator can significantly improve your range of career options. Within the general category of illustration, many Illustrator experts specialize in certain types of work: logo design, technical drawing, and editorial illustration are only a few subcategories of artwork you can create with Illustrator.

Adobe Illustrator is the industry-standard application for creating digital drawings or **vector images** (graphics composed of mathematically defined lines instead of pixels). Although not intended as a page-layout application, you can also use the tools in Illustrator to combine type, graphics, and images into a single cohesive design. Many people create flyers, posters, and other one-page projects entirely within Illustrator. With the ability to work with multiple artboards (explained in Project 3: Identity Package), we will likely see more of this type of Illustrator work in the future.

1. **With sfaa5.indd open (from your WIP>InterfaceCC14 folder), use the Selection tool (the solid arrow) to select the "SFCT" graphic on Page 1.**

2. **Control/right-click the selected object and choose Edit Original from the contextual menu.**

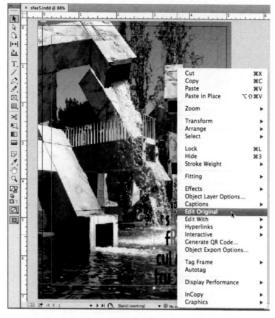

Choosing Edit Original opens the placed file in its native application. This graphic is a native Adobe Illustrator file (with the extension ".ai"), so it opens in the latest possible version of Adobe Illustrator.

If Adobe Illustrator is not already running on your computer, it might take a moment while the application launches. If you have multiple versions of Illustrator running on your computer, the placed graphic will open in the first available version. If CS6 is already launched, for example, the graphic opens in that version instead of launching Illustrator CC.

3. **Macintosh users: Open the Window menu in Illustrator. If Application Frame is not checked (active), choose that command in the menu.**

Note:

You can press Command-Option-Shift/Control-Alt-Shift while launching the application to reset the Illustrator preferences.

4. **Choose Essentials in the Workspace switcher, then choose Reset Essentials.**

Remember that in InDesign, calling a workspace restores the workspace to its last-used state; to restore the saved state of a workspace, you have to choose Reset [Workspace] in the Workspace switcher. The same is true of Illustrator.

Note:

The Manage Workspaces option opens a dialog box where you can rename or delete user-defined custom workspaces. You can't alter the default workspaces that come with the application.

Illustrator panels are arranged and accessed using the same techniques you already learned, and saved workspaces in Illustrator serve the same function as in InDesign. The Essentials workspace includes the Tools panel on the left of the screen, the Control panel at the top, and a set of iconized and docked panels on the right. (The Tools panel defaults to one-or two-column mode, depending on the size of your screen.)

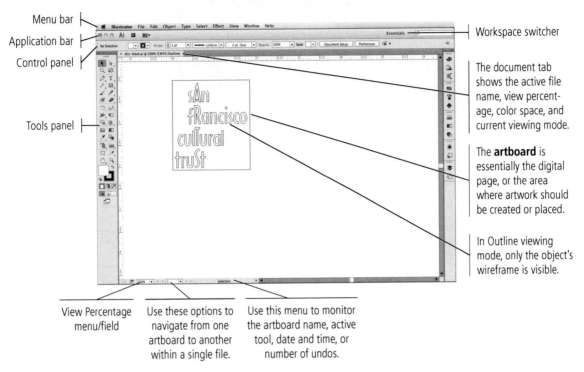

Menu bar
Application bar
Control panel
Tools panel

Workspace switcher

The document tab shows the active file name, view percentage, color space, and current viewing mode.

The **artboard** is essentially the digital page, or the area where artwork should be created or placed.

In Outline viewing mode, only the object's wireframe is visible.

View Percentage menu/field

Use these options to navigate from one artboard to another within a single file.

Use this menu to monitor the artboard name, active tool, date and time, or number of undos.

5. **With nothing selected in the open file, review the options in the Control panel.**

We will not discuss all 30+ Illustrator panels here, but the Control panel deserves mention. This panel appears by default at the top of the workspace below the Menu bar (and the Application bar on Macintosh systems). It is context sensitive, which means it provides access to different options depending on which tool is active and what is selected in the document.

When nothing is selected in the file, the most important Control panel options open the Document Setup dialog box and the Preferences dialog box (more about these specific elements in the projects).

Note:

For now, don't worry about the specific options that are available. You only need to realize that the Control panel changes depending on what is selected.

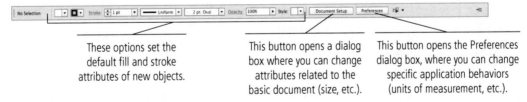

These options set the default fill and stroke attributes of new objects.

This button opens a dialog box where you can change attributes related to the basic document (size, etc.).

This button opens the Preferences dialog box, where you can change specific application behaviors (units of measurement, etc.).

6. **With the sfct-black.ai file open, choose File>Open.**

In many cases, you will open Illustrator files from directly within an InDesign file (as you did for the sfct-black.ai file). Of course, you can also simply open a file from directly within Illustrator. How you open a file does affect what happens to instances that are placed in an InDesign layout. In Project 10 you will see how opening a file from within an InDesign layout offers distinct advantages in an integrated workflow.

7. **Navigate to the WIP>InterfaceCC14>Links folder. Click `sfaa.ai` to select that file, and then click Open.**

This file was saved in Preview mode, which shows the artwork in color.

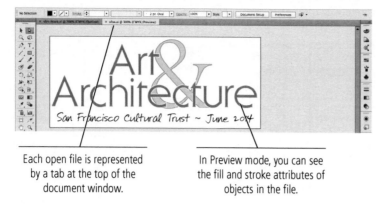

Note:

You can zoom an Illustrator document from 3.13% to 6400%.

Each open file is represented by a tab at the top of the document window.

In Preview mode, you can see the fill and stroke attributes of objects in the file.

Note:

Macintosh users: If you turn off the Application frame, the new document will have its own title bar.

8. **Click the Selection tool at the top of the Tools panel to make sure that tool is active.**

The Selection tool (the solid arrow) is used to select entire objects in the file.

9. **Click any of the black letter shapes at the bottom of the artwork, then review the options in the Control panel.**

When an object is selected in the file, the Control panel shows the attributes of the selected object. In this case, the entire set of black letter shapes is a group, so the Control panel shows options related to groups.

The Control panel shows options and attributes of the selected object (in this case, a group of shapes).

Selected object (indicated by **bounding box handles** on all four sides of the object)

Selection tool

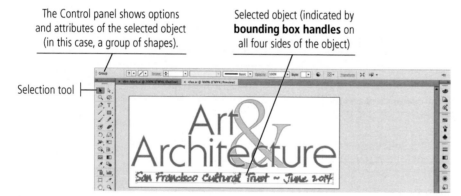

10. **Click the ampersand character to select that object.**

The selected object is a single path (not part of a group). The Control panel changes to show options related to paths.

The Control panel shows options related to the selected object (in this case, a compound path).

Selected object

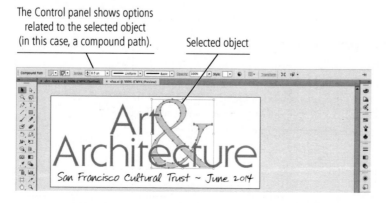

11. **Click the button at the bottom of the Tools panel to show the screen mode options.**

Illustrator has three different **screen modes**, which change the way the document window displays on the screen. The default mode, which you saw when you opened these three files, is called Normal Screen Mode.

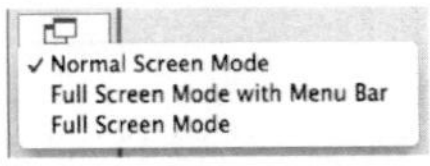

```
✓ Normal Screen Mode
  Full Screen Mode with Menu Bar
  Full Screen Mode
```

Identifying Illustrator Tools

ILLUSTRATOR FOUNDATIONS

The chart below offers a quick reference of nested tools, as well as the keyboard shortcut for each tool (if any). Nested tools are shown indented and in italics.

Selection tool (V)	Paintbrush tool (B)	Gradient tool (G)
Direct Selection tool (A)	Pencil tool (N)	Eyedropper tool (I)
Group Selection tool	*Smooth tool*	*Measure tool*
Magic Wand tool (Y)	*Path Eraser tool*	Blend tool (W)
Lasso tool (L)	Blob Brush tool (Shift-B)	Symbol Sprayer tool (Shift-S)
Pen tool (P)	Eraser tool (Shift-E)	*Symbol Shifter tool*
Add Anchor Point tool (+)	*Scissors tool (C)*	*Symbol Scruncher tool*
Delete Anchor Point tool (-)	*Knife tool*	*Symbol Sizer tool*
Convert Anchor Point tool (Shift-C)	Rotate tool (R)	*Symbol Spinner tool*
Type tool (T)	*Reflect tool (O)*	*Symbol Stainer tool*
Area Type tool	Scale tool (S)	*Symbol Screener tool*
Type on a Path tool	*Shear tool*	*Symbol Styler tool*
Vertical Type tool	*Reshape tool*	Column Graph tool (J)
Vertical Area Type tool	Width tool (Shift-W)	*Stacked Column Graph tool*
Vertical Type on a Path tool	*Warp tool (Shift-R)*	*Bar Graph tool*
Touch Type tool (Shift-T)	*Twirl tool*	*Stacked Bar Graph tool*
Line Segment tool (\\)	*Pucker tool*	*Line Graph tool*
Arc tool	*Bloat tool*	*Area Graph tool*
Spiral tool	*Scallop tool*	*Scatter Graph tool*
Rectangular Grid tool	*Crystallize tool*	*Pie Graph tool*
Polar Grid tool	*Wrinkle tool*	*Radar Graph tool*
Rectangle tool (M)	Free Transform tool (E)	Artboard tool (Shift-O)
Rounded Rectangle tool	Shape Builder tool (Shift-M)	Slice tool (Shift-K)
Ellipse tool (L)	*Live Paint Bucket tool (K)*	*Slice Selection tool*
Polygon tool	*Live Paint Selection tool (Shift-L)*	Hand tool (H)
Star tool	Perspective Grid tool (Shift-P)	*Print Tiling tool*
Flare tool	*Perspective Selection tool (Shift-V)*	Zoom tool (Z)
	Mesh tool (U)	

12. **Choose Full Screen Mode with Menu Bar from the Screen Mode menu.**

Note:

Press F to switch between screen modes.

In Full Screen Mode with Menu Bar, the document tabs are hidden behind the Menu bar.

In Full Screen Mode with Menu Bar, the document window fills the entire workspace and extends behind the docked panels.

13. **Click the Screen Mode button at the bottom of the Tools panel and choose Full Screen Mode.**

In Full Screen Mode, the Menu bar, title bar, and all panels are hidden.

Move your mouse cursor to the edges of the screen to temporarily show docked panels.

14. **Press the Escape key to exit Full Screen Mode and return to Normal Screen Mode.**

15. **Click the Close button on the sfaa.ai tab to close that file.**

As in InDesign, all open Illustrator files can be accessed and closed using the document tabs at the top of the document window. A file does not need to be active before you close it using the document tab.

Note:

All open files are listed at the bottom of the Window menu. You can use these menu options to navigate from one file to another, which is particularly useful if you're working in Full Screen Mode with Menu Bar because the document tabs are not visible in this mode.

16. **Click the Close button on the sfct-black.ai document tab. If asked to save changes, click Don't Save in the warning message.**

17. **Return to the open InDesign file (sfaa5.indd) and then continue to the next exercise.**

Most Illustrator projects require some amount of zooming in and out to various view percentages, as well as navigating around the document within its window. As we show you how to complete different stages of the workflow, we usually won't tell you when to change your view percentage because that's largely a matter of personal preference. But you should understand the different options for navigating around an Illustrator file so you can efficiently get to what you want.

To change the view percentage, you can type a specific percent in the **View Percentage field** of the document window or choose from the predefined options in the related menu.

You can also click with the **Zoom tool** to increase the view percentage in specific, predefined intervals (the same intervals you see in the View Percentage menu in the bottom-left corner of the document window). Pressing Option/Alt with the Zoom tool allows you to zoom out in the same defined percentages. If you drag a marquee with the Zoom tool, you can zoom into a specific location; the area surrounded by the marquee fills the available space in the document window.

The **View menu** also provides options for changing view percentage. (The Zoom In and Zoom Out options step through the same predefined view percentages as clicking with the Zoom tool.)

Zoom In	Command/Control-plus (+)
Zoom Out	Command/Control-minus (-)
Fit Artboard in Window	Command/Control-0 (zero)
Fit All in Window	Command-Option-0/ Control-Alt-0 (zero)
Actual Size (100%)	Command/Control-1

Whatever your view percentage, you can use the **Hand tool** to drag the file around in the document window. The Hand tool changes what is visible in the window; it has no effect on the actual content of the image.

The Navigator Panel

The **Navigator panel** (Window> Navigator) is another method of adjusting what you see, including the view percentage and the specific area that is visible in the document window. The Navigator panel shows a thumbnail of the active file; a red rectangle (called the Proxy Preview Area) represents exactly how much of the document shows in the document window.

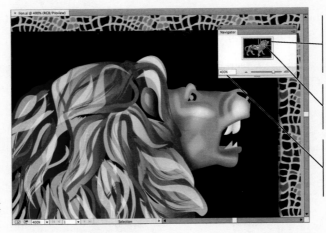

The red rectangle shows the area of the file that is visible in the document window.

Drag the red rectangle to change the visible portion of the file.

Use the slider and field at the bottom of the panel to change the view percentage.

Saved Views

Named views can be helpful if you repeatedly return to the same area and view percentage. By choosing View>New View, you can save the current view with a specific name.

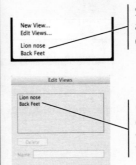

Saved views can be accessed at the bottom of the View menu.

Change view names or delete specific views by choosing View>Edit Views.

Adobe Photoshop is the industry-standard application for working with pixels — both manipulating existing ones and creating new ones. Many Photoshop experts specialize in certain types of work. Photo retouching, artistic painting, image compositing, color correction, and Web site design are only a few subcategories of work you can create with Photoshop. Our goal in this book is to teach you how to use the available tools to create different types of work that you might encounter in your professional career.

Although not intended as a layout-design application, you can also use the Photoshop tools to combine type, graphics, and images into a finished design; many people create advertisements, book covers, and other projects entirely in Photoshop. Others argue that Photoshop should never be used for layout design, maintaining that InDesign is the preferred page-layout application.

Project 4: Composite Movie Ad, and Project 5: Vintage Car Montage result in finished composite designs. We do not advocate doing *all* or even *most* layout composite work in Photoshop. But because many people use the application to create composite designs, we feel the projects in this book portray a realistic workflow. Project 6: Menu Image Correction, focuses specifically on image manipulation or creation — which is the true heart of the application.

As you move forward in your career, it will be your choice to determine which application is appropriate for which task; it is our job to teach you how to use the tools so you can make the best possible decision when that need arises.

1. **With sfaa5.indd open in InDesign, use the Selection tool (the solid arrow) to select the background image on Page 1.**

2. **Control/right-click the selected image and choose Edit With>Adobe Photoshop CC 2014 in the contextual menu.**

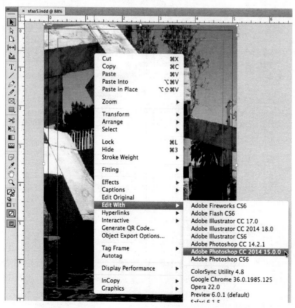

3. **Macintosh users: Open the Window menu. If Application Frame is not checked (active), choose that command in the menu.**

4. Choose Essentials in the Workspace switcher, then choose Reset Essentials to restore the deault user interface settings.

Photoshop panels are arranged and accessed using the same techniques you already learned, and saved workspaces in Photoshop serve the same function as in InDesign. Also like InDesign, calling a saved workspace calls the last-used version of the workspace; you have to use the Reset option to call the saved version of the workspace.

Menu bar

Application title bar

Options bar

Workspace switcher

Panel dock

Docked, expanded panel group

Docked, iconized panels

Tools panel

View Percentage field

On Windows, the Minimize, Restore, and Close buttons appear on the right end of the Menu bar.

Menu bar

Options bar

If you have used previous versions of Photoshop, you will notice that the Application bar has been removed from the user interface. The features that were available in the Application bar are still available in other locations.

5. Click the Zoom tool in the Tools panel, and then review the options in the Options bar.

The Options bar appears by default at the top of the workspace below the Menu bar. It is context sensitive, providing different options depending on which tool is active.

Note:

In Photoshop, the Arrange Documents options are available in the Window>Arrange submenu.

Identifying Photoshop Tools

The following chart offers a quick reference of nested tools, as well as the shortcut for each tool (if any). Nested tools are shown indented and in italics.

⊹ Move tool (V)	
⬚ Rectangular Marquee tool (M)	
○ *Elliptical Marquee tool (M)*	
--- *Single Row Marquee tool*	
⫶ *Single Column Marquee tool*	
⬭ Lasso tool (L)	
⬭ *Polygonal Lasso tool (L)*	
⬭ *Magnetic Lasso tool (L)*	
⬭ Quick Selection tool (W)	
⬭ *Magic Wand tool (W)*	
⬚ Crop tool (C)	
⬚ *Perspective Crop tool (C)*	
⬭ *Slice tool (C)*	
⬭ *Slice Select tool (C)*	
⬭ Eyedropper tool (I)	
⬭ *3D Material Eyedropper tool (I)*	
⬭ *Color Sampler tool (I)*	
⬭ *Ruler tool (I)*	
⬭ *Note tool (I)*	
1₂³ *Count tool (I)*	

Spot Healing Brush tool (J)
- *Healing Brush tool (J)*
- *Patch tool (J)*
- *Content Aware Move tool (J)*
- *Red Eye tool (J)*

Brush tool (B)
- *Pencil tool (B)*
- *Color Replacement tool (B)*
- *Mixer Brush tool (B)*

Clone Stamp tool (S)
- *Pattern Stamp tool (S)*

History Brush tool (Y)
- *Art History Brush tool (Y)*

Eraser tool (E)
- *Background Eraser tool (E)*
- *Magic Eraser tool (E)*

Gradient tool (G)
- *Paint Bucket tool (G)*
- *3D Material Drop tool (G)*

Blur tool
- *Sharpen tool*
- *Smudge tool*

Dodge tool (O)
- *Burn tool (O)*
- *Sponge tool (O)*

Pen tool (P)
- *Freeform Pen tool (P)*
- *Add Anchor Point tool*
- *Delete Anchor Point tool*
- *Convert Point tool*

T Horizontal Type tool (T)
- *Vertical Type tool (T)*
- *Horizontal Type Mask tool (T)*
- *Vertical Type Mask tool (T)*

Path Selection tool (A)
- *Direct Selection tool (A)*

Rectangle tool (U)
- *Rounded Rectangle tool (U)*
- *Ellipse tool (U)*
- *Polygon tool (U)*
- *Line tool (U)*
- *Custom Shape tool (U)*

Hand tool (H)
- *Rotate View tool (R)*

Zoom tool (Z)

6. Click the Fit Screen button in the Options bar.

When the Zoom tool is active, the Fit Screen button (the same as the Fit on Screen command in the View menu) changes the image view to whatever percentage is necessary to show the entire image in the current document window.

The Fill Screen button resize the image to fill the available space in the document window; the entire image might not be visible.

If Resize Windows to Fit is checked, zooming in a floating window affects the size of the actual document window.

If Zoom All Windows is checked, zooming in one window affects the view percentage of all open files.

The Options bar shows options related to the active tool.

Fit Screen resizes the view percentage as necessary to show the entire image in the document window.

Zoom tool

7. In the Options bar, click the 100% button.

This option is the same as the View>100% menu command.

8. **Using the Zoom tool, press Option/Alt, and then click two times anywhere in the document window.**

   Clicking with the Zoom tool enlarges the view percentage in specific, predefined percentage steps. Pressing Option/Alt while clicking with the Zoom tool reduces the view percentage in the reverse sequence of the same percentages.

Option/Alt-clicking with the Zoom tool reduces the view in the predefined sequence of percentages.

With the Zoom tool active, pressing Option/Alt changes the cursor to the Zoom Out icon.

<aside>
Note:

In Photoshop, you can zoom a document between approximately 0.098% and 3200%. We say "approximately" because the actual smallest size depends on the original image size; you can zoom out far enough to "show" the image as a single tiny square, whatever that percentage of the image.
</aside>

9. **In the Tools panel, Control/right-click the Hand tool and choose the Rotate View tool from the list of nested tools. Click in the document window and drag left to turn the document counterclockwise.**

   The Rotate View tool turns an image without permanently altering the orientation of the file; the actual image data remains unchanged. This tool allows you to more easily work on objects or elements that are not oriented horizontally (for example, working with text that appears on an angle in the final image).

   If you are unable to rotate the image view, your graphics processor does not support OpenGL — a hardware/software combination that makes it possible to work with complex graphics operations. If your computer does not support OpenGL, you will not be able to use a number of Photoshop CC features (including the Rotate View tool).

Type a specific angle in this field to rotate the image view.

Click and drag around this icon to rotate the image view.

Clicking Reset View restores the original image orientation.

If Rotate All Windows is checked, dragging in one window affects the view angle of all open files.

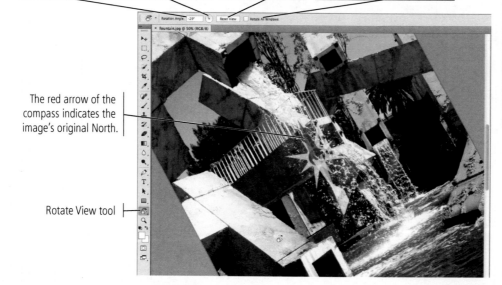

The red arrow of the compass indicates the image's original North.

Rotate View tool

<aside>
Note:

The Hand tool in Photoshop and Illustrator serves the same purpose as the Hand tool in InDesign. Simply click and drag to reposition the document within the document window.
</aside>

10. **In the Control panel, click the Reset View button.**

As we said, the Rotate View tool is non-destructive. You can easily use the tool's options to define a specific view angle or to restore an image to its original orientation.

Resetting the view restores the image's original orientation.

Note:

*Like Illustrator, Photoshop has three **screen modes** that change the way the document window displays on the screen. In Photoshop, you can access these options using the Screen Mode button in the Tools panel.*

11. **Click the Close button on the fountain.jpg tab.**

12. **Return to InDesign. Close the sfaa5.indd file without saving, and then continue to Project 1.**

Summing Up the Photoshop View Options

PHOTOSHOP FOUNDATIONS

You should understand the different options for navigating around a Photoshop file so you can easily and efficiently get to what you want, when you want to get there.

View Percentage Field

You can type a specific percentage in the View Percentage field in the bottom-left corner of the document window.

View Menu

The View menu also provides options for changing the view percentage, including the associated keyboard shortcuts.

Zoom In	Command/Control-plus (+)
Zoom Out	Command/Control-minus (-)
Fit On Screen	Command/Control-0 (zero)
Actual Pixels (100%)	Command/Control-1

Zoom Tool

You can click with the **Zoom tool** to increase the view percentage in specific, predefined intervals. Pressing Option/Alt allows you to zoom out in the same predefined steps. If you drag a marquee with the Zoom tool, you can zoom into a specific location; the area surrounded by the marquee fills the available space in the document window.

If you activate the Scrubby Zoom option in the Options bar, you can click and drag left to reduce the view percentage, or drag right to increase the view percentage.

Hand Tool

Whatever your view percentage, you can use the **Hand tool** to drag the file around in the document window. The Hand tool changes only what is visible in the window; it has no effect on the actual pixels in the image.

Mouse Scroll Wheel

If your mouse has a scroll wheel, rolling the scroll wheel up or down moves the image up or down within the document window. If you press Command/Control and scroll the wheel, you can move the image left (scroll up) or right (scroll down) within the document window. You can also press Option/Alt and scroll the wheel up to zoom in or scroll the wheel down to zoom out.

(In the General pane of the Preferences dialog box, the Zoom with Scroll Wheel option is unchecked by default. If you check this option, scrolling up or down with no modifier key zooms in or out and does not move the image within the document window.)

Navigator Panel

The **Navigator panel** is another method of adjusting how close your viewpoint is and what part of the page you're currently viewing. The Navigator panel shows a thumbnail of the active file; a red rectangle represents exactly how much of the document shows in the document window.

The red rectangle shows the area that is visible.

Drag the red rectangle to change the visible portion of the file.

Use the slider and field to change the view percentage.

As part of your Adobe Creative Cloud membership, you can use the Sync Settings options to share certain application assets between different computers. This means that you can access those same assets on any computer where you are logged in to your Creative Cloud account.

First, you must be logged into your Creative Cloud account and connected to the Internet for the sync process to work. You can open the Help menu to verify that you are signed in to your Creative Cloud account. (If you see an option to Sign In, choose that option and follow the instructions with your user name and password.)

In all three applications, you can open the Sync Settings pane of the Preferences dialog box to customize which assets will be synchronized.

Photoshop

Once you have determined what options to synchronize, you can click the Upload button in the Sync Settings pane of the Preferences dialog box. The settings that are active on your computer become the ones that are stored in your Creative Cloud account.

You can also click the Download button to pull the saved settings, which are synced in your Creative Cloud account, onto the machine you are currently using.

You can also use menu commands to upload or download synced settings. On Macintosh, your personal user name in the Photoshop menu provides access to a submenu with Upload Settings and Download Settings options. Choosing either of these options synchronizes the settings that are currently active in the Preferences dialog box.

On Windows, the same option is available near the bottom of the Edit menu.

InDesign & Illustrator

When a file is open in InDesign or Illustrator, you can use the Sync button in the bottom-left corner of the document window to initiate the sync process.

Sync button

If you sync the settings from a computer other than the one where you performed the last sync, you'll see a message in InDesign that updated settings are ready. You can click the Apply Now button to load the sync settings onto your local machine.

Depending on which options you choose to sync in Illustrator, you might need to relaunch the application. In that case, a message appears after the sync settings are finished downloading.

If you try to sync settings and a conflict exists between your local and Creative Cloud settings, you are asked how you want to resolve the conflict.

- Clicking **Sync Local** overwrites the settings on the Cloud with the settings from your local computer.
- Clicking **Sync Cloud** overwrites the settings on your local computer with the settings in your Creative Cloud account.
- (Illustrator only) Clicking **Keep Latest File** applies whichever settings files are more recent — local or Cloud.

International Symbols

Biotech Services manages large-scale manufacturing facilities specializing in everything from digital photographic equipment to large earth-moving machines used to build new roads. The company builds plants all over the world that in many cases handle hazardous chemicals and undertake dangerous tasks — which means they must prominently display appropriate warnings. Biotech Services hired you to create a digital collection of universal symbols that they can use to create signs, print on the side of large machines, and place as icons on their Web site.

This project incorporates the following skills:

❏ Placing raster images into an Illustrator file to use as drawing templates

❏ Creating and managing simple shapes and lines

❏ Using various tools and panels to transform objects' color, position, and shape

❏ Cloning objects to minimize repetitive tasks

❏ Using layers to organize and manage complex artwork

❏ Drawing complex shapes by combining simple shapes

Project Meeting

client comments

We have a set of universal warning symbols on our Web site, but we need to use those same icons in other places as well. Our printer told us that the symbols on our Web site are "low res," so they can't be used for print projects. The printer also said he needs vector graphics that will scale larger and still look good. The printer suggested we hire a designer to create digital versions of the icons so we can use them for a wide variety of purposes, from large machinery signs to small plastic cards to anything else that might come up. We need you to help us figure out exactly what we need and then create the icons for us.

art director comments

Basically, we have the icons, but they're low-resolution raster images, so they only work for the Web, and they can't be enlarged. The good news is that you can use the existing icons as templates and more or less trace them to create the new icons.

The client needs files that can be printed cleanly and scaled from a couple of inches up to several feet. Illustrator vector files are perfect for this type of job. In fact, vector graphics get their resolution from the printer being used for a specific job, so you can scale them to any size you want without losing quality.

project objectives

To complete this project, you will:

- ❏ Create a grid that will eventually hold all icons in one document
- ❏ Control objects' stroke, fill, and transparency attributes
- ❏ Import and use the client's raster images as templates, which you can then trace
- ❏ Use layers to manage complex artwork
- ❏ Use the Line Segment tool to create a complex object from a set of straight lines
- ❏ Lock, unlock, hide, and show objects to navigate the objects' stacking order
- ❏ Rotate and reflect objects to create complex artwork from simple shapes
- ❏ Use the Pathfinder to combine simple shapes into a single complex object

Stage 1 Setting up the Workspace

There are two primary types of digital artwork: raster images and vector graphics. (**Line art**, sometimes categorized as a third type of image, is actually a type of raster image.)

Raster images are pixel-based, made up of a grid of individual **pixels** (**rasters** or **bits**) in rows and columns (called a **bitmap**). Raster files are **resolution dependent**; their resolution is determined when you scan, photograph, or create the file. As a professional graphic designer, you should have a basic understanding of the following terms and concepts:

- **Pixels per inch (ppi)** is the number of pixels in one horizontal or vertical inch of a digital raster file.

- **Lines per inch (lpi)** is the number of halftone dots produced in a linear inch by a high-resolution imagesetter, which simulates the appearance of continuous-tone color.

- **Dots per inch (dpi)** or **spots per inch (spi)** is the number of dots produced by an output device in a single line of output.

Drawing objects that you create in Illustrator are **vector graphics**, which are composed of mathematical descriptions of a series of lines and points. Vector graphics are **resolution independent**; they can be freely scaled and are output at the resolution of the output device.

CREATE A NEW DOCUMENT

In this project, you work with the basics of creating vector graphics in Illustrator using a number of different drawing tools, adding color, and managing various aspects of your artwork. The first step is to create a new document for building your artwork.

1. **Download `Symbols_Print14_RF.zip` from the Student Files Web page.**

2. **Expand the ZIP archive in your WIP folder (Macintosh) or copy the archive contents into your WIP folder (Windows).**

   This results in a folder named **Symbols**, which contains all of the files you need for this project. You should also use this folder to save the files you create in this project.

3. **In Illustrator, choose File>New.**

4. **In the resulting New Document dialog box, type `icons` in the Name field.**

   The New Document dialog box defaults to the last-used settings.

5. **Choose Print in the New Document Profile menu, and make sure the Number of Artboards field is set to 1.**

   Illustrator includes the ability to create multiple **artboards** (basically, Illustrator's version of "pages"). For this project, however, you need only a single artboard.

6. **Choose Letter in the Size menu, choose Points in the Units menu, and choose the Portrait Orientation option.**

   The **point** is a standard unit of measurement for graphic designers. There are 72 points in an inch. As you complete this project, you will work with other units of measurement; you will convert the units later.

7. **Set all four bleed values to `0`.**

   Bleed is the amount an object needs to extend past the edge of the artboard or page to meet the mechanical requirements of commercial printing.

Note:

If necessary, refer to Page 1 of the Interface chapter for specific information on expanding or accessing the required resource files.

Note:

To begin this project, we reset the built-in Essentials workspace. Feel free to work with whatever settings you are most comfortable using.

Note:

You learn more about bleeds in Project 3: Identity Package.

8. **If the Advanced options aren't visible, click the arrow button to the left of the word Advanced.**

9. **Make sure the Color Mode is set to CMYK and the Preview Mode is set to Default.**

   CMYK is the standard color mode for printing, and RGB is the standard color mode for digital distribution.

   Don't worry about the other Advanced options for now. You will learn about those in later projects when they are more relevant.

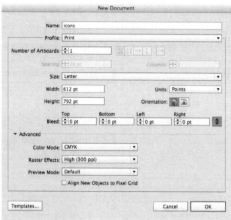

Note:

Our screen shots show the Macintosh operating system using the Application frame. If you're on a Macintosh system and your screen doesn't look like our screen shots, choose Window>Application Frame to toggle on that option.

10. **Click OK to create the new file.**

    In the resulting document window, the letter-size "page" (or artboard) is represented by a dark black line. As we explained in the Interface chapter, the panels you see depend on what was done the last time you (or someone else) used the application. Because workspace arrangement is such a personal preference, we tell you what panels you need to use, but we don't tell you where to place them.

    In our screen shots, we typically float panels over the relevant area of the document so we can focus the images on the most important part of the file at any particular point. As you complete the projects in this book, feel free to dock the panels, grouped or ungrouped, iconized or expanded, however you prefer.

Note:

The color of the pasteboard (the area around the artboard) defaults to match the brightness of the user interface. You can change this setting to show a white pasteboard in the User Interface pane of the Preferences dialog box.

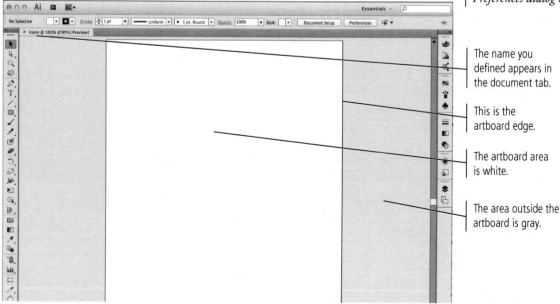

The name you defined appears in the document tab.

This is the artboard edge.

The artboard area is white.

The area outside the artboard is gray.

11. **Choose File>Save As and navigate to your WIP>Symbols folder.**

If you assign a name in the New Document dialog box (as you did in Step 4), that name becomes the default file name in the Save As dialog box.

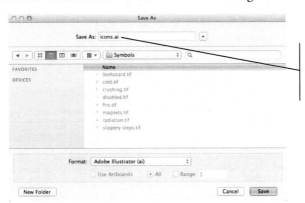

The file name defaults to the name you defined when you created the file, including the ".ai" extension.

Note:

Press Command/Control-S to save a document, or press Command/Control-Shift-S to open the Save As dialog box.

12. **Click Save in the Save As dialog box. Review the options in the resulting Illustrator Options dialog box.**

This dialog box determines what is stored in the resulting file. The default options are adequate for most files.

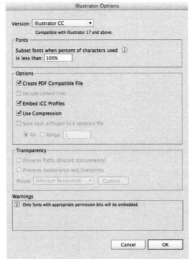

- Use the **Version** menu to save files to be compatible with earlier versions of the software. (Keep in mind that many features are not supported by earlier versions; if you save a file for an earlier version, some file information will probably be lost.)

- **Subset Fonts when Percent of Characters Used Is Less Than** determines when to embed an entire font instead of just the characters that are used in the file. Embedding the entire font can significantly increase file size.

- Make sure **Create PDF Compatible File** is checked if you want to use the file with other Adobe applications (such as placing it into an InDesign layout). This does not create a separate PDF file; it simply includes PDF preview data in the file.

- **Include Linked Files** embeds files that are linked to the artwork.

- **Embed ICC Profiles** stores color information inside the file for use in a color-managed workflow.

- **Use Compression** compresses PDF data in the Illustrator file.

- **Save Each Artboard to a Separate File** saves each artboard as a separate file; a separate master file with all artboards is also created.

- **Transparency** options determine what happens to transparent objects when you save a file for Illustrator 9.0 or earlier. Preserve Paths discards transparency effects and resets transparent artwork to 100% opacity and Normal blending mode. Preserve Appearance and Overprints preserves overprints that don't interact with transparent objects; overprints that interact with transparent objects are flattened.

13. **Click OK to save the file, and then continue to the next exercise.**

DEFINE SMART GUIDE PREFERENCES

Adobe Illustrator provides many tools to help you create precise lines and shapes. **Smart Guides** are temporary snap-to guides that help you create, align, and transform objects. Smart Guides also show you when the cursor is at a precise angle relative to the original position of the object or point you're moving. In this exercise, you will make sure the correct Smart Guides are active.

1. **With icons.ai open, click the Preferences button in the Control panel.**

2. **Choose Smart Guides in the list of categories on the left.**

3. **Make sure the Alignment Guides, Object Highlighting, Anchor/Path Labels, and Measurement Labels options are selected and click OK.**

Note:

When nothing is selected in the file, you can access the Preferences dialog box directly from the Control panel.

If something is selected in the file, you have to choose Illustrator> Preferences on Macintosh or Edit>Preferences on Windows.

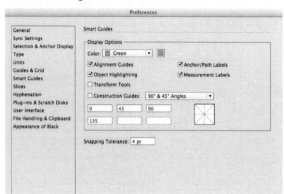

4. **Choose View>Smart Guides to make sure that option is toggled on (checked).**

   If the option is already checked, simply move your mouse away from the menu and click to dismiss the menu without changing the active option.

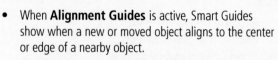

5. **Continue to the next exercise.**

Using Smart Guides

You can change the appearance and behavior of Smart Guides in the Preferences dialog box. The Display options determine what is visible when Smart Guides are active:

- When **Alignment Guides** is active, Smart Guides show when a new or moved object aligns to the center or edge of a nearby object.

- When **Object Highlighting** is active, moving the mouse over any part of an unselected object shows the anchors and paths that make up that object.

- When **Transform Tools** is active, Smart Guides display when you scale, rotate, or shear objects.

- When **Anchor/Path Labels** is active, Smart Guides include labels that show the type of element (path or anchor) under the cursor.

This anchor is being dragged with the Direct Selection tool.

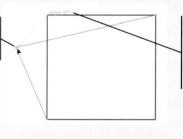

The Smart Guide shows that the anchor is being moved at a 45-degree angle from the original position.

- When **Measurement Labels** is active, Smart Guides show the distance and angle of movement.

- When **Construction Guides** is active, Smart Guides appear when you move objects in the file at or near defined angles (0°, 45°, 90°, and 135° are the default angles). A number of common angle options are built into the related menu, or you can type up to six specific angles in the available fields.

ILLUSTRATOR FOUNDATIONS

 **DRAW ROUNDED RECTANGLES**

Now that you have a place to draw (the artboard), you're ready to start creating the icon artwork. The first step of this project requires a set of background shapes — simple rectangles with rounded corners — to contain each icon. Illustrator includes a number of shape tools that make it easy to create this kind of basic shape — rectangles (or squares), ellipses (or circles), and so on.

1. **With icons.ai open, click the Rectangle tool in the Tools panel and hold down the mouse button until the nested tools appear. Choose the Rounded Rectangle tool from the list of nested tools.**

   When you choose a nested tool, that variation becomes the default option in the Tools panel. You don't need to access the nested menu to select the Rounded Rectangle tool again as long as the application remains open. (If you quit and relaunch Illustrator, the regular Rectangle tool again becomes the default tool in that position.)

2. **Click the Default Fill and Stroke button at the bottom of the Tools panel.**

   In Illustrator, the default fill is white and the default stroke is 1-pt black.

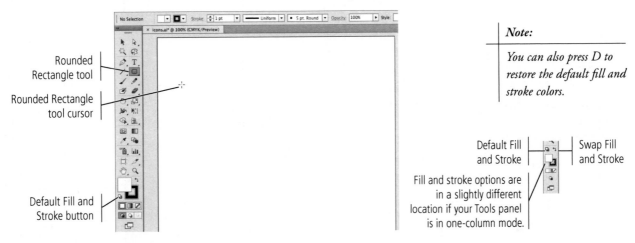

Rounded Rectangle tool

Rounded Rectangle tool cursor

Default Fill and Stroke button

Note:

You can also press D to restore the default fill and stroke colors.

Default Fill and Stroke

Swap Fill and Stroke

Fill and stroke options are in a slightly different location if your Tools panel is in one-column mode.

3. **With the Rounded Rectangle tool active, click anywhere on the artboard.**

   The resulting dialog box asks how big you want to make the new rectangle, defaulting to the last-used measurements. The default measurement system is points, as you defined when you created this file.

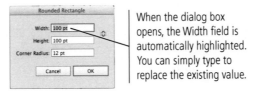

When the dialog box opens, the Width field is automatically highlighted. You can simply type to replace the existing value.

4. **Type 1.5″ in the Width field and then press Tab to move to the Height field.**

Regardless of what unit you see in the dialog box, you can enter values in whatever system you prefer, as long as you remember to type the correct unit in the dialog box fields (use ″ for inches, mm for millimeters, and pt for points; there are a few others, but they are rarely used). Illustrator automatically translates one unit of measurement to another.

When you move to the next field, Illustrator calculates the conversion of 1.5 inches (the value you placed in the Width field) to 108 pt (the value that automatically appears in the Width field after you move to the Height field).

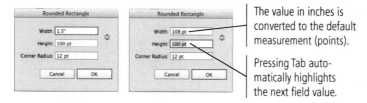

The value in inches is converted to the default measurement (points).

Pressing Tab automatically highlights the next field value.

5. **Type 1.5″ in the Height field.**

Because you are making a shape with the same height and width, you could also click the Constrain icon (the broken chain) on the right side of the dialog box to make the Height field match the modified Width field.

6. **Make sure the corner radius field is set to 12 pt.**

A rounded-corner rectangle is simply a rectangle with the corners cut at a specific distance from the end (the corner radius). The two sides are connected with one-fourth of a circle, which has a radius equal to the amount of the rounding.

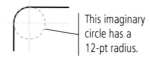

This imaginary circle has a 12-pt radius.

7. **Click OK to create the new shape.**

A shape appears on the artboard with its top-left corner exactly where you clicked with the Rounded Rectangle tool. (If you Option/Alt-click with any of the shape tools, the place where you click becomes the center of the new shape.)

8. **Click the Selection tool in the Tools panel and zoom in to 200%.**

When the object is selected, the rectangular **bounding box** marks the outermost edges of the shape. **Bounding box handles** mark the corners and exact horizontal and vertical center of the shape. (If you don't see the bounding box, choose View>Show Bounding Box.) Because this shape has rounded corners, the corner bounding-box handles actually appear outside the shape edges.

Four small circles inside each corner of the shape are Live Corner widgets, which allow you to click and drag to change the shape of object corners.

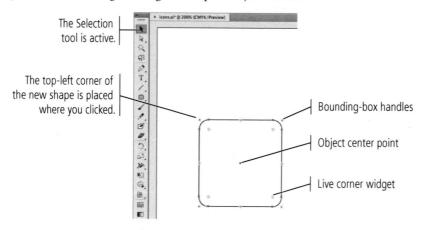

The Selection tool is active.

The top-left corner of the new shape is placed where you clicked.

Bounding-box handles

Object center point

Live corner widget

9. **Click the Rounded Rectangle tool in the Tools panel and hold down the mouse button until the nested tools appear. Choose the Rectangle tool from the list of nested tools.**

10. **Move the cursor to the right of the top edge of the existing shape. When you see a green line connected to the top edge of the first shape, click, hold down the mouse button, and drag down and right to begin creating a second shape. Do not release the mouse button.**

The green line is a function of the Smart Guides feature, which provides instant feedback while you draw. As you drag, notice the cursor feedback showing the size of the new shape. Also notice that as you drag near the bottom edge of the first shape, a Smart Guide appears to indicate your position.

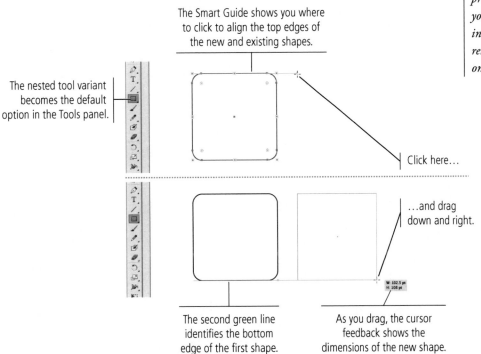

The Smart Guide shows you where to click to align the top edges of the new and existing shapes.

The nested tool variant becomes the default option in the Tools panel.

Click here…

…and drag down and right.

The second green line identifies the bottom edge of the first shape.

As you drag, the cursor feedback shows the dimensions of the new shape.

W: 102.5 pt
H: 108 pt

11. **While still holding down the mouse button, press the Shift key. When the cursor feedback shows both Width and Height values of 108 pt, release the mouse button to create the second shape.**

Pressing Shift **constrains** the shape to equal height and width. Although you can accomplish the same result by carefully monitoring the cursor feedback, pressing the Shift key makes the process faster and easier.

Because you are using the Rectangle tool instead of the Rounded Rectangle tool, the second shape does not have rounded corners; the bounding-box handles match the actual shape corners.

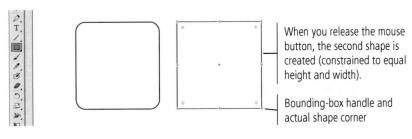

When you release the mouse button, the second shape is created (constrained to equal height and width).

Bounding-box handle and actual shape corner

12. Using the Selection tool, click one of the Live Corner widgets and drag toward the center of the shape. When cursor feedback shows a corner radius of approximately 12 pt, release the mouse button.

The Live Corner widgets allow you to manually adjust the corner radius of corners on the selected shape. Dragging in toward the shape center increases the corner radius; dragging out toward the corner decreases the corner radius.

Because the entire object is selected (with the Selection tool), dragging any of the widgets applies the same change to all corners on the shape. To change only certain corners, you can use the Direct Selection tool to select the corner points you want to affect before dragging a Live Corner widget.

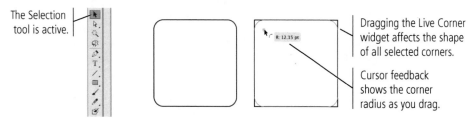

The Selection tool is active.

Dragging the Live Corner widget affects the shape of all selected corners.

Cursor feedback shows the corner radius as you drag.

13. With the adjusted shape still selected, open the Transform panel.

The Transform panel shows the corner radius of all four corners on the shape. If you find it difficult to achieve an exact radius by dragging, you can always use these fields to adjust the corner radius to specific values.

14. Make sure the Constrain icon between the Corner Radius fields is active (a linked chain). Highlight any of the Corner Radius fields and type 12, then press Return/Enter to finalize the change.

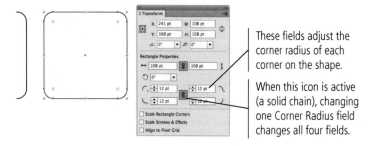

These fields adjust the corner radius of each corner on the shape.

When this icon is active (a solid chain), changing one Corner Radius field changes all four fields.

Note:

Corner radius fields are only available in the Transform panel if the shape is a rectangle (with four 90° corner angles).

15. Using the Selection tool, press Option/Alt, then click the second shape and drag right.

When you drag an object with the Selection tool, you move it to another location. If you press Option/Alt while dragging, you clone the original object (make a copy of it) and move the clone.

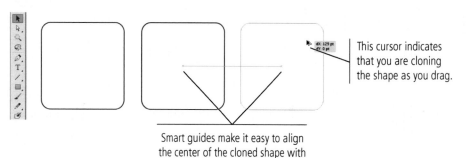

This cursor indicates that you are cloning the shape as you drag.

Smart guides make it easy to align the center of the cloned shape with the center of the original.

Note:

Don't worry about the spaces between the objects. You'll adjust the object spacing in a later exercise.

16. Save the file and continue to the next exercise.

If a shape is an actual rectangle (with all 90° corners), the Live Corner widgets appear whenever the shape is selected with either Selection tool. For any other shape, including a four-cornered polygon with different-angled corners, the widgets appear only when the shape is selected with the Direct Selection tool.

Select the shape with the Direct Selection tool to access the Live Corner widgets.

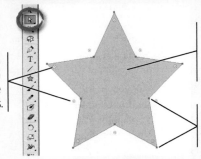

Click inside the shape to select the entire object (and all shape corners).

Click specific corner points to select only those corners.

If the entire object is selected, dragging any one Live Corner widget affects all corners on the same shape (below left). If you want to affect only specific corners, you can select those points first and then drag any of the visible widgets to change only the selected corners (below right).

Option/Alt-clicking a Live Corner widget toggles through the available corner shapes (round, inverted round, and chamfer/beveled). Again, only selected corners are affected by the shape change.

Round corner	Inverted Round corner	Chamfer corner

Corner shapes have two rounding options, relative and absolute (the default). Using absolute corners, the radius between two connecting points exactly matches the defined value. Using relative corners, the corner curve is extended slightly to create a more natural-seeming shape.

In the example here, the red circle has the same radius value as the rounded corner on the underlying shape. The Absolute rounding method shows that the rounded corner exactly matches the same-radius circle; the Relative method shows how the corner curve extends slightly beyond the edge of the same-radius circle.

Relative corner   Absolute corner

The Corners subpanel, available in the Control panel, can be used to change the shape, corner radius, and rounding of selected corners on non-rectangular shapes. (If you have a wide enough application frame, the Corner  Radius field might appear directly in the Control panel. If you don't see it, you must click the Corners hot-text link to open the subpanel and its Corner Radius field.)

Most Illustrator objects (including shapes like rounded-corner rectangles) contain two basic building blocks: anchor points and paths. These building blocks are the heart of vector graphics. Fortunately, you don't need to worry about the geometric specifics of vectors because Illustrator manages them for you — but you do need to understand the basic concept of how Illustrator works with anchor points and paths. You should also understand how to access those building blocks so you can do more than create basic shapes.

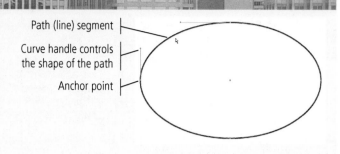

Path (line) segment

Curve handle controls the shape of the path

Anchor point

When you select an object with the **Selection tool** (the solid arrow), you can see the bounding box that identifies the outermost dimensions of the shape. Around the edges of the bounding box you see the bounding box handles, which you can use to resize the shape. (Press Command/Control-Shift-B to show or hide the bounding box of selected objects.)

When you select an object with the **Direct Selection tool** (the hollow arrow), you can see the anchor points and paths that make up the selected object rather than the object's bounding box. As you work with Illustrator, keep this distinction in mind: use the Selection tool to select an entire object; use the Direct Selection tool to edit the points and paths of an object.

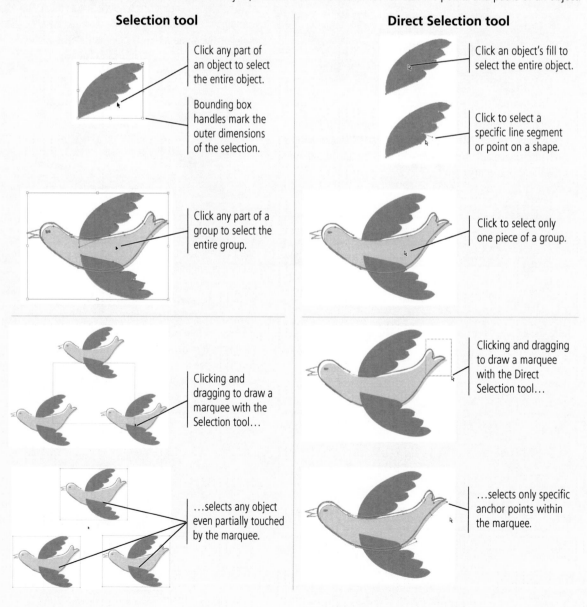

Selection tool

Click any part of an object to select the entire object.

Bounding box handles mark the outer dimensions of the selection.

Click any part of a group to select the entire group.

Clicking and dragging to draw a marquee with the Selection tool…

…selects any object even partially touched by the marquee.

Direct Selection tool

Click an object's fill to select the entire object.

Click to select a specific line segment or point on a shape.

Click to select only one piece of a group.

Clicking and dragging to draw a marquee with the Direct Selection tool…

…selects only specific anchor points within the marquee.

ILLUSTRATOR FOUNDATIONS

Bounding box handles make it easy to transform an object on the artboard. You can resize an object by dragging any handle, and even rotate an object by placing the cursor directly outside a corner handle. (If Smart Guides are active, cursor feedback helps if you want to make specific transformations, or you can work freestyle and drag handles until you're satisfied with the results.)

Drag a left- or right-center handle
to change the object's height.

Shift-drag to maintain an object's original
height-to-width aspect ratio as you transform it.

Drag a top- or bottom-center handle
to change the object's height.

Option/Alt-drag a handle to transform
the object around its center point.

Drag a corner handle to change both the
height and shape of an object at once.

Click directly outside an object's
corner handle to rotate the object.

The Free Transform tool allows you to change the shape of selected objects by dragging the transformation handles.

The **Touch widget**, which you can use to change the active transformation mode, appears when the Free Transform tool is active. To move the Touch bar in the workspace, click away from the three buttons and drag to another location.

Transformation handles

When the cursor is over a transformation handle, the icon shows which distortions can be made.

Free Transform Touch widget

Constraint

Free Transform

Perspective Distort

Free Distort

Moving the mouse cursor over a handle shows the transformation that can be made by dragging that handle. Clicking one of the transformation handles shows a larger icon to indicate the possible transformation.

When you first select the Free Transform tool, the widget shows that the **Free Transform** mode is active. Larger transformation handles appear over all eight of the selected object's bounding box handles. In this case, most of the available transformations are the same as those you can make when the Selection tool is active (see Page 49).

Drag a corner handle diagonally in or out to scale the selection horizontally and vertically at the same time.	Drag a center handle perpendicular to the bounding box edge to scale the selection in one direction.	Drag a center handle parallel to the bounding box edge to skew the selection.
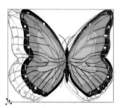	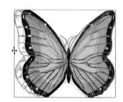	
Click a corner handle and drag around to rotate the selection.	Press Option/Alt to apply the transformation around the center point.	Press Shift, or activate the Constraint option, to transform the selection proportionally (maintaining the original height-to-width aspect ratio).

If you activate the **Perspective Distort** option in the Touch widget, you can drag the object's corner transformation handles to change the object's perspective. (The Constraint option is not available when the Perspective Distort option is active.)

When the Free Transform mode is active, you can accomplish the same goal by clicking a corner handle, then pressing Command-Option-Shift/Control-Alt-Shift and dragging.

If you activate the **Free Distort** option, you can drag the corner transformation handles to distort the selection. When the Constraint option is active, you can only drag the corner exactly horizontal or vertical from its previous position.

When the Free Transform mode is active, you can accomplish the same goal by clicking a corner handle, then pressing Command/Control and dragging.

CONTROL FILL AND STROKE ATTRIBUTES

At the beginning of the previous exercise, you clicked the Default Fill and Stroke button in the Tools panel to apply a white fill and 1-pt black stroke to the objects you created. Obviously, most artwork requires more than these basic attributes. Illustrator gives you almost unlimited control over the fill and stroke attributes of objects on the artboard.

As you complete the projects in this book, you will learn about styles, patterns, gradients, effects, and other attributes that can take an illustration from flat to fabulous. In this exercise, you learn about a number of options for changing the basic fill, stroke, and color attributes for objects on the page.

1. **With icons.ai open, choose the Selection tool at the top of the Tools panel. Click the left rectangle on the artboard to select it.**

   The Selection tool is used to select entire objects.

2. **Choose View>Hide Corner Widget.**

   These widgets can be distracting, so it's useful to turn them off when they are no longer needed.

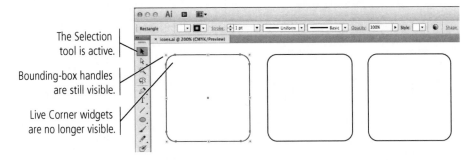

The Selection tool is active.

Bounding-box handles are still visible.

Live Corner widgets are no longer visible.

3. **Open the Swatches panel. If the panel shows a list of items including the color names, open the Swatches panel Options menu and choose Small Thumbnail View.**

   The Swatches panel includes a number of predefined and saved colors, which you can use to change the color of the fill and stroke of an object. You can also save custom swatches to more efficiently apply custom colors as you create artwork.

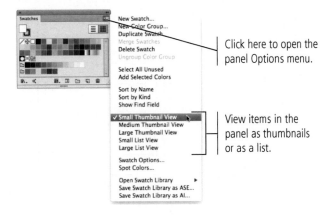

Click here to open the panel Options menu.

View items in the panel as thumbnails or as a list.

Note:

Remember, panels can always be accessed in the Window menu.

4. **Near the bottom of the Tools panel, click the Stroke icon to bring it to the front of the stack.**

The fill and stroke icons in the Tools panel are used to change the color of the related attributes. Clicking one of these buttons brings it to the front of the stack (makes it active) so you can change the color of that attribute.

Use these pop-up panels to change the fill or stroke color of the selected object.

Clicking the Stroke icon brings it in front of the Fill icon, and makes the Stroke attribute active.

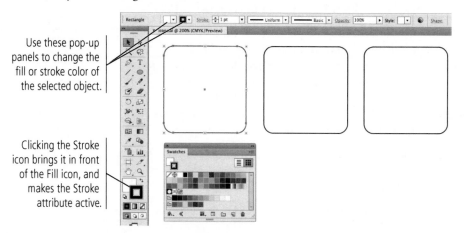

Note:

If your Swatches panel is docked and iconized, and if Auto-Collapse Iconic Panels is active, clicking the Stroke icon in the Tools panel collapses the Swatches panel back into the dock. Before completing Step 5, you need to either re-expand the Swatches panel, turn off the Auto-Collapse Iconic Panels option, or float the panel away from the dock.

5. **In the Swatches panel, click the gold swatch at the end of the first row.**

Because the Stroke icon is active in the Tools panel, the color of the selected object's stroke (border) changes to gold.

6. **In the Tools panel, click the Fill icon to bring it to the front of the stack. In the Swatches panel, click the black swatch in the first row.**

Because the Fill icon is active in the Tools panel, clicking the black color swatch changes the fill color of the selected object.

These swatches reflect the colors that are applied to the selected object.

Make sure the correct attribute is selected if you use the stand-alone Swatches panel to change attribute colors.

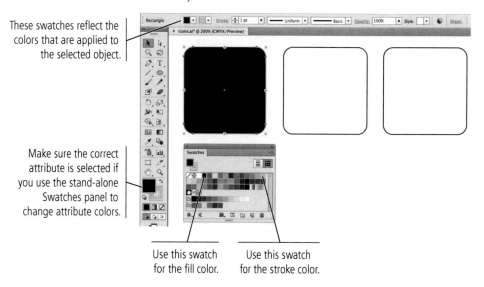

Use this swatch for the fill color.

Use this swatch for the stroke color.

Note:

It is very easy to forget to check which icon (fill or stroke) is on top of the stack. If you forget and accidentally change the color of the wrong attribute, simply undo the change (press Command/Control-Z) and bring the correct attribute to the front before changing colors.

7. **Open the Stroke panel. With the rounded rectangle selected, change the Stroke Weight field to 3 pt and press Return/Enter to apply the change.**

The Stroke icon in the Tools panel does not need to be active to change the stroke weight. The Tools panel icons relate only to color changes made with the stand-alone Swatches or Color panels.

Change the Stroke Weight field to 3 pt.

The Stroke icon doesn't need to be on top to change an object's stroke weight.

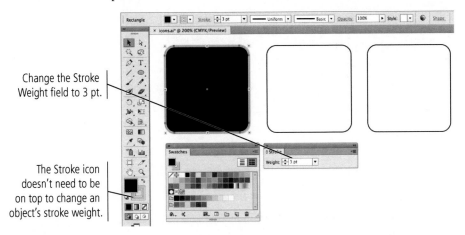

8. **With the rectangle still selected, click the Swap Fill and Stroke button in the Tools panel.**

This button makes it easy to reverse the fill and stroke colors of an object; the stroke weight remains unaffected when you swap the colors.

Click the Swap Fill and Stroke button to reverse the color attributes of the selected object.

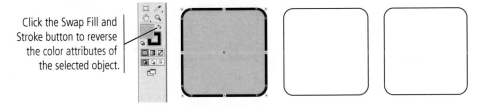

9. **Using the Selection tool, click the second rectangle on the artboard.**

The Fill and Stroke icons change to reflect the colors of the selected objects.

10. **Click the Fill color swatch in the Control panel. Choose the gold swatch in the second row to change the fill color for the selected object.**

When an object is selected with the Selection tool, the Control panel provides quick access to the stroke and fill attributes of the selected object.

Clicking the Fill color swatch opens an attached Swatches panel so you can change the fill for the selected object without opening the separate Swatches panel.

Click this color swatch to change the fill color of the selected object.

Click this color swatch to change the stroke color of the selected object.

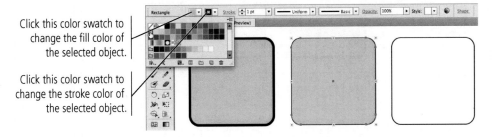

Note:

When you use the Control panel options, you don't need to worry about which icon is active in the Tools panel.

11. In the Control panel, change the Stroke Weight value to 3 pt.

Again, the Control panel options allow you to change the attribute value without opening the Stroke panel. The Control panel can be a significant time-saver for common operations such as changing stroke and fill attributes.

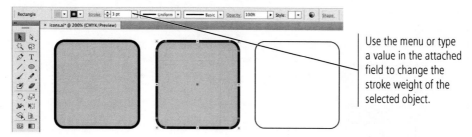

Use the menu or type a value in the attached field to change the stroke weight of the selected object.

12. Using the Selection tool, click the third rectangle on the artboard.

Again, the Fill and Stroke icons in the Tools panel change to reflect the colors of the selected object.

13. Select the Eyedropper tool in the Tools panel, and then click the first or second rectangle on the artboard.

The Eyedropper tool copies fill and stroke attributes from one object (the one you click) to another (the one you first selected).

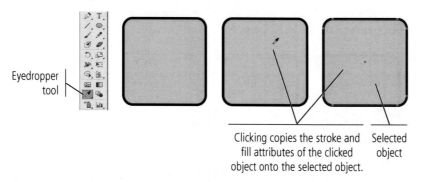

Eyedropper tool

Clicking copies the stroke and fill attributes of the clicked object onto the selected object.

Selected object

Note:

You can double-click the Eyedropper tool in the Tools panel to define which attributes are picked up and applied by clicking with the tool.

14. Press and hold the Command/Control key, and click anywhere on the artboard away from the three rectangles.

Pressing Command/Control temporarily switches to the Selection tool. By clicking on the empty artboard area while holding down the modifier key, you can quickly deselect the selected object(s). When you release the Command/Control key, the tool reverts to the one you last used — in this case, the Eyedropper tool.

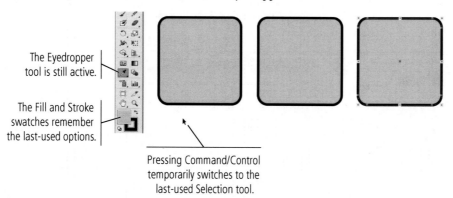

The Eyedropper tool is still active.

The Fill and Stroke swatches remember the last-used options.

Pressing Command/Control temporarily switches to the last-used Selection tool.

15. Release the Command/Control key.

16. **Choose the Rounded Rectangle tool in the Tools panel.**

17. **To the right of the third shape on the artboard, draw a fourth rounded rectangle that is 108 pt square.**

    The Fill and Stroke swatches remember the last-used options, so the new rectangle has the same heavy black stroke and gold fill as the others. Don't worry if your shapes aren't entirely on the artboard; you will define their precise position in the next exercise.

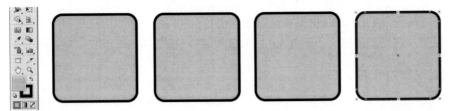

18. **Save the file (File>Save or Command/Control-S) and continue to the next exercise.**

CONTROL OBJECT POSITIONING

The ability to move objects around on the artboard is one of the advantages of digital drawing. On paper, you have to manually erase items and then redraw them in their new locations. Illustrator offers a number of tools that make it easy to move objects around the artboard, either as isolated objects or in relation to other elements on the page. In this exercise, you learn several techniques for moving objects on the artboard.

1. **With icons.ai open, change your zoom percentage so you can see all four shapes and the entire top of the artboard.**

2. **Choose View>Rulers>Show Rulers to show the rulers at the top and left edges of the document window.**

    Because you created this file using points as the default unit of measurement, the rulers — and fields in dialog boxes and panels — show measurements in points.

3. **Control/right-click the top ruler and choose Inches from the contextual menu.**

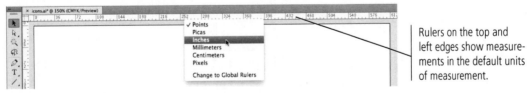

Rulers on the top and left edges show measurements in the default units of measurement.

4. **Choose the Selection tool from the top of the Tools panel. Click the left rectangle on the artboard to select it.**

5. With the left rectangle selected, look at the right side of the Control panel. If you have a smaller monitor and see the word "Transform," click it to open the pop-up Transform panel.

What you see in the Control panel depends on the size of your monitor (or the size of your Application Frame if you've made it smaller than your monitor).

If you have a wide monitor, the reference point proxy and the X, Y, W, and H fields of the Transform panel are available directly in the Control panel.

If you have a smaller monitor that does not allow these fields to fit, the Control panel includes a hot-text link to the Transform panel. Clicking the link opens the Transform panel as a pop-up, directly below the Control panel; after you make a change in the pop-up panel, it collapses back into the Control panel.

Note:

You could also use the stand-alone Transform panel (Window>Transform) to access these same options.

Monitor width might limit the contents of your Control panel.

Click these hot-text links to open the related pop-up panel.

With a wider monitor, you can access most Transform panel options directly in the Control panel.

Click these hot-text links to open the full pop-up panel.

6. Review the Transform options.

The reference points correspond to the bounding box handles of the selected object. The selected square in this icon identifies which point of the object is being measured.

If you use the W or H fields to resize an object, you can constrain the object's height-to-width aspect ratio by clicking the chain icon (right of the W and H fields in the Transform panel, or between the W and H fields in the Control panel).

Note:

The Change to Global Rulers option is only relevant when you work with multiple artboards.

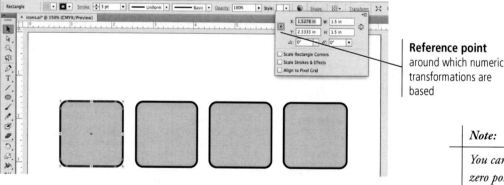

Reference point
around which numeric transformations are based

In Illustrator, the default **zero point** (the source of measurements) is the top-left corner of the artboard; the X and Y positions of an object are measured relative to that location. (The X axis is the horizontal value and the Y axis is the vertical value.) Keep these ideas in mind when you move something in an Illustrator file:

- Moving up requires subtracting from the Y value.
- Moving down requires adding to the Y value.
- Moving left requires subtracting from the X value.
- Moving right requires adding to the X value.

Note:

You can change the zero point by clicking where the horizontal and vertical rulers meet and dragging to a new position. If you do reposition the zero point, you can double-click the intersection of the rulers to restore the default zero point.

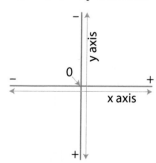

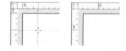

7. Using either the pop-up Transform panel or the option directly in the Control panel, click the top-left reference point to select it.

The X and Y fields now show the exact position of the top-left bounding box handle for the selected object.

8. Highlight the X field and type .5. Press Return/Enter to apply the change.

You don't need to type the measurement unit ("), or the preceding "0". Because the rulers are showing inches, Illustrator automatically applies inches as the unit of value.

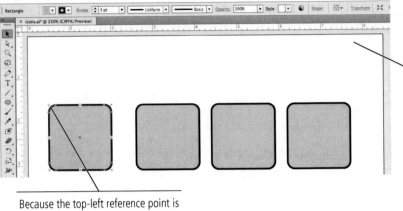

The pop-up panel collapses when you press Return/Enter to apply the change.

Because the top-left reference point is selected, measurements correspond to this point of the selected shape.

If you used the pop-up Transform panel, the panel collapses as soon as you press Return/Enter. You will have to click the Transform link again to complete the next step.

9. Highlight the Y field and type .5. Press Return/Enter to apply the change.

The top-left handle of the selected object is now 1/2″ from the top and left edges. The numbers you typed correspond to the measurements you see on the rulers.

As with dialog boxes, you can enter values in a unit of measurement other than the default, as long as you remember to type the unit abbreviation.

Rulers show that the selected point of the object is at X: 0.5″, Y: 0.5″.

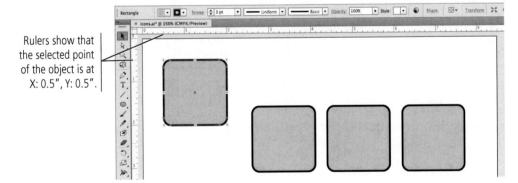

10. **Using the Selection tool, click the second rectangle on the artboard and drag until a green line appears, connecting the center points of the first and second shapes.**

As you drag the cursor, feedback shows the relative position of the object. In other words, you can see the change (<u>difference</u>) in the object's position, both horizontally (<u>X</u>) and vertically (<u>Y</u>) — hence the "dX" and "dY" values.

In addition to providing cursor feedback, Smart Guides can be very useful for aligning objects on the artboard. As you drag, Illustrator identifies and highlights relative alignment, and snaps objects to those alignment points as you drag.

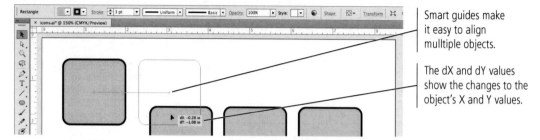

Smart guides make it easy to align mulltiple objects.

The dX and dY values show the changes to the object's X and Y values.

11. **Release the mouse button while the center Smart Guide is visible.**

If you don't see the alignment guides as you drag, make sure that option is checked in the Smart Guides preferences.

12. **Click the fourth shape on the page. In the Control or Transform panel, select the top-right reference point, type 8 in the X field, and type .5 in the Y field.**

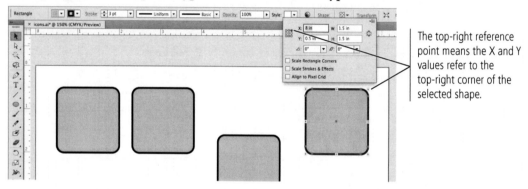

The top-right reference point means the X and Y values refer to the top-right corner of the selected shape.

Because you changed the reference point, you defined the X/Y position for the top-right bounding box handle of the fourth rectangle.

13. **Save the file and continue to the next exercise.**

ALIGN AND DISTRIBUTE OBJECTS

In addition to dragging objects around the artboard, the Illustrator Align panel makes it very easy to align and distribute selected objects relative to one another, to a specific key object in the file, or to the overall artboard. In this exercise, you learn how to use the Align panel to align shapes.

1. **With icons.ai open, click and drag with the Selection tool to draw a marquee that touches some part of all four objects on the artboard.**

   The Selection tool selects objects, so the selection marquee only needs to touch the objects you want to select. The marquee doesn't need to surround the objects entirely.

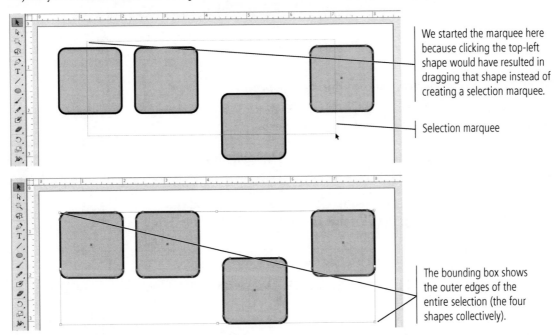

We started the marquee here because clicking the top-left shape would have resulted in dragging that shape instead of creating a selection marquee.

Selection marquee

The bounding box shows the outer edges of the entire selection (the four shapes collectively).

2. **Open the Align panel (Window>Align) and click the Vertical Align Top button.**

   By default, alignment and distribution functions occur relative to the selected objects. In other words, when you click the Vertical Align Top button, Illustrator determines the topmost edge of the selected objects, and then moves the top edges of all other selected objects to that position.

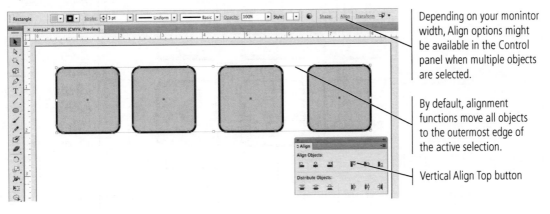

Depending on your monintor width, Align options might be available in the Control panel when multiple objects are selected.

By default, alignment functions move all objects to the outermost edge of the active selection.

Vertical Align Top button

3. **With all four objects selected, click the Horizontal Distribute Center button.**

By default, the distribution functions create equal distance between the selected point of the selected objects. In this case, Illustrator distributed the center points along the horizontal axis by determining the center positions of the outermost selected objects, and then moving the middle two objects to create equal distance between the centers of all four selected objects; the positions of the two outer objects remained unchanged.

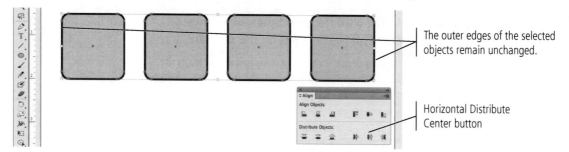

The outer edges of the selected objects remain unchanged.

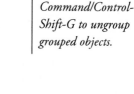

Horizontal Distribute Center button

4. **With all four objects selected, choose Object>Group.**

When you group multiple objects, the group is essentially treated as a single object. A single bounding box surrounds all objects within the group.

5. **Click inside any of the grouped objects; while still holding down the mouse button, press Option/Alt and drag down.**

6. **Use the Smart Guides and cursor feedback to drag exactly vertical (the dX value should be 0). When the dY value in the cursor feedback is 2 in, release the mouse button.**

Remember, pressing Option/Alt while you drag clones the original selection.

Note:

Press Command/Control-G to group selected objects. Press Command/Control-Shift-G to ungroup grouped objects.

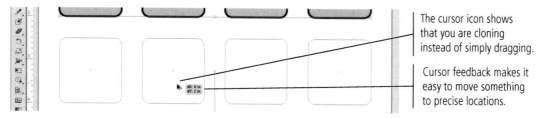

The cursor icon shows that you are cloning instead of simply dragging.

Cursor feedback makes it easy to move something to precise locations.

7. **With the second group of rectangles selected, choose Object>Transform> Transform Again.**

This command repeats the last-used transformation. In this case, the last transformation was the cloning movement, so it creates the third row of rectangles.

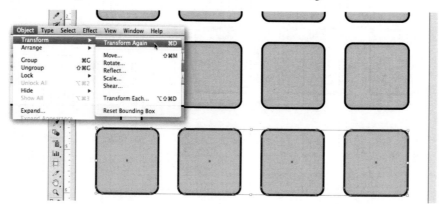

Note:

There is almost always more than one way to accomplish a specific task. The Align panel is useful for certain functions (especially distribution), but Smart Guides make object-to-object alignment very easy.

Note:

Press Command/Control-D to repeat the last-used transformation.

8. **Click anywhere outside the rectangle shapes to deselect all objects and groups.**

9. **Save the file and continue to the next exercise.**

EDIT INDIVIDUAL GROUPED ELEMENTS

The client in this project requested only ten icons, so you don't need two of the rectangles in the third row. As you know, the Selection tool selects entire objects on the page. You also know that grouped objects are treated as a single object — which means you can't use the Selection tool to select part of a group. In this exercise, you use two techniques to work with component pieces of a group.

Note:

Think carefully about your ultimate goal when you group objects, especially for alignment purposes. If the objects in a group don't need to stay together, it's often a good idea to ungroup them.

1. **With icons.ai open, use the Selection tool to click the fourth rectangle in the third row.**

   Because the four objects are grouped, the Selection tool selects the entire group. You need to use a different method to select certain elements within the group.

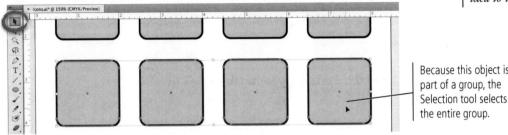

Because this object is part of a group, the Selection tool selects the entire group.

2. **Click anywhere outside the rectangle shapes to deselect the group, then choose the Direct Selection tool in the Tools panel.**

   The Direct Selection tool selects pieces of an object — specific paths, anchor points, or individual elements in a grouped object.

3. **Click the gold fill of the fourth rectangle in the third row.**

   Because you clicked the fill, you selected the entire object. If you had clicked along the object's stroke, you would have selected that particular segment of the shape's edge.

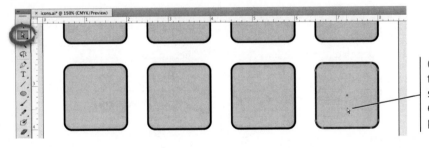

Clicking an object's fill with the Direct Selection tool selects only that object, even though the object is part of a group.

4. **Press Delete to remove the selected object.**

   Easy enough, especially because this is a very simple group of objects that don't overlap. When you start working with complex files that have multiple levels of grouping, however, it can be challenging to manipulate objects within a group using only the Direct Selection tool.

5. **Choose the Selection tool in the Tools panel, and then double-click the third rectangle in the third row.**

Double-clicking a group enters into **Isolation mode**, where only objects within the selected group are available. Basically, Isolation mode provides access to objects in the group without ungrouping the objects on the main artboard.

"Breadcrumbs" in the Edit bar show the path to the active selection.

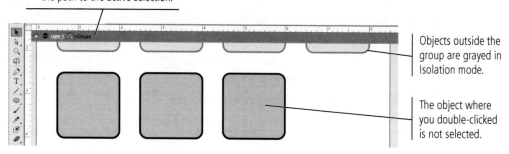

Objects outside the group are grayed in Isolation mode.

The object where you double-clicked is not selected.

6. **Using the Selection tool, click the third rectangle in the third row to select it, and then press Delete.**

Because you created only a single level of grouping, you can now use the Selection tool to select individual objects.

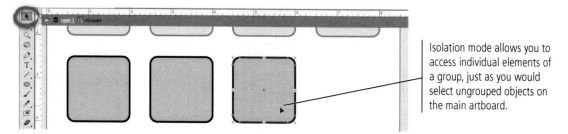

Isolation mode allows you to access individual elements of a group, just as you would select ungrouped objects on the main artboard.

7. **At the top of the document window, click the Arrow button twice to return to the main artboard.**

You can also double-click away from the isolated artwork, or press the ESC key, to exit Isolation mode.

Click this button to exit Isolation mode.

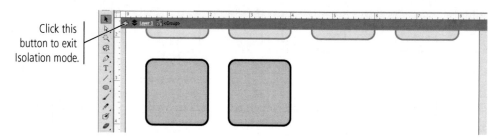

The third row, now with two rectangles, is still a single group on the main artboard.

8. **Save the file and continue to the next exercise.**

ILLUSTRATOR FOUNDATIONS

You can create more than one level of group, called **nesting**, by selecting an existing group and grouping it with other objects or groups. You can use the **Group Selection tool** to help navigate complex levels of nested groups.

The first click with the Group Selection tool selects an individual object in a group. The second click selects that object's containing group. The third click adds the next containing group to the selection, and so on until the entire parent group is selected.

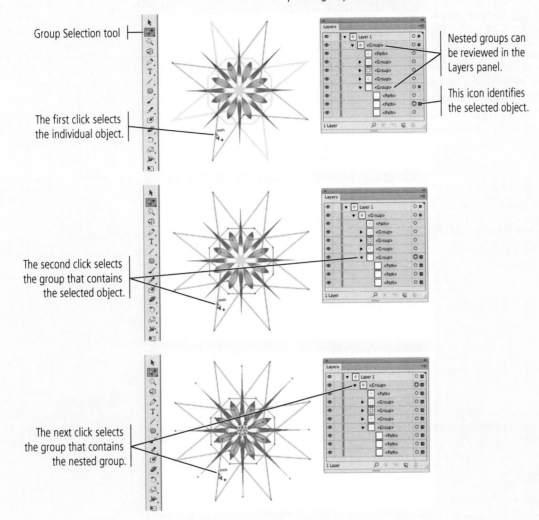

Group Selection tool

The first click selects the individual object.

Nested groups can be reviewed in the Layers panel.

This icon identifies the selected object.

The second click selects the group that contains the selected object.

The next click selects the group that contains the nested group.

IMPORT TEMPLATE IMAGES

Many Illustrator projects require you to start with something that has already been captured — a sketch, photograph, or low-resolution image (which is the case in this project). Illustrator makes it easy to place existing digital files to use as templates for your new artwork. You will use this feature in this exercise.

1. **With icons.ai open, choose File>Place. Navigate to your WIP>Symbols folder and click cold.tif to select that file.**

2. **At the bottom of the Place dialog box, check the Template option.**

   If you check the Link option, the placed file does not become a part of the actual file where you're working; for the file to output properly, Illustrator must be able to locate the linked file in the same location (hard drive, CD, etc.) as when you placed it. If the Link option is *not* checked, the placed file is **embedded** — it becomes part of the file where it's placed; the original external file is not necessary for the artwork to output properly. We will explore the details of placed files in later projects.

   In the case of this project, you are going to delete the template images after you create the artwork; it doesn't matter if the images are linked or embedded.

   When you place an object as a template, it's added to the file on a separate, non-printing layer that is partially grayed, making it easier to work with.

Make sure this option is checked.

If this option is checked, the placed file is not stored (embedded) as a part of your Illustrator file.

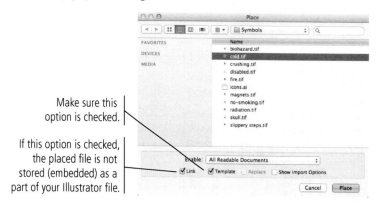

3. **Click Place.**

   When you place an object into Illustrator as a Template, it is automatically centered in the current document window.

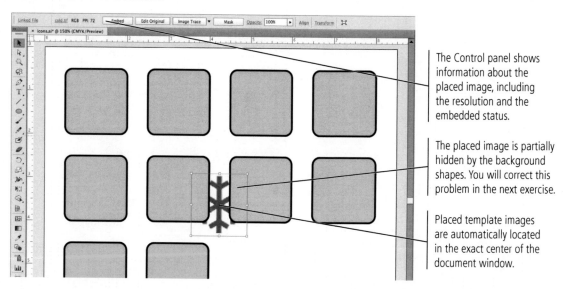

The Control panel shows information about the placed image, including the resolution and the embedded status.

The placed image is partially hidden by the background shapes. You will correct this problem in the next exercise.

Placed template images are automatically located in the exact center of the document window.

4. **Choose File>Place a second time. Select `radiation.tif` in the list, check the Template option, and click Place.**

The Place dialog box remembers the last-used location, so you don't have to re-navigate to the Symbols folder. The Link option also remembers the last-used settings. The Template option, however, always defaults to off, so you have to manually check this box for each template object.

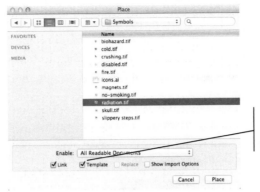

Make sure you remember to check the Template option.

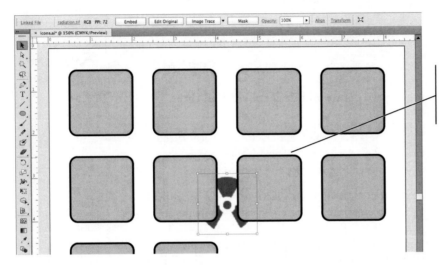

This image is also placed in the center of the document window, directly on top of the first placed image.

Note:

If you change the view percentage or scroll the document in the window before placing the second image, the second file will not be centered over the first. Instead, it will be centered in the docuemnt window based on the current view.

5. **Repeat Step 4 to place `fire.tif` into your file as a template image.**

6. **Save the file and continue to the next exercise.**

MANAGE MULTIPLE LAYERS

When you create artwork in Illustrator, you almost always end up with more than one object on the artboard. In many cases, a completed file has dozens or hundreds of objects, arranged in specific order on top of one another. As files become more and more complex, it can be difficult to find and work with exactly the pieces you need. Illustrator layers are one of the most powerful tools available for solving this problem.

1. **In the open icons.ai file, open the Layers panel.**

   By default, all files have a single layer, named Layer 1. Your file has three additional layers — the template layers — below Layer 1. Template layers are locked by default, which means you can't select or modify objects on those layers.

   Click in this column to show or hide a layer.

   Click in this column to lock or unlock a layer.

   Double-click the layer thumbnail to open the Layer Options dialog box.

   Note:

   If you don't see all three locked template layers, you forgot to check the Template option when you placed one of the images. You can select and delete the placed file from the artboard, then replace the necessary image as a template.

2. **In the Layers panel, click the Layer 1 name and drag it below all three template layers in the stack.**

   The top-to-bottom position of objects or layers is called the **stacking order**. Objects and layers typically appear in the stack based on the order in which they are created — the first-created is at the bottom, the last-created is at the top, and so on in between.

   Placed template objects are the exception; these layers are placed *below* the currently selected layer (i.e., lower in the stacking order). In this case, the rectangle shapes are filled with a color, which obscures the template images on the underlying layers. To see the template images, you need to move the template object layers above the layer containing the background shapes. Rather than moving three layers above Layer 1, you can save a few clicks by moving Layer 1 below all of the template layers.

   Note:

   For a template layer, the Visibility icon is a small square instead of an eye.

   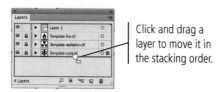

   Click and drag a layer to move it in the stacking order.

3. **Using the Selection tool, click the top-left rounded rectangle to select it.**

   Remember, this object is grouped with the other rectangles in the same row. You need to align the placed object to only the first rectangle, which means you need to be able to select only that object.

   As you saw in an earlier exercise, you can use Isolation mode to access a single element of a group. However, each rectangle shape is ultimately going to be a separate icon; you're simply creating them all in the same workspace. The best choice here is to simply ungroup the rectangles, returning them to individual objects.

4. **With the top-row group selected, choose Object>Ungroup.**

5. **Click away from the selected objects to deselect them, and then click the top-left rectangle to select that object only.**

   Note:

   Press Command/Control-Shift-G to ungroup objects in a group.

6. **In the Layers panel, click the Lock icon for the Template cold.tif layer.**

   Because you need to move the placed template object into the correct position, you first need to unlock the layer.

7. **With the Selection tool still active, press Shift and click anywhere inside the area where the template images are placed.**

   Pressing Shift allows you to add objects to the current selection. The first rectangle and the image should both be selected. (Remember, the other two template object layers are still locked. Even though you can't see it, you can select the cold.tif image by clicking in the area where it is placed.)

8. **With both objects selected, click the Align To button in the Control panel.**

Click this button to access the Align To options.

The placed template images are stacked on top of each other in the order you placed them.

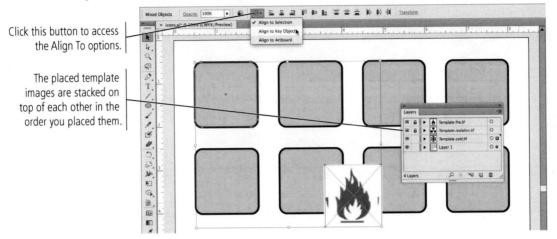

9. **Choose Align to Key Object in the menu.**

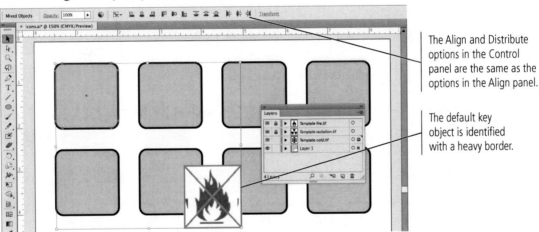

The Align and Distribute options in the Control panel are the same as the options in the Align panel.

The default key object is identified with a heavy border.

10. **Click the selected rounded rectangle on the artboard.**

   Key Object alignment allows you to define where you want other objects to align. By selecting the key object, you're telling Illustrator which object to use as the basis for alignment.

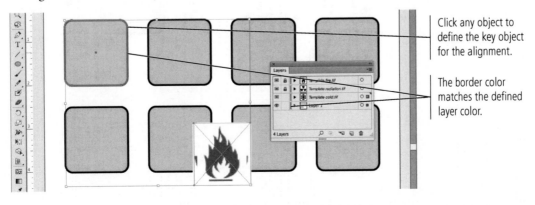

Click any object to define the key object for the alignment.

The border color matches the defined layer color.

11. **Click the Horizontal Align Center and Vertical Align Center buttons in the Control panel.**

    Because you selected the rounded rectangle as the key object, the placed template image moves to the horizontal and vertical center of the rounded rectangle; the rectangle — the key object — remains in the same place.

12. **In the Layers panel, click the empty space to the left of the Template cold.tif layer to relock that layer.**

    Now that the template object is in place, it's a good idea to lock it again so you don't accidentally move the object.

13. **Double-click the layer thumbnail of the Template cold.tif layer.**

    Double-clicking a layer thumbnail opens the Layer Options dialog box for that layer, where you can change a number of attributes for the selected layer.

14. **Change the Dim Images To field to 30, and then click OK to close the Layer Options dialog box.**

    Dimming the template image will make it easier to see your artwork when you draw.

15. Repeat Steps 6–14 to position the other two template images in the first-row rectangles (as shown in the following image).

16. In the Layers panel, double-click the Layer 1 name to highlight the name. Type Background Shapes to change the layer name, then press Return/Enter.

Whenever you have more than one working layer, it's a good idea to use names that tell you what is on each layer. Doing so prevents confusion later when you or someone else needs to change a particular item.

Double-click the layer name to highlight it, so you can type a new name.

Press Return/Enter to finalize the new layer name.

17. In the Layers panel, click the empty space immediately left of the Background Shapes layer.

This step — locking the Background Shapes layer — is simply a safeguard to avoid accidentally changing the background rectangles while you're drawing the icon artwork.

Lock the Background Shapes layer to protect the objects on that layer.

18. In the Layers panel, click the Create New Layer button.

In the next stage of the project, you will start tracing the object in the template. The completed icon will be a black icon on top of the rounded rectangle with the gold background color.

Create New Layer button

At this point, most of the gold color in the background shapes is obscured by the placed images, because the template layers are above the layer containing the rectangles. If you tried to draw the icon shapes on the existing non-template layer, you would be drawing *behind* the template — in other words, you wouldn't be able to see what you were drawing. Instead, you need a layer above the template layers, where you can create the icon artwork.

19. In the Layers panel, drag Layer 5 to the top of the layer stack.

New layers are automatically placed immediately above the selected layer. You need this new layer to be above the template layers so you can see what you're drawing.

20. **Double-click the Layer 5 thumbnail in the Layers panel. In the Layer Options dialog box, change the layer name to Icon Art and choose Magenta from the Color menu, then click OK.**

The Color option has nothing to do with the stroke or fill colors used in the artwork on that layer; instead, it simply determines the color of bounding box handles and other visual indicators for objects on a layer. (The default for Layer 5, Yellow, can be very difficult to see. We chose Magenta because it shows better in our screen shots.)

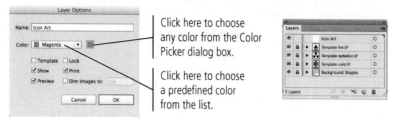

Click here to choose any color from the Color Picker dialog box.

Click here to choose a predefined color from the list.

21. **Save the file and continue to the next stage of the project.**

Stage 2 Drawing Basic Shapes

If you remember from the client meeting, the client's bitmap icons work fine on the Web, but they look terrible in print. After you redraw the icons in Illustrator, the client will be able to print them anywhere, with no loss in quality — which is the primary advantage of vector-based artwork vs. raster-based images. A number of tools and utilities can be used to create complex Illustrator artwork. Creating the icons in this project gives you an opportunity to experiment with some of these options. As you complete the other projects in this book, you will delve deeper into complex drawing techniques.

 CREATE ARTWORK WITH LINES

The snowflake icon is really nothing more than a series of straight lines — which makes it ideal for introducing the Line Segment tool. In this exercise, you create simple lines, and then use some basic modification techniques to create the final icon.

1. **With icons.ai open, make sure the Icon Art layer is selected. Zoom in to the top-left rectangle (with the snowflake image).**

2. **In the Tools panel, select the Line Segment tool, and then click the Default Fill and Stroke button.**

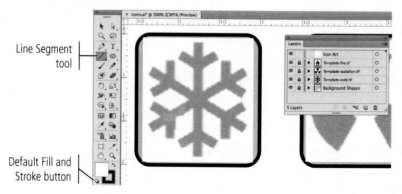

Line Segment tool

Default Fill and Stroke button

3. **Click at the bottom of the vertical line in the snowflake image, and then drag up to the top of the snowflake image. Release the mouse button while the cursor feedback shows the line at 90°.**

As you drag, the cursor feedback shows the length and — more importantly in this case — the angle of the line you're drawing. If you don't see the cursor feedback, choose View>Smart Guides to toggle on that option.

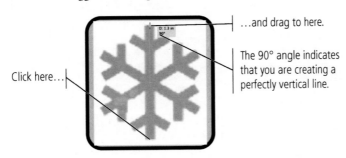

...and drag to here.

The 90° angle indicates that you are creating a perfectly vertical line.

Click here...

Note:

You can also press Shift to constrain a line to increments of 45°.

4. **With the Line Segment tool still active, click the cursor on the top of the left flake branch in the template image; while holding down the mouse button, drag down and right until you see the word "path" appear near the cursor, then release the mouse button.**

The word "path" is another function of Illustrator's Smart Guides; when you drag near an existing path, Illustrator identifies the path so you can place a point exactly on top of the existing path.

Click here and hold down the mouse button...

...drag to here, and then release the mouse button.

The word "path" is a function of Smart Guides.

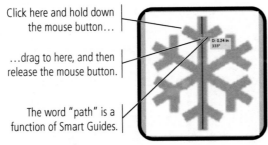

5. **Move the cursor to the top of the right flake branch until you see a green line connecting to the top of the left branch that you drew in Step 4.**

6. **Click and hold the mouse button, drag down and left until the word "anchor" appears next to the cursor, and then release the mouse button.**

The "anchor" label indicates that you have dragged to the position of an existing anchor point (in this case, the endpoint of the left flake branch). As you can see, Illustrator makes it easy to create precise lines and shapes in relation to other objects on the page.

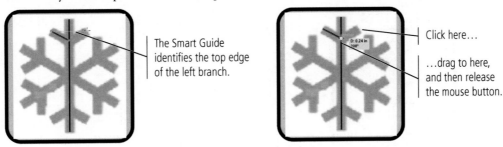

The Smart Guide identifies the top edge of the left branch.

Click here...

...drag to here, and then release the mouse button.

7. **Choose the Selection tool from the Tools panel, and then click the vertical line that you drew in Step 3. Choose Object>Lock>Selection.**

When an object is locked, you can't select or change it — just as locking a template layer protects the template object from being moved. In the next few steps, you select and join the endpoints of the two angled lines, which is much easier if the vertical line can't be selected (you want the vertical line to remain unchanged).

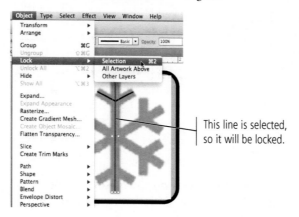

This line is selected, so it will be locked.

8. **Using the Direct Selection tool, drag a marquee around the bottom points of both angled lines.**

You want to join the lines' endpoints, so you need to select only those specific points (instead of the entire lines). As mentioned earlier, you need the Direct Selection tool to select specific points on a path.

Direct Selection tool

Click in an empty area to start drawing the selection marquee.

The marquee should surround the endpoints of these two lines.

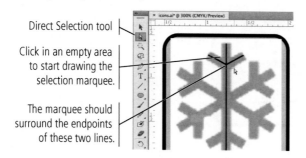

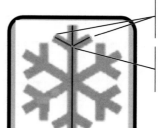

These anchor points are hollow, which means they are not selected.

These anchor points are solid, which means they are selected.

9. **Choose Object>Path>Join.**

This command connects any two selected open endpoints. If the selected points overlap, as in this exercise, the two points are simply combined into a single corner endpoint. If the two selected points do not overlap, Illustrator automatically connects them with a straight line segment.

10. **Choose the Selection tool to reveal the bounding box for the selected object.**

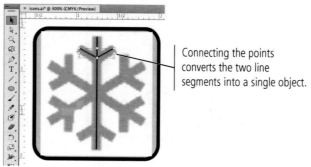

Connecting the points converts the two line segments into a single object.

11. **Save the file and continue to the next exercise.**

REFLECT DRAWING OBJECTS

Illustrator includes four important transformation tools — Rotate, Reflect, Scale, and Shear. Each of these transformations can be applied by hand using the related tool in the Tools panel, as well as numerically using the appropriate dialog box from the Object>Transform menu.

Much of the work you do in Illustrator requires changing objects that already exist. In this exercise, you use reflection to create additional sections of the snowflake icon.

1. **With icons.ai open, choose the Selection tool in the Tools panel. Make sure the angled-branch object is selected on the artboard.**

   Because the Selection tool is active, you can now see the bounding box of the selected object — both angled lines, which have been joined into a single object.

2. **Choose Object>Transform>Reflect.**

   You can reflect objects around the vertical or horizontal axis at specific degrees. In this case, you want to make the branches at the bottom of the snowflake, so you need to reflect the object around the horizontal axis.

3. **In the Reflect dialog box, make sure the Preview check box is active.**

   The Preview option, which is available in all of the Illustrator transformation dialog boxes, allows you to see the effects of your changes before you commit them.

4. **Choose the Horizontal option and click Copy.**

   If you click OK in any of the transformation dialog boxes, the transformation directly affects the selected object. Because you want another branch for the bottom of the flake, you are using the Copy function instead of simply clicking OK.

When Preview is checked, you can see the result of clicking OK.

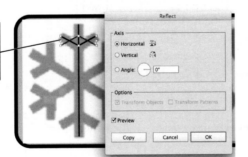

The original object remains in position.

The Copy option reflects the new object.

5. **With the Selection tool still active, click the reflected branches and drag them to the bottom of the flake. Place the object appropriately, using the template image as a guide.**

   Again, the Smart Guides help you place the object; the green line and cursor feedback show the angle at which you're moving the selected object, so you can more easily maintain the same horizontal position.

Use cursor feedback to move the shape to the exact horizontal position (dX = 0).

Note:

Reflecting on the horizontal axis flips the object top over bottom. Reflecting around the vertical axis flips the object left to right.

6. Choose Object>Unlock All.

Remember, you locked the original vertical line to protect it while you worked with the endpoints of the angled branches. Now that you have one complete set of branches, you can use the existing objects to create the remaining icon elements — which means you need to unlock the vertical line so you can access and copy it.

7. Choose Select>All.

All three objects — the vertical line and the two branch objects — are now selected.

8. In the Control panel, change the stroke width to 7 pt.

9. Choose Object>Group.

Because these three objects are basically a single entity in the icon, it's a good idea to treat them as a single object.

10. Save the file and continue to the next exercise.

 ROTATE DRAWING OBJECTS

Very few projects are entirely horizontal, making rotating objects a foundational Illustrator skill. In this exercise, you use several rotation techniques to create the rest of the snowflake artwork.

1. With icons.ai open, make sure the grouped object is selected.

2. Activate the Rotate tool in the Tools panel.

When you select the Rotate tool, an **origin point** appears by default at the center of the selected object. This origin point is the point around which rotation occurs. If you want to rotate an object around some other point, you can single-click anywhere to define a different origin point.

Origin point for rotation

Rotate tool

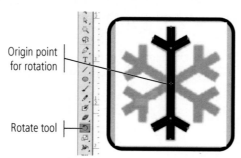

3. **Click near the top of the vertical line, hold down the mouse button, and then drag left and down until the line appears over the next branch in the snowflake. Note the angle in the cursor feedback, and then release the mouse button.**

As you can see, the rotation moved the selected objects around the origin point. Unfortunately, the vertical line is no longer there because you just rotated it.

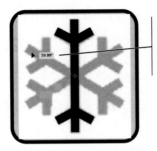

When you drag with the Rotate tool, the cursor feedback shows the angle of rotation.

When you release the mouse button, the original object rotates.

Note:

You can Option/Alt-click and drag to clone an object while you transform it. In other words, if you press Option/Alt while dragging with the Rotate tool, you can create a rotated copy.

4. **Press Command/Control-Z to undo the rotation.**

5. **With the group still selected, double-click the Rotate tool to open the Rotate dialog box.**

This dialog box is the same one you would see by choosing Object>Transform>Rotate. Transformation dialog boxes, which default to the last-used settings for that transformation, make it easy to apply very specific numeric transformations to selected objects.

6. **Type 60 in the Rotate field, and then click Copy.**

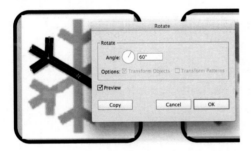

7. **Choose Object>Transform>Transform Again to create the third branch of the snowflake icon.**

As before, the Transform Again command repeats the last-used transformation — in this case, the copy-rotate transformation from Step 6.

8. **Choose Select>All. Using the Align or Control panel, click the Vertical Align Center and Horizontal Align Center buttons.**

Because each "branch" is a group, the three sets of branches are now exactly centered in both directions. This step might not cause a noticeable change, depending on how precisely you placed the lines, but it's a good idea to be certain that the groups align properly.

Note:

The Transform Again command applies the last-used transformation of any type to a selected object without opening a dialog box. This command might result in movement, rotation, reflection, shear, or scale, depending on the last transformation you applied.

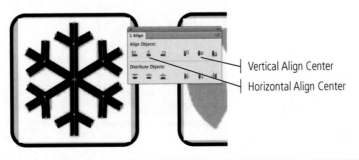

Vertical Align Center

Horizontal Align Center

9. **With all snowflake objects selected, choose Object>Lock>Selection.**

10. **In the Layers panel, select the Template cold.tif layer and click the Delete Selection button at the bottom of the panel. Click Yes in the confirmation message.**

   Since the snowflake drawing is complete, you no longer need the template image.

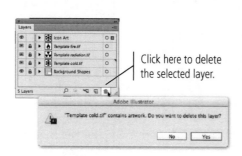

Click here to delete the selected layer.

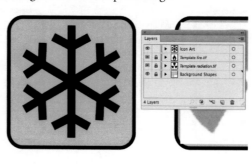

11. **Save the file and continue to the next exercise.**

DIVIDE BASIC SHAPES INTO COMPONENT PIECES

Using the Illustrator Pathfinder panel, you can combine multiple shapes in a variety of ways, or you can use one object as a "cookie cutter" to remove or separate one shape from another. As you work with more complicated artwork in Illustrator, you will find many different ways to use the Pathfinder functions, either alone or in combination.

1. **With icons.ai open, make sure the Icon Art layer is selected in the Layers panel. Zoom into the second rectangle in the first row of background shapes.**

2. **Select the Ellipse tool (nested under the Rounded Rectangle tool) in the Tools panel. Set the fill color to black and the stroke color to None.**

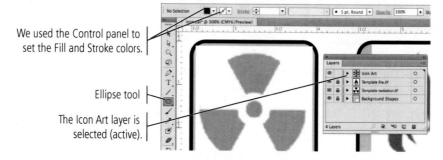

We used the Control panel to set the Fill and Stroke colors.

Ellipse tool

The Icon Art layer is selected (active).

3. **Click in the center of the radiation icon, press Option/Alt-Shift, and then drag to create a circle that covers the entire template icon.**

   Remember, pressing Option/Alt allows you to draw a shape from the center out. Pressing Shift constrains the shape to equal height and width.

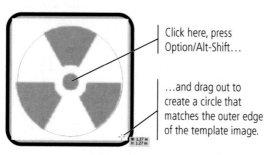

Click here, press Option/Alt-Shift...

...and drag out to create a circle that matches the outer edge of the template image.

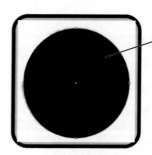

The fill color appears when you release the mouse button.

Note:

The fill color does not appear until you release the mouse button.

4. **With the new circle selected, change the Opacity field in the Control panel to 50.**

Opacity defines the transparency of the selected object. In this case, you're reducing the opacity from 100% (entirely solid or opaque) so you can see the template image behind the circle you just drew.

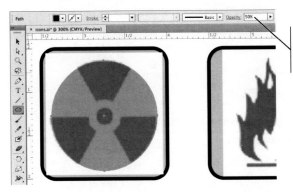

Change the shape's Opacity value so you can see the underlying template image.

Note:

You can also use the Transparency panel to change an object's opacity.

5. **Using the Ellipse tool, click again in the center of the template image, press Option/Alt-Shift, and drag to create the smaller circle in the center of the shape.**

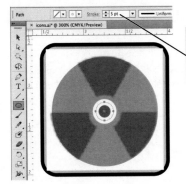

By default, the Opacity value resets to 100% for new objects.

The Fill and Stroke values remember the last-used settings.

The second circle has a black fill, no stroke, and 100% opacity.

6. **With the smaller circle selected, change the fill color to None and the stroke color to white. Change the stroke weight to 5 pt.**

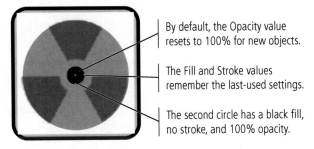

We used the Control panel to change the Fill and Stroke attributes for the selected object.

7. **Open the Stroke panel (Window>Stroke). If you only see the Stroke Weight field, open the panel's Options menu and choose Show Options.**

Because you used the template image to draw the small circle shape, the default position of the path does not accomplish the goal of creating the white ring. You can use the Stroke panel options to change the position of the stroke relative to the path, which better meets your needs in this artwork.

Click here to open the panel Options menu.

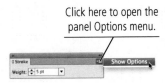

8. **With the small circle selected, click the Align Stroke to Outside button in the Stroke panel.**

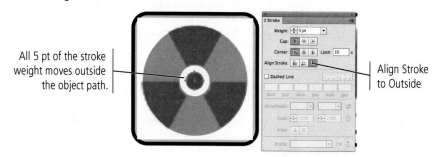

All 5 pt of the stroke weight moves outside the object path.

Align Stroke to Outside

9. **Press and hold Command/Control to temporarily access the Selection tool, and click away from the existing shapes to deselect them.**

If you don't deselect the circle, changing the Fill and Stroke attributes in the next step will change the attributes of the selected shape.

10. **Choose the Line Segment tool in the Tools panel, and then click the Default Fill and Stroke button at the bottom of the Tools panel.**

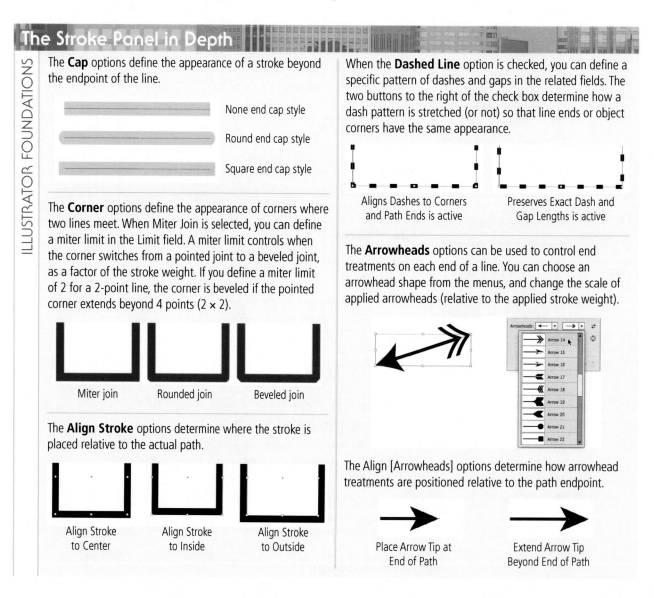

11. **Move the cursor below the circles you created until you see the Smart Guide connecting to the existing shapes' center points. Click and drag up to create a vertical line that extends past the top edge of the outer circle.**

Note:

To create the vertical line, use the cursor feedback to drag a 90° line, or press Shift to constrain the line to 90°.

Although none of the icon wedges have a vertical line, it's easier to start at vertical and rotate the objects as necessary.

Clicking the Default Fill and Stroke button in the Tools panel resets the options in the Control panel.

Line Segment tool

Smart Guides indicate when you are in line with the center of the existing circles.

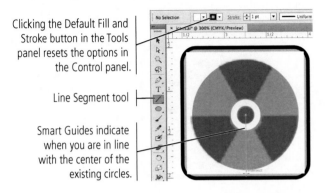

Extend the line past the top of the outer circle.

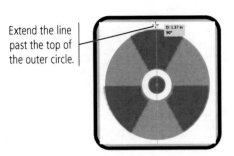

12. **Using the Selection tool, draw a marquee around the three objects that you have created to select them all. Use the options in the Align or Control panel to align the selected objects horizontally and vertically.**

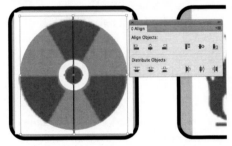

13. **Click away from the selected objects, and then select only the vertical line.**

The icon has six wedges, which means each half of the circle needs to be divided into three pieces. You will use precise rotation to slice the larger circle into the necessary parts.

14. **With the vertical line selected, choose Object>Transform>Rotate. Type 60 in the Angle field and click Copy.**

This menu command has the same result as double-clicking the Rotate tool, but you don't have to switch tools.

A full circle has 360 degrees. You're cutting the circle into six equal pieces; one sixth of 360° is 60°, so this is the exact angle that you need to create the correct number of pieces.

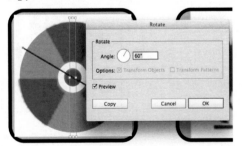

15. **Choose Object>Transform>Transform Again to make a third line.**

The Transform Again command applies the last-used transformation of any type to a selected object without opening a dialog box. Because you used the Rotate dialog box with the Copy button in the previous step, the Transform Again command copies the current selection and rotates it by the same angle you used in Step 14.

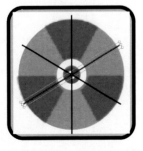

16. Using the Selection tool, select the smaller circle only and choose Object>Path>Outline Stroke.

This command changes the object stroke to a filled object. You drew the white circle to "cut out" the smaller black circle from the wedges. The Pathfinder functions recognize strokes for cutting apart shapes, but the stroke weight is not considered when the new paths are generated. To create the thick white space in the actual icon, you need to convert the heavy stroke to a filled shape.

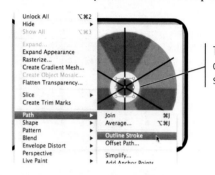

The original object had a 5-pt stroke weight.

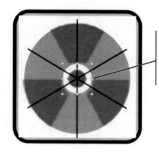

The Outline Stroke command changes the selected object to a filled shape with no visible stroke attributes.

17. Select all the objects in the icon, and then open the Pathfinder panel (Window>Pathfinder).

You can drag a marquee with the Selection tool, or choose Select>All. Because you locked the snowflake artwork in the first icon, those objects are not selected.

Note:

Press Command/ Control-A to select all unlocked objects on the artboard.

18. In the Pathfinder panel, click the Divide button.

Options in the Pathfinder panel allow you to cut shapes out of other shapes and merge multiple shapes into a single shape.

It's important to realize that many Pathfinder options can be applied in more than one way. We're using the Divide and Unite options in this exercise to give you an idea of what you can accomplish with the Pathfinder.

Divide button

The Divide function slices apart all possible shapes of the selected objects. Everywhere two objects overlap, a new shape is created.

Because the straight lines are open shapes, they divide the circles into sixths, but the open ends of the lines (outside the area of the larger circle) are removed.

19. Save the file and continue to the next exercise.

ILLUSTRATOR FOUNDATIONS

In the Pathfinder panel, the top row of buttons — the Shape Modes — create complex shapes by combining the originally selected shapes. (You can press Option/Alt and click a Shape Mode to maintain the paths from the original objects.)

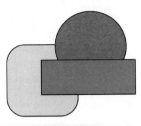

Original objects

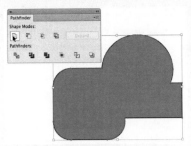

Unite combines all selected objects into a single shape. By default, the Shape options result in a single new object.

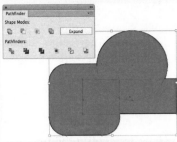

If you Option/Alt-click a shape mode button, the result maintains the original paths unless you manually expand it.

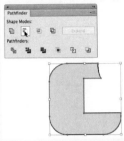

Minus Front removes overlapping areas from the backmost shape in the selection.

Intersect creates a shape of only areas where all selected objects overlap.

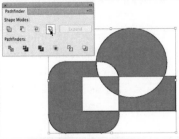

Exclude removes any areas where two objects overlap.

The second row of options — the Pathfinders — do exactly that. The resulting shapes are some combination of the paths that made up the originally selected objects.

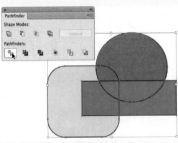

Divide creates separate shapes from all overlapping areas of selected objects.

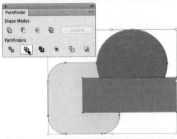

Trim removes underlying areas of overlapping objects. Objects of the same fill color are not combined.

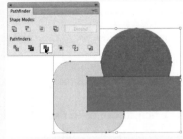

Merge removes underlying areas of overlapping objects. Objects of the same fill color are combined.

Crop returns the areas of underlying objects that are within the boundary of the topmost object.

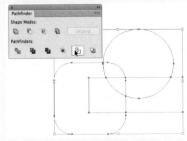

Outline divides the selected objects, then returns unfilled, open paths.

Minus Back removes the area of underlying objects from the front object.

WORK IN ISOLATION MODE

Groups can be invaluable when you need to treat multiple items as a single object. When items are grouped, it is easy to move and manipulate the entire group as a single object. In many cases, however, you will need to make changes to only part of a group. Depending on the complexity of the file, this can be very difficult without first breaking apart the group ("ungrouping"). Illustrator's Isolation mode offers a convenient workspace, where you can work with grouped objects as if they were stand-alone objects.

1. **With icons.ai open, hide the Template radiation.tif layer.**

2. **Use the Selection tool to double-click any of the shapes in the radiation icon to enter Isolation mode.**

   When you use the Pathfinder panel, the resulting shapes are automatically grouped. Because all of these shapes make up the icon artwork, it's a good idea to leave them grouped. Isolation mode allows you to work with the constituent objects without ungrouping.

3. **Using the Selection tool, click the outer wedge shape in the top-left area of the icon, and then press Delete.**

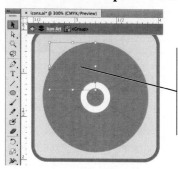   Because you're working in Isolation mode, you can use the Selection tool to select one object, even though the object is part of a group on the main artboard.

4. **Select and delete every other wedge in the outside area of the group.**

5. **Choose View>Outline.**

   Outline mode allows you to see and work with the basic shapes only; object fills don't obscure the shapes that you need to see clearly.

6. **Click in the center set of wedges and drag a marquee that encompasses the center points of all six center wedges.**

   If you tried to do this in Preview mode, clicking one of the filled shapes and dragging would actually move the shape you clicked. Because the fills are not technically present in Outline mode, you can use the click-drag method to select all six shapes instead of Shift-clicking each one individually.

   Be sure you don't click on any actual line when you begin to draw the selection marquee. If necessary, zoom in so you can clearly see the empty spaces in the small wedge shapes.

Note:

If the template layer was visible, it would show crossed diagonal lines through the file area. Because this would confuse the issue of which lines you want to select here, you hid the template layer in Step 1.

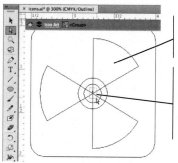   In Outline mode, you can't see or interact with the objects' Fill attributes.

   Because you can't select an object's fill, you can drag a selection marquee to select only the six small shapes in the icon center.   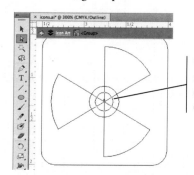   When you release the mouse button, you can see that all six objects are selected.

7. In the Pathfinder panel, click the Unite button.

This function merges the selected shapes into a single object.

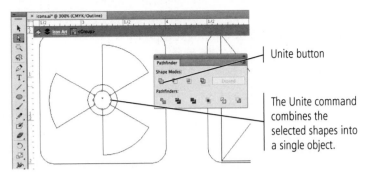

Unite button

The Unite command combines the selected shapes into a single object.

8. Choose View>Preview to exit Outline mode and display the normal artwork.

9. Using the Selection tool, click the fill of one of the white shapes to select it, then choose Select>Same>Fill Color.

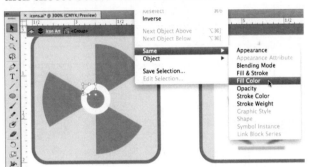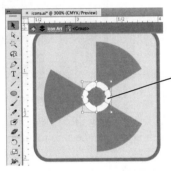

All six white-filled objects are selected because the original selection had a white fill.

10. With all six white shapes in the icon selected, press Delete.

11. Using the Selection tool, click to select any one of the black (partially transparent) objects, then choose Select>Same>Opacity.

The options in this menu are very useful for finding objects that share specific attributes.

12. Change the Opacity (in the Control panel) to 100 for the selected objects.

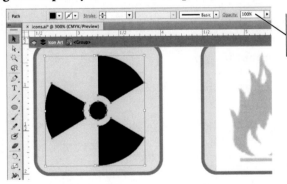

Use this field to restore the artwork to 100% opacity.

13. At the top of the document window, click the arrow button twice to return to the main artboard.

Your icon is almost complete; you only need to rotate the shape to match the image.

14. Save the file and continue to the next exercise.

Note:

You can also use the Select Similar Objects menu in the Control panel to select objects with like attributes.

Note:

Be careful when you use the Select Similar functions. They select all similar unlocked objects on the entire artboard. If the art for another unlocked icon had a white fill, for example, it would also be selected.

USE MEASUREMENTS TO ADJUST YOUR ARTWORK

Depending on the type of work you do, Illustrator drawings can be entirely freeform, precisely measured, or a combination of the two (as in this case). The Measure tool evaluates different dimensional attributes of objects on the page. As you might expect from the name, the Measure tool acts like a digital tape measure. In addition to sizes and positions, the tool also measures angles — an important feature for technical drawing that requires precise detail.

1. **With icons.ai open, show the Template radiation.tif layer.**

2. **Choose the Measure tool in the Tools panel (under the Eyedropper tool).**

3. **Click at the outside corner of the left wedge, and then drag down and right along the shape edge (as shown in the following image).**

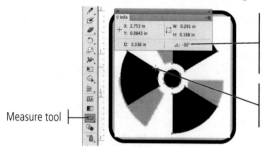

Measure tool

When you use the Measure tool, measurements appear in the Info panel (which opens automatically).

Click and drag along this line (down and right) to find the angle of the line.

Note:

If you drag from the inside out, the Info panel shows an angle of 150°. This provides the same information, because 180° — your goal — minus 150° equals 30°.

The Measure tool tells you that the angle of this line is –30°. You need it to be 180° (horizontal), which means you need to rotate the shape by 30°.

4. **Select the group with the Selection tool, and then choose Object>Transform>Rotate.**

5. **Change the Angle field to 30 and click OK.**

6. **In the Layers panel, delete the Template radiation.tif layer.**

7. **Center the radiation icon artwork in the background shape if necessary, then choose Object>Lock>Selection.**

This step protects the completed icon artwork from inadvertently being changed while you work on the rest of this project.

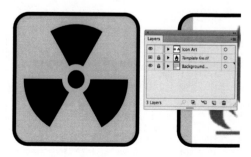

8. **Save the file and continue to the next exercise.**

DRAW WITH THE PENCIL TOOL

At this point, you have used a number of basic shapes to create finished icon artwork. As you might already realize, however, not all artwork can be created from basic shapes and lines. Illustrator includes everything you need to create artwork in any form, from a basic square to irregular shapes without a single visible straight edge. The Pencil tool is one method for creating custom shapes. Like a regular pencil on a piece of paper, the Pencil tool creates lines that follow the path of your cursor. (If you have a digital drawing tablet, the Pencil tool can be particularly useful for drawing custom artwork.)

1. **With icons.ai open, make sure the Icon Art layer is selected in the Layers panel. Zoom in to the third rectangle in the first row of background shapes.**

2. **Choose the Pencil tool and click the Default Fill and Stroke button in the Tools panel.**

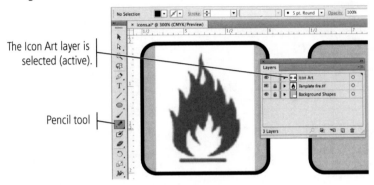

The Icon Art layer is selected (active).

Pencil tool

3. **Double-click the Pencil tool in the Tools panel.**

   Double-clicking certain tools in the Tools panel opens an Options dialog box, where you can control the default behavior for the selected tool. The Pencil tool options include:

   - **Fidelity.** This option determines how far apart anchor points are added as you drag. Smooth results in fewer points and smoother curves, but also less accurately matching the path you draw. More accurate means more anchor points and a path closer to what you draw, although this can make the lines appear choppy.

   - **Fill New Pencil Strokes.** By default, pencil paths are not filled regardless of the fill color defined in the Tools panel.

   - **Keep Selected.** If this option is checked, the line you draw is automatically selected when you release the mouse button.

   - **Option Key Toggles to Smooth Tool.** As the name suggests, this allows you to quickly and temporarily switch to the Smooth tool while drawing with the Pencil tool. (The Smooth tool can be used to remove unnecessary points along a pencil-drawn path, removing small or jagged jumps in the path.)

   - **Edit Selected Paths.** If this option is checked, drawing near a selected path (based on the Within value) can change the existing path. This is an important distinction — especially when Keep Selected is checked — because you can accidentally edit the first path instead of creating a second shape.

4. **Set the Fidelity slider to the midpoint, uncheck all options in the lower half of the dialog box, then click OK.**

5. **Click at the bottom-left point of the fire icon, hold down the mouse button, and begin dragging around the shape of the fire.**

6. **When you get near your original starting point and a hollow circle appears in the cursor icon, release the mouse button.**

   As you drag, a colored line indicates the path you're drawing. Don't worry if the path isn't perfect; when you release the mouse button, Illustrator automatically smoothes the path.

   When you release the mouse button, the shape shows the defined stroke color but not the fill color because you unchecked the Fill New Pencil Strokes option in Step 4.

Drag to trace the shape of the template image.

Click here to start drawing.

The hollow circle in the cursor icon indicates that releasing the mouse button will create a closed shape.

7. **Click near the top point of the white flame area (inside the first path) and drag to create the white inner shape in the fire icon.**

Use the Pencil tool to draw this shape. Press Option/Alt before releasing the mouse button to create a closed shape.

Note:

In previous versions of Illustrator, you had to press Option/Alt to create a closed path with the Pencil tool. This is no longer necessary in the 2014 release of Illustrator CC.

8. **Using the Rectangle tool, draw the gray bar below the fire shape.**

9. **In the Layers panel, delete the Template fire.tif layer.**

10. **Use the Selection tool to select all three shapes of the icon art. Change the fill color to black and the stroke color to None.**

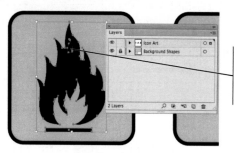

When all three objects are filled, you can't see the inner shape at the top of the flame.

11. **Choose Object>Compound Path>Make.**

   This option combines all three selected shapes into a single shape; the area of the smaller shape is removed from the larger shape behind it.

As a compound path, the inner shape is removed from the outer shape.

Note:

*A **compound path** is a single shape made up of more than one path. Compound paths usually have inner "empty" areas, such as the letter O or Q.*

12. **Save the file and close it.**

fill in the blank

1. _____ are composed of mathematical descriptions of a series of lines and points; they are resolution independent, can be freely scaled, and are automatically output at the resolution of the output device.

2. _____ are pixel-based, made up of a grid of individual pixels (rasters or bits) in rows and columns.

3. The _____ is a rectangle that marks the outermost edges of an object, regardless of the actual object shape.

4. _____ is the relative top-to-botom order of objects on the artboard, or of layers in the Layers panel.

5. The _____ is used to select entire objects or groups.

6. The _____ is used to select individual paths and points of a shape, or to select component pieces within a group.

7. The _____ is used to draw freeform paths defined by dragging the mouse cursor.

8. Press _____ to temporarily access the Selection tool; releasing the modifier key restores the previously selected tool.

9. The _____ is used to create complex shapes by combining multiple selected objects.

10. A(n) _____ is a single object that is made up of more than one shape.

short answer

1. Briefly explain the difference between vector graphics and raster images.

2. Briefly explain the difference between the Selection tool and the Direct Selection tool.

3. Briefly explain the difference between Shape Mode and Pathfinder operations in the Pathfinder panel.

Use what you learned in this project to complete the following freeform exercise.
Carefully read the art director and client comments, then create your own design to meet the needs of the project.
Use the space below to sketch ideas; when finished, write a brief explanation of your reasoning behind your final design.

The client is pleased with the first three icons, and they want you to complete the rest of the warning icons. They also want you to create an additional set of icons for travel and outdoor activities that they offer as benefits during their international corporate conferences.

To complete this project, you should:

❏ Complete the remaining international warning icons. The bitmap versions are in your WIP>Symbols folder.

❏ Carefully consider the best approach for each icon and use whichever tool (or tools) you feel is most appropriate.

❏ Create a second Illustrator file for the six new recreation icons.

We host a number of large, international conventions and conferences every year, and many attendees bring their families along for a working vacation. To keep everyone happy, we have started offering different outdoor activities for the families while their spouses are attending sessions, but the international crowd means that many people need visual help getting to the right place.

Since you did such a good job on the first three icons, we would like you to finish those. But first, we want you to create icons for horseback riding, sailing, swimming, hiking, rock climbing, and nature walks.

We don't have the images for these ones, so we would like you to come up with something. Remember, icons need to be easily recognizable, so they should very clearly convey visually what each one is for.

_____

_____

_____

_____

_____

_____

_____

_____

_____

_____

_____

_____

The skills that you learned in this project will serve as the foundation for most work you create in Illustrator. You learned how to place raster images as templates, from which you created scalable vector graphics that will work in virtually any printed application. You learned a number of techniques for selecting objects and component pieces of objects, as well as various options for aligning objects relative to one another and to the artboard.

You learned how to draw primitive geometric shapes, and how to control the color of objects' fill and stroke attributes. You used a number of transformation options, including cloning methods to copy existing objects. Finally, you learned how to draw freeform shapes to suit more complex needs. As you move forward in this book, you will build on the basic skills you learned in this project to create increasingly complex artwork.

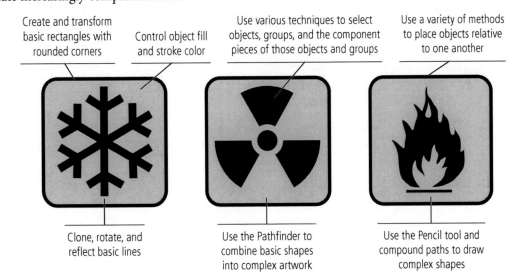

Create and transform basic rectangles with rounded corners

Control object fill and stroke color

Use various techniques to select objects, groups, and the component pieces of those objects and groups

Use a variety of methods to place objects relative to one another

Clone, rotate, and reflect basic lines

Use the Pathfinder to combine basic shapes into complex artwork

Use the Pencil tool and compound paths to draw complex shapes

Regatta Artwork

Your client is the marketing director for the Long Beach Regatta, which attracts tens of thousands of visitors to the beach community throughout the four-day event. You have been hired to create the primary artwork for this year's event, which will be used in a variety of different products (ads, posters, etc.).

This project incorporates the following skills:

❏ Drawing complex custom shapes with the Pen tool

❏ Editing anchor points and handles to control the precise position of vector paths

❏ Drawing irregular shape outlines by painting with the Blob Brush tool

❏ Creating a custom color scheme using saved swatches

❏ Adding interest and depth with color gradients

❏ Adjusting color, both globally and in specific selections

❏ Working with a file that uses Typekit fonts

❏ Saving a PDF file for print distribution

client comments

The poster to promote the Regatta is basically the "play bill," and we will place it in store windows, public sites, and on bulletin boards all over the city. It will also be placed in local newspapers and entertainment magazines, and used as the cover for the souvenir program that we produce for the event.

We want the artwork to be very colorful and vivid, so the main focus — and most of the poster real estate — should be on the graphics. The only text for the poster is the event name, date, and location.

art director comments

I sketched a mock-up of a sailboat that you can use as the basis for the artwork. You should use the Pen tool to draw the necessary paths because simple shapes won't work and the Pencil tool doesn't provide fine enough control to efficiently achieve what you need.

I assigned the ocean background artwork to another designer, so you will have to incorporate your artwork into that file. The poster file includes several text objects that use Adobe Typekit fonts, so you'll have to install those on your computer for the type to appear correctly when you open the file.

This is going to be a complex piece of artwork, so you should pay close attention to the layer content when you organize the various pieces. That will make it far easier to edit specific components as necessary if the client decides to make changes.

project objectives

To complete this project, you will:

❏ Use the Pen tool to draw precise curves

❏ Adjust anchor points and handles to precisely control the shape of vector objects

❏ Reshape line segments with the Anchor Point tool

❏ Use the Blob Brush tool to "paint" the area of vector shapes

❏ Define custom color swatches to allow easy universal changes

❏ Create color gradients to blend multiple colors in a single object

❏ Adjust gradients in context on the artboard

❏ Install fonts from Adobe Typekit

❏ Manage artwork with sublayers

❏ Save the file as PDF

Stage 1 Drawing Complex Artwork

Much of the artwork you create will require far more complexity than simple lines and geometric shapes. When you need to produce custom artwork — whether from scratch or by tracing a hand-drawn sketch or photo — Illustrator includes a powerful set of tools to create and manipulate every point and path in the illustration. In the first stage of this project, you begin exploring the Pen tool, as well as other options for building and controlling custom shapes.

 PREPARE THE DRAWING WORKSPACE

As with any project, setting up the workspace is an important first step. This project requires a single artboard to contain the entire illustration.

1. Download `Regatta_Print14_RF.zip` from the Student Files Web page.

2. **Expand the ZIP archive in your WIP folder (Macintosh) or copy the archive contents into your WIP folder (Windows).**

   This results in a folder named **Regatta**, which contains the files you need for this project. You should also use this folder to save the files you create in this project.

3. **In Illustrator, choose File>New. Type `sailboat` in the Name field, choose Letter in the Size menu, and choose Inches in the Units menu.**

4. **If the Advanced options are not visible, click the right-arrow button to show those options. Choose CMYK in the Color Mode menu and choose High (300 PPI) in the Raster Effects menu.**

   This illustration will be printed in various documents, so you should design the job in the CMYK color mode. Some Illustrator functions, such as effects and gradient meshes, will be rasterized for commercial output; the High (300 PPI) raster effects setting results in sufficient resolution for those elements.

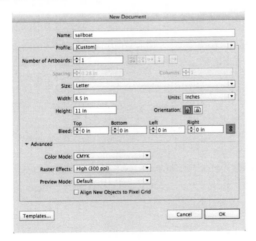

5. **Click OK to create the file.**

6. **Choose File>Place. Navigate to the file sketch.jpg in your WIP>Regatta folder. Make sure the Link option is not checked and the Template option is checked, and then click Place.**

You will use this client-supplied sketch to create the primary artwork for this illustration.

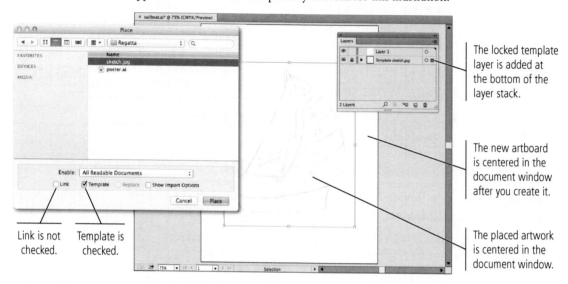

Link is not checked.

Template is checked.

The locked template layer is added at the bottom of the layer stack.

The new artboard is centered in the document window after you create it.

The placed artwork is centered in the document window.

7. **Double-click the template layer icon in the Layers panel to open the Layer Options dialog box. Uncheck the Dim Images option and click OK.**

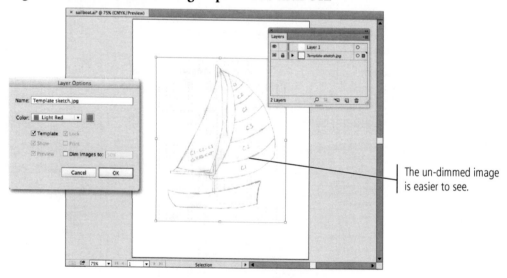

The un-dimmed image is easier to see.

8. **Double-click the Layer 1 name in the Layers panel to highlight it. Rename the layer Boat Drawing, then press Return/Enter to finalize the new name.**

9. **Click away from the placed sketch image to deselect it.**

10. **Save the file as an Illustrator file named sailboat.ai in your WIP>Regatta folder, and then continue to the next exercise.**

USE THE PEN TOOL TO TRACE THE SKETCH

In this project, you use the Pen tool, which provides far more power to control the precise position of every line in a drawing. In fact, many believe the Pen tool is the most powerful and important tool in the Illustrator Tools panel.

Note:

*The lines you create by connecting anchor points and pulling handles are called **Bézier curves**.*

When you draw with the Pen tool, an anchor point marks the end of a line segment, and the point handles determine the shape of that segment. That's the basic definition of a geometric vector. Fortunately, you don't need to be a mathematician to master the Pen tool because Illustrator handles the underlying geometry for you.

Each segment in a path has two anchoring end points and two associated handles. In the image shown to the right, we first clicked to create Point A and dragged to the right (without releasing the mouse button) to create Handle A1. We then clicked and dragged to create Point B and Handle B1; Handle B2 was automatically created as a reflection of B1 (Point B is a smooth symmetrical point).

The image to the right shows the result of dragging Handle B1 to the left instead of to the right. Notice the difference in the curve, as compared to the curve above. When you drag the handle, the segment arcs away from the direction of the handle.

It's important to understand that every curved segment is connected to two handles. In this image, dragging the handle to the right pulls out the arc of the connected segment. You could change the shape of Segment A by dragging either Handle A1 or B2.

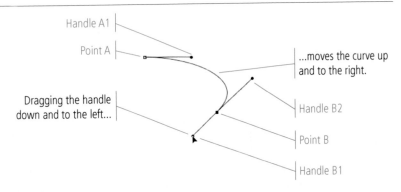

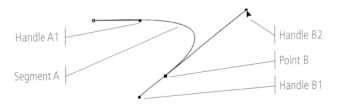

The final concept you should understand about anchors and handles (for now, at least) is that clicking and dragging to create a point creates a smooth symmetrical point. Dragging one handle of a smooth point also changes the other handle of that point. In the image shown below, dragging Handle B1 also moves Handle B2, which affects the shape of Segment A.

You can create corner points by simply clicking with the Pen tool instead of clicking and dragging. Corner points do not have their own handles; the connected segments are controlled by the handles of the other associated anchor points.

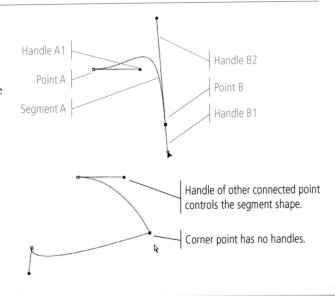

1. With **sailboat.ai** open, zoom in so you can clearly see the shape of the boat in the sketch.

2. Choose the Pen tool in the Tools panel. Using the Control panel, set the stroke to 1-pt black and the fill to None.

Note:

As you draw, zoom in as necessary to view different parts of the sketch.

3. Click the arrow button to the right of the Brush Definition menu and choose the Basic brush.

4. Click with the Pen tool to place the first anchor point on the top-left corner of the boat shape.

We typically find it easier to start drawing at a corner (if one exists).

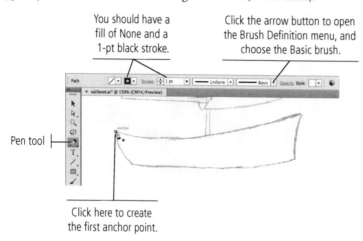

You should have a fill of None and a 1-pt black stroke.

Click the arrow button to open the Brush Definition menu, and choose the Basic brush.

Pen tool

Click here to create the first anchor point.

Note:

The words "anchor" and "path" near the cursor icon are a function of Illustrator Smart Guides. If you find them distracting, you can toggle those off by choosing View>Smart Guides.

5. Click again at the bottom-left corner of the boat shape and immediately drag down and right to create handles for the second point. When the preview of the connecting segment matches the line in the sketch, release the mouse button.

When you click and drag without releasing the mouse button, you create symmetrical handles, which determine the shape of the segment that connects the two points.

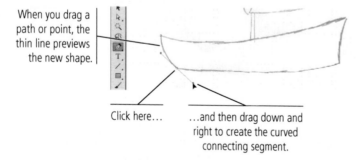

When you drag a path or point, the thin line previews the new shape.

Click here…

…and then drag down and right to create the curved connecting segment.

6. Click and drag again from the bottom-right corner of the boat shape.

Again, clicking and dragging creates a smooth, symmetrical point. Equal-length, exactly opposing handles are created on both sides of the point.

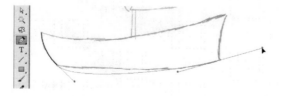

Note:

When we say "click and drag," you should hold down the mouse button until the end of the step.

7. **Click again on the second anchor point and release the mouse button without dragging.**

Clicking a smooth point as you draw converts it to a corner point, removing the outside handle from the point; the inside handle that defines the shape of the connecting segment remains in place. This allows you to change direction as you draw.

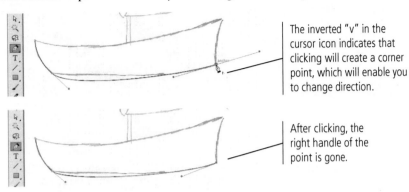

The inverted "v" in the cursor icon indicates that clicking will create a corner point, which will enable you to change direction.

After clicking, the right handle of the point is gone.

Note:

Don't worry if the connecting segment doesn't exactly match the sketch. The bottom of the boat will be obscured by other artwork in the final poster.

8. **Click and drag to create a new point (with handles) from the top-right corner of the boat shape. Drag the handles until the connecting segment matches the shape of the sketched line.**

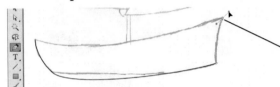

Click here and immediately drag up and right until the connecting segment matches the shape of the sketched line.

Note:

While drawing with the Pen tool, you can Option/Alt-click an anchor point, hold down the mouse button, and drag to add a non-symmetrical handle to one side of a corner point.

9. **Click the original point without dragging to close the shape.**

When you return to the original point, the cursor shows a small hollow circle. This indicates that clicking the existing point will close the shape.

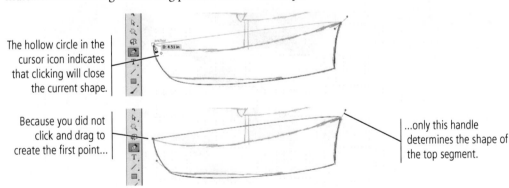

The hollow circle in the cursor icon indicates that clicking will close the current shape.

Because you did not click and drag to create the first point...

...only this handle determines the shape of the top segment.

10. **Using the Direct Selection tool, click the top-right point on the shape to select only that anchor point.**

You can use the Direct Selection tool to edit any specific anchor point or segment.

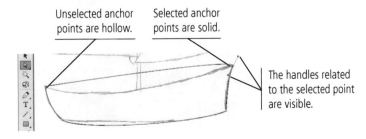

Unselected anchor points are hollow.

Selected anchor points are solid.

The handles related to the selected point are visible.

11. Press Option/Alt, then click and drag the top handle of the selected point. Drag the handle left until the top segment matches the line in the sketch.

Remember, the Direct Selection tool allows you to adjust individual anchor points and handles. Option/Alt-dragging one handle of a smooth point converts the point to a corner point, but leaves both handles in place. This method allows you to change the direction of an existing point, but leave the opposite curve intact.

Note:

A diagonal line in the Pen tool cursor icon indicates that clicking will connect to an open endpoint so you can continue drawing the shape.

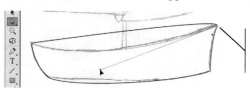

Option/Alt-dragging the handle converts the point to a corner point.

12. Save the file and continue to the next exercise.

Understanding Anchor Point and Bézier Curve Tools

Keep the following points in mind as you work with the Pen tool (and its nested variations) and Bézier curves.

Using the Direct Selection tool...

Click a specific anchor point to select it and show all handles that relate to that point.

Click a specific segment to select it and show all handles that relate to that segment.

Option/Alt drag a handle of a smooth point to convert it to a corner point.

Using the Pen tool...

Place the cursor over an existing point to temporarily access the Delete Anchor Point tool.

Place the cursor over an existing segment to temporarily access the Add Anchor Point tool.

Press Option/Alt and place the cursor over an existing point to temporarily access the Anchor Point tool.

ILLUSTRATOR FOUNDATIONS

RESHAPE LINE SEGMENTS

In Illustrator, you have numerous options to create, select, and modify shapes — or parts of shapes — so you can create exactly what you need, regardless of what is already on the artboard. In this exercise you use a new method to easily behind line segments in the shapes you need.

1. **With sailboat.ai open, make the right sail in the sketch visible in the document window.**

2. **Using the Pen tool, click to place three connected anchor points at the corners of the sail.**

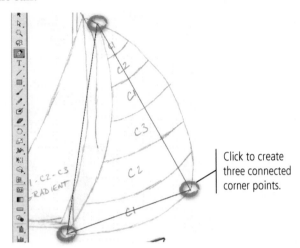

Click to create three connected corner points.

Note:

As a general rule, use as few points as necessary to create a shape with the Pen tool.

3. **Press the Option/Alt key to temporarily access the Anchor Point tool.**

The Anchor Point tool, nested under the Pen tool, can be used to change anchor points from corner to smooth (or vice versa):

The Pen tool is technically active.

Anchor Point tool cursor

- Click a smooth point to convert it to a corner point.
- Click and drag a corner point to convert it to a smooth point with symmetrical handles.
- Option/Alt-click a handle to move only that handle, even if the related point has an opposing handle; a smooth point is converted to a corner point as you drag the handle.

4. **While holding down the Option/Alt key, click the right segment of the sail and drag until the segment matches the sketch.**

You can click and drag a segment to bend it into a different shape; handles are added to or adjusted as necessary for the related points. This method of reshaping a line segment makes it very easy to edit your artwork without manually manipulating anchor points or handles.

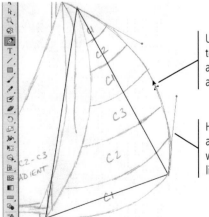

Using the Anchor Point tool, click a segment and drag to push it into a different shape.

Handles are added or adjusted as necessary when you reshape a line segment.

5. **Still holding down the Option/Alt key, adjust the other two lines that make up the sail shape.**

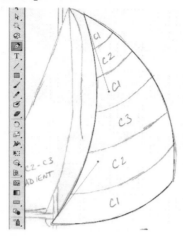

6. **Repeat Steps 2–4 to create the shape of the left sail.**

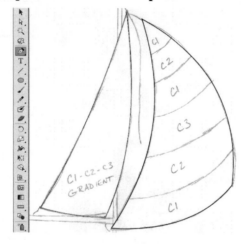

7. **Using the Pen tool, click to place a new anchor point to the left of the bottom horizontal line in the right sail, starting and stopping past the edges of the sail shape (as shown in the following image).**

You are going to use the Shape Builder tool to divide the sail into the necessary shapes. For this process to work properly, the dividing lines need to be at least on top of the outside shape; to be sure, you should extend the lines farther than they need to be.

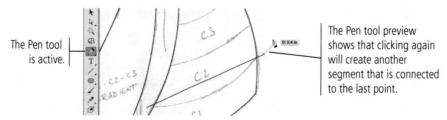

The Pen tool is active.

The Pen tool preview shows that clicking again will create another segment that is connected to the last point.

8. **Press Option/Alt, then use the Anchor Point tool to reshape the segment to match the line in the sketch.**

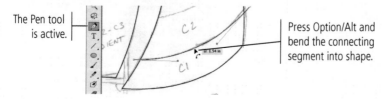

The Pen tool is active.

Press Option/Alt and bend the connecting segment into shape.

9. **While the Pen tool is still active, press Command/Control to temporarily access the Selection tool and click away from the line to deselect it.**

You can simply click away from selected objects with the Selection or Direct Selection tool to deselect the current selection. You can also press Command/Control-Shift-A to deselect the current selection.

Pressing Command/Control while drawing temporarily switches to the last-used Selection tool. This technique allows you to easily deselect the current path and then continue to draw another unconnected path, all without manually switching tools.

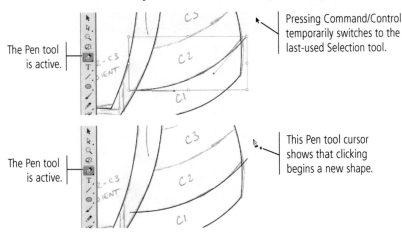

The Pen tool is active.

Pressing Command/Control temporarily switches to the last-used Selection tool.

The Pen tool is active.

This Pen tool cursor shows that clicking begins a new shape.

10. **Still using the Pen tool, draw the second horizontal line on the sail.**

If you don't deselect the previous path before clicking to draw the next line, the third click would create a segment that is connected to the last place you clicked (on the first line). In the context of this exercise, a single line with multiple anchor points is much more difficult to control than two separate lines with open endpoints.

11. **Press Option/Alt, then use the Anchor Point tool to reshape the segment to match the line in the sketch.**

12. **Press the ESC key.**

When drawing with the Pen tool, this key disconnects your drawing from the current shape. You can then click to begin a new shape that is not part of the previously suggested shape.

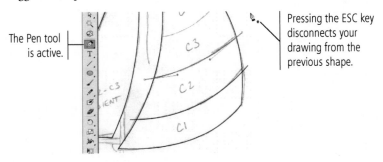

The Pen tool is active.

Pressing the ESC key disconnects your drawing from the previous shape.

13. **Repeat Steps 10–12 to draw the rest of the curved horizontal lines on the sail.**

14. **Save the file and continue to the next exercise.**

BUILD SHAPES FROM OVERLAPPING PATHS

The Shape Builder tool makes it easy to break apart overlapping objects into component pieces. This tool offers similar functionality as the Pathfinder, but on a piece-by-piece basis rather than for entire selected shapes. In this exercise, you will use the Shape Builder tool to break up the sail into the individual strips that are shown on the sketch.

1. **With sailboat.ai open, use the Selection tool to draw a marquee that selects all lines that make up the right sail.**

2. **Choose the Shape Builder tool in the Tools panel, and then reset the default fill and stroke colors.**

3. **Move the cursor over the bottom section of the sail.**

   The Shape Builder tool identifies overlapping areas of selected objects, which is why you had to select the pieces in Step 1.

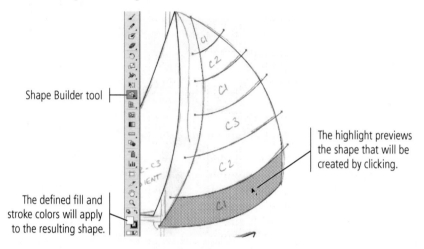

Shape Builder tool

The defined fill and stroke colors will apply to the resulting shape.

The highlight previews the shape that will be created by clicking.

4. **Click the highlighted area to create the new shape.**

   Clicking with the Shape Builder tool changes the fill of the resulting shape to the active fill color — white, in this case, because you reset the default fill and stroke colors in Step 2. The resulting shape now obscures the sketch behind it; this helps to identify which pieces you have already created.

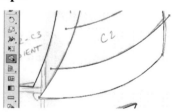

5. **Repeat Steps 3–4 for the remaining five strips on the sail.**

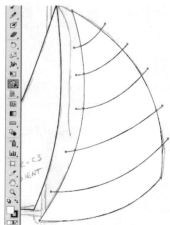

Note:

When the Shape Builder tool divides the objects into separate shapes, it creates anchor points as necessary at the intersections, and also maintains the original points.

6. **Press Option/Alt, and move the cursor over the bottom line segment outside the right sail edge. When the line segment is highlighted and the cursor shows a minus sign in the icon, click the segment to remove it.**

The Shape Builder tool can be used to both create and remove shapes. Pressing Option/Alt switches the tool into Erase mode so you can remove paths or shapes.

The area that will be removed is highlighted.

7. **Repeat Step 6 to remove the remaining extraneous line segments.**

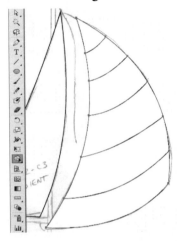

More on the Shape Builder Tool

The Shape Builder tool offers a number of options that can significantly enhance your ability to create complex artwork.

If a small opening exists in a path, you can activate **Gap Detection** settings to overlook small, medium, large, or custom-sized gaps in open paths. This option is especially useful if the Consider Open Filled Paths as Closed option is not checked.

The **Pick Color From** menu determines whether the tool recognizes all swatches in the file or only colors that are actually used in the artwork.

You can also use the **Highlight** options to determine what, if anything, is highlighted when you move the tool cursor over a shape.

Click and drag with the Shape Builder tool to combine multiple pieces into a single shape:

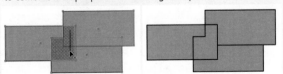

Option/Alt-click and drag with the Shape Builder tool to remove multiple pieces at once:

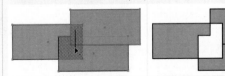

When In Merge Mode, Clicking Stroke Splits the Path is active, click a path to cut apart the path at the nearest anchor points:

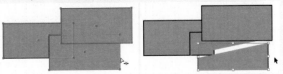

When Cursor Swatch Preview is active, three available swatches appear above the tool cursor. Use the Left and Right Arrow keys to move through those swatches:

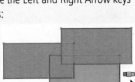

8. **Deselect all objects by clicking away from the current selection.**

9. **Using the Direct Selection tool, click the right edge of the shape and drag slightly out to create a slightly bulged appearance.**

   When the Direct Selection tool is active, you can click and drag a line segment on a closed path to access the same path-reshaping functionality as you have using the Anchor Point tool.

10. **Repeat Step 9 to adjust the right edges of the other shapes in the sail.**

    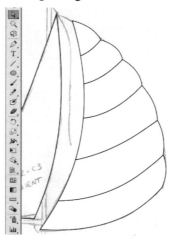

11. **Save the file and continue to the next exercise.**

Editing Anchor Points with the Control Panel

When you are working with Bézier paths, the Control panel provides a number of options for editing selected anchor points.

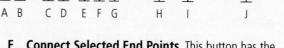

A **Convert Selected Anchor Points to Corner.** This button removes the direction handles from both sides of the selected point(s).

B **Convert Selected Anchor Points to Smooth.** This button adds symmetrical direction handles to both sides of the selected point(s).

C **Show Handles for Multiple Selected Anchor Points.** If this option is toggled on, direction handles display for all selected points.

D **Hide Handles for Multiple Selected Anchor Points.** If this option is toggled on, direction handles are not visible when more than one point is selected.

E **Remove Selected Anchor Points.** This button removes the selected point from the path. If the removed point was between two other points, the connecting segment is not removed.

F **Connect Selected End Points.** This button has the same effect as the Object>Path>Join command.

G **Cut Path at Selected Anchor Points.** This button results in two overlapping, open endpoints where the selected point was previously a single point.

H **Corner Radius.** Use this field to define a specific corner radius for the selected point.

I **Isolate Selected Object.** This button enters isolation mode with the object containing the selected anchor point(s). If points are selected on more than one object, this button is not available.

J **Point Position.** Use the X and Y fields to define a specific position for the selected point. You can also use mathematical operations to move a point relative to its current position (e.g., move it left by typing "-1" after the current X value).

USE THE DRAW BEHIND MODE

Illustrator's three drawing modes allow you to create new shapes in different ways relative to other existing shapes. In the Draw Normal method (the default), new objects are simply created on top of one another in sequential order; you can rearrange them using commands in the Object>Arrange submenu or drag them in the Layers panel. Alternatively, you can use the Draw Behind mode to automatically create new shapes behind existing objects, which eliminates a few steps in reaching the accurate object stacking order.

1. **With sailboat.ai open, use any method you prefer to fill the left sail with white and fill the boat shape with black.**

2. **Deselect everything on the artboard.**

3. **Choose the Pen tool in the Tools panel. In the Control panel, set the fill color to a dark brown from the built-in swatches and the stroke to None.**

4. **At the bottom of the Tools panel, choose the Draw Behind option.**

   If your Tools panel is in one-column mode, the Drawing Mode options are available in a pop-up menu. If your Tools panel is in two-column mode, the Drawing Mode options are presented as three buttons (from left to right: Draw Normal, Draw Behind, and Draw Inside).

   When you use the Draw Behind mode, new objects are automatically placed behind the selected object(s), or at the bottom of the stacking order if nothing is selected.

5. **Using the sketch as a guide, use the Pen tool to click four times without dragging to create the mast shape (use the following image as a guide).**

   Remember, when you see a small round circle in the cursor icon, clicking creates a closed shape. Because you aren't dragging when you click to place the anchor points, you are creating four corner points and a closed polygon shape.

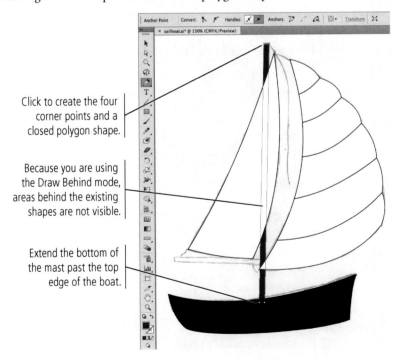

Click to create the four corner points and a closed polygon shape.

Because you are using the Draw Behind mode, areas behind the existing shapes are not visible.

Extend the bottom of the mast past the top edge of the boat.

6. **Use the Pen tool to create the boom (the horizontal pole sticking out from the mast).**

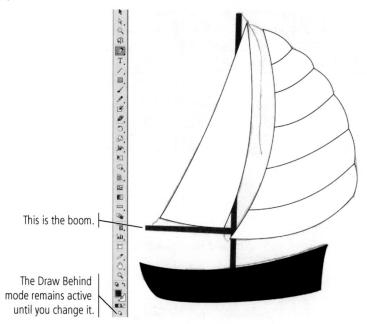

This is the boom.

The Draw Behind mode remains active until you change it.

7. **Deselect the shape you just created.**

8. **In the Tools panel, click the Drawing Mode button and choose Draw Normal.**

The drawing mode remains at the last-used setting. To draw the rope shapes in font of the sails and mast, you need to restore the Draw Normal mode.

9. **Choose the Pencil tool in the Tools panel. In the Control panel, change the fill color to None, choose a medium brown swatch as the stroke color, and define a stroke weight of 2 pt.**

10. **Use the Pencil tool to draw the ropes on the sketch.**

11. **If necessary, adjust the anchor points of the ropes until you are satisfied with the results.**

12. **Save the file and continue to the next stage of the project.**

The Draw Inside mode, which is only available when an existing object is already selected, is an easy way to create new objects inside a **clipping path** (a shape that defines areas of other objects that will be visible; anything outside the area of the clipping path is not visible).

If you select the clipped object with the Selection tool, you can use the Edit Clipping Path and Edit Contents buttons in the Control panel to edit either shape without ungrouping and without entering isolation mode.

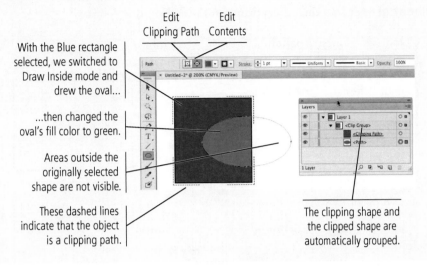

Edit
Clipping Path

Edit
Contents

With the Blue rectangle selected, we switched to Draw Inside mode and drew the oval...

...then changed the oval's fill color to green.

Areas outside the originally selected shape are not visible.

These dashed lines indicate that the object is a clipping path.

The clipping shape and the clipped shape are automatically grouped.

Stage 2 Coloring and Painting Artwork

The CMYK color model, also called "process color," recreates the range of printable colors by overlapping layers of cyan, magenta, yellow, and black inks in varying percentages from 0–100.

Using theoretically pure pigments, a mixture of equal parts of cyan, magenta, and yellow would produce black. Real pigments, however, are not pure; the actual result of mixing these three colors usually appears as a muddy brown. The fourth color, black (K), is added to cyan, magenta, and yellow to extend the range of printable colors and allow much purer blacks to be printed. (Black is abbreviated as "K" because it is the "key" color to which others are aligned on the printing press. Using K for black also avoids confusion with blue in the RGB color model, which is used for digitally distributed files.)

In process-color printing, each of the four process colors — cyan, magenta, yellow, and black — is imaged, or separated, onto an individual printing plate. Each color separation is printed on a separate unit of a printing press. When printed on top of each other in varying percentages, the semitransparent inks produce the range of colors in the CMYK **gamut**. Other special colors (called spot colors) are printed using specifically formulated inks as additional color separations.

 +  +  +  =

Different color models have different ranges or gamuts of possible colors. A normal human visual system is capable of distinguishing approximately 16.7 million different colors; color reproduction systems, however, are far more limited. The RGB model has the largest gamut of the output models. The CMYK gamut is much more limited; many of the brightest and most saturated colors that can be reproduced using light (in the RGB model) cannot be reproduced using CMYK inks.

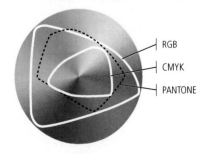

RGB

CMYK

PANTONE

CREATE GLOBAL CUSTOM COLOR SWATCHES

As you saw in the original sketch, the sail in this project will be filled using three different colors (indicated as C1, C2, and C3). In this exercise, you are going to create these colors and then save them as swatches that can be changed at any time to dynamically modify the colors in the artwork.

1. **With sailboat.ai open, deselect everything on the artboard.**

2. **Open the Color and Swatches panels.**

   If you don't see four color fields/sliders in the Color panel, open the panel options menu and choose Show Options.

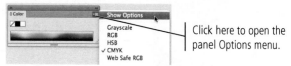

Click here to open the panel Options menu.

Because you defined CMYK as the color mode for this document, the Color panel shows ink value sliders for those four primary colors.

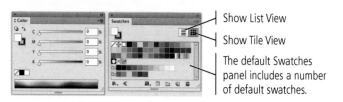

Show List View

Show Tile View

The default Swatches panel includes a number of default swatches.

Note:

We dragged both panels out of the panel dock so we could work with both panels at once.

Note:

The default swatches appear in every new file you create, even if you delete them from a specific file.

3. **Open the Swatches panel Options menu and choose Select All Unused.**

   The default Swatches panel includes a number of basic swatches that provide a good starting point for some artwork; you already used two of these to color the mast, boom, and rope shapes. When you build custom swatches, it can be a good idea to delete any default swatches that you don't need so your panel isn't too cluttered.

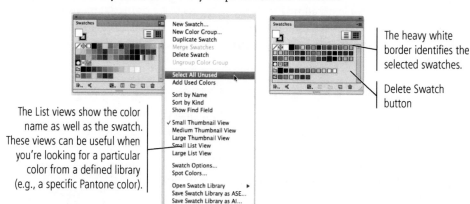

The List views show the color name as well as the swatch. These views can be useful when you're looking for a particular color from a defined library (e.g., a specific Pantone color).

The heavy white border identifies the selected swatches.

Delete Swatch button

4. **Click the Swatches panel Delete button, and then click Yes in the resulting warning dialog box.**

   You used two of the built-in swatches to create the mast and ropes, so those swatches remain in the panel and file.

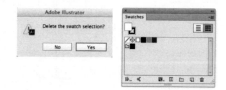

Note:

If you delete a swatch that you applied to objects in a project, there is no effect on the existing objects; you simply can't apply that color to any new objects in the project.

5. **Select all of the white-filled objects and change their fill to 50% opacity.**

   The easiest method to accomplish this is to select one of the white-filled shapes, then use the Select Same Fill Color option. Alternatively, you can Shift-click each white-filled object to select them individually. Changing the objects' opacity allows you to see the color indicators on the original sketch.

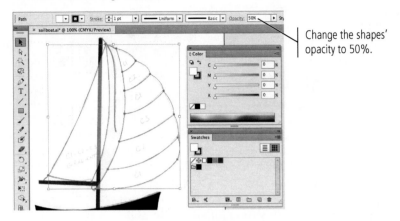

Change the shapes'
opacity to 50%.

6. **Deselect everything, and then use the Selection tool to select only the top stripe in the sail (labeled C1 in the sketch).**

7. **Press Shift and click the other two C1 shapes to add them to the selection.**

   By pressing Shift, you can click to add other objects to the current selection. Shift-clicking an object that is already selected removes it from the active selection.

8. **In the Color panel, make sure the Fill icon is on top of the Stroke icon.**

   Like the options in the Tools panel, the Fill and Stroke icons determine which attribute you are currently changing. Whichever icon is on top will be affected by changes to the color values.

9. **In the Color panel, click a green area in the color spectrum bar.**

   All three selected objects fill with the green color you clicked. They seem lighter because they are still semi-transparent.

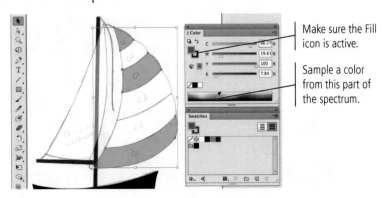

Make sure the Fill
icon is active.

Sample a color
from this part of
the spectrum.

Note:

Press Shift while dragging any of the sliders in the Color panel to drag all four sliders at once. Their relative relationship to each other remains the same while you drag.

10. **With the Fill icon still active in the Color panel, click the New Swatch button in the Swatches panel.**

Because the Fill icon is
active, the fill color is the
one that will be stored in
the new swatch.

Click this button to make
a new swatch from the
currently active color.

11. **Check the Global option in the New Swatch dialog box and click OK.**

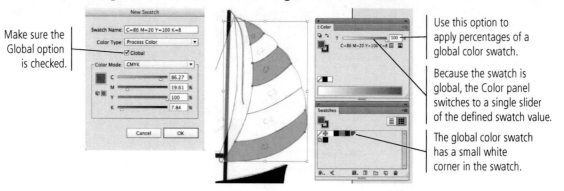

Make sure the Global option is checked.

Use this option to apply percentages of a global color swatch.

Because the swatch is global, the Color panel switches to a single slider of the defined swatch value.

The global color swatch has a small white corner in the swatch.

12. **Select the two shapes marked C2 in the sketch.**

13. **Repeat the process from Steps 8–11 to fill the C2 shapes with a blue color and then create a global swatch from the color.**

14. **Select the shape marked C3 in the sketch, fill it with a purple color, and then create a third global swatch from the color.**

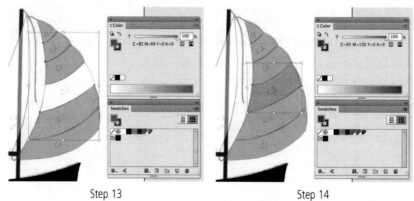

Step 13

Step 14

Note:

When an object is colored with a global swatch, you can click the process button under the percentage field to convert the applied swatch to the component color percentages (i.e., breaking the link to the global swatch).

15. **With the purple shapes still selected, choose Select>Same>Opacity. Return the selected objects' opacity to 100%.**

You no longer need to see the color markers on the sketch, so you can return these objects to full opacity.

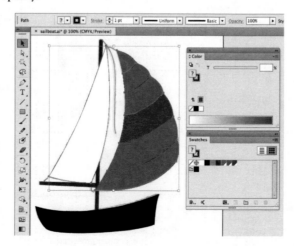

16. **Deselect all objects in the file, then save the file and continue to the next exercise.**

ADD A COLOR GRADIENT

The original sketch shows that the left sail needs to be a gradient of the three colors in the other sail. Illustrator's Gradient tool makes it easy to create this gradient based on the three custom swatches you defined in the previous exercise.

1. **With sailboat.ai open, use the Selection tool to select the left sail shape.**

2. **Open the Gradient panel (Window>Gradient). If you see only a gradient sample in the panel, open the panel Options menu and choose Show Options.**

   If you don't see the gradient stops under the ramp, click the ramp once to show the stops.

3. **Click the swatch in the top-left corner of the Gradient panel.**

   Clicking the swatch applies the linear gradient to the selected object.

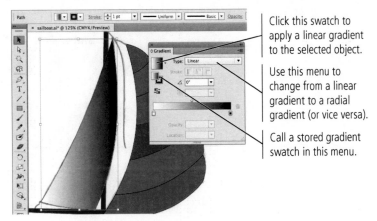

   Click this swatch to apply a linear gradient to the selected object.

   Use this menu to change from a linear gradient to a radial gradient (or vice versa).

   Call a stored gradient swatch in this menu.

4. **In the Gradient panel, double-click the left gradient stop on the gradient ramp.**

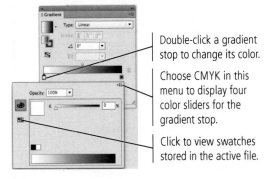

   Double-click a gradient stop to change its color.

   Choose CMYK in this menu to display four color sliders for the gradient stop.

   Click to view swatches stored in the active file.

5. **In the pop-up panel, click the Swatches button to display the swatches stored in the current document.**

6. **Click the green global swatch you created in the previous exercise, and then press Return/Enter to close the pop-up panel.**

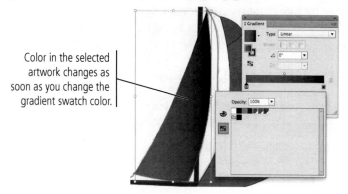

Color in the selected artwork changes as soon as you change the gradient swatch color.

7. **Double-click the right gradient stop to open the pop-up panel. Apply the purple custom swatch to this stop.**

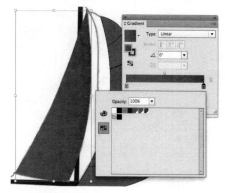

Note:

You can also drag a swatch from the Swatches panel onto a particular gradient stop to change the color of that stop.

Note:

You can remove a stop by dragging it down and off the gradient ramp.

8. **Click once below the gradient ramp to add another stop to the gradient. With the new stop selected, type 40 in the Location field.**

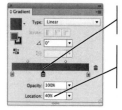

Click below the ramp to add stops to the gradient.

Use the Location field to define a precise position along the ramp.

9. **Double-click the middle stop and apply the blue swatch.**

10. **Click the left gradient stop and drag right until the Location field shows approximately 5%.**

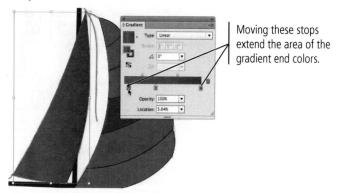

Moving these stops extend the area of the gradient end colors.

Note:

The Gradient panel remembers the last-used gradient, so you can simply click the sample to apply the gradient to another object.

12. **Click the marker above the gradient ramp between the left and middle stops. Drag left until the Location field shows approximately 30%.**

This point indicates where the colors of the two surrounding stops are equally mixed. Dragging the point extends the gradient on one side of the point and compresses the gradient on the other side. (You can also simply select the midpoint icon and then type a specific position in the Location field.)

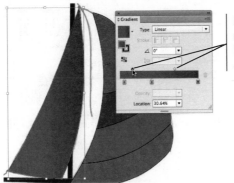

Dragging these markers moves the midpoint between the two adjacent color stops.

13. **Save the file and continue to the next exercise.**

 ## EDIT GLOBAL COLOR SWATCHES

Global swatches offer a particular advantage when you need to change the colors used in your artwork. In the case of this project, you are going to place this artwork into a stylized ocean illustration, in which blues are the predominant color. To make the boat more prominent in the final poster, you are going to use a yellow-orange scheme — complementary colors to blue — for the boat sails.

Note:

Complementary color refers to opposing colors on a color wheel.

1. **With sailboat.ai open, deselect all objects on the artboard.**

2. **In the Swatches panel, double-click the green custom swatch.**

3. **In the resulting Swatch Options dialog box, make sure the Preview option is checked.**

4. **Change the color values to C=0 M=75 Y=75 K=10, and then click OK to change the swatch definition.**

Because this is a global color swatch, any objects that use the color — including the gradient — reflect the new swatch definition. Locked objects are also affected by the change.

Everything colored with the previously green swatch is now filled with the orange you just defined.

5. **Repeat Steps 2–4 to change the blue swatch definition to C=0 M=10 Y=100 K=0.**

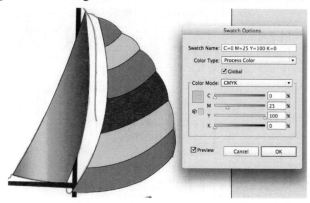

6. **Repeat Steps 2–4 to change the purple swatch definition to C=0 M=60 Y=100 K=0.**

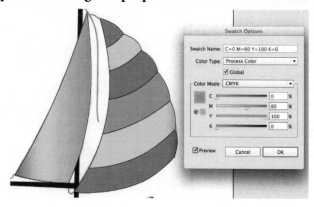

7. **Save the file and continue to the next exercise.**

 ## USE THE GRADIENT TOOL

In addition to simply applying a gradient with the Gradient panel, you can also use the Gradient tool to define the gradient directly in the context of the artwork.

1. **With sailboat.ai open, select only the left sail shape.**

2. **Choose the Gradient tool in the Tools panel.**

   When a selected object is filled with a gradient, choosing the Gradient tool reveals the Gradient Annotator for that shape. The Gradient Annotator is simply a visual tool for applying most of the same options that are available in the Gradient panel.

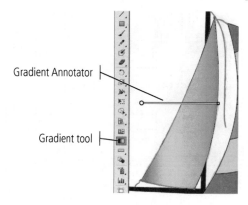

Gradient Annotator

Gradient tool

3. **Move your cursor over the Gradient Annotator to show the associated stops.**

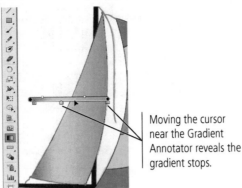

Moving the cursor near the Gradient Annotator reveals the gradient stops.

Note:

You can turn off the Gradient Annotator in the View menu (View>Hide Gradient Annotator).

4. **Using the Gradient tool, click the bottom-right corner of the sail, then drag up and left until the gradient width is slightly less than the shape's actual width (use the following image as a guide).**

Clicking and dragging with the Gradient tool defines the width and angle of the gradient within a selected object.

When working with a linear gradient, the first place you click with the Gradient tool defines the location for the starting color of the gradient; where you release the mouse button marks the location for the ending color of the gradient. Any areas beyond the two ends fill with the end-stop colors of the gradient.

As you drag, the marquee shows a preview of the gradient width. When you release the mouse button, the gradient annotator snaps back to the object's center; its angle matches the angle you defined.

Note:

Click and drag the gradient endpoint (the smaller circle) on the annotator to change the gradient width.

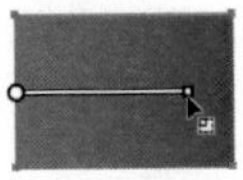

Place the cursor just outside the gradient endpoint on the annotator to reveal the rotation cursor; click and drag to change the angle of the gradient.

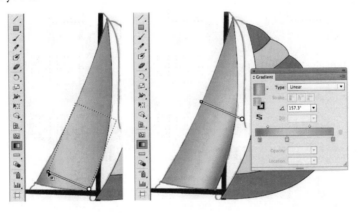

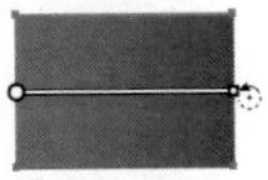

5. **Save the file and continue to the next stage of the project.**

Many vague and technical-sounding terms are mentioned when discussing color. Is hue the same as color? The same as value? As tone? What's the difference between lightness and brightness? What is chroma? And where does saturation fit in?

This problem has resulted in several attempts to normalize color communication. A number of systems have been developed to define color according to specific criteria, including Hue, Saturation, and Brightness (HSB); Hue, Saturation, and Lightness (HSL); Hue, Saturation, and Value (HSV); and Lightness, Chroma, and Hue (LCH). Each of these models or systems plots color on a three-dimensional diagram, based on the elements of human color perception — hue, colorfulness, and brightness.

Hue is what most people think of as color — red, green, purple, and so on. Hue is defined according to a color's position on a color wheel, beginning from red (0°) and traveling counterclockwise around the wheel.

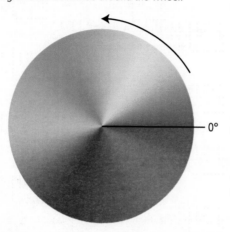

0°

Saturation (also called "intensity") refers to the color's difference from neutral gray. Highly saturated colors are more vivid than those with low saturation. Saturation is plotted from the center of the color wheel. Color at the center is neutral gray and has a saturation value of 0; color at the edge of the wheel is the most intense value of the corresponding hue and has a saturation value of 100.

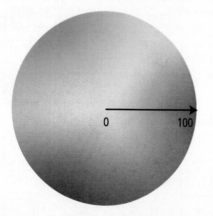

0   100

If you bisect the color wheel with a straight line, the line creates a saturation axis for two complementary colors. A color is dulled by the introduction of its complement. Red, for example, is neutralized by the addition of cyan (blue and green). Near the center of the axis, the result is neutral gray.

−100   0   +100

Chroma is similar to saturation, but chroma factors in a reference white. In any viewing situation, colors appear less vivid as the light source dims. The process of chromatic adaptation, however, allows the human visual system to adjust to changes in light and still differentiate colors according to the relative saturation.

Brightness is the amount of light reflected off an object. As an element of color reproduction, brightness is typically judged by comparing the color to the lightest nearby object (such as an unprinted area of white paper).

Lightness is the amount of white or black added to the pure color. Lightness (also called "luminance" or "value") is the relative brightness based purely on the black-white value of a color. A lightness value of 0 means there is no addition of white or black. Lightness of +100 is pure white; lightness of −100 is pure black.

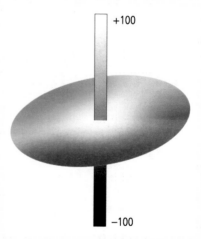

+100

−100

All hues are affected equally by changes in lightness.

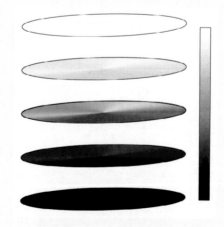

Stage 3 Working with Adobe Typekit

When you work with type in an Illustrator file, it is important to understand that fonts are external files of data that describe the font for on-screen display and for the output device. The fonts you use in a layout need to be available on any computer that will be used to open the file. Illustrator stores a reference to used fonts, but it does not store the actual font data.

Adobe Typekit is an online library of high-quality fonts. The Typekit Portfolio Plan, which provides access to the full font library and allows you to sync up to 100 fonts at a time to your desktop, is included in your Adobe Creative Cloud subscription.

You can use the Typekit Web site to browse through a large number of available fonts, and even filter those fonts based on specific attributes and/or uses (for example, show only serif fonts that are available for desktop use). When you find fonts you want to use, you can sync them to your desktop through the Adobe Creative Cloud application; synced fonts will be available for use in any application on your device.

VERIFY YOUR ADOBE ID IN ILLUSTRATOR

In the next exercises you are going to select and install fonts from Adobe Typekit, which is part of your Adobe Creative Cloud subscription services. For that process to work, you must be signed in to your Creative Cloud account in Illustrator, and have an active internet connection. In this exercise, you will verify that you are signed in to your Adobe Creative Cloud account.

1. **In Illustrator, open the Help menu.**

2. **If you see an option to Sign In, skip to Step 5.**

If this option shows "Sign In," you are not yet signed in to your Creative Cloud account.

3. **If you see an option to Sign Out, verify that the listed email is the Adobe ID linked to your Creative Cloud account.**

If this option shows "Sign Out," someone is already signed in to a Creative Cloud account.

This is the email (Adobe ID) that is currently signed in to the Adobe Creative Cloud.

4a. **If the email address listed in the Help menu is yours, continue to the next exercise.**

4b. **If the email in the menu is not yours, choose the Sign Out option. Read the resulting message and then click Sign Out.**

If you sign out of any Adobe CC application, this message informs you that you are also signing out of *all* Adobe CC applications.

5. **In Illustrator, choose Help>Sign In.**

6. **Read the message in the resulting dialog box, then click Sign In Now.**

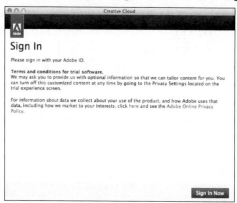

7. **In the Sign In screen, enter your Adobe ID and password, then click Sign In.**

8. **Read the message in the final screen, then click Continue.**

9. **Open the Adobe Creative Cloud application.**

   On Macintosh, this is accessed on the right side of the Menu bar at the top of the screen. On Windows, it is accessed on the right side of the Taskbar at the bottom of the screen.

   Macintosh   Windows

10. **Click the Assets tab in the Creative Cloud window, and choose the Fonts option in the secondary list. If you see a Start Syncing button, click that button.**

    Font syncing through Adobe Typekit is part of your Creative Cloud subscription. In the next exercises, you will use the Typekit Web site to sync fonts in your Creative Cloud account.

    However, you have to first enable syncing functionality in your Creative Cloud account for the process to work properly.

11. **Continue to the next exercise.**

Note:

This dialog box is actually a function of the Creative Cloud application, which is part of your Creative Cloud subscription. If you switch to another application, you have to choose the Adobe Application Manager (Macintosh) or Creative Cloud application (Windows) to return to this screen.

Macintosh

Windows

Note:

On Macintosh, the Creative Cloud application is attached to the Menu bar icon by default. On Windows, it typically appears as a floating window.

INSTALL FONTS FROM ADOBE TYPEKIT

As we explained in the beginning of this stage, fonts used in artwork must be available on the computer used to work with the Illustrator file. In this exercise, you are going to a font that is used in the poster artwork for this project.

1. **Open the Creative Cloud application and display the Assets>Fonts screen.**

   After syncing has been enabled in your account, the Fonts screen of the Creative Cloud application shows all fonts that have been synced for your account. If you have not yet synced fonts in your account, you see a default screen; if you have already synced fonts, the application shows a list of the synced fonts.

Note:

You can click the Manage Fonts button to show the "Your Account" page on the Typekit Web site, where you can use the Remove option to unsync specific fonts from your account.

Note:

You can also choose Type>Add Fonts from Typekit in Illustrator to access this Web page.

2. **Click the Add Fonts from Typekit button.**

   This launches your default browser and shows the Browse Fonts page of the Adobe Typekit Web site. Because you launched the site from your Creative Cloud application, you are automatically logged in to your Typekit account.

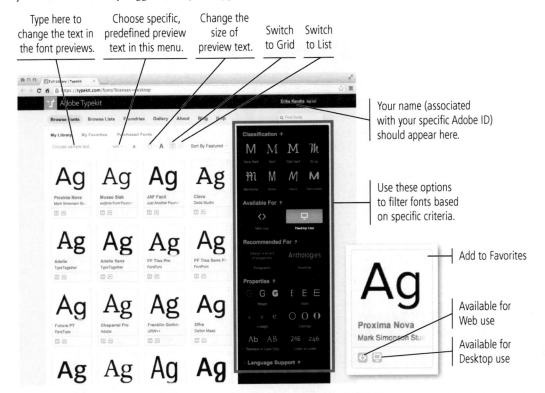

Type here to change the text in the font previews.

Choose specific, predefined preview text in this menu.

Change the size of preview text.

Switch to Grid

Switch to List

Your name (associated with your specific Adobe ID) should appear here.

Use these options to filter fonts based on specific criteria.

Add to Favorites

Available for Web use

Available for Desktop use

3. **On the right side of the browser, make sure the Desktop Use filter is active (green). Click the Script button in the Classification section.**

The right side of the Typekit page allows you to filter the available fonts based on a number of criteria:

- **Classification** — Show only fonts that are serif, sans-serif, slab serif, script, blackletter, micro, hand, or decorative.

- **Available For** — Show fonts that can be used in a Web site or on your desktop (for layout design, illustration, etc.).

- **Recommended For** — Show fonts that are best suited for paragraphs or headings.

- **Properties** — Show fonts that fit specific criteria, including:
    - weight, or the thickness of strokes in the letterforms
    - width of the individual letterforms (narrow, medium, wide)
    - x-height, or the ratio of lowercase letter height compared to uppercase
    - contrast, or the ratio of thin strokes compared to thick strokes in individual letterforms
    - type case, or whether a font includes both upper- and lowercase or all capitals/small caps and all caps
    - number positioning, which refers to whether numbers all align to the baseline or extend above or below the baseline

- **Language Support** — Show fonts that include special glyphs for non-Roman alphabetic characters and diacritical marks.

Filter buttons on the right side of the screen are toggles; when they are green, they are active (toggled on). Active filters remain active until you intentionally turn them off.

Only one button in any section can be active at a time (for example, you can't find fonts that are both thin and bold weight). However, you can use multiple categories at once to filter fonts down to a very specific set.

4. **Move your mouse over the Lush Script font preview to reveal the Use Fonts button for that font.**

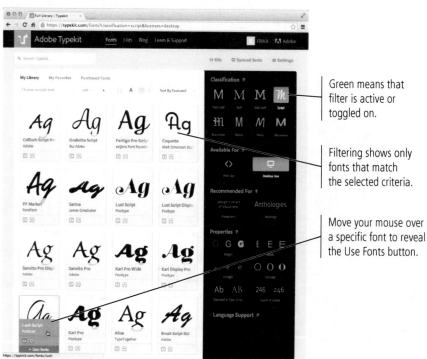

Green means that filter is active or toggled on.

Filtering shows only fonts that match the selected criteria.

Move your mouse over a specific font to reveal the Use Fonts button.

5. **Click the Lush Script font preview to open the detail screen for that font.**

   Clicking a font preview in the list shows that font's details page.

   - The **Weights & Styles** tab shows a previews of any variants in the family
   - The **Specimens** tab shows samples of the font at various sizes (from 9 to 36 pt.), as well as in reverse (white text on a black background, also called knockout type)
   - The **Type Tester** tab allows you to enter specific type so you can see a preview of your exact copy in the selected font.
   - The **Browser Samples** tab shows a preview of the selected font as rendered by different browsers (important for Web design).

   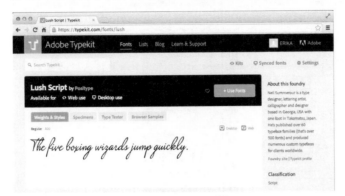

6. **Click the Use Fonts button at the top of the page. In the Use This Family window, click the Sync Selected Fonts button.**

   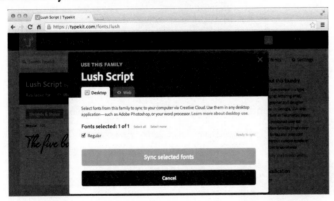

7. **Read the resulting message, then click the Close button.**

   Once you sync a font to your account in the Typekit Web site, it will be available in the Illustrator Font menus.

   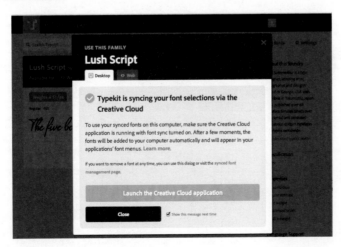

8. When you return to the Font Detail page, click the Fonts link at the top of the screen.

9. In the main Typekit interface, toggle on the San Serif button (in the Classification section) and click the Desktop Use button (in the Available For section).

10. Move your mouse over the Bree font preview to reveal the Use Fonts button for that font.

11. Click the Use Fonts button for the Bree font. In the Use This Family screen, uncheck all but the Regular option.

Because this font family has more than one variant, you have the option to select which variations you want to sync. By default, all fonts in the family are selected; you can uncheck specific fonts if you do not want to sync them in your account.

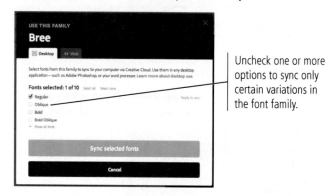

Uncheck one or more options to sync only certain variations in the font family.

12. **Click the Sync Selected Fonts button, then read the resulting message.**

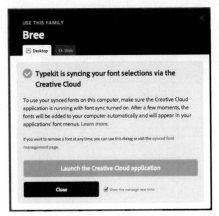

13. **Click the Launch the Creative Cloud Application button.**

    The Fonts screen of the Creative Cloud application should now show all three synced font families.

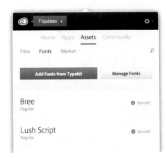

14. **Return to Illustrator and open the Character panel (Window>Type> Character).**

15. **Click to open the Font Family menu in the Character panel. At the top of the menu, click the Apply Typekit Filter button.**

    When this filter is active, only Typekit fonts appear in the Font menu.

16. **Click the Clear [Typekit] Filter button to toggle off the filter.**

17. **Continue to the next stage of the project.**

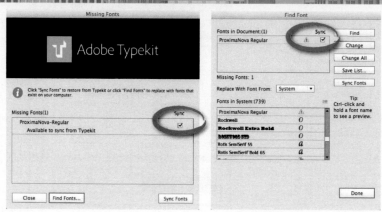

ILLUSTRATOR FOUNDATIONS

If you open a file that uses fonts not available on your computer, you will see a Missing Fonts dialog box listing that fonts that are not installed.

Clicking the Find Fonts button opens the Find Font dialog box, where all fonts used in the file are listed in the top half of the dialog box. You can select the missing font (identified by the warning icon) and replace it with another font that is available on your device.

In either dialog box, the Sync option is checked by default if the missing fonts are available on the Adobe Typekit Web site. You can click the Sync Fonts button to automatically sync the required fonts in your Creative Cloud account, making them available on your computer.

Stage 4 Creating a Finished Poster

The final step in the process is to place your finished sailboat in the background illustration that was created by a colleague; this type of collaborative workflow is common in the graphic design world. Although there are many ways to accomplish this task, you are going to use the most basic — copying and pasting — in this project. When all of the pieces are together in the same file, you will make necessary adjustments to make all pieces of the file work together as a single composition.

 MANAGE ARTWORK WITH SUBLAYERS

In the first stage of this project you created the entire sailboat on a single layer. When you paste it into the background artwork you need to be able to manage the entire illustration as a single object. In this exercise, you work with sublayers to accomplish this goal.

1. **With sailboat.ai open, open the Layers panel.**

2. **Click the arrow to the left of the Boat Drawing layer to reveal the sublayers.**

   Individual objects are listed as sublayers in the Layers panel. Because you created all of the artwork in this file on a single layer, every object appears as a sublayer of the Boat Drawing layer.

Click this arrow to expand the layer.

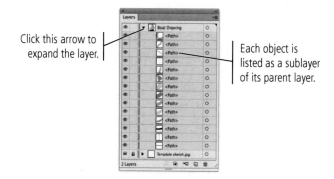

Each object is listed as a sublayer of its parent layer.

3. Click the empty space to the right of any of the available sublayers.

You can use sublayers to select individual objects on a specific layer; the Selected Art icon (the larger rectangle) identifies selected objects. The parent layer of selected art shows a smaller Selected Art icon, which makes it easier to identify which layer contains a specific object.

Note:

This technique also works to select individual components of a group.

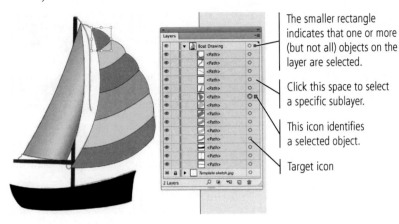

The smaller rectangle indicates that one or more (but not all) objects on the layer are selected.

Click this space to select a specific sublayer.

This icon identifies a selected object.

Target icon

Note:

You can also click the Target icon for a specific layer or sublayer to select specific objects.

4. Choose Select>All.

This command selects all unlocked objects on the artboard. The Layers panel now shows a Selected Art icon for all objects on the Boat Drawing layer. The Selected Art icon for the parent layer is now larger, which means all objects on that layer are selected.

Note:

Press Command/ Control-A to select all objects in the file.

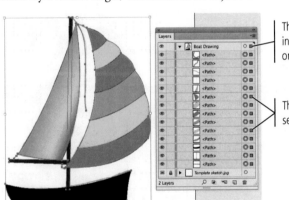

The larger rectangle indicates that all objects on the layer are selected.

These icons identify selected objects.

Note:

You can click the space to the right of a specific layer name to select all objects on that layer.

5. Choose Object>Group. In the Layers panel, click the arrow to expand the Group.

Grouping multiple objects creates a second level of nesting: the Boat Drawing layer is the parent of the Group, which is the parent of the individual objects in the artwork. You can use the Selected Art icons in Layers panel to select individual objects in a group, just as you can to select those objects when they are not grouped.

6. **In the Layers panel, double-click the <Group> name to highlight it. Type Sailboat to rename the group, then press Return/Enter to finalize the new name.**

You can rename sublayers — including groups and individual objects — just as you would rename actual layers. This type of descriptive naming can help you to better organize and manage the elements in a complex file.

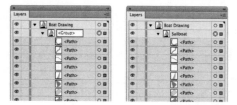

7. **With the group selected on the artboard, choose Edit>Copy.**

You can press Command/Control-C to copy the selected objects.

8. **Save the sailboat.ai file, then choose File>Open. Navigate to poster.ai in the WIP>Regatta folder and click Open.**

9. **Choose View>Fit Artboard in Window so you can see the entire poster file.**

10. **Choose Edit>Paste.**

The group you copied in Step 7 is pasted into the poster file, in the center of the document window.

Because you grouped the sailboat objects before you copied them, they are pasted as a group. If you had not grouped them, each object that makes up the sailboat artwork would be pasted as a separate sublayer in the poster file.

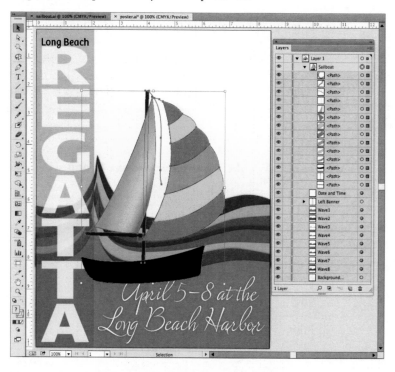

11. **In the Layers panel, click the arrow to the left of the Sailboat sublayer to collapse it.**

12. Using the Selection tool, drag the selected group into the empty space at the top-right section of the poster (use the following image as a guide.

The arrow indicates that this is a group, contianing more than one object.

13. In the Layers panel, drag the Sailboat sublayer down. When a heavy line appears below the Wave6 sublayer, release the mouse button.

When you use the Edit>Paste command, the pasted objects are placed at the top of the stacking order on the active layer. You can use this method to easily reorder sublayers as necessary.

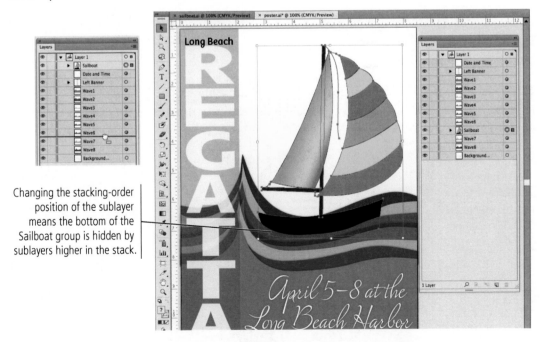

Changing the stacking-order position of the sublayer means the bottom of the Sailboat group is hidden by sublayers higher in the stack.

14. If necessary, adjust the position of the sailboat artwork so the entire bottom edge is hidden by the third wave from the top.

15. Save the file and continue to the next exercise.

LOCK AND HIDE ARTWORK

The final required adjustment for this poster is to change the shape of the highest wave so it looks like a splash. If you review the existing artwork and Layers panel, you can see that the wave nearest the top of the artboard is also the lowest in the sublayer stacking order — Wave8, according to the object names assigned in the Layers panel. To make this task easier, you are going to lock and hide certain sublayers to avoid accidentally changing elements that you don't want to change.

1. **With poster.ai open, click the empty space to the left of the Date and Time sublayer. Hold down the mouse button and drag down the same column for all other sublayers.**

Individual objects in a file can be locked by clicking the empty space immediately left of the object name in the Layers panel. If a Lock icon already appears in that space, you can click the lock icon to unlock a specific object.

You can also select an object on the artboard and choose Object>Lock.

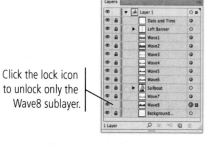

Click here and drag down over the empty space to lock all sublayers.

2. **Click the Lock icon to the left of the Wave8 sublayer to unlock only that element.**

The Object>Unlock All menu command is an all-or-nothing option; it unlocks all locked objects on all layers. The Layers panel allows you to unlock only certain objects, which provides better control over your workflow.

Because all other objects in the file are locked, you can now edit the Wave8 shape without affecting the other elements.

Click the lock icon to unlock only the Wave8 sublayer.

Note:

When an object is locked, you can't select it — which means you can't change it.

3. **In the Layers panel, click the Eye icon for the Left Banner sublayer.**

The Eye icons identify visible layers and sublayers; you can click any Eye icon to hide an entire layer, or hide only specific sublayers. If an element is already hidden, you can click the empty space in the Layers panel to show that element.

You can also select an object on the artboard and choose Object>Hide>Selection. The Object>Show All command, however,

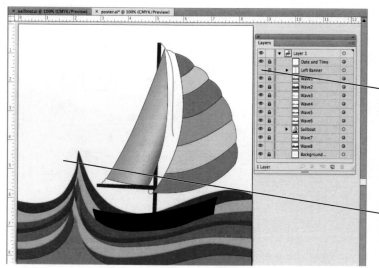

Click an Eye icon to hide a specific layer or sublayer.

Hidden artwork is no longer visible on the artboard.

unlocks all hidden objects on all layers in the file. As with locking and unlocking objects, it is often better to use the icons in the Layers panel to show and hide exactly and only the elements you need.

4. Choose Select>All.

Because all the other sublayers are locked and/or hidden, you selected only the artwork on the Wave8 sublayer.

You can't select hidden or locked objects.

Only the Wave8 sublayer object is selected.

5. Save the file and continue to the next exercise.

CREATE SHAPES WITH THE BLOB BRUSH TOOL

The Blob Brush tool is used to paint filled shapes, which you can manipulate just as you would any other shape made up of anchor points and handles. In this exercise, you use the Blob Brush tool to paint a splashing wave shape, which you will then merge with the top wave shape to create a single object.

1. With sailboat.ai open, deselect everything on the artboard.

2. Double-click the Blob Brush tool in the Tools panel to open the Blob Brush Tool Options dialog box.

3. Check the Keep Selected option and uncheck Merge Only with Selection.

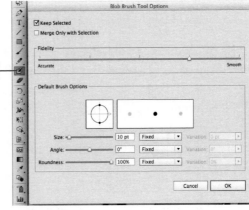

Blob Brush tool

Overlapping Blob Brush strokes merge to create a single object. If Merge Only with Selected is active, overlapping strokes will not merge unless the previous strokes are selected.

4. Set the Fidelity slider to the three-quarter point, close to the Smooth end of the scale.

Like the Pencil tool, the Blob Brush tool Tolerance options determine the accuracy of the resulting shape. Fidelity settings nearer the Accurate end of the scale result in more points to better match the path you drag with the tool; a setting closer to the Smooth end of the scale results in fewer points and smoother edges on the shape you draw.

5. Leave the remaining options at their default values, then click OK.

The lower half of the dialog box defines the size, angle, and roundness of the brush cursor.

6. **Reset the default fill and stroke colors, then move the Blob Brush tool cursor near the peak of the top wave shape. Align the right side of the brush to the right side of the wave peak, as shown here:**

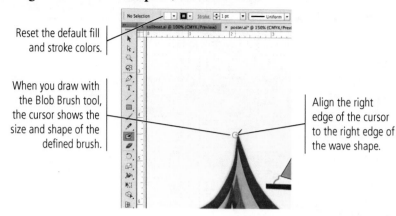

Reset the default fill and stroke colors.

When you draw with the Blob Brush tool, the cursor shows the size and shape of the defined brush.

Align the right edge of the cursor to the right edge of the wave shape.

Note:

Press the right bracket key ( ]) to increase the brush size by one point. Press the left bracket key ([ ) to decrease the brush size by one point.

7. **Click and drag to create an arch shape that approximately matches the curve of the existing wave.**

You are essentially painting a shape that matches the brush stroke you see while you drag. As you paint, the path might look a bit sketchy; however, the resulting path is smoothed based on the Fidelity setting defined in the tool options.

When you release the mouse button, the result is a single shape that fills the entire area where you drew. The shape is still selected because you activate the Keep Selected option in the tool options.

It is important to note that the resulting path is filled with the default *stroke* color you defined in Step 4. When you "paint" with the Blob Brush tool, the defined fill color has no effect on the resulting shape unless the stroke color is set to None.

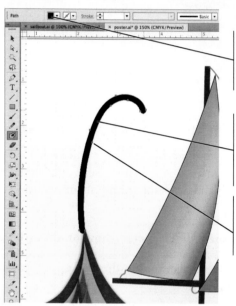

The previous Stroke color becomes the Fill color of the resulting shape.

When you release the mouse button, the result is a filled shape based on where you dragged the brush cursor.

Anchor points are automatically created to define the outside edge of the shape.

8. **With the path still selected, click and drag to create another path near the top of the splash, using a slightly different arch.**

As you complete the rest of this exercise, use our images as a guide. You do not have to match the exact shape you see in our images, but your end result should be similar.

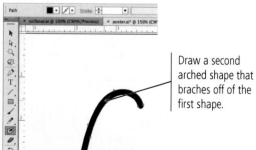

Draw a second arched shape that braches off of the first shape.

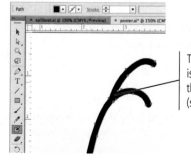

The second path is merged with the previous (selected) path.

9. **Continue adding brush strokes to the selected path to create more branches off the splash shape.**

   As you draw, you can press the right bracket key ( ]) to increase the brush size by one point; press the left bracket key ([ ) to decrease the brush size by one point. Feel free to enlarge or reduce the brush size to create different thicknesses throughout the shape.

10. **Where the splash shape meets the top wave, make sure the left edge of the splash shape matches the left edge of the wave shape.**

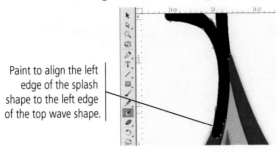

Paint to align the left edge of the splash shape to the left edge of the top wave shape.

11. **Paint several shapes that do not overlap the main splash shape.**

    When you paint a shape that does not overlap the existing selection, it is created as a new, separate shape.

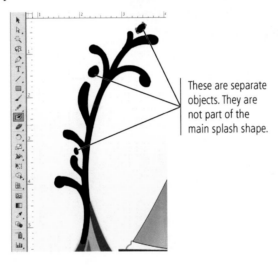

These are separate objects. They are not part of the main splash shape.

12. **Deselect everything in the layout.**

13. **In the Layers panel, click the top <Path> sublayer to select it in the panel. Press Shift and click the bottom <Path> object to add it and all in-between sublayers to the previous selection.**

    Selecting an element in the Layers panel is not the same thing as selecting it on the artboard. The right side of the panel shows no Selected Art icons, which means nothing is selected on the artboard.

14. **In the Layers panel, click any of the selected elements and drag them below the Wave8 sublayer.**

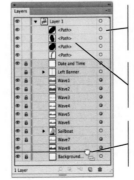

Our splash shape includes four separate paths (objects).

Shift-click to select multiple consecutive sublayers in the panel.

Drag all selected sublayers below the Wave8 sublayer.

Note:

You can Command/Control-click to select multiple, nonconsecutive layers or sublayers in the Layers panel.

15. Choose Select>All.

Because most objects are locked, only the top wave and splash shapes are selected.

16. In the Pathfinder panel, click the Unite button.

The Unite function merges overlapping shapes into a single object; non-overlapping objects are grouped with the merged shape. All elements affected by the unification adopt the appearance attributes (fill color, etc.) of the top-most selected object — which is why you reordered the sublayers in Step 14.

Unite button

The resulting group contains all objects in the wave shape.

17. In the Layers panel, click the empty space to the left of the Left Banner sublayer to show that layer.

Click here to reshow the Left Banner sublayer.

18. Save the file and continue to the final exercise.

SAVE THE FILE AS PDF

Adobe PDF (or simply PDF, for Portable Document Format) has become a universal method of moving files to virtually any digital destination. One of the most important uses for the PDF format is the ability to create perfectly formatted digital documents, exactly as they would appear if printed on paper. You can embed fonts, images, drawings, and other elements into the file so all the required bits are available on any computer. The PDF format can be used to move your artwork to the Web as a low-resolution RGB file or to a commercial printer as a high-resolution CMYK file.

1. **With `poster.ai` open, choose File>Save As.**
   If necessary, navigate to your WIP>Regatta folder as the target location.

2. **Choose Adobe PDF in the Format/Save As Type menu and click Save.**

Again, the extension automatically changes to reflect the selected format (.pdf).

3. **Choose Illustrator Default in the Adobe PDF Preset menu.**

4. **Review the options in the General pane.**

   Read the description area to see what Adobe has to say about these options.

Use this menu to call a group of saved settings (called a preset).

Choose a category from this menu to see related options.

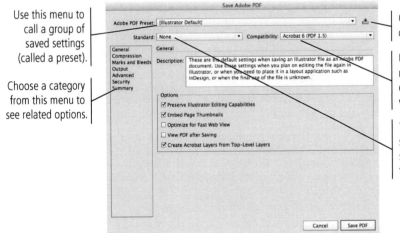

Click here to save your current options as a preset.

Use the Compatibility menu to save the file to be compatible with older versions of Acrobat Reader.

You can save PDFs using several different technical standards (PDF/X formats) for printing applications.

5. **Click Compression in the list of categories on the left and review the options.**

These options allow you to reduce the resulting file size by compressing color, grayscale, and/or monochrome bitmap (raster) images. You can also compress text and line art by clicking the check box at the bottom.

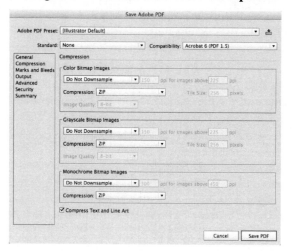

6. **Review the Marks and Bleeds options.**

These options add different marks to the output page:

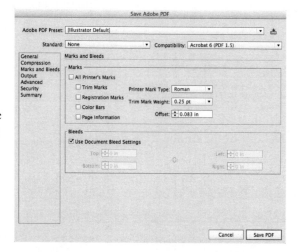

- **Trim marks** indicate the edge of the page, where a page printed on a larger sheet will be cut down to its final size. You can also define the thickness (weight) of the trim marks, as well as how far from the page edge the lines should appear (offset).

- **Registration marks** resemble a small crosshair. These marks are added to each ink unit on a printing press to make sure the different inks are properly aligned to one another.

- **Color bars** are rows of small squares across the sheet, used to verify press settings for accurate color reproduction.

- **Page information** adds the file name, date, and time of output.

- **Bleeds** define how much of elements outside the page boundaries will be included in the final output. Most printers require at least a 0.125″ bleed on each side, but you should always ask before you create the final file.

7. **Click Save PDF.**

8. **Close any open Illustrator files.**

Note:

The other categories of options are explained in later projects that discuss transparency and color management.

Note:

Most printers require trim marks to be created outside the bleed area. Always check with your service provider when saving a PDF for commercial output.

1. The _____ tool is used to place anchor points that are connected by line segments.

2. The _____ tool is used to change a smooth anchor point to a corner anchor point (and vice versa).

3. The _____ tool is used to edit individual anchor points (and their related handles) on a vector path.

4. _____ is the range of possible colors within a specific color model.

5. _____ are the four component colors in process-color output.

6. The _____ panel includes value sliders for each component in the defined color model.

7. The _____ is used to paint shapes of solid color based on the defined brush size and the area you drag with a single mouse click.

8. The _____ appears over a gradient-filled object when selected with the Gradient tool; you can use it to control the position and direction of color in the gradient-filled object.

9. Changes made to a _____ color swatch are reflected in all elements where that color is applied.

10. Individual objects on a layer appear as _____ in the Layers panel.

1. Describe three ways to deselect the current selection on the artboard.

2. Briefly explain the significance of "process color" related to Illustrator artwork.

3. Briefly explain the advantage of using the PDF format for creating printable files.

Use what you learned in this project to complete the following freeform exercise.
Carefully read the art director and client comments, then create your own design to meet the needs of the project.
Use the space below to sketch ideas; when finished, write a brief explanation of your reasoning behind your final design.

art director comments

Your local animal shelter hosts an annual fundraising gala on the first Saturday in October. You have been hired to create a poster advertising this year's theme — a classic, black-tie masquerade ball.

❑ Design an 11″ × 17″ poster to promote the event in local storefronts and other public venues.

❑ Develop a creative type treatment for the event name: "Barking Mad for the Masquerade"

❑ Find or create imagery and graphics to support the event theme.

❑ Include the event date (look at this year's calendar to find out the exact date) prominently in the poster design.

❑ Include the contact information (phone number and Web address) for your local animal shelter.

client comments

We raise a considerable portion of our annual operating budget during this annual event. This year the theme is a very classic masquerade in the style of Victorian-England opulence... Think "Phantom of the Opera," the state dining room on the Titanic, that sort of thing. Men in tuxes and women in flowing gowns, everyone masked in some fashion until the traditional 'reveal' at midnight.

Every year the event includes a silent auction with some incredible prizes that are donated by local businesses, as well as a gourmet four-course meal prepared by a celebrity chef.

If there is any way you can tastefully incorporate a couple of animal photos into the poster, we would like that. But it isn't really a requirement as long as the shelter's name and contact information is clearly displayed.

project justification

_____
_____
_____
_____
_____
_____
_____
_____
_____
_____
_____
_____
_____
_____

Project Summary

This project incorporated more advanced drawing techniques that allow you to exercise precise control over every point and path in a file. The Pen tool is arguably one of the most important tools you will use throughout your career as an illustrator; although it can be challenging at first, practice is the best way to master this skill.

This project also explored working with color in Illustrator: applying color, saving global color swatches to make changes more efficiently, and using gradients to add visual interest.

Finally, you saved your artwork in a file format that is commonly used to share Illustrator artwork with other applications. The PDF format is an invaluable part of design workflows using software applications that can't import native Illustrator files.

Use the Pen tool to create custom artwork based on lines in a hand-drawn sketch

Use the Anchor Point tool to reshape specific line segments

Use the Blob Brush tool to paint the outline of custom shapes

Use the Shape Builder tool to divide overlapping objects into individual shapes

Use the Gradient Annotator to control the content and position of gradients within specific objects

Use global swatches to allow universal changes to all objects where that color is applied

Use layers and sublayers to manage the various elements in a complex file

Long Beach

REGATTA

April 5–8 at the Long Beach Harbor

Identity Package

Your client, Graham Apple, owns an organic orchard in Central Florida. He hired you to create a corporate identity package so he can begin branding his products to reach a larger consumer base in gourmet groceries throughout the Southeast. He asked you to develop a logo, and then create the standard identity pieces (letterhead and envelope) that he will use for business promotion and correspondence.

This project incorporates the following skills:

❏ Developing custom logo artwork based on an object in a photograph

❏ Using a gradient mesh to create realistic color blends

❏ Converting type to outlines and manipulating letter shapes to create a finished logotype

❏ Using layers to easily manage complex artwork

❏ Creating multiple artboards to contain specific projects and layouts

❏ Building various logo versions to meet specific output requirements

❏ Saving EPS files for maximum flexibility

❏ Printing desktop proofs of individual artboards

It's just a coincidence that my last name is Apple and I own an organic orchard, but I might as well take advantage where I can. I want my logo to be — surprise! — an apple, with some creative type treatment for the name of the farm (Apple Organics).

Once the logo is complete, I want you to use it to create letterhead and envelopes that I will have preprinted; I want a more professional feel than I can create using my laser printer. The printer I spoke with said I could do this for less money if I go "four-color" for the letterhead, but "two-color" for the envelope; I really don't know what that means — I'm hoping you do.

The logo is the first part of this project because you will use it on the other two pieces. The client told you exactly what he wants, so that part is taken care of. I had our photographer take a good apple picture; use that as the basis for the one you draw in the logo art.

The client wants to print the letterhead in four-color and the envelope in two-color, so you will have to create two different versions of the logo. Since logos are used on far more than just these two jobs in this one application, you should also create a one-color version because the client will inevitably ask for it at some point.

To complete this project, you will:

- [ ] Use the Pen tool to trace the outline of a photograph
- [ ] Create a gradient mesh
- [ ] Use Smart Guides to manage a gradient mesh
- [ ] Use effects to add object highlights
- [ ] Create and control point-type objects
- [ ] Convert text to outlines so you can manipulate the letter shapes
- [ ] Use the Appearance panel to revert gradient mesh objects back to regular paths
- [ ] Apply spot-color inks for special printing applications
- [ ] Create versions of the final logo for one-color, two-color, and four-color printing
- [ ] Print desktop proofs of the completed identity pieces

Stage 1 Working with Gradient Meshes

There are several important points to keep in mind when you design a logo. First, logos need to be scalable. A company might place its logo on the head of a golf tee or on the side of a building. This is a strong argument for using the simpler line-art approach instead of photography. Vector graphics — the kind you typically create in Illustrator — can be scaled as large or small as necessary without losing quality; photographs are raster images, and they can't be greatly enlarged or reduced without losing quality. That's why you're converting a photograph (a raster image) into a vector graphic in this project.

Second, you almost always need more than one version of any given logo — very often in more than one file format. Different kinds of output require different formats (specifically, one set of files for print and one for the Web), and some types of jobs require special options saved in the files — such as the four-color, two-color, and one-color versions of the logo that you will create in this project.

SET UP THE WORKSPACE

Your client needs several versions of a new logo, including one with realistic color. Illustrator includes a number of tools ideally suited for creating lifelike illustrations. In this project, you will work from a photograph to create a vector-based apple graphic that will be part of your client's logo. You will start with the full-color version, and then work from there to create the other variations that are part of a typical logo package.

1. **Download `Organics_Print14_RF.zip` from the Student Files Web page.**

2. **Expand the ZIP archive in your WIP folder (Macintosh) or copy the archive contents into your WIP folder (Windows).**

   This results in a folder named **Organics**, which contains the files you need for this project. You should also use this folder to save the files you create in this project.

3. **In Illustrator, choose File>New.**

4. **Type `apple` in the Name field, choose Letter as the page size, and choose Inches as the unit of measurement.**

   At this point, you are simply using the artboard as a drawing space, so you only need to make it large enough to draw. Later, you will adjust the artboard to meet the specific needs of the finished logo.

5. **Make sure the Number of Artboards field is set to 1.**

   Later in this project, you will add multiple artboards to hold various versions of the logo. For now, you only need one artboard, which will serve as a drawing board.

6. **In the Advanced options, choose CMYK in the Color Mode menu and choose High (300 ppi) in the Raster Effects menu.**

   Because the CMYK gamut is smaller than the RGB gamut, you are starting with the smaller gamut to avoid the color shift that could occur if you started with RGB and converted the colors to CMYK. You are also creating the file to meet the high-resolution requirements of commercial printing. While not part of this project, you can easily use the Save For Web utility to export low-resolution RGB versions of the file for digital media.

   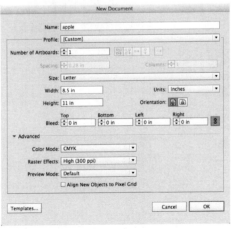

7. **Click OK to create the new file.**

8. **Choose File>Place. Navigate to `apple.jpg` in your WIP>Organics folder. Make sure the Template option is checked, and click Place.**

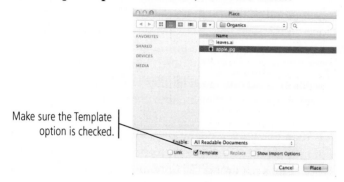

Make sure the Template option is checked.

9. **In the Layers panel, double-click the template layer icon to open the Layer Options dialog box. Uncheck the Dim Images option and click OK.**

Choosing the Template option places an image onto a template layer that is automatically dimmed. You want the photograph to appear at full visibility so you can extract colors from the photo.

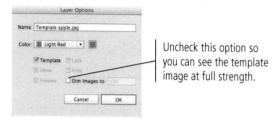

Uncheck this option so you can see the template image at full strength.

For most of the drawing process, you will use the apple photo as the basis of your artwork. You will draw on other layers, and then delete the template layer when your apple graphic is complete.

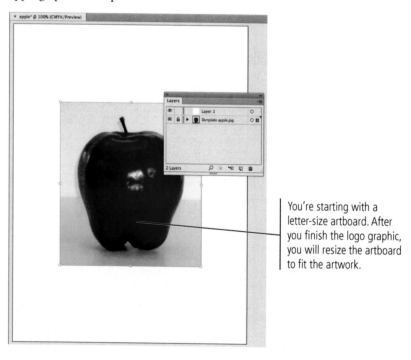

You're starting with a letter-size artboard. After you finish the logo graphic, you will resize the artboard to fit the artwork.

10. **Save the file as a native Illustrator file named `apple.ai` in your WIP>Organics folder, and then continue to the next exercise.**

DRAW THE APPLE SHAPES

The apple shape in this logo is another example of a custom shape composed of lines and paths. In this project you use a photo as your guide, and use the Pen tool to create the necessary paths. The first step is to determine what shapes you need to create.

1. **With apple.ai open, double-click the Layer 1 name and type** `Apple Front`. **Press Return/Enter to finalize the new layer name.**

2. **Using the Pen tool with a 1-pt black stroke and no fill, draw the outline of the front part of the apple. Follow the shape of the apple as it curves in front of the stem.**

   We started our contour line at the bottom part of the apple where there is a sharp corner because starting a contour line on a curve often creates less than perfect results. Use our image as a rough guide for where to place the anchor points; yours doesn't have to match exactly, but it should come close.

Note:

Refer back to Project 2: Regatta Artwork for details about drawing and editing Bézier curves.

Pen tool

We started drawing here (at a corner).

Skip over the area that wraps behind the stem.

3. **If necessary, use the Direct Selection tool to adjust the anchor points and handles until the outline matches the shape of the apple.**

4. **Create another new layer and rename it** `Apple Back`. **In the Layers panel, drag this layer below the Apple Front layer.**

5. **On the Apple Back layer, use the Pen tool to draw the shape of the back part of the apple (where the apple curves behind the stem).**

   Be sure to overlap this shape with the Apple Front shape so no blank space will show between the two elements later.

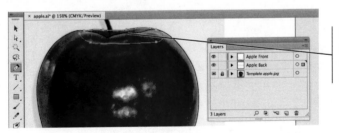

Overlap this line to ensure complete coverage when you start adding color.

6. **Create a new layer and rename it Stem.**

   Since you were just working on the Apple Back layer, the new Stem layer should automatically reside between the Apple Front and Apple Back layers in the Layers panel (which is where you want it to reside). If not, drag the Stem layer to the correct position before continuing.

7. **Draw the outline of the stem on the active Stem layer. Again, overlap the bottom of the Stem shape with the Apple Front shape.**

   You now have all the outlines for the apple, with each outline on its own layer. When you start adding gradient meshes in the next exercises, you will see how important it is to use a different layer for each element.

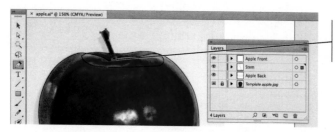

The Stem shape overlaps the Apple Front shape.

8. **Save the file and continue to the next exercise.**

CREATE A GRADIENT MESH

A gradient mesh is basically a special type of fill. Each point in the mesh can have a different color value; the colors of adjacent mesh points determine the colors along the gradient between the two points. When you paint objects with a mesh, it's similar to painting with ink or watercolor. It takes considerable practice to become proficient with gradient meshes.

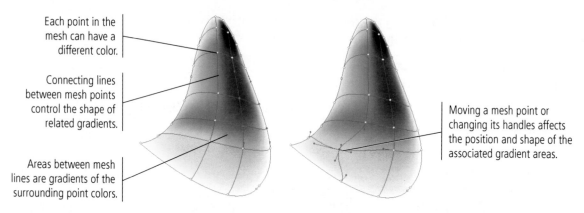

Each point in the mesh can have a different color.

Connecting lines between mesh points control the shape of related gradients.

Areas between mesh lines are gradients of the surrounding point colors.

Moving a mesh point or changing its handles affects the position and shape of the associated gradient areas.

One of the techniques you will explore in this project is Illustrator's Outline mode. Outline mode allows you to see the points and paths of an object without the colors and fills. This viewing mode can be very useful when you need to adjust anchor points of one shape while viewing the underlying objects.

1. **With apple.ai open, click the eye icons in the Layers panel to hide the Apple Back and Stem layers, and then select the Apple Front layer.**

2. **Using the Selection tool, select the outline shape on the Apple Front layer.**

3. **Using the Eyedropper tool, click a medium-red color in the apple image to fill the selected apple shape with the sampled color.**

You can add a gradient mesh to a path without filling it with color first, but if you don't choose a color, the mesh will automatically fill with white. It's easier to create a good mesh if you start with a fill that colors most of the object.

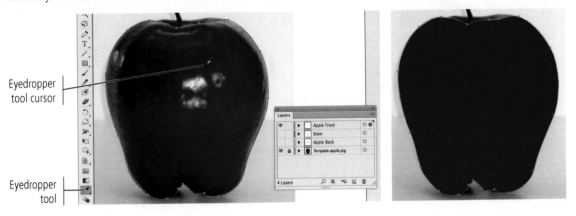

Eyedropper tool cursor

Eyedropper tool

4. **Choose Object>Create Gradient Mesh.**

Understanding Gradient Mesh Options

When creating a gradient mesh, the number of rows and columns you create depends on the size and shape of the object you want to shade. You might want to experiment with these settings before you click OK and create the mesh. If you add too many mesh points, the colors blend incorrectly and take a long time to paint; if you add too few mesh lines, it can be difficult — if not impossible — to add enough depth to the illustration. (Even though you can use the Mesh tool to add and delete mesh lines later, it's more efficient to create a mesh as close as possible to what you need as the final result.)

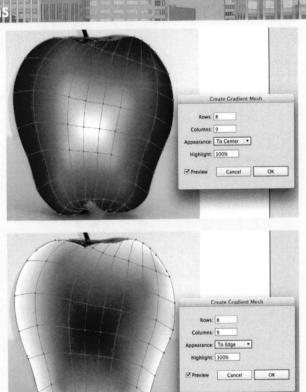

The Appearance option in the Create Gradient Mesh dialog box determines how colors affect the mesh you create:

- The **Flat** option, which you used in this exercise, spreads a single color to all points in the mesh. If you don't fill the shape with a color before creating the mesh, the mesh object will fill with solid white.

- The **To Center** option (upper right) creates a white highlight at the center of the mesh and gradually spreads the highlight color outward toward the object edges. The Highlight (%) field controls the strength of the white in the resulting mesh.

- The **To Edge** option (lower right) is essentially the opposite of the To Center option; the white highlight appears around the edges of the mesh, blending to the solid color in the center of the mesh object.

5. **In the Create Gradient Mesh dialog box, activate the Preview option. Set the Rows value to 8 and the Columns value to 9, and make sure the Appearance menu is set to Flat.**

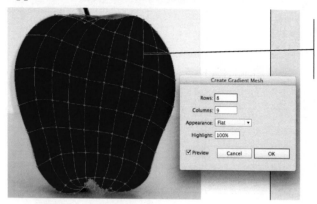

The Rows and Columns settings determine how many lines will make up the resulting mesh.

Note:

When you convert a path to a mesh, the shape is no longer a path. You cannot apply a stroke attribute to a gradient mesh object.

6. **Click OK to create the mesh.**

7. **Choose View>Outline.**

In Outline mode, you see only the edges or **wireframes** of the objects in the file.

Template layers are not affected when you view the file in Outline mode. You can now see the mesh wireframe and the actual pixels of the apple image, enabling you to sample colors directly from the apple image, and then use those colors to paint the mesh points.

(Your mesh might appear different than ours, based on where you placed your anchor points on the shape edges. Don't worry — you will still be able to achieve the same overall effect as what you see in our examples.)

Note:

In our screen shots, we have the bounding box turned off to better show only the mesh points. You can turn off the bounding box by choosing View>Hide Bounding Box.

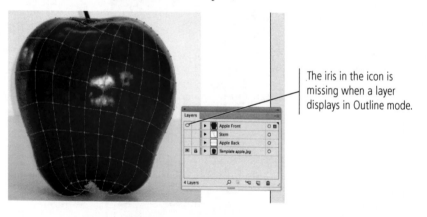

The iris in the icon is missing when a layer displays in Outline mode.

8. **Using the Direct Selection tool, click the top-left point on the inside of the mesh object to select only that mesh point.**

Don't select one of the mesh points on the outside edge of the shape.

9. **With the mesh point selected, choose the Eyedropper tool in the Tools panel, and then click next to the selected mesh point to sample the color from the apple photo.**

   Because the mesh object is still displayed in Outline mode, you can't see the effect of the color sampling.

   Selected anchor point

   Use the Eyedropper tool to sample the color next to the anchor point.

   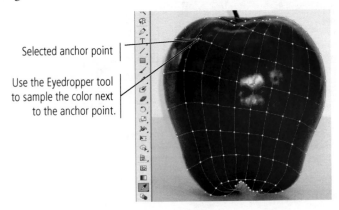

10. **Press and hold the Command/Control key to temporarily access the Direct Selection tool, and then click the next mesh point on the same vertical mesh line.**

    Selected anchor point

    The Eyedropper tool is still technically active.

    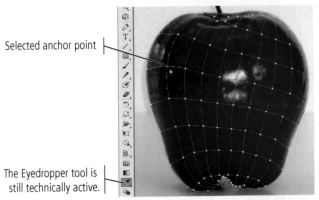

    Note:

    You can use the Opacity field in the Control panel to define a different opacity for every point in a gradient mesh.

11. **Release the Command/Control key to return to the Eyedropper tool, and then click to sample the color next to the selected mesh point.**

    When you release the Command/Control key, you return to the previously active tool.

12. **Continue this process to change the color of the mesh points in the first column of the mesh.**

13. **Choose View>Preview to see the actual content of the visible layers.**

14. **Deselect everything on the page and review your progress.**

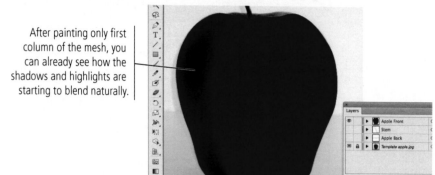

After painting only first column of the mesh, you can already see how the shadows and highlights are starting to blend naturally.

15. **Command/Control-click the eye icon for the Apple Front layer to change only that layer back to Outline mode.**

    When working in Outline mode, Command/Control-clicking a layer's visibility icon (the eye icon) returns only that layer to Preview mode.

16. **Using the same technique from the previous steps, finish painting all the mesh points in the mesh object.**

    This task might seem tedious because there are so many points in the mesh, but with this process, you can create realistic depth in a flat vector object in a matter of minutes. To accomplish the same result using manual techniques would require many hours of time and a high degree of artistic skill.

17. **Command/Control-click the Apple Front layer eye icon to return the layer to Preview mode, and then deselect the mesh object and review your results.**

18. **Save the file and continue to the next exercise.**

WORK WITH A MESH USING SMART GUIDES

It can be difficult to select and manipulate points in a mesh in Preview mode because you can't see the actual mesh lines and points until the mesh object is selected. You could move your cursor around until you locate the exact mesh point you want to work with, or you could continue switching back and forth between Preview and Outline modes. Both methods, however, can be time consuming (and frustrating).

Fortunately, Smart Guides solve this problem. Using Smart Guides, you can see the entire mesh wireframe as soon as your cursor touches any part of the object — providing a temporary outline/preview combination.

1. **With apple.ai open, choose View>Smart Guides to make sure that option is turned on.**

2. **Make sure the Snap to Point option is toggled off in the View menu.**

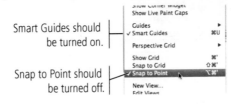

Smart Guides should be turned on.

Snap to Point should be turned off.

3. **Command/Control-click the visibility icon for the Apple Front layer so you can see the photo behind the mesh object.**

4. **Make sure everything in the file is deselected, and then roll the Direct Selection tool over the apple shape.**

   You can now see the mesh points and lines, as well as the precise location of the Direct Selection tool.

With Smart Guides turned on, you can easily view and select specific anchors in the mesh.

5. **Using the Eyedropper tool, sample the highlight color on the top-left side of the apple shape.**

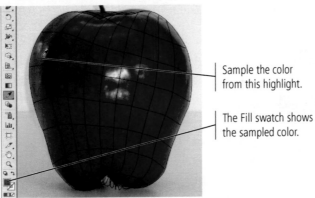

Sample the color from this highlight.

The Fill swatch shows the sampled color.

6. **Command/Control-click the visibility icon for the Apple Front layer to restore that layer to Preview mode.**

7. **Choose the Mesh tool from the Tools panel.**

   The Mesh tool adds new gridlines to an existing mesh, or it creates a mesh if you click inside a basic shape that doesn't currently have a mesh.

8. **Click the third horizontal mesh line, between the first and second vertical mesh lines, to create a new vertical mesh line (as shown in the following image).**

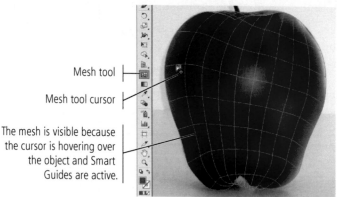
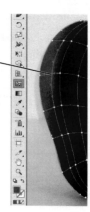

Mesh tool

Mesh tool cursor

The mesh is visible because the cursor is hovering over the object and Smart Guides are active.

Clicking this horizontal mesh line adds a new vertical mesh line, colored with the highlight color you sampled in the previous step.

9. **Press Command/Control and click away from the mesh object to deselect it.**

10. **Change the Apple Front layer to Outline mode.**

11. **Using the Direct Selection tool, drag the points in the second horizontal mesh line to better align to the highlight in the apple photograph.**

   Use the following image as a guide.

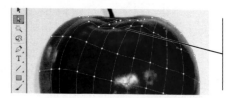

Using the Direct Selection tool, adjust the points on the second horizontal mesh line so it more closely matches the contour of the highlight.

12. **Using the Mesh tool, click three times along the vertical mesh line directly below the stem to add three horizontal mesh lines between the first two rows of the existing mesh.**

   Clicking a horizontal mesh line with the Mesh tool creates a new vertical mesh line. To add a horizontal mesh line, click the Mesh tool on a vertical mesh line.

   It isn't necessary to return the layer to Preview mode before adding lines to the mesh.

Click this vertical mesh line twice to add three horizontal mesh lines.

Note:

It might be helpful to deselect the mesh after adding the first new mesh line, and then click again to add the second and third mesh lines.

13. **Using the Direct Selection tool, select the point on the (now) third horizontal mesh line, directly below the stem.**

   This is one of the mesh lines you created with the Mesh tool in the previous step.

14. **With the mesh point selected, use the Eyedropper tool to sample the light red of the apple's highlight to change the color of the point.**

    When you change the color of a mesh point, you change the way surrounding colors blend into that point's color. By changing this point to a medium red, you reduce the distance over which the highlight color (in the lower point) can blend — effectively shortening the highlight area.

    Changing this anchor point to a lighter red adds a highlight to the apple graphic, more closely matching the highlight in the original image.

15. **Command/Control-click to select the mesh point to the immediate left of the point where you placed the highlight.**

    Remember, pressing Command/Control with another tool selected temporarily accesses the last-used Selection tool.

16. **Release the mouse button to return to the Eyedropper tool, and then sample the highlight color again to spread the highlight horizontally across the apple.**

17. **Repeat Steps 15–16 for the point to the right of the one you changed in Step 13.**

    By filling these two anchors with the highlight color, you extend the highlight horizontally along the mesh line.

18. **Deselect the mesh object, return the Apple Front layer to Preview mode, and review your work.**

    The highlight area — which you only defined on the third mesh line — only extends from the between the second and fourth horizontal gridlines. Because the space between the mesh lines you added is narrow, the highlight is equally narrow.

19. **Continue adjusting the positions and colors of the mesh points until you are satisfied with the result.**

20. **Save the file and continue to the next exercise.**

Building and coloring the shape for the apple's front should have given you a good idea of how mesh points control color blending from one point to another. Because you set up the file using layers for the individual shapes that make up the apple, it will be fairly easy to create additional meshes for the remaining pieces of the apple.

1. With **apple.ai** open, hide the Apple Front layer and show the Apple Back layer.

2. Using the Selection tool, select the shape on the Apple Back layer.

3. Using the Eyedropper tool, click a darker part of the apple to fill the selected shape with the sampled color.

4. Choose Object>Create Gradient Mesh and add a 3-row, 5-column mesh with the Appearance menu set to Flat.

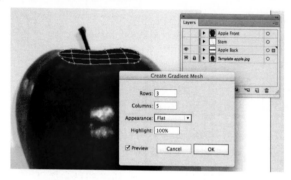

5. Use the same method you learned in the previous exercise to color the mesh points for the Apple Back shape.

Switch the Apple Back layer to Outline mode, and then use the Eyedropper tool to sample colors from the photo for each point in the mesh.

6. Show the Apple Front layer and review your work.

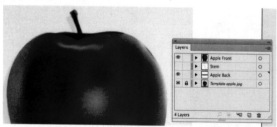

7. Lock the Apple Back layer, and then show the Stem layer.

8. Select the stem shape and fill it with a color sampled from the lightest color near the top of the stem.

9. Change the Stem layer to Outline mode.

10. Convert the stem path to a Gradient Mesh object with 2 rows and 2 columns, using a flat appearance.

11. Using the Direct Selection tool, select the center mesh point in the stem shape. Drag the selected point to a more central position within the shape.

12. With the same point selected, use the Eyedropper tool to sample the dark color of the stem.

Move and recolor the center mesh point in the object.

13. Return the Stem layer to Preview mode.

14. Deselect everything, and then hide the template layer to review your work.

15. Select the template layer in the Layers panel, then click the Delete Selection button to remove the template layer. When asked to confirm the deletion, click Yes.

Delete Selection button

16. Save the file, and then continue to the next stage of the project.

Stage 2 Working with Type

To create a complete logo, you pair logo artwork with text that makes up the corporate brand (the company name and tagline, if there is one). Illustrator includes sophisticated tools for controlling type — from changing the font and size to controlling the appearance of quotes and using styles to format long blocks of text.

In this stage of the project, you will use some of the basic type formatting options to set your client's company name. You will also use illustration techniques to manipulate the individual letter shapes in the company name to create the finished logotype.

Type Terminology

Before you begin the exercises in the second stage of this project, you should understand the terms that are commonly used when people talk about type. Keep the following terms in mind as you work through the next exercises.

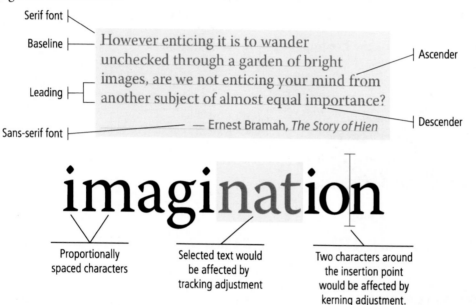

Type is typically divided into two basic categories: serif and sans serif. **Serif type** has small flourishes on the ends of the letterforms; **sans-serif** has no such decorations (sans is French for "without"). There are other categories of special or decorative fonts, including script, symbol, dingbat, decorative, and image fonts.

The actual shape of letters is determined by the specific **font** you use; each character in a font is referred to as a **glyph**. Fonts can be monospaced or proportionally spaced. In a monospace font, each character takes up the same amount of space on a line; in other words, a lowercase i and m occupy the same horizontal space. In a proportionally spaced font, different characters occupy different amounts of horizontal space as necessary.

The **x-height** of type is the height of the lowercase letter x. Elements that extend below the baseline are called **descenders** (as in g, j, and p); elements that extend above the x-height are called **ascenders** (as in b, d, and k).

The size of type is usually measured in **points** (there are approximately 72 points in an inch). When you define a type size, you determine the distance from the bottom of the descenders to the top of the ascenders (plus a small extra space above the ascenders called the **body clearance**).

When you set type, it rests on a non-printing line called the **baseline**. If a type element has more than one line in a single paragraph, the distance from one baseline to the next is called **leading** (pronounced "ledding"). Most applications set the default leading as 120% of the type size.

CREATE POINT-TYPE OBJECTS

Creating type in Illustrator is fairly simple; simply click with the Type tool and begin typing. Many advanced options are also available, such as importing type from an external file, using type areas to control long blocks of text, and so on. In this project, you concentrate on the basic type formatting controls.

1. **With apple.ai open (from your WIP>Organics folder), lock and hide all three layers in the file.**

2. **Create a new layer named Logotype at the top of the layer stack, and make sure the new layer is selected.**

3. **Choose the Type tool in the Tools panel, and then click an empty area of the artboard to create a new point-type object.**

   You can create two basic kinds of type (or text) objects in Illustrator: **point-type objects** (also called **path type**), where the text usually resides on a single line or path; and **area-type objects,** where the text fills a specific shape (usually a rectangle).

   When you single-click with the Type tool, you create **point type**. You will see a flashing **insertion point** where text will appear when you begin typing.

4. **With the insertion point flashing, type apple.**

   When you add a new type object (either point type or area type) without changing anything in Illustrator, the type is automatically set in the last-used font and type settings, which will probably be different from one computer to the next.

Note:

We used Magenta as the layer color so it would be more visible in our screen captures.

When you click the
Type tool, Illustrator
automatically switches
to a default black fill
and no stroke.

Wherever you click with the
Type tool, you'll see this
flashing insertion point.

When working with text, the
Control panel includes some
common text formatting options.

Type tool

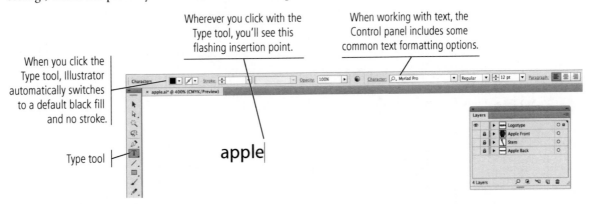

apple

5. **Choose the Direct Selection tool in the Tools panel.**

When selected with the Direct
Selection tool, you can see the point
and path that make up the type object.

New type objects default to
left paragraph alignment.

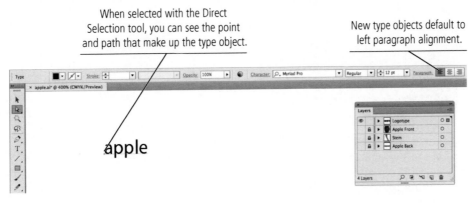

apple

6. **With the type object selected, click the Paragraph Align Center button in the Control panel.**

Remember, different options are available in the Control panel, depending on the width of your monitor. If the Paragraph Align buttons are not available in the Control panel, you can click the Paragraph hot-text link, or open the stand-alone Paragraph panel (Window>Type>Paragraph).

Individual characters do not need to be selected to change text formatting. Changes made while a type *object* is selected apply to all text in that type object.

Note:

Hot text *is any text in the user interface that appears blue and underlined. Clicking these hot-text links opens a panel or dialog box where you can change the related settings.*

Click the hot-text link to open the Paragraph panel.

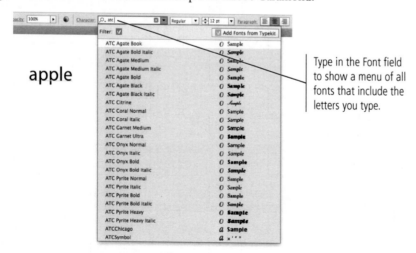

The point shows how the type object is aligned.

Align Center button

7. **In the Control panel, click the Font Family field to highlight the active font. Type atc.**

When you type in the Font Family field, a menu shows all fonts that include the letters you type. By default, the menu includes any font containing those letters, regardless of the position of the letters within the font name. In other words, typing "gar" would show fonts named both "Garamond" and "Adobe Garamond."

If you click the magnifying glass icon to the left of the field, you can choose Search First Word Only (Legacy). In that case, the letters you type automatically scroll the Font Family list to the first font with the typed letters at the beginning of the name; typing "gar" would scroll to Garamond and skip over Adobe Garamond.

Note:

You can also open the regular Character panel by choosing Window>Type>Character.

Type in the Font field to show a menu of all fonts that include the letters you type.

If your Control panel does not include the Font menu, click the Character hot-text link to open the Character panel; then use the Font field in the panel to complete Steps 7 and 8.

8. Click ATC Onyx Normal in the Font menu to select that font.

After you select the font, you should notice that the Font Family menu shows "ATC Onyx" and the secondary Font Style menu shows "Normal." When you use the Font Search option (as in Step 7), the resulting menu shows all font variations that include the letters you type —including different styles within the same family.

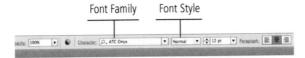

apple

ILLUSTRATOR FOUNDATIONS

The Character panel, accessed either from the Control panel hot text or as an independent panel by choosing Window>Type>Character, includes all the options you can use to change the appearance of selected text characters.

If these options are not visible, choose Show Options in the panel Options menu.

Touch Type tool
Font Family
Size
Kerning
Horizontal Scale
Baseline Shift
Language Dictionary

Font Style
Leading
Tracking
Vertical Scale
Character Rotation
Type Styles
Anti-Aliasing

- The **Touch Type tool** is used to change the shape and position of individual characters in a text object.

- **Leading** is the distance from one baseline to the next. Adobe applications treat leading as a character attribute, even though leading controls the space between lines of an individual paragraph. (Space between paragraphs is controlled using the Space Before option in the Paragraph panel.) To change leading for an entire paragraph, you must first select the entire paragraph. This approach means you can change the leading for a single line of a paragraph by selecting any character(s) in that line; however, changing the leading for any character in a line applies the same change to the entire line that contains those characters.

- **Kerning** increases or decreases the space between pairs of letters. Kerning is used in cases where particular letters in specific fonts need to be manually spread apart or brought together to eliminate a too-tight or too-spread-out appearance. Manual kerning is usually necessary in headlines or other large type elements. (Many commercial fonts have built-in kerning pairs, so you won't need to apply much hands-on intervention with kerning. Adobe applications default to the kerning values stored in the **font metrics**.)

- **Tracking**, also known as "range kerning," refers to the overall tightness or looseness across a range of characters. Tracking and kerning are applied in

thousandths of an **em** (or the amount of space occupied by an uppercase "M," which is usually the widest character in a typeface).

- **Vertical Scale** and **Horizontal Scale** artificially stretch or contract the selected characters. This scaling is a quick way of achieving condensed or expanded type if those variations of a font don't exist. (Type that has been artificially condensed or expanded too much looks bad because the scaling destroys the type's metrics; if possible, use a condensed or expanded version of a font before resorting to horizontal or vertical scaling.)

- **Baseline Shift** moves the selected type above or below the baseline by a specific number of points. Positive numbers move the characters up; negative values move the characters down.

- **Character Rotation** rotates only selected letters, rather than rotating the entire type object.

- Type Styles — **All Caps, Small Caps, Superscript, Subscript, Underline**, and **Strikethrough** — change the appearance of selected characters.

- **Language Dictionary** defines the language that is used to check spelling in the story.

- **Anti-Aliasing** can be used to help smooth the apparent edges of type that is exported to a bitmap format that does not support vector information.

9. **Click the Selection tool in the Tools panel.**

When the Selection tool is active, you can see the bounding box of the type object. Like any other object, you can use the bounding box handles to stretch, scale, or rotate the type object (including the characters in the type object).

If you don't see the bounding box, choose View>Show Bounding Box to toggle it on.

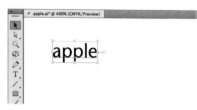

10. **Click any of the type object's corner handles and drag out to make the type larger. When the cursor feedback shows the object's height of approximately 0.5 in, release the mouse button.**

When you resize a type object with the Selection tool, you'll probably notice that the baseline of the letters moves when you drag the bottom-right handle. You might need to reposition the type object and resize it a couple of times to achieve the desired result.

Note:

You can press Shift after you begin dragging to constrain the object's original proportions.

Note:

We turned Smart Guides on (View>Smart Guides) to show the cursor feedback in our screen shots.

11. **In the Control panel, click the Character hot text to open the Character panel directly below the hot text.**

In addition to the font and size values in the main Control panel, the Character panel provides access to all character formatting options that can be applied in Illustrator.

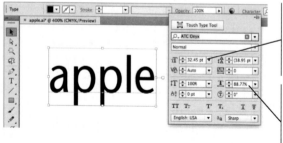

The Size menu shows the new size that results from resizing the object by dragging its bounding box handles.

If you do not constrain the resizing process, you might have a horizontal or vertical scale other than 100% of the font size.

Some argue that you should never artificially scale type horizontally or vertically (as you did in Step 8) because it distorts the spacing and shape of characters, and requires more processing time for an output device to accurately output the non-standard type sizes.

However, in this case the type will eventually be converted to vector outlines, so artificially scaling the type will cause no problems.

12. In the Character panel, change the Size field to 72. Make sure both the horizontal and vertical scale values are set to 100%.

Pressing Tab moves through the panel fields; as soon as you move to a new field, your changes in the previous field are reflected in the document. You can also press Return/Enter to apply a change and collapse the Character panel back into the Control panel.

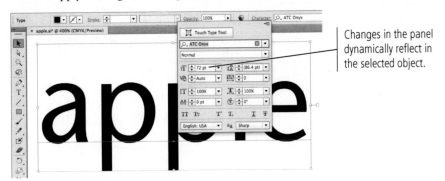

Changes in the panel dynamically reflect in the selected object.

13. Using the Type tool, double-click the word "apple" to select all the letters in the word, and then open the stand-alone Character panel (Window>Type>Character).

Tracking and kerning are two terms related to the horizontal spacing between characters in a line of text. **Kerning** is the spacing between two specific characters; **tracking** refers to the spacing between all characters in a selection.

Most industrial-quality font families come with built-in kern and track values. Smaller type does not usually pose tracking and kerning problems; when type is very large, however, spacing often becomes an issue. To fix spacing problems, you need to adjust the kerning and/or tracking values.

Note:

Kerning and tracking are largely matters of personal preference. Some people prefer much tighter spacing than others.

14. Change the Tracking field to -25 to tighten the space between all selected letters.

You can change the field manually, choose a pre-defined value from the Tracking menu, or click the up- or down-arrow button to change the tracking by 1 unit with each click.

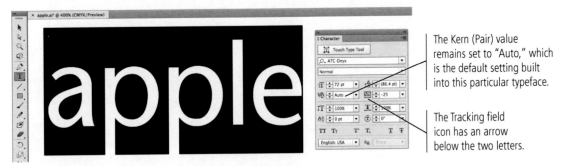

The Kern (Pair) value remains set to "Auto," which is the default setting built into this particular typeface.

The Tracking field icon has an arrow below the two letters.

15. Click with the Type tool to place the insertion point between the "a" and the "p".

This is a good example of a **kern pair** that needs adjustment. The Auto setting built into the font leaves a little too much space between the two characters — even after you have tightened the tracking considerably.

Clicking with the Type tool creates a point-type object. Clicking and dragging with the Type tool creates an area-type object. **Point type** (or path type) starts at a single point and extends along or follows a single path. **Area type** fills up an area (normally a rectangle). The following images show point type on the left and area type on the right.

The difference between the two kinds of type becomes obvious when you try to resize them or otherwise modify their shapes using the Selection tool. Area type is contained within an area. If you resize that area, the type doesn't resize; it remains within the area but simply flows (or wraps) differently. If you scale or resize point type by dragging a bounding box handle, the type within the object resizes accordingly.

This point-type object is selected with the Direct Selection tool. You can see the paths that make up the single type object. | This is a point type object, which is created by clicking once with the Type tool. | This is an area type object, which is created by clicking and dragging with the Type tool. | This area-type object is selected with the Direct Selection tool. You can see the edges of the type object, but no bounding box handles appear.

The object is selected with the Selection tool. You can now see the object's bounding box handles. | This is a point type object, which is created by clicking once with the Type tool. | This is an area type object, which is created by clicking and dragging with the Type tool. | The object is selected with the Selection tool. You can see the edges of the type object, as well as the object's bounding box handles.

Resizing the bounding box with the Selection tool resizes the text in the point-type object. | This is a point-type object, which is created by clicking once with the Type tool. | This is an area type object, which is created by clicking and dragging with the Type tool. dragging with the Type tool. | Resizing the bounding box with the Selection tool resizes the object; the text rewraps inside the new object dimensions.

Another consideration is where the "point" sits on the type path. When you change the paragraph alignment of point type, the point remains in the same position; the text on the point moves to the appropriate position, relative to the fixed point.

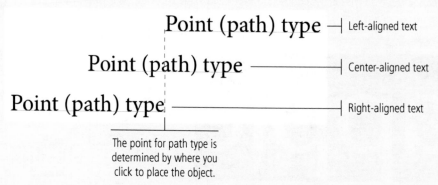

Point (path) type — Left-aligned text

Point (path) type ——— Center-aligned text

Point (path) type ——— Right-aligned text

The point for path type is determined by where you click to place the object.

When you're working with type, it can be easier — at least at first — to work with bounding boxes turned off. You can turn off the bounding boxes for all objects — including type objects — by choosing View>Hide Bounding Box.

Converting Type Objects

When the Selection tool is active, the handle on the right side of the type-object bounding box indicates whether that object contains point type or area type. A hollow handle identifies a point-type object; a solid handle identifies an area-type object. When you move the cursor over a type object, an icon in the cursor indicates that double-clicking will convert the object to the other kind of type object.

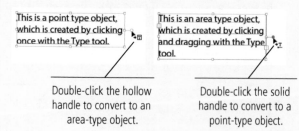

This is a point type object, which is created by clicking once with the Type tool.

This is an area type object, which is created by clicking and dragging with the Type tool.

Double-click the hollow handle to convert to an area-type object.

Double-click the solid handle to convert to a point-type object.

16. **Change the Kerning value to -20.**

Like tracking, you can change this value manually, choose a value from the pop-up menu, or use the Kerning field buttons to change kerning by 1 unit.

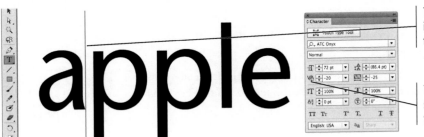

The insertion point is placed between these two letters.

The Kerning field icon shows a slash between the two letters.

These slight modifications to tracking and kerning improve the overall appearance and readability of the logo. Later in the project, you will use a different technique to adjust letter spacing. For now, however, you should become familiar with making this type of manual adjustment.

17. **Save the file and continue to the next exercise.**

 MANIPULATE TYPE OBJECTS

When you work with type in Illustrator, you need to be aware of a few special issues that can affect the way you interact with the application. This exercise explores some common problems that can arise when you work with type, as well as some tricks you can use to work around them.

1. **With apple.ai open, select the Type tool in the Tools panel. Click at the end of the existing type object to place the insertion point.**

2. **Move the Type tool cursor below the existing type object and click.**

When the insertion point is already flashing, you can't click with the Type tool to create a new point-type object.

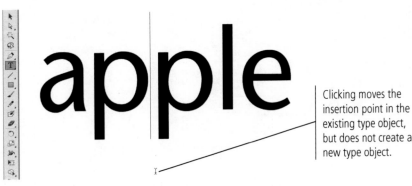

Clicking moves the insertion point in the existing type object, but does not create a new type object.

Note:

When the insertion point is flashing in a type object, you can't use the keyboard shortcuts to access tools; instead, pressing a key adds that letter to the current type object, at the location of the insertion point.

Note:

If you want to add another type object, you have to first deselect the one where the insertion point is flashing. To accomplish this, you can Command/Control-click away from the currently active type object.

Remember, pressing Command/Control temporarily switches to the Selection or Direct Selection tool (whichever was last used); when you release the Command/Control key, you return to the previously active tool — in this case, the Type tool.

You can also choose Select>Deselect, and then click again with the Type tool to create a new type object.

3. **With the insertion point flashing, press Command/Control.**

As you know, this modifier key temporarily switches the active tool to the Selection tool. The bounding box of the type object remains visible as long as you hold down the Command/Control key.

4. **While still holding down the Command/Control key, click within the bounding box of the type object.**

When you click, you select the actual type object. The point and path become active, and the insertion point no longer flashes. You can use this method to move or modify a type object without switching away from the Type tool.

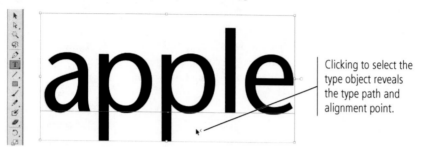

Clicking to select the type object reveals the type path and alignment point.

5. **Release the Command/Control key to return to the Type tool.**

6. **Click below the existing type object to create a new type object.**

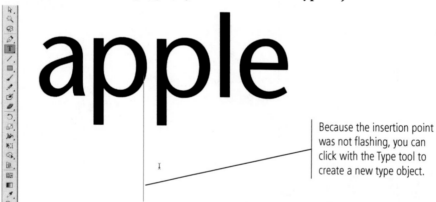

Because the insertion point was not flashing, you can click with the Type tool to create a new type object.

7. **Type** organics.

When you add a new type object, the type is automatically set using the last-used formatting options.

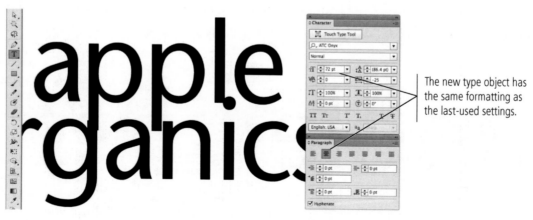

The new type object has the same formatting as the last-used settings.

8. **Press Command/Control. Click the new type object and drag it up until the descender of the second "p" in apple aligns with the stem of the "g" in the word "organics."**

   Leave approximately 0.125″ between the baseline of "apple" and the x-height of the letters in "organics."

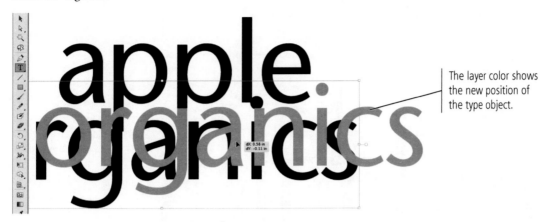

The layer color shows the new position of the type object.

9. **Release the mouse button to reposition the type object, and then release the Command/Control key to return to the Type tool.**

10. **Save the file and continue to the next exercise.**

CONVERT TYPE TO OUTLINES

In Illustrator, fonts — and the characters that compose them — are like any other vector objects. They are made up of anchors and paths, which you can modify just as you would any other vector object. To access the anchor points, however, you must first convert the text to outlines.

1. **With apple.ai open, use the Selection tool to select both type objects in the file.**

2. **Choose Type>Create Outlines.**

   When you convert the type to outlines, the anchor points and paths that make up the letter shapes appear. Each type object (in this case, one for "apple" and one for "organics") is a separate group of letter shapes.

3. **Click away from the objects to deselect them, and then click the word "apple."**

4. **In the Layers panel, click the arrow to the left of the Logotype layer name to expand the layer.**

5. **In the Layers panel, click the arrow to the left of the bottom group to expand that group.**

6. **Click the Target icon of the first (lowest) "p" to select only that object.**

   By expanding the individual layers and sublayer groups, you can use the Layers panel to access and work with individual objects in a group, without ungrouping the objects.

Click the Target icon to select or deselect a specific object within a group.

7. **Press the Right Arrow key to nudge the selected object right (narrowing the space between the letter shapes).**

   You could have fine-tuned the letter spacing with the tracking and kerning controls before you converted the letters to outlines. Since you're working with these letters as graphics, however, you are accessing and nudging individual pieces of a group to adjust the spacing in the overall logotype.

Note:

*Open the General pane of the Preferences dialog box to change the distance an object moves when you press the arrow keys (called the **keyboard increment**).*

Press Shift and an arrow key to move an object 10 times the default keyboard increment.

8. **Repeat Step 7 to move the "a" shape right, and again to move the "l" and "e" shapes left.**

   As mentioned previously, letter spacing is largely a matter of personal preference. You might prefer more or less space between the letters than what you see in our images.

9. **In the Layers panel, collapse the apple group and expand the organics group.**

10. **Using the Target icons in the Layers panel, click to select the "s" shape, and then Shift-click to also select the "c", "i", "n", and "a" shapes.**

Just as Shift-clicking objects selects multiple objects on the artboard, Shift-clicking in the Layers panel allows you to easily select multiple objects within a group.

In this case, you have to Shift-click the icon for each item in the panel individually; Shift-clicking does not select all in-between layers when you add more than one object to the selection.

11. **Press the Left Arrow key to nudge the selected shapes left.**

12. **In the Layers panel, Shift-click the Target icon for the selected "a" letter shape.**

Shift-clicking a selected object (Target icon) deselects that object only.

13. **Press the Left Arrow key to nudge the remaining selection left.**

14. **Continue selecting and nudging the letter shapes to reduce the spacing between all letters in the word "organics." Use the following image as a guide.**

Don't worry about the overlap between the two lines of text at this point; you will fix those issues in the next exercise.

15. **Save the file and continue to the next exercise.**

CREATE CUSTOM GRAPHICS FROM LETTER SHAPES

Because you converted the letter shapes to outlines, the logo text no longer behaves as type. You can now apply your drawing skills to adjust the vector shapes and create a unique appearance for your client's logotype. Remember, you can use the Add Anchor Point tool to add points to a vector path, use the Delete Anchor Point tool to remove points from a vector path, and use the Anchor Point tool to convert smooth points to corner points (and vice versa). All three of these tools are nested below the Pen tool in the Tools panel.

1. **With apple.ai open, use the Direct Selection tool to adjust the anchor points at the bottom of the "p" to follow the same arch as the lowercase "r".**

   Remember, click directly on an anchor point to select and move only that point. The selected point appears solid, while unselected points appear hollow.

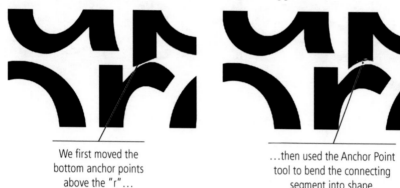

We first moved the bottom anchor points above the "r"…

…then used the Anchor Point tool to bend the connecting segment into shape.

Note:

It is helpful to zoom in very close to complete this part of the project.

2. **Using the Direct Selection tool, click the second "p" in the word "apple". Press Shift, and then click the "g" in the word "organics".**

3. **Using the Shape Builder tool, click and drag to merge the two shapes that make up the "p" and "g".**

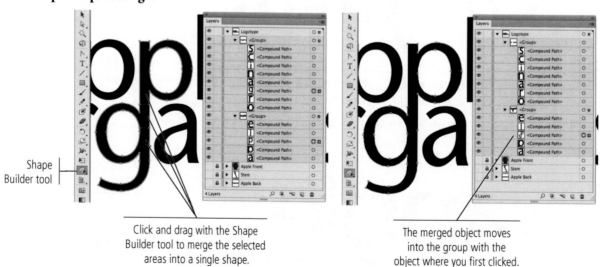

Shape Builder tool

Click and drag with the Shape Builder tool to merge the selected areas into a single shape.

The merged object moves into the group with the object where you first clicked.

4. **Using the Direct Selection tool, click the edge of the dot (above the letter "i") to show the anchor points of that shape. Use what you know about points and handles to change the dot to a leaf shape.**

5. In the Layers panel, click the Target icon for the "i" shape to select the entire compound path. Change the fill color of the selected object to a medium green from the built-in swatches.

6. Select both groups of type shapes and group them.

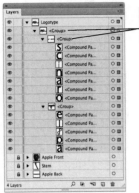

The Layers panel shows nested levels of groups.

7. Press Command/Control-0 to show the entire artboard in the document window.

8. Make sure the entire logotype group selected with the Selection tool. In the Control panel, click the Transform hot text to open the Transform panel. Make sure the W and H fields are linked, and type **250%** in the W field.

Remember: The appearance of the Transform hot text depends on the width of your Application frame; if you have enough horizontal screen space, the Transform hot text is replaced by individual X, Y, W, and H fields. In that case, you can click any of those field names to open the Transform panel.

Click the hot-text link in the Control panel to access the related panel.

You can resize this group just as you would any other object.

When you press Return/Enter (or simply click away from the Transform panel), the logotype group is scaled proportionally to 250% of its original size.

9. **Show the three locked Apple layers.**

10. **Select all objects on the Logotype layer, then drag the logotype group so the "a" and "o" closely align with the outer contour of the apple shape. Use the following image as a guide.**

11. **Save the file and continue to the next stage of the project.**

Stage 3 Working with Multiple Artboards

For all intents and purposes, the Apple Organics logo is now complete. However, you still need to create the alternate versions that can be used in other applications. You need a two-color version for jobs that will be printed with spot colors, and you need a one-color version for jobs that will be printed with black ink only.

Rather than generating multiple files for individual versions of a logo, you can use Illustrator's multiple-artboard capabilities to create a single file that manages the different logo variations on separate artboards.

In this stage of the project, you adjust the artboard to fit the completed logo. You then duplicate the artwork on additional artboards, and adjust the colors in each version to meet the specific needs of different color applications.

ADJUST THE DEFAULT ARTBOARD

When you place an Illustrator file into another file (for example, a page-layout file in InDesign or even another Illustrator file) you can decide how to place that file — based on the artwork boundaries (the outermost bounding box), on the artboard boundaries, or on other specific dimensions. To make the logo artwork more placement-friendly, you should adjust the Illustrator artboard to fit the completed logo artwork.

1. **With apple.ai open, make the entire artboard visible in the document window.**

2. **Unlock all layers in the file, and select everything on the artboard.**

ILLUSTRATOR FOUNDATIONS

When the Artboard tool is active, the Control panel presents a number of options for adjusting the active artboard.

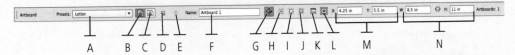

A Use this menu to change the artboard to a predefined size (letter, tabloid, etc.)

B Click to change the artboard to portrait orientation

C Click to change the artboard to landscape orientation

D Click to add a new artboard at the currently defined size. The cursor is "loaded" with the new artboard; you can click to place the new artboard in the workspace.

E Click to delete the active artboard

F Type here to define a name for the active artboard

G Click to toggle the Move/Copy Artwork with Artboard option. When active, objects on the artboard move along with the artboard being moved (or cloned).

H Click **Show Center Mark** displays a point in the center of the crop area.

I Click **Show Cross Hairs** displays lines that extend into the artwork from the center of each edge.

J Click **Show Video Safe Areas** displays guides that represent the areas inside the viewable area of video.

K Click to open the Artboard Options dialog box

L Choose a registration point for changes in size or position

M Use these fields to define the position of the artboard. (The first artboard always begins at X: 0, Y: 0.)

N Use these fields to change the size of the artboard. If the link icon is active, the height and width will be constrained.

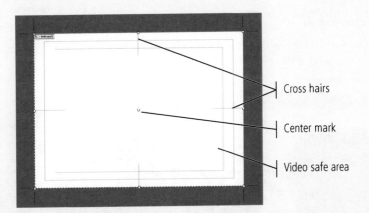

Cross hairs

Center mark

Video safe area

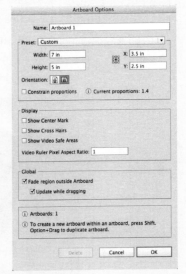

Clicking the Artboard Options button opens a dialog box where you can further manage and control the selected artboard. Most of these options (Preset, Width, Height, Orientation, and Position) are the same as those available in the Control panel. The remaining choices are explained here:

- **Constrain Proportions** maintains a consistent aspect ratio (height to width) if you resize the artboard.
- **Video Ruler Pixel Aspect Ratio** specifies the pixel aspect ratio used for artboard rulers.

- **Fade Region Outside Artboard** displays the area outside the artboard darker than the area inside the artboard.
- **Update While Dragging** keeps the area outside the artboard darker as you move or resize the artboard.

3. **Using the Control or Transform panel, choose the top-left reference point. Change the X and Y positions to 0.1 in.**

4. **Review the W and H values of the selected artwork.**

You created this file with a letter-size artboard. As you can see, the size is both too narrow and too high for the finished artwork.

Note:

Your W and H values might be slightly different than what you see in our screen shots, but they should be in the same general ballpark.

5. **Select the Artboard tool in the Tools panel.**

When the Artboard tool is active, the artboard edge is surrounded by marching ants; you can drag the side and corner handles to manually resize the artboard in the workspace.

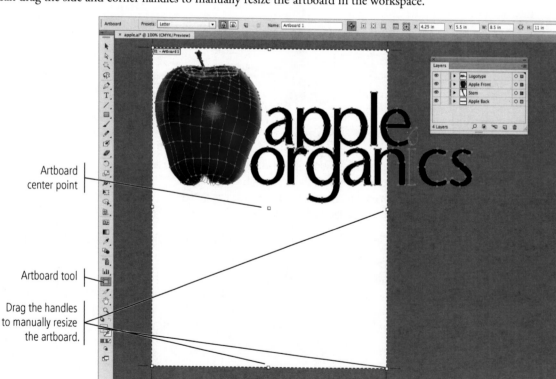

Artboard center point

Artboard tool

Drag the handles to manually resize the artboard.

6. **In the Control panel, select the top-left reference point and then change the artboard width to 11.9 in and the height to 5.4 in.**

    If your Control panel does not show the W and H fields, click the Artboard Options button in the Control panel and use the Artboard Options dialog box to change the artboard width and height.

    These dimensions are large enough to entirely encompass the logo artwork. If your dimensions are different than ours, use whatever values you need to fit your artwork and leave a bit of white space on all four sides.

7. **Click the Selection tool to exit the Artboard-editing mode.**

8. **Save the file and continue to the next exercise.**

USE THE LAYERS PANEL TO ORGANIZE ARTWORK

Your goal is to create three separate versions of the logo — the four-color version that's already done, a two-color version for spot-color applications, and a one-color version that will be used in jobs that are printed black-only.

As you created the artwork, you used five layers to manage the arrangement and stacking order of the various elements. The Apple Back layer is behind the Stem layer, which is behind the Apple Front layer. This precise order produces the effect you need to create a realistic illustration.

Now that the drawing is complete, however, you will use layers for a different purpose — to create, isolate, and manage multiple versions of the logo in a single file.

1. **With apple.ai open, make sure all layers are unlocked in the Layers panel.**

2. **In the Layers panel, click the Target icon of the Stem layer to select the objects on that layer.**

3. **Click the Selected Art icon to the right of the Target icon and drag down to the Apple Back layer.**

Dragging the Selected Art icon is an easy way to move objects from one layer to another without manually cutting and pasting.

Target icon

The Selected Art icon indicates what is selected in the file.

Drag the Selected Art icon to a different layer to move selected objects without affecting their position on the artboard.

4. **Expand the Apple Back layer.**

The mesh object that was on the Stem layer is now on the Apple Back layer, at the top of the sublayer stack.

The stem object guides now show the color of the Apple Back layer instead of the color of the Stem layer.

5. **Repeat Steps 2–3 for the Apple Front and Logotype layers.**

6. **Shift-click to select the three empty layers in the Layers panel, and then click the panel's Delete button.**

7. **Rename the Apple Back layer `Four Color`.**

You can access the sublayers, so you can still use the panel to select, arrange, and manage individual objects.

8. **Collapse the Four Color layer to hide the sublayers.**

9. **Save the file and continue to the next exercise.**

COPY THE ARTBOARD AND ARTWORK

Now that all the logo artwork resides on a single layer, the final step is to create the two alternate versions of the logo. This process is largely a matter of cloning the existing artboard and artwork — but you need to complete a few extra steps to convert the mesh objects to standard filled paths.

Note:

You might want to zoom out so you can see the entire original artboard and the empty space below it.

1. With **apple.ai** open, choose the Artboard tool in the Tools panel.

2. With the only artboard currently active, highlight the contents of the Name field in the Control panel and type **Four Color Apple**.

3. Make sure the Move/Copy Artwork with Artboard option is toggled on.

4. Place the cursor inside the artboard area. Press Option/Alt-Shift and then click and drag down to clone the existing artboard.

The Artboard name appears in the Name field and in the artboard tag.

The Move/Copy Artwork with Artboard option should be toggled on.

Pressing Option/Alt clones the existing artboard, just as you would clone a regular drawing object.

Because Move/Copy Artwork with Artboard is toggled on, the logo artwork and the artboard are cloned at the same time.

5. When the new artboard/artwork is entirely outside the boundaries of the first artboard, release the mouse button.

The second (cloned) artboard is named "Four Color Apple Copy."

6. **With the second artboard active, change the Name field to Two Color Apple.**

7. **In the Layers panel, click the Create New Layer button.**

New layers are added above the previously selected layer. Because the Four Color layer was the only layer in the file, the new layer is added at the top of the layer stack.

Create New
Layer button

8. **Double-click the new layer name in the panel, then type Two Color to rename the layer.**

9. **Using the Selection tool, drag a marquee to select all the objects on the second artboard.**

10. **In the Layers panel, drag the Selected Art icon from the Four Color layer to the Two Color layer.**

The second version
of the artwork
should now be on
the Two Color layer.

11. **Save the file and continue to the next exercise.**

CONVERT MESH OBJECTS TO REGULAR PATHS

When you created the gradient meshes in the first stage of this project, you saw that adding the mesh removed the original path you drew. When you worked on the mesh, you might have noticed that the Control panel showed that the selected object was transformed from a path object to a mesh object.

To create the flat two-color version of the logo, however, you need to access the original paths you drew to create the mesh objects. There is no one-step process to convert the mesh object back to a flat path object, so you need to take a few extra steps to create the flat version of the logo.

Note:

Because the black-only version of the logo is also flat, you are going to create the flat two-color version first, and then clone it. Doing so avoids unnecessary repetition of the process presented in this exercise.

1. **With apple.ai open, deselect everything in the file and then open the Artboards panel (Window>Artboards).**

   The Artboards panel can be used to access and arrange the various artboards in a file.

2. **Double-click Two Color Apple in the panel.**

   This forces the selected artboard to fill the space available in the document window.

3. **Expand the Two Color layer in the Layers panel.**

4. **Use the Layers panel to select the mesh object that represents the Front Apple shape, and then open the Appearance panel.**

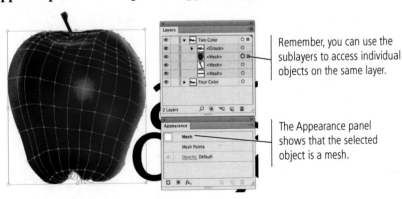

Remember, you can use the sublayers to access individual objects on the same layer.

The Appearance panel shows that the selected object is a mesh.

Note:

When working with a mesh object, it can be helpful to turn off object bounding boxes (View>Hide Bounding Box).

5. **With the mesh object selected, click the Add New Stroke button at the bottom of the Appearance panel.**

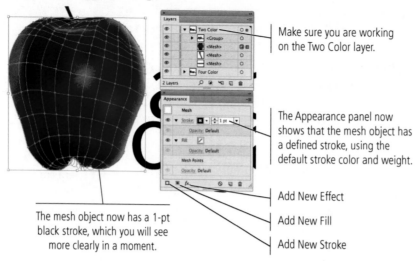

Make sure you are working on the Two Color layer.

The Appearance panel now shows that the mesh object has a defined stroke, using the default stroke color and weight.

Add New Effect

Add New Fill

Add New Stroke

The mesh object now has a 1-pt black stroke, which you will see more clearly in a moment.

Note:

In addition to changing the existing attributes of an object, you can also use the Appearance panel to compound effects and attributes. In other words, you can add a new stroke to any object, including an object that already has a defined stroke.

6. **With the mesh object still selected, choose Object>Expand Appearance.**

This command converts the selected object into separate constituent objects — one path for the shape's stroke attribute and one for the object's mesh fill — which are automatically grouped together.

7. **In the Layers panel, expand the new group.**

8. **Use the Layers panel to select only the mesh object in the group.**

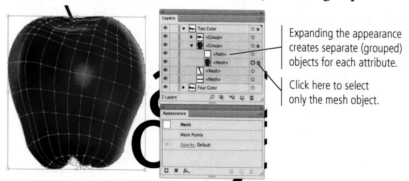

Expanding the appearance creates separate (grouped) objects for each attribute.

Click here to select only the mesh object.

Note:

New appearance attributes are created on top of the currently selected appearance. You can drag the appearance names in the panel to change their stacking sequence, which can have a significant impact on the end result.

9. **Press Delete/Backspace to remove the selected mesh object.**

You now have a simple path object that is essentially the Apple Front shape. However, you need to complete one more step because the path is still part of the group that was created by the Expand Appearance command.

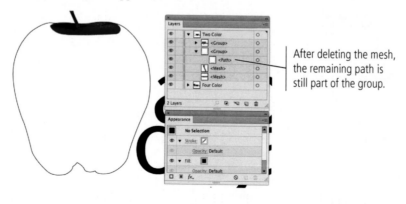

After deleting the mesh, the remaining path is still part of the group.

10. **Use the Layers panel to select the path in the group, and then choose Object>Ungroup.**

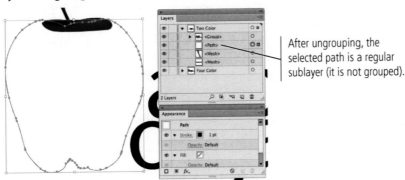

After ungrouping, the selected path is a regular sublayer (it is not grouped).

11. **Repeat this process to convert the other two mesh objects (the Stem shape and the Apple Back shape) back into standard paths with the default stroke attributes.**

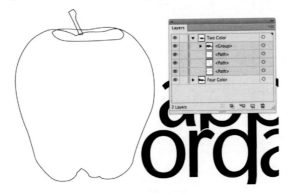

13. **Save the file and continue to the next exercise.**

The Appearance Panel in Depth

The Appearance panel allows you to review and change the appearance attributes of objects, including stroke, fill, transparency, and applied effects.

As you know, the last-used settings for fill color, stroke color, and stroke weight are applied to new objects. Other attributes, such as the applied brush or effects, are not automatically applied to new objects. If you need to create a series of objects with the same overall appearance, you can turn off the **New Art Has Basic Appearance** option in the Appearance panel Options menu.

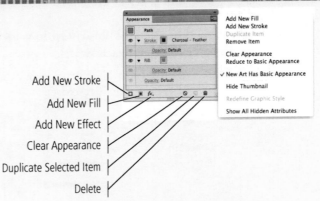

Add New Stroke
Add New Fill
Add New Effect
Clear Appearance
Duplicate Selected Item
Delete

Add New Fill
Add New Stroke
Duplicate Item
Remove Item

Clear Appearance
Reduce to Basic Appearance

✓ New Art Has Basic Appearance

Hide Thumbnail

Redefine Graphic Style

Show All Hidden Attributes

Clicking the **Clear Appearance** button reduces the selected object to a fill and stroke of None. Choosing **Reduce to Basic Appearance** in the panel Options menu resets an object to only basic fill and stroke attributes; fill color and stroke weight and color are maintained, but all other attributes are removed.

You can use the **Duplicate Selected Item** button to create multiple versions of the same attribute for an object, such as two stroke weights/colors — allowing you to compound the effect without layering multiple objects. If you want to remove a specific attribute, simply select that item and click the panel's **Delete** button.

Spot colors are created with special premixed inks that produce a certain color with one ink layer; spot colors are not built from the standard process inks used in CMYK printing. When you output a job with spot colors, each spot color appears on its own separation. Spot inks are commonly used to reproduce colors you can't get from a CMYK build, in two- and three-color documents, and as additional separations in a process color job when an exact color (such as a corporate color) is needed.

You can choose a spot color directly from the library on your screen, but you should look at a printed swatch book to verify that you're using the color you intend. Special inks exist because many of the colors can't be reproduced with process inks, nor can they be accurately represented on a monitor. If you specify spot colors and then convert them to process colors later, your job probably won't look exactly as you expect.

Note:

In the United States, the most popular collections of spot colors are the Pantone Matching System (PMS) libraries. TruMatch and Focoltone are also used in the United States. Toyo and DICColor (Dainippon Ink & Chemicals) are used primarily in Japan.

1. **With apple.ai open, choose Window>Swatch Libraries>Color Books>Pantone+ Solid Coated.**

   Illustrator includes swatch libraries of all the common spot-color libraries. You can open any of these libraries to access the various colors available in each collection.

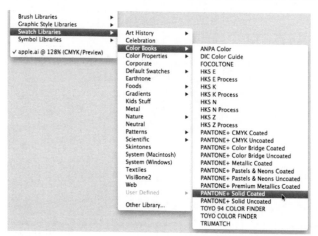

2. **In the Pantone+ Solid Coated library Options menu, choose Small List View to show the color names for each swatch.**

   It is often easier to view swatches with their names and samples, especially when you need to find a specific swatch (as in this exercise).

Note:

The View options in the panel Options menu are available for all swatch panels, including colors, patterns, and brushes.

3. **On the Two Color artboard/layer, select the shape that represents the apple front.**

4. **In the Find field of the color library panel, type 188.**

   You could simply scroll through the panel to find the color you want, but typing a number in the Find field automatically scrolls the panel to that color.

5. **Make sure the Fill icon is active in the Tools panel, and then click Pantone 188 C in the swatch Library panel.**

Note:

To restore all spot color to the panel, simply delete the characters from the panel's Search field.

6. **Review the Swatches panel (Window>Swatches).**

When you apply a color from a swatch library, that swatch is added to the Swatches panel for the open file.

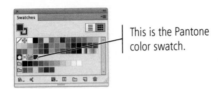

This is the Pantone color swatch.

7. **Using whichever method you prefer, change the stroke color of the selected object to None.**

8. **Select the Apple Back shape. Apply Pantone 188 C as the fill color and None as the stroke color.**

9. **Select the Stem shape. Swap the current stroke and fill colors so the shape is filled with black and has no stroke.**

10. **Select the shape that comprises the "p" and "g" in the logotype and change the fill color to Pantone 188 C.**

Because this shape is part of a group, you must use the Direct Selection tool or the sublayers in the Layers panel to select only this shape.

11. **Select the "i" shape. Change the fill color to white (not None) and change the stroke to 2-pt Pantone 188 C.**

Because our leaf slightly overlaps the "e," we used white as the fill color instead of None.

12. **Choose the Artboard tool. With the Move/Copy Artwork with Artboard option still active, press Option/Alt-Shift and then click and drag down to clone the flat version. Rename the new artboard One Color Apple.**

13. **Move the artwork on the third artboard to a new layer named One Color. Change all Pantone 188 C elements in the third version to black.**

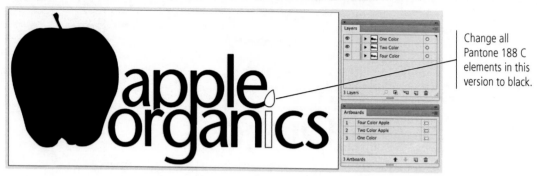

Change all Pantone 188 C elements in this version to black.

14. **Save the file, close it, and then continue to the next stage of the project.**

Stage 4 Combining Text and Graphics

The final stage of this project requires two additional layouts: a letterhead and a business envelope. Rather than adding more artboards to the logo file, you are going to create a new file that will contain both pieces of stationery. This means you must place the logos from the original apple.ai file, and understand how to work with objects that are placed from external files.

WORK WITH PLACED GRAPHICS

Some production-related concerns dictate how you design a letterhead. In general, there are two ways to print a letterhead: commercially in large quantities or one-offs on your desktop laser or inkjet printer. (The second method includes a letterhead template, which you can use to write and print your letters from directly within a page-layout program. While this method is quite common among designers, it is rarely done using Illustrator.)

If your letterhead is being printed commercially, it's probably being printed with multiple copies on a large press sheet, from which the individual letterhead sheets will be cut. (In fact, most commercial printing happens this way.) This type of printing typically means that design elements can run right off the edge of the sheet, called **bleeding**. If you're using a commercial printer, always ask the output provider whether it's safe (and cost-effective) to design with bleeds, and find out how much bleed allowance to include.

If you're designing for a printer that can only run letter-size paper, you need to allow enough of a margin area for your printer to hold the paper as it moves through the device (called the **gripper margin**); in this case, you can't design with bleeds.

1. **Open the New Document dialog box (File>New). Name the new file stationery, with 1 artboard that is letter-size in portrait orientation. Define 0.125 in bleeds on all four sides, CMYK color mode, and 300 PPI raster effects.**

Note:

When you create a new file, the Raster Effects setting determines the resolution of raster objects that are created by Illustrator to output effects like gradient meshes and feathering.

2. **Click OK to create the new file.**

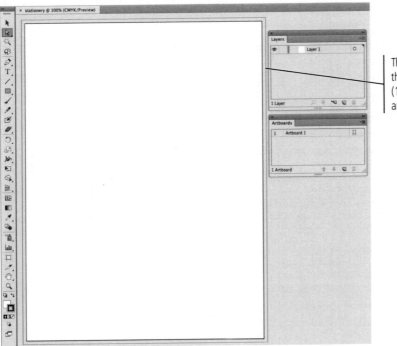

The red line indicates the defined bleed (1/8″ outside the artboard edge).

3. **Choose File>Place. Navigate to the file apple.ai in your WIP>Organics folder, and make sure Link and Template are both unchecked. Check the Show Import Options box, then click Place.**

Until now, you have placed raster images in the JPEG format. Different types of files, however, have different options that determine what is imported into your Illustrator file.

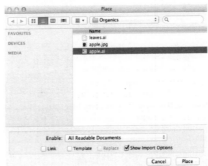

4. **Review the options in the Place PDF dialog box.**

Although you're placing a native Illustrator (.ai) file, the dialog box shows options for placing PDF files. Illustrator files use PDF as the underlying structure (which is what enables multiple artboard capability), so the options are the same as the ones you would see if you were placing a PDF file.

Use these arrows to select which artboard you want to place.

Note:

If Show Import Options is not checked in the Place dialog box, the Illustrator file is placed based on the last-used Crop To option.

The **Crop To** option determines exactly what is placed into an Illustrator file. (If you are placing an Illustrator file, many of these options produce the same result.)

- The **Bounding Box** setting places the file's bounding box, or the minimum area that encloses the objects on the page or artboard.

- The **Art** setting crops incoming files relative to the size and position of any objects selected at the time of the cropping. For example, you can create a frame and use it to crop an incoming piece of artwork.

- Use the **Crop** setting when you want the position of the placed file to be determined by the location of a crop region drawn on the page (when placing an Illustrator file, this refers to the defined artboard).

- The **Trim** setting identifies where the page will be physically cut in the production process, if trim marks are present.

- The **Bleed** setting places only the area within bleed margins (if a bleed area is defined). This is useful if the page is being output in a production environment. (The printed page might include page marks that fall outside the bleed area.)

- The **Media** setting places the area that represents the physical paper size of the original PDF document (for example, the dimensions of an A4 sheet of paper), including printers' marks.

5. **Choose Bounding Box in the Crop To menu, and then click OK to place the four-color logo.**

6. **If you get a warning about an unknown image construct, click OK to dismiss it.**

For some reason, gradient mesh objects *created in Illustrator* are unrecognized *by Illustrator*, which is the case with this logo file. Gradient meshes are imported into the new file as "non-native art" objects that can't be edited in the new file unless you use the Flatten Transparency command to turn them into embedded raster objects.

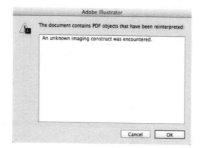

After dismissing the warning message, the selected file is loaded into the Place cursor. A small preview of the loaded file appears in the cursor.

The selected file is loaded into the Place cursor.

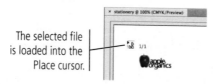

7. **Click near the top-left corner of the artboard to place the loaded image.**

8. **Open the General pane of the Preferences dialog box. Make sure the Scale Strokes & Effects option is checked, and then click OK.**

   If this option is checked, scaling an object also scales the applied strokes and effects (including the Feather effect you used to create the front highlight objects) proportionally to the new object size. For example, reducing an object by 50% changes a 1-pt stroke to a 0.5-pt stroke. If this option is unchecked, a 1-pt stroke remains a 1-pt stroke, regardless of how much you reduce or enlarge the object.

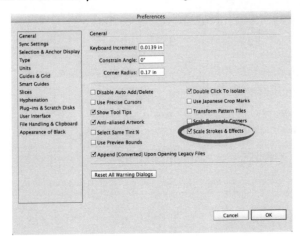

Note:

On Macintosh, open the Preferences dialog box in the Illustrator menu. On Windows, open the Preferences dialog box in the Edit menu.

9. **With the placed artwork selected, use the Transform panel to scale the artwork to 3 in wide (constrained). Using the top-left reference point, position the artwork 0.125 in from the top and left edges (as shown in the following image).**

Constrain the width and height before changing the object size.

Use the Transform panel to scale the image to 3 in wide and position the group at X: 0.125 in, Y: 0.125 in.

Note:

Remember, your original artwork might be a slightly different size than ours, so your resized height might also be slightly different than what is shown here.

10. **Using the Type tool, click to create a new point-type object. Type 564 Orchard Way. Format the type as 10-pt ATC Onyx Normal. Apply a medium-red swatch as the type fill color and define no stroke color.**

11. **Using the Selection tool, position the type object directly to the left of the "g" descender (use the following image as a guide).**

12. **Option/Alt-click-drag the type object to clone it to the right. Press the Shift key after you begin dragging to constrain the clone's movement to exactly horizontal. Move the clone immediately to the right of the "g" descender, and then release the mouse button.**

13. **Change the text in the cloned object to Orange, FL 35682.**

14. **Activate the Selection tool, then choose File>Place. Navigate to the file leaves.ai in your WIP>Organics folder and click Place.**

The Show Import Options check box remembers the last-used setting, so it should still be checked. After clicking Place, the Place PDF dialog box automatically appears.

The Place PDF dialog box also defaults to the last-used option, so Bounding Box should already be selected in the Crop To menu.

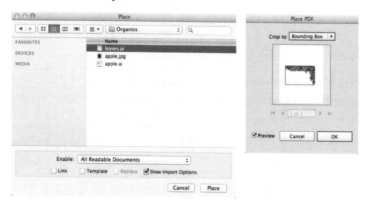

Again, the selected file is loaded into the Place cursor.

15. **Click the loaded Place cursor to place the leaves.ai file.**

16. Using the Selection tool, drag the placed graphic so the edges of the artwork align with the top and right bleed guides.

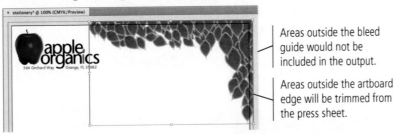

Areas outside the bleed guide would not be included in the output.

Areas outside the artboard edge will be trimmed from the press sheet.

17. Save the file as an Illustrator file named stationery.ai in your WIP>Organics folder, and then continue to the next exercise.

CREATE THE ENVELOPE LAYOUT

In general, printed envelopes can be created in two ways. You can create and print the design on a flat sheet, which will be specially **die cut** (stamped out of the press sheet), and then folded and glued into the shape of the finished envelope. Alternatively (and usually at less expense), you can print on pre-folded and -glued envelopes.

Both of these methods for envelope design have special printing requirements, such as ensuring no ink is placed where glue will be applied (if you're printing on flat sheets), or printing far enough away from the edge (if you're printing on pre-formed envelopes). Whenever you design an envelope, consult with the output provider that will print the job before you get too far into the project.

In this case, the design will be output on pre-folded #10 business-size envelopes (4-1/8″ by 9-1/2″). The printer requires a 1/4″ gripper margin around the edge of the envelope where you cannot include any ink coverage.

1. With stationery.ai open, zoom out until you can see the entire artboard and an equal amount of space to the right.

2. Choose the Artboard tool. With the current artboard active, type Letterhead in the Name field of the Control panel.

3. Place the cursor to the right of the existing artboard, click, and drag to create a new artboard.

Note:

*The **live area** is the "safe" area inside the page edge, where important design elements should remain. Because printing and trimming are mechanical processes, there will always be some variation, however slight. Elements too close to the page edge run the risk of being accidentally trimmed off.*

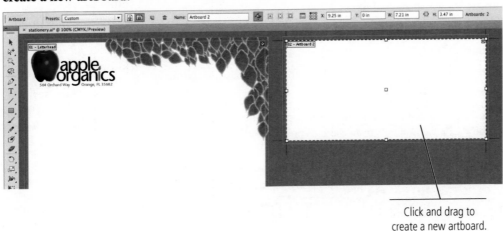

Click and drag to create a new artboard.

4. **With the second artboard active, use the fields in the Control panel to change the artboard dimensions to W: 9.5 in, H: 4.13 in.**

   If the W and H fields are not visible in your Control panel, click the Artboard Options button in the Control panel and use the resulting dialog box to change the artboard size.

5. **With the second artboard active, type Envelope in the Name field of the Control panel.**

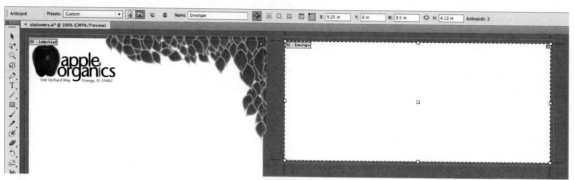

6. **Choose File>Place. Navigate to the file apple.ai in your WIP>Organics folder. Make sure Show Import Options is checked, then click Place.**

7. **In the Place PDF dialog box, click the right-arrow button to show 2 of 3, then click OK.**

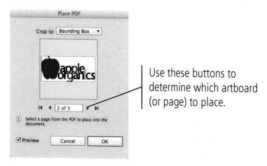

Use these buttons to determine which artboard (or page) to place.

8. **Click with the loaded Place cursor to place the loaded file on the Envelope artboard.**

9. **Make the Selection tool active. If rulers are not visible in your document window, choose View>Show Rulers.**

10. **Choose View>Rulers and make sure the menu option reads "Change to Global Rulers".**

    When Artboard rulers are active — which you want for this exercise — the menu command reads to "Change to Global Rulers".

    Artboard rulers show all measurements from the zero-point of the active artboard. Global rulers show all measurements from the zero-point of Artboard 1 (unless you reset the zero-point when a different artboard is active).

Note:

You can't switch between Artboard and Global rulers while the Artboard tool is active.

11. **Select the placed object with the Selection tool. Scale it to 2.5 in wide (constrained) and place it 0.25 in from the top and left edges of the envelope artboard.**

Because Artboard rulers are active, each artboard has its own zero point.

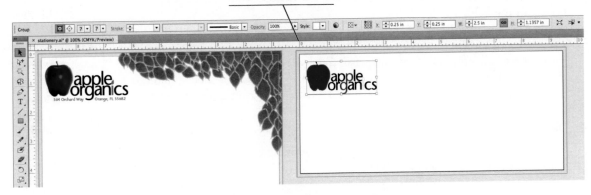

12. **Copy the type objects from the letterhead and paste them onto the envelope layout. Change the size of the type in the pasted objects to 8 pt and change the fill to Pantone 188 C (the same color you used in the two-color logo artwork).**

13. **Save the file and continue to the next exercise.**

PRINT DESKTOP PROOFS OF MULTIPLE ARTBOARDS

Before you send a file to a commercial output provider, it's a good idea to print a sample to see how the artwork looks on paper. Illustrator provides a large number of options for outputting files, including the ability to define the area of the actual artwork.

There are two important points to remember about using inkjet and laser proofs. First, inkjet printers are usually not PostScript driven; because the commercial output process revolves around the PostScript language, proofs should be created using a PostScript-compatible printer if possible (if not, the proofs might not accurately represent what will appear in final output). Second, inkjet and laser printers typically do not accurately represent color.

1. **With stationery.ai open, choose File>Print.**

   The Print dialog box is divided into eight sections or categories, which display in the window on the left side of the dialog box. Clicking one of the categories in the list shows the associated options in the right side of the dialog box.

2. **In the Printer menu, choose the printer you want to use, and then choose the PPD for that printer in the PPD menu (if possible).**

   If you are using a non-PostScript printer, complete as much of the rest of this exercise as possible based on the limitations of your output device.

3. **With the General options showing, choose the Range radio button and type 1 in the field.**

   By default, all artboards in the file are output when you click Print.

   If your printer can only print letter-size paper, you need to tile the letterhead artboard to multiple sheets so you can output a full-size proof. Tiling is unavailable when printing multiple artboards, so in this exercise you are printing each artboard separately.

4. **In the Options section, make sure the Do Not Scale option is selected.**

   As a general rule, proofs — especially final proofs that would be sent to a printer with the job files — should be output at 100%.

5a. **If your printer is capable of printing oversize sheets, choose Tabloid/ A3/11×17 in the Media menu. Choose the Portrait orientation option.**

Note:

The most important options you'll select are the Printer and PPD (PostScript printer description) settings, located at the top of the dialog box. Illustrator reads the information in the PPD to determine which of the specific print options are available for the current output.

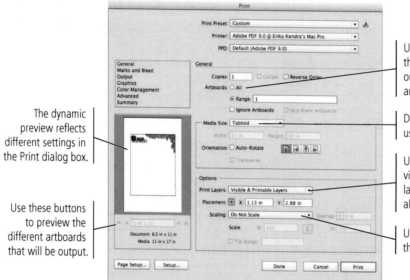

The dynamic preview reflects different settings in the Print dialog box.

Use these buttons to preview the different artboards that will be output.

Use these options to print more than one copy and reverse the output order of the multiple artboards (last to first).

Define the paper size used for the output.

Use this menu to output visible and printable layers, visible layers, or all layers.

Use these options to scale the output (if necessary).

5b. **If you can only print to letter-size paper, turn off the Auto-Rotate option and choose the Landscape orientation option. Choose Tile Full Pages in the Scaling menu and define a 1 in Overlap.**

   To output a letter-size page at 100% on letter-size paper, you have to tile to multiple sheets of paper; using the landscape paper orientation allows you to tile to 2 sheets instead of 4 (as shown in the preview area).

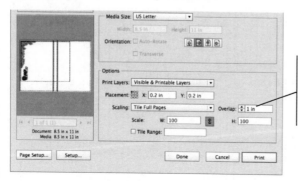

When tiling a page to multiple sheets, you can define a specific amount of space that will be included on both sheets.

Note:

The Tile options are not available if you are printing multiple artboards at one time.

Note:

The Auto-Rotate option is useful if you are printing multiple artboards; when this option is active, the application automatically positions each artboard to take best advantage of the available paper.

6. **Click the Marks and Bleed option in the list of categories on the left. Activate the All Printer's Marks option, and then change the Offset value to 0.125 in.**

If you type the value in the Offset field, Illustrator automatically rounds up to the nearest two-decimal value. Since 0.13″ is larger than the 0.125″ bleed, this offset position is fine.

7. **In the Bleeds section, check the Use Document Bleed Settings option.**

When you created the stationery file, you defined 1/8″ bleeds on all four sides of the artboard. Checking this box in the Print dialog box includes that same 1/8″ extra on all four sides of the output.

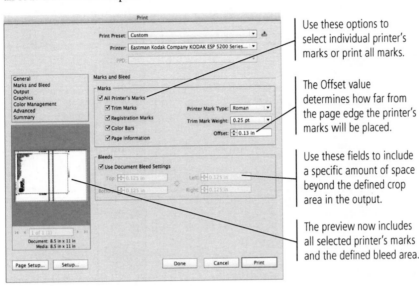

Use these options to select individual printer's marks or print all marks.

The Offset value determines how far from the page edge the printer's marks will be placed.

Use these fields to include a specific amount of space beyond the defined crop area in the output.

The preview now includes all selected printer's marks and the defined bleed area.

8. **Click the Output option in the list of categories on the left.**

Depending on the type of output device you are using, you can print all colors to a single sheet by choosing Composite in the Mode menu, or print each color to an individual sheet by choosing Separations (Host-based). The third option — In-RIP Separation — allows the file data to be separated by the output device instead of by the software.

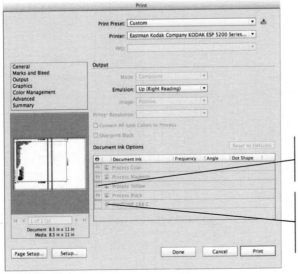

When printing separations, click any of these icons to stop that ink separation from outputting.

If a job includes spot colors, click the icon in this column to convert the spot color to process color for the output.

9. **Click Print to output the artwork.**

10. **Choose File>Print again. Choose the Range radio button and type 2 in the field to print the envelope layout.**

11. **Choose Letter/US Letter in the Size menu and choose the Landscape orientation option. Choose Do Not Scale in the Scaling menu.**

    In this case, a letter-size sheet is large enough to print the envelope artboard without scaling. (Some of the printer's marks might be cut off by the printer's gripper margin, but that is fine for the purpose of a desktop proof.)

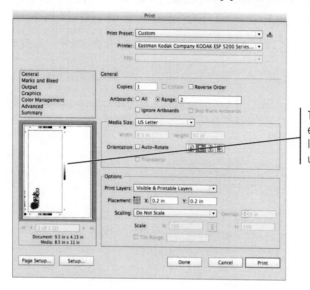

The preview area shows that the envelope artboard will fit on a letter-size page at 100% if you use landscape orientation.

12. **Click Print to output the envelope proof.**

13. **When the document comes back into focus, save and close it.**

Project Review

fill in the blank

1. The _____ provide access to handles that you can use to manually resize the artboard in the workspace.

2. Press _____ and click the eye icon on a specific layer to switch only that layer between Preview and Outline mode.

3. When _____ are active, moving your cursor over an unselected object reveals the paths that make up that object.

4. The _____ tool is used to sample colors from an object already placed in the file.

5. The _____ is used to monitor and change the individual attributes (fill, stroke, etc.) of the selected object.

6. The _____ is the imaginary line on which the bottoms of letters rest.

7. _____ is the spacing between specific pairs of letters (where the insertion point is placed).

8. The _____ command makes the vector shapes of letters accessible to the Direct Selection tool.

9. A _____ is a special ink used to reproduce a specific color, typically used for one- or two-color jobs.

10. Click the _____ in the Layers panel to select a specific sublayer.

short answer

1. Explain the advantages of using a gradient mesh, compared to a regular gradient.

2. Briefly explain two primary differences between point-type objects and area-type objects.

3. Explain the potential benefits of using multiple artboards rather than different files for different pieces.

Use what you learned in this project to complete the following freeform exercise.
Carefully read the art director and client comments, then create your own design to meet the needs of the project.
Use the space below to sketch ideas; when finished, write a brief explanation of your reasoning behind your final design.

art director comments

The Cincinnati Zoo has hired you to create a series of graphics that will be used to rebrand the facility at next spring's Grand Reopening. Your work will be used for everything from printed collateral, to park signage, to the zoo's Web site, and even embroidered on clothing.

❏ Create a new logo to identify the re-designed zoo.

❏ Create a series of icons for each of the zoo's seven main sections: Tropics, Desert, Arctic, Forest, Ocean, Sky, and Kids Kingdom.

❏ Create an invitation for the Grand Reopening celebration incorporating the new logo. Research the best size for a printed invitation that will be sent through the U.S. Postal Service. Include placeholder text for the date and time of the event, as well as the zoo's phone number and Web address.

client comments

Our facility received a significant grant from an anonymous donor to update the entire facility — everything from the animal enclosures to the guest facilities to the walking paths and water fountains. Basically, we've rebuilt from the ground up and are very excited to reveal our efforts to the public next spring at the Grand Reopening.

Since everything is new, we felt it was also time to update our corporate identity. The previous logo was designed more than 20 years ago and is little more than the words "Cincinnati Zoo." We want something fresh that incorporates more than just two words in a fancy typeface. Remember though, it has to look good on a 15-foot sign or embroidered on the pocket of a T-shirt.

For the section icons, try to keep them simple. We don't want visitors to have to work to figure out what they mean. You can include the actual words, but we're an international facility, so not everyone will be able to read the English explanations.

project justification

_____
_____
_____
_____
_____
_____
_____
_____
_____
_____
_____
_____
_____

Logos are one of the most common types of artwork that you will create in Illustrator. These can be as simple as text converted to outlines, or as complex as a line drawing based on an object in a photograph. Most logos will actually be some combination of drawing and text-based elements. As you learned throughout this project, one of the most important qualities of a logo is versatility — a good logo can be used in many different types of projects and output in many different types of print processes. To accomplish this goal, logos should work equally well in grayscale, four-color, and spot-color printing.

By completing this project, you worked with complex gradients to draw a realistic apple, then added creative type treatment to build the finished logotype. After completing the initial logo, you converted it to other variants that will work with different output processes (two-color and one-color). Finally, you incorporated the logo artwork into completed stationery to help solve your client's communication needs as he expands his business.

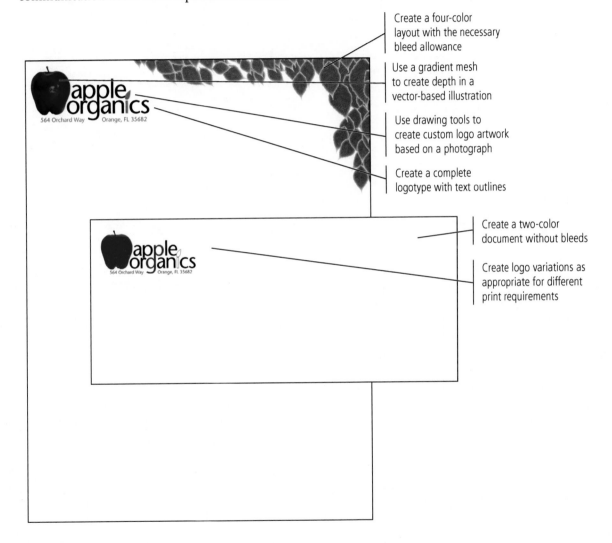

Create a four-color layout with the necessary bleed allowance

Use a gradient mesh to create depth in a vector-based illustration

Use drawing tools to create custom logo artwork based on a photograph

Create a complete logotype with text outlines

Create a two-color document without bleeds

Create logo variations as appropriate for different print requirements

Composite Movie Ad

Tantamount Studios, one of the largest film production companies in Hollywood, is developing a new movie called "Aftermath." You have been hired to develop an advertisement that will be used to announce the movie in several different trade magazines.

This project incorporates the following skills:

❑ Creating a single composite ad from multiple supplied images

❑ Compositing multiple photographs, using various techniques to silhouette the focal object in each image

❑ Incorporating vector graphics as rasterized layers and Smart Object layers

❑ Scaling and aligning different objects in relation to the page and to each other

❑ Managing individual layout elements using layers and layer groups

❑ Saving multiple versions of a file to meet different output requirements

client comments

Here's a basic synopsis of the movie:

A massive hurricane, unlike anything ever seen on the West Coast of the United States, takes aim at San Francisco. The category 6 hurricane sparks tidal waves, fires, floods — the resulting destruction dwarfs even the earthquake and fire of 1906. The movie follows the storm survivors through the process of rebuilding, both personally and politically.

This movie is going to be one of our summer blockbusters, and we're throwing a lot of resources behind it. We'll be putting the same ad in multiple magazines, and they all use different software to create the magazine layouts. We need the ad to work for all of our placements, regardless of what software is being used by the magazine publishers.

art director comments

The client loved the initial concept sketch I submitted last week, so we're ready to start building the files. I've had the photographer prepare the images we need, and the client has provided the studio and rating logo files. They also sent me the first two magazines' specs:

Magazine 1

- Bleed size: 8.75 × 11.25″

- Trim size: 8.5 × 11″

- Live area: 8 × 10.5″

- Files should be submitted as native layout files or layered TIFF

Magazine 2

- Sizes are the same as Magazine 1

- Files should be submitted as flattened TIFF or PDF

project objectives

To complete this project, you will:

❏ Resize a raster image to change resolution

❏ Composite multiple images into a single background file

❏ Incorporate both raster and vector elements into the same design

❏ Transform and arrange individual layers to create a cohesive design

❏ Create layer groups to easily manage related layer content

❏ Use selection techniques to isolate images from their backgrounds

❏ Save two different types of TIFF files for different ad requirements

Stage 1 **Compositing Images and Artwork**

Technically speaking, **compositing** is the process of combining any two or more objects (images, text, illustrations, etc.) into an overall design. When we talk about compositing in Photoshop, we're typically referring to the process of combining multiple images into a single cohesive image. Image compositing might be as simple as placing two images into different areas of a background file; or it could be as complex as placing a person into a group photo, carefully clipping out the individual's background, and adjusting the shadows to match the lighting in the group.

Types of Images

There are two primary types of digital artwork: vector graphics and raster images.

Vector graphics are composed of mathematical descriptions of a series of lines and shapes. Vector graphics are **resolution independent**; they can be freely enlarged or reduced, and they are automatically output at the resolution of the output device. The shapes that you create in Adobe InDesign, or in drawing applications such as Adobe Illustrator, are vector graphics.

Raster images, such as photographs or files created in Adobe Photoshop, are made up of a grid of independent pixels (rasters or bits) in rows and columns (called a **bitmap**). Raster files are **resolution dependent** — their resolution is fixed, determined when you scan, photograph, or otherwise create the file. You can typically reduce raster images, but you cannot enlarge them without losing image quality.

Line art is a type of raster image that is made up entirely of 100% solid areas; the pixels in a line-art image have only two options: they can be all black or all white. Examples of line art are UPC bar codes or pen-and-ink drawings.

Screen Ruling

The ad that you will be building in this project is intended to be placed in print magazines, so you have to build the new file with the appropriate settings for commercial printing. When reproducing a photograph on a printing press, the image must be converted into a set of printable dots that fool the eye into believing it sees continuous tones. Prior to image-editing software, pictures that were being prepared for printing on a press were photographed through a screen to create a grid of halftone dots. The result of this conversion is a halftone image; the dots used to simulate continuous tone are called **halftone dots**. Light tones in a photograph are represented as small halftone dots; dark tones become large halftone dots.

The screens used to create the halftone images had a finite number of available dots in a horizontal or vertical inch. That number was the **screen ruling**, or **lines per inch (lpi)** of the halftone. A screen ruling of 133 lpi means that in a square inch there are 133 × 133 (17,689) possible locations for a halftone dot. If the screen ruling is decreased, there are fewer total halftone dots, producing a grainier image; if the screen ruling is increased, there are more halftone dots, producing a clearer image.

Line screen is a finite number based on a combination of the intended output device and paper. You can't randomly select a line screen. Ask your printer what line screen will be used before you begin creating your images.

Note:

The ad you're building in this project requires compositing four digital photographs. You will also incorporate title treatment and logo files that were created in Adobe Illustrator by other members of your creative team. The various elements that make up the ad are fairly representative of the type of work you can (and probably will) create in Photoshop.

Note:

Despite their origins in pre-digital print workflows, these terms persist in the digital environment.

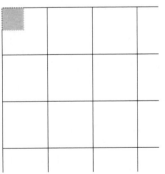

72 ppi

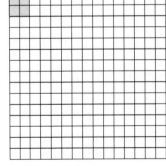

300 ppi

Each white square represents a pixel. The highlighted area shows the pixel information used to generate a halftone dot. If an image only has 72 pixels per inch, the output device has to generate four halftone dots per pixel, resulting in poor printed quality.

If you can't find out ahead of time, or if you're unsure, follow these general guidelines:

- Newspaper or newsprint: 85–100 lpi

- Magazine or general commercial printing: 133–150 lpi

- Premium-quality-paper jobs (such as art books or annual reports): 150–175 lpi; some specialty jobs might use 200 lpi or more

Image Resolution

When a printer creates halftone dots, it calculates the average value of a group of pixels in the raster image and generates a spot of appropriate size. A raster image's resolution — measured in **pixels per inch (ppi)** — determines the quantity of pixel data the printer can read. Regardless of their source — camera, scanner, or files created in Photoshop — images need to have sufficient resolution so the output device can generate enough halftone dots to create the appearance of continuous tone. In the images to the right, the same raster image is reproduced at 300 ppi (top) and 72 ppi (bottom); notice the obvious degradation in quality in the 72-ppi version.

Ideally, the printer will have four pixels for each halftone dot created. The relationship between pixels and halftone dots defines the rule of resolution for raster-based images — the resolution of a raster image (ppi) should be two times the screen ruling (lpi) that will be used for printing.

For line art, the general rule is to scan the image at the same resolution as the output device. Many laser printers and digital presses image at 600–1200 dots per inch (dpi); imagesetters used to make printing plates for a commercial press typically output at much higher resolution, possibly 2400 dpi or more.

OPEN AND RESIZE AN IMAGE

Every raster image has a defined, specific resolution that is established when the image is created. If you scan an image to be 3″ high by 3″ wide at 150 ppi, that image has 450 pixels in each vertical column and 450 pixels in each horizontal row. Simply resizing the image stretches or compresses those pixels into a different physical space, but does not add or remove pixel information. If you resize the 3 × 3″ image to 6 × 6″ (200% of the original), the 450 pixels in each column or row are forced to extend across 6″ instead of 3″, causing a marked loss of quality.

The **effective resolution** of an image is the resolution calculated after any scaling is taken into account. This number is equally important as the original image resolution — and perhaps moreso. The effective resolution can be calculated with a fairly simple equation:

Original resolution ÷ (% magnification ÷ 100) = Effective resolution

If a 300-ppi image is magnified 150%, the effective resolution is:

300 ppi ÷ 1.5 = 200 ppi

In other words, the more you enlarge a raster image, the lower its effective resolution becomes. In general, you can make an image 10% or 15% larger without significant adverse effects; the more you enlarge an image, however, the worse the results. Even Photoshop, which offers very sophisticated formulas (called "algorithms") for sizing images, cannot guarantee perfect results.

Effective resolution can be a very important consideration when working with client-supplied images, especially those that come from consumer-level digital cameras. Many of those devices capture images with a specific number of pixels rather than a number of pixels per inch (ppi). In this exercise, you will explore the effective resolution of an image to see if it can be used for a full-page printed magazine ad.

1. **Download Movie_Print14_RF.zip from the Student Files Web page.**

2. **Expand the ZIP archive in your WIP folder (Macintosh) or copy the archive contents into your WIP folder (Windows).**

   This results in a folder named **Movie**, which contains all of the files you need for this project. You should also use this folder to save the files you create in this project.

3. **Choose File>Open and navigate to your WIP>Movie folder. Select Bricks.jpg and click Open.**

4. **If the rulers are not visible on the top and left edges, choose View>Rulers.**

   As you can see in the rulers, this image has a very large physical size.

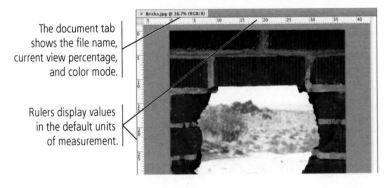

The document tab shows the file name, current view percentage, and color mode.

Rulers display values in the default units of measurement.

5. **Choose Image>Image Size.**

   The Image Size dialog box shows the number of pixels in the image, as well as the image dimensions and current resolution. You can change any value in this dialog box, but you should understand what those changes mean before you do so.

   As you can see, this image is currently 37.5 inches wide and 50 inches high, but it was photographed at 72 pixels/inch. For most commercial printing, you need at least 300 ppi. You can use the principle of effective resolution to change the file to a high enough resolution for printing.

The actual number of pixels in the image is the most important information.

When the cursor is over the preview area, you can drag to show a different area.

Use this widget to change the view percentage in the preview area.

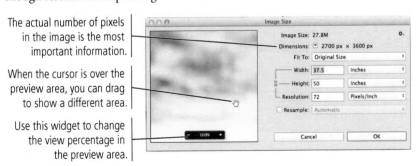

Note:

We are intentionally overlooking issues of color space for the sake of this project. You will learn about color spaces and color management in Project 6: Menu Image Correction.

Note:

Although designers trained in traditional (non-digital) methods are sometimes comfortable talking about picas or ciceros, most people use inches as the standard unit of measurement in the U.S.

You can change the default unit of measurement in the Units & Rulers pane of the Preferences dialog box. Double-clicking either ruler opens the appropriate pane of the Preferences dialog box.

Note:

Press Command-Option-I/Control-Alt-I to open the Image Size dialog box.

6. **Check the Resample option at the bottom of the dialog box.**

The options in this dialog box remember the last-used choices. The Resample option might already be checked in your dialog box.

Resampling means maintaining the existing resolution in the new image dimensions; in other words, you are either adding or deleting pixels to the existing image. When this option is turned on, you can change the dimensions of an image without affecting the resolution, or you can change the resolution of an image (useful for removing excess resolution or **downsampling**) without affecting the image size.

7. **Change the Resolution field to 300 pixels/inch.**

When you change the resolution with resampling turned on, you do not change the file's physical size. To achieve 300-ppi resolution at the new size, Photoshop needs to add a huge number of pixels to the image. You can see at the top of the dialog box that this change would increase the total number of pixels from 2700 × 3600 to 11250 × 15000.

You can also see that changing the resolution of an image without affecting its physical dimensions would have a significant impact on the file size. Changing the resolution to 300 ppi at the current size would increase the file size to nearly 483 megabytes.

Note:

When the Resample option is checked, you can use the attached menu to tell Photoshop how to generate extra pixel data when increasing the image size, or which pixels to discard when reducing the image size. Each option also includes a parenthetical notation about when it is best used (enlargement, smooth gradients, etc.).

When Resample is checked, changing the Resolution value adds or removes pixels.

Higher resolution means larger file sizes, which translates to longer processing time for printing or longer download time over the Internet. When you scale an image to a smaller size, simply resizing can produce files with far greater effective resolution than you need. Resampling allows you to reduce physical size without increasing the resolution, resulting in a smaller file size.

The caveat is that once you discard (delete) pixels, they are gone. If you later try to re-enlarge the smaller image, you will not achieve the same quality as the original (before it was reduced). You should save reduced images as copies instead of overwriting the originals.

8. **Press Option/Alt and click the Reset button to restore the original image dimensions in the dialog box.**

In many Photoshop dialog boxes, pressing the Option/Alt key changes the Cancel button to Reset. You can click the Reset button to restore the original values that existed when you opened the dialog box.

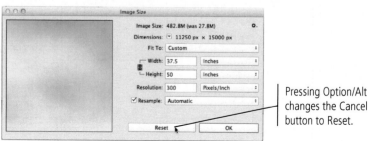

Pressing Option/Alt changes the Cancel button to Reset.

9. **Uncheck the Resample option at the bottom of the dialog box.**

10. **Change the Resolution field to `300` pixels/inch.**

   Resizing *without* resampling basically means distributing the same number of pixels over a different amount of physical space. When you resize an image without resampling, you do not change the number of pixels in the image. (In fact, those fields in the dialog box become simple text; the fields are unavailable and you cannot change the number of pixels in the image.)

   You can see how changing one of the linked fields (Resolution) directly affects the other linked fields (Width and Height). By resizing the image to be 300 ppi — enough for commercial print quality — you now have an image that is 9″ × 12″.

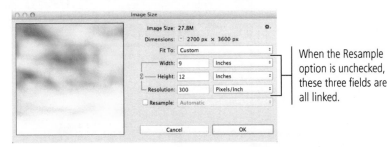

   When the Resample option is unchecked, these three fields are all linked.

11. **Click OK to apply the change and return to the document window.**

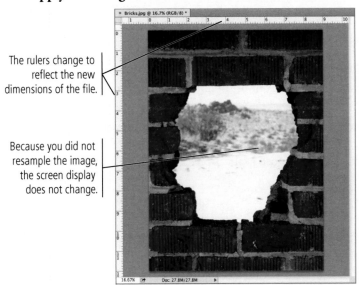

   The rulers change to reflect the new dimensions of the file.

   Because you did not resample the image, the screen display does not change.

   Note:

   Although many magazines are printed at 133 lpi, some are printed at 150 lpi. By setting the resolution to 300, your file will work for any magazine that prints at 133 or 150 lpi.

12. **Choose File>Save As. If necessary, navigate to your WIP>Movie folder as the target location. Change the file name (in the Save As field) to `aftermath`.**

   Since this is a basic image file with only one layer (so far), most of the other options in the Save As dialog box are grayed out (not available).

13. **Choose Photoshop in the Format menu and then click Save.**

You can save a Photoshop file in a number of different formats, all of which have specific capabilities, limitations, and purposes. While you are still working on a file, it's best to keep it as a native Photoshop (PSD) file. When you choose a different format, the correct extension is automatically added to the file name.

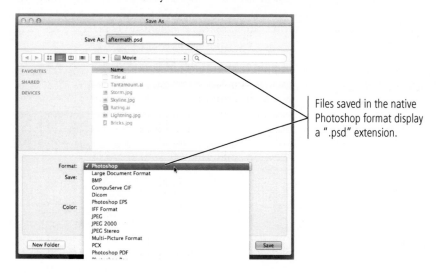

Files saved in the native Photoshop format display a ".psd" extension.

Note:

Also called "native", the PSD format is the most flexible format to use while building files in Photoshop.

14. **Continue to the next exercise.**

 CROP THE CANVAS AND PLACE RULER GUIDES

The final step in preparing the workspace is defining the live area of the page. **Trim size** is the actual size of a page once it has been cut out of the press sheet. According to your client, the magazine has a trim size of 8.5″ × 11″.

Any elements that print right to the edge of a page (called **bleeding**) must actually extend beyond the defined trim size. The **bleed allowance** is the amount of extra space that should be included for these bleed objects; most applications require at least 1/8″ bleed allowance on any bleed edge.

Because of inherent variation in the mechanical printing and trimming processes, most magazines also define a safe or **live area**; all important design elements (especially text) should stay within this live area. The live area for this project is 8 × 10.5″.

1. **With aftermath.psd open, choose the Crop tool in the Tools panel.**

When you choose the Crop tool, a crop marquee appears around the edges of the image. The marquee has eight handles, which you can drag to change the size of the crop area.

Note:

You should familiarize yourself with the most common fraction-to-decimal equivalents:

1/8 = 0.125

1/4 = 0.25

3/8 = 0.375

1/2 = 0.5

5/8 = 0.625

3/4 = 0.75

7/8 = 0.875

Set Overlay Options   Set Additional Crop Options

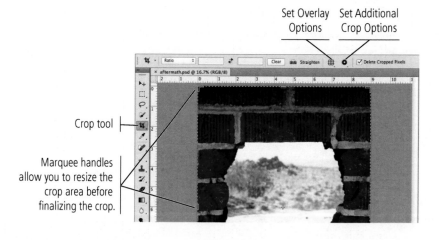

Crop tool

Marquee handles allow you to resize the crop area before finalizing the crop.

PHOTOSHOP FOUNDATIONS

You can control a number of options related to saving files in the File Handling pane of the Preferences dialog box.

Image Previews.
You can use this menu to always or never include image thumbnails in the saved file. If you choose Ask When Saving in this menu, the Save As dialog box includes an option to include the image preview/thumbnail.

Macintosh

Windows

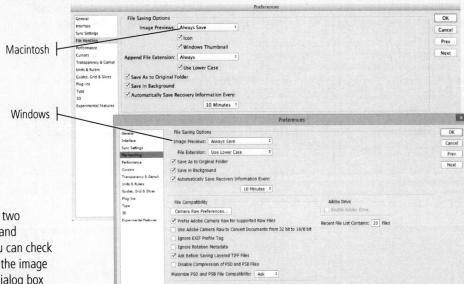

On Macintosh, you have two additional options: Icon and Windows Thumbnail. You can check the Icon option to show the image thumbnail in the Open dialog box and Finder (instead of the default Photoshop file icon). Although Macintosh can almost always read Windows information, Windows sometimes has trouble with certain Macintosh data — specifically, file thumbnails; you can check the Windows Thumbnail option to include a thumbnail that will be visible in the Windows Open dialog box.

Append File Extension. On Macintosh, you can use this menu to always or never include the file extension in the saved file. If the Ask When Saving option is selected in this menu, the Save As dialog box includes options to append the file extension (in lower case or not). On Windows, file extensions are always added to saved files; this preference menu has only two options: Use Upper Case and Use Lower Case.

If Ask When Saving is selected in the File Handling preferences, the Save As dialog box presents options to include Image Previews and File Extension.

Save As to Original Folder. When this option is checked, choosing File>Save As automatically defaults to the location where the original file is located.

Save in Background. The Save process occurs by default in the background — in other words, you can continue working even while a file is being saved. In versions prior to CS6, you could not interact with the application while a file was being saved. Especially when you work with large files, this can be a significant time saver because you don't have to sit and wait the several minutes it might take to save a very large file. (The only thing you can't do while a file is being saved is use the Save As command; if you try, you will see a warning advising you to wait until the background save is complete.)

When a file is being saved in the background, the completed percentage appears in the document tab.

Automatically Save Recovery Information Every... When checked, this option means that your work is saved in a temporary file, every 10 minutes by default; if something happens — a power outage, for example — you will be able to restore your work back to the last auto-saved version. In other words, the most you will lose is 10 minutes' work!

2. **In the Options bar, make sure the Delete Cropped Pixels option is checked.**

When this option is checked, areas outside the cropped areas are permanently removed from all layers in the file. If this option is not checked, cropped pixels remain in the file, but exist outside the edges of the file canvas. The Background layer, if one exists, is converted to a regular layer (you'll learn more about Background layers later in this project).

This is an important distinction — by maintaining cropped pixels, you can later transform or reposition layers to reveal different parts of the layer within the newly cropped canvas size.

3. **Click the right-center handle of the crop marquee and drag left until the cursor feedback shows W: 8.750 in.**

When you drag certain elements in the document window, live cursor feedback (also called "heads-up display") shows information about the transformation. When dragging a side crop marquee handle, for example, the feedback shows the new width of the area.

You might need to zoom into at least 66.7% or 100% view percentage to achieve the exact dimensions needed for this project.

Note:

You can press the Escape key to cancel the crop marquee and return to the uncropped image.

Note:

You can rotate a crop marquee by placing the cursor slightly away from a corner handle.

Click and drag the marquee handle to resize the marquee area.

Use the cursor feedback to find the appropriate measurement.

4. **Repeat Step 3 with the bottom-center handle until feedback shows the area of H: 11.250 in.**

Remember, the defined trim size for this ad is 8.5″ × 11″. Anything that runs to the page edge has to incorporate a 0.125″ bleed allowance, so the actual canvas size must be large enough to accommodate the bleed allowance on all edges:

[Width]   8.5″ + 0.125″ + 0.125″ = 8.75

[Height]   11″ + 0.125″ + 0.125″ = 11.25

5. Click inside the crop area and drag to reposition the image so that it is approximately centered in the crop area.

When you change the size of the marquee, the area outside the marquee is "shielded" by a darkened overlay so you can get an idea of what will remain after you finalize the crop.

You can drag the image inside the crop area to change the portion that will remain in the cropped image. By default, the crop area remains centered in the document window; instead, the image moves behind the crop area.

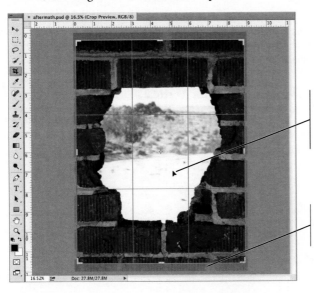

Click and drag inside the crop area to change the portion of the image inside the crop.

Areas outside the crop marquee are partially obscured.

6. Press Return/Enter to finalize the crop.

7. Choose the Move tool, and then open the Info panel (Window>Info).

As we explained in the Interface chapter, the panels you see depend on what was done the last time you (or someone else) used the Photoshop application. Because workspace arrangement is such a personal preference, we tell you what panels you need to use, but we don't tell you where to put them.

8. Click the horizontal page ruler at the top of the page and drag down to create a guide positioned at the 1/8″ (0.125″) mark.

If you watch the vertical ruler, you can see a marker indicating the position of the cursor. In addition to the live cursor feedback, the Info panel also shows the precise numeric position of the guide you are dragging.

Here again, it helps to zoom in to a higher view percentage if you want to precisely place guides. We found it necessary to use at least 100% view before the Info panel reflected exactly the 0.125″ position. If you zoom in, you can press the Spacebar to temporarily access the Hand tool to reposition the image so you can see the top-left corner.

Click and drag from the horizontal ruler to add a horizontal guide.

The blue line indicates the location of the guide you're dragging.

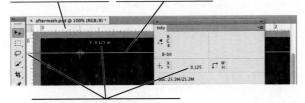

Watch the ruler, cursor feedback, or Info panel to see the location of the guide you're dragging.

9. **Click the vertical ruler at the left and drag right to place a guide at the 0.125″ mark.**

Watch the marker on the horizontal ruler to judge the guide's position.

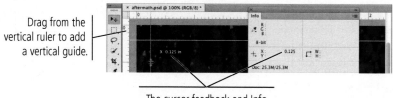

Drag from the vertical ruler to add a vertical guide.

The cursor feedback and Info panel show the exact X location of the guide you're dragging.

Note:

Use the Move tool to reposition placed guides. Remove individual guides by dragging them back onto the ruler.

If you try to reposition a guide and can't, choose View>Lock Guides. If this option is checked, guides are locked; you can't move them until you toggle this option off.

10. **Choose View>New Guide. In the resulting dialog box, choose the Vertical option and type 8.625 in the field and click OK.**

You don't need to type the unit of measurement because the default unit for this file is already inches. Photoshop automatically assumes the value you type is in the default unit of measurement.

11. **Choose View>New Guide again. Choose the Horizontal option and type 11.125 in the field. Click OK.**

At this point you should have four guides – two vertical and two horizontal, each 1/8″ from the file edges. These mark the trim size of your final 8.5 × 11″ file.

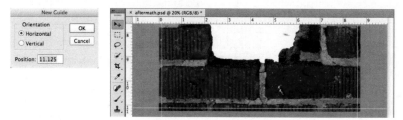

Note:

Press Option/Alt and click a guide to change it from vertical to horizontal (or vice versa). The guide rotates around the point where you click, which can be useful if you need to find a corner based on the position of an existing guide.

12. **In the top-left corner of the document window, click the zero-point crosshairs and drag to the top-left intersection of the guides.**

You can reposition the zero point to the top-left corner of the bleed allowance by double-clicking the zero-point crosshairs.

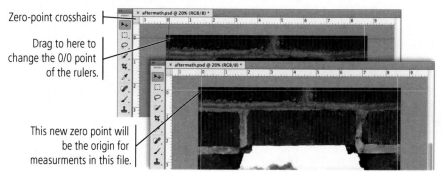

Zero-point crosshairs

Drag to here to change the 0/0 point of the rulers.

This new zero point will be the origin for measurments in this file.

13. Drag new guides 0.25″ inside each trim guide to mark the live area of the page.

These guides mark the defined live area of the ad (8 × 10.5″). This is how we determined where to put these guides:

[Width] $8.5'' - 8.0'' = 0.5 \div 2 = 0.25''$

[Height] $11'' - 10.5'' = 0.5'' \div 2 = 0.25''$

Notice that this step says "drag new guides." It is important to realize that the View>New Guide dialog box always positions guides from the original document zero-point (top-left corner); if you use that method, you would have to place the guides 0.375″ from each edge of the file — 0.125″ for the existing bleed guide plus 0.25″ for the live area.

14. Click the View menu and make sure a checkmark appears to the left of Lock Guides. If no checkmark is there, choose Lock Guides to toggle on that option.

After you carefully position specific guides, it's a good idea to lock them so you don't accidentally move or delete them later. If you need to move a guide at any point, simply choose View>Lock Guides to toggle off the option temporarily.

The outside guides mark the trim edge.

The inside guides mark the live area.

The option should be checked.

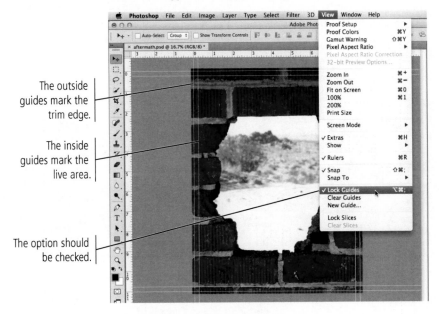

Note:

You can press Command/Control-; to toggle the visibility of page guides.

15. Save the file and continue to the next exercise.

Because you have already saved this working file with a new name, you can simply choose File>Save, or press Command/Control-S to save without opening a dialog box. If you want to change the file name, you can always choose File>Save As.

The Crop Tools in Depth

When the Crop tool is selected, the Options bar can be used to define a number of settings related to the cropped area.

The left menu includes a number of common aspect ratios as presets. If you choose one of these options, the crop marquee is constrained to the aspect ratio defined in the preset. It's important to note that these presets do not define the actual size of the resulting crop, only the aspect ratio.

You can also choose the **W x H x Resolution** option to define custom settings for the result of a crop. For example, if you define the width and height of a crop area as 9″ × 9″ at 300 ppi, when you click and drag to draw, the crop area will be restricted to the same proportions defined in the Width and Height fields (in this example, 1:1).

When you finalize the crop, the resulting image will be resized to be 9″ × 9″, regardless of the actual size of the crop marquee. This presents a problem if you remember the principles of resolution.

Enlarging a 3″ × 3″ area (for example) to 9″ × 9″ means the application needs to create enough pixels to fill in the 6 extra inches — at 300 ppi, Photoshop needs to create ("interpolate") more than 1800 pixels per linear inch. Although Photoshop can slightly enlarge images with reasonable success, such a significant amount of new data will not result in good quality. As a general rule, you should avoid enlarging raster images, and certainly no more than about 10%.

The crop area is constrained to the aspect ratio of the defined width and height.

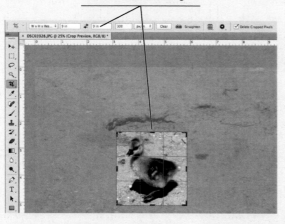

The resulting cropped image is the actual size defined in the Crop Image Size & Resolution dialog box.

You can use the **Set Overlay Options** menu to show a variety of overlays within the crop area; these follow basic design principles, such as the Rule of Thirds and the Golden Spiral.

You can also use the commands in this menu to turn the overlay on or off. If you choose Auto Show Overlay, the selected overlay only appears when you drag the marquee handles or click inside the marquee area to move the image inside the crop area.

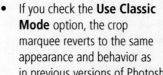

You can also click the **Set Additional Crop Options** button to access a variety of crop-related choices.

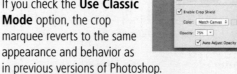

- If you check the **Use Classic Mode** option, the crop marquee reverts to the same appearance and behavior as in previous versions of Photoshop.

- When **Show Cropped Area** is checked, the area outside the crop marquee remains visible in the document window until you finalize the crop.

- When **Auto Center Preview** is checked, the crop area will always be centered in the document window; the image dynamically moves in the document window as you resize the crop area.

- When **Enable Crop Shield** is checked, areas outside the crop marquee are partially obscured by a semi-transparent solid color. You can use the related options to change the color and opacity of the shielded area.

The Crop Tools in Depth (continued)

When the Crop tool is selected, you can click the **Straighten** button in the Options bar and then draw a line in the image to define what should be a straight line in the resulting image. The image behind the crop marquee rotates to show what will remain in the cropped canvas; the line you drew is adjusted to be perfectly horizontal or vertical.

Click the Straighten button, then draw a line representing what you want to be "straight" in the cropped image.

The image is rotated behind the crop marquee to be "straight" based on the line you drew.

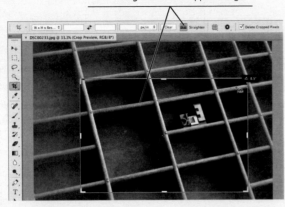

The **Perspective Crop tool** (nested under the Crop tool) can be used to draw a non-rectangular crop area. To define the area you want to keep, simply click to place the four corners of the area, then drag the corners in any direction as necessary. When you finalize the crop, the image inside the crop area is straightened to a front-on viewing angle. You should use this option with care, however, because it can badly distort an image.

In this first example, we used the actual lines in the photograph to draw the perspective crop marquee. After finalizing the crop, the type case appears to be perfectly straight rather than the original viewing angle at which it was photographed.

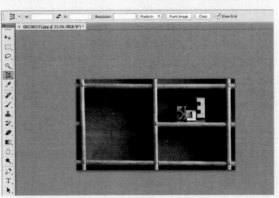

In this second example, we used the Perspective Crop tool to try to adjust the photograph of an historic hop kiln. You can see the obvious distortion in the resulting image.

DRAG A FILE TO COMPOSITE IMAGES

Compositing multiple images in Photoshop is a fairly simple process — or at least, it starts out that way. There are, of course, a number of technical and aesthetic issues that you must resolve when you combine multiple images in a single design.

1. **With aftermath.psd open, open the file Storm.jpg from your WIP>Movie folder.**

2. **With storm.jpg the active file in the document window, open the Image Size dialog box (Image>Image Size).**

   Remember: You can press Command-Option-I/Control-Alt-I, to open the dialog box.

   This image is only 180 ppi, but it has a physical size much larger than the defined ad size. As with the original bricks image, the principle of effective resolution might make this image usable in the composite ad.

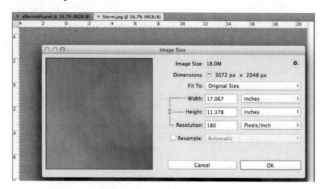

3. **Click Cancel to close the Image Size dialog box.**

4. **Open the Window>Arrange menu and choose 2-up Vertical to show both open files at one time.**

   As you saw in the Interface chapter, these options are useful for arranging and viewing multiple open files within your workspace.

5. **Choose the Move tool in the Tools panel.**

6. **Click in the Storm.jpg image window and drag into the aftermath.psd image window, then release the mouse button.**

   Basic compositing can be as simple as dragging a selection from one file to another. If no active selection appears in the source document, this action moves the entire active layer from the source document.

Move tool —

This cursor shows that you are dragging a layer. In this case, you're dragging it into another document window. —

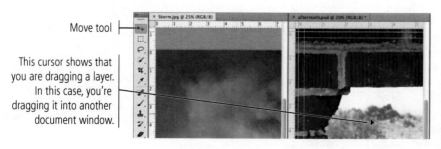

7. **Click the Close button on the Storm.jpg document tab to close that file.**

   After closing the storm file, the aftermath.psd document window expands to fill the available space.

   If you remember from the Image Size dialog box, the storm image was 17.1″ × 11.4″ at 180 ppi. Photoshop cannot maintain multiple resolutions in a single file. When you move the image content into the aftermath file, it adopts the resolution of the target file (in this case, 300 ppi). The concept of effective resolution transforms the storm image/layer to approximately 10.25″ × 6.825″ at 300 ppi.

8. **Open the Layers panel (Window>Layers).**

   The original aftermath.psd file had only one layer — Background. Before editing, every scan and digital photograph has this characteristic. When you copy or drag content from one file into another, it is automatically placed on a new layer with the default name "Layer *n*", where "n" is a sequential number.

   When a file contains more than one layer, the document tab shows the name of the active layer.

   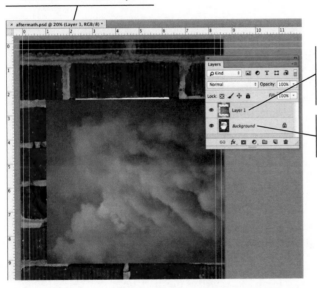

   A new layer (Layer 1) is added to contain the contents that you dragged from the storm.jpg file.

   The Background layer contains the original bricks file content.

9. **Choose File>Save, and read the resulting message.**

   Because this is the first time you have saved the file after adding new layers, you should see the Photoshop Format Options dialog box with the Maximize Compatibility check box already activated. It's a good idea to leave this check box selected so that your files will be compatible with other Adobe applications and other versions of Photoshop.

   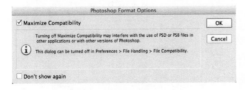

Note:

If you don't see this warning, check the File Handling pane of the Preferences dialog box. You can set the Maximize PSD and PSB File Compatibility menu to Always, Never, or Ask.

10. **Make sure the Maximize Compatibility check box is selected and click OK.**

11. **Continue to the next exercise.**

COPY AND PASTE SELECTED PIXELS

In the previous exercise, you used the Move tool to drag an entire layer. You can also use a variety of selection tools to choose only certain areas of a layer that will be moved. In this exercise, you will use the most basic selection tool — the Rectangle Marquee tool.

1. **With aftermath.psd open, choose View>Fit on Screen to show the entire image centered in the document window.**

2. **Open the file Skyline.jpg from your WIP>Movie folder.**

3. **Choose the Rectangular Marquee tool in the Tools panel and review the options in the Options bar.**

   By default, dragging with a marquee tool creates a new selection. You can use the buttons on the left end of the Options bar to add to the current selection, subtract from the current selection, or intersect with the current selection.

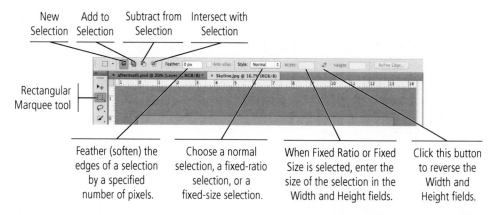

| New Selection | Add to Selection | Subtract from Selection | Intersect with Selection |

Rectangular Marquee tool

Feather (soften) the edges of a selection by a specified number of pixels.

Choose a normal selection, a fixed-ratio selection, or a fixed-size selection.

When Fixed Ratio or Fixed Size is selected, enter the size of the selection in the Width and Height fields.

Click this button to reverse the Width and Height fields.

4. **Choose the New Selection option in the Options bar. Click outside of the top-left corner, drag down past the bottom edge of the image, and drag right to create a selection area that is approximately 8.5" wide.**

   You can't select an area larger than the current canvas, so the top, left, and bottom edges of the selection snap to the canvas edges. The live cursor feedback, as well as the mark on the horizontal ruler, help to determine the selection area's width.

Selection marquee

Rectangular Marquee tool cursor

Note:

The edges of this image will be hidden by the bricks, so you don't need the full 8.75" width of the overall ad.

Note:

Press Shift while dragging a new marquee to constrain the selection to a square (using the Rectangular Marquee tool) or circle (using the Elliptical Marquee tool).

5. Click inside the selection marquee and drag it to the approximate center of the image.

You can move a selection marquee by clicking inside the selected area with the Marquee tool and dragging to the desired area of the image.

The live cursor feedback shows how far you have moved the area.

Note:

If you want to move a marquee, make sure the Marquee tool is still selected. If the Move tool is active, clicking inside the marquee and dragging will actually move the contents within the selection area.

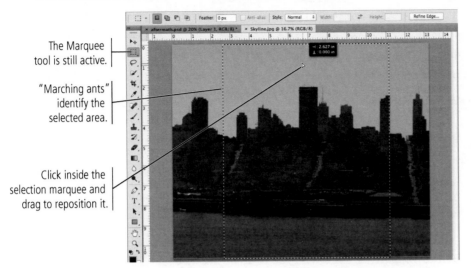

The Marquee tool is still active.

"Marching ants" identify the selected area.

Click inside the selection marquee and drag to reposition it.

Note:

When creating a new selection with a marquee tool, pressing Option/Alt places the center of the selection marquee at the point where you click; when you drag out, the marquee is created around that point.

6. In the Options bar, choose the Subtract from Selection option.

7. Click near the waterline at the left edge of the existing selection, drag down past the bottom edge of the image, and right past the right edge of the existing selection.

Note:

Press Shift to add to the current selection or press Option/Alt to subtract from the current selection.

Subtract from Selection is active.

Click here...

...and drag to here.

The cursor shows a minus sign because you are subtracting from the existing selection.

You only want the city to appear in the ad, so you don't need the water area of this image. When you release the mouse button, the selection is the area of the first marquee, minus the area of the second marquee. (This two-step process isn't particularly necessary in this case, but you should know how to add to and subtract from selections.)

8. **Choose Edit>Copy.**

The standard Cut, Copy, and Paste options are available in Photoshop, just as they are in most applications. Whatever you have selected will be copied to the Clipboard, and whatever is in the Clipboard will be pasted.

9. **Click the Close button on the Skyline.jpg document tab to close the file. When asked, click Don't Save.**

10. **With the aftermath.psd file active, choose Edit>Paste.**

The copied selection is pasted in the center of the document window. Because you used the Fit on Screen option at the beginning of this exercise, the pasted image is centered in the document. Another new layer is automatically created to store the pasted content.

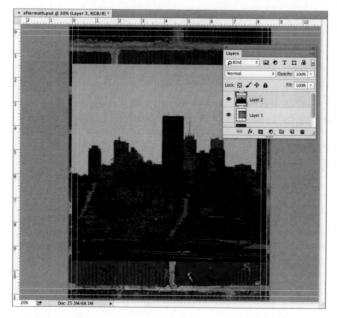

11. **Save the file and continue to the next exercise.**

RASTERIZE A VECTOR FILE

As you learned earlier, vector graphics are based on a series of mathematical descriptions that tell the computer processor where to draw lines. Logos and title treatments — such as the ones you will use in this project — are commonly created as vector graphics. Although Photoshop is typically a "paint" (pixel-based) application, you can also open and work with vector graphics created in illustration programs like Adobe Illustrator.

1. **With aftermath.psd open, choose File>Open and navigate to your WIP>Movie folder.**

2. **Select Title.ai in the list of files and then click Open.**

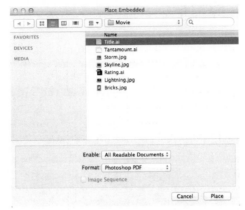

This is an Adobe Illustrator file of the movie title text treatment. The Format menu defaults to Photoshop PDF because Illustrator uses PDF as its underlying file structure.

When you open a vector file (Illustrator, EPS, or PDF) in Photoshop, it is rasterized (converted to a raster graphic). The Import PDF dialog box allows you to determine exactly what and how to rasterize the file. The default values in this box are defined by the contents of the file you're opening.

The Crop To options determine the size of the opened file. Depending on how the file was created, some of these values might be the same as others:

- **Bounding Box** is the outermost edges of the artwork in the file.
- **Media Box** is the size of the paper as defined in the file.
- **Crop Box** is the size of the page including printer's marks.
- **Bleed Box** is the trim size plus any defined bleed allowance.
- **Trim Box** is the trim size as defined in the file.
- **Art Box** is the area of the page as defined in the file.

3. **Highlight the Width field and type 8, and make sure the Resolution field is set to 300 pixels/inch.**

The Image Size fields default to the settings of the bounding box you select. You can change the size, resolution, color mode, and bit depth by entering new values.

You know the live area of the ad you're building is 8″ wide, so you can import this file at a size small enough to fit into that space. Because the Constrain Proportions option is checked by default, the height changes proportionally to match the new width.

If you're opening a multi-page PDF or an Illustrator file with more than one artboard, this window shows previews of each "page" in the file.

When this chain icon appears, the width and height are constrained.

4. Click OK.

The title treatment file opens in Photoshop. The checkered area behind the text indicates that the background is transparent. If you look at the Layers panel, you will see that Layer 1 isn't locked; because it's transparent, it is not considered a background layer.

5. Choose Select>All.

This command creates a marquee for the entire canvas.

The gray-and-white checked pattern identifies areas of transparency in the layer content.

Using the Select>All command surrounds the entire canvas in a selection marquee.

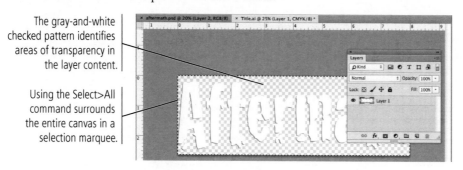

6. Choose Edit>Copy, then click the Close button on the Title document tab to close that file. Click Don't Save if asked.

7. With the aftermath.psd file active, choose Edit>Paste.

8. Save aftermath.psd and continue to the next exercise.

 PLACE FILES AS SMART OBJECT LAYERS

As you have seen in the last few exercises, copying layer content from one file to another results in new regular layers for the pasted content. Photoshop also supports Smart Object layers, in which you place one file into another instead of pasting layer content. Smart Objects provide a number of advantages over regular layers, which you will explore later in this project. In this exercise, you will create the Smart Object layers for the remaining image elements.

1. With aftermath.psd open, choose File>Place Embedded.

Two options in the File menu — Place Embedded and Place Linked — give you have the option to embed the placed file data into active file, or to place smart objects as links to the original placed file. (See Page 219 For more about placing linked files.)

2. **Choose the Lightning.jpg file (in your WIP>Movie folder) and click Place.**

The placed file appears with bounding box handles and crossed diagonal lines. The placement isn't final until you press Return/Enter; if you press the Escape key, the file will not be placed.

In the Options bar, you can see that the placed image has been scaled to approximately 45% to fit into the document where it is being placed.

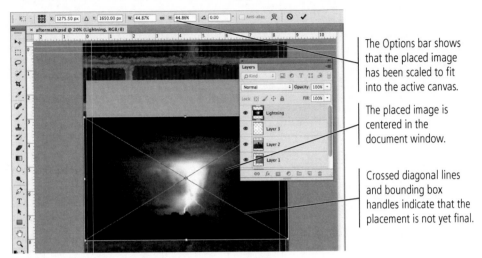

The Options bar shows that the placed image has been scaled to fit into the active canvas.

The placed image is centered in the document window.

Crossed diagonal lines and bounding box handles indicate that the placement is not yet final.

3. **Press Return/Enter to finalize the placement.**

After you finalize the placement, the bounding box handles and crossed diagonal lines disappear. In the Layers panel, the placed file has its own layer (just as the copied layers do). This layer, however, is automatically named, based on the name of the placed file.

The layer's thumbnail indicates that this layer is a **Smart Object** — it is linked to the file that you placed. Changes in the original file will also be reflected in the file where the original is placed.

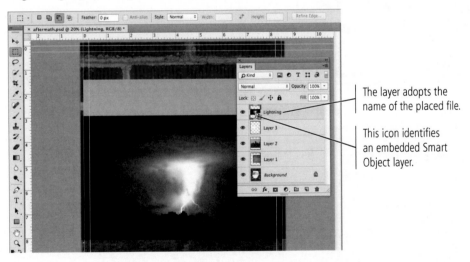

The layer adopts the name of the placed file.

This icon identifies an embedded Smart Object layer.

4. **Choose File>Place Embedded again. Select Rating.ai and click Place.**

Vector graphics offer several advantages over raster images, including sharper edges and free scaling without deteriorating image quality. To take advantage of these benefits, you might want to maintain vector files as vector objects instead of rasterizing them. Photoshop gives you the option to do exactly that — maintaining vector information and raster information in the same file.

5. **In the resulting dialog box, choose Bounding Box in the Crop To menu, then click OK.**

Because this is a native Illustrator file (identified by the ".ai" extension), you have the same Crop To options as when you actually open an Illustrator file in Photoshop.

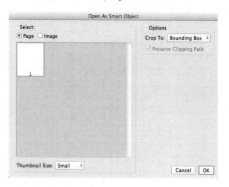

6. **In the Options bar, change the W and H fields to 100%.**

Placed files are not always scaled exactly proportionally; it's a good idea to check and (if necessary) restore the original height-to-width aspect ratio.

7. **Press Return/Enter to finalize the placement of the first file.**

Change both fields to 100%.

8. **Repeat Steps 4–7 to place Tantamount.ai as a Smart Object layer.**

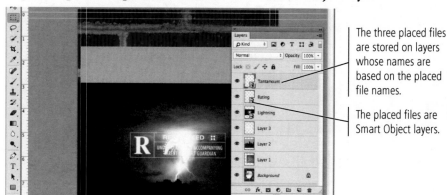

The three placed files are stored on layers whose names are based on the placed file names.

The placed files are Smart Object layers.

9. **Save the file and continue to the next stage of the project.**

Right now, you have a fairly incomprehensible mess of four raster images and three vector objects all piled on top of one another. You will start to make sense of these files in the next stage.

In the previous exercise you used the Place Embedded option to create Smart Object layers that contain the placed file data. Using that method the embedded file data becomes a part of the parent file.

If you double-click the thumbnail icon of an embedded Smart Object, the embedded file opens in an application that can edit the stored data — AI files open in Illustrator; PSD, TIFF, and JPEG files open in Photoshop.

When you first open a Smart Object file, the application provides advice for working with Smart Objects:

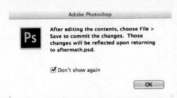

After you make necessary changes, you can save the file and close it, then return to Photoshop (if necessary). Your changes in the Smart Object file will automatically reflect in the parent file where the Smart Object layer is placed.

Important note: Do not use the Save As option when editing Smart Object layers. The changes will not reflect in the parent file if you save changes with a different file name.

If you choose the Place Linked option in the File menu, Smart Object layer stores a link to the original file data rather than embedding that data inside the parent file.

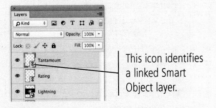

This icon identifies a linked Smart Object layer.

This provides an opportunity for maintaining consistency because you only need to change one instance of a file to reflect those changes anywhere the file is placed.

Say you place a logo created in Illustrator into a Photoshop file. The same logo is also placed as a link in a number of InDesign documents. If you open the logo in Illustrator and change the main color (for example), then save the changes in the original logo file, the new color automatically reflects in any file — whether InDesign or Photoshop — that is linked to the edited logo.

If you use the Place Embedded option in Photoshop, the Smart Object layer is not linked to the original, edited logo file; you would have to open the embedded Smart Object and make the same color change a second time.

Linked files also have potential disadvantages. As we mentioned previously, double-clicking a Smart Object layer thumbnail opens the linked or embedded file in an application that can edit the relevant data. If you are working with *linked* Smart Object layers, any changes you make affect the original file data. This means your changes appear not only in the parent Photoshop file where it is linked, but also any other file that links to the same data.

For a file to output properly, linked Smart Object layers must be present and up to date at the time of output.

If the linked file has been modified while the parent file is open, the changes automatically reflect in the parent file when you return to that document. If the parent file is not open in Photoshop when the linked file is edited, you will see a Modified icon for the linked Smart Object layer.

If the linked file is deleted or moved to another location after it has been placed, the parent file will show a Missing icon for the linked Smart Object layer.

If a linked Smart Object has been moved while the parent file is not open, you will see a warning dialog box when you open the parent Photoshop file. You can use that dialog box to locate the missing link, or close it and use the options in the Layers panel to correct the problem.

Control/right-clicking a linked Smart Object layer name opens a contextual menu with options to update modified content and resolve broken links.

This icon identifies a linked, missing Smart Object layer.

This icon identifies a linked, modified Smart Object layer.

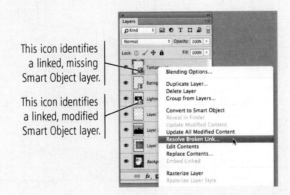

To avoid potential problems with missing linked files, you can use the File>Package command to create a job folder. The parent file is copied to a new folder, along with a Links subfolder containing any files that are placed as linked Smart Object layers.

Stage 2 Managing Layers

Your ad file now has most of the necessary pieces, but it's still not an actual design — just a pile of images. When you composite images into a cohesive design, you almost certainly need to manipulate and transform some of the layers to make all of the pieces work together.

Photoshop includes a number of options for managing layers: naming layers for easier recognition, creating layer groups so multiple layers can be manipulated at once, moving layers around on the canvas, transforming layers both destructively and non-destructively, controlling individual layer visibility, and arranging the top-to-bottom stacking order of layers to determine exactly what is visible. You will use all of these options in this stage of the project.

NAME LAYERS AND LAYER GROUPS

It's always a good idea to name your layers because it makes managing the file much easier — especially when you work with files that include dozens of layers. Even with only four unnamed layers in this file (counting the Background layer), it would be tedious to have to toggle each layer on to find the one you want.

1. **With aftermath.psd open, review the Layers panel.**

2. **Option/Alt-click the eye icon for Layer 1 to hide all other layers.**

   Toggling layer visibility is an easy way to see only what you want to see at any given stage in a project.

   Clicking the eye icon for a specific layer hides that layer; clicking the empty space where the eye icon should be shows the hidden layer. To show or hide a series of consecutive layers, click the visibility icon (or empty space) for the first layer you want to affect, hold down the mouse button, and drag down to the last layer you want to show or hide.

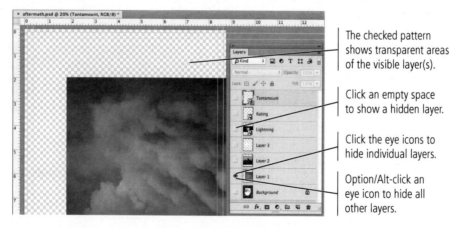

The checked pattern shows transparent areas of the visible layer(s).

Click an empty space to show a hidden layer.

Click the eye icons to hide individual layers.

Option/Alt-click an eye icon to hide all other layers.

3. **Double-click the Layer 1 layer name, and then type Storm.**

   You can rename any layer by simply double-clicking the name and typing.

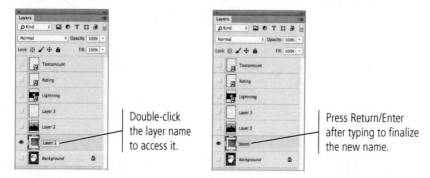

Double-click the layer name to access it.

Press Return/Enter after typing to finalize the new name.

4. Click the eye icon to hide the renamed Storm layer, and then click the empty space to the left of Layer 2 to show only that layer.

5. Double-click the Layer 2 name and then type Skyline to rename the layer.

6. Repeat Steps 4–5 to rename Layer 3 as Title.

7. Click the spaces on the left side of the Layers panel (where the eye icons were) to show all hidden layers.

8. In the Layers panel, click the Tantamount layer to select it.

9. Press Shift and click the Rating layer to select that layer as well.

Since the Tantamount layer was already selected, the Rating layer should now be a second selected (highlighted) layer.

10. Click the button in the top-right corner of the panel to open the Layers panel Options menu. Choose New Group from Layers.

This option creates a group that automatically contains the selected layers. You can also create an empty group by choosing New Group (this option is available even when no layer is selected) or by clicking the New Group button at the bottom of the panel.

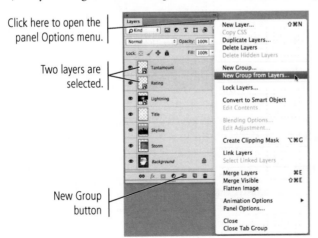

Click here to open the panel Options menu.

Two layers are selected.

New Group button

Note:

Press Shift and click to select consecutive layers in the Layers panel.

Press Command/Control and click to select non-consecutive layers in the Layers panel.

Note:

You can create a group from selected layers by dragging the selected layers onto the New Group button at the bottom of the panel. In this case, the new group is automatically named "Group N" (N is a placeholder for a sequential number); of course, you can rename a layer group just as easily as you can rename a layer.

11. **In the New Group from Layers dialog box, type Logos in the Name field and click OK.**

As with any other layer, you should name groups based on what they contain so you can easily identify them later.

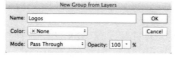 

12. **Click the arrow to the left of the Logos group name to expand the layer group.**

You have to expand the layer group to be able to access and edit individual layers in the group. If you select the entire layer group, you can move all layers within the group at the same time. Layers in the group maintain their position relative to one another.

13. **Save the file and continue to the next exercise.**

MOVE AND TRANSFORM SMART OBJECT LAYERS

Photoshop makes scaling, rotating, and other transformations fairly easy to implement, but it is important to realize the potential impact of your transformations.

1. **With aftermath.psd open, click the Tantamount layer (in the Logos folder) in the Layers panel to select only that layer.**

2. **Choose the Move tool in the Tools panel.**

As the name suggests, the Move tool is used to move a selection around on the canvas. You can select a specific area, and then click and drag to move only the selection on the active layer. If there is no active selection area, you can click and drag to move the contents of the entire active layer.

3. **In the Options bar, make sure the Auto-Select option is not checked.**

When Auto-Select is checked, you can click in the image window and drag to move the contents of the layer containing the pixels where you click; you do not need to first select the layer in the Layers panel before moving the layer content. This is very useful in some cases, as you will see later in this project. However, the Auto-Select option is *not* very useful when the contents of multiple layers are stacked on top of each other (as is the case in your file as it exists now).

4. **Click in the image window and drag until the Tantamount layer content snaps to the bottom-right live-area guides.**

If you toggled off the Snap feature when you used the Crop tool, you should turn it back on now by choosing View>Snap.

This option should
not be checked.

Move tool

With no marching ants in
the image window, select
the layer you want to move,
then click and drag in the
document window to move
the layer's contents.

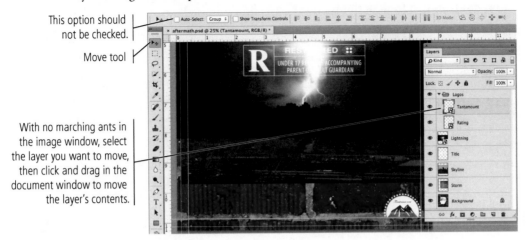

5. **Click the Rating layer in the Layers panel to select that layer.**

6. **Click in the image window and drag until the Rating layer content snaps to the bottom-left live-area guides.**

7. **With the Rating layer still active, choose Edit>Free Transform.**

When you use the transform options, bounding box handles surround the selection.

8. **Press Shift, click the top-right bounding box handle, and then drag down and left until the layer content is approximately two-thirds the original size.**

The selection (in this case, the entire Rating layer) dynamically changes as you scale the layer. Pressing Shift while you drag a handle constrains the image proportions as you resize it. When you release the mouse button, the handles remain in place until you finalize ("commit") the transformation.

The live cursor feedback shows the new dimensions of the transformed selection.

Note:

You can also use the Edit>Transform submenu to apply specific transformations to a layer or selection.

Reference   Horizontal   Vertical   Horizontal   Vertical
Point   Position   Position   Scale   Scale   Rotate   Warp

Cancel Transform

Commit Transform

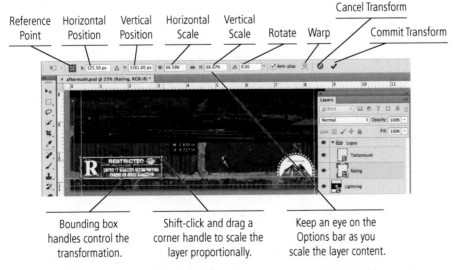

Bounding box
handles control the
transformation.

Shift-click and drag a
corner handle to scale the
layer proportionally.

Keep an eye on the
Options bar as you
scale the layer content.

While you're manually transforming a layer or selection, the Options bar shows the specifics. You can also type into these fields to apply specific numeric transformations.

9. **Press Return/Enter to finalize the transformation.**

   After finalizing the transformation, the bounding-box handles disappear.

10. **With the Rating layer still active, press Command/Control-T to enter Free Transform mode again and look at the Options bar.**

    Because the rating layer is a Smart Object layer, the W and H fields still show the scaling percentage based on the original.

The W and H fields still show the scaling you applied in Step 8.

11. **In the Options bar, choose the bottom-left reference point location.**

    The selected reference point defines the point around which transformations are made. By selecting the bottom-left point, for example, the bottom-left corner of the active selection will remain in place when you scale the selection in the next steps; the top-right corner will move based on the scaling you define.

12. **Click the Link icon between the W and H fields to constrain proportions during the transformation.**

13. **Type 50 in the Options bar W field.**

The bottom-left reference point is selected.

Click the Lock icon to constrain the height and width proportionally.

14. **Click the Commit Transform button on the Options bar (or press Return/Enter) to finalize the transformation.**

    If you press Return/Enter, you have to press it two times to finalize the transformation. The first time you press it, you apply the change to the active field; the second time, you finalize the transformation and exit Free Transform mode.

15. **Collapse the layer group by clicking the arrow at the left of the group name.**

16. **Save the file and continue to the next exercise.**

Understanding Smart Guides

As you dragged the layers in the previous exercise, you might have noticed a series of pink lies appearing in different locations while you moved the layer content. These lines are a function of Smart Guides, which make it easier to align layer content to other layers or to the overall canvas.

Smart Guides are active by default, but you can toggle them on and off in the View>Show submenu.

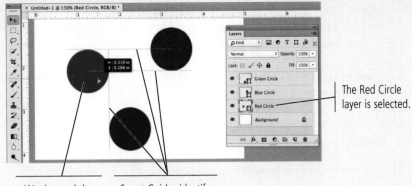

The Red Circle layer is selected.

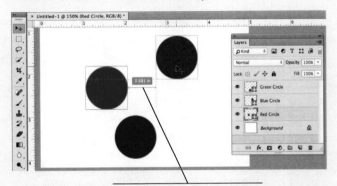

We dragged the Red Circle layer with the Move tool.

Smart Guides identify the center and edges of content on other layers.

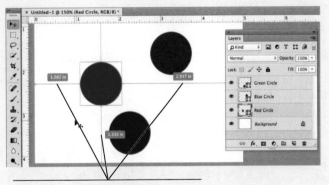

Press Command/Control and hover over an object to find the distance between it and the selected layer.

Press Command/Control and hover over the canvas find the distance between the selected layer content and the canvas edges.

TRANSFORM A REGULAR LAYER

Smart Object layers enable non-destructive transformations, which means those transformations can be changed or undone without affecting the quality of the layer content. Transforming a regular layer, on the other hand, is destructive and permanent.

1. **With aftermath.psd open, hide all but the Storm layer. Click the Storm layer in the Layers panel to select it.**

2. **If necessary, drag the layer content so it is approximately centered on the canvas.**

3. **Choose Edit>Transform>Flip Horizontal.**

   The Transform submenu commands affect only the selected layer.

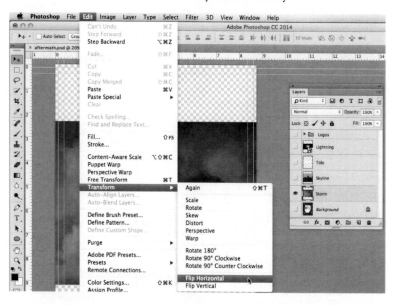

4. **Press Command/Control-T to enter Free Transform mode.**

   Some handles might not be visible within the boundaries of the document window. If necessary, zoom out so you can see all eight handles of the layer content.

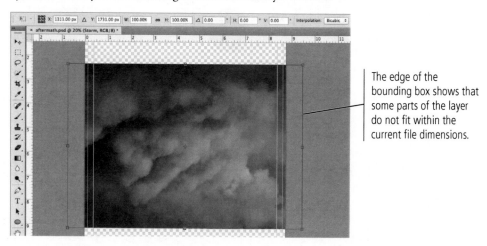

The edge of the bounding box shows that some parts of the layer do not fit within the current file dimensions.

5. **In the Options bar, choose the center reference point if it is not already selected.**

6. **Click the Link icon between the W and H fields to constrain the proportions.**

7. **Place the cursor over the W field label to access the scrubby slider for that field.**

   When you see the scrubby slider cursor, you can drag right to increase or drag left to decrease the value in the related field.

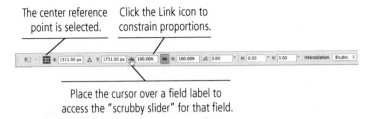

The center reference point is selected. | Click the Link icon to constrain proportions.

Place the cursor over a field label to access the "scrubby slider" for that field.

8. **Click and drag left until the W field shows 90%.**

9. **Press Return/Enter to finalize the transformation.**

10. **With the Storm layer still active, press Command/Control-T to re-enter Free Transform mode.**

    Once you commit the transformation on a regular layer, the transformation is final. Looking at the Options bar now, you can see that it shows the layer at 100% instead of the 90% from Step 8.

    If you transform a Smart Object layer, the scale percentage is maintained even after you finalize the change — unlike scaling a regular layer, where the layer re-calibrates so the new size is considered 100% once you finalize the scaling.

Re-entering Free Transform mode shows that the regular layer is again 100%, even after scaling.

11. **Press Esc to exit Free Transform mode without changing anything.**

12. **Save the file and continue to the next exercise.**

TRANSFORM THE BACKGROUND LAYER

Your file currently has a number of layers, most of which were created by pasting or placing external files into the original file. Because every photograph and scan (and some images that you create from scratch in Photoshop) begins with a default locked Background layer, it is important to understand the special characteristics of that layer:

- You can't apply layer transformations, styles, or masks to the Background layer.

- You can't move the contents of the Background layer around in the document.

- If you delete pixels from the Background layer, you must determine the color that will be used in place of the deleted pixels.

- The Background layer cannot include transparent pixels, which are necessary for underlying layers to be visible.

- The Background layer is always the bottom layer in the stacking order; you can't add or move layers lower than the Background layer.

Note:

If you crop an image that includes a Background layer, the Background layer is automatically converted to a regular layer if the Delete Cropped Pixels option is not checked.

In the final composite file for this project, you need to flip the bricks image from top to bottom, remove the desert area from the hole in the bricks, and place the other photographs to appear through the hole in the wall. For any of these options to work properly, you need to convert the default Background layer to a regular layer.

1. **With aftermath.psd open, hide the Storm layer and then show the Background layer.**

2. **Click the Background layer to select it and then choose Edit>Transform.**

   The Transform submenu commands are not available for the locked Background layer.

Many commands are not available because the Background layer is locked.

3. **With the Background layer still selected, choose Image>Image Rotation> Flip Canvas Vertical.**

   To affect the locked background layer, you have to flip the actual canvas.

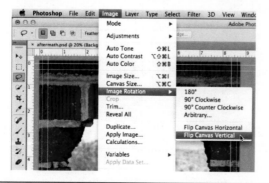

4. **Show the Logos layer group.**

   Because you flipped the canvas, the Tantamount and Ratings layers are also flipped upside-down. Rotating or flipping the entire canvas affects all layers in the file; this is obviously not what you want to do.

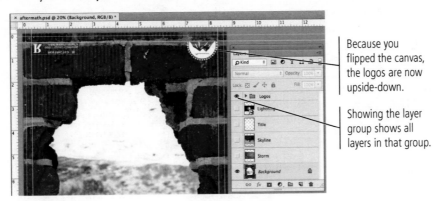

Because you flipped the canvas, the logos are now upside-down.

Showing the layer group shows all layers in that group.

5. **Choose Edit>Undo Flip Canvas Vertical.**

   The Undo command affects the last action you performed; the actual command changes to reflect the action that will be undone. Showing or hiding a layer is not considered an "action," so the Undo command simply un-flips the canvas. The Logos group is again hidden, as it was when you flipped the canvas in Step 3.

6. **In the Layers panel, click the Lock icon on the Background layer.**

   Clicking the Lock icon unlocks the layer and immediately converts the previous Background layer to a regular layer named "Layer 0."

7. **Double-click the Layer 0 layer name to highlight it, then type Bricks to rename the layer.**

Click the lock icon to unlock the Background layer.

The layer is automatically converted to a regular layer named Layer 0.

8. **With the Bricks layer selected in the panel, choose Edit>Transform>Flip Vertical.**

   Because the layer is no longer locked, you can now access and apply the transform commands that affect only the selected layer.

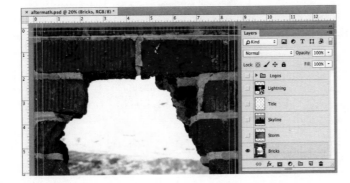

Note:

Although the Background layer exists by default in many files, it is not a required component.

9. **Show all layers in the file.**

10. **Save the file and continue to the next stage of the project.**

The Undo command (Edit>Undo or Command/Control-Z) only steps back to the last action completed; after you use the Undo command, it toggles to Redo. You can also use the Step Backward command (Edit>Step Backward or Command-Option-Z/Control-Alt-Z) to move back in the history one step at a time, or use the History panel (Window>History) to navigate back to earlier stages.

Every action you take is recorded as a state in the History panel. You can click any state to return to that particular point in the document progression. You can also delete specific states or create a new document from a particular state using the buttons at the bottom of the panel.

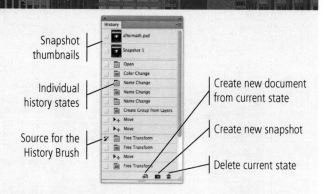

Snapshot thumbnails

Individual history states

Source for the History Brush

Create new document from current state

Create new snapshot

Delete current state

By default, the History panel stores the last 20 states; older states are automatically deleted. You can change that setting in the Performance pane of the Preferences dialog box. Keep in mind, however, that storing a larger number of states will increase the memory that is required to work with a specific file.

Keep the following in mind when using the History panel:

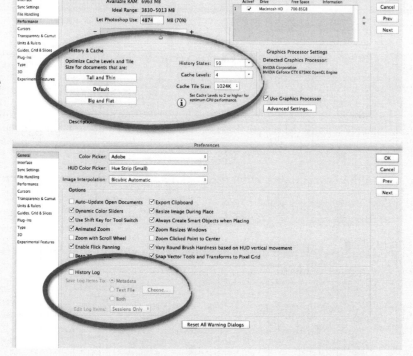

- The default snapshot is the image state when it was first opened.

- The oldest state is at the top of the list; the most recent state appears at the bottom.

- The History State slider identifies the active state.

- You can save any particular state as a snapshot to prevent it from being deleted when that state is no longer within the number of states that can be stored.

- The history is only stored while the file is open; when you close a file, the history and snapshots are not saved.

- When you select a specific state, the states below it are dimmed so you can see which changes will be discarded if you go back to a particular history state.

- Selecting a state and then changing the image eliminates all states that come after it.

- Deleting a state deletes that state and those after it. If you choose Allow Non-Linear History in the History Options dialog box (accessed in the History panel Options menu), deleting a state deletes only that state.

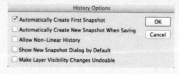

If you need to keep a record of a file's history even after you close the file, you can activate the History Log option in the General pane of the Preferences dialog box. When this option is checked, you can save the history log as metadata, in a text file, or both. You can also determine the level of detail that will be recorded in the history log.

- Sessions Only records each time you launch or quit and each time you open and close individual files.

- Concise adds the text that appears in the History panel to the Sessions information.

- Detailed gives you a complete history of all changes made to files.

Stage 3 Creating Complex Selections

At this stage of the project, you still have a few issues to resolve: some of the images are still randomly stacked on top of one another, and some images have areas that are hiding other images (the blue sky in the Skyline layer, for example). In this stage, you start fixing these problems.

Virtually any Photoshop project involves making some kind of selection. Making selections is so important, in fact, that there are no fewer than nine tools dedicated specifically to this goal, as well as a whole Select menu and a few other options for making and refining selections.

In an earlier lesson you learned how to use the Rectangular Marquee tool to draw simple selections. In the next series of exercises, you use several other selection methods to isolate pixels from their backgrounds (called **silhouetting**).

MAKE A FEATHERED SELECTION IN A SMART OBJECT

Smart Object layers are actually links to the files that are placed. If you open the linked file and make changes, those changes are automatically reflected in the file where the Smart Object layer exists. In this exercise, you will explore one of the advantages and disadvantages of Smart Object layers.

1. **With aftermath.psd open, hide all but the Lightning layer.**

2. **Double-click the Lightning layer thumbnail to open the Smart Object file in its own window. If you see a warning message, click OK.**

   This message tells you that you must save the Smart Object with the same name for the changes to reflect in the aftermath file. You can't use the Save As function to save the file with a different name or in a different location.

Double-click the Smart Object layer thumbnail to open the linked file.

Note:

If you don't see this message, you can open the General pane of the Preferences dialog box and click the Reset All Warning Dialogs button.

   The Lightning.jpg file opens separately, appearing by default as a separate tab at the top of the document window. This is a JPEG file, which means it is a flat file with only a locked Background layer.

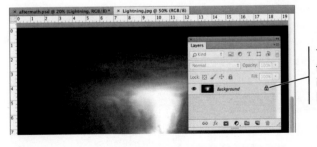

The Lightning image is a flat image, which means it has only a Background layer that is locked.

3. **Close the Lightning.jpg file.**

   Your goal in this exercise is to create a transparent area around the actual lightning bolt.

   Flat files (including JPEG) do not support transparency. To save the file with transparency, you would need to save it as a native Photoshop file with the PSD extension. However, as the warning message indicated, you must save the Smart Object file with the same name — which includes the file extension.

   Because you can't save transparency in a JPEG file, you need to break the link to the original JPEG file before you can create that transparency in the composite file.

4. **With aftermath.psd still open, Control/right-click the Lightning layer name in the Layers panel. Choose Rasterize Layer in the contextual menu.**

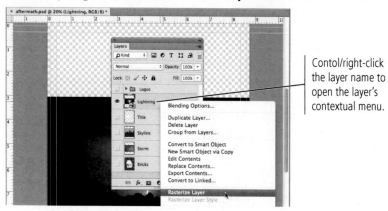

Contol/right-click the layer name to open the layer's contextual menu.

Rasterizing the Smart Object basically removes the link to any external file, making the Smart Object a part of the file in which it has been placed.

After rasterizing the layer, the thumbnail shows that this layer is a regular image layer instead of a Smart Object layer.

Note:

If the original placed file was a native Photoshop file, you would not need to rasterize the Smart Object layer to accomplish your goal.

5. **Select the Lasso tool in the Tools panel.**

6. **Drag a rough shape around the lightning in the photo.**

The lasso tools allow you to make irregular selections — in other words, selections that aren't just rectangular or elliptical. When you release the mouse button, the end point automatically connects to the beginning point of the selection.

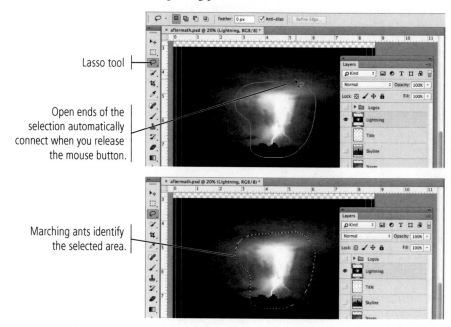

Lasso tool

Open ends of the selection automatically connect when you release the mouse button.

Marching ants identify the selected area.

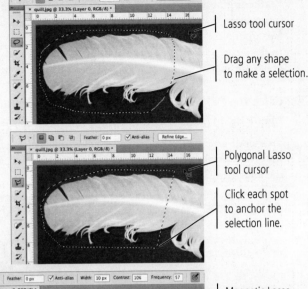

The Lasso Tools

The basic **Lasso tool** works like a pencil, following the path where you drag the mouse.

The **Polygonal Lasso tool** creates selections with straight lines, anchoring a line each time you click the mouse. To close a selection area, you must click the first point in the selection.

Lasso tool cursor

Drag any shape to make a selection.

The **Magnetic Lasso tool** snaps to high-contrast edges; you can use the Options bar to control the way Photoshop detects edges of an image.

- **Width** is the distance away from the edge the cursor can be and still detect edges; if you set this value higher, you can move the cursor farther from edges.

Polygonal Lasso tool cursor

Click each spot to anchor the selection line.

- **Contrast** is how different the foreground can be from the background and still be detected; if there is a sharp distinction between the foreground and background, you can set this value higher.

- **Frequency** is the number of points that will be created to make the selection; setting this number higher creates finer selections, while setting it lower creates smoother edges.

Magnetic Lasso tool cursor

Drag near the edges of the object and the selection snaps to the edges.

It isn't uncommon for a mouse to unexpectedly jump when you don't want it to — which can be particularly troublesome if you're drawing a selection with the Polygonal or Magnetic Lasso tools. If you aren't happy with your Polygonal or Magnetic Lasso selection, press Escape to clear the selection and then try again.

7. **With the marching ants active, choose Select>Modify>Feather.**

Photoshop offers a number of options for modifying an exiting selection marquee. In the Select>Modify menu:

Border creates a selection of a defined number of pixels around the edge of the active marquee.

Smooth helps to clean up stray pixels at the edge of a selection. Within a defined radius from the selection edge, pixels with less than half of the surrounding pixels are excluded from the selection.

Expand and **Contract** enlarge and shrink a selection (respectively) by a defined number of pixels.

Feather creates a blended edge to the active selection area.

Select>Grow expands the selection to include all adjacent pixels that fall within the tolerance defined for the Magic Wand tool.

Select>Similar expands the selection to include all pixels throughout the image that fall within the tolerance range, even if they are not adjacent to the active selection.

Select>Transform Selection shows bounding box handles around the selection marquee, which you can use to transform the selection just as you would transform layer content.

8. **In the resulting dialog box, type 35 in the Feather Radius field. Click OK to return to the image window.**

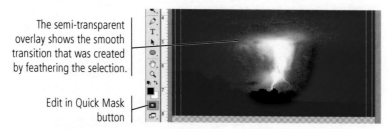

   Feathering means to soften the edge of a selection so the image blends into the background instead of showing a sharp line around the edge. The Feather Radius defines the distance from solid to transparent. In the image window, there's no apparent difference in the selection because the marching ants can't show shades of a selection.

9. **Click the Edit in Quick Mask button at the bottom of the Tools panel to toggle into Quick Mask mode.**

   This mode creates a temporary red overlay (called an Alpha channel) that shows the feathered selection. By default, the overlay is semi-transparent, which allows you to see the underlying image.

The semi-transparent overlay shows the smooth transition that was created by feathering the selection.

Edit in Quick Mask button

10. **Click the Edit in Standard Mode button at the bottom of the Tools panel to toggle off the Quick Mask.**

   When Quick Mask mode is active, the Edit in Quick Mask mode toggles to become the Edit in Standard Mode button.

11. **Choose Select>Inverse.**

   You want to remove the area around the lightning, so you have to select everything *other than* what you originally selected — in other words, the inverse of the previous selection.

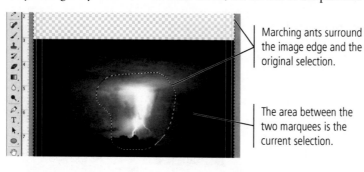

Marching ants surround the image edge and the original selection.

The area between the two marquees is the current selection.

12. **With the Lightning layer selected in the Layers panel, press Delete/Backspace.**

   Selection marquees are not particular to a specific layer. You have to make sure the correct layer is active before you use the selection to perform some action.

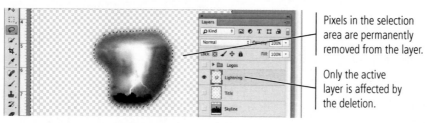

Pixels in the selection area are permanently removed from the layer.

Only the active layer is affected by the deletion.

13. **Choose Select>Deselect to turn off the active selection (marching ants).**

14. **Save the file and continue to the next exercise.**

Note:

*You could also create a feathered selection by typing in the Feather field of the Options bar **before** drawing the selection marquee.*

Keep in mind, however, that if you draw a feathered selection (using the tool option setting), you can't undo the feather without also undoing the selection area.

Note:

Press Command/Control-Shift-I to invert the active selection.

Note:

Press Command/Control-D to deselect the active selection.

Understanding Channels

You need a bit of background about channels to understand what's happening in the Quick Mask you will use in the next exercise. (You will use channels extensively in later projects.)

Every image has one channel for each component color. An RGB image has three channels: Red, Green, and Blue; a CMYK image has four channels: Cyan, Magenta, Yellow, and Black. Each channel contains the information for the amount of that component color in any given pixel.

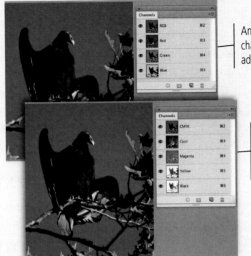

An RGB image has three channels, one for each additive primary.

A CMYK image has four channels, one for each subtractive primary plus one for black.

In RGB images, the three additive primaries can have a value of 0 (none of that color) to 255 (full intensity of that color). Combining a value of 255 for each primary results in white; a value of 0 for each primary results in black.

In CMYK images, the three subtractive primaries plus black are combined in percentages from 0 (none of that color) to 100 (full intensity of that color) to create the range of printable colors. Channels in a CMYK image represent the printing plates or separations required to output the job.

When you work in Quick Mask mode, an extra Alpha channel is created to temporarily store the selection area. An Alpha channel functions like a regular channel, in that it has the same range of possible values (0–255 in an RGB image, 0–100 in a CMYK image). However, the Alpha value determines the degree of transparency of a pixel. In other words, a 50% value in the Alpha channel means that area of the image will be 50% transparent.

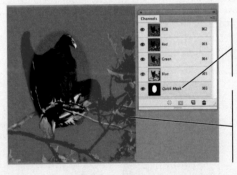

The Quick Mask channel stores the degree of transparency based on the current selection.

The semi-transparent red overlay shows areas being masked (i.e., the areas outside the current selection).

Alpha channels allow you to design with degrees of transparency. You can blend one image into another, blend one layer into another, or blend an entire image into a background in a page-layout application.

You can change the appearance of Alpha channel masks by double-clicking the Quick Mask button in the Tools panel, or double-clicking the Quick Mask thumbnail in the Channels panel.

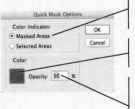

Change the mask to overlay the masked area instead of the selected area.

Click here to change the color of the mask in the image window.

Use this option to make the mask more or less transparent. (This setting only affects the appearance of the mask in Photoshop.)

Quick Masks are useful when you need to work with a temporary selection or if you are still defining the exact selection area. As long as you stay in Quick Mask mode, the temporary Alpha channel remains in the Channels panel (listed in italics as "Quick Mask"). If you return to Standard mode, the Quick Mask disappears from the window and the panel.

Once you have created a complex selection, you can save it as a permanent Alpha channel by dragging the Quick Mask channel onto the New Channel button at the bottom of the Channels panel. This adds a channel named "Quick Mask copy" (not in italics), which will be a permanent part of the file even if you exit Quick Mask mode.

Permanent Alpha channel

Temporary Quick Mask channel

New Channel button

As we said earlier, there are many selection options in Photoshop, each with its own advantages and disadvantages. You have already used the marquee tools and lasso tools to select general areas of images.

Many images have both hard and soft edges, and/or very fine detail that needs to be isolated from its background (think of a model's blowing hair overlapping the title on the cover of a magazine). In this type of image, other tools can be used to create a very detailed selection based on the color in the image.

Rather than simply deleting pixels, as you did for the lightning image, another option for isolating an object with a path is to create a **layer mask** that hides unwanted pixels. Areas outside the mask are hidden but not deleted, so you can later edit the mask to change the visible part of the image.

1. **With aftermath.psd open, hide all but the Skyline layer. Click the Skyline layer to make it active.**

2. **Choose the Magic Wand tool (under the Quick Selection tool). In the Options bar, make sure the New Selection button is active and set the Tolerance field to 32.**

   The Magic Wand tool is an easy way to select large areas of solid color. The first four options in the Options bar are the same as those for the Marquee tools (New Selection, Add to Selection, Subtract from Selection, and Intersect with Selection).

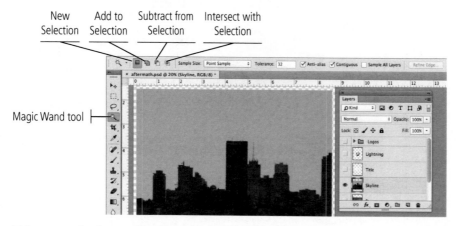

Tolerance is the degree of variation between the color you click and the colors Photoshop will select; higher tolerance values select a larger range based on the color you click. If you're trying to select a very mottled background (for example), you should increase the tolerance; be careful, however, because increasing the tolerance might select too large a range of colors if parts of the foreground object fall within the tolerance range.

The **Anti-alias** check box, selected by default, allows edges to blend more smoothly into the background, preventing a jagged, stair-stepped appearance.

When **Contiguous** is selected, the Magic Wand tool only selects adjacent areas of the color; unchecking this option allows you to select all pixels within the color tolerance, even if some pixels are non-contiguous (for example, inside the shape of the letter Q).

By default, selections relate to the active layer only. You can check **Sample All Layers** to make a selection of all layers in the file.

The **Refine Edge** button opens a dialog box where you can use a number of tools to fine-tune the selection edge.

Note:

Anti-aliasing is the process of blending shades of pixels to create the illusion of sharp lines in a raster image.

3. **Click anywhere in the blue sky area of the image.**

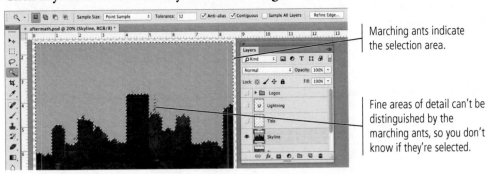

Marching ants indicate the selection area.

Fine areas of detail can't be distinguished by the marching ants, so you don't know if they're selected.

4. **Choose Select>Deselect to turn off the current selection.**

   Although you could keep adding to the selection with the Magic Wand tool, the marching ants can't really show the fine detail.

5. **Choose Select>Color Range.**

6. **Make sure the Localized Color Clusters option is unchecked.**

7. **Choose White Matte in the Selection Preview menu (if it is not already).**

   By changing the Selection Preview, you can more easily determine exactly what is selected. You can preview color range selections in the image window as:

   • **None** shows the normal image in the document window.

   • **Grayscale** shows the entire image in shades of gray; selected areas are solid white and unselected areas are solid black.

   • **Black Matte** shows unselected areas in solid black; selected areas appear in color.

   • **White Matte** shows unselected areas in solid white; selected areas appear in color.

   • **Quick Mask** adds a partially transparent overlay to unselected areas.

8. **Set the Fuzziness value to 25 and click anywhere in the blue sky (in the document window).**

   Fuzziness is similar to the Tolerance setting for the Magic Wand tool. Higher Fuzziness values allow you to select more variation from the color you click.

   Depending on where you clicked, your selection might not exactly match what you see in our screen shot. For now, the important point is to know that the visible areas indicate the current selection.

Note:

Because the dialog box preview is so small, we prefer to rely on the preview in the document window, which is controlled in the Selection Preview menu at the bottom of the dialog box.

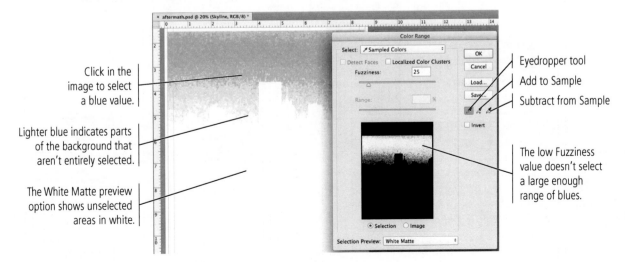

Click in the image to select a blue value.

Lighter blue indicates parts of the background that aren't entirely selected.

The White Matte preview option shows unselected areas in white.

Eyedropper tool

Add to Sample

Subtract from Sample

The low Fuzziness value doesn't select a large enough range of blues.

Selecting Localized Color Clusters

The **Localized Color Clusters** option in the Color Range dialog box can be used to select specific areas of a selected color. When this option is checked, the Range slider defines how far away (in physical distance) a color can be located from the point you click and still be included in the selection.

The same colors in other jellyfish are not selected because they are outside the reduced Range value.

We used a number of clicks with different Fuzziness values to sample the colors in this jellyfish.

Using Localized Color Clusters and a reduced Range value, we were able to isolate this jellyfish from its school.

Selection Presets

The Select menu at the top of the dialog box includes several presets for isolating specific ranges of primary colors (Reds, Yellows, Greens, Cyans, Blues, or Magentas), or specific ranges of color (highlights, midtones, or shadows).

If you select the **Skin Tones** preset, you can then activate the Detect Faces option at the top of the dialog box. By adjusting the Fuzziness slider, you can use this dialog box to make reasonably good selections of people's skin.

As you can see in this example, however, no automatic option is a perfect substitute when subjective decision-making is required. The tones in the rolling pin's reflection are very close to the color of skin, so they are included in the selection. This automatic selection method is still a good starting point, though, for making the complex selection of only a person's (or people's) skin.

Choose a preset from this menu.

When you choose the Skin Tones preset, you can also activate the Detect Faces option.

Some colors are close to skin tones, but are are not skin. You will have to manually edit the mask to correct these areas.

9. **Change the Fuzziness value to 80 and watch the effect on the dialog box preview.**

Changing the Fuzziness value expands (higher numbers) or contracts (lower numbers) the selection. Be careful, though, since higher fuzziness values can eliminate fine lines and detail.

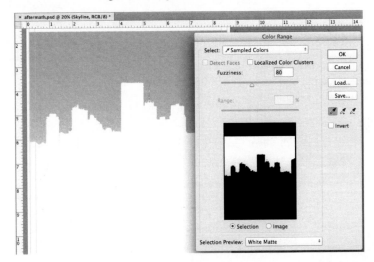

10. **In the Color Range dialog box, click the Add to Sample eyedropper. In the document window, click where parts of the blue sky are not shown in full strength.**

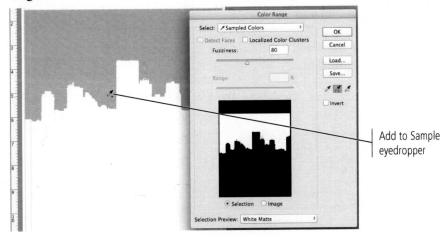

Add to Sample eyedropper

11. **Check the Invert box in the Color Range dialog box.**

Because your goal is to isolate the city and not the sky, it helps to look at what you want to keep instead of what you want to remove.

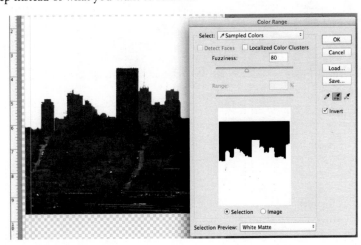

Note:

When the Color Range dialog box is open, you can press Command/ Control to switch between the Selection and Image previews within the dialog box.

Note:

For the purposes of this exercise, don't worry if you have small unselected areas in the city or sky areas. You will fix these in the next exercise.

12. **Continue adding to (or subtracting from, if necessary) your selection until you are satisfied that all the blue sky is gone.**

    You can also adjust the Fuzziness slider if necessary, but be sure you don't adjust it too far to include areas of the city.

13. **Click OK when you're satisfied with your selection.**

    When you return to the image window, the marching ants indicate the current selection. In the Color Range dialog box, you selected the blue and inverted the selection — in other words, your selection is everything that isn't blue.

    If you zoom out to see the entire file, you see the marching ants surround the canvas as well as the blue sky. Since the transparent area is not blue, it is included in the selection.

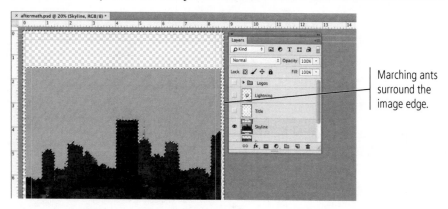

Marching ants surround the image edge.

14. **Choose the Magic Wand tool in the Tools panel and choose the Subtract from Selection option on the Options bar.**

15. **Click anywhere in the transparent area (the gray-and-white checkerboard) to remove that area from the selection.**

New Selection   Add to Selection   Subtract from Selection   Intersect with Selection

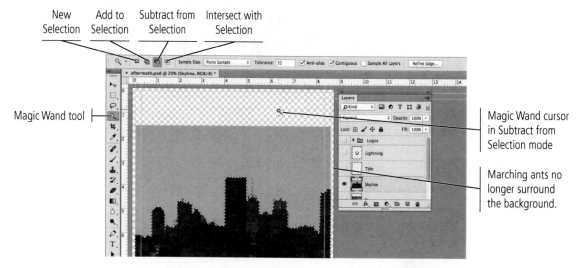

Magic Wand tool

Magic Wand cursor in Subtract from Selection mode

Marching ants no longer surround the background.

16. In the Layers panel, click the Add Layer Mask button.

A **layer mask** is a map of areas that will be visible in the selected layer. The mask you just created is a raster-based pixel mask, based on the active selection when you created the mask. This is a non-destructive way to hide certain elements of a layer without permanently deleting pixels; you can edit or disable the layer mask at any time.

Note:

A layer mask is basically an Alpha channel connected to a specific layer.

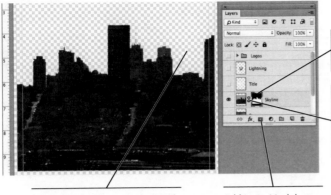

The layer mask thumbnail shows the masked (hidden) areas in black.

As long as the mask is linked to the layer, the mask will move along with the layer. You can click this icon to unlink the layer from its mask.

On the masked layer, pixels outside the original selection are hidden.

Add Layer Mask button

17. Control/right-click the mask thumbnail and choose Disable Layer Mask from the contextual menu.

Note:

In the Layers panel, the Add Layer Mask option is not available if the Background layer is selected. You can't apply a layer mask to the Background layer of a file, so you first have to convert the Background layer to a regular layer.

You have to click the mask thumbnail to open the contextual menu for the mask.

When you disable the mask, the background pixels are again visible. This is one of the advantages of using masks — the background pixels are not permanently removed, they are simply hidden.

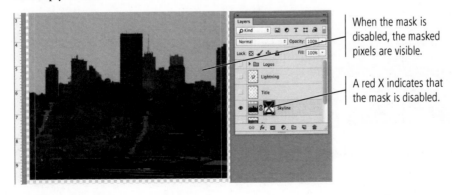

When the mask is disabled, the masked pixels are visible.

A red X indicates that the mask is disabled.

18. **Control/right-click the mask thumbnail and choose Apply Layer Mask from the contextual menu.**

Note:

Creating selections, reversing them, and then deleting the pixels surrounding an object is a common method for creating silhouettes — but not necessarily the best method. Masks protect the original pixels while providing exactly the same result.

This option applies the mask to the attached layer, permanently removing the masked pixels from the layer.

The masked pixels are permanently removed from the layer.

The mask is removed from the layer.

19. **Choose Edit>Undo Apply Layer Mask to restore the layer mask.**

As you saw in the previous step, applying a mask permanently removes the masked pixels. This essentially defeats the purpose of a mask, so you are restoring it in this step.

20. **Control/right-click the mask thumbnail and choose Enable Layer Mask from the contextual menu.**

21. **Save the file and continue to the next exercise.**

EDIT A LAYER MASK

In the previous exercise, you created a mask based on a selected color range. Depending on how you clicked to select the color range, you might have small areas of selected color in the city area, or small areas of unselected color in the sky. Rather than trying to isolate small spots of color in the Color Range dialog box, you can manually edit the mask using the built-in painting tools.

1. **With aftermath.psd open, click the Skyline layer mask thumbnail to select it.**

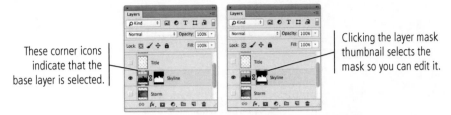

These corner icons indicate that the base layer is selected.

Clicking the layer mask thumbnail selects the mask so you can edit it.

2. **In the Channels panel (Window>Channels), make the Skyline Mask channel visible.**

   Layer masks are not visible by default; you have to turn them on in the Channels panel to see them. This isn't strictly necessary, since you can paint a mask without seeing it, but it is easier (at least when you're first learning) to be able to see what you're painting. By painting on a layer mask, you're not really "painting" anything; instead, you're actually "painting" the visibility of the associated layer.

Making the mask channel visible allows you to see the red overlay in the image.

3. **In the Channels panel, double-click the Skyline Mask channel thumbnail. Change the Opacity value to 100% in the Layer Mask Display Options dialog box, then click OK.**

   Remember, this change only affects the transparency of the mask, not the degree of transparency applied to the layer. By setting the mask opacity to 100%, you know that anything solid red will be hidden and anything with no red will be visible.

4. Carefully review the image to find any problems with the existing mask.

Changing the mask opacity makes it easier to find areas in the sky that need to be masked, as well as areas in the city that need to be removed from the mask.

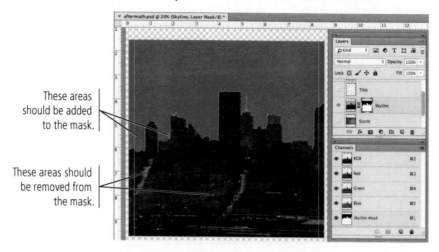

These areas should be added to the mask.

These areas should be removed from the mask.

5. Choose the Brush tool in the Tools panel. In the Options bar, open the Brush Preset picker to access the tool options.

This panel shows the different brushes that are included with Photoshop. The default brush set includes a number of specific-diameter hard- and soft-edge brushes, as well as some artistic options. A number below a brush icon shows the size of the brush; if you click a specific brush in the panel, the same number displays in the Size field.

6. Click the Hard Round brush icon in the lower half of the panel, then change the Size value to 50 px.

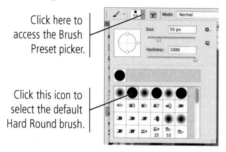

Click here to access the Brush Preset picker.

Click this icon to select the default Hard Round brush.

7. Click the Default Foreground and Background Colors button at the bottom of the Tools panel.

If you look at the layer mask thumbnail for the layer, you can see it's just a black-and-white shape. White areas of the thumbnail show which parts of the layer are visible in the main document; the black parts of the mask hide the associated areas of the layer. This is an important distinction: painting with black on a layer mask hides those areas; painting with white on a layer mask reveals those areas.

8. **With the Brush tool active and Black as the active foreground color, click and drag over those pixels to add to the mask area.**

The Brush tool paints with whatever is defined as the foreground color, which is black in this case. Remember: When painting on a mask, black adds to the mask and hides pixels on the masked layer.

Note:

Even though you're painting with black, the stroke appears as red because that's the defined mask color.

Brush tool

Brush tool cursor

Paint with black to remove pixels from the image (add to the mask).

Default Foreground and Background Colors

9. **Click the Switch Foreground and Background Colors button near the bottom of the Tools panel.**

10. **Paint over any masked areas inside the city area.**

Painting on a mask with white removes from the mask area, revealing more of the masked layer's pixels.

As you paint to fine-tune a mask, keep the following points in mind:

- You can use the bracket keys to enlarge (]) or reduce ([) the brush size.

- You can press X to switch the current foreground and background colors. This is very useful to remember when you are painting on a mask, because you can reset the default (black and white) colors and switch them as necessary depending on what you want to accomplish.

- You can also use the Eraser tool on a mask. Be careful, though, because erasing an area of the mask when the foreground color is white has the same effect as painting with the background color.

Paint on the mask with white to reveal the city areas.

The Brush tool cursor reflects the size of the brush you're using.

Switch Foreground and Background Colors

11. **Open the Properties panel (Window>Properties).**

The Properties panel contains different options for different types of selections. When a mask is available for the active layer, the panel shows options related to that mask. You can use the buttons at the top of the panel to select the mask on the active layer, or add a new vector mask.

The Density slider changes the opacity of the overall mask. If you reduce the density to 80%, for example, underlying layers will be 20% visible through the mask. (Don't confuse this with the opacity of an alpha channel, which only affects the appearance of the mask on screen.)

Note:

The Mask Edge and Color Range buttons in the Properties panel open the Refine Mask and [Select] Color Range dialog boxes (respectively).

12. **In the Properties panel, change the Feather value to 25 px.**

If you feather a selection and then make a layer mask from that selection, the feathering becomes a permanent part of the mask.

The Properties panel allows you to adjust the feathering of a hard-edge mask, and then later change or even remove the feathering if necessary, without painting on the mask.

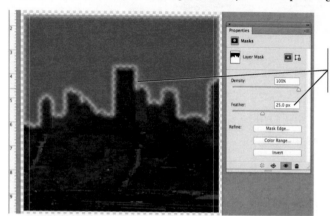

Use the Properties panel to feather the mask edge non-destructively.

13. **Change the Feather value to 1 px.**

This small feathering value will help to remove (or at least minimize) any remaining background artifacts around the edges of your mask.

14. **Save the file and continue to the next exercise.**

MAKE AND REFINE A QUICK SELECTION

As you just saw, you can make selections based on the color in an image. This technique is useful when you want to select large areas of solid color, or in photos with significant contrast between the foreground and background. When the area you want to select has a complex edge, refining the selection edge can produce very detailed results.

1. **With aftermath.psd open, hide all but the Bricks layer. Click the Bricks layer to select it as the active layer.**

2. **Choose the Quick Selection tool (nested under the Magic Wand tool).**

3. **In the Options bar, make sure the Sample All Layers option is not checked.**

   You only want to select the area in the bricks layer (the hole in the wall), so you do not want to make a selection based on the content of other layers in the file.

4. **Click at the top area of the hole in the wall and drag down to the bottom edge of the hole.**

   The Quick Selection tool essentially allows you to "paint" a selection. As you drag, the selection expands and automatically finds the edges in the image.

Note:

If you stop dragging and then click in a nearby area, the selection grows to include the new area.

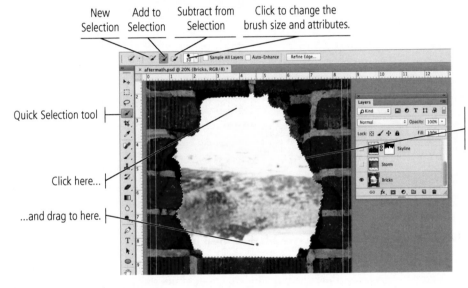

New Selection | Add to Selection | Subtract from Selection | Click to change the brush size and attributes.

Quick Selection tool

Click here...

...and drag to here.

Marching ants surround the selected area.

5. **Click the Refine Edge button in the Options bar.**

6. **Click the View button. Choose the On White option from the menu if it is not already selected.**

   The preview options allow you to change the way your image appears in the document window while you refine the edges within the dialog box.

   - **Marching Ants** shows the basic standard selection.
   - **Overlay** shows the unselected areas with a Quick Mask overlay.
   - **On Black** shows the selection in color against a black background.
   - **On White** shows the selection in color against a white background.
   - **Black & White** shows the selected area in white and the unselected area in black.
   - **On Layers** shows only the selected area; unselected areas are hidden.
   - **Reveal Layer** shows the entire layer, with no visual indication of the selection.

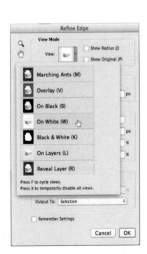

7. Experiment with the adjustments until you're satisfied with the selection edge.

You want to include a small amount of darkness around the edge so that when you invert the selection to remove the hole in the wall, there is no light halo effect left by the selection edge. We used the Shift Edge slider to slightly expand the selection edge.

- **Radius** is the number of pixels around the edge that are affected. Higher radius values (up to 250 pixels) improve the edge in areas of fine detail.

- **Smooth** reduces the number of points that make up your selection and, as the name suggests, makes a smoother edge. You can set smoothness from 0 (very detailed selection) to 100 (very smooth selection).

- **Feather** softens the selection edge, resulting in a transition that does not have a hard edge (in other words, blends into the background). You can feather the selection up to 250 pixels.

- **Contrast** is the degree of variation allowed in the selection edge. Higher Contrast values (up to 100%) mean sharper selection edges.

- **Shift Edge** shrinks or grows the selection edge by the defined percentage (from −100% to 100%).

- **Decontaminate Colors** can be checked to remove a certain percentage of color from the edge of a selection.

Note:

It might help to work with a closer view while you refine edges. You can use the Zoom and Hand tools in the Refine Edge dialog box to change the image view behind the open dialog box.

The On White preview shows the selected area on a white background.

The dark edge should be easily visible using the On White preview.

8. At the bottom of the dialog box, choose the Layer Mask option in the Output To menu.

This menu can be used to create a new layer or file (with or without a mask) from the selection. You want to mask the existing layer, so you are using the Layer Mask option.

9. Click OK to accept your refined selection.

The resulting layer mask hides areas that were not selected.

10. **Click the mask thumbnail in the Layers panel to select only the mask, and then open the Properties panel (Window>Properties).**

As you know, you want to remove the hole in the wall and not the wall. You selected the area in the hole to create the mask, but you now need to invert the mask.

Like the Options bar, the Properties panel is contextual. Different options are available in the panel depending on what is selected in the Layers panel.

When a layer mask is selected, you can manipulate a variety of properties related to the selected mask. (You will use different aspects of the Properties panel in later projects.)

11. **In the Properties panel, click the Invert button.**

This button reverses the mask, so now only the bricks are visible.

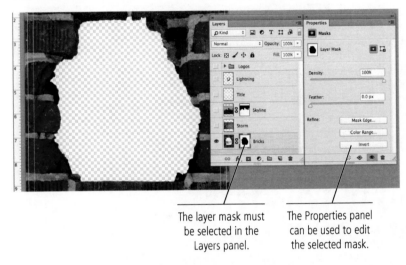

The layer mask must be selected in the Layers panel.

The Properties panel can be used to edit the selected mask.

12. **Save the file and continue to the next exercise.**

 ARRANGE LAYER POSITION AND STACKING ORDER

The ad is almost final, but a few pieces are still not quite in position. You already know you can use the Move tool to move the contents of a layer around on the canvas. You can move a layer to any position in the **stacking order** (the top-to-bottom position of a layer) by simply dragging it to a new position in the Layers panel.

1. **With aftermath.psd open, make all layers visible.**

2. **Click the Bricks layer in the Layers panel and drag up. When a heavy bar appears below the Title layer, release the mouse button.**

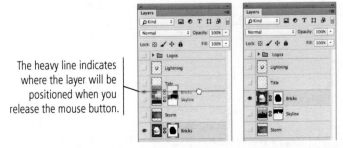

The heavy line indicates where the layer will be positioned when you release the mouse button.

Note:

Press Command/Control-[(left bracket) to move a layer down in the stacking order.

Press Command/Control-] (right bracket) to move a layer up in the stacking order.

Be careful when dragging layers near a layer group: If the border appears around a layer group, releasing the mouse button would place the dragged layer inside of the group.

3. **Repeat the process to move the Lightning layer below the Skyline layer.**

4. **With the Move tool active, check the Auto-Select option in the Options bar. Open the attached menu (to the right of the Auto-Select check box) and choose Layer.**

When Layer is selected in the Auto-Select menu, only the relevant layer will move even if it is part of a layer group. If you want all layers in a group containing the selected layer to move, you can choose Group in the menu.

5. **In the document window, click any pixel in the movie title and drag down until the title appears in the bottom half of the canvas.**

Your layers should appear in the same order as shown in the following image, with the Logos layer group at the top of the layer stack.

Check the Auto-Select option and choose Layer in the menu.

Click any pixel in the storm image and drag to move that layer's content.

Be careful to not click an area where the layer is transparent.

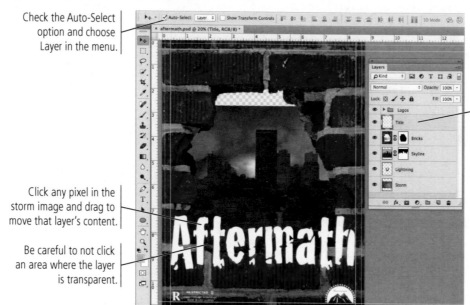

When Auto-Select is active, clicking in the document window automatically selects the relevant layer.

6. **If necessary, drag the Storm layer until the image fills any transparent area behind the bricks and skyline.**

Make sure you click an area where no pixels from another layer are visible.

7. **With the Move tool still active, uncheck the Auto-Select option in the Optons bar.**

8. **Click the Lightning layer in the Layers panel to select that layer. Click and drag in the document window to move the layer content so the lightning appears to strike one of the buildings.**

Uncheck the Auto-Select option.

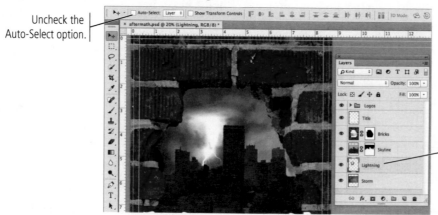

When Auto-Select is not active, remember to first select the layer you want to move.

Note:

When the Move tool is active, you can move the selected object or layer 1 pixel by pressing the Arrow keys. Pressing Shift with any of the Arrow keys moves the selected object/layer by 10 pixels.

9. **Save the file and continue to the final stage of the project.**

PHOTOSHOP FOUNDATIONS

When you work with complex files, you might find yourself with dozens — or even hundreds — of layers. Descriptive names can help you navigate through the layers, but you still have to scroll through the panel to find what you need.

Layer filtering, available at the top of the Layers panel, allows you to narrow down the panel to only layers that meet certain criteria — making it much easier to locate a specific layer.

Use this menu to filter layers by kind, name, effect, mode, attribute, or color.

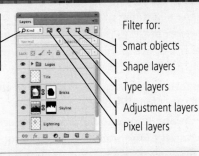

Filter for:

Smart objects
Shape layers
Type layers
Adjustment layers
Pixel layers

When **Kind** is selected in the menu, you can use the associated buttons to show only certain types of layers (adjustment layers, smart objects, etc.).

Use this switch to turn filtering on and off.

Only layers matching the applied filter appear in the panel.

When **Name** is selected, you can type in the attached field to find layers with names that include the text you enter in the field. The defined text string does not need to be at the beginning of the layer name; for example, typing "ti" would return both Rating and Title layers in the file for this project.

When **Effect** is selected, you can use the secondary menu to find only layers with a specified effect (applied using the Layer>Layer Style submenu).

When **Attribute** is selected, you can choose from a number of layer attributes — visible, linked, clipped, masked, etc.

When **Color** is selected, you can choose any of the built-in colors from the secondary menu. (These colors, which appear around the layer's visibility icon, can be assigned to individual layers in each layer's contextual menu.)

When **Mode** is selected, you can use the secondary menu to find only layers to which a certain blending mode has been assigned.

When **Smart Object** is selected, you can use the buttons at the top of the panel to find linked layers, layers with modified source data, layers with missing source data, or embedded layers. These buttons are non-exclusive, which means you can select more than one option at a time (for example, all layers with missing and modified source data).

The **Selected** option shows a subset of layers that exist in Isolation mode, a new option in Photoshop CC. To create a subset, select one or more layers in the Layers panel and then choose Select>Isolate Layers. The Layers panel automatically shows a subset of only the selected layers, and Selected appears in the Filter By menu.

Stage 4 Saving Photoshop Files for Print

At the beginning of the project, you saved this file in Photoshop's native format (PSD). However, many Photoshop projects require saving the completed file in at least one other format. Many artists prefer to leave all files in the PSD format since there is only one file to track. Others prefer to send only flattened TIFF files of their artwork because the individual elements can't be changed. Ultimately, the format (or formats, if the file is being used in multiple places) you use will depend on where and how the file is being placed.

Many Photoshop projects are pieces of a larger composition; the overall project defines the format you need to use when you save a complete project. The ad you just created, for example, will be placed in magazine layouts, which will be built in a page-layout application such as Adobe InDesign or QuarkXPress. Although the current versions of both industry-standard page-layout applications can support native layered PSD files, older versions can't import those native files. As the Photoshop artist, you have to save your work in a format that is compatible with the magazine layout.

As you know, the ad you created will be placed in multiple magazines, and different publishers have provided different file requirements. You need to save two different versions of the ad to meet those requirements.

 ## SAVE A LAYERED TIFF FILE

Some software that can't use native PSD files can use layered TIFF files, which allow you to maintain as much of the native information as possible in the resulting file.

1. **With aftermath.psd open, choose File>Save As.**

2. **If necessary, navigate to your WIP>Movie folder as the target location.**

   The Save As dialog box defaults to the last-used location. If you continued the entire way through this project without stopping, you won't have to navigate.

3. **In the Save As field, type _layered at the end of the current file name (before the .psd extension).**

4. **Click the Format menu and choose TIFF.**

Common File Formats

Photoshop, with the extension PSD, is the native format.

Photoshop EPS can maintain vector and raster information in the same file, and can maintain spot-color channels.

JPEG is a lossy compressed file format that does not support transparency.

Large Document Format, using the extension PSB, is used for images larger than 2 GB (the limit for PSD files); this format supports all Photoshop features including transparency and layers.

Photoshop PDF can contain all required font and image information in a single file, which can be compressed to reduce file size.

Photoshop 2.0 saves a flattened file that can be opened in Photoshop 2.0; all layer information is discarded.

Photoshop Raw supports CMYK, RGB, and grayscale images with alpha channels, and multichannel and LAB images without alpha channels; this format does not support layers.

PNG is a raster-based format that supports both continuous-tone color and transparency. It is sometimes used for print applications, but is more commonly used in digital publishing (specifically, Web design).

TIFF is a raster-based image format that supports layers, alpha channels, and file compression.

5. **Make sure the Layers check box is selected in the lower half of the dialog box.**

Because this file contains layers, this option is probably checked by default. If your file contained alpha channels, annotations, or spot colors, those check boxes would also be available. The As a Copy check box can be used if you want to save multiple versions of the same file with different options (which you will do in the next exercise).

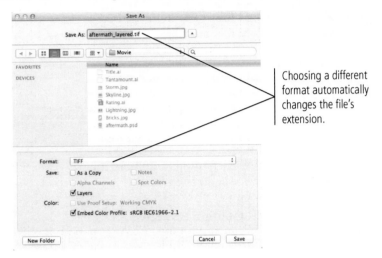

Choosing a different format automatically changes the file's extension.

6. **Leave the remaining options at their default values and click Save.**

7. **In the resulting TIFF Options dialog box, make sure the None image compression option is selected.**

TIFF files can be compressed (made smaller) using one of three methods:

- **None** (as the name implies) applies no compression to the file. This option is safe if file size is not an issue, but digital file transmission often requires files to be smaller than a full-page, multi-layered Photoshop file.

- **LZW** (Lempel-Ziv-Welch) compression is **lossless**, which means all file data is maintained in the compressed file.

- **ZIP** compression is also lossless, but is not supported by all desktop-publishing software (especially older versions).

- **JPEG** is a **lossy** compression scheme, which means some data will be thrown away to reduce the file size. If you choose JPEG compression, the Quality options determine how much data can be discarded. Maximum quality means less data is thrown out and the file is larger. Minimum quality discards the most data and results in a smaller file size.

8. **Leave the Pixel Order radio button at the default value, and choose the Byte Order option for your operating system.**

Pixel Order determines how channel data is encoded. The Interleaved (RGBRGB) option is the default; Per Channel (RRGGBB) is called "planar" order.

Byte Order determines which platform can use the file, although this is somewhat deceptive. On older versions of most desktop-publishing software, Macintosh systems can read the PC byte order but Windows couldn't read the Macintosh byte order — which is why even the Macintosh system defaults to the IBM PC option. This option is becoming obsolete because most newer software can read either byte order. Nonetheless, some experts argue that choosing the order for your system can improve print quality, especially on desktop output devices.

Save Image Pyramid creates a tiered file with multiple resolution versions; this isn't widely used or supported by other applications, so you can typically leave it unchecked.

If your file contains transparency, the Save Transparency check box will be available. If you don't choose this option, transparent areas will be white in the saved file.

9. **In the Layer Compression area, make sure the RLE option is selected.**

These three options explain — right in the dialog box — what they do.

10. **Click OK to save the file.**

Photoshop warns you that including layers will increase the file size.

11. **Click OK to dismiss the warning and save the file.**

12. **Continue to the next exercise.**

Note:

If you don't see the warning, it's possible that someone checked the Don't Show Again check box. If you want to make sure that you see all warnings and messages, click Reset All Warning Dialogs in the General pane of the Preferences dialog box.

 ## SAVE A FLATTENED TIFF FILE

Magazines using older page-layout applications need files that no longer maintain the layer information — called **flattened** files. You can flatten a file's layers manually using the Layers panel Options menu, or simply flatten the file during the Save As process.

1. **With aftermath_layered.tif open in Photoshop, choose File>Save As.**

If you continued directly from the previous exercise, this is the version you just saved. If you quit before you began this exercise, make sure you open the TIFF version and not the PSD version from your WIP>Movie folder.

Assuming that you started this exercise with the TIFF file from the previous exercise, the format and file name extension already reflect the TIFF options.

Note:

You can manually flatten a file by choosing Layer>Flatten Image.

2. **Uncheck the Layers check box.**

The As a Copy box is now selected by default. A warning shows that the file must be saved as a copy when the Layers option is unchecked. This is basically a failsafe built into Photoshop that prevents you from overwriting your layered file with a flattened version.

Note:

Older desktop-publishing software doesn't always support compressed TIFF files. When saving for those workflows, you might have to save the file without compression, regardless of the resulting file size.

3. **In the Save As field, highlight the words "layered copy" and type** flat.

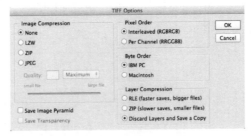

4. **Click Save. In the resulting TIFF Options dialog box, make sure the None compression option is selected and the Byte Order is set to IBM PC. At the bottom of the dialog box, make sure the Discard Layers and Save a Copy option is checked.**

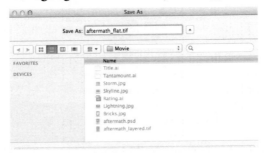

5. **Click OK to save the second version of the file.**

6. **When the save is complete, close the active file.**

1. _____ is likely to cause degradation of a raster image when it's reproduced on a printing press.

2. A _____ is an external file that you placed into another Photoshop document.

3. The _____ is context sensitive, providing access to different functions depending on what tool is active.

4. The _____ is the final size of a printed page.

5. The _____ tool is used to draw irregular-shaped selection marquees.

6. The _____ tool is used to select areas of similar color by clicking and dragging in the image window.

7. The _____ tool can be used to drag layer contents to another position within the image, or into another open document.

8. When selecting color ranges, the _____ value determines how much of the current color range falls into the selection.

9. A _____ can be used to non-destructively hide certain areas of a layer.

10. _____ is a lossy compression method that is best used when large file size might be a problem.

1. Briefly describe the difference between raster images and vector graphics.

2. Briefly explain three separate methods for isolating an image from its background.

3. Briefly explain the concept of a layer mask.

Portfolio Builder Project

Use what you learned in this project to complete the following freeform exercise.
Carefully read the art director and client comments, then create your design to meet the needs of the project.
Use the space below to sketch ideas; when finished, write a brief explanation of the reasoning behind your design.

Tantamount Studios is pleased with your work on the *Aftermath* ad, and they would like to hire you again to create the ad concept and final files for another movie that they're releasing early next year.

To complete this project, you should:

❏ Download the **Airborne_Print14_PB.zip** archive from the Student Files Web page to access the client-supplied title artwork and rating placeholder file.

❏ Find appropriate background and foreground images for the movie theme (see the client's comments at right).

❏ Incorporate the title artwork, logos, and rating placeholder that the client provided.

❏ Composite the different elements into a single completed file; save both a layered version and a flattened version.

The movie is titled *Above and Beyond*. Although the story is fictionalized, it will focus on the men who led the first U.S. Airborne unit (the 501st), which suffered more than 2,000 casualties in the European theater of World War II.

We don't have any other images in mind, but the final ad should reflect the time period (the 1940s) of the movie. The 501st Airborne was trained to parachute into battle, so you should probably incorporate some kind of parachute image.

This movie is a joint venture between Sun and Tantamount, so both logos need to be included in the new ad. It isn't rated yet, so please use the "This Movie Is Not Yet Rated" artwork as a placeholder.

Create this ad big enough to fit on an 8.5 × 11″ page, but keep the live area an inch inside the trim so the ad can be used in different-sized magazines.

Making selections is one of the most basic, and most important, skills that you will learn in Photoshop. Selections are so important that Photoshop dedicates an entire menu to the process.

As you created the movie ad in this project, you used a number of skills and techniques that you will apply in many (if not all) projects you build in Photoshop. You learned a number of ways to make both simple and complex selections — and you will learn additional methods in later projects. You also learned how to work with multiple layers, which will be an important part of virtually every Photoshop project you create, both in this book and throughout your career.

Composite images by dragging from one document to another

Transform a regular layer

Composite images by copying and pasting

Incorporate vector graphics into a raster image

Move layer content around on the canvas

Composite images by placing from Mini Bridge

Transform a Smart Object layer

Make a basic selection with a Marquee tool

Create a feathered selection to blend one layer into another

Create a silhouette using the Select Color Range utility

Create a silhouette using the Quick Selection tool

Refine a selection using the Refine Edges utility

Use a layer mask to hide pixels on a layer

Vintage Car Montage

Your client hosts an annual vintage car show that draws more than 20,000 visitors over a two-week period. You have been hired to create a composite image for the cover of the event program.

This project incorporates the following skills:

- ❏ Resizing and resampling supplied images
- ❏ Creating complex vector paths and shape layers
- ❏ Compositing images as Smart Objects
- ❏ Applying non-destructive styles, effects, and filters
- ❏ Developing custom artistic background

client comments

We need an image to use on the cover of a program for this year's Vintage Car Show. The main layout is fixed — we keep it constant from year to year. The area available for the image is 7″ wide by 8″ high.

We don't have any specific images or concepts in mind, but we would like the image to be a composite instead of just a single image. We had thought about hiring a traditional artist to create a painting, but we don't have time.

Hopefully you can come up with something that highlights the "vintage" concept of the Vintage Car Show.

art director comments

I think we'll go with a montage to highlight one primary car and several smaller inset photos. I've located a number of great vintage car images at www.publicdomainpictures.net.

The main car needs to be knocked out of its background so it can be more prominent. A vector path will work well to meet this goal because you can edit it at any time without losing quality.

The main image is a bit small for the defined canvas size, so you'll need to enlarge it a bit so it fills more of the space.

The client wants an overall artistic effect. I think you can use styles, filters, and effects on the background objects and inset images to solve those problems. Photoshop's Smart Object capabilities will be a significant advantage in this task because we can edit the effects and filters if the client isn't thrilled with the initial effort.

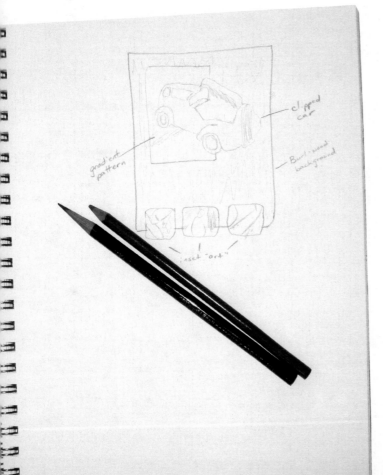

project objectives

To complete this project, you will:

- ❏ Resize and resample an existing source image
- ❏ Edit the canvas size
- ❏ Create a vector-based layer mask
- ❏ Create a vector shape layer
- ❏ Create a clipping mask
- ❏ Add texture to a shape layer
- ❏ Apply custom layer effects
- ❏ Use the Filter Gallery
- ❏ Liquify a layer
- ❏ Use the Eyedropper tool
- ❏ Create a custom gradient
- ❏ Create a gradient fill layer
- ❏ Create a pattern fill layer
- ❏ Print a composite proof

Stage 1 Enlarging Source Files

Any project that you build in Photoshop requires some amount of zooming in and out to various view percentages, as well as navigating around the document within its window. As we show you how to complete different stages of the workflow, we usually won't tell you when to change your view percentage because that's largely a matter of personal preference. Nonetheless, you should understand the different options for navigating around a Photoshop file so you can easily and efficiently get to what you want, when you want to get there.

To review information from the Interface chapter, keep in mind that you have a number of options for navigating around a document:

- Click with the Hand tool to drag the image around in the document window.

- Click with the Zoom tool to zoom in; Option/Alt-click to zoom out.

- Use the View Percentage field in the bottom-left corner of the document window.

- Use the options in the View menu (or the corresponding keyboard shortcuts).

- Use the Navigator panel.

Note:

As you complete the exercises in this project, use any of these methods to zoom in or out on different areas of the file.

RESIZE AND RESAMPLE THE EXISTING SOURCE IMAGE

This project — like many others you will build throughout your career — starts with an existing image, which you will open and use as the basis for the rest of the project. Whenever you start with an existing file, it's best to evaluate what you already have before you make any changes.

1. Download **Montage_Print14_RF.zip** from the Student Files Web page.

2. Expand the ZIP archive in your WIP folder (Macintosh) or copy the archive contents into your WIP folder (Windows).

   This results in a folder named **Montage**, which contains the files you need for this project. You should also use this folder to save the files you create in this project.

3. In Photoshop, choose File>Open. Navigate to the file **hot-rod.jpg** in the WIP>Montage folder and click Open.

4. Choose View>Fit on Screen so you can see the entire image, and make sure rulers are visible (View>Rulers).

5. Choose Image>Image Size.

   The hot-rod.jpg file is 17.778″ wide by 13.333″ high, with a resolution of 72 pixels/inch. Commercial printing typically requires 300 pixels/inch, so this image would not be considered "print quality" at its current size.

   The first step is to resize the image using the principle of effective resolution to achieve the 300 pixels/inch required for commercial printing.

6. **At the bottom of the dialog box, uncheck the Resample option and change the Resolution field to 300.**

Remember: When resampling is not active, the image retains the same number of pixels when you change the size or resolution fields.

Uncheck the Resample option.

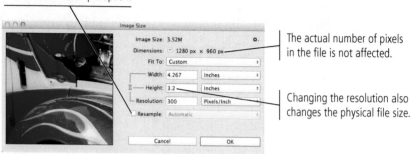

The actual number of pixels in the file is not affected.

Changing the resolution also changes the physical file size.

7. **Click OK to resize the source image.**

As you can see, the image view in the document window does not change because the image still has the same number of pixels. The rulers at the left and top edges of the document window show the new measurements that are associated with the resized image.

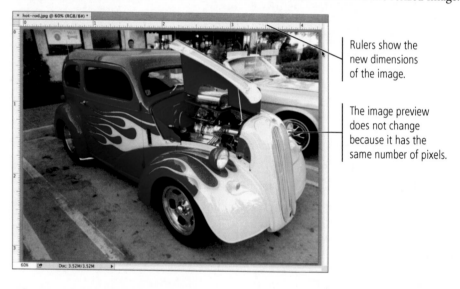

Rulers show the new dimensions of the image.

The image preview does not change because it has the same number of pixels.

8. **Choose Image>Image Size again.**

Because you already defined the appropriate resolution for this image, you now need to make the image large enough to meet the overall job requirements.

Resampling adds or removes pixels to create the size you define, without affecting the defined resolution.

9. **Click in the Preview window and drag until the car's engine is visible.**

Areas of greater detail are the most prone to distortion when you enlarge an image. The Image Size preview area allows you to review the results before finalizing the process.

10. **At the bottom of the dialog box, check the Resample option.**

When the Resample option is checked, you can change the actual number of pixels in the image without affecting its resolution.

11. **Open the Resample menu and choose Preserve Details (enlargement).**

Although you should try to capture images at the size you will need them, this is not always possible when working with client-supplied images. The Preserve Details option significantly improves the results of artificially enlarging an existing image.

12. **With the units menus set to Inches, change the Width field to 7.**

The overall project requires a finished image that is 7″ wide by 8″ high. If you enlarged the picture to match the required height, it would be too wide for the entire car to fit into the composition. Instead, you are enlarging the image to match the required width; you will later adjust the canvas to suit the project's height requirement.

As you can see, increasing the image's physical size with resampling adds more pixels to the image. This also significantly increases the file weight (its size in bytes).

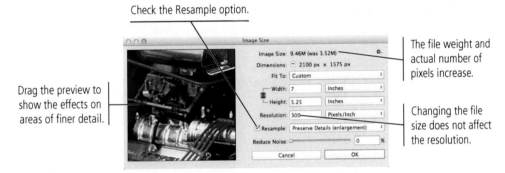

Check the Resample option.

Drag the preview to show the effects on areas of finer detail.

The file weight and actual number of pixels increase.

Changing the file size does not affect the resolution.

13. **Drag in the Preview window to show an area with flat areas of color near a high-contrast edge.**

Artificially enlarging an image often results in small pixels of varying color, especially in areas of solid color and near high-contrast edges. When you choose the Preserve Details option, you can use the Reduce Noise slider to help reduce those artifacts.

14. **Change the Reduce Noise slider to 20%.**

The Preview window shows the results that will be achieved when you finalize the resampling.

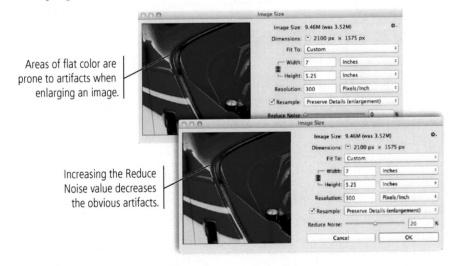

Areas of flat color are prone to artifacts when enlarging an image.

Increasing the Reduce Noise value decreases the obvious artifacts.

15. **Click OK to finalize the resampling.**

Resampling the image (enlarging) adds pixels to the file. The image no longer fits in the document window at the current view percentage.

The image now has more pixels, so less of the image is visible in the document window.

16. **Choose View>Fit On Screen to show the entire image.**

17. **Choose File>Save As. Save the file as a native Photoshop file named montage.psd in your WIP>Montage folder.**

18. **Continue to the next exercise.**

Note:

You're adding a sizeable amount of information to this file, so the resampling process might take a few seconds. Depending on the power and speed of your computer, you might see a progress bar as the image size is remapped.

SHARPEN THE ENLARGED IMAGE

When you enlarge an image in Photoshop, the application must generate new data. The algorithm underlying the Preserve Details option does a significantly better job of generating new pixels than was available in previous versions, but the pixels are still not original to the image. This can result in a loss of detail, especially near apparent edges or areas of high contrast. Whenever you enlarge an image, **sharpening** can help to restore detail and make the image appear more crisp.

1. **With montage.psd open, choose Filter>Sharpen>Unsharp Masking.**

2. **Make sure the Preview check box is active in the dialog box.**

Unsharp masking sharpens an image by increasing contrast along the edges in an image.

- **Amount** determines how much the contrast in edges will increase; typically, 150–200% creates good results in high-resolution images.

- **Radius** determines how many pixels will be included in the edge comparison; higher radius values result in more pronounced edge effects.

- **Threshold** defines the difference that is required for Photoshop to identify an edge. A threshold of 15 means that colors must be more than 15 levels different.

Note:

The Sharpen, Sharpen More, and Sharpen Edges filters apply sharpening with no user control.

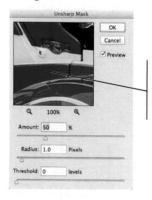

Drag here or click in the document window to change the visible area in the preview window.

3. Change the Amount to 100%, the Radius to 2.0 pixels, and the Threshold to 5 levels.

4. Toggle the Preview option off and on to review the results in the document window.

Sharpening is most obvious in areas of high contrast.

5. Click OK to apply the Unsharp Mask filter.

6. Save the file and continue to the next exercise.

EDIT THE CANVAS SIZE

As you learned in the project meeting, the final artwork for this project needs to be 7" wide by 8" high. You already accomplished the required width when you resampled the source file. In this exercise, you are going to enlarge the canvas to meet the project's height requirement.

1. With montage.psd open, make the Layers panel visible.

   Photos and scans almost always default to exist on the Background layer when you first open them.

2. Choose Image>Canvas Size.

In Photoshop, **canvas** refers to the overall image area — like the surface of a canvas used by traditional artists. It is not directly connected to the content of most layers (except for the Background layer, as you will see shortly).

You can use this dialog box to change the size of the canvas to specific measurements.

Note:

If you define smaller measurements, you are basically accomplishing the same thing as using the Crop tool.

3. Choose the top-center anchor option.

The Anchor area shows the reference point around which the canvas will be enlarged or cropped. Using this option, all new pixels will be added at the bottom of the image.

4. Change the Height field to 8 [inches], and choose White in the Canvas Extension Color menu.

This menu defines what color will appear in the new pixels on the Background layer.

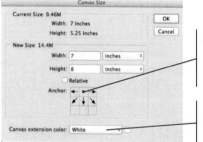

Anchoring the top edge means new pixels will be added to the bottom of the existing canvas.

Use this menu to define the color of new pixels on the Background layer.

5. Click OK to apply the change, then choose View>Fit On Screen.

As you can see, new pixels were added to the bottom of the canvas. Because the existing image content exists on the Background layer, and the Background layer cannot contain transparent pixels, the new pixels are filled with white.

Because the photo existed on the locked Background layer, new pixels are filled with white.

6. **Choose Edit>Undo Canvas Size.**

   Press Command/Control-Z to undo the previous action.

   Press Command-Option-Z/Control-Alt-Z to step backward one action at a time through the file history.

7. **In the Layers panel, click the Lock icon to unlock the Background layer.**

8. **Double-click the Layer 0 name, type `Car` to rename the layer, then press Return/Enter.**

9. **Choose Image>Canvas Size again. Select the top-center Anchor option, then change the Height field to `8` [inches].**

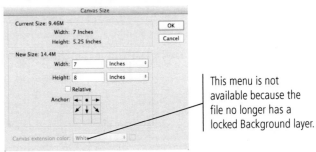

This menu is not available because the file no longer has a locked Background layer.

10. **Click OK to apply the change.**

    Regular layers support transparency, so the new pixels are not filled with a solid color. The gray-and-white checked pattern identifies transparent areas of the visible layer.

Because regular layers can include transparency, no color appears in the area of the new pixels.

11. **Save the file. With Maximize Compatibility checked, click OK in the Photoshop Format Options dialog box.**

    Because you converted the Background layer to a regular image layer, you see the dialog box that asks if you want to maximize compatibility the first time you save the file.

12. **Continue to the next stage of the project.**

Stage 2 Working with Vector Tools

Vector paths, also called Bézier curves, are defined mathematically based on the position of anchor points and the length and angle of direction handles that are connected to those anchor points. Unlike the pixels in a raster image, vector paths do not have a defined resolution until they are output. Because of this, vector paths can be edited at any time without any loss of quality.

Photoshop includes a number of tools for creating vector paths:

- The **Pen tool** places individual anchor points each time you click; line segments connect each point. If you click and drag, you create a point with direction handles, which precisely control the shape of the connecting segments.

- The **Freeform Pen tool** draws vector paths wherever you drag, just as you would draw with a pencil on paper.

- The **Rectangle** and **Ellipse tools** create shapes that you would expect based on the tool names. If you press Shift while you click and drag, you create a shape with equal height and width (a square or circle, respectively).

Note:

The Type tool is also technically a vector-based tool because digital type uses vectors to define the character shapes.

- The **Polygon tool** creates a shape with any number of sides. Clicking once opens a dialog box where you can define the number of sides.

  If you check the Smooth Corners option, each anchor point has direction handles that make the corners rounded instead of sharp.

  If you choose the Star option, the Indent Sides By value determines where the inner points of the star appear relative to the overall shape diameter.

  You can also check the Smooth Indents option to create smooth curves on the inside points of the shape (instead of corner points).

Polygon created with all options unchecked

Polygon created with the Star option checked

Polygon (star) created with the Smooth Corners option checked

Polygon (star) created with the Smooth Corners and Smooth Indents options checked

- The **Line tool** creates open straight lines with two points, one at each end. When first created, the points have no direction handles and the connecting segment is a straight line.

- The **Custom Shape tool** creates vector-based shapes from built-in or external libraries.

When you use the vector drawing tools, you have the option to create a new shape, path, or pixels.

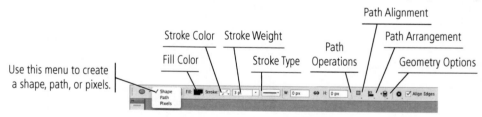

Use this menu to create a shape, path, or pixels.

Fill Color · Stroke Color · Stroke Weight · Stroke Type · Path Operations · Path Alignment · Path Arrangement · Geometry Options

- If you choose Shape, the shape is placed on a vector-based shape layer.

- If you choose Path, the shape exists only as a work path in the Paths panel.

- If you choose Pixels, the resulting shape is created as pixels on the previously selected layer. No vector path is created.

Note:

The Pixels option is not available when you are using the Pen tools.

USE THE FREEFORM PEN TOOL

The Freeform Pen tool creates a vector path based on where you drag the cursor. The application creates anchor points and direction handles as necessary to create the shape that you draw.

1. **With montage.psd open, show the image at 100% in the document window.**

   Ideally, you should work at 100% while you complete this exercise.

2. **Choose the Freeform Pen tool (nested under the Pen tool) in the Tools panel.**

3. **In the Options bar, choose the Path option in the left menu.**

   When you choose Path in the tool mode menu, the vector path that you draw is stored in the Paths panel.

4. **Check the Magnetic option in the Options bar, then click the Geometry Options button.**

   Curve Fit determines how closely the curves will match the path that you drag with the mouse cursor. When the Magnetic option is active, you can also define settings that control how the magnetic function behaves:

   Width determines how far from an edge you have to drag (1–256 pixels) for Photoshop to still find the edge.

   Contrast determines how much variation (1–100%) must exist between pixels for Photoshop to define an edge.

   Frequency determines the rate at which Photoshop places anchor points. Higher values (up to 100) create anchor points faster than lower values (down to 0).

5. **Set the Curve Fit to 2 px, Width to 50, the Contrast to 10%, and the Frequency to 25. Press Return/Enter to apply your settings.**

Note:

The Pen Pressure option only applies if you have a pressure-sensitive graphics tablet. When this option is turned on, higher pressure decreases the Width tolerance.

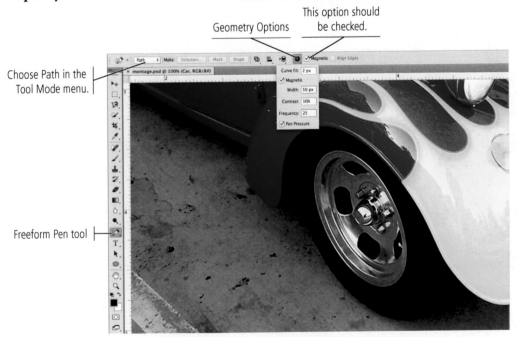

Geometry Options

This option should be checked.

Choose Path in the Tool Mode menu.

Freeform Pen tool

6. **Click at the corner where the running board meets the front fender to place the first anchor point. Drag down and around the fender.**

You don't have to hold down the mouse button when you draw with the Freeform Pen tool in Magnetic mode.

As you drag, the magnetic function creates anchor points to define a vector path around obvious edges where you drag.

Magnetic Freeform Pen tool cursor

Click here to place the first anchor point for the path.

The path snaps to the high-contrast edges near where you drag.

7. **Continue dragging around the car shape to create the initial outline.**

Skip the tires for now, and don't worry if the path is not perfect as you outline the car shape. You will fine-tune the path in the next few exercises.

8. **If you can't see the entire car in the document window, press the Spacebar to temporarily access the Hand tool and move the image so you can see the edges that you need to follow.**

The Spacebar temporarily switches to the Hand tool, so you can drag the image in the window even while working on another task. When you release the Spacebar, you return to the previously selected tool, so you can continue drawing the path of the car's shape.

If you drag past the edge of the document window, Photoshop automatically scrolls the visible area of the image. Manually repositioning with the Hand tool gives you better control over exactly what you see.

Press the Spacebar to temporarily access the Hand tool.

9. **When you reach an obvious corner in the car's outline, click to place a specific anchor point.**

Although Photoshop automatically creates anchor points based on the defined magnetic behavior, you can also click to place anchor points in specific locations.

Click to manually place an anchor point at apparent corners.

10. **Continue outlining the car shape. When you get back to your original starting point, click to create a closed path.**

For now, skip the exhaust pipe and the rear tire; you wil use another technique to add those shapes later.

When the tool cursor is over the original starting point, a hollow circle in the icon indicates that clicking will close the path.

The hollow circle indicates that clicking will close the path.

If you use the Pen tool in Paths mode, the vector path that you create is stored in the Paths panel rather than attached to a specific layer.

When you first create a path, it is stored as the work path. If you use the Combine Shapes geometry option, drawing another shape adds to the current work path, which is stored temporarily until you deselect the path.

If you want to be able to access a path later in your work, you can save the work path with a custom name. Saved paths are stored in the Paths panel until you intentionally delete them.

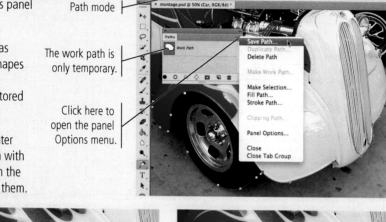

Path mode

The work path is only temporary.

Click here to open the panel Options menu.

If you click a saved path name in the panel, the path becomes visible in the document window. You can then use the vector drawing and editing tools to edit the path.

Click a saved path to select it and reveal the path in the document window.

Click the empty area of the panel to deselect the active path and hide it in the document window.

In the Paths panel options menu, you can choose **Make Selection** to make a marching-ants selection based on the path shape. You can use the resulting dialog box to define the details of the selection.

If you choose **Fill Path** in the Options menu, you can use the resulting dialog box to determine how the fill will be created. You can choose the color or pattern, the blending mode and opacity, and whether to feather the edge of the resulting fill so it blends smoothly into underlying layers.

If you choose the **Stroke Path** option, you must also choose which tool will create the stroke; the applied stroke will have the last-used settings for the selected tool. In other words, you have to define the tool options (brush size, hardness, etc.) that you want before using this option.

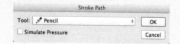

The Fill Path and Stroke Path options add the resulting pixels to the currently active layer — an important distinction from the Shape Layer option, which automatically creates a new layer when you begin drawing the vector path. It is also important to remember that although the path remains a vector path, color that is applied to the fill or stroke of the path is raster or pixel-based; it does not have the same scalability as a vector shape layer.

If you choose the **Clipping Path** option, the selected path will become a clipping path, which is essentially a vector mask that defines the visible area of an image if the file is placed into a page-layout application such as Adobe InDesign. (The white area in the path thumbnail defines what areas will be visible in the image.)

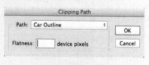

Buttons across the bottom of the Paths panel provide quick access to many of the features explained here. They are, from left:

- Fill Path with Foreground Color
- Stroke Path with Brush
- Load Path as a Selection
- Make Work Path from Selection
- Add Layer Mask
- Create New Path
- Delete Path

11. Open the Layers and Paths panels.

As you can see, no layer has been added. The path you drew is stored in the Paths panel as the Work Path, which is a temporary path that exists only until you create another path.

The path you drew is stored as the Work Path.

No layer is added to the file.

Some parts of the car are not included inside the path.

12. With the Work Path selected in the Paths panel, open the panel Options menu and choose Save Path.

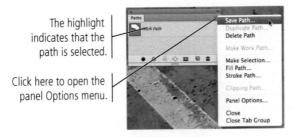

The highlight indicates that the path is selected.

Click here to open the panel Options menu.

13. Type `Car Outline` in the resulting dialog box, then click OK.

After you save the path, the new name appears in regular type instead of italics. This path will remain in the file even if you create a different temporary Work Path.

The saved path is permanent, so the name does not appear in italics.

14. Click the bottom area of the Paths panel to deselect the path.

When the path is not selected, you can't see its anchor points and connecting segments in the document window.

When the path is not selected, you can't see it in the document window.

15. Save the file and continue to the next exercise.

In the previous exercise, you used the Freeform Pen tool in magnetic mode to draw a rough outline of the car's shape. You intentionally skipped the wheels because the tool's magnetic properties perform better with higher-contrast edges, such as the red-to-gray transitions where the car body meets the pavement and tires. In this exercise, you will use the Pen tool to add the car wheels to the existing path.

Note:

The Photoshop Pen tool (and its variants) work in the same manner as the Pen tool in Illustrator. If necessary, refer to Page 95 for a refresher.

1. **With montage.psd open, make sure the view percentage is 100% and position the image so the front wheel is entirely visible.**

2. **Choose the Pen tool (nested under the Freeform Pen tool) in the Tools panel.**

   When you choose a nested tool, it becomes the default option in that position of the Tools panel. To access the original default tool — the Pen tool in this case — you have to click the tool and hold down the mouse button to access the nested tools menu.

3. **In the Paths panel, click the Car Outline path to make it visible in the document window.**

   You want to add more shapes to the existing path, so the path needs to be selected and visible in the document window.

4. **In the Options bar, choose Path in the Tool Mode menu.**

5. **Click the Path Operations button and choose Combine Shapes.**

The Pen tool is active.

Clicking the path name selects it.

The selected path is visible in the document window.

These options define how a new path will interact with any existing paths. (Illustrator and InDesign users might recognize these as options from the Pathfinder panel.)

- **New Layer**, available when Layer is selected in the Tool Mode menu, creates a new shape layer every time you draw a new path.

- **Combine Shapes** adds new paths to an already selected path or shape layer. Each path's shape is maintained as a separate vector path.

- **Subtract Front Shape** removes the area of secondary shapes from existing shapes.

- **Intersect Shape Areas** results in a shape that is only the area where a new shape overlaps an existing shape.

- **Exclude Overlapping Shapes** is similar to Subtract; overlapping areas are removed from the existing shape, but non-overlapping areas of the new shape are filled with the shape color.

- The **Merge Shape Components** option, available when a single path contains more than one shape, results in a single (possibly compound) shape. Any overlapping paths are combined into one shape/path.

6. **Click the Pen tool in the Tools panel to hide the anchor points of the existing path.**

   If the existing path's anchor points are visible, you can use the Pen tool to add anchor points to the existing path. You want to create a second shape in the same path, so you need to turn off the existing path's anchor points.

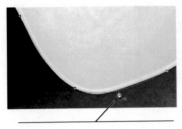 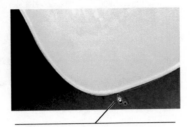

   If the existing path's anchor points are visible, clicking would add a new point to the existing path.

   If the existing path's anchor points are not visible, clicking creates a new shape that is part of the same path.

7. **Click with the Pen tool cursor where the front tire meets the yellow bumper.**

   Clicking once with the Pen tool creates a corner anchor point with no direction handles.

8. **Move the cursor down and left near the tire edge (as shown after Step 9).**

9. **Click to create an anchor point, hold down the mouse button, and drag down and left to create direction handles for the point.**

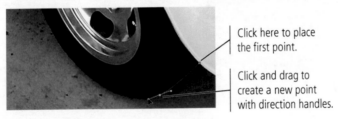

   Click here to place the first point.

   Click and drag to create a new point with direction handles.

   > **Note:**
   >
   > *Don't worry if the curve isn't quite perfect; you will learn how to edit anchor points and handles in the next exercise.*

10. **When the shape of the connecting segment between the two points matches the shape of the tire, release the mouse button.**

    When you click and drag with the Pen tool, you create a smooth point with symmetrical direction handles. As you drag, you can see the handles extend equal distances from both sides of the point you just created. The length and angle of the direction handles control the shape of segments that connect two anchor points.

    As long as you hold down the mouse button, you can continue dragging to change the length and angle of the point's handles, which also changes the shape of the connecting segment.

11. **Move the cursor up and left, again following the edge of the tire. Click and drag to create another anchor point with symmetrical direction handles. When the connecting segment matches the shape of the tire, release the mouse button.**

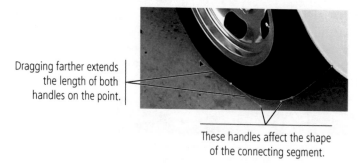

Dragging farther extends the length of both handles on the point.

These handles affect the shape of the connecting segment.

12. **Add two more smooth points to the shape, placing the final point where the rear of the tire meets the red car bumper.**

Add a point where the tire meets the bumper.

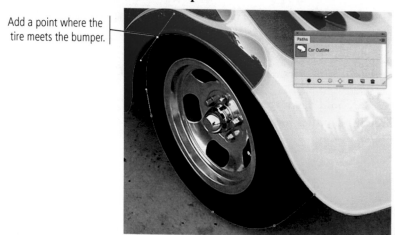

13. **Click and drag to place another smooth point inside the area of the bumper.**

You are intentionally overlapping the new path with the existing one. Later you will combine the multiple separate shapes into a single path.

14. **Move the cursor over the original starting point. When you see a hollow circle in the cursor icon, click to close the path.**

Add a point in the car area so the second path overlaps the first.

Click the original point to close the second shape.

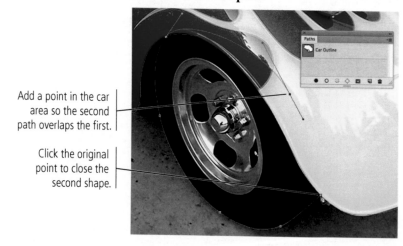

15. Repeat the process from this exercise to add another path around the rear tire and exhaust pipe.

Remember, clicking without dragging creates a corner point, which does not have direction handles.

The Car Outline path is still selected.

Overlap the tire shape with the existing path.

Include the exhaust pipe in the third shape.

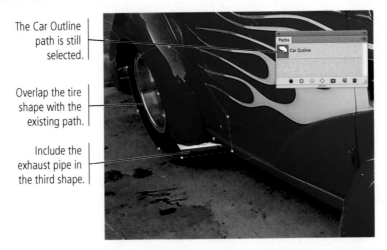

16. Change your view percentage so you can see the entire car in the document window.

17. With the Car Outline path selected in the Paths panel, make sure the Pen tool is still active.

18. Open the Path Operations menu in the Options bar and choose Merge Shape Components.

The three original paths are combined into a single shape. Photoshop adds anchor points where necessary and removes overlapping segments from the original paths.

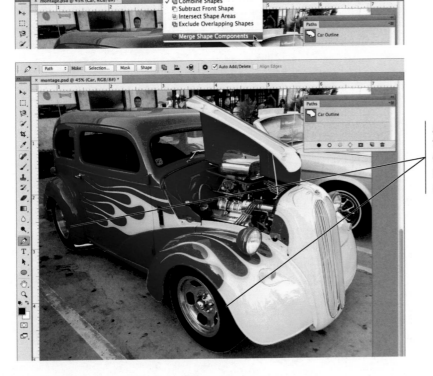

After merging shapes, the three separate paths are combined into a single path that is the outermost path of each component.

19. Save the file and continue to the next exercise.

You probably noticed that the path you created in the previous exercises is not a perfect outline of the car. The Freeform Pen tool can be a very good starting point for creating odd-shaped paths, but you will almost always need to edit and fine-tune the resulting paths to accurately reflect the path you want. Fortunately, Photoshop offers a number of options for editing vector paths.

You can use the **Path Selection tool** (▐▶▐) to select an entire path, or use the **Direct Selection tool** (▐▶▐) to select a specific anchor point or segment.

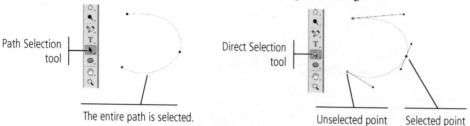

Path Selection tool

The entire path is selected.

Direct Selection tool

Unselected point   Selected point

You can use the **Add Anchor Point tool** (▐✑▐) to add a new anchor point to an existing path. Photoshop automatically creates handles for the new point and adjusts handles for existing points to maintain the existing path shape.

You can use the **Delete Anchor Point tool** (▐✑▐) to remove an existing point from a path. Photoshop removes the selected point and adjusts the handles of remaining points to try to maintain the original path shape.

Clicking a smooth point with the **Convert Point tool** (▐◥▐) converts that point to a corner point by removing its handles (below left). Clicking and dragging from a corner point with this tool converts it to a smooth, symmetrical point (below right).

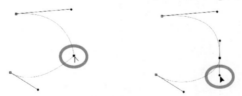

You can add a handle to only one side of a corner point by Option/Alt-clicking a point with the Convert Point tool and dragging (below left). You can also click a handle with the Convert Point tool and drag to move only one handle of the point, resulting in a corner point with asymmetrical handles (below right).

Note:

When the Pen tool is active, placing the cursor over an existing selected path automatically shows the Add Anchor Point tool cursor.

Note:

When the Pen tool is active, placing the cursor over an existing point on a selected path automatically shows the Delete Anchor Point tool cursor.

Note:

When the Pen tool is active, you can press Option/Alt to temporarily access the Convert Point tool cursor.

1. **With montage.psd open, set your view percentage to at least 100%.**

2. **Drag around the image to review the Car Outline path.**

   Although your results might differ from our screen shots, the path almost certainly does not accurately outline the car. You must use what you learned on Page 278 to edit the path to exactly match the car's shape.

The Magnetic Freeform Pen tool path excluded some areas that must be inside the path.

3. **Use the following information to finetune your Car Outline path.**

   This is one place where we can't give you specific instructions because everyone's path will be a bit different. Keep the following points in mind as you refine your shape:

   - Use the Direct Selection tool to select and edit specific segments or points on the path. You can move points to a new position by dragging (or using the Arrow keys), or move their handles to change segment shapes.
   - Use the Add Anchor Point tool to add a point to the path.
   - Use the Delete Anchor Point tool to remove a point from the path.
   - Use the Convert Point tool to change a corner point to a smooth point, and vice versa.

4. **Save the file and continue to the next exercise.**

Now that your car outline shape is nearly complete, you are going to use the path to create a vector-based layer mask, which will remove the car from the surrounding background. The edges of a vector mask are defined by a vector path, which means they cannot have degrees of transparency. To edit the mask edge, you have to edit the vector path.

1. **With montage.psd open, set your view percentage so you can see the entire car in the document window.**

2. **Select the Car Outline path in the Paths panel and select the Car layer in the Layers panel.**

3. **Choose Layer>Vector Mask>Current Path.**

The path you want to use as the mask is selected.

The layer you want to mask is selected.

As you can see, a new path is added to the Paths panel. The name "Car Vector Mask" identifies this path as a vector mask for the layer named Car. The name in italics indicates that it is a temporary path, which only appears in the panel when the masked layer is selected.

Nothing is added to the Channels panel because channels are raster-based; they do not store vector-based path information.

The mask path is visible in the Paths panel when the masked layer is selected.

The mask thumbnail is added to the masked layer.

No alpha channel is added to the file.

4. Click the empty area at the bottom of the Layers panel to deselect the layer.

When the masked layer is not selected, the mask path does not appear in the Paths panel. This is an important distinction — if you want to edit the mask path, you have to make sure the correct path is selected first. Editing the original Car Outline path will have no effect on the mask path.

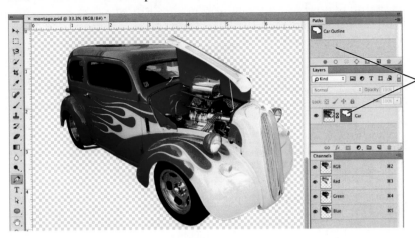

When the masked layer is not selected, the mask path does not appear in the Paths panel.

5. Save the file and continue to the next exercise.

CREATE A VECTOR SHAPE LAYER

A shape layer is a special type of Photoshop layer that retains vector path information. The vector shape functions as a mask, revealing the defined fill color for the shape. Any vector paths can have defined stroke properties (color, width, and type/style), and can be edited using the same tools that you used to edit the paths in the previous exercises.

In this exercise, you will build a compound vector shape that will exist behind the car, creating the visual effect of a "window" from which the car is emerging.

1. With montage.psd open, make the rulers visible (View>Rulers).

2. In the Tools panel, choose the Rounded Rectangle tool (nested under the Rectangle tool).

3. In the Options bar, choose Shape in the Tool Mode menu.

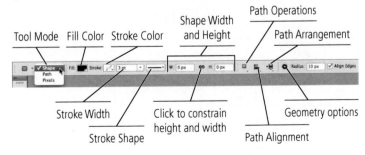

4. **Click the Fill color swatch to open the pop-up Swatches panel. Click the White swatch to select it as the fill color.**

   You can define separate fill and stroke colors of a vector shape layer, just as you might do for an object you create in Adobe Illustrator or InDesign. Clicking the Fill or Stroke color swatch opens a pop-up panel, where you can select a specific swatch to use as the attribute's color. Four buttons at the top of the panel change the attribute to (from left) None, Solid, a Gradient, or a Pattern. You can also click the Color Picker button to define any color that is not already in the Swatches panel.

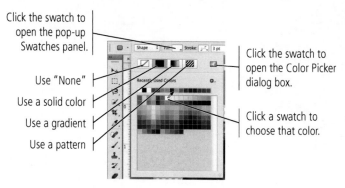

Click the swatch to open the pop-up Swatches panel.

Use "None"
Use a solid color
Use a gradient
Use a pattern

Click the swatch to open the Color Picker dialog box.

Click a swatch to choose that color.

5. **Click the Stroke swatch and choose None in the pop-up Swatches panel.**

6. **Change the Radius field to 50 px.**

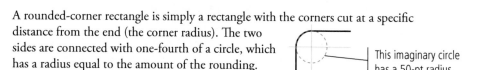

   A rounded-corner rectangle is simply a rectangle with the corners cut at a specific distance from the end (the corner radius). The two sides are connected with one-fourth of a circle, which has a radius equal to the amount of the rounding.

   This imaginary circle has a 50-pt radius.

7. **Click near the top-left corner of the document window, then drag down and right to create the new shape.**

   When you release the mouse button, the shape you drew fills with the defined Fill color. Because you chose None as the Stroke color, the shape you drew has no applied stroke.

   When you use the Shape option in the Tool Mode menu, the resulting vector shape exists by default on its own layer.

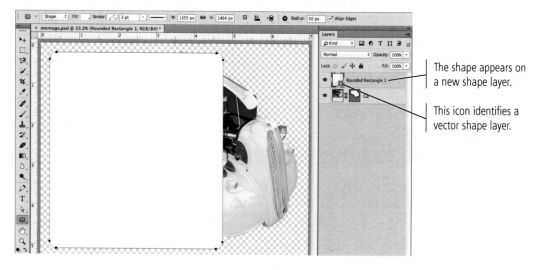

The shape appears on a new shape layer.

This icon identifies a vector shape layer.

8. Review the information in the Properties panel.

This panel automatically appears when you create a new shape with one of the vector shape tools. It shows the dimensions and position of the resulting shape, as well as other properties that were available in the Options bar before you created the shape.

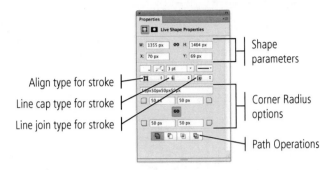

Shape parameters

Align type for stroke
Line cap type for stroke
Line join type for stroke

Corner Radius options

Path Operations

Note:

Because you are creating a vector shape, you can edit its properties at any time without losing quality or pixel integrity (as would happen for pixel-based raster data).

9. Highlight the current X field and type 0. Press Tab to highlight the Y field, then type 0 again. Press Return/Enter to apply the change.

The X and Y fields define the object's position based on its top-left corner.

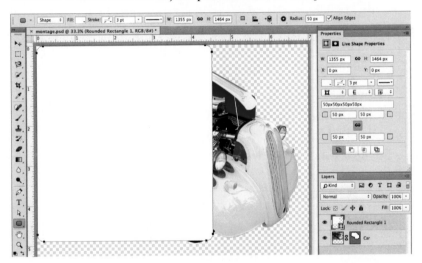

Note:

Fields in the Properties panel only recognize measurements in pixels. You can't type other units of measurement.

10. Place the Mouse cursor over the W field until you see the scrubby slider cursor. Click and drag right until the rectangle is approximately 1/8″ narrower than the canvas.

Scrubby sliders, available in most Photoshop panels, offer a dynamic way to change field values. You can click the field name and drag left to decrease the value or drag right to increase the value.

When you see this scrubby slider, click and drag to change the related field value.

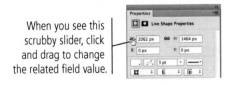

11. **Place the Mouse cursor over the H field until you see the scrubby slider cursor. Click and drag right until the rectangle is approximately 1/2″ shorter than the canvas.**

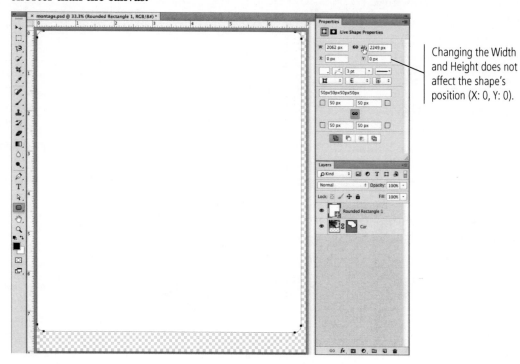

Changing the Width and Height does not affect the shape's position (X: 0, Y: 0).

12. **Click the Rounded Rectangle tool in the Tools panel to deselect the existing path.**

Although the actual vector path is deselected, the shape layer is still selected in the Layers panel.

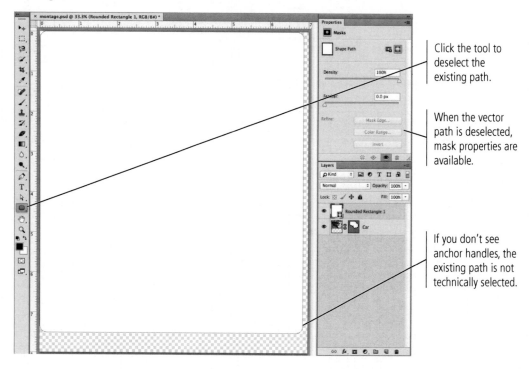

Click the tool to deselect the existing path.

When the vector path is deselected, mask properties are available.

If you don't see anchor handles, the existing path is not technically selected.

13. **In the Options bar, open the Path Operations menu and choose Subtract Front Shape.**

If no shape layer is currently selected, the Path Operations menu defaults to New Layer. As long as a shape layer is selected and one of the shape layer tools is active, the menu retains the last-used option. You can continue subtracting (for example) as many new shapes as you like until you switch to a different tool — say, the Direct Selection tool to modify a specific anchor point.

Note:

The Path Operations menu retains the last-used selection as long as the same tool remains active. If you switch to a different tool, the path operation reverts back to the New Layer option.

14. **Click and drag to create another rectangle inside the area of the first.**

Using the Subtract Front Shape option, the second shape removes the overlapping area of underlying shapes, creating a compound path that results in a "window" effect.

Options for the basic Shape tools remember the last-used settings, so the new shape automatically has the 50-px corner radius that you defined for the first shape.

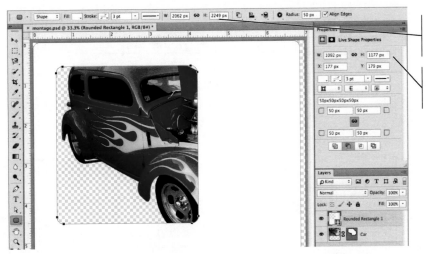

The Options panel shows options for the overall shape layer.

The Properties panel shows options for the selected vector path.

Note:

*A **compound path** is any single shape made up of more than one closed path.*

15. **In the Properties panel, change the new shape's parameters to:**

> W: 1250 px   H: 1550 px
>
> X: 150 px   Y: 150 px

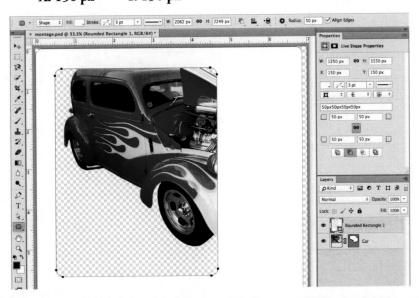

Stroke Types

When a vector drawing tool is active, you can use the Stroke Type menu in the Options bar to choose a preset stroke style (solid, dashed, or dotted).

- The Align menu changes the stroke's alignment relative to the path. The icons in the menu suggest the result.

- The Caps menu determines how the stroke aligns to the ends of the path.

- The Corners menu defines the way the stroke appears at corners on the path.

If you click the More Options button, you can define a custom dash pattern.

Align

- Align stroke to inside of path
- Align stroke to center of path
- Align stroke to outside of path

Caps

- No end cap
- Rounded end cap
- Square end cap

Corners

- Miter join
- Rounded join
- Beveled join

Path Alignment

You can use the **Path Alignment** to align or distribute multiple shapes on the same layer. For these options to work properly, you must use the Path Selection tool to select the paths you want to align, then choose an option from the menu. When Align to Canvas is selected, you can align one or more paths in relation to the overall canvas.

Geometry Options

Pen Tool

For the Pen tool, you can check the Rubber Band option in the Geometry Options menu to show a preview of the path curve as you move the cursor.

When the Rubber Band option is active, you can see a preview of the curve that will be created when you click to place an anchor point.

Rectangle, Rounded Rectangle, and Ellipse Tools

When **Unconstrained** is selected, you can simply click and drag to create a rectangle of any size.

If you choose the **Square** option (or Circle for the Ellipse tool), the shape you draw will be constrained to equal width and height (1:1 aspect ratio).

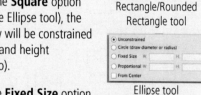

Rectangle/Rounded Rectangle tool

Ellipse tool

You can use the **Fixed Size** option to create a shape at a specific width and height. When you click in the canvas, you see a preview of the shape that will be created; you can drag around to determine where the shape will be placed when you release the mouse button.

You can also use the **Proportional** option to define the aspect ratio of the shape you will create. When you click and drag, the shape is constrained to the proportions you define.

If you choose the **From Center** option, the center of the shape you create will be placed where you first click.

Polygon Tool

Geometry options for this tool are the same as those that are available when you double-click the tool to define the shape you want to create (see Page 268).

Line Tool

When you draw with the Line tool, you can use the Geometry Options menu to add arrowheads to the start and/or end of the line. The Width and Length fields define those attributes of the arrowheads as a percentage of the line weight; the Concavity field defines the arrowheads' inset as a percentage of its length.

Custom Shape Tool

The Custom Shape tool makes it easy to create custom vector shapes from one of several defined libraries. You can open the Shape panel in the Options bar to access the built-in libraries of shapes.

Geometry options for the Custom Shape tool are the same as for the Rectangle and Ellipse tools.

PHOTOSHOP FOUNDATIONS

New Layer

When you first choose one of the vector drawing tools — Pen, Freeform Pen, or one of the Shape tools — the Path Operations menu defaults to **New Layer**. When this option is active, every new path will be created on a separate layer.

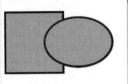

Combining Shapes

Combine Shapes creates the new path on the existing (selected) shape layer.

Subtract Front Shape creates the new path on the existing (selected layer), and removes overlapping areas of the new shape from the existing shape.

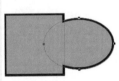

Intersect Shape Areas results in the shape of only overlapping areas in the existing and new shapes.

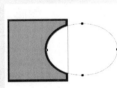 

Exclude Overlapping Areas removes overlapping areas between the existing and new shapes.

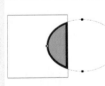 

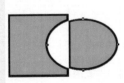

Merge Shape Components

It is important to note that with the four Combine options explained to the left, the result is the appearance of a single shape, but the original paths of each shape are maintained. You can still select and manipulate each component path independently.

To make the interaction of overlapping shapes permanent, you can select the paths you want to affect and choose **Merge Shape Components**. This results in a single shape that is the combination of any selected paths; unselected paths are not affected.

The actual result of this command depends on the interaction of the selected paths. In the example below, the top shape had been created with the Intersect Shape Areas operation. After applying the Merge Shape Components operation, anchor points were removed where the original paths did not intersect (as you can see in the right image).

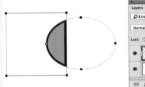

Merging Shape Layers

If multiple shape layers are selected in the Layers panel, you can combine them by choosing Merge Shapes in the Layers panel Options menu.

This command combines the shapes on all selected layers into a single shape layer — basically the same as using the Combine Shapes path operation. The new combined layer adopts the name of the highest layer in the previous selection.

Important note: Don't confuse this Merge option with the Merge Shape Components option in the Path Operations menu. The Merge Shapes option in the Layers panel actually combines the various shapes into a single layer, but maintains all of the existing paths.

16. In the lower half of the Properties panel, makes sure the four corner radius fields are linked.

Although rounded-corner shapes always start with four identical corners, you can use this panel to change each corner radius individually.

17. Type 0 in the top-left field, then press Return/Enter to apply your changes.

Note:

When the link icon is highlighted (active), changing any one radius value affects the other three corners.

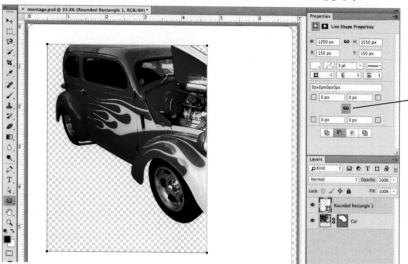

When this icon is highlighted, changing one corner radius changes all four corners.

Selecting and Modifying Paths

When you draw vector paths, you can use the Path Selection tool to select and move specific paths on a layer.

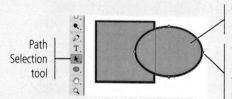

Path Selection tool

We clicked the oval to select only that path.

When a path is selected, you can see the anchor points that make up that path.

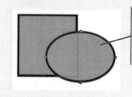

Click and drag with the Path Selection tool to move the selected path.

You can also select a specific shape to change the path operation that applies to it (in either the Options or Properties panel). In the example to the right, the rectangle was created first and then the oval was created with the Combine Shapes path operation. We then used the Path Selection tool to select the oval, and chose the Subtract Front Shape operation. Unless you merge the paths into a single shape, you can always select an individual path and change the way it interacts with underlying shapes.

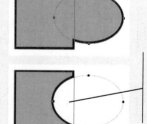

Changing the path operation of the selected path changes the way it interacts with the bottom path.

Because the path operations affect underlying shapes, you should also understand the concept of **stacking order**. When you create multiple shapes on the same shape layer, they exist from bottom to top in the order in which you create them — the first shape is on the bottom, then the next shape, and so on until the last shape created is at the top of the stack. You can use the **Path Arrangement** menu to control the stacking order of selected paths on the same shape layer.

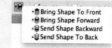

18. **Unlink the four corner radius fields, then change the top-left field to**
    100 px.

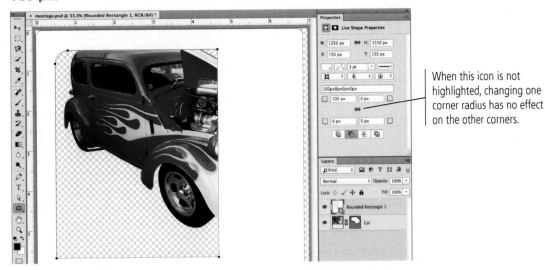

When this icon is not highlighted, changing one corner radius has no effect on the other corners.

19. **Choose the Path Selection tool in the Tools panel, then click the outer path**
    of the compound shape to select it.

    Each component path of the overall shape is still an independent vector path, which means you can select and edit its properties in the Properties panel at any time.

20. **Change the bottom-right corner radius for the outer path to 100 px and**
    change the other three corners to 0 px.

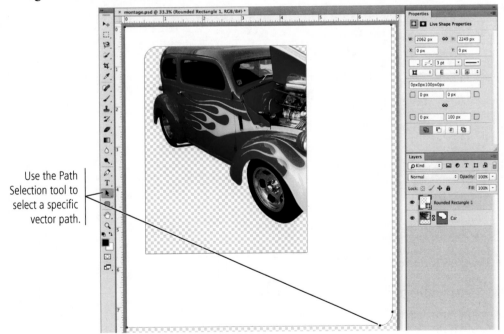

Use the Path Selection tool to select a specific vector path.

21. **Save the file and continue to the next exercise.**

If you need more than one version of the same layer, you can create a copy by choosing Duplicate Layer in the layer's contextual menu. This command results in a copy of the original layer in the exact same position as the original.

You can also use the Move tool to **clone** a layer, which results in a duplicate copy of the original layer, in the position where you drag to make the clone. In this exercise, you will use cloning to create three rounded-rectangle shape layers across the bottom of the canvas. You will then use built-in options to distribute the shape layers evenly across the image.

Note:

These shapes will be used to hold additional inset photos to enhance the visual interest of the overall composition.

1. **With `montage.psd` open, click the empty area at the bottom of the layers panel to deselect the existing shape layer.**

   If you don't first deselect the shape layer, your stroke color changes in the next few steps would affect the existing shape.

2. **Choose the Rounded Rectangle tool. In the Options bar, click the Stroke Color swatch to open the pop-up Swatches panel. Click the Color Picker button to open the related dialog box.**

   When the Color Picker dialog box is open, you can use the Eyedropper cursor to sample a color from the existing image.

3. **Move the cursor over a medium red in the car layer and click to sample it.**

Click here to open the Color Picker dialog box.

Use the Eyedropper cursor to sample color from the image.

4. **Change the Stroke Width field to 3 pt.**

5. **Open the Path Operations menu and review the options.**

   The Path Operations menu defaults to the New Layer option if an existing shape layer is not selected.

6. **Click and drag to create a rounded rectangle in the lower half of the canvas. Using the Properties panel, define the new shape's parameters as:**

   W: 600 px   H: 575 px

   X: 75 px   Y: 1760 px

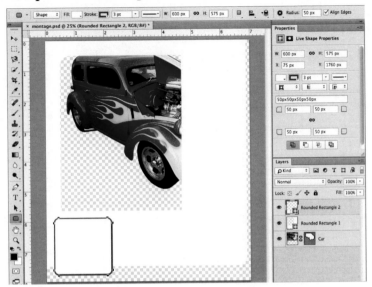

7. **Choose the Move tool in the Tools panel. Press Option/Alt, then click inside the smaller rectangle shape and drag right to clone it.**

   Pressing Option/Alt while dragging a selection clones that selection. Because the shape layer is the active selection, the entire shape layer is cloned. The Smart Guides help you maintain the cloned layer's horizontal alignment to the original. (If you decide to hide Smart Guides, pressing Shift constrains the movement to 45° angles.)

   The new cloned layer appears immediately above the original in the Layers panel, with the name "Rounded Rectangle 2 Copy."

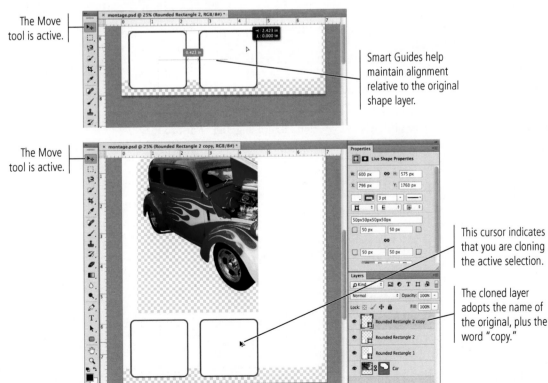

The Move tool is active.

Smart Guides help maintain alignment relative to the original shape layer.

The Move tool is active.

This cursor indicates that you are cloning the active selection.

The cloned layer adopts the name of the original, plus the word "copy."

8. **Double-click the name of the Round Rectangle 2 layer to highlight it. Type** `Left Inset`, **then press Return/Enter to change the layer name.**

   Even though you will have only three copies of this shape layer, it could become very confusing later if you don't use meaningful names to differentiate the layers.

9. **Double-click the name of the cloned layer to highlight it. Type** `Center Inset`, **then press Return/Enter to change the layer name.**

10. **Repeat Steps 7–8 to create a third shape layer at the bottom of the canvas. Name this new layer** `Right Inset`.

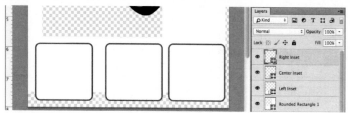

11. **Choose the Path Selection tool, then click the edge of the right vector shape to select the shape. In the Properties panel, change the X position of the active shape to** `1400 px`.

    Remember: The Path Selection tool is used to select and modify entire paths.

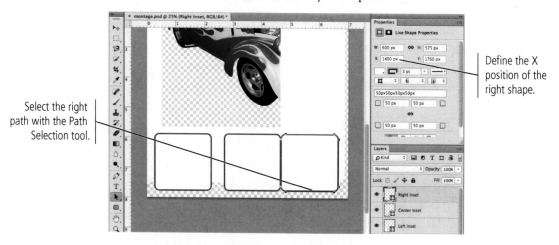

Select the right path with the Path Selection tool.

Define the X position of the right shape.

12. **In the Layers panel, Shift-click to select all three Inset shape layers.**

    When multiple layers are selected in the Layers panel, a number of alignment options become available in the Options bar. These are very useful for aligning or distributing the content of multiple layers relative to one another.

13. Choose the Move tool in the Tools panel. In the Options bar, click the Distribute Horizontal Centers button.

When the Move tool is active and multiple layers are selected, you can use the Options bar to align the contents of the selected layers relative to one another. The Distribute Horizontal Centers option places an equal amount of space between the center pixel of each selected layer; the positions of layers containing the outermost pixels in the selection are not affected.

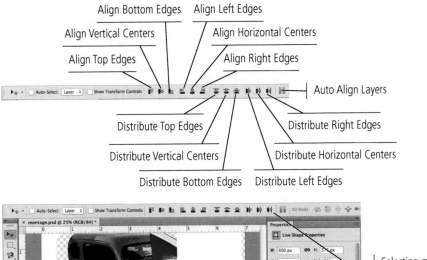

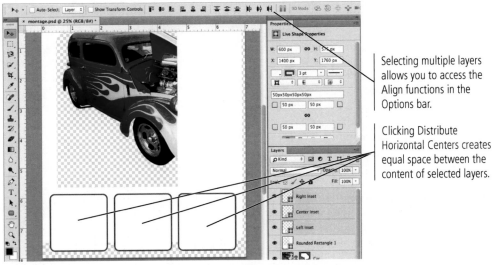

Selecting multiple layers allows you to access the Align functions in the Options bar.

Clicking Distribute Horizontal Centers creates equal space between the content of selected layers.

14. Save the file and continue to the next exercise.

When your files have more than a few layers — a common occurrence — selecting exactly the layer you want can be difficult. As you already learned, the Move tool defaults to affect whatever layer is selected in the Layers panel. Using the Auto-Select option, you can automatically select a specific layer by clicking pixels in the document window rather than manually selecting a layer in the panel first.

1. **With montage.psd open, choose File>Place Embedded.**

2. **Navigate to inset1.jpg (in your WIP>Montage folder) and click place. When the image appears on the canvas, press Return/Enter to finalize the placement.**

   The new Smart Object layer appears immediately above the previously selected layer. In this case, it is at the top of the layer stack.

3. **Repeat Steps 1–2 to place inset2.jpg and inset3.jpg as embedded Smart Object layers in the file.**

4. **In the Layers panel, drag inset1 to appear immediately above the Left Inset layer and drag inset2 to appear immediately above the Center Inset layer.**

5. **Choose the Move tool in the Tools panel. In the Options bar, check the Auto-Select option.**

6. **Click the placed image in the center of the canvas.**

   When Auto-Select is active, clicking in the canvas automatically selects the layer containing the pixel where you clicked. Because the inset3 image is on top of the other two, clicking in the area of the placed images automatically selects the inset3 layer.

Check the Auto-Select option.

All three Smart Object layers were placed in the center of the document window.

Clicking automatically selects the layer containing the pixel where you clicked.

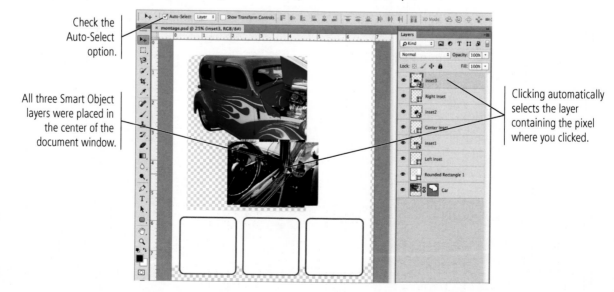

7. **Click in the area of the placed images and drag until the inset3 image entirely obscures the bottom-right rounded rectangle shape.**

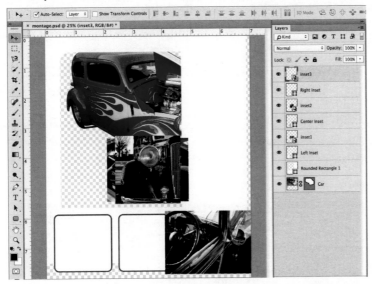

8. **Click again in the original area of the placed images.**

   Again, clicking automatically selects the relevant layer. Using the Auto-Select option makes it easier to manage layer contents even when you are not sure which layer contains the pixels you want to affect.

9. **Move the inset2 image until it entirely obscures the center rounded rectangle.**

10. **Move the inset1 image until it entirely obscures the left rounded rectangle.**

11. **Save the file and continue to the next exercise.**

CREATE CLIPPING MASKS

As you can see, the placed images completely hide the underlying layer content. To make the inset images appear only within the area of the underlying shapes, you need to create clipping masks. This task is relatively easy to accomplish.

1. **With montage.psd open, Control/right-click the inset1 layer to open the layer's contextual menu.**

2. **Choose Create Clipping Mask from the contextual menu.**

   A clipping mask is another way to show only certain areas of a layer; in this case, using the shape of one layer (Left Inset) to show parts of the layer above it (inset1).

   The Layers panel shows that the inset1 layer is clipped by the Left Inset layer.

Note:

Remember, to access the contextual menu for a specific layer, you have to Control/right-click in the area to the right of the layer name.

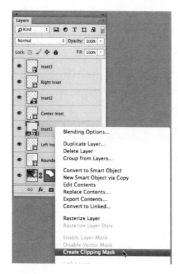
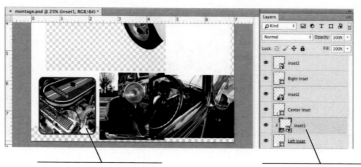

The only visible area is where the image overlaps the shape.

The inset1 layer is indented from and clipped by the Left Inset layer.

3. **If any of the rounded rectangle's white fill area is visible, use the Move tool to reposition the inset1 layer content.**

   Even though a layer is clipped, you can still move it without affecting the position of the clipping layer. Unlike a layer mask, the clipping and clipped layers are not automatically linked.

Note:

As with layer masks, clipping masks do not permanently modify the pixels in the layer. You can choose Release Clipping Mask in the clipped layer's contextual menu to undo a clipping mask without altering the affected layers.

Use the Move tool to reposition the clipped image.

The clipping layer still defines the visible area of the clipped image.

4. **Repeat Steps 1–3 to clip the inset2 and inset3 images to their underlying layers.**

5. **In the Layers panel, move the Car layer above the Rounded Rectangle 1 layer.**

6. **Using the Move tool, position the car so it seems to come out of the empty space in the underlying layer.**

   Use the following image as a guide.

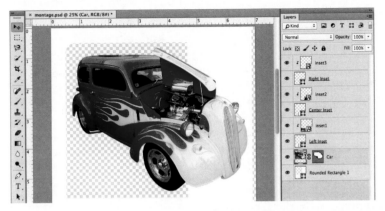

Note:

Remember, if the Auto-Select option is checked in the Options bar, you can simply click pixels of the layer you want to move without first selecting the layer.

   If you created a clipping mask for the Car layer, the car would only be visible within the area of the underlying compound shape. To make the car appear to drive out from the cut-out interior shape, you can simply rearrange and move the layers.

7. **Save the file and continue to the next stage of the project.**

Stage 3 Applying Styles and Filters

Photoshop includes a large number of options for creating artistic effects, including built-in patterns, styles, and filters. You can add texture to the flat fill color of a vector shape layer. You can apply effects such as drop shadows or beveling to add the appearance of depth. You can make images look like pencil sketches, paintings, or any of dozens of other options. You can even compound these filters and styles to create unique effects that would require extreme skill in traditional art techniques such as oil painting. In this stage of the project, you will use a number of these options to enhance your overall composition.

ADD TEXTURE TO A SHAPE LAYER

Aside from their usefulness as scalable vector paths, shape layers can be filled with solid colors (as the background shape is now), with other images (as the smaller inset shapes are now), or with styles or patterns (which you will add in this exercise).

1. **With montage.psd open, choose Window>Styles to open the Styles panel.**

   This panel shows the predefined styles that can be applied to a shape layer. The icons give you an idea of what the styles do, but these small squares can be cryptic.

2. **Click the arrow in the top-right corner of the Styles panel and choose Large List from the Options menu.**

   We prefer the list view because the style names provide a better idea of what the styles do. The Large List option displays a bigger style thumbnail than the Small List view.

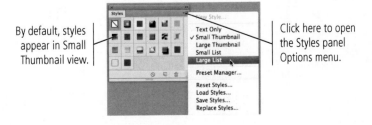

By default, styles appear in Small Thumbnail view.

Click here to open the Styles panel Options menu.

3. **Open the Styles panel Options menu again and choose Textures near the bottom of the list.**

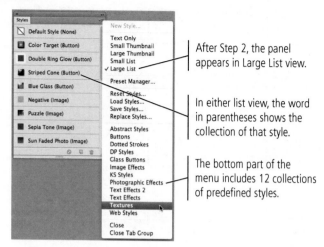

After Step 2, the panel appears in Large List view.

In either list view, the word in parentheses shows the collection of that style.

The bottom part of the menu includes 12 collections of predefined styles.

4. **Click OK to replace the current set with the Textures set.**

When you call a new set of styles, Photoshop asks if you want to replace the current set or append the new set to the existing set(s).

If you select Append, the new styles will be added to the existing ones. This can result in a very long list, which makes it difficult to find what you want. By replacing the current set, you will only see the styles in the texture set. This does not delete the previous styles, it only removes them from the panel; you can recall the previous styles by choosing Reset Styles in the panel Options menu.

Note:

Some users report seeing a message asking if they want to save changes to the current styles before replacing them, even if they did not make changes to the default set. This is a minor bug in the software. If you see this message, click No.

5. **Select the Rounded Rectangle 1 shape layer in the Layers panel, then click the Oak style in the Styles panel to apply the style to the shape layer.**

The layers panel shows that a series of effects — the ones that make up the style — has been applied to the layer.

Photoshop styles are non-destructive, which means you can change or delete them without affecting the original layer content. You can temporarily disable all effects by clicking the eye icon to the left of the word "Effects," or disable individual effects by clicking the icon for a specific item in the panel.

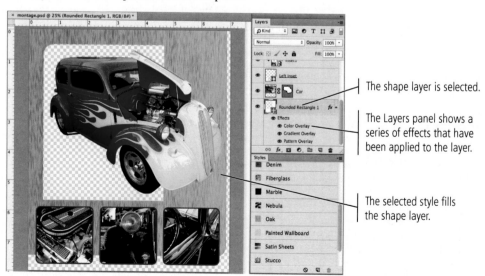

The shape layer is selected.

The Layers panel shows a series of effects that have been applied to the layer.

The selected style fills the shape layer.

6. **In the Layers panel, click the arrow to the right of the fx icon of the Rounded Rectangle 1 layer.**

   This collapses the list of applied effects, which helps keep the Layers panel easier to manage.

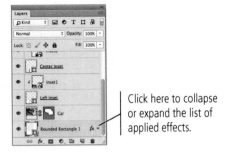

Click here to collapse or expand the list of applied effects.

7. **Save the file and continue to the next exercise.**

 ## APPLY CUSTOM LAYER EFFECTS

A style is simply a saved group of effects that can be applied with a single click. You can also create your own styles using the Layer Effects dialog box, which you will do in this exercise.

1. **With montage.psd open, choose the Left Inset layer.**

2. **Choose Layer>Layer Style>Drop Shadow.**

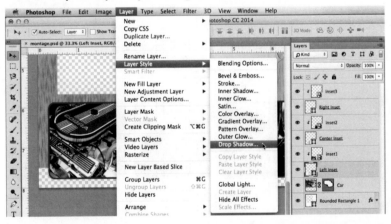

3. **In the resulting dialog box, make sure the Preview option is checked.**

   The Preview option allows you to see the results of your settings while the dialog box is still open.

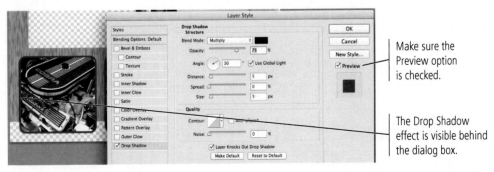

Make sure the Preview option is checked.

The Drop Shadow effect is visible behind the dialog box.

4. **In the Layer Style dialog box, make sure the Use Global Light option is checked.**

   This option is checked by default, so you should not have to make any change.

   The Angle field defines the position of the effect in relation to the layer. When the Global Light option is checked, changing the style Angle applies the same change to any other layer where an effect is applied using the Use Global Light option.

5. **Make the following changes to the default settings in the dialog box:**

   > **Distance: 10 px**

   > **Spread: 5 px**

   > **Size: 10 px**

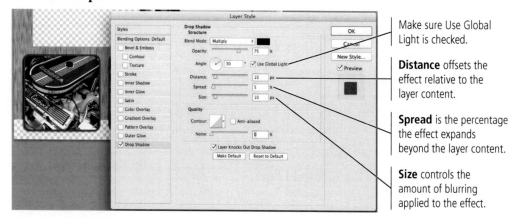

Make sure Use Global Light is checked.

Distance offsets the effect relative to the layer content.

Spread is the percentage the effect expands beyond the layer content.

Size controls the amount of blurring applied to the effect.

6. **Click OK to apply the layer style.**

   In the Layers panel, the drop shadow style appears as an effect for the Left Inset layer. As with the built-in style you applied in the previous exercise, custom layer styles are non-destructive.

The applied Drop Shadow effect is non-destructive.

7. **Press Option/Alt, then click the Drop Shadow effect in the Layers panel and drag it to the Center Inset layer.**

   Just as you cloned a layer in an earlier exercise, pressing Option/Alt allows you to clone effects from one layer to another. This offers an easy way to apply the exact same effect to multiple layers in your file.

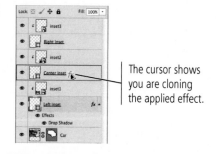

The cursor shows you are cloning the applied effect.

8. **Repeat Step 7 to add the Drop Shadow effect to the Right Inset and Car layers.**

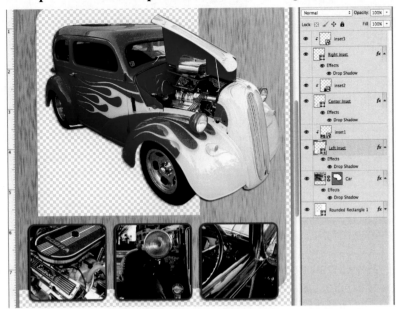

9. **In the Layers panel, double-click the Drop Shadow effect for the Car layer.**

   Double-clicking an effect in the panel opens the dialog box, where you can make changes to the settings that define the effect for the active layer.

10. **Click in the document window (behind the dialog box) and drag until the drop shadow is much more prominent behind the car layer.**

    When you drag in the document window, the dialog box dynamically changes to reflect the new angle and distance for the effect.

    As you dynamically change the angle, you should also notice the effect on the three Inset layers. Because the Use Global Light option is checked for all four layers, changing the angle for one of these layers applies the same change to all four layers.

    You should also notice, however, that the altered Distance value does not apply to the other three layers where the Drop Shadow effect is applied. Only the Angle of the effects is synchronized between the various layers.

Note:

If you double-click the word "Effects" in the Layers panel, the dialog box opens to the Blending Options: Default screen. Double-clicking a specific effect opens the dialog box directly to the settings for the effect you clicked.

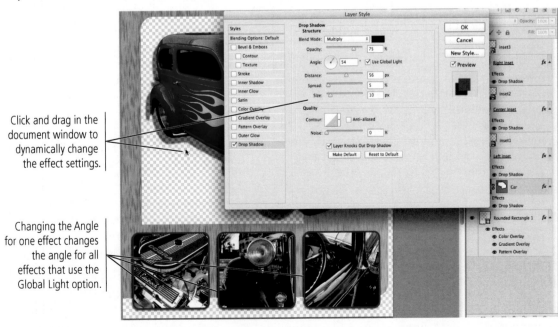

Click and drag in the document window to dynamically change the effect settings.

Changing the Angle for one effect changes the angle for all effects that use the Global Light option.

Photoshop offers ten layer style options, which you can apply individually or in various combinations to create unique flat and dimensional effects for any layer.

Bevel and Emboss

This style has five variations: Outer Bevel, Inner Bevel, Emboss, Pillow Emboss, and Stroke Emboss:

- **Outer Bevel** creates a bevel on the outside edges of the layer contents.

- **Inner Bevel** creates a bevel on the inside edges.

- **Emboss** creates the effect of embossing the layer contents against the underlying layers.

- **Pillow Emboss** creates the effect of stamping the edges of the layer into the underlying layers.

- **Stroke Emboss** applies an embossed effect to a stroke applied to the layer. (The Stroke Emboss effect is not available if you haven't applied a stroke to the layer.)

Any of these styles can be applied as **Smooth** (blurs the edges of the effect), **Chisel Hard** (creates a distinct edge to the effect), or **Chisel Soft** (creates a distinct but slightly blurred edge to the effect).

You can change the **Direction** of the bevel effect. **Up** creates the appearance of the layer coming out of the image; **Down** creates the appearance of something stamped into the image.

The **Size** slider makes the effect smaller or larger, and the **Soften** slider blurs the edges of the effect.

In the Shading area, you can control the light source **Angle** and **Altitude** (think of how shadows differ as the sun moves across the sky). You can also apply a **Gloss Contour** (see the following explanation of Contours). Finally, you can change the Blending Mode, Opacity, and Color settings of both highlights and shadows created in effects.

When a Bevel and Emboss style is applied, you can also apply Contour and Texture effects.

Stroke

The **Stroke** style adds an outline of a specific number of pixels to the layer. The Stroke effect can be added at the outside or inside of the layer edge, or it can be centered over the edge (half the stroke will be inside and half outside the actual layer edge). You can adjust the Blending Mode and Opacity setting of the stroke, and you can also define a specific color, gradient, or pattern to apply as the stroke.

Satin

The Satin options apply interior shading to create a satiny appearance. You can change the Blending Mode, Color, and Opacity settings of the effect, as well as the Angle, Distance, and Size settings.

Drop Shadow and Inner Shadow

Drop Shadow adds a shadow behind the layer; **Inner Shadow** adds a shadow inside the edges of the layer's content. For both types, you can define the blending mode, color, opacity, angle, distance, and size of the shadow.

- **Distance** is the offset of the shadow, or how far away the shadow will be from the original layer.

- **Spread** (for Drop Shadows) is the percentage the shadow expands beyond the original layer.

- **Choke** (for Inner Shadows) is the percentage the shadow shrinks into the original layer.

- **Size** is the blur amount applied to the shadow.

You can also adjust the Contour, Anti-aliasing, and Noise settings in the shadow effect. (See the Contours section later in this discussion for further explanation.)

When checked, the Layer Knocks Out Drop Shadow option removes the drop shadow underneath the original layer area. This is particularly important if you convert a shadow style to a separate layer that you move to a different position, or if the layer is semi-transparent above its shadow.

Global Light. The Use Global Light check box is available for Drop Shadow, Inner Shadow, and Bevel and Emboss styles. When this option is checked, the style is linked to the "master" light source angle for the entire file. Changing the global light affects any linked style applied to any layer in the entire file. You can change the Global Light setting in any of the Layer Style fields, or by choosing Layer>Layer Style>Global Light.

Outer Glow and Inner Glow

Outer Glow and **Inner Glow** styles add glow effects to the outside and inside edges (respectively) of the original layer. For either kind of glow, you can define the Blending Mode, Opacity, and Noise values, as well as whether to use a solid color or a gradient.

- For either kind of glow, you can define the **Technique** as Precise or Softer. **Precise** creates a glow at a specific distance; **Softer** creates a blurred glow and does not preserve detail as well as Precise.

- For Inner Glows, you can also define the **Source** of the glow (Center or Edge). **Center** applies a glow starting from the center of the layer; **Edge** applies the glow starting from the inside edges of the layer.

- The **Spread** and **Choke** sliders affect the percentages of the glow effects.

- The **Size** slider makes the effect smaller or larger.

Contours

Contour options control the shape of the applied styles. Drop Shadow, Inner Shadow, Inner Glow, Outer Glow, Bevel and Emboss, and Satin styles all include Contour options. The default option for all but the Satin style is Linear, which applies a linear effect from solid to 100% transparent.

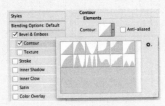

The easiest way to understand the Contour options is through examples. In the following series of images, the same Inner Bevel style was applied in all three examples. In the top image, you can clearly see the size and depth of the bevel. In the center and bottom images, the only difference is the applied contour. If you look carefully at the shape edge, you should be able to see how the applied contour shape maps to the beveled edge in the image.

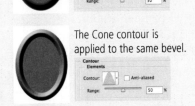

The Linear contour is applied to the bevel.

The Gaussian contour is applied to the same bevel.

The Cone contour is applied to the same bevel.

When you apply a contour, the **Range** slider controls which part of the effect is contoured. For Outer Glow or Inner Glow, you can add variation to the contour color and opacity using the **Jitter** slider.

Textures

The Textures options allow you to create texture effects using the built-in patterns.

- The **Scale** slider varies the size of the applied pattern.

- The **Depth** slider varies the apparent depth of the applied pattern.

- The **Invert** option (as the name implies) inverts the applied pattern.

- If you check the **Link with Layer** option, the pattern's position is locked to the layer so you can move the two together. If this option is unchecked, different parts of the pattern are visible if you move the associated layer.

- When you create a texture, you can drag in the image window (behind the Layer Style dialog box) to move the texture. When the Link with Layer option is checked, clicking the **Snap to Origin** button positions the pattern origin at the upper-left corner of the layer. If Link with Layers is unchecked, clicking the Snap to Origin button positions the pattern at the image origin point.

Color Overlay, Gradient Overlay, Pattern Overlay

A **color overlay** is simply a solid color with specific Blending Mode and Opacity value applied. A color overlay can be used to change an entire layer to a solid color (with the Normal blending mode at 100% opacity), or to create unique effects using different Blending Mode and Opacity settings.

A **gradient overlay** is basically the same as a color overlay, except you use a gradient instead of a solid color. You can choose an existing gradient or define a new one, change the Blending Mode and Opacity value of the gradient, apply any of the available gradient styles (Linear, Radial, etc.), and change the Angle and Scale values of the gradient.

A **pattern overlay** is similar to the Texture options for a Bevel and Emboss style. You can choose a specific pattern, change the Blending Mode and Opacity value, and change the applied pattern scale. You can also link the pattern to the layer and snap the pattern to the layer or the file origin.

11. Change the Size field to 50 px, then click OK to apply the changed settings.

12. In the Layers panel, click the fx buttons to collapse the effects for all layers.

13. Save the file and continue to the next exercise.

USE THE FILTER GALLERY

Filters can be used for a variety of purposes, from purely aesthetic to technically functional. You can apply filters to specific selections, individual layers, or even individual channels depending on what you need to accomplish. If you combine filters with Smart Objects, you can apply nondestructive filters and then change the settings or turn off the filters to experiment with different results.

In addition to the options in the Filter Gallery, a wide range of other filters can be accessed in the various Filter submenus. You will use a number of these in other projects throughout this book, but we encourage you to explore the various settings. Any filter that includes an ellipsis (...) in the menu command opens a secondary dialog box, where you can control the filter's specific settings.

Keep the following points in mind when you use filters:

Note:

Photoshop ships with more than 100 filters divided into 13 categories; some of these are functional while others are purely decorative.

- Filters can be applied to the entire selected layer or to an active selection.

- Some filters work only on RGB images; if you are in a different color mode, some or all filter options — including the Filter Gallery — will be unavailable.

- All filters can be applied to 8-bit images; available filter options are limited for 16-bit and 32-bit images.

- If you don't have enough available RAM to process a filter effect, you might get an error message.

1. With **montage.psd** open, select the inset3 layer in the Layers panel.

Like styles and effects, filters apply to the selected layer, not to the entire file.

2. Choose Filter>Filter Gallery.

If the Filter menu includes the Filter Gallery at the top of the list, that top command applies the last-used filter gallery settings to the selected layer. To open the actual Filter Gallery dialog box, you have to choose the Filter Gallery command that appears at the third spot in the menu.

This command applies the last-used filter without opening the Filter Gallery dialog box.

This command opens the Filter Gallery dialog box with the last-used settings applied.

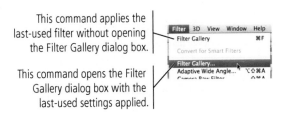

3. If necessary, adjust the view percentage and position in the dialog box so you can see the inset3 image.

4. In the middle pane of the dialog box, expand the Artistic collection of filters and click the Cutout thumbnail.

The left side of the Filter Gallery dialog box shows a preview of the applied filter(s). You can use the menu and field in the bottom-left corner to change the view percentage of the preview.

In the middle column of the dialog box, the available filters are broken into six categories; inside each folder, thumbnails show a small preview of each filter.

The top half of the right side of the dialog box shows settings that are specific to the selected filter (from the middle column).

The bottom half of the right side shows the filters that are applied to the selected layer.

Note:

You can apply more than one filter to a layer by clicking the New Effect Layer button in the bottom-right corner of the Filter Gallery dialog box.

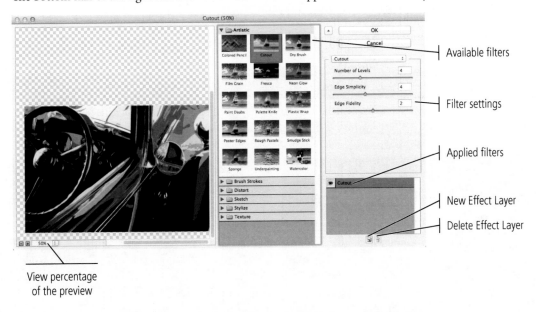

Available filters

Filter settings

Applied filters

New Effect Layer

Delete Effect Layer

View percentage of the preview

5. Adjust the filter options until you are satisfied with the result, then click OK to apply the filter.

Because the inset1 layer is a Smart layer, the filter is applied non-destructively as a Smart Filter. If you apply a filter to a regular layer, it is destructive and cannot be changed or turned off.

The filter is applied to the Smart Object layer as a Smart Filter.

6. **Press Option/Alt, then click the Filter Gallery listing in the Layers panel and drag it to the inset2 layer.**

As with layer styles, this method allows you to apply the exact same Smart Filter to multiple layers, without opening any dialog box.

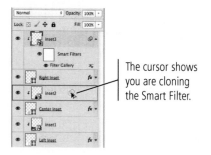

The cursor shows you are cloning the Smart Filter.

7. **Repeat Step 6 to apply the Smart Filter to the inset1 layer.**

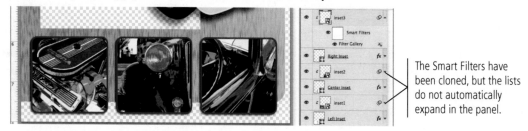

The Smart Filters have been cloned, but the lists do not automatically expand in the panel.

8. **Collapse the Smart Filters listing for the inset3 layer.**

9. **Save the file and continue to the next exercise.**

Fading Filters

The Fade option (Edit>Fade [Filter]) changes the opacity and blending mode of the last-used filter, painting tool, or color adjustment; you can also fade the effects of the Brush Strokes and Liquify filters. The example here shows the result of fading the Glowing Edges filter (from the Filter Gallery) that was applied to the left image.

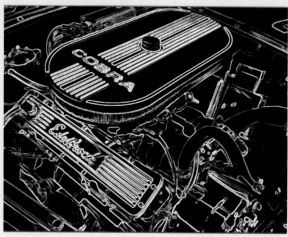
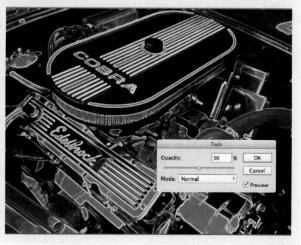

PHOTOSHOP FOUNDATIONS

LIQUIFY A LAYER

The oak effect in the shape around the car has a strong patterned feel — which makes sense, since the style uses a pattern fill. In this exercise, you use the Liquify filter to push around the layer pixels in a freeform style to create a unique, non-patterned background.

1. **With `montage.psd` open, hide all but the Rounded Rectangle 1 layer. Expand the fx listing for that layer.**

   You can Option/Alt-click the eye icon for a layer to hide all other layers.

2. **With the Rounded Rectangle 1 layer selected, choose Layer>Layer Style>Create Layers.**

   This option results in three separate layers — one for each applied effect — that are clipped by the original vector shape.

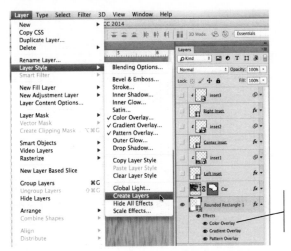

Three effects make up the applied style.

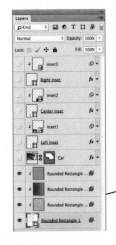

Three clipped layers result from the applied effects.

3. **Control/right-click the visible shape layer and choose Rasterize Layer.**

   The Liquify filter does not work on vector-based shape layers. Keep in mind, however, that once you rasterize a vector shape layer, you can no longer edit the shape with the vector-based tools.

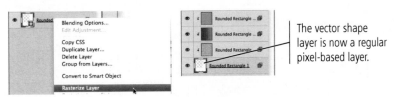

The vector shape layer is now a regular pixel-based layer.

4. **Select all four visible layers in the Layers panel.**

5. **Control/right-click any of the selected layers and choose Merge Layers from the contextual menu.**

   When you merge selected layers, the resulting single layer adopts the name of the selected layer that was highest in the stacking order.

Note:

You could have accomplished the same goal by selecting the original shape layer and choosing Rasterize Layer Style in the layer's contextual menu. The steps in this exercise explain the process underlying this command.

The Rasterize Layer option rasterizes the vector shape but maintains the Smart Effects settings.

6. **Change the name of the resulting layer to** Wood Cutout.

7. **With the Wood Cutout layer still selected, choose Filter>Liquify.**

   The Liquify filter has its own interface and tools. Depending on which tool you select, different options become available in the right side of the dialog box.

8. **In the bottom-left corner of the dialog box, open the View Percentage menu and choose Fit In View.**

9. **Check the Advanced Mode box in the right side of the dialog box.**

   For any of the distortion tools, you have to define a brush size, density (feathering around the edges), and pressure. Some tools also allow you to define the brush rate (how fast distortions are made); using the Turbulence tool, you can set the Turbulent Jitter (how tightly pixels are scrambled by the effect).

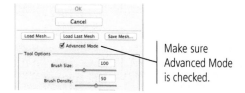

Make sure Advanced Mode is checked.

10. **In the Mask Options area, open the Replace Selection menu and choose Transparency.**

11. **Click the Forward Warp tool in the top-left corner. On the right side of the dialog box, select a large brush size, medium density, and high pressure.**

12. **Click and drag in the preview to warp the oak pattern away from exactly vertical lines.**

    As you drag near the edges, notice that the mask prevents you from pushing pixels into the masked area. It does not, however, prevent you from pushing pixels away from the mask edges.

Note:

The mask, visible as 50% Red by default, defines areas that will not be affected by your painting in the left side of the dialog box.

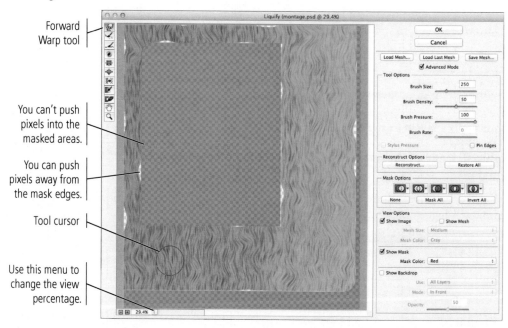

Forward Warp tool

You can't push pixels into the masked areas.

You can push pixels away from the mask edges.

Tool cursor

Use this menu to change the view percentage.

PHOTOSHOP FOUNDATIONS

Tools in the Liquify filter distort the brush area when you drag; the distortion is concentrated at the center of the brush area, and the effect intensifies as you hold down the mouse button or repeatedly drag over an area. (The **Hand** and **Zoom tools** have the same function here as in the main Photoshop interface.)

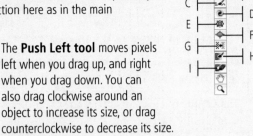

A. The **Forward Warp tool** pushes pixels as you drag.

B. The **Reconstruct tool** restores distorted pixels.

C. The **Smooth tool** helps smooth out jagged edges.

D. The **Twirl Clockwise tool** rotates pixels clockwise as you hold down the mouse button or drag. Press Option/Alt to twirl pixels counterclockwise.

E. The **Pucker tool** moves pixels toward the center of the brush, creating a zoomed-out effect if you simply hold down the mouse button without dragging.

F. The **Bloat tool** moves pixels away from the center of the brush, creating a zoomed-in effect.

G. The **Push Left tool** moves pixels left when you drag up, and right when you drag down. You can also drag clockwise around an object to increase its size, or drag counterclockwise to decrease its size.

H. The **Freeze Mask tool** protects areas where you paint.

I. The **Thaw Mask tool** removes the protection created by the Freeze Mask tool.

Reconstructing Pixels

When you manipulate pixels in the Liquify dialog box, you can press Command/Control-Z to undo your last brush stroke in the dialog box. Clicking the **Restore All** button has the same effect as using the Undo keyboard shortcut.

You can also use the **Reconstruct** button to affect the last-applied stroke. Rather than undoing the entire stroke, you can use the resulting Revert Reconstruction dialog box to lessen the effect by a specific percentage.

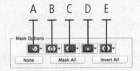

Using Masks in the Liquify Filter

Mask Options allow you to freeze areas in the Liquify preview to protect them from distortion. You can use the Mask options to freeze areas based on existing selections, transparent areas, or layer masks in the original image.

A. **Replace Selection** creates a new mask from the selection, transparency, or mask.

B. **Add to Selection** adds the selection, transparency, or mask to the currently thawed area.

C. **Subtract from Selection** adds the selection, transparency, or mask to the currently frozen area.

D. **Intersect with Selection** creates a mask with areas that are frozen in the preview, and in the selection, transparency, or mask from the original image.

E. **Invert Selection** inverts the mask in the preview image within the boundaries of the selection, transparency, or mask from the original image.

You can click the **None** button to thaw all masked areas; click the **Mask All** button to mask the entire image; or click the **Invert All** button to reverse the current mask.

Changing the Filter View

The **Show Image** option, active by default, shows the active layer in the filter's preview area. If you check the **Show Mesh** option, the preview also shows a grid that defaults to small, gray lines. You can use the Mesh Size and Mesh Color menus to change the appearance of the grid.

When the **Show Mask** option is checked, any mask you paint with the Freeze Mask tool appears in the filter's preview area. You can use the Mask Color menu to change the color of the visible mask.

When the **Show Backdrop** option is checked, you can include other layers in the filter's preview area. The Use menu, which defaults to All Layers, also lists individual layers in the file so that you can show only a certain layer in the preview. You can use the Mode and Opacity menus to change the way extra layer(s) appear in the preview.

13. Continue clicking and dragging to push pixels so that all non-masked areas are filled.

If necessary, you can press Command/Control-Z to undo your last brush stroke in the Liquify dialog box.

14. Click OK to return to the image.

Depending on the size of the layer you are liquifying, the process might take a while to complete; be patient.

The Liquify filter is not a smart filter, and cannot be applied to a Smart Object layer; it permanently alters the pixels in the layer where it is applied.

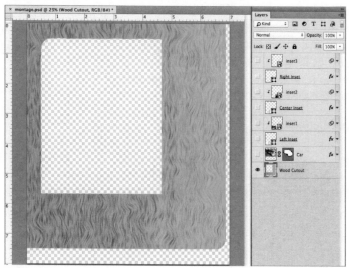

15. Save the file and continue to the next exercise.

 ## USE THE EYEDROPPER TOOL

In Photoshop, there is almost always more than one way to complete a task. In this exercise, you use the Eyedropper tool to change the Foreground and Background colors by sampling from the original car image. You will then use those colors to create a gradient background for the overall composition.

1. With montage.psd open, hide all but the Car layer.

You can hide multiple layers by clicking and dragging over the eye icons of each layer that you want to hide.

2. Choose the Eyedropper tool in the Tools panel.

3. In the Options bar, choose 5 by 5 Average in the Sample Size menu and choose All Layers in the Sample menu. Make sure the Show Sampling Ring option is checked.

The default eyedropper option — Point Sample — selects the color of the single pixel where you click. Using one of the average values avoids the possibility of sampling an errant artifact color because the tool finds the average color in a range of adjacent pixels.

By default, the sample will be selected from All [visible] Layers. You can choose Current Layer in the Sample menu to choose a color from only the active layer.

4. **Move the cursor over the blue accent in the front fender and click to change the foreground color.**

When you click with the Eyedropper tool, the sampling ring appears and shows the previous foreground color on the bottom and the current sample color on the top half.

If you hold down the mouse button, you can drag around the image to find the color you want. The sampling ring previews what color will be selected if you release the mouse button.

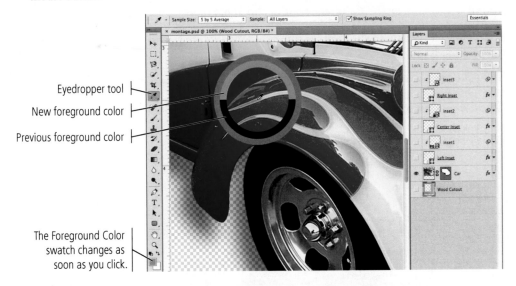

Eyedropper tool

New foreground color

Previous foreground color

The Foreground Color swatch changes as soon as you click.

5. **Move the cursor over the edge of the reflection area in the hubcap (as shown in the image below). Option/Alt-click to change the background color.**

Pressing Option/Alt while you click with the Eyedropper tool changes the Background color. In this case, the sampling ring shows the previous background color on the bottom and the current selection on the top.

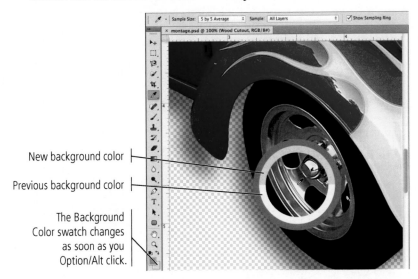

New background color

Previous background color

The Background Color swatch changes as soon as you Option/Alt click.

6. **Save the file and continue to the next exercise.**

CREATE A CUSTOM GRADIENT

A **gradient** (sometimes called a blend) is a fill that creates a smooth transition from one color to another or across a range of multiple colors. Photoshop can create several different kinds of gradients (linear, radial, etc.) from one color to another, and you can access a number of built-in gradients. You can also create your own custom gradients, which you will do in this exercise.

1. **With montage.psd open, choose the Gradient tool in the Tools panel.**

2. **In the Options bar, click the arrow to the right of the gradient sample bar to show the Gradient Picker panel.**

   The Gradient Picker panel shows a set of predefined gradients, including black-to-white, foreground-to-transparent, foreground-to-background, and several other common options. You can also access additional gradient libraries in the panel Options menu.

3. **Open the Gradient Picker panel Options menu and choose Small List view.**

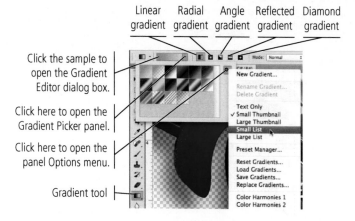

4. **Open the Gradient Picker panel again (if necessary) and choose Foreground to Background from the list of gradients. Press Return/Enter to close the Gradient Picker panel.**

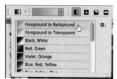

5. **Click the gradient sample in the Options bar to open the Gradient Editor dialog box.**

   You can use this dialog box to edit existing gradients or create new ones.

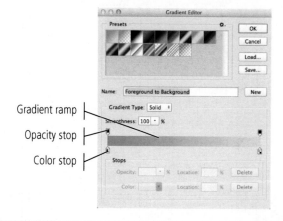

6. **Click the left color stop below the gradient ramp. Drag right until the Location field shows 40%.**

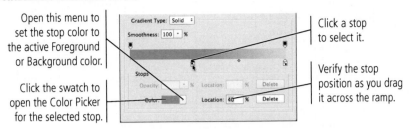

Open this menu to set the stop color to the active Foreground or Background color.

Click the swatch to open the Color Picker for the selected stop.

Click a stop to select it.

Verify the stop position as you drag it across the ramp.

Note:

As soon as you click the color stop, the name changes to Custom because you're defining a custom gradient.

7. **Click the right color stop and drag left until the Location field shows 60%.**

8. **Click below the left side of the ramp. Drag the new stop until the location field shows 20%.**

This adds a new stop with the same settings as the last-selected stop.

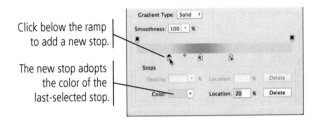

Click below the ramp to add a new stop.

The new stop adopts the color of the last-selected stop.

Note:

Drag a stop off the gradient ramp to remove it from the gradient.

9. **Add another new stop to the left end of the ramp. Set its location to 0%.**

10. **Double-click the new stop to open the Color Picker dialog box. Change the stop color to white, then click OK.**

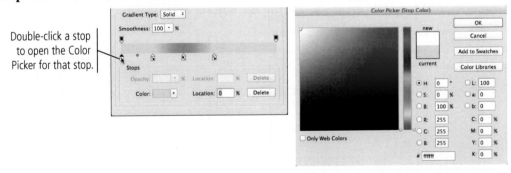

Double-click a stop to open the Color Picker for that stop.

11. **Click the left stop to make it the active color stop, then click the right end of the ramp to add a fifth stop to the ramp at Location: 100%.**

If you don't click the new stop first, the new stop would have the same color as the last selected stop from Step 8.

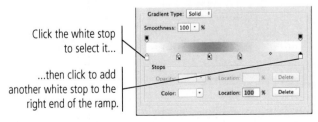

Click the white stop to select it...

...then click to add another white stop to the right end of the ramp.

12. Type `Car Background` in the Name field and click the New button.

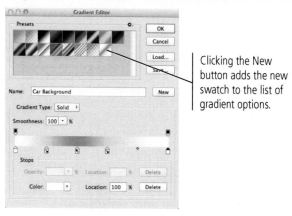

Clicking the New button adds the new swatch to the list of gradient options.

13. Click OK to close the dialog box.

14. Save the file and continue to the next exercise.

 ## CREATE A GRADIENT FILL LAYER

Once you define the gradient you want, applying it is fairly easy: add a layer (if necessary), select the type of gradient you want to create, and then click and drag.

1. With `montage.psd` open, click the New Layer button at the bottom of the Layers panel.

When you add a new layer, it is automatically added directly above the selected layer.

2. Name the new layer `Background`, then move it to the bottom of the layer stack.

Simply naming a layer "Background" does not automatically convert it to the Background layer that you see when you open a flattened image file.

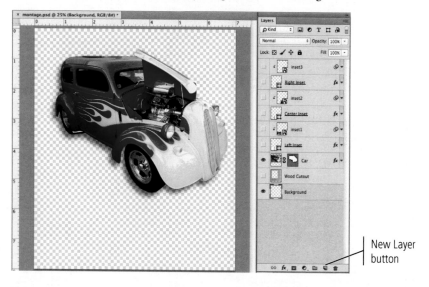

New Layer button

3. Show all layers, and then click the Background layer to select it.

4. Make sure the Gradient tool is selected. In the Options bar, make sure the Car Background gradient is selected and the Linear gradient option is active.

5. **Click in the top edge of the cutout area and drag to the bottom outside edge of the cutout layer (as shown in the following image).**

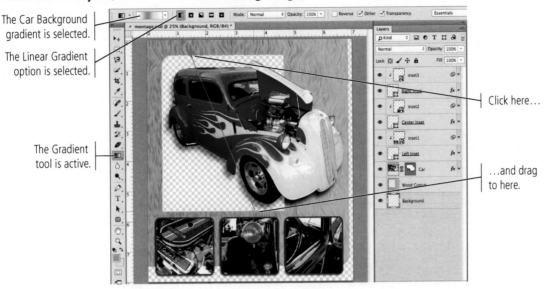

The Car Background gradient is selected.

The Linear Gradient option is selected.

The Gradient tool is active.

Click here...

...and drag to here.

When you release the mouse button, the layer fills with the gradient. Areas before and after the line drawn with the Gradient tool fill with the start and stop colors of the gradient (in this case, they're both white).

6. **Save the file and continue to the next exercise.**

CREATE A PATTERN FILL LAYER

The gradient layer is a good start for your art background, but it needs some texture to look more like a painting. A pattern fill will create the texture you need.

1. **With montage.psd open, create a new layer named** Background Pattern **above the Background layer.**

2. **Choose the Paint Bucket tool (nested under the Gradient tool) and review the Options bar.**

   When you click with the Paint Bucket tool, it fills areas of similar color. You can define the Paint Bucket tool tolerance in the Options bar.

3. **Choose Pattern in the left menu of the Options bar, and then open the Pattern panel.**

4. **In the Pattern panel Options menu, choose Small List to see the names of the various patterns.**

Use this menu to fill with a color or pattern.

Click this button to open the Pattern panel.

Click here to open the panel Options menu.

Paint Bucket tool

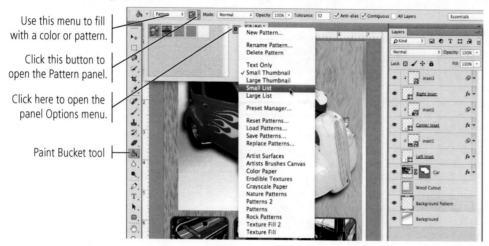

5. **Choose Grayscale Paper in the Options menu to show that set of patterns.**

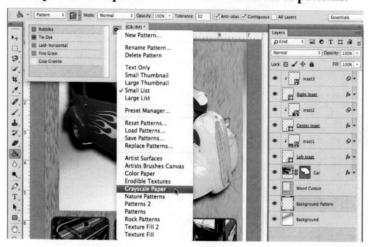

6. **When you see a warning that the patterns will replace the current set, click OK.**

7. **Scroll through the list and click Crepe to select that pattern.**

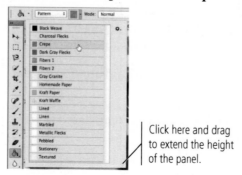

Click here and drag to extend the height of the panel.

8. **In the Options bar, make sure the All Layers option is not checked.**

   The Paint Bucket tool creates fills based on the defined sample tolerance. If the All Layers option is checked, clicking would fill an area (on the active layer) within the defined tolerance based on the color values on *all layers* instead of only sampling color values only on the layer where you want to add the texture fill.

9. **Place the cursor anywhere in the image window and click.**

   Because there is nothing on the currently selected layer, every pixel in the layer is within the tool's tolerance — the entire layer fills with the pattern. As you can see, the pattern fill completely obscures the gradient. To blend the two layers together, you have to change the top layer's blending mode and opacity.

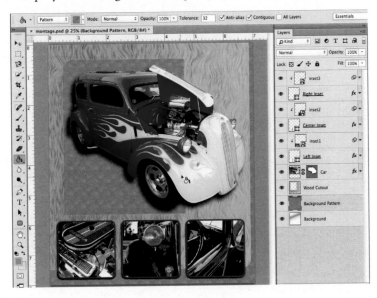

10. **With the Background Pattern layer selected, choose Darken in the Blending Mode menu at the top of the Layers panel.**

   Photoshop provides access to 27 different layer blending modes; the default is Normal, or no blending applied. Using the Darken mode, the gradient is now visible behind the texture of the pattern, but the pattern is still overpowering.

11. **Change the Opacity of the active layer to 15%.**

Change the layer opacity in this field.

Use this menu to change the blending mode.

12. **Save the file and continue to the final exercise.**

Distinguishing Photoshop Blending Modes

When working with blending modes, think of the top layer as the "blend" layer and the next lowest layer as the "base".

- **Normal** is the default mode (no blending applied).

- **Dissolve** results in a random scattering of pixels of both the blend and base colors.

- **Darken** returns the darker of the blend or base color. Base pixels that are lighter than the blend color are replaced; base pixels that are darker than the blend color remain unchanged.

- **Multiply** multiplies (hence the name) the base color by the blend color, resulting in a darker color. Multiplying any color with black produces black; multiplying any color with white leaves the color unchanged (think of math — any number times 0 equals 0).

- **Color Burn** darkens the base color by increasing the contrast. Blend colors darker than 50% significantly darken the base color by increasing saturation and reducing brightness; blending with white has no effect.

- **Linear Burn** darkens the base color similar to Color Burn; using Linear Burn, the brightness is reduced about twice as much for blend colors in the mid-tone range.

- **Darker Color** compares the channel values of the blend and base colors, resulting in the lower value.

- **Lighten** returns whichever is the lighter color (base or blend). Base pixels that are darker than the blend color are replaced; base pixels that are lighter than the blend color remain unchanged.

- **Screen** is basically the inverse of Multiply, always returning a lighter color. Screening with black has no effect; screening with white produces white.

- **Color Dodge** brightens the base color. Blend colors lighter than 50% significantly increase brightness; blending with black has no effect.

- **Linear Dodge (Add)** is similar to Color Dodge, but creates smoother transitions from areas of high brightness to areas of low brightness.

- **Lighter Color** compares channel values of the blend and base colors, resulting in the higher value.

- **Overlay** multiplies or screens the blend color to preserve the original lightness or darkness of the base.

- **Soft Light** darkens or lightens base colors depending on the blend color. Blend colors lighter than 50% lighten the base color (as if dodged); blend colors darker than 50% darken the base color (as if burned).

- **Hard Light** combines the Multiply and Screen modes. Blend colors darker than 50% are multiplied, and blend colors lighter than 50% are screened.

- **Vivid Light** combines the Color Dodge and Color Burn modes. Blend colors lighter than 50% lighten the base by decreasing contrast; blend colors darker than 50% darken the base by increasing contrast.

- **Linear Light** combines the Linear Dodge and Linear Burn modes. If the blend color is lighter than 50%, the result is lightened by increasing the base brightness. If the blend color is darker than 50%, the result is darkened by decreasing the base brightness.

- **Pin Light** preserves the brightest and darkest areas of the blend color; blend colors in the mid-tone range have little (if any) effect.

- **Hard Mix** pushes all pixels in the resulting blend to either all or nothing. The base and blend values of each pixel in each channel are added together (e.g., R 45 [blend] + R 230 [base] = R 275). Pixels with totals over 255 are shown at 255; pixels with a total lower than 255 are dropped to 0.

- **Difference** inverts base color values according to the brightness value in the blend layer. Lower brightness values in the blend layer have less of an effect on the result; blending with black has no effect.

- **Exclusion** is very similar to Difference, except that mid-tone values in the base color are completely desaturated.

- **Subtract** removes the blend color from the base color.

- **Divide** looks at the color information in each channel and divides the blend color from the base color.

- **Hue** results in a color with the luminance and saturation of the base color and the hue of the blend color.

- **Saturation** results in a color with the luminance and hue of the base color and the saturation of the blend color.

- **Color** results in a color with the luminance of the base color and the hue and saturation of the blend color.

- **Luminosity** results in a color with the hue and saturation of the base color and the luminance of the blend color (basically the opposite of the Color mode).

PRINT A COMPOSITE PROOF

The last stage of most jobs — after the client has approved the work — is printing a proof. A printed proof is basically the output provider's roadmap of how the final job should look. As more processes move to all-digital workflows, a printed proof is not always required — especially if you're submitting files digitally. But some output providers still require a printed proof, and you might want to print samples of your work at various stages of development.

To output this file at 100%, you need a sheet at least tabloid size (11 × 17″). If you don't have that option, you can use the Photoshop Print dialog box to fit the job onto letter-size paper. Keep in mind, however, that many of the effects that you created with filters will lose some of their impact when you reduce the file to fit onto a letter-size page.

1. **With montage.psd open, choose File>Print.**

2. **In the Printer menu of the Print dialog box, choose the printer you're using.**

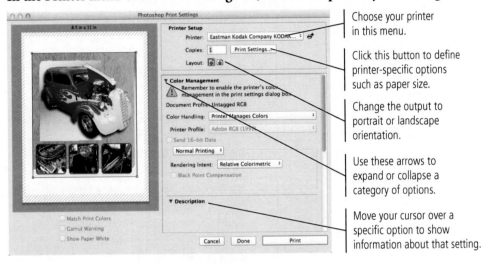

Choose your printer in this menu.

Click this button to define printer-specific options such as paper size.

Change the output to portrait or landscape orientation.

Use these arrows to expand or collapse a category of options.

Move your cursor over a specific option to show information about that setting.

3. **Choose the Portrait layout option (below the number of copies).**

    Ideally, you should always print proofs at 100%. If this is not possible, however, you can print a sample content proof by scaling the page to fit the available paper size.

4. **Review the options in the scrolling pane below the Printer Setup options.**

    Different types of output jobs require different settings. If you are simply printing a desktop proof, you can leave most of these options at their default values.

    As a general rule, proofs should be printed at 100% of the actual file size. If you are printing a file that is larger than the paper size your printer can handle, you can use the Scaled Print Size options to fit the job on the available paper size. Alternatively, you can use the Print Selected Area option to output different portions of the image onto separate sheets, and then manually assemble the multiple sheets into a single page.

Note:

If you submit a scaled proof with a print job, make sure you note the scale percentage prominently on the proof.

5. **Click Print to output the file.**

6. **When the output process is complete, close the file.**

Use the following as a guide to help you decide which options to include in your output:

Color Management options

(Color management is explained in detail in Project 6: Menu Image Correction.)

- Color Handling determines whether color management is applied by the printer or by Photoshop.

- Printer Profile defines the known color characteristics of the output device you are using.

- Normal Printing simply prints the file to your printer, using no defined output profile for color management.

  - Rendering Intent defines how colors are shifted to fit inside the printer's output capabilities.

  - Black Point Compression adjusts for differences in the black point (the darkest possible black area) between the file and the output device.

- Hard Proofing simulates the color output properties of another printer, based on the defined profile in the Proof Setup menu.

  - Simulate Paper Color applies the absolute colorimetric rendering intent to simulate the appearance of color on the actual paper that would be used on the defined output device (for example, newsprint on a web press).

  - Simulate Black Ink simulates the brightness of dark colors as they would appear on the defined output device. If this option is not checked, dark colors are simply printed as dark as possible on the actual printer you are using.

Position and Size Options

- **Position** defines the location of the output on the paper. It is centered by default; you can use the Top and Left fields to position the output at a specific distance from the paper corner. You can also click in the preview area and drag to reposition the image on the paper.

- **Scale** defaults to 100%, creating a full-size print; the **Height** and **Width** fields define the size of the image being printed. If you change the Scale field, the Height and Width fields reflect the proportional size. You can also define a specific size in the Height and Width fields; in this case, the Scale field is adjusted accordingly.

- If you check **Scale to Fit Media**, the image is automatically scaled to fit inside the printable area on the selected paper size.

- **Print Resolution** defines the resolution that will be sent to the output device. Remember the principle of effective resolution; if you print a 300-ppi image at 200%, the printer has only 150 ppi to work with.

- If you check **Print Selected Area**, handles appear in the preview area. You can drag those handles to define the image area that will be output.

Printing Marks

- **Corner Crop Marks** adds crop marks to show the edges of the image (where it should be cut).

- **Center Crop Marks** adds a crop mark at the center of each edge of the image.

- **Registration Marks** adds bulls-eye targets and star targets that are used to align color separations on a printing press. (Calibration bars and star target registration marks require a PostScript printer.)

- **Description** adds description text (from the File>File Info dialog box) outside the trim area in 9-pt Helvetica.

- **Labels** adds the file name above the image.

Functions

- **Emulsion Down** reverses the image on the output. This option is primarily used for output to a filmsetter or imagesetter.

- **Negative** inverts the color values of the entire output. This option is typically used if you are outputting directly to film, which will then be used to image a photo-sensitive printing plate (a slowly disappearing workflow).

- The **Background** option allows you to add a background color that will print outside the image area.

- The **Border** option adds a black border around an image. You can define a specific width (in points) for the border.

- The **Bleed** option moves crop marks inside the image by a specific measurement.

PostScript Options

(If your printer is not PostScript compatible, the PostScript options will not be available.)

- **Calibration Bars** adds swatches of black in 10% increments (starting at 0% and ending at 100%).

- The **Interpolation** option can help reduce the jagged appearance of low-resolution images by automatically resampling up when you print. This option is only available on PostScript Level 2 or 3 printers.

- The **Include Vector Data** option sends vector information in the output stream for a PostScript printer, so the vector data can be output at the highest possible resolution of the output device.

Project Review

fill in the blank

1. _____ sharpens an image by increasing contrast along the edges in an image.

2. _____ refers to the overall image area, like the surface used by traditional painters.

3. The _____ tool is used to draw freeform vector-based shapes and paths.

4. A _____ is a special type of Photoshop layer that retains vector path information.

5. The _____ tool can be used to change a smooth point to a corner point.

6. The _____ tool can be used to fill areas with solid colors or patterns.

7. A _____ is a smooth transition from one color to another.

8. The _____ command is used to show only areas of one layer that fall within the area of the underlying layer.

9. In the Liquify filter, the _____ tool can be used to protect specific areas from being liquified.

10. The _____ allows you to experiment with different filters and filter settings, and to compound multiple filters to create unique artistic effects.

short answer

1. Briefly explain the difference between vectors and pixels.

2. Briefly describe two different tool modes when using a vector drawing tool.

3. Briefly explain the difference between the Path Selection tool and the Direct Selection tool.

Portfolio Builder Project

Use what you learned in this project to complete the following freeform exercise.
Carefully read the art director and client comments, then create your own design to meet the needs of the project.
Use the space below to sketch ideas; when finished, write a brief explanation of your reasoning behind your final design.

art director comments

Against The Clock is considering a new design for the covers of its Professional Portfolio series of books. You have been hired to design a new cover comp for the Photoshop CC book.

❑ Measure the cover of the existing Photoshop CC book to determine the required trim size.

❑ Incorporate the same elements that currently appear on the book cover — title, publisher logo, and the text in the bottom-right corner. (The logo file is included in the **Covers_Print14_PB.zip** archive on the Student Files Web page.)

❑ Create compelling images and artwork to illustrate the concept of the book title.

❑ Design the cover to meet commercial printing requirements.

client comments

We really like the existing cover design, but after five editions we're starting to think a fresh look might be a good thing.

Obviously, the most important element of the cover is the title. However, it seems that Adobe is going to stop using version numbers in its software releases, so we're also going to need a way to differentiate editions; your design should include an edition number (2nd edition, etc.).

In the existing covers, we chose the cityscapes as a representation of places where graphic design students find jobs. We don't really have any set ideas for new imagery, but there should be some connection between graphic design and the imagery you choose.

Finally, keep in mind that the design should allow for repurposing for the other titles in the series.

project justification

Vectors offer an advantage over pixel-based images because they can be freely scaled and edited without losing quality. This project focused on many different options related to working with vectors in Photoshop — drawing paths, creating shape layers, and editing vector shape properties. You used vectors in this project to create a custom layer mask, as well as vector shapes that you filled with other images and a custom artistic pattern.

This project also introduced some of the creative tools that can turn photos and flat colors into painting-like artwork. You learned to use the Filter Gallery, the Liquify filter, custom gradients, gradient and pattern fill layers, and layer blending modes. You will use these options many times in your career as you complete different types of projects in Photoshop.

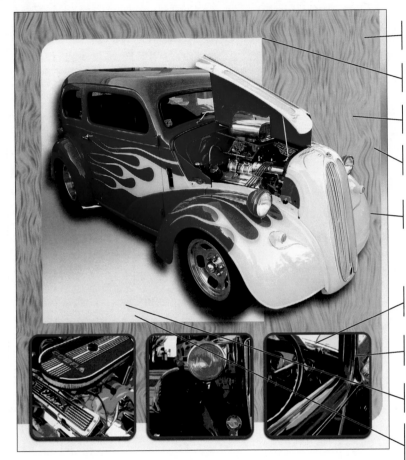

Create a compound vector shape layer

Edit corner properties of vector shapes

Apply a style to a vector shape layer

Liquify pixels to create unique effects

Use a vector mask to remove an image from its background

Composite multiple images using Smart Objects

Apply filters to images to create a "painting" effect

Use gradients and patterns to create a custom background

Adjust blending mode and opacity to blend one layer into another

Menu Image Correction

Your client is the owner of The Chateau, a five-star gourmet restaurant that has been operating in northern Los Angeles County for over five decades. The restaurant changes its menu frequently, so they currently use a chalkboard menu, presented on an easel at each table when guests are seated. The owner recently received a number of comments about the chalkboard menu being difficult to read, so he decided to create printed menus with the standard offerings and use the chalkboard to display the chef's daily specials.

This project incorporates the following skills:

❑ Repairing damaged images

❑ Understanding the relationship between tonal range and contrast

❑ Correcting image lighting and exposure problems

❑ Understanding how gray balance affects overall image color

❑ Correcting minor and severe image color problems

❑ Preparing corrected images for printing

❑ Combining exposures into an HDR image

client comments

The Chateau is a unique destination restaurant that consistently wins awards from local and national food and wine reviewers. The restaurant was first opened in 1952 by Paul and Gina Roseman as a rest stop and diner for travelers along the Sierra Highway. While the restaurant remains in the family, it has evolved from home-style comfort food to more exotic fare such as wild game with a French twist.

The history of the restaurant is important to us. We have a Roseman family portrait — my great-grandparents — that we'd like to include on the back of the menu. The picture is a bit grainy and has some damage, though, and we'd like you to clean it up as much as possible. We also want to include a picture of the current executive chef, who is Paul and Gina's great-grandniece, in the same section. The only picture we have of her is very dark though, and we're hoping you can make it look better.

In addition, we've taken several pictures of different meals that Suzanne created. We want you to make sure they will look as good as possible when printed. You're the expert, so we trust that you know what needs to be done.

art director comments

Digital images come from a wide variety of sources: scanned photographs and digital cameras are the two most common, as is the case for the client's images for this project. Some images can be used as is, or at least with only minor correction. Realistically, most professional photographers reshoot an image until they have one that doesn't need your help.

Unfortunately, however, not every project involves a professional photographer. Consumer-level cameras have come down in price and gone up in quality to the point where many non-professionals shoot their own photos without proper skill or knowledge. That means many of those images require a bit of help — and some require a lot.

Even when a professional photographer is involved, not every image comes from a perfectly lit studio. Location shots — where a subject is photographed in a "real-world" setting — can't always be captured perfectly. Those images usually need work as well. Fortunately, Photoshop provides a powerful toolset for solving most image problems, or at least improving the worst of them.

project objectives

To complete this project, you will:

- ❏ Remove grain with blur and sharpen techniques
- ❏ Heal severe scratches
- ❏ Clone out major damage
- ❏ Correct minor problems with the Brightness/Contrast adjustment
- ❏ Correct tonal range with the Levels adjustment
- ❏ Correct lighting problems with the Exposure adjustment
- ❏ Correct overall color problems with the Color Balance adjustment
- ❏ Correct precise color values with the Curves adjustment
- ❏ Correct an RGB image to CMYK gamut limits
- ❏ Embed color profile information in a file
- ❏ Combine multiple exposures with the Merge to HDR Pro utility

① Rosemans — touch up, fix damage

② Buffalo steak — fix brightness/contrast

③ Suzanne — lighten overall, add detail in shadows

④ Chicken — fix muddy/exposure problem

⑤ Salmon — fix green cast throughout

⑥ Flan — fix red cast in plate

⑦ Pasta — bump contrast in midtones

⑧ Salad — correct color shift in reds/greens

⑨ Mill... exposures for better detail

Stage 1 Retouching Damaged Images

Image repair is the process of fixing scratches, removing dust, making tears disappear, and generally putting broken or damaged pictures back together again. **Retouching**, on the other hand, is the technique of changing an image by adding something that wasn't there or removing something that was there. Damage can come from a wide range of sources: creases, scratches from any number of abrasive objects, water spots, and tape marks to name just a few. Other image problems such as photographic grain are a natural part of photographs (especially old ones), and dust is common (if not inevitable) whenever photographs are scanned.

There are many different ways to approach image repairs. As you complete the exercises in this stage of the project, you will use several tools — from basic to complex — to clean up damage in the client's family portrait from the early 1940s.

REMOVE GRAIN WITH BLUR AND SHARPEN TECHNIQUES

Photographic film is made up of microscopic grains of light-sensitive material. These grains capture the image information, which is eventually processed into a print or transparency. While not usually apparent in a standard photographic print, the grain in a photograph can become pronounced when scanned with a high-resolution scanner. Enlarging an image during scanning further enhances any grain that already exists.

When grain is evident in a digital image, the grain pattern can destroy fine detail and create a mottled appearance in areas of solid color or subtle tone variation. Slower-rated film typically has the smallest and least-evident grain, while faster film can produce significant graininess.

Blurring and Sharpening techniques are the best methods for removing photographic grain. The techniques you use in this exercise work for any image with grain. Older images — such as the one your client wants to use — almost always have obvious grain problems that can be fixed to some degree; antique images can be fixed only just so much. The techniques you learn in this project produce very good results if you need to remove grain from modern scanned images.

1. **Download Menu_Print14_RF.zip from the Student Files Web page.**

2. **Expand the ZIP archive in your WIP folder (Macintosh) or copy the archive contents into your WIP folder (Windows).**

   This results in a folder named **Menu**, which contains the files you need for this project. You should also use this folder to save the files you create in this project.

3. **Open the file rosemans.jpg from your WIP>Menu folder.**

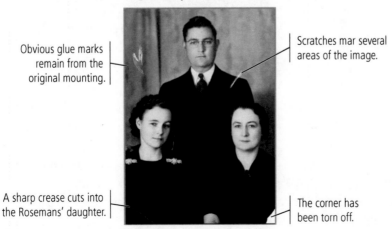

Obvious glue marks remain from the original mounting.

Scratches mar several areas of the image.

A sharp crease cuts into the Rosemans' daughter.

The corner has been torn off.

4. Choose View>100% to show the image at the actual size.

Grain is most obvious in large areas of solid (or nearly solid) color.

Grain in lighter areas can produce a sickly appearance in a person's face.

The Noise Filters

Noise is defined as random pixels that stand out from the surrounding pixels, either hurting the overall appearance of the image (as in the case of visible grains in an old photograph) or helping to prevent printing problems (as in the case of a gradient that extends across a large area). Photoshop includes several filters (Filters>Noise) that can add or remove noise.

The **Add Noise filter** applies random pixels to the image. Uniform distributes color values of noise between 0 and the defined amount. Gaussian distributes color values of noise along a bell-shaped curve. Monochromatic adds random pixels without affecting the colors in the image.

The **Despeckle** filter detects the edges in an image and blurs everything except those edges.

The **Dust & Scratches filter** reduces noise by comparing the contrast of pixels within the defined radius; pixels outside the defined threshold are adjusted.

The **Median filter** reduces noise by blending the brightness of pixels within a selection. The filter compares the brightness of pixels within the defined radius, and replaces pixels that differ too much from surrounding pixels with the median brightness value of the compared pixels.

The **Reduce Noise** filter provides far greater control over different aspects of noise correction. In Basic mode, you can remove luminance noise and color noise in the composite image.

In Advanced mode, you can remove noise from individual color channels. (**Luminance noise**, also called grayscale noise, makes an image appear grainy; **color noise** usually appears as color artifacts in the image.)

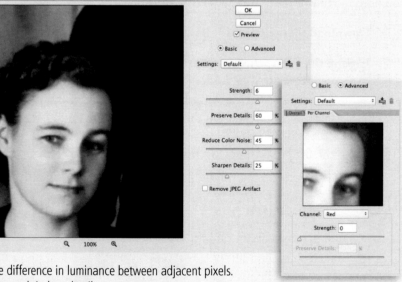

- **Strength** controls the amount of luminance noise reduction.

- **Preserve Details** controls how carefully the filter compares the difference in luminance between adjacent pixels. Lower values remove more noise but result in less detail.

- **Reduce Color Noise** removes random color pixels from the image.

- **Sharpen Details** sharpens the image. Because the noise reduction process inherently blurs the image, this option applies the same kind of sharpening that is available in the Photoshop Sharpen filters.

- **Remove JPEG Artifacts** removes artifacts and halos caused by saving an image with a low JPEG quality setting (in other words, using a high lossy compression scheme).

5. **Choose Filter>Blur>Gaussian Blur.**

   All Photoshop blur filters work in essentially the same way: they average the brightness values of contiguous pixels to soften the image.

6. **In the image behind the dialog box, click the area where the girl's face meets the man's jacket.**

   When many filter dialog boxes are open, clicking the image (behind the dialog box) changes the visible preview area in the dialog box. You can also click inside the dialog box preview area and drag to change the visible preview area.

7. **Make sure Preview is checked in the dialog box and change the Radius field to 1.5 pixels.**

   The **Radius** field defines (in pixels) the amount of blurring that will be applied. Photoshop uses this value to average the brightness of a pixel with that of surrounding pixels. A radius value near 1 can soften an image and remove most photographic grain.

Click the image to change the visible preview area in the dialog box.

A small amount of Gaussian blur removes most of the photographic grain.

Areas of fine detail are also slightly blurred by the Gaussian Blur filter.

8. **Click OK to apply the Gaussian Blur to the image.**

   To remove the photographic grain, you had to blur the entire image; this means that areas of fine detail were also blurred. You can use a second technique — sharpening — to restore some of the lost edge detail.

9. **Choose Filter>Sharpen>Smart Sharpen.**

   The Smart Sharpen filter allows you to sharpen an image based on a specific amount and radius. You can also limit the sharpening that occurs in shadow and highlight areas.

10. **If you don't see the entire dialog box, click the arrow to the left of Shadows/ Highlights to show all the available options.**

11. **Make the girl's face visible in the dialog box preview area.**

12. **Define the following settings in the dialog box:**

    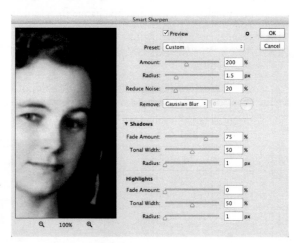

    - **Choose Gaussian Blur in the Remove menu.**

      The **Remove** menu defines the type of blur you want to remove. Because you applied a Gaussian blur to remove the heavy noise, you are now using the Smart Sharpen filter to remove that blur and restore image detail.

      Lens Blur detects edges and detail, and provides finer sharpening of detail and reduced halos. Motion Blur attempts to reduce the effects of blur that is caused by camera movement; you can also define a specific angle of the blur to remove.

    - **Set the Amount to 200%.**

      Amount defines how much sharpening to apply; a higher amount increases contrast between edge pixels, giving the appearance of greater sharpness. (Be careful, because a too-high amount can result in halos at apparent edges.)

    - **Set the Radius to 1.5 px.**

      Radius defines the number of pixels around edge pixels that will be affected by the sharpening. Higher radius values result in more obvious sharpening.

    - **Set the Reduce Noise slider to 20%.**

      Reduce Noise helps to avoid sharpening any noise that still exists in the image.

    - **In the Highlights section, set the Fade Amount to 75%.**

      In the Shadows and Highlights sections, you can adjust sharpening that will be applied in those areas of the image.

      - **Fade Amount** adjusts the amount of sharpening. By reducing the sharpening in the highlights of this image, you help to further remove the noise that remains in the lighter portions (the faces and background).

      - **Tonal Width** controls the range of tones that will be modified. Smaller values restrict the adjustments to only darker regions for shadows and only lighter regions for highlights.

      - **Radius** defines the size of the area around each pixel used to determine whether a pixel is in the shadows or highlights.

12. **Click OK to apply sharpen the image.**

13. **Choose File>Save As. Save the file as a native Photoshop file named rosemans_working.psd in your WIP>Menu folder. Continue to the next exercise.**

    Remember, you have to choose File>Save As to save the file with a different name or format.

PHOTOSHOP FOUNDATIONS

As the name suggests, the Shake Reduction filter (Filter>Sharpen>Shake Reduction) was designed to reduce the blur caused by a shaking camera — for example, images that were photographed with a slow shutter speed or without a flash.

Keep in mind that the filter was also not designed to remove blur caused by a moving camera, not a moving subject. The filter also does not work well on images with specular highlights or noise. Finally, it works best to reduce shake in specific areas of an image, not over an entire image.

Blur Estimation tool
Blur Direction tool

Blur Estimation region pin

Blur Estimation region

Add Suggested Blur Trace

Delete Blur Trace

Enhance at Loupe Location

Undock Detail

Unlock Detail

When you first open the filter, the image is automatically analyzed. The software determines a "region of interest" and calculates the shape and direction of the blur.

If necessary, you can adjust the automatically defined settings on the right side of the dialog box:

- Blur Trace Bounds is the extent of blur size introduced by the camera shake.
- Source Noise defines the noise level of the Source image (Auto, Low, Medium, High)
- Smoothing reduces high-frequency sharpening noise.
- Artifact Suppression reduces larger artifacts that might be enhanced by sharpening.

You can use the Blur Estimation tool to add more than one blur estimation region to the image, or use the Blur Direction tool to manually specify the direction and length of a straight blur.

When Advanced options are expanded, the small icons show previews of the blur shape that was defined for each region.

You can select a specific region in this area to make it active in the larger preview pane. Click the handles on the blur region marquee to resize it, and click the pin in the center of a region to move it.

Using the Detail Loupe

You can use the Detail loupe (pane) to analyze specific areas of the image. You can enlarge the detail preview using the options at the bottom of the pane (.5x, 1x, 2x, 4x).

While the pane is docked, click inside the preview area to change the preview area. You can also undock the Detail pane and drag it over the image to enhance a specific area.

If you click the Enhance at Loupe Location button, the filter creates a new blur estimation region based on what is visible in the Detail pane.

Click the Close button to redock the detail pane.

Drag the detail pane to enhance a specific area.

Change the enlargement in the detail pane.

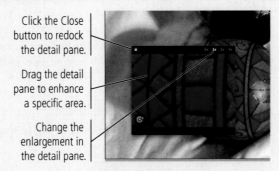

HEAL SEVERE SCRATCHES

The blur and sharpen routine from the previous exercise improved the client's image — the obvious grain is gone. Even though the edges are slightly less sharp than the original scan, they are sharp enough to produce good results when the image is printed. If you're working with images that aren't 70 years old, you will be able to produce far sharper edges using these same techniques.

There are still a number of problems in the image that require intervention. Photoshop includes several tools for changing the pixels in an image — from painting with a brush to nudging selections on a layer to using repair tools specifically designed for adjusting pixels based on other pixels in the image.

The **Spot Healing Brush tool** allows you to remove imperfections by blending the surrounding pixels. The **Healing Brush tool** has a similar function, except you can define the source pixels that will be used to heal a specific area. The **Patch tool** allows you to repair a selected area with pixels from another area of the image by dragging the selection area.

Note:

Throughout this project, you are going to clean up blemishes on images and make other adjustments that require looking at very small areas. It can be very helpful to clean your monitor so you don't mistake on-screen dust and smudges with flaws in the images you are adjusting.

1. **With rosemans_working.psd open, view the image at 100%. Set up the document window so you can see the lower half of the image.**

2. **Select the Spot Healing Brush tool in the Tools panel.**

3. **In the Options bar, open the Brush Preset picker and choose a 20-pixel hard-edge brush. Choose the Proximity Match option.**

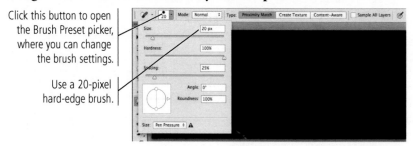

Click this button to open the Brush Preset picker, where you can change the brush settings.

Use a 20-pixel hard-edge brush.

The **Proximity Match** method uses the pixels around the edge of the selection to find an image area to use as a patch for the selected area. The **Create Texture** method uses all the pixels in the selection to create a texture for repairing the area. **Content Aware** mode attempts to match the detail in surrounding areas while healing pixels (this method does not work well for areas with hard edges or sharp contrast). If you select **Sample All Layers**, the tool pulls pixel data from all visible layers.

4. **Place the cursor over the small white spot in the bottom-left corner of the image. Click immediately over the white spot to heal it.**

The Spot Healing Brush tool shows the size of the selected brush.

5. **Using the same technique, remove the remaining white spots from the dark areas of the Rosemans' clothing.**

6. **Choose the Healing Brush tool (nested under the Spot Healing Brush tool).**

7. **In the Options bar, open the Brush Preset picker. Choose a small brush size that's slightly larger than the white spot on the girl's chin (we used 9 pixels).**

When using the Healing Brush tool, the Mode menu determines the blending mode used to heal an area. The default option (Normal) samples the source color and transparency to blend the new pixels smoothly into the area being healed. The Replace mode preserves texture in the healed area when you use a soft-edge brush.

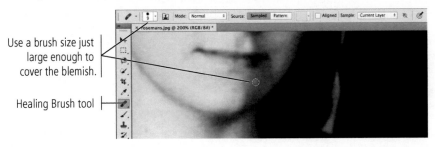

Use a brush size just large enough to cover the blemish.

Healing Brush tool

Note:

Multiple, Screen, Darken, Lighten, Color, and Luminosity modes have the same function as the blending modes for specific layers and brushes (refer to Project 5: Vintage Car Montage for an explanation of each blending mode).

8. **Place the cursor directly below the spot you want to heal. Press Option/Alt and click to define the healing source.**

Pressing Option/Alt with the Healing Brush tool changes the cursor icon to a crosshair, which you can click to select the source of the brush (the pixels that will be used to heal the spot where you next click).

Pressing Option/Alt allows you to define the source pixels that will be used to heal the next spot you click.

Note:

You can use the bracket keys to enlarge (]) or reduce ([) the Healing Brush tool brush size.

Aligning the Healing Source

PHOTOSHOP FOUNDATIONS

When you work with the Healing Brush and Clone Stamp tools, you have the option to align the source to the cursor. If the Align option is turned off, the source starting point will be relative to the image. If the Align option is turned on, the source starting point will be relative to the cursor. The following images illustrate this idea.

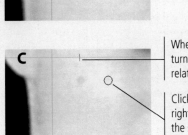

A We first Option/Alt-clicked at the guide intersection to define the healing source.

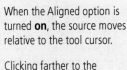

C When the Aligned option is turned **on**, the source moves relative to the tool cursor.

Clicking farther to the right moves the source the same distance from its defined origin.

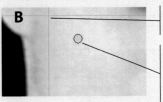

B The crosshair shows the source of the healing.

This circle shows the cursor location where we clicked with the Healing Brush tool.

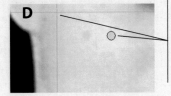

D When the Aligned option is turned **off**, the source remains in the same position even when the Healing Brush tool is clicked farther to the right.

9. **Place the cursor over the blemish on the girl's chin and click.**

Unlike the Spot Healing Brush tool, the Healing Brush tool allows you to define the source of the healing. By choosing nearby pixels as the healing source, the blemish on the girl's chin disappears, and that spot blends nicely into the surrounding pixels.

The Healing Brush tool blends colors from the source pixels (which you defined in Step 8) with colors in the area where you click. You can also change the source from Sampled (the pixels you defined by Option/Alt-clicking) to Pattern, which uses pixels from a defined pattern to heal the area. The Pattern option is a good choice for creating artistic effects, rather than healing blemishes in an existing photo.

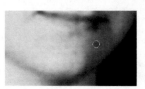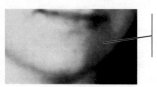

After clicking, the spot is healed using the source pixels.

10. **Save the file and continue to the next exercise.**

CLONE OUT MAJOR DAMAGE

The client's image has definitely been improved by removing the grain and healing the small blemishes, but four major areas of damage still need to be fixed. These larger areas require more control over the healing process, which the Clone Stamp tool provides.

The Clone Stamp tool paints one part of an image over another part, which is useful for duplicating objects or removing defects in an image. As with the Healing Brush tool, you can define the source that will be cloned when you click with the tool; the difference is that whole pixels are copied, not just their color values.

1. **With the file rosemans_working.psd open, zoom into the bottom-left corner (where the crease marks the image) and select the Clone Stamp tool.**

2. **In the Brush Preset picker (in the Options bar), choose a soft-edge brush large enough to cover the crease.**

When you are using the Clone Stamp tool, the Options bar combines brush options (brush size, blending mode, opacity, and flow) with healing options (alignment and sample source, which you used in the previous exercise).

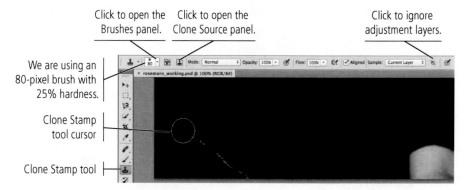

Click to open the Brushes panel.

Click to open the Clone Source panel.

Click to ignore adjustment layers.

We are using an 80-pixel brush with 25% hardness.

Clone Stamp tool cursor

Clone Stamp tool

3. **In the Options bar, make sure the Aligned option is turned on (checked).**

In this case, you want the cloning source to remain relative to the cursor, even if you stop and start several times. If you clone a large area relative to the same source origin (in other words, with the Align option turned off), you could end up with an unwanted pattern in the area you clone.

Note:

Using the Sample menu in the Options bar, you can sample source pixels from the current layer, from all layers including and below the current layer, or from all visible layers.

Note:

It might help to zoom in when you want to heal small areas such as this spot on the girl's chin. We are working at 200% in these screen shots.

4. **Place the cursor directly above and to the right of the crease. Option/Alt-click to define the cloning source.**

Option/Alt-click to define the cloning source, just as you did with the Healing Brush tool.

Note:

When using the Clone Stamp tool, hard-edge brushes can result in harsh lines where you clone pixels; soft-edge brushes can help prevent harsh lines from appearing.

5. **Click over an area of the crease and drag to clone out the crease.**

As you drag, notice that the source crosshairs move in relation to the Clone Stamp cursor. Because you turned on the Aligned Sample option in Step 3, you can stop and restart cloning, and the source will retain the same relative position to the tool cursor.

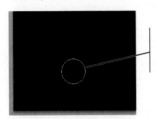

Drag with the Clone Stamp tool until the crease is no longer visible.

Note:

You can use the bracket keys to enlarge (]) or reduce ([) the Clone Stamp brush size.

6. **Use the same process to fill in the torn area in the bottom-right corner of the image.**

7. **Zoom into the scratch on the man's left shoulder.**

Cloning out damage in areas of solid color is fairly simple. This area presents a more difficult problem since the area you need to fix has an edge that must be maintained.

8. **In the Brush Preset picker, select a brush that just barely covers the edge of the man's jacket, and turn off the Aligned option.**

To prevent cloning a hard edge, we used a 30-pixel brush with a 50% Hardness value.

9. **Place the cursor over the edge you want to reproduce and Option/Alt-click to define the source.**

Because the Aligned Sample option is turned off, each successive click uses the same source point.

Note:

When you are cloning — especially large areas — it's usually a good idea to clone in small strokes or even single clicks. This method can help you avoid cloning in patterns or "railroad tracks" that do as much damage as good. When cloning large areas, it's also a good idea to frequently resample the clone source to avoid cloning the same pixels into a new noticeable pattern.

Turn off the Aligned option.

Option/Alt-click to define the clone source.

10. **Place the cursor over the scratched pixels on the man's shoulder.**

As you move the Clone Stamp tool cursor, the source pixels move along with the tool cursor to give you a preview of what will happen when you click.

11. **Click without dragging when the cloned pixels appear to align properly with the area behind the scratch.**

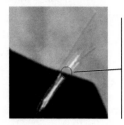

Clicking without dragging clones a 30-pixel area. Because the brush we chose has 50% hardness, the center (where the shoulder edge is) is clear, but the outside parts of the brush are feathered into the surrounding area.

Note:

If you're not happy with the result of a clone, simply undo the action (Command/Control-Z, or using the History panel) and try again. Cloning — especially edges — often takes more than one try to achieve the desired result.

12. **Move the cursor slightly to the left, again centering the cursor preview over the would-be edge, and click without dragging.**

With the Aligned Sample option turned off, you can click again to clone pixels from the same source.

13. **Repeat this process as necessary to clone out the remaining scratch along the man's shoulder.**

We clicked two more times to completely remove the scratch along the shoulder line.

14. **Choose the Lasso tool in the Tools panel. Draw a marquee around the scratches in the background, above the man's shoulder.**

Be careful to avoid the man's shoulder in the selection area.

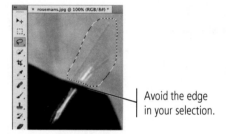

Avoid the edge in your selection.

15. **Choose Edit>Fill. Choose Content-Aware in the Use menu and click OK.**

Photoshop evaluates the image and determines what should be created inside the selection area. The fill might take a few seconds to process, so be patient.

16. **Choose Select>Deselect to turn off the selection marquee.**

Content-Aware Fill works very well on areas of subtle shading, such as the backdrop in this image, or other areas where you do not need to maintain fine detail or edges in the selected area. If you try to use this option on a sharp edge, however, the Content-Aware Fill results are unpredictable. Other tools, such as the Clone Stamp tool, work better for retouching distinct edges.

Note:

Press Command/Control-D to turn off a selection marquee.

17. **Use the same method as in Steps 14–15 to remove the scratches from the man's coat, and the scratches and glue residue on the left side of the photo.**

At the ends of the image, it's okay to drag outside the edge of the canvas; Photoshop identifies the edge and snaps the selection edge to the canvas edge.

18. **Choose File>Save As and choose TIFF in the Format menu. Change the file name to `rosemans_fixed.tif` and save it with the default TIFF options in your WIP>Menu folder.**

19. **Close the file and continue to the next stage of the project.**

The Clone Source Panel in Depth

The Clone Source panel (Window>Clone Source) allows you to store up to five sources for the Clone Stamp or Healing Brush tool. These sources can be from any layer of any open image, which allows you to create unique blended effects by combining pixels from multiple layers or multiple files.

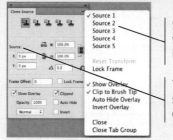

Store and access up to five sources from any layer of any open image.

Transform the offset, size, and angle of the clone source.

The Show Overlay options allow you to show (at the defined opacity) the source pixels on top of the area where you are cloning. For example, let's say you want to clone the gorilla into the giraffe photo. You would first define a clone source in the gorilla image, and then make the giraffe image active.

With the Show Overlay option checked, placing the Clone Stamp cursor over the giraffe image shows the gorilla on top of the giraffe. When you click in the giraffe image with the Clone Stamp tool, that area of the gorilla image will be cloned into the giraffe image; the overlay allows you to preview the areas of the source that will be cloned into the giraffe image.

If the Auto Hide option is checked, the overlay is only visible when the mouse button is not clicked. The Invert option reverses the overlay into a negative representation of the source image. You can also change the blending mode of the overlay from the default Normal to Darken, Lighten, or Difference.

We defined a clone source here.

Using the Show Overlay option, you can see the Clone Stamp cursor in relation to the clone source.

When the Clipped option is checked, the clone source appears only within the tool cursor area.

We turned off the Clipped option and reduced the opacity to 50% to show the entire source file over the image where the cloning is taking place.

Stage 2 Correcting Lighting Problems

Before you start correcting problems with lighting and color, you should understand the different parts of an image, as well as the terms used to describe these areas.

- **Highlights** are defined as the lightest areas of the image that include detail. Direct sources of light such as a light bulb or reflected sunlight on water are called **specular highlights**; they should not be considered the highlights of an image.

- **Shadows** are the darkest areas of the image that still contain some detail; areas of solid black are not considered shadow tones.

- The shades between the highlights and shadows are the **midtones** (or **gamma**) of the image.

Contrast and saturation play an integral role in reproducing high-quality images. **Contrast** refers to the tonal variation within an image; an image primarily composed of highlights and shadows is a high-contrast image, while an image with more detail in the midtones is a low-contrast image.

Contrast is closely linked to **saturation**, which refers to the intensity of a color or its variation away from gray. The saturation of individual colors in an image, and the correct saturation of different colors in relation to one another, affects the overall contrast of the image. If an image is under- or oversaturated, the contrast suffers — detail is lost and colors appear either muted or too bright.

Note:

Image adjustments can be applied directly to the image pixels or as non-destructive adjustment layers using the Adjustments panel. In this project, you edit the actual image pixels; you use the adjustment layer method in Project 6: Advertising Samples.

Correct Problems with Brightness/Contrast

Depending on the image, several tools are available for correcting problems related to images that are either too dark or too light. The most basic adjustment option — Brightness/Contrast — can fix images that need overall adjustment to brightness, contrast, or both. If an image requires more sophisticated adjustment, you should use one of the other adjustment options.

1. **Open the file buffalo.jpg from your WIP>Menu folder.**

   This image has an overall dark feel, probably caused by poor lighting or underexposure. The Brightness/Contrast adjustment can correct this problem.

2. **Choose Image>Adjustments>Brightness/Contrast and make sure the Preview option is checked.**

3. **Drag the Brightness slider to +35.**

   Increasing the overall brightness creates an immediate improvement in this image, although some areas of detail are still muddy.

4. Drag the Contrast slider to +10.

Increasing the contrast brings out more detail in the food texture, which is the focal point of the image (pay particular attention to the meat).

5. Click OK to apply the change.

6. Save the file in your WIP>Menu folder as a TIFF file named buffalo_fixed.tif using the default TIFF options.

7. Close the file and continue to the next exercise.

CORRECT CONTRAST AND TONAL RANGE WITH LEVELS

The **tonal range** of an image is the amount of variation between the lightest highlight and the darkest shadow in a particular image. A grayscale image can contain 256 possible shades of gray. Each channel of a color image can also contain 256 possible shades of gray. To achieve the best contrast in an image, the tonal range of the image should include as many levels of gray as are available.

While the Brightness/Contrast option is a good choice for making basic adjustments, the Levels adjustment is the best approach for enhancing image detail throughout the entire tonal range. Using Levels, adjusting contrast is a three-step process:

- Determine the image's highlight areas (the lightest areas that contain detail).

- Determine the image's shadow areas (the darkest areas that contain detail).

- Adjust the gamma (the contrast in midtones of an image) to determine the proportion of darker tones to lighter tones.

1. Open the file chef.jpg from the WIP>Menu folder.

2. **Display the Histogram panel (Window>Histogram), and then choose Expanded View from the panel Options menu.**

The Histogram panel can help you identify problems that need to be corrected. When you first display the panel, it probably appears in Compact view, which shows only the graphs for the individual color channels and the composite image.

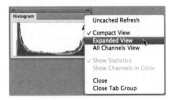

3. **In the Histogram panel, change the Channel menu to RGB.**

The histogram — the chart that shows the distribution of tones — can display a single graph for the entire composite image (all channels combined) or for individual channels.

In Expanded view, the panel shows the distribution of pixels from the darkest to the lightest portion of the image, for the entire image or for individual color channels.

If you see a warning icon, click it to reset the cache.

Choose from this menu to view and modify the histogram for individual channels.

These shadow values are pushing out of the histogram "container," which shows that there is a problem in the shadow tones.

The empty space at the left of the histogram indicates that some tones in the available range are not being used.

Histogram Statistics

The Histogram panel (Window>Histogram) shows the distribution of pixels — or more accurately the tonal values of those pixels — from the darkest to the lightest portions of an image, for the entire image or for individual color channels. The Histogram panel can help identify problems that need to be corrected. In Expanded view, you can see more information about how pixels are distributed in the image (from shadows on the left to highlights on the right).

- The **Mean** value is an average point of the brightness values. A Mean of 128 usually identifies a well-balanced image. Images with a Mean of 170 to 255 are light; images with a Mean lower than 90 are very dark.

- The **Standard Deviation** (Std Dev) value represents how widely the brightness values vary.

- The **Median** value shows the middle value in the range of color values.

- The **Pixels** value displays the total number of pixels used for the graphic displayed on the histogram.

- The **Level** statistic displays the intensity level of the pixels below the mouse cursor.

- **Count** shows the number of pixels in the area below the cursor.

- Values displayed as a **Percentile** represent the percentage of pixels **below or to the left** of the cursor location. Zero represents the left edge of the image and 100% is the right edge.

- The **Cache Level** is determined by the Performance preferences and is related to the Cache Refresh icon (and Warning icon). The larger your cache, the more you can do before the image and the disk cache don't match. On the other hand, a larger cache requires more RAM for the application to run smoothly.

4. If you see one, click the Warning icon in the upper-right corner of the Histogram panel to reset the cache.

Every time you zoom in or out of an image, Photoshop stores the results of the display in a **cache** (a drive location that keeps track of what you're doing). The image you're looking at on the histogram often doesn't match the results on the drive. The Warning icon shows there's a problem; clicking the icon resets the image and rereads the cache.

Note:

If you see the Warning icon in the Histogram panel, click the icon to match the disk cache with what's happening in the live image.

5. Choose Image>Adjustments>Levels and make sure Preview is checked.

The Levels dialog box shows a histogram like the one shown in the Histogram panel.

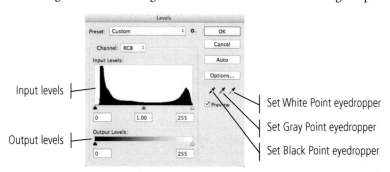

The Levels dialog box has two sets of sliders to control input levels and output levels. Each set has a black slider for adjusting the shadows in an image and a white slider to adjust highlights. The Input Levels slider also has a gray triangle in the center of the slider bar for adjusting gamma or midtones.

The Input sliders in the Levels dialog box correspond to the tonal range of the image. Any pixels that exist to the left of the Input Shadow slider are reproduced as solid black, and they have no detail; any pixels that exist to the right of the Input Highlight slider are reproduced as pure white.

Identifying Shadows and Highlights

PHOTOSHOP FOUNDATIONS

When you move the Shadow and Highlight sliders in the Levels dialog box, you change the **black point** and **white point** of the image — the points at which pixels become black or white. The goal is to find highlight and shadow points that maintain detail. Choosing a point that has no detail causes the area to turn totally white (highlight) or black (shadow) with no detail reproduced. In some images, it can be difficult to visually identify the black and white points in an image; in these cases you can use the Levels dialog box to help you find those areas.

If you press Option/Alt while dragging the Input Shadow or Input Highlight slider, the image turns entirely white or black (respectively). As you drag, the first pixels that become visible are the darkest shadow and the lightest highlight.

Once you identify the highlight and shadow points in the image, select the White Point eyedropper and click the highlight, and then select the Black Point eyedropper and click the shadow to define those two areas of the image.

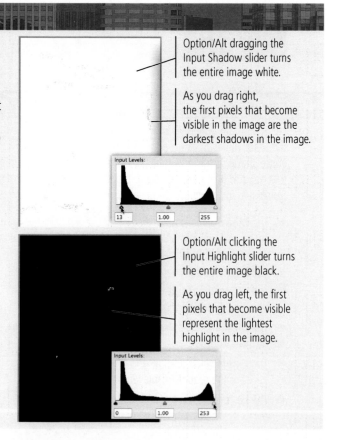

Option/Alt dragging the Input Shadow slider turns the entire image white.

As you drag right, the first pixels that become visible in the image are the darkest shadows in the image.

Option/Alt clicking the Input Highlight slider turns the entire image black.

As you drag left, the first pixels that become visible represent the lightest highlight in the image.

6. **Move the Input Shadow slider to the right until it touches the left edge of the curve.**

This simple adjustment extends the colors in the image to take advantage of all 256 possible tones. This adjustment has a small effect on the shadow area of the image, but the majority of the colors in the image are still clustered near the shadow point (as you can see by the spike in the histogram).

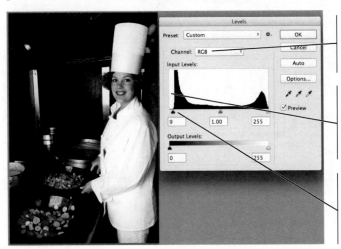

Choose from this menu to view and modify the histogram for an individual channel.

The white space at the left of the histogram indicates that some of the tones in the available range are not being used.

Dragging the Input Shadow slider to the left edge of the histogram extends the shadows into the full tonal range.

7. **Move the Input Gamma slider to the left until the middle box below the slider shows approximately 1.50.**

The Input Gamma slider controls the proportion of darker tones to lighter tones in the midtones of an image. If you increase gamma, you increase the proportion of lighter grays in the image; this effectively increases contrast in lighter shades and lightens the entire image. If you decrease gamma, you extend the tonal range of darker shades; this allows those areas of the image to be reproduced with a larger range of shades, which increases the contrast in darker shades.

Note:

You can change input and output levels by moving the sliders, entering actual values in the boxes below the slider sets, or by using the eyedroppers to select the brightest and darkest points in the image.

Dragging the Input Gamma slider extends the range between the midtone and the highlights, creating greater contrast and showing more detail throughout the image.

To decrease contrast in an image, you can adjust the Output sliders. This method effectively compresses the range of possible tones that can be reproduced, forcing all areas of the image into a smaller tonal range. Areas originally set to 0 are reproduced at the value of the Output Shadow slider; areas originally set to 255 are output at the value of the Output Highlight slider.

8. **Click OK to close the Levels dialog box.**

9. Save the file in your WIP>Menu folder as a TIFF file named `chef_fixed.tif`.

10. Close the file and then continue to the next exercise.

The Gradient Map Adjustment

The **Gradient Map adjustment** (Image>Adjustments>Gradient Map) enables you to create interesting artistic effects by mapping the tones of an image to the shades in a defined gradient.

In the Gradient Map dialog box, you can apply any defined gradient by clicking the arrow to the right of the gradient sample and choosing from the pop-up menu, or you can edit the selected gradient by clicking the sample gradient ramp. The **Dither** option adds random noise to the effect. If you check the **Reverse** option, image highlights map to the left end of the gradient, and image shadows map to the right end of the gradient, effectively reversing the gradient map.

The composite histogram of an RGB image starts at the darkest point and ends at the lightest point with 256 total possible tonal values. If you think of the gradient as having 256 steps from one end to the other, then you can see how the shades of the selected gradient map to the tones of the original image.

CORRECT LIGHTING PROBLEMS WITH THE EXPOSURE ADJUSTMENT

Many images are either over- or underexposed when photographed. If an image is under-exposed, it appears dark and lacks detail in the shadows. If an image is overexposed, it appears too light and lacks detail in the highlights. You can use the Exposure adjustment to correct exposure — and thus, the overall detail and contrast in the image.

Keep in mind, however, that Photoshop cannot create information that doesn't exist. If you have an underexposed image with no detail in the shadow areas, Photoshop cannot generate that detail for you. Some problems are simply beyond fixing.

The Exposure dialog box is designed to make tonal adjustments to 32- and 64-bit HDR (high dynamic range) images, but it also works with 8-bit and 16-bit images. The Exposure adjustment works by performing calculations in a linear color space (gamma 1.0) rather than the image's current color space.

Note:

HDR refers to high-density range (32- or 64-bit) images.

1. **Open chicken.jpg from your WIP>Menu folder.**

2. **Choose Image>Adjustments>Exposure and make sure Preview is checked.**

White Point eyedropper
Gray Point eyedropper
Black Point eyedropper

3. **Click the White Point eyedropper, and then click the white area on the top edge of the plate.**

The eyedroppers in the Exposure dialog box adjust the image's luminance (or the degree of lightness, from white to black). By adjusting the luminance only, you can change the lightness of the image without affecting the color.

Note:

The White Point and Gray Point eyedroppers affect the Exposure value. The Black Point eyedropper affects the Offset value.

- Clicking with the Black Point eyedropper shifts the point you click to black (0 luminance).

- Clicking with the White Point eyedropper shifts the point you click to white (100 luminance).

- Clicking with the Gray Point eyedropper shifts the point you click to gray (50 luminance).

Click here with the White Point eyedropper to define the white area of the image.

Clicking with the White Point eyedropper changes the Exposure setting.

4. **Drag the Gamma Correction slider left to extend the midtone range, which increases contrast and brings out detail in the image. (We used a setting of 1.25.)**

The Gamma slider adjusts the image midtones. Dragging the slider left lightens the image, improving contrast and detail in the midtones and highlights. Dragging the slider right darkens the image, extending the range and increasing detail in the shadows.

Extending the Gamma Correction value into the shadow range brings out more detail in the midtones.

5. **Click the Offset slider and drag very slightly left to add detail back into the midtones and shadows.**

The Offset slider lightens (dragged to the right) or darkens (dragged to the left) the shadows and midtones of the image. The white point (highlight) remains unaffected, but all other pixels are affected.

Decreasing the Offset value adds detail back into the shadows.

6. **Click OK to finalize the adjustment.**

7. **Save the file as a TIFF file named `chicken_fixed.tif` in your WIP>Menu folder.**

8. **Close the file and continue to the next stage of the project.**

Stage 3   Correcting Color Problems

You can't accurately reproduce color without a basic understanding of color theory, so we present a very basic introduction in this project. Be aware that there are entire, weighty books written about color science; we're providing the condensed version of what you absolutely must know to work effectively with files in any color mode.

Before starting to color-correct an image, you should understand how different colors interact with one another. There are two primary color models — RGB and CMYK — used to output digital images. (Other models such as LAB and HSB have their own purposes in color conversion and correction, but they are not typically output models.)

Additive vs. Subtractive Color

The most important thing to remember about color theory is that color is light, and light is color. You can easily prove this by walking through your house at midnight; you will notice that what little you can see appears as dark shadows. Without light, you can't see — and without light, there is no color.

The **additive color** model (RGB) is based on the idea that all colors can be reproduced by combining pure red, green, and blue light in varying intensities. These three colors are considered the **additive primaries**. Combining any two additive primaries at full strength produces one of

the **additive secondaries** — red and blue light combine to produce magenta, red and green combine to produce yellow, and blue and green combine to produce cyan. Although usually considered a "color," black is the absence of light (and, therefore, of color). White is the sum of all colors, produced when all three additive primaries are combined at full strength.

Reproducing color on paper requires **subtractive color theory**, which is essentially the inverse of additive color. Instead of adding red, green, and blue light to create the range of colors, subtractive color begins with a white surface that reflects red, green, and blue light at equal and full strength. To reflect (reproduce) a specific color, you add pigments that subtract or absorb only certain wavelengths from the white light. To reflect only red, for example, the surface must subtract (or absorb) the green and blue light.

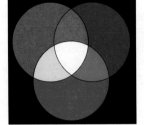 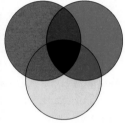

Additive color model   Subtractive color model

Remember that the additive primary colors (red, green, and blue) combine to create the additive secondaries (cyan, magenta, and yellow). Those additive secondaries are also called the **subtractive primaries**, because each subtracts one-third of the light spectrum and reflects the other two-thirds:

- Cyan absorbs red light, reflecting only blue and green light.

- Magenta absorbs green light, reflecting only red and blue light.

- Yellow absorbs blue light, reflecting only red and green light.

A combination of two subtractive primaries, then, absorbs two-thirds of the light spectrum and reflects only one-third. As an example, a combination of yellow and magenta absorbs both blue and green light, reflecting only red.

Color printing is a practical application of subtractive color theory. The pigments in the cyan, magenta, yellow, and black (CMYK) inks are combined to absorb different wavelengths of light. By combining different amounts of the subtractive primaries, it's possible to produce a large range (or gamut) of colors.

Note:

Additive color theory is practically applied when a reproduction method uses light to reproduce color. A computer monitor is black when turned off. When the power is turned on, light in the monitor illuminates at different intensities to create the range of colors you see.

Although the RGB and CMYK models handle color in different ways, these two color models are definitely linked. RGB colors are directly inverse (opposite) to CMY colors, referring to the position of each color on a color wheel. The relationship between primary colors is the basis for all color correction.

Referencing a basic color wheel can help you understand how RGB colors relate to CMY colors. If you center an equilateral triangle over the color wheel, the points of the triangle touch either the RGB primaries or the CMY primaries. Adding together two points of the triangle results in the color between the two points. Red and blue combine to form magenta, yellow and cyan combine to form green, and so on.

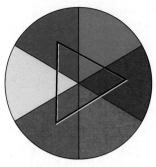

Note:

Because white is a combination of all colors of light, white paper should theoretically reflect equal percentages of all light wavelengths. However, different papers absorb or reflect varying percentages of some wavelengths, thus defining the paper's apparent color. The paper's color affects the appearance of inks printed on that paper.

Opposite colors on the color wheel are called **color complements**. Using subtractive color theory, a color's complement absorbs or subtracts that color from visible white light. For example, cyan is opposite red on the color wheel; cyan absorbs red light and reflects green and blue. If you know green and blue light combine to create cyan, you can begin to understand how the two theories are related.

How does all this apply to color correction?

If you want to add a specific color to an image, you have three options: add the color, add equal parts of its constituent colors, or remove some of its complement color. For example, to add red to an image, you can add red, add yellow and magenta, or remove cyan. Conversely, this means that to remove a color from an image, you can remove the color itself, remove equal parts of its constituents, or add its complement. To remove cyan from an image, for example, you can remove cyan, remove blue and green, or add red.

Make sure you understand the relationships between complementary colors:

- To add red, add yellow and magenta or remove cyan.
- To add blue, add cyan and magenta or remove yellow.
- To add green, add cyan and yellow or remove magenta.
- To remove cyan, remove blue and green or add red.
- To remove yellow, remove green and red or add blue.
- To remove magenta, remove blue and red or add green.

Note:

It might seem easiest to simply add or subtract the color in question, but a better result might be achieved by adding one color and subtracting another. For example, if an image needs less blue, simply removing cyan can cause reds to appear pink or cyan to appear green. Adding magenta and yellow to balance the existing cyan creates a better result than simply removing cyan.

Understanding Gray Balance

Understanding the concept of neutral gray is also fundamental to effective color correction. Once you correct the contrast (tonal range) of an image, many of the remaining problems can be at least partially (if not entirely) corrected by correcting the **gray balance**, or the component elements of neutral grays within an image.

In the RGB color model, equal parts of red, green, and blue light combine to create a shade of gray that is equal to the percentage of each component — R=0 G=0 B=0 creates pure black, while R=255 G=255 B=255 creates pure white. To correct an image in RGB mode, you should evaluate and correct the neutral grays so that they contain equal percentages of the three primary colors.

Using the CMYK color model, equal percentages of cyan, magenta, and yellow theoretically combine to produce an equal shade of gray — C=0 M=0 Y=0 creates pure white, while C=100 M=100 Y=100 theoretically creates pure black. In practice,

Note:

An important point to remember is that any color correction requires compromise. If you add or remove a color to correct a certain area, you also affect other areas of the image.

however, the impurities of ink pigments — specifically cyan — do not live up to this theory. When you print an area of equal parts cyan, magenta, and yellow, the result is a muddy brown because the cyan pigments are impure. To compensate for the impurities of cyan, neutral grays must be adjusted to contain equal parts of magenta and yellow, and a slightly higher percentage of cyan.

CORRECT COLOR CAST WITH THE COLOR BALANCE ADJUSTMENT

Color cast is the result of improper gray balance, when one channel is significantly stronger or weaker than the others. An image with improper gray balance has an overall predominance of one color, which is most visible in the highlight areas. The image that you will correct in this exercise has a strong green cast that needs to be removed.

1. **Open the file salmon.jpg from your WIP>Menu folder.**

2. **Display the Info panel (Window>Info).**

3. **If you don't see both RGB and CMYK color modes in the Info panel, choose Panel Options in the Info panel Options menu. In the resulting dialog box, choose Actual Color for the First Color Readout and CMYK Color for the Second Color Readout, then click OK.**

Note:

This exercise relies purely on numbers to correct gray balance. To see an accurate preview of image color on screen, you should calibrate your monitor and create a monitor profile that you can load into Photoshop.

4. **Choose the Color Sampler tool (nested under the Eyedropper tool).**

5. **In the Options bar, choose 3 by 3 Average in the Sample Size menu.**

   Instead of correcting based on individual pixel values, you can average a group of contiguous pixels as the sample value. Doing so prevents accidentally correcting an image based on a single anomalous pixel (a dust spot, for example).

Use this menu to define the sample size.

Color Sampler tool

Color Sampler tool cursor

The Info panel shows color values for the current cursor location, in both RGB and CMYK modes.

6. **Click the cursor on the lower-left plate lip to place a color sample.**

7. **Click to add a second sample point to the top-right plate lip.**

    The two samples show a strong predominance of green; the numbers in the Info panel reflect the visible color cast in the image.

Sample points are numbered in order of creation.

This is the color sample that we placed in Step 6.

The Info panel shows the values associated with each of the sample points you created.

8. **Choose Image>Adjustments>Color Balance.**

    Color Balance is a basic correction tool that can effectively remove overall color cast. The Color Balance dialog box presents a separate slider for each pair of complementary colors. You can adjust the highlights, shadows, or midtones of an image by selecting the appropriate radio button; the Preserve Luminosity check box ensures that only the colors shift, leaving the tonal balance of the image unchanged.

9. **Click the Highlights radio button in the Tone Balance section at the bottom of the Color Balance dialog box.**

    The focal point of this image is green spinach, which you don't want to affect. Instead, you need to remove the green cast from the highlight, where it is most obvious.

10. **Drag the Magenta/Green slider left until the middle field shows –10.**

    Remember, adding a color's complement is one method for neutralizing that color. Increasing magenta in the highlight areas neutralizes the green color cast.

Note:

The Color Sampler tool can place up to ten sample points per image.

Note:

To delete an existing sample point, make the Color Sampler tool active, press Option/Alt, and click a point when the cursor icon changes to a pair of scissors.

The values after the "/" show the result of the changes; these will become the actual sample values if you click OK.

Changing the color balance brings the three values much closer to equal (called "in balance").

These fields correspond to the three color sliders. The middle field shows the Magenta/Green adjustment.

11. **Click OK to apply the adjustment.**

12. **Save the file in your WIP>Menu folder as a TIFF file named salmon_fixed.tif.**

13. **Close the file and continue to the next exercise.**

CORRECT GRAY BALANCE WITH CURVES

The Curves adjustment is the most powerful color-correction tool in Photoshop. If you understand the ideas behind curves, you can use this tool to remove color cast, enhance overall contrast, and even modify color values in individual channels.

The diagram in the Curves dialog box is the heart of the Curves adjustment. When you open the Curves dialog box, a straight diagonal line in the graph represents the existing color in the image.

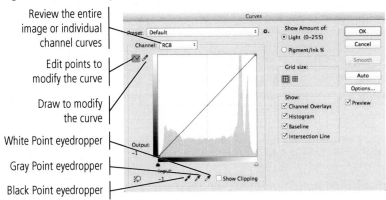

Review the entire image or individual channel curves

Edit points to modify the curve

Draw to modify the curve

White Point eyedropper

Gray Point eyedropper

Black Point eyedropper

The horizontal axis represents the input color value, and the vertical axis represents the output color value. The upper-right point is the maximum value for that color mode (255 for RGB images and 100 for CMYK images). The bottom-left corner of the curves grid is the zero point.

The color mode of the image determines the direction of the input and output scales. In both CMYK and RGB, 0 means "none of that color." However, remember the difference between the two different color modes:

- The additive RGB color model starts at black and adds values of each channel to produce different colors, so 0, 0, 0 in RGB equals black.

- The subtractive CMYK model starts with white (paper) and adds percentages of each ink (channel) to produce different colors, so 0, 0, 0, 0 in CMYK equals white.

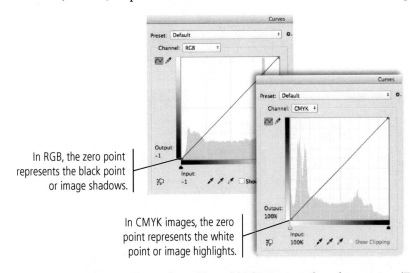

In RGB, the zero point represents the black point or image shadows.

In CMYK images, the zero point represents the white point or image highlights.

Note:

Remember, the additive colors (RGB) at full strength combine to create pure white, while the subtractive colors (CMYK) at full strength combine to create pure black.

Every curve is automatically anchored by a black point and a white point. (For RGB, the black point is at the bottom left and the white point is at the top right.) You can add points along the curve by simply clicking the curve. You can also move any point on the curve by clicking and dragging.

When you move points on the curve of an image (whether for the whole image or for an individual channel), you are telling Photoshop to, "Map every pixel that was [this] input value to [that] output value." In other words, using the following image as an example, a pixel that was 128 (the input value) will now be 120 (the output value). Because curves are just that — curves, and not individual points — adjusting one point on a curve changes the shape of the curve as necessary.

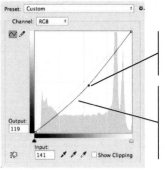

This point changes the input value of 141 to an output value of 119.

On either side of the adjusted point, the curve is adjusted to smoothly meet the other points on the curve (in this case, the black and white points).

1. **Open the file flan.jpg from the WIP>Menu folder.**

2. **Using the Color Sampler tool, place a sample point on the left plate lip.**

   This image has a strong red cast that needs to be neutralized. You can correct cast by removing the cast color or adding the other two primaries; the goal is equal (or nearly equal) parts of red, green, and blue in the neutral areas such as the plate lip.

   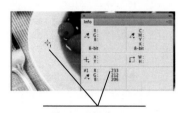

   In the Info panel, the sample values show that the red channel has a value of 233, the green channel has a value of 212, and the blue channel has a value of 206. To fix the cast in this image, you will use the middle of these values (the green channel) as the target and adjust the other two curves.

   The sample shows a strong red cast in what should be neutral areas.

3. **Choose Image>Adjustments>Curves and make sure the Preview option is checked in the Curves dialog box.**

4. **Choose Red in the Channel menu to display the curve for only the Red channel, and then click the line on the graph to place a point near the three-quarter grid intersection.**

Click here to add a point to the curve.

Numbers before the slash are the original values. Numbers after the slash are the values that result from your changes in the Curves dialog box.

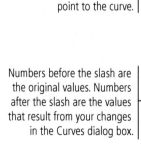

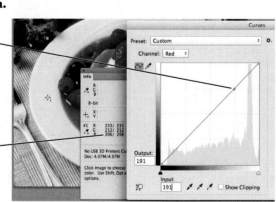

5. **With the new point selected on the curve, type the original Red value in the Input field (ours is 233).**

6. **Type the target value in the Output field (ours is the Green value of 212).**

The number after the slash shows that the Red value for this sample will be equal to the Green value when you click OK.

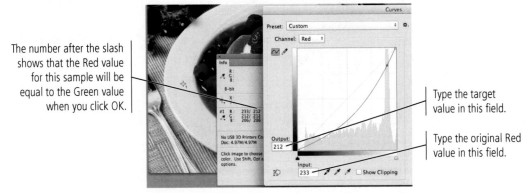

Type the target value in this field.

Type the original Red value in this field.

7. **In the Channel menu, choose the other channel that you need to adjust based on your sample values (ours is Blue). Add a point to the curve, and then adjust the input value to match your target output value (the original Green value, in our example). Using our sample point, we adjusted the 206 Input value to a 212 Output value.**

You can add the point anywhere along the curve; when you change the Input and Output values, the point automatically moves to that location along the curve.

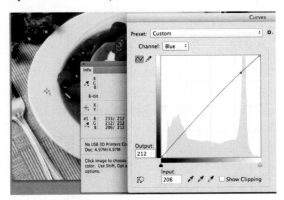

8. **Click OK to apply the changes and close the Curves dialog box.**

You can see how simply correcting gray balance has a significant impact on the image:

9. **Save the file in your WIP>Menu folder as a TIFF file named** flan_fixed.tif.

10. **Close the file and continue to the next exercise.**

The On-Image Adjustment tool in the Curves dialog box allows you to make curve adjustments by interacting directly with the image (behind the dialog box).

When the On-Image Adjustment tool is active, clicking in the image places a point on the curve based on the pixel data where you clicked; you can then drag up or down within the image area to move that point of the curve (in other words, to change the output value of the selected input value).

You can add 14 points on a curve, and delete points by pressing Command/Control-delete.

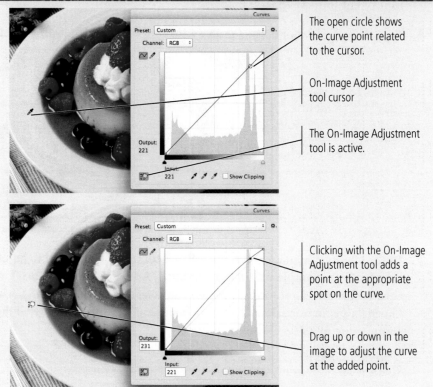

The open circle shows the curve point related to the cursor.

On-Image Adjustment tool cursor

The On-Image Adjustment tool is active.

Clicking with the On-Image Adjustment tool adds a point at the appropriate spot on the curve.

Drag up or down in the image to adjust the curve at the added point.

CORRECT CONTRAST WITH CURVES

Remember, contrast is essentially the difference between the values in an image. By adjusting the points on the curve, you increase the tonal range between those points — which means you also increase the contrast in that same range.

In the following image, Point A has an Input value of 167 and an Output value of 182. Point B has an Input value of 87 and an Output value of 62. Mathematically:

- Original tonal range (Input values): 167 to 87 = 80 available tones

- New tonal range (Output values): 182 to 62 = 120 available tones

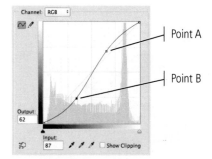

Point A

Point B

By making these two curve adjustments, we significantly increased the tonal range available for the image's midtones, which means we also significantly increased the contrast in the midtones. A steeper curve indicates increased tonal range and increased contrast. Notice, however, that the curves before Point B and after Point A are much shallower than the original curves, which means this change also significantly reduces the contrast in the shadow and highlight areas.

Points to Remember about Curves

Curves are very powerful tools, and they can be intimidating. To simplify the process and make it less daunting, keep these points in mind:

- Aim for neutral grays.
- You can adjust the curve for an entire image, or you can adjust the individual curves for each channel of the image.
- The horizontal tone scale shows the Input value, and the vertical tone scale shows the Output value.
- Changes made to one area of a curve affect all other areas of the image.
- The steeper the curve, the greater the contrast.
- Increasing contrast in one area inherently decreases contrast in other areas.

Understanding Curve Display Options

PHOTOSHOP FOUNDATIONS

Options on the right side of the dialog box allow you to control what is visible in the graph.

The Show Amount Of radio buttons reverse the input and output tone scales. Light is the default setting for RGB images; Pigment/Ink % is the default setting for CMYK images.

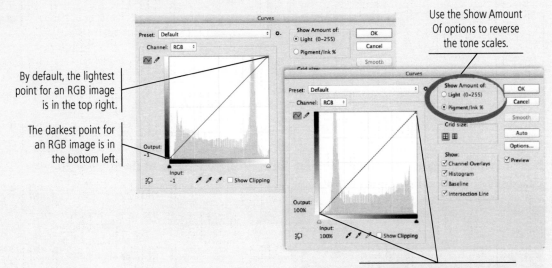

By default, the lightest point for an RGB image is in the top right.

The darkest point for an RGB image is in the bottom left.

Use the Show Amount Of options to reverse the tone scales.

For an RGB image, the lightest point moves to the bottom left and the darkest point moves to the top right.

The Show options determine what is visible in the actual graph:

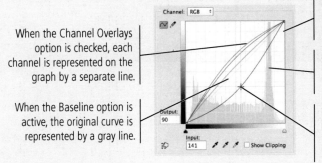

When the Channel Overlays option is checked, each channel is represented on the graph by a separate line.

When the Baseline option is active, the original curve is represented by a gray line.

Use the Grid Size options to show the grid in quartertone or 10% increments.

When the Histogram option is active, the image's tonal range is represented behind the graph.

When the Intersection Line option is active, crosshairs appear when you drag a point in the graph, which can help you more precisely adjust curve points.

1. **Open the file pasta.jpg from the WIP>Menu folder.**

2. **Choose Image>Adjustments>Curves and make sure Preview is checked.**

3. **Activate the Show Clipping option, click the black point on the bottom-left corner of the graph, and then drag until some pixels start to appear in the image (behind the dialog box).**

   We dragged the Input Black point just past the point where the histogram shows the darkest shadows in the image. (You performed this same action in the Levels dialog box when you adjusted the Input Shadow slider.) The Input and Output fields show that any pixels with an Input value of 14 will be output as 0; in other words, anything with an Input value lower than 14 will be clipped to solid black.

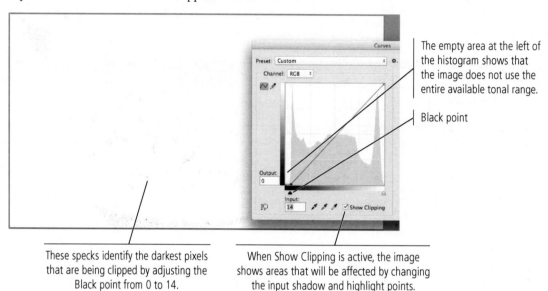

The empty area at the left of the histogram shows that the image does not use the entire available tonal range.

Black point

These specks identify the darkest pixels that are being clipped by adjusting the Black point from 0 to 14.

When Show Clipping is active, the image shows areas that will be affected by changing the input shadow and highlight points.

4. **Repeat Step 3, dragging the White point left until the lightest areas of the image start to appear behind the dialog box.**

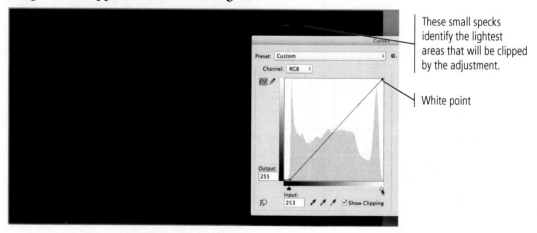

These small specks identify the lightest areas that will be clipped by the adjustment.

White point

5. **Turn off the Show Clipping option so you can see the actual image behind the dialog box.**

Even this small change improved the image, but the midtones — especially in the pasta, which is the focal area of the image — need some additional contrast. To accomplish that change, you need to steepen the curve in the middle of the graph.

Note:

Contrast adjustments can have a major impact on color as well as on sharpness. Take particular note of the green basil leaves; no direct color adjustment was done to these two images, but the leaves are noticeably greener and brighter after you adjust the curves.

6. **Click the curve to create a point at the quartertone gridline and drag it slightly to the right.**

We adjusted the curve point from an Input value of 81 to an Output value of 62.

Three-quartertone gridlines

Quartertone gridlines

7. **Click the curve at the three-quartertone gridline and drag the point to the left.**

We adjusted the 180 Input value to a 190 Output value.

The adjusted points steepen the curve, increasing contrast between the two points.

8. **Click OK to apply the changes and close the dialog box.**

   Adjusting the contrast with curves improved the detail in the image and enhanced the overall image color.

9. **Save the file in your WIP>Menu folder as a TIFF file named `pasta_fixed.tif`.**

10. **Close the file and continue to the next stage of the project.**

Automatic Color Correction

Clicking Options in the right side of the Curves dialog box opens the Auto Color Correction Options dialog box. These settings will apply if you click the Auto button in the Levels or Curves dialog box, or if you choose one of the automatic adjustments in the Image>Adjustments menu (Auto Tone, Auto Contrast, or Auto Color). The Algorithms options determine how Photoshop will adjust the image's tonal range.

- **Enhance Monochromatic Contrast** is applied if you choose Auto Contrast. This option clips all channels identically, preserving overall color while making highlights appear lighter and shadows darker.

- **Enhance Per Channel Contrast** is applied if you choose Auto Levels. This option maximizes the tonal range in each channel by moving the darkest shadow to 0 (or 100 for CMYK images) and the lightest highlight to 255 (or 0 for CMYK images). The overall color relationship is not maintained, which might result in color cast in the adjusted image.

- **Find Dark & Light Colors** is applied if you choose Auto Color. This option uses the average lightest and darkest pixels to maximize contrast and minimize clipping. **Snap Neutral Midtones** also relates to the Auto Color adjustment; this option finds an average neutral color in an image, and then adjusts midtone (gamma) values to make that color neutral.

- **Enhance Brightness and Contrast** allows Photoshop to use content-aware monochromatic adjustments to produce smoother results across the entire tonal range.

In the **Target Colors & Clipping** options, you can define the target shadow, midtone, and highlight values by clicking the appropriate color swatch. The Clip fields determine how much of the darkest shadow and lightest highlight will be clipped when you apply an automatic adjustment. In other words, a Shadow Clip setting of 1% means Photoshop will ignore the first 1% of the darkest pixels when adjusting the image. If you change the Target Colors & Clipping settings, you can check the Save As Defaults option; you can then apply those settings by clicking the Auto button in the Levels or Curves dialog box.

The Match Color Adjustment

The Match Color adjustment (Image>Adjustments>Match Color) allows you to match colors between multiple RGB images, layers, or selections. In the Match Color dialog box, the Target shows the image, layer, or selection you are modifying. The changes are based on values from the source image and layer selected in the Image Statistics area. You can change the luminance or color intensity of the target image, fade the adjustment, and neutralize color cast caused by the adjustment.

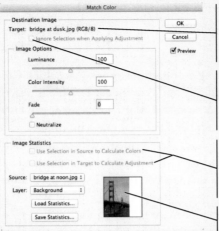

The Destination Image Target is the active image (and selected layer, if applicable) when you open the dialog box.

If the target image has an active selection area, click this check box to apply the change to the entire target image instead of the selected area only.

If the target or source image has an active selection area, click these check boxes to apply changes based on the selected area only.

Choose the source image and layer to which the target will be matched.

- The **Luminance** slider affects the brightness in the target image; higher values lighten the image.
- The **Color Intensity** slider adjusts the color saturation in the target image; higher values increase the color saturation.
- The **Fade** slider changes the amount of adjustment applied to the target image; higher values (i.e., more fade) reduce the amount of the adjustment.
- The **Neutralize** check box automatically removes color cast in the target image.

Stage 4   Preparing Images for Print

You might have noticed that all the images for this project are in the RGB color mode. Printing, however, relies on the CMYK mode to output color images.

Although a full discussion of color science and management can be extremely complex, and is beyond the needs of most graphic designers, applying color management in Photoshop is more intimidating than difficult. We believe this foundational information on color management will make you a more effective and practically grounded designer.

Color Management in Brief

Remember, different color models have different ranges or **gamuts** of possible colors. **Color management** is intended to preserve color predictability and consistency as a file is moved from one color mode to another throughout the reproduction process. Color management can also eliminate ambiguity when a color is only specified by some numbers. For example, you might create a royal purple in the Photoshop Color Picker; but without color management, that same set of RGB numbers might look more lilac (or even gray) when converted to CMYK for printing. A well-tuned color-management system can translate the numbers that define a color in one space to numbers that can better represent that same color in another space.

It's important to have realistic expectations for color management, and to realize that color management isn't a replacement for a thorough knowledge of the color-reproduction process. Even at its best, color management can't fix bad scans or bad photos — all it can do is introduce consistency and predictability to a process that otherwise rarely has either.

Color management relies on **color profiles**, which are simply data sets that define the reproduction characteristics of a specific device. A profile is essentially a recipe that contains the ingredients for reproducing a specific color in a given color space. The color recipes in profiles are known as **look-up tables** (LUTs), which are essentially cross-reference systems for finding matching color values in different color spaces.

Source profiles are the profiles of the devices (scanner, camera, or monitor in the case of original digital artwork) used to capture or generate the image. **Destination profiles** are the profiles of output devices used in the process. Most professional-level devices come with profiles you can install when you install the hardware; a number of generic and industry-specific destination profiles are also built into Photoshop.

> **Note:**
>
> *Color profiles are sometimes also called "ICC profiles," named after the International Color Consortium (ICC), which developed the standard for creating color profiles.*

Understanding Color Modes

Bitmap color reproduces all pixels in the image as either black or white; there are no shades of gray.

Grayscale color reproduces all tones in the file as shades of gray. This type of image has only one channel (you were introduced to color channels in Project 4: Composite Movie Ad, and will learn more in subsequent projects).

RGB creates color by combining different intensities of red, green, and blue light (collectively referred to as the "additive primaries"). Computer monitors and television sets display color in RGB, which has a **gamut** or range of more than 16.7 million different colors. An RGB file has three color channels, one for each of the additive primaries.

LAB color is device independent; the colors it describes don't depend upon the characteristics of a particular printer, monitor, or scanner. In theory, LAB bridges the gap between the various color models and devices; it is used in the background when converting images from one color space to another.

CMYK ("process") **color** is based on the absorption and reflection of light. Four process inks — cyan, magenta, yellow, and black — are used in varying combinations and percentages to produce the range of printable colors in most commercial printing. A CMYK file has four color channels, one for each subtractive primary and one for black.

Theoretically, a mixture of equal parts of cyan, magenta, and yellow would produce black. Pigments, however, are not pure, so the result of mixing these colors is a muddy brown (called **hue error**). To obtain vibrant colors (and so elements such as type can be printed cleanly), black ink is added to the three primaries. Black is represented by the letter "K" for "key color."

The problem with using RGB for print jobs is that the RGB colors eventually need to be converted to CMYK separations for a commercial printing press. Photoshop includes sophisticated tools that allow you to control this conversion.

LAB (or L*a*b*, or CIELAB) is a theoretical color space that represents the full visible spectrum. This device-independent color space can represent any possible color. By moving device-dependent RGB and CMYK colors into LAB as an intermediary space, you can convert color from any one space to any other space.

The **Color Management Module** (CMM) is the engine that drives color conversions via the LUT numbers. The engine doesn't do much other than look up numbers and cross-reference them to another set of numbers. The mechanics of color-managed conversions are quite simple. Regardless of the specific input and output spaces in use, the same basic process is followed for every pixel:

1. The CMM looks up the color values of a pixel in the input-space profile to find a matching set of LAB values.

2. The CMM looks up the LAB values in the output-space profile to find the matching set of values that will display the color of that pixel most accurately.

Your client's menu will be printed, which means the image files ultimately have to be in the CMYK color mode. In this stage of the project, you will learn how to control and correct for the conversion process from RGB to CMYK — a very common process in professional graphic design. (In a professional environment, you would actually have to convert all of the images you have used in this project; we are only working with one for the sake of illustration.)

Color Management in Theory and Practice

PHOTOSHOP FOUNDATIONS

RGB and CMYK are very different entities. The two color models have distinct capabilities, advantages, and limitations. There is no way to exactly reproduce RGB color using the CMYK gamut because many of the colors in the RGB gamut are simply too bright or too saturated. Rather than claiming to produce an exact (impossible) match from your monitor to a printed page, the true goal of color management is to produce the best possible representation of the color using the gamut of the chosen output device.

A theoretically ideal color-managed workflow resembles the following:

- Image-capture devices (scanners and digital cameras) are profiled to create a look-up table that defines the device's color-capturing characteristics.

- Images are acquired using a calibrated, profiled device. The profile of the capturing device is tagged to every image captured.

- The image is opened in Photoshop and viewed on a calibrated monitor. The monitor's profile is defined in Photoshop as your working space.

- Photoshop translates the image profile to your working space profile.

- You define a destination (CMYK) profile for the calibrated output device that will be used for your final job.

- The image is converted from RGB to CMYK, based on the defined working space and destination profiles.

Notice that three of the "ideal workflow" steps mention a form of the word "calibrate." To **calibrate** something means to check and correct a device's characteristics. Calibration is an essential element in a color-managed workflow; it is fundamentally important to achieving consistent and predictable output.

You cannot check or correct the color characteristics of a device without having something to compare the device against. To calibrate a device, a known target — usually a sequence of distinct and varying color patches — is reproduced using the device. The color values of the reproduction are measured and compared to the values of the known target. Precise calibration requires adjusting the device until the reproduction matches the original.

As long as your devices are accurately calibrated to the same target values, the color acquired by your RGB scanner will exactly match the colors displayed on your RGB monitor and the colors printed by your desktop printer. Of course, most devices (especially consumer-level desktop devices that are gaining a larger market share in the commercial graphics world) are not accurately calibrated, and very few are calibrated to the same set of known target values.

Keeping in mind these ideals and realities, the true goals of color management are to:

- Compensate for variations in the different devices

- Accurately translate one color space to another

- Compensate for limitations in the output process

- Better predict the result when an image is reproduced

DEFINE COLOR SETTINGS

Photoshop's color management system allows you to set up a fully managed color workflow — from input device through output device. You can use Adobe's predefined color settings or create custom settings that pertain to the equipment you use.

1. **With no file open in Photoshop, choose Edit>Color Settings.**

   The Color Settings dialog box defines default working spaces for RGB, CMYK, gray, and spot colors, as well as general color management policies.

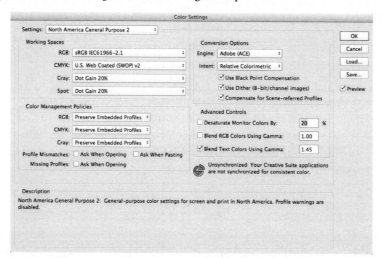

Note:

Your default options might be different than what you see here, depending on what previous users have defined.

2. **Choose North America Prepress 2 in the Settings menu.**

   Photoshop includes four saved groups of options that are common in North America, which can be accessed in the Settings menu. You can also make your own choices and save those settings as a new preset by clicking Save, or you can import settings files created by another user by clicking Load.

Note:

*In Photoshop, a **working space** is the default profile used for each of the different color modes.*

3. **In the Working Spaces area, choose the RGB profile for your monitor. If your specific monitor isn't available, choose Adobe RGB (1998).**

   If you use a color-managed workflow, each color mode must be defined as a particular type of color space. Because there are different types of monitors, there are different types of RGB color spaces; the same is true of the other color spaces. The Working Space menus define exactly which version of each space is used to define color within that space.

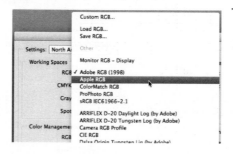

Note:

When you choose a profile that isn't part of the saved settings, the Settings menu automatically changes to "Custom."

Note:

If you convert an image's color space using the Image>Mode menu, Photoshop converts the image to the default working space for the mode you choose.

For color management to work properly, you must have accurate, device-specific profiles for every device in the workflow. However, you can use generic settings such as Adobe RGB (1998) in a "better-than-nothing" color environment — which is almost a direct contradiction to the concept of color management. We're showing you *how* to use the tools in Photoshop, but it's up to you to implement true color management by profiling your devices and using those profiles for specific jobs.

4. In the CMYK menu, choose U.S. Sheetfed Coated v2.

There are many CMYK profiles — each different printer and press has a gamut unique to that individual device.

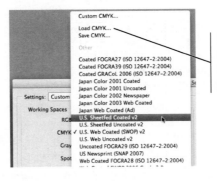

Use the Load CMYK option to access profiles that are supplied by your output provider.

This is a United States industry-standard profile for a common type of printing (sheetfed printing on coated paper). In a truly color-managed workflow, you would actually use a profile for the specific printing press/paper combination being used for the job. Again, we're using the default profiles to show you how the process works.

5. Leave the Gray and Spot working space menus at their default settings.

The Gray working space defines how grayscale images will translate when the images are printed. Gray working space options include:

- **Dot Gain** (of varying percentages). These options compensate for the spread of a halftone dot in a grayscale image.

- **Gray Gamma.** This option allows you to set the monitor's gamma to compensate for differences between the monitor's presentation of an image and the actual grayscale image on press.

The Spot working space is similar to the Gray working space, but you can only specify dot gain percentages (not gamma).

6. In the Color Management Policies area, make sure RGB is turned off; Preserve Embedded Profiles is selected for CMYK and Gray; and all three check boxes are selected.

These options tell Photoshop what to do when you open an existing image. When an option here is turned off, color is not managed for that mode. If you choose Preserve Embedded Profiles, images that have a defined profile retain that

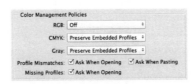

profile; images with no profile use the current working space. If you choose Convert to Working Space, all images, even those with an embedded profile, are converted to the current working profile; images with no profile are assigned the current working profile.

For profile mismatches, you can display a warning when opening or pasting an image with an embedded profile that does not match the working profile. When an image doesn't have an embedded profile, you can display a warning by checking the Missing Profiles Ask When Opening option.

7. **Review the options in the right side of the dialog box.**

Engine determines the system and color-matching method used to convert between color spaces – **Adobe (ACE)** or Adobe Color Engine; **Apple CMM** (Macintosh only); or **Microsoft ICM** (Windows only).

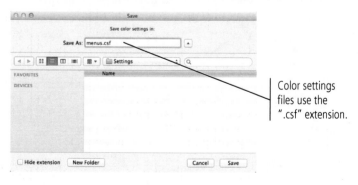

The **Intent** menu defines how the engine translates source colors outside the gamut of the destination profile (see the box below).

- **Perceptual** presents a visually pleasing representation of the image, preserving visual relationships between colors. All colors — including those available in the destination gamut — shift to maintain a proportional relationship within the image.

- **Saturation** compares the saturation of colors in the source profile and shifts them to the nearest-possible saturated color in the destination profile. The focus is on saturation instead of actual color value; this method can produce drastic color shift.

- **Relative Colorimetric** maintains any colors that are in both the source and destination profiles; source colors outside the destination gamut shift to fit. This method adjusts for the media whiteness of the media.

- **Absolute Colorimetric** maintains colors in both the source and destination profiles. Colors outside the destination gamut are shifted to a color within the destination gamut, without considering the white point of the media.

When **Use Black Point Compensation** is selected, the full range of the source space is mapped into the destination space. This method is most useful when the black point of the source is darker than that of the destination.

When **Use Dither** is selected, colors in the destination space are mixed to simulate missing colors from the source space. (This can result in larger file sizes for Web images.)

Compensate for Scene-Referred Profiles relates to the increasingly popular use of Photoshop to perform color correction (and profile matching) for video enhancement.

Desaturate Monitor Colors is useful for visualizing the full range of color, including colors outside the monitor's range. When this option is deselected, colors that were previously distinct might appear as a single color.

Blend RGB Colors Using Gamma inputs a gamma curve to avoid artifacts. (A gamma of 1.00 is considered "colorimetrically correct.")

Blend Text Colors Using Gamma applies the defined gamma to text layers.

8. **Click Save in the Color Settings dialog box. In the resulting navigation dialog box, change the Save As/File Name field to menus and click Save.**

By default, custom color settings are saved in a Settings folder in a specific location where your system stores user preferences for different applications. Settings files saved in the application's default location are available in the Settings menu of the Color Settings dialog box.

Color settings files use the ".csf" extension.

If you are working on a shared computer or a network where you can't save to the system files, you might want to save the custom Color Settings file in your WIP folder. In this case, you would have to click the Load button to locate the CSF file.

9. **In the Color Settings Comment dialog box, type** Use this option for Photoshop menu image adjustment project.

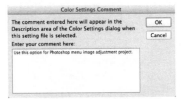

10. **Click OK to return to the Color Settings dialog box.**

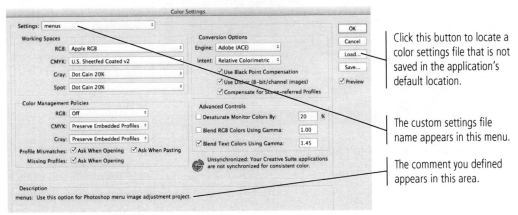

Click this button to locate a color settings file that is not saved in the application's default location.

The custom settings file name appears in this menu.

The comment you defined appears in this area.

11. **Click OK to close the Color Settings dialog box and apply your settings, and then continue to the next exercise.**

 IDENTIFY OUT-OF-GAMUT COLORS

Fortunately, Photoshop contains the necessary tools for previewing out-of-gamut colors, which means you can correct colors *before* converting an image. If you have no out-of-gamut colors, then there is nothing to shift, and you can be fairly confident that your color images will be reproduced as you intended.

1. **Open the file salad.jpg from the WIP>Menu folder.**

2. **If you see a profile mismatch warning, choose Use the Embedded Profile and click OK.**

   As a general rule, you should use the embedded profile whenever one is available.

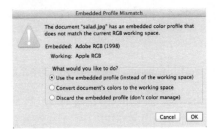

If you do not see a profile mismatch warning, choose Edit>Assign Profile once the image is open. With the Profile option selected, click OK.

You can use this dialog box to change the profile for an image. If an image has an embedded profile, the third radio button is selected and the embedded profile appears in the list. You can choose to not color manage the image, change to your working profile, or choose any other available profile from the Profile menu.

3. Choose View>Proof Colors to toggle that option on.

This toggle provides a quick preview of what will happen when the image is converted to the CMYK working-space profile — without affecting the actual file data.

Note:

Command/Control-Y toggles the Proof Colors view on or off.

Shift-Command/Control-Y toggles the Gamut Warning View.

Original color

Proof color

View>Proof Colors shows that converting this image will result in a color shift, especially in the red areas.

4. Choose View>Proof Colors again to toggle the option off.

5. Choose View>Gamut Warning.

The areas that shifted are now highlighted with a gray overlay. This overlay shows you exactly what you need to correct; when this image is printed on a commercial sheetfed press, those regions will not reproduce as expected.

Note:

You can change the color of the gamut warning overlay in the Transparency & Gamut pane of the Preferences dialog box.

6. Save the file as a native Photoshop file named salad.psd, then continue to the next exercise.

For images that will be commercially printed, some allowance must be made in the highlight and shadow areas for the mechanics of the printing process. In CMYK images, shades of gray are reproduced using combinations of four printing inks. In theory, a solid black would be printed as 100% of all four inks, and pure white would be 0% of all four inks. This, however, does not take into consideration the limitations of mechanical printing.

Images are printed as a pattern of closely spaced dots called a **halftone**. Those dots create the illusion of continuous color. Different sizes of dots create different shades of color — larger dots create darker shades and smaller dots create lighter shades.

There is a limit to the smallest size dot that can be consistently reproduced. A 1% dot is so small that the mechanical aspect of the printing process causes anything specified as a 1% dot to drop out, resulting in highlights that lack detail and contrast. The **minimum printable dot**, then, is the smallest printable dot, and should be specified for highlights in a CMYK image. There is some debate over the appropriate highlight setting because different presses and imaging equipment have varying capabilities. To be sure your highlights will work on most printing equipment, you should define the highlight as C=5 M=3 Y=3 K=0.

Maximum printable dot is the opposite of minimum printable dot. Paper's absorption rate, speed of the press, and other mechanical factors limit the amount of ink that can be placed on the same area. If too much ink is printed, the result is a dark blob with no visible detail; heavy layers of ink also result in drying problems and a number of other issues.

Total ink coverage is the largest percentage of ink that can be safely printed on a single area, and therefore dictates the shadow dot you define in Photoshop. This number, similar to minimum printable dot, varies according to the ink/paper/press combination being used for a given job. The Specifications for Web Offset Publications (SWOP) indicates a 300% maximum value. Many sheetfed printers require 280% maximum, while the number for newspapers is usually around 240% because the lower-quality paper absorbs more ink.

Unless your images will be printed in a newspaper, 290% is an acceptable shadow for most applications. You can safely define shadows as C=80 M=70 Y=70 K=70. If you need to adjust a lower or higher number for specific projects, you can do so at any time.

1. **With salad.psd open and the gamut warning visible, choose Image>Adjustments>Curves.**

2. **Double-click the White Point eyedropper.**

3. **In the resulting Color Picker (Target Highlight Color) dialog box, change the CMYK values to C=5 M=3 Y=3 K=0 and click OK.**

Note:

Even though you are working on an RGB image, you can still correct it to target CMYK white and black values.

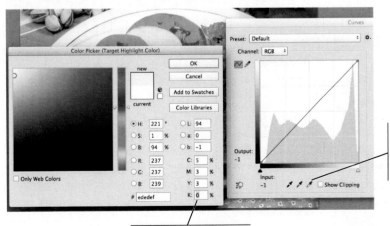

Change the Target Highlight Color in these fields.

Double-click the White Point eyedropper to open the Color Picker (Target Highlight Color) dialog box.

4. **With the White Point eyedropper selected, click the lightest highlight in the image where you want to maintain detail.**

We used this plate edge as the white point.

5. **Double-click the Black Point eyedropper. Change the target CMYK values to C=80 M=70 Y=70 K=70, and then click OK.**

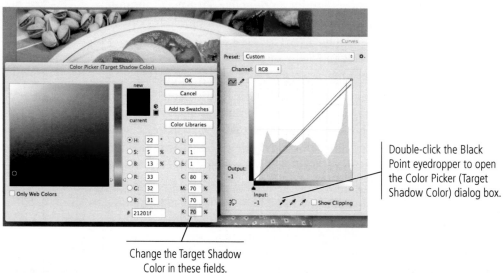

Double-click the Black Point eyedropper to open the Color Picker (Target Shadow Color) dialog box.

Change the Target Shadow Color in these fields.

6. **With the Black Point eyedropper selected, click the darkest area of the image where you want to maintain shadow detail.**

By defining the target highlight and shadow points in the image, you can see that the gray gamut warning is nearly gone from the green areas, and it's significantly reduced in the red areas.

We used this shadow as the black point.

7. **Display the curve for the Red channel only.**

8. **Add a point near the midpoint, and then drag the point down to steepen the overall Red curve.**

   Just a slight adjustment, from 140 Input to 115 Output, removes nearly all the gamut warning from the tomatoes.

Use this menu to show the curve for only one channel.

Note:

You can turn the gamut warning off and on while the Curves dialog box is open. Simply choose the option from the View menu and toggle the gray overlay off and on.

9. **Display the curve for the Green channel and make adjustments until most or all of the gamut warning is gone.**

   Experiment with points along the curve until you are satisfied with the result.

10. **Click OK to apply your changes.**

11. **Click No in the warning message.**

    If you change the target Black Point, Gray Point, or White Point eyedropper values, Photoshop asks if you want to save the new target values as the default settings when you click OK to close the Curves dialog box.

12. **Choose View>Gamut Warning to toggle that option off.**

13. Save the file and continue to the next exercise.

Because the RGB gamut is so much larger than the CMYK gamut, you can expect colors to be far less brilliant (especially in the outer ranges of saturation) when corrected to the CMYK gamut. It's better to know this will happen and control it, rather than simply allowing the color management engine to shift colors where it deems best.

CONVERTING IMAGE COLOR MODES

Although many modern workflows convert RGB images to CMYK during the output process (called "on-the-fly" or "in-RIP conversion"), there are times when you need to manually convert RGB images to CMYK. This is a fairly simple process, especially if you have corrected your images to meet the requirements of the printing process.

1. With the corrected salad image open from the previous exercise, choose Image>Mode>CMYK Color.

This menu option converts the image to the CMYK color mode using the current working space profile. Since you intentionally defined the working profile and corrected the image to that profile, you can safely use this menu option to convert the RGB image to CMYK.

2. Click OK in the resulting warning dialog box.

If you had not completed the process in the previous series of exercises, you shouldn't convert the image color mode. Color mode is not something that should be simply switched on a whim; rather, it is the final stage of a specific process.

If you didn't precisely follow this workflow, but you are certain the image colors are correct, you can convert an image to a different model by choosing Edit>Convert to Profile and choosing any available profile in the Destination Space Profile menu.

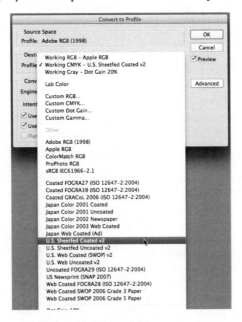

3. **Choose File>Save As. If necessary, navigate to your WIP>Menu folder as the target location.**

4. **Change the Format menu to TIFF, and then add _CMYK to the end of the existing file name (before the extension).**

5. **Macintosh users: In the bottom half of the Save As dialog box, make sure the Embed Color Profile: U.S. Sheetfed Coated v2 option is checked.**

   Windows users: In the bottom half of the Save As dialog box, make sure the ICC Profile: U.S. Sheetfed Coated v2 option is checked.

   This image has been corrected and converted to the U.S. Sheetfed Coated v2 color profile. By embedding the profile into the TIFF file, other applications and devices with color management capabilities will be able to correctly process the image color data in the file, based on the embedded profile.

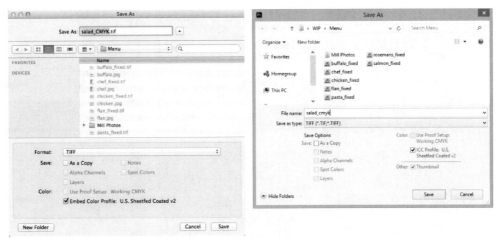

6. **Click Save, and then click OK to accept the default TIFF options.**

7. **Close the file, then continue to the final stage of the project.**

Converting Images to Grayscale

An RGB image has three channels and a CMYK image has four channels; each channel is a grayscale representation of the tones of that color throughout the image. A grayscale image has only one channel; the grayscale tones in that channel are the tones in the entire image. Choosing Image>Mode>Grayscale simply flattens the component color channels, throwing away the color information to create the gray channel.

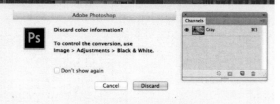

The Desaturate adjustment (Image>Adjustments>Desaturate) has a similar effect, but maintains the same number of channels as the original image. This adjustment averages the individual channel values for each pixel and applies the average value in each channel. (Remember, equal values of red, green, and blue combine to create a neutral gray value.)

If you need to convert a color image to grayscale, you might want to carefully consider which data to use for generating the gray channel. The Black & White adjustment (Image>Adjustments>Black & White) enables you to control the conversion process. In the Black and White dialog box, you can either choose one of the built-in presets, or you can drag the individual color sliders to determine how dark that color component will be in the resulting image.

When you move the mouse cursor over the image, it changes to an eyedropper icon. You can click an area in the image to highlight the predominant color in that area. Click within the image and drag to dynamically change the slider associated with that area of the image.

Remember, equal parts red, green, and blue combine to create a neutral gray. Applying the Black & White filter maintains the existing color channels, with the exact same data in all three channels. Because the adjusted image is still technically in a color mode (not Grayscale), you can also use the Tint options in the Black & White dialog box to apply a hue or saturation tint to the grayscale image. After using the Black & White dialog box to control the conversion of colors to grayscale, you can safely discard the color data by choosing Image>Mode>Grayscale.

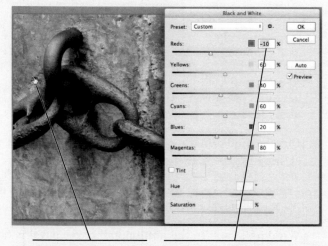

Clicking here and dragging left or right changes the associated Reds slider.

The Reds slider is highlighted, indicating that red is the predominant color where you clicked in the image.

	Red channel	Green channel	Blue channel
Original channel data			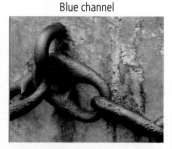
Channel data after Black & White adjustment			

The Channel Mixer Adjustment

You can use the Channel Mixer adjustment to change the values of individual channels in an image, affecting overall color balance and contrast. The Output Channel menu determines which channel you are changing; the Source Channels sliders determine how much of the original channels will be used to create the new output channel values.

 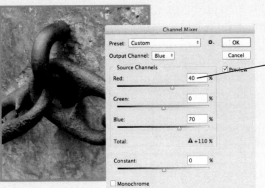 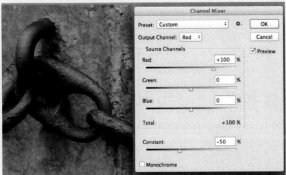

Replacing 40% of the Blue channel with information from the Red channel significantly affects the overall color and contrast in the image.

The Constant slider adjusts the overall grayscale value of the output channel. Negative values add more black to the channel (reducing the target color in the overall image), and positive values add more white to the channel (increasing the target color in the overall image).

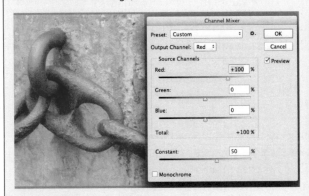

You can also use the Channel Mixer to control the conversion to grayscale. If you check the Monochrome option, the output channel automatically changes to gray.

When the Monochrome option is checked, you can change the percentage of each component channel that will be used to generate the grayscale values. If the combined channel values are higher than 100%, Photoshop displays a warning icon next to the total.

The "Output Channel:Gray" option is deceptive, since there is no Gray channel in either an RGB or CMYK image. As

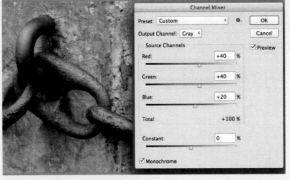

with the Black and White adjustment, the Channel Mixer results in a color image with the same color channels that it had before you applied the adjustment. All the color channels have equal data, however, so you can safely discard color data by choosing Image>Mode>Grayscale.

Stage 5 Working with HDR Images

The human eye is extremely sensitive to subtle changes in light. In general, we can perceive detail in both light and dark areas — and areas in between — with a single glance. Camera sensors, on the other hand, are not so sensitive. If you look at most photographs, they typically have sharp detail in one of the ranges — highlights, midtones, or shadows, depending on the exposure and other settings used to capture the image. If a photograph favors highlights, details in shadow areas are lost (and vice versa).

To solve this problem, the concept of HDR (**high dynamic range**) images combines multiple photographs of different exposures into a single image to enhance the detail throughout the entire image — combining highlight, shadow, and midtone detail from various exposures to create an image more like what the human eye is capable of observing, rather than the more limited range that characterizes a digital camera's sensors.

The phrase "dynamic range" refers to the difference between the darkest shadow and the lightest highlight in an image.

- A regular 8-bit RGB photo has a dynamic range of 0–255 for each color channel (2^8 or 256 possible values). In other words, each pixel can have one of 256 possible values to describe the lightness of that color in that specific location.

- A 16-bit RGB photo allows 16 bits of information to describe the information in each pixel, allowing a dynamic range of 2^{16} or 65,536 possible values in each color channel.

- A 32-bit or HDR image allows 2^{32} possible values — more than 4 billion, which is signficantly larger than the visible spectrum of 16.7 million colors (thus, 32-bit dynamic range is sometimes referred to as "infinite").

USE MERGE TO HDR PRO

The last piece required to complete this project is an image of the antique waterwheel that is one of the hallmarks of the restaurant's exterior. Its location makes it very difficult to capture because the surrounding trees cast shadows even when the sun is at the best lighting angle. The photographer suggested using high dynamic range (HDR) photo techniques to capture the most possible detail in the scene, and has provided you with five photos taken at the same time, using different exposure settings.

1. **With no file open, choose File>Automate>Merge to HDR Pro.**

2. **In the resulting Merge to HDR Pro dialog box, choose Folder in the Use menu and then click the Browse button.**

   This option makes it easy to identify the folder that contains all component images for the HDR merge.

3. **Navigate to WIP>Menu>Mill Photos, then click Open/OK.**

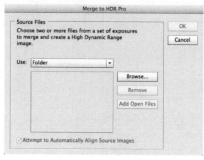
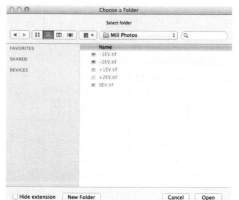

You can merge up to seven images with the Merge to HDR Pro utility.

4. **Make sure the Attempt to Automatically Align Source Images box at the bottom of the dialog box is checked, then click OK.**

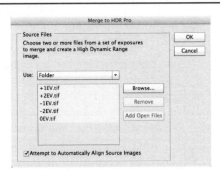

Because you are merging multiple images into a single one, there is a chance that one or more images might be slightly misaligned. (Even using a tripod, a stiff breeze can affect the camera just enough to make the different exposures slightly different.) When Attempt to Automatically Align Source Images is checked, Photoshop compares details in each image and adjusts them as necessary to create the resulting merged image.

5. **Read the resulting message, then click OK.**

HDR images are best created from Camera RAW files, which can maintain significantly more data than the TIFF or JPEG formats. In many cases, however, you will have to use non-RAW files because that is what your photographer or client will provide to you. The merge process still works very well with JPEG and TIFF files.

6. **If you don't see a histogram on the right side of the dialog box, open the Mode menu and choose 32 Bit.**

The resulting dialog box shows each selected image as a thumbnail at the bottom. By default, all selected images are included in the merge. You can exclude specific exposures by unchecking the box for that image.

If you work with HDR, you need to realize that most computer monitors are not capable of displaying 32-bit image depth. When you merge to a 32-bit image, you can use the White Point Preview slider to change the dynamic range that is visible on your screen, but this has no effect on the actual data in the file — it affects only the current display of the image data.

Note:

The merge process might take a minute or two to complete, so be patient.

7. **Check the Remove Ghosts option on the right side of the dialog box.**

When an HDR image contains movement, merging the individual exposures can blur the areas where that movement occurs — such as the water dripping off the wheel in this image. When you check Remove Ghosts, the software uses one of the exposures (highlighted in green) to define detail in the area of motion; you can change the key exposure by simply clicking a different image in the lower pane.

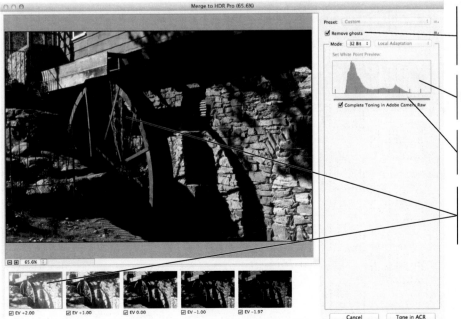

Check Remove Ghosts to eliminate blurring in areas that differ from one exposure to another.

Tones to the right of the white point will be displayed as white.

Drag this slider to change the white point for the active display.

When Remove Ghosts is checked, details in areas of movement are defined by the selected exposure.

8. Open the Mode menu and choose 8 Bit.

32-bit images can store a tremendous amount of information, which creates images with far more detail than you see in a conventional 8-bit photograph. However, one significant disadvantage of such images is that they cannot be separated for commercial printing. If you're going to use an HDR image in a print application — such as the cover of this menu — you need to apply the process of **tone mapping** to define how the high dynamic range will be compressed into the lower dynamic range that is required by the output process.

9. Leave the secondary menu set to Local Adaptation.

You can use the other options to apply less specific tone mapping to the image. Equalize Histogram and Highlight Compression have no further options. The Exposure and Gamma option allows you to define specific values for only those two settings.

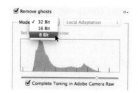
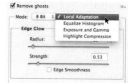

When the Local Adaptation method is selected, you can change the values for a number of specific options to map the tones in the HDR image to a lower dynamic range.

10. Open the Preset menu and choose Photorealistic.

The application includes a number of standard settings, including several variations of monochromatic, photorealistic, and surrealistic. Each preset changes the values of the Local Adaptation sliders to create the desired effect.

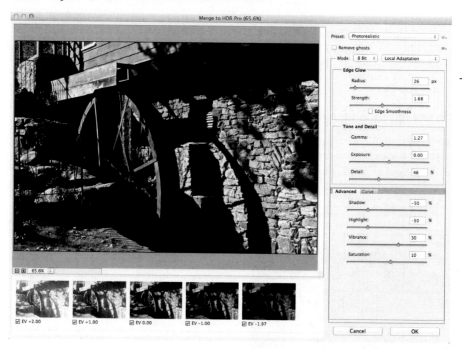

Note:

You can create your own presets by clicking the button to the right of the Preset menu and choosing Save Preset in the resulting menu.

11. **Experiment with the different sliders until you are satisfied with the result.**

Tone mapping is a largely subjective process, and different end uses can influence the settings that you apply to a specific image. You should understand the following information as you experiment with the various settings:

- **Radius** defines the size of the glowing effect in areas of localized brightness.

- **Strength** determines the required tolerance between tonal values before pixels are no longer considered part of the same brightness region.

- **Gamma** values lower than 1.0 increase details in the midtones, while higher values emphasize details in the highlights and shadows.

- **Exposure** affects the overall lightness or darkness of the image.

- **Detail** increases or decreases the overall sharpness of the image.

- **Shadow** and **Highlight** affect the amount of detail in those areas of the image. Higher values increase detail and lower values reduce detail.

- **Vibrance** affects the intensity of subtle colors, while minimizing clipping of highly saturated colors.

- **Saturation** affects the intensity of all colors from –100 (monochrome) to +100 (double saturation).

12. **Click OK to finalize the process.**

Because you chose 8 Bit in the Mode menu of the Merge to HDR Pro dialog box, the resulting image is an 8-bit RGB image (as you can see in the document tab).

13. **Save the file in your WIP>Menu>Mill Images folder as a native Photoshop file named mill_merged.psd, then close it.**

1. The _____ filter locates pixels that differ in value from surrounding pixels by the threshold you specify; it sharpens an image by increasing contrast along the edges in an image.

2. _____ is defined as random pixels that stand out from the surrounding pixels.

3. The _____ blends colors from user-defined source pixels with colors in the area where you click.

4. The _____ paints one part of an image over another part, which is useful for duplicating specific objects or removing defects in an image.

5. _____ are direct sources of light such as a light bulb or reflected sunlight on water; they should not be considered the highlights of an image.

6. _____ refers to the tonal variation within an image.

7. A _____ is a visual depiction of the distribution of colors in an image.

8. The _____ menu command can be used to see an on-screen preview of the way colors will look when the job is printed on a specific output device.

9. The _____ menu command can be used to convert an image to a specific profile other than the current working profile.

10. The _____ is the color profile of the output device that is being used for a particular job.

1. Explain the concept of neutral gray.

2. List three important points to remember when working with curves.

3. Briefly explain the concepts of minimum printable dot and maximum ink coverage.

Use what you learned in this project to complete the following freeform exercise.

Carefully read the art director and client comments, then create your design to meet the needs of the project.

Use the space below to sketch ideas; when finished, write a brief explanation of the reasoning behind your design.

art director comments

The tourism board director dined at The Chateau recently. In a conversation with the restaurant owner, he mentioned a new project about local architecture. Mr. Roseman, pleased with your work on the menu images, recommended you for the job.

To complete this project, you should:

❏ Find at least 10 photos of different architectural styles throughout the Los Angeles metropolitan area.

❏ Use photo retouching techniques to clean up any graffiti and trash that is visible in the images.

❏ Use correction techniques to adjust the tonal range and gray balance of the images.

❏ Correct and convert all images based on the U.S. Sheetfed Coated v2 CMYK destination profile.

client comments

Over the next year, we're planning on publishing a series of promotional booklets to show tourists that L.A. is more than just Hollywood.

Each booklet in the series will focus on an 'interest area' such as fine art or — for the first one — architecture. The city has a diverse architectural mix, from eighteenth-century Spanish missions to 1920s bungalows to the Walt Disney Concert Hall designed by Frank Gehry in the 1990s.

We'd like at least ten pictures of different landmarks or architectural styles, corrected and optimized for printing on a sheetfed press. If possible, we'd also like some historical images to include in a "building a metropolis" section on the first couple of pages.

Of course, Los Angeles is a large city, and cities have their problems — not the least of which are graffiti and garbage. We are trying to attract tourists, not turn them away. Make sure none of the images show any graffiti or blatant litter; if these problems are visible in the images you select, give them a good digital cleaning.

project justification

_____

_____

_____

_____

_____

_____

_____

_____

_____

_____

_____

_____

_____

As with many other skills, it takes time and practice to master image correction techniques. Understanding the relationship between brightness and contrast, and how these two values affect the quality of reproduction in digital images, is the first and possibly most critical factor in creating a high-quality image. An image that has too much contrast (a "sharp" image) or not enough contrast (a "flat" image) translates to an unsatisfactory print.

A basic understanding of color theory (specifically complementary color) is the foundation of accurate color correction. Effective color correction relies on the numbers, rather than what you think you see on your monitor. As you gain experience in correcting images, you will be better able to predict the corrections required to achieve the best possible output.

Remove photographic grain with blur and sharpen techniques

Use the Healing Brush and Spot Healing Brush tools to correct scratches

Use the Clone Stamp tool to remove major damage

Correct contrast and tonal range using the Levels adjustment

Use Merge to HDR Pro to find detail in multiple exposures

Correct minor color problems using the Brightness/Contrast adjustment

Correct gray balance using the Curves adjustment

Correct lighting problems with the Exposure adjustment

Correct overall color cast using the Color Balance adjustment

Correct contrast with the Curves adjustment

Correct and convert the image using the defined destination CMYK profile

Letterhead Design

Your client, Amelia Crowe, is a local photographer. She hired you to create a letterhead design that incorporates her personal logo and a set of images representing the kind of work she does. She is going to have the letterhead printed commercially so she can use it to print letters, invoices, and other business correspondence.

This project incorporates the following skills:

❑ Creating a new file to meet defined project requirements

❑ Using the basic InDesign drawing tools to develop visual interest

❑ Selecting objects and object contents

❑ Creating and formatting basic text attributes

❑ Placing and manipulating external graphics files

❑ Printing a desktop proof sample

client comments

Until now, I've just added my logo and address at the top of a Word document whenever I sent out correspondence. My business has been growing lately, and I want something more professional and more indicative of my work in photographing urban architecture and natural landscapes.

I sent you my logo, which was created in Adobe Illustrator. I also selected a bunch of images that I really like; I want to include at least a few of those on the letterhead to give people an idea of my work.

Can you get my contact information from my email sig file, or do I need to send that to you as a separate document?

art director comments

I've looked over the client's images, and I think we should use all of them. Since she's a photographer, a filmstrip across the bottom of the page will make a nice container; InDesign has everything you need to create the necessary graphics directly on the page layout. I already sized the photos down to thumbnails that should be close to the right size, so you won't have to manipulate the actual image files.

I also copied the client's contact info into a file for you. Since she specifically mentioned two areas of photographic specialty, I want you to include the words "urban architecture & natural landscapes" as a tag line.

It might feel like there's a lot involved in creating this piece, but it's not too complicated. The client liked the initial sketch, so putting in the effort at this point will be worth it.

project objectives

To complete this project, you will:

- ❏ Create a new document based on the requirements of a commercial printer.
- ❏ Place ruler guides to define "safe" areas on the page.
- ❏ Draw basic shapes using native InDesign tools
- ❏ Edit shapes using the Pathfinder and Align panels
- ❏ Work with anchor points and handles to create a complex shape
- ❏ Apply color to fills and strokes
- ❏ Create and format basic text elements
- ❏ Import external text and graphics files
- ❏ Print a desktop proof

Stage 1 Setting up the Workspace

The best way to start any new project is to prepare your workspace. As you learned in the Interface chapter, InDesign gives you extensive control over your workspace — you can choose where to place panels, whether to collapse or expand open panels, and even to save workspaces with sets of panels in specific locations. Because workspace issues are largely a matter of personal preference, we tell you what tools to use, but we don't tell you where to keep the various panels. Many of our screen captures show floating panels so that we can maximize the available space and clearly focus on a specific issue. Likewise, we typically don't tell you what view percentage to use; you should use whatever you are comfortable with to accomplish the specific goal of an exercise.

DEFINE A NEW LAYOUT FILE

Some production-related concerns will dictate how you design a letterhead. In general, there are two ways to print letterhead: one-offs on a desktop laser or inkjet printer, or commercially in large quantities. (The first method typically involves creating a letterhead template, which you then use to write and print letters from directly within InDesign — a fairly common practice among graphic designers.)

If letterhead is being printed commercially, it's probably being printed with multiple copies on a large press sheet, from which the individual letterhead sheets will be cut. Most commercial printing happens this way. This type of printing typically means that design elements can run right off the edge of the sheet, called **bleeding**.

If you're designing for a printer that can only run letter-size paper, you have to allow enough of a margin area for your printer to hold the paper as it moves through the device (called the **gripper margin**); in this case, you can't design with bleeds.

The most basic process in designing a layout is creating a new InDesign file. The New Document dialog box has a large number of options, and the following exercise explains all of those. Don't be overwhelmed by the length of this process; in later projects, we simply tell you what settings to define without re-explaining every field.

Note:

Some desktop printers have a minimum margin at the page edges; you're usually safe with 3/8". Many newer inkjet printers have the capability to print 8.5 × 11" with full bleed. Consult your printer documentation to be sure.

1. **Download Letterhead_Print14_RF.zip from the Student Files web page.**

2. **Expand the ZIP archive in your WIP folder (Macintosh) or copy the archive contents into your WIP folder (Windows).**

   This results in a folder named **Letterhead**, which contains all of the files you need for this project. You should also use this folder to save the files you create in this project.

3. **In InDesign, choose File>New>Document.**

   The New Document dialog box opens with the last-used document preset; if no user-defined preset exists, the dialog box opens with the settings that are stored in the Default preset.

   Some of the options we define in the following steps might already be reflected in the New Document dialog box, but we can't be sure because someone might have modified the default settings on your computer. If something is already set to the value we define, simply leave that value as is.

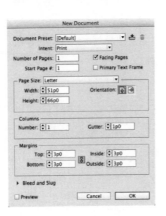

Note:

You can create a new file by pressing Command/Control-N.

4. Choose Print in the Intent menu.

InDesign uses picas as the default unit of measurement for print documents; measurements in this dialog box are shown in picas and points, using the "ApB" notation (for A picas and B points). Colors in a print-intent document default to the CMYK color model.

If you choose Web or Digital Publishing, InDesign changes the default unit of measurement to pixels, which is more appropriate for Web design. Colors in a Web-intent document default to the RGB color model.

Note:

Picas are the measuring units traditionally used in typography; they are still used by many people in the graphic communications industry.

1 point = 1/72 inch

12 points = 1 pica

1 pica = 1/6 inch

6 picas = 1 inch

5. Set the Number of Pages field to 1.

A letterhead is a single page, usually printed on only one side. A one-sided, one-page document needs only a single layout page in the InDesign file.

6. Set the Start Page # field to 1.

This option is useful when you work with multi-page files. Odd-numbered pages always appear on the right, as you see in any book or magazine; you can define an even-numbered starting page number to force the first page of a layout to the left.

7. Uncheck the Facing Pages check box.

Facing pages are used when a printed job will be read left to right like a book — with Page 1 starting on the right, then Page 2 facing Page 3, and so on. Facing-page layouts are based on **spreads**, which are pairs of left-right pages as you flip through a book (e.g., Page 6 facing Page 7).

8. Uncheck the Primary Text Frame option.

When this option is checked, InDesign creates a text frame that automatically fills the area created by the defined page margins. A letterhead design primarily focuses on the area outside of the margins, so you don't need to add a primary text frame to this file.

9. Choose Letter in the Page Size menu.

This menu includes a number of common sizes based on the selected intent. Choosing any of these options automatically changes the width and height fields to match the selected size.

Note:

Choosing Custom in the Page Size menu has no real effect. This setting is automatically reflected as soon as you change the Width or Height field from the standard measurements.

10. Choose the Portrait Orientation option.

Portrait documents are higher than they are wide; **landscape** documents are wider than they are high. If you click the orientation option that is not currently selected, the Width and Height values are automatically reversed.

Width and Height are automatically defined by the Page Size menu selection.

Portrait Landscape

11. At the bottom of the dialog box, check the Preview option.

When this option is active, you can see the result of your choices (behind the dialog box) before you click OK to create the new file.

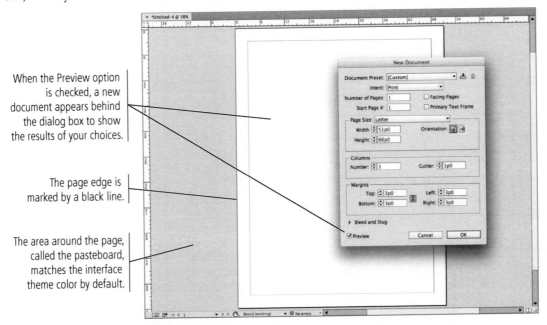

When the Preview option is checked, a new document appears behind the dialog box to show the results of your choices.

The page edge is marked by a black line.

The area around the page, called the pasteboard, matches the interface theme color by default.

12. If the chain icon between the Margin fields shows two connected links, click the icon to break the link between the fields.

When the chain icon is active (connected links or highlighted dark gray), all four margin fields will be the same; changing one field changes all margin values to the same value. For this project, you need to define different values for the top and bottom than for the left and right, so you need to unlink (unconstrain) the fields if they are currently linked.

13. Highlight the first Margins field (Top) and type 1.25″.

Even though the default measurement is picas, you can type values in any unit as long as you type the appropriate unit along with the value; InDesign makes the necessary conversion for you, so the values will still be displayed in the default units.

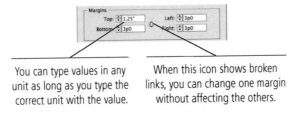

You can type values in any unit as long as you type the correct unit with the value.

When this icon shows broken links, you can change one margin without affecting the others.

If you enter a value in a unit other than the default, you have to include the alternate unit. This technique works in dialog boxes and panels — anywhere that you can enter a measurement.

Note:

When you work with non-facing pages, the Inside and Outside margin fields change to Left and Right respectively. Technically, non-facing pages do not have an inside (spine edge) or outside (face or trim edge), so there are only left and right sides.

14. Press Tab to move to the Bottom field.

Pink guides represent the defined margins.

Because the Preview option is checked, the document automatically shows the modified top margin of 7p6 (2").

When you move to the next field, InDesign converts the Top value to the default unit of measurement (picas).

Note:

You can tab through the fields of most dialog boxes and panels in InDesign. Press Shift-Tab to move the highlight to the previous field in the tab order.

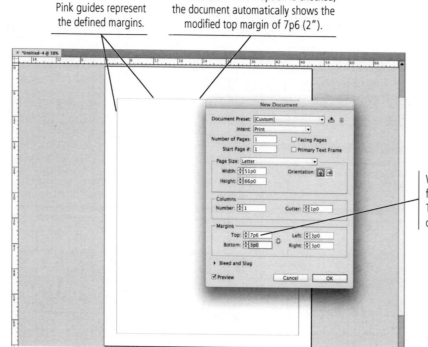

15. Change the Bottom field to 2", then press Tab two times.

The first time you press Tab from the Bottom field highlights the chain icon. You have to press Tab a second time to highlight the Left field.

16. Change the Left field to 1", press Tab, and then change the Right field to 1".

All four margin guides are changed.

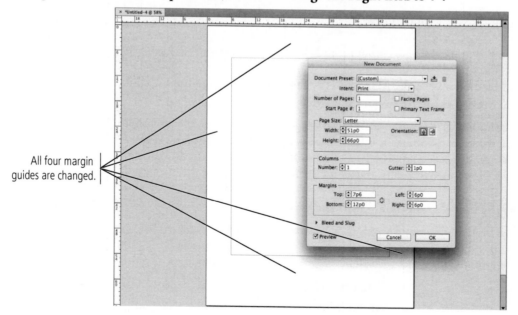

17. **Click the arrow button to the left of the Bleed and Slug heading.**

18. **Make sure the chain icon to the right of the Bleed fields is active (unbroken links), then change the first Bleed field to 0.125″ (the decimal equivalent of 1/8). Press Tab to apply the new Bleed value to all four sides.**

    The letterhead for this project will be printed commercially; the printer said the design can safely bleed on all four sides, and its equipment requires a 1/8″ bleed allowance. In this case, you want all four edges to have the same bleed, so the chain icon should be active to constrain all four Bleed fields to the same value.

19. **Make sure all four Slug fields are set to 0.**

    A **slug** is an area outside of the bleed, where designers typically add job information that will not appear in the final printed piece.

    You don't need to type the full "0p0" notation when you change measurements using the default units. Zero pica is still zero, so you don't need to worry about converting units.

Note:

*A **slug** is an element entirely outside the page area, but included in the final output. The slug area can be used for file/plate information, special registration marks, color bars, and/or other elements that need to be printed on the press sheet, but do not appear within the job area.*

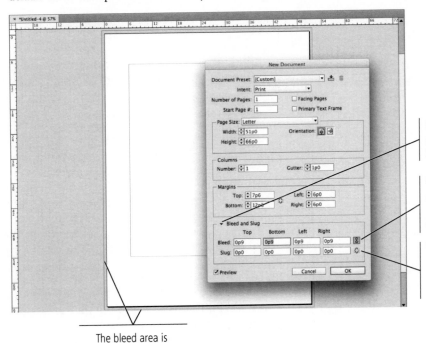

Click this button to show the Bleed and Slug options.

When this icon shows two unbroken links, changing any linked field will apply the same value to the other three fields.

When a chain icon shows two broken links, you can change any one field without affecting the other related fields.

The bleed area is represented by a red line.

20. **Click OK to create the new document.**

    The document appears, filling the available space in the document window. Your view percentage might appear different than what you see in our images.

21. **Choose File>Save As. In the Save As dialog box, navigate to your WIP>Letterhead folder as the target location for saving the file.**

    The Save As dialog box follows a system-standard format. Macintosh and Windows users see slightly different options, but the basic InDesign functionality is the same.

22. Change the file name (in the Save As field) to crowe.indd and click Save.

If the Hide Extension option is checked at the bottom of the dialog box, the ".indd" will not appear in the file name.

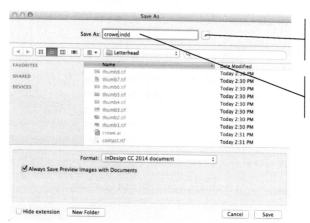

Click here if you don't see the full navigation options on Macintosh.

The extension ".indd" is automatically added to the file name.

Note:

The first time you save a file, the Save command opens the same dialog box as the File>Save As command. After saving the file once, you can use Save to save changes to the existing file, or use Save As to create an additional file under a new file name.

23. Continue to the next exercise.

Understanding Document Presets

INDESIGN FOUNDATIONS

A **preset** stores groups of common settings; you define a preset once, and then you can access the same group of settings later with a single click. You'll often use this concept while building InDesign documents — when you use text styles, table styles, object styles, and output documents for printing.

If you frequently define the same document settings, you can save those choices as a preset so that you can create the same document settings with minimal repetition. Clicking the Save Document Preset button in the New Document dialog box opens a secondary dialog box where you can name the preset.

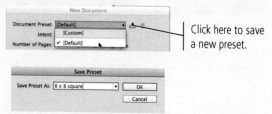

Click here to save a new preset.

When you return to the New Document dialog box, your new preset appears as the selection in the Document Preset menu. Any time you need to create a file with the same settings, you can choose the saved preset from this menu.

You can also access and manage document presets in the File>Document Presets submenu.

If you choose one of the existing presets in the menu, the New Document dialog box opens, defaulting to the values in the preset that you called (instead of defaulting to the application-default letter-size page). All the settings you saved in the preset automatically reflect in the dialog box.

You can also create, edit, and manage presets by choosing Define in the Document Presets submenu; this opens a dialog box that lists the existing presets.

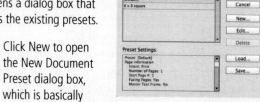

- Click New to open the New Document Preset dialog box, which is basically the same as the New Document dialog box, except the Preset menu is replaced with a field where you type the preset name instead of clicking the Save Preset button.

- Select a preset and click Edit to change the preset's associated options.

- Select a preset and click Delete to remove the preset from the application.

- Click Load to import presets created on another computer.

- Click Save to save a preset (with the extension ".dcst") so that it can be sent to and used on another computer.

 Project 7: Letterhead Design

In addition to the margin and bleed guides that you defined when you created the document, you can also place ruler guides to mark whatever other positions you need to identify in your layout.

The **live area** is the "safe" area inside the page edge where important design elements should reside. Because printing and trimming are mechanical processes, there will always be some variation — however slight. Elements placed too close to the page edge run the risk of being accidentally trimmed off. The printer for this job recommended a 1/8″ live-area margin. You defined the margins for this file to describe the area that would typically occupy the content of a letter; in this exercise you will create ruler guides to mark the live area.

Note:

You should become familiar with the common fraction-to-decimal equivalents:

> *1/8 = 0.125*
>
> *1/4 = 0.25*
>
> *3/8 = 0.375*
>
> *1/2 = 0.5*
>
> *5/8 = 0.625*
>
> *3/4 = 0.75*
>
> *7/8 = 0.875*

1. **With crowe.indd open, choose View>Show Rulers if you don't see rulers at the top and left edges of the document window.**

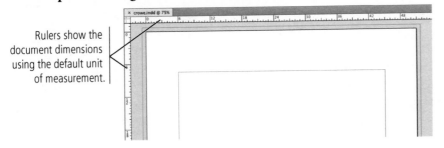

Rulers show the document dimensions using the default unit of measurement.

2. **Open the Units & Increments pane of the Preferences dialog box (from the InDesign menu on Macintosh or the Edit menu on Windows).**

Since most people (in the United States, at least) think in terms of inches, we use inches throughout the projects in this book.

3. **In the Ruler Units area, choose Inches in both the Horizontal and Vertical menus, and then click OK.**

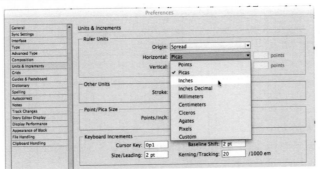

When you return to the document window, the rulers now display in inches.

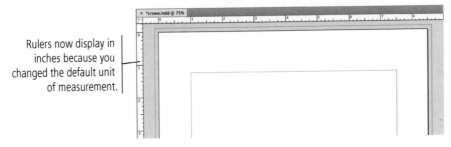

Rulers now display in inches because you changed the default unit of measurement.

4. **Click the horizontal page ruler (at the top of the document window) and drag down until the cursor feedback indicates that the guide is positioned at Y: 0.125 in. With the cursor inside the page area, release the mouse button.**

As you drag, cursor feedback shows the current position of the guide you are placing; this makes it very easy to precisely position guides.

Click and drag from the horizontal ruler to add a horizontal guide.

The Control panel, ruler, and cursor feedback all show the location of the guide you're dragging.

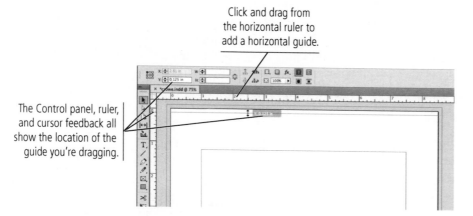

Note:

Y values define vertical (top-to-bottom) position; X values define horizontal (left-to-right) position.

5. **Click the horizontal page ruler again and drag a guide to Y: 10.875 in.**

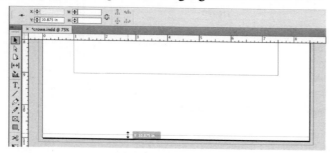

Note:

If you drag a guide outside of the page edge, the guide will extend across the entire pasteboard. You can also press Command/Control while dragging a guide onto the page to extend the guide the entire width of the pasteboard.

6. **Click the vertical ruler and drag a guide to X: 0.125 in.**

Watch the marker on the horizontal ruler to judge the guide's position.

Drag from the vertical ruler to add a vertical guide.

Note:

If the Control panel is not visible, you can show it by choosing Window>Control.

7. **Click the vertical ruler again and drag a second vertical guide to X: 8.375 in.**

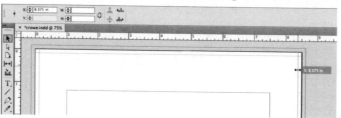

Note:

You can click the intersection of the rulers and drag to reposition the zero point away from the top-left corner of the page. If you do reposition the zero point, you can double-click the ruler intersection to reset the original zero point.

8. **Using the Selection tool, click anywhere in the document space to deselect the guide you just created.**

9. **Save the file and continue to the next stage of the project.**

Stage 2 Creating Basic Page Elements

Based on the approved sketch, the client's letterhead includes several elements:

- A "filmstrip" graphic to frame a number of thumbnails of the client's work

- A logo that was created in Adobe Illustrator

- A tag line, separated from the logo with a curved line

- Contact information, which was provided to you as a rich-text file

- Actual thumbnails of the client's photographs, which were supplied to you as ready-to-print TIFF files.

Other than the logo and the supplied photos, you need to create these elements directly in the InDesign file. Fortunately, the software includes sophisticated drawing tools that can create everything you need. Before you begin, however, you should understand the different types of elements that you will encounter when you design files in InDesign.

Vector graphics are composed of mathematical descriptions of a series of lines and shapes. Vector graphics are resolution independent; they can be freely scaled, and they are automatically output at the resolution of the output device. The shapes that you create in Adobe InDesign, or in drawing applications such as Adobe Illustrator, are vector graphics.

Raster images, such as photographs or files created in Adobe Photoshop, are made up of a grid of independent pixels (rasters or bits) in rows and columns (called a bitmap). Raster files are resolution dependent — their resolution is determined when you scan, photograph, or otherwise create the file. You can typically reduce raster images, but you cannot enlarge them without losing image quality.

Line art is a type of raster image that is made up entirely of 100% solid areas; the pixels in a line-art image have only two options: they can be all black or all white. Examples of line art are UPC bar codes or pen-and-ink drawings.

CREATE BASIC FRAMES

Although much drawing and illustration work is done in a dedicated illustration program such as Adobe Illustrator, you can use the drawing tools in InDesign to create vector artwork. In fact, the drawing tools in InDesign are actually a limited subset of the more comprehensive Illustrator toolset, which means you can create fairly sophisticated artwork entirely within the layout application. In this exercise, you are going to use the basic InDesign drawing tools to create a filmstrip graphic, which will serve as the background for the client's image samples.

1. **With crowe.indd open, choose View>Grids & Guides>Smart Guides to make sure this option is toggled on. If the option is already checked, move the cursor away from the menu and click to dismiss it.**

   Smart guides are a useful function of the application, making it easy to create and precisely align objects. Smart guides show the dimensions of an object when you create it; the position of an object when you drag it; the edge and center position of nearby objects; and the distance between nearby similar objects.

Note:

You can turn off specific Smart Guide functions in the Guides & Pasteboard pane of the Preferences dialog box.

This option should be checked (active).

2. **Click the button at the right end of the Control panel to open the panel Options menu.**

3. **If the Dimensions Include Stroke Weight option is checked, choose that item to toggle the option off.**

   When this option is active, the size of an object's stroke is factored as part of the overall object size. Consider, for example, a frame that is 72 points wide by 72 points high with a 1-point stroke. If you remove the stroke from the frame, the frame would then be only 70 points by 70 points.

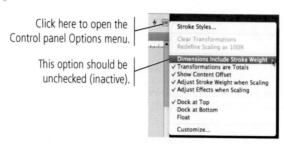

Click here to open the Control panel Options menu.

This option should be unchecked (inactive).

Note:

These options remember the last-used settings.

4. **Choose the Rectangle tool in the Tools panel.**

   If you don't see the Rectangle tool, click and hold the default shape tool until the nested tools appear; slide over and down to select the Rectangle tool.

Note:

Tools with nested options default to show the last-used variation in the main Tools panel.

5. **Click the Default Fill and Stroke button at the bottom of the Tools panel.**

   In InDesign, the default fill is None, and the default stroke is 1-pt black.

6. **Click anywhere on the page, and drag down and right to draw a rectangle that is about 1″ high and 2″ wide.**

   As you draw, cursor feedback shows the size of the shape you are creating.

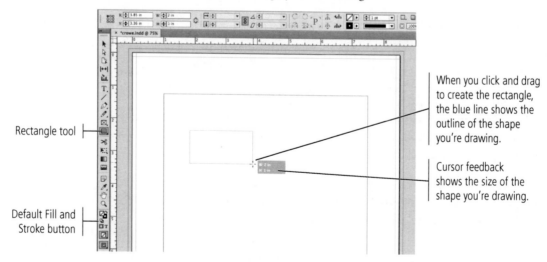

Rectangle tool

Default Fill and Stroke button

When you click and drag to create the rectangle, the blue line shows the outline of the shape you're drawing.

Cursor feedback shows the size of the shape you're drawing.

7. Release the mouse button to create the rectangle.

Every shape you create in an InDesign document has a **bounding box**, which is a non-printing rectangle that marks the outer dimensions of the shape. (Even a circle has a square bounding box, marking the largest height and width of the object.) The bounding box has eight handles, which you can drag to change the size of the rectangle. If you can see an object's bounding box handles, that object is selected.

Note:

Press Shift while drawing a shape to constrain the horizontal and vertical dimensions of the shape (in other words, to create a perfect square or circle).

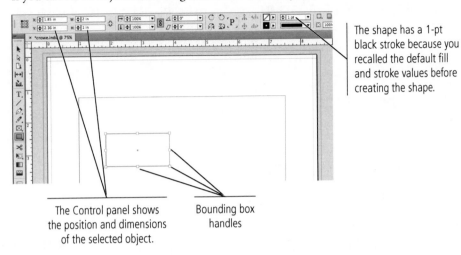

The shape has a 1-pt black stroke because you recalled the default fill and stroke values before creating the shape.

The Control panel shows the position and dimensions of the selected object.

Bounding box handles

8. At the bottom of the Tools panel, click the Swap Fill and Stroke button.

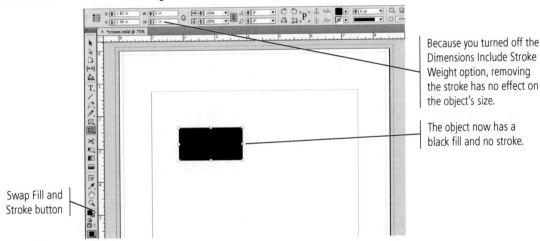

Because you turned off the Dimensions Include Stroke Weight option, removing the stroke has no effect on the object's size.

The object now has a black fill and no stroke.

Swap Fill and Stroke button

9. At the left end of the Control panel, select the top-left reference point.

The Control panel is context-sensitive, which means different options are available depending on what is selected in the document. This panel consolidates the most common options from multiple InDesign panels.

The **reference point** determines how transformations will occur (in other words, which point of the object will remain in place if you change one of the position or dimension values). These points correspond to the object's bounding box handles, as well as to the object's exact center point.

Constrain object width and height   Constrain object scale

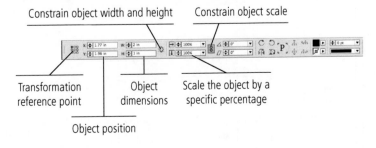

Transformation reference point

Object dimensions

Scale the object by a specific percentage

Object position

INDESIGN FOUNDATIONS

The Control panel is one of the most versatile, productive tools in the InDesign workspace, combining all of the most common formatting options into a single, compact format across the top of the workspace. It is context sensitive, which means different options are available depending on what is selected in the layout. Finally, it is customizable, which means you can change the options that are available in the panel.

It is also important to note that the options available in the Control panel might be limited by the active workspace, as well as by the width of your monitor or Application frame.

Essentials Control panel when a graphics frame is selected:

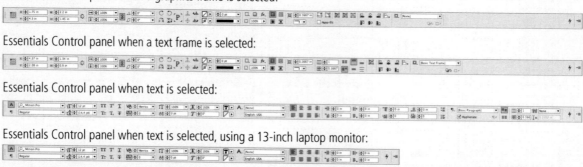

Essentials Control panel when a text frame is selected:

Essentials Control panel when text is selected:

Essentials Control panel when text is selected, using a 13-inch laptop monitor:

When anything other than text is selected (or nothing is selected), the panel Options menu includes options for controlling the position of the panel (top, bottom, or floating), as well as how transformations affect selected objects:

Quick Apply button

Click here to open the panel Options menu.

- **Stroke Styles.** This opens a dialog box where you can edit or define custom styles for lines and object strokes.

- **Clear Transformations.** Choosing this option resets an object to its original position (including rotation).

- **Dimensions Include Stroke Weight.** When checked, width and height values include the object width as well as the defined stroke width. For example, if this option is checked, a square that is 72 points wide with a 1-pt stroke would be 73 points wide (using the default stroke position that aligns the stroke on the center of the object edge).

- **Transformations are Totals.** When checked, transformations such as rotation are cumulative for the frame and the frame contents. For example, an image frame is rotated 10°...

  - When Transformations are Totals is checked, the image in the frame also shows 10° rotation; you can change the content rotation to 0° to return the image (but not the frame) to horizontal.

  - When not checked, the image in the frame shows 0° because the content is not rotated relative to its container. You have to rotate the content −10° to return it to horizontal without affecting the frame's rotation.

- **Show Content Offset.** When checked, the Control panel shows X+ and Y+ values for a graphic placed within a frame when the actual graphic (not the frame) is selected.

- **Adjust Stroke Weight when Scaling.** When checked, resizing an object changes the stroke weight proportionally. For example, resizing an object with a 1-pt stroke to 50% results in a 0.5-pt stroke.

Choosing **Customize** in the panel Options menu opens a dialog box where you can define the available options in the panel; anything with a checkmark will be available when it's relevant to the selection in the document.

Clicking the Quick Apply button (to the left of the panel Options button) opens a special navigation dialog box. This feature enables you to easily find and apply what you want (menu commands, user-defined styles, and so on) by typing a few characters in the text entry field and then clicking the related item in the list.

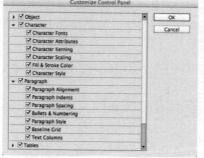

10. **Highlight the X field in the Control panel and type −0.25, then press Tab to move the highlight to the Y field.**

   As in dialog boxes, you can use the Tab key to move through the fields in the Control panel. The X and Y fields determine the position of the selected object. X defines the horizontal (left-to-right) position, and Y defines the vertical (top-to-bottom) position.

11. **With the Y field highlighted, type 9.5 and then press Return/Enter.**

   Pressing Return/Enter applies your changes in the Control panel. You can also simply click away from the object to apply the changes, but then you would have to reselect the object to make further changes.

Note:

Because inches are now the default unit of measurement for this file, you don't need to type the unit in the field.

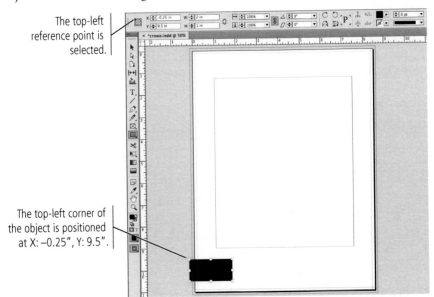

The top-left reference point is selected.

The top-left corner of the object is positioned at X: −0.25″, Y: 9.5″.

Note:

You can use math operators to add (+), subtract (-), divide (/), or multiply (*) existing values in the Control panel. This is useful when you want to move or change a value by a specific amount.

Type +.5 after the value to move the object down half an inch.

12. **In the Control panel, make sure the chain icon for the W and H fields is inactive (not linked). Change the W (width) field to 9″, change the H (height) field to 1.2″, and then press Return/Enter to apply the change.**

   Remember, you don't need to type the units if you are working with the default units.

Note:

The Transform panel (Window>Object & Layout>Transform) includes the same options that are available in the Control panel when an object is selected with the Selection tool. You can change an object's position or dimensions, scale an object to a specific percentage, and apply rotation or shear to the selected object. The Transform panel Options menu includes the same options that are available in the Control panel Options menu, as well as commands to rotate and flip the selected object.

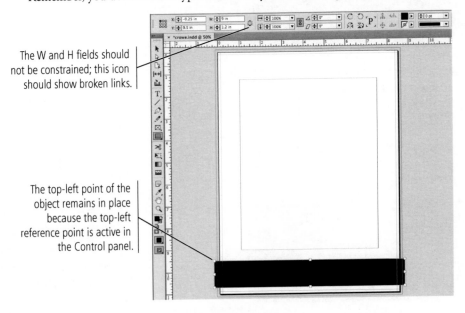

The W and H fields should not be constrained; this icon should show broken links.

The top-left point of the object remains in place because the top-left reference point is active in the Control panel.

13. **Save the file and continue to the next exercise.**

CREATE A ROUNDED RECTANGLE

In addition to basic rectangles, you can create frames with a number of special corner treatments. The Rounded Rectangle tool automatically creates frames with special corners, but you can also easily modify the corners of an existing frame to create the effect you want.

1. **With crowe.indd open, make sure the Rectangle tool is active, then zoom into the left end of the black rectangle.**

2. **Press Command/Control, then click away from the existing shape to deselect it.**

   If you don't deselect the existing shape, the changes you make in the next step would affect the selected object.

   Pressing Command/Control temporarily switches to the last-used Selection tool (Selection or Direct Selection). This allows you to easily make selections — or, in this case, deselect an object — without changing the active tool.

   When you click to deselect the active object, be careful that you don't accidentally click a white-filled object instead of the empty page or pasteboard area.

3. **In the Control panel, click the arrow button to the right of the Fill swatch to open the attached Swatches panel. Choose Paper from the pop-up panel.**

   There is a difference between no fill and 0% of a color. Using 0% of a color — or using the Paper color — effectively creates a solid "white" fill. (In printing, solid white areas **knock out** or hide underlying shapes.)

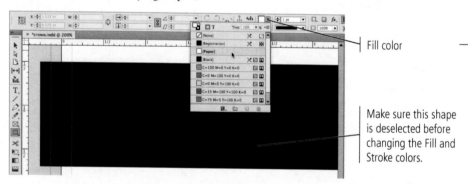

Fill color

Make sure this shape is deselected before changing the Fill and Stroke colors.

4. **In the Control panel, click the arrow button to the right of the Stroke swatch and choose None from the pop-up panel.**

   The "None" color option essentially removes color from that attribute. Underlying objects will be visible in areas where None is applied.

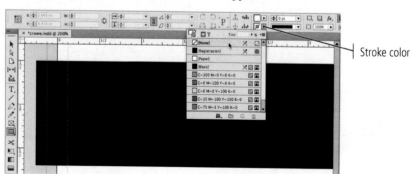

Stroke color

5. **Click once on the page to open the Rectangle dialog box.**

Single-clicking with a shape tool opens a dialog box where you can define specific measurements for the new shape.

6. **In the Rectangle dialog box, set the Width to 0.125 in and the Height to 0.08 in, and then click OK.**

The new rectangle is placed with the selected reference point where you clicked.

7. **Zoom in so you can more clearly see the small rectangle you just created.**

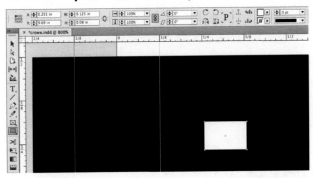

8. **With the new rectangle selected, open the Corner Shape menu in the Control panel and choose the rounded option.**

Leave the Corner Radius field at its default value of 0.1667″ (the equivalent of 1 pica).

Even though the object now has rounded corners, the **bounding box** still marks the outermost corners of the shape. (You might need to zoom in to see the effect of the new corner shape.)

Note:

If you don't see the Corner Shape menu in the Control panel, choose Object>Corner Options to modify the shape of an object's corners. (See Editing Corner Options on Page 398.)

Corner Shape menu   Corner Radius

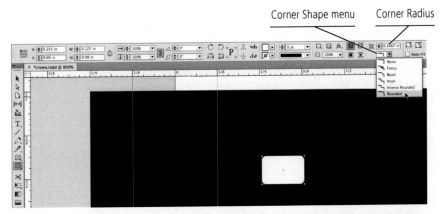

A rounded-corner rectangle is simply a rectangle with the corners cut at a specific distance from the end (the corner radius). The two sides are connected with one-fourth of a circle, which has a radius equal to the amount of the rounding.

Radius

In this case, the rectangle is so small that the corner radius field is not relevant. The application applied the largest possible radius, which is just large enough to see the effect on the corners of the shape.

9. **Save the file and continue to the next exercise.**

When a rectangular frame is selected in the layout, a small yellow square appears on the right edge of the shape's bounding box. You can click this button to enter Live Corner Effects edit mode, where you can dynamically adjust the appearance of corner effects for all corners or for one corner at a time. Simply clicking away from the object exits the edit mode.

You can also edit the corners numerically in the Corner Options dialog box, which you can open by Option/Alt clicking the icon in the Control panel.

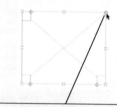

Option/Alt-click this icon to open the Corner Options dialog box.

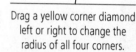

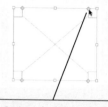

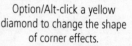

Click this yellow square to enter Live Corner Effects edit mode.

Drag a yellow corner diamond left or right to change the radius of all four corners.

Option/Alt-click a yellow diamond to change the shape of corner effects.

Shift-click a yellow diamond to change the radius of only one corner (Option/Alt-Shift-click to change the shape of one corner).

 ## CLONE, ALIGN, AND DISTRIBUTE MULTIPLE OBJECTS

As you should have already noticed, there is often more than one way to accomplish the same task in InDesign. Aligning multiple objects on a page is no exception. In fact, InDesign offers a number of methods for aligning objects, both to the page and to each other. In this exercise you will explore a number of those options as you create sprocket-hole shapes that will turn the black rectangle into a strip of film.

1. **With crowe.indd open, choose the Selection tool in the Tools panel.**

   The Selection tool is used to select entire objects; the Direct Selection tool is used to select parts of objects or the contents of a frame.

2. **Click inside the area of the rounded rectangle, press the Option/Alt key, and drag right. Release the mouse button when the preview shows a small space between the two objects.**

   Pressing Option/Alt as you drag moves a copy of the selected object (called **cloning**). As you drag, a series of green lines mark the top, center, and bottom of the original object. These green lines are a function of InDesign's Smart Guides, which make it easy to align objects to each other by simply dragging.

Note:

You can also press Shift to constrain the cloning movement to 45° angles.

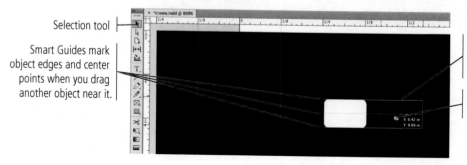

Selection tool

Smart Guides mark object edges and center points when you drag another object near it.

Pressing Option/Alt while you drag clones the selected object.

"Clone" Selection tool cursor

3. **Click the second shape, press Option/Alt, and drag right. Release the mouse button when you see opposing arrows below/between the first and second pair, and the second and third pair of shapes.**

Smart Guides identify equal
spacing between multiple objects.

Note:

Smart Guides also identify equal dimensions when you create a new object near an existing one.

4. **Press Shift and then click the first and second shapes to add them to the current selection.**

   You can Shift-click an object to select it in addition to the previously selected object(s), or Shift-click an already selected object to deselect it without deselecting other objects.

5. **Click inside the area of any of the selected shapes. Drag the selected objects (the three rounded rectangles) so that a small amount of the black background rectangle is visible above the rounded rectangles, and the left rounded rectangle is centered on the bleed guide.**

Click inside the area of
any selected object to
drag all selected objects.

Align the center of the
left shape to the bleed
guide and leave a small
amount of space above
the rounded rectangles.

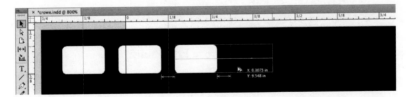

6. **Click away from the active objects to deselect them, then click only the third rounded rectangle. Option/Alt-click and drag right; release the mouse button when the fourth object is evenly spaced with the first three.**

   This step re-establishes the cloning movement as the last-applied transformation.

7. **With the fourth object still selected, choose Object>Transform Again> Transform Again.**

   This command applies the last-used transformation to the selected object. Because you used the cloning movement in the previous step, the result is a fifth copy that is spaced at the same distance you moved the copy in Step 6. (The Transform Again command can be used to re-apply rotation, scaling, sizing, and other transformations.)

Note:

You could also choose Edit>Duplicate, which makes a copy of the selected object using the last-applied movement distance.

8. **Zoom out so you can see the entire width of the document.**

9. **With the new fifth object selected, choose Edit>Step and Repeat. Activate the Preview option in the resulting dialog box. Type 45 in the Count field, then press Tab to initiate the change in the document (behind the dialog box).**

The Step and Repeat dialog box makes a defined number of copies, spaced according to the defined Offset values. By default, these values are set to the last-used movement that you applied in the layout. As you can see, the 50 copies (the original 5 and the 45 that will result from the Step and Repeat process) are all equally spaced, but not enough to fill the filmstrip.

Note:

For the dialog box Preview option to work properly, you have to move the highlight away from the field you changed. Pressing Tab while the dialog box is open allows you to see the results of your changes.

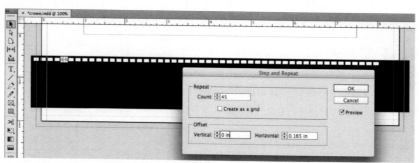

10. **Click OK to make the copies, then click away from the resulting shapes to deselect them.**

11. **Zoom in to the right end of the black rectangle, and select only the right-most rounded rectangle.**

12. **Press Shift, then drag horizontally until the center of the object snaps to the bleed guide.**

Because this object ends up entirely outside the page edge, the Smart Guides no longer appear to mark exact horizontal movement. Pressing Shift while dragging constrains the movement to 45° angles.

As you drag, the bleed guide acts as a magnet; the object's center point snaps to that guide.

13. **Zoom out so you can see the entire page width, then choose Edit>Select All.**

14. **Press Shift and click the black rectangle to deselect only that object.**

When you are working with a large number of objects, it is often easier to deselect what you don't want than to select the ones you do want. Steps 13 and 14 show a very easy way to select most, but not all, of the objects on a page.

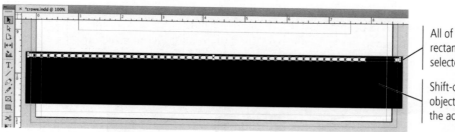

All of the rounded rectangles are still selected.

Shift-clicking a selected object removes it from the active selection.

You can also use the Align panel to align multiple objects relative to one another, to the page margins, to the page, or to the spread.

The Align Objects options are fairly self explanatory; when multiple objects are selected, the objects align based on the edge(s) or center(s) you click.

Align Right Edges
Align Horizontal Centers
Align Left Edges
Distribute Top Edges
Distribute Vertical Centers
Distribute Bottom Edges

Align Top Edges
Align Vertical Centers
Align Bottom Edges
Distribute Right Edges
Distribute Horizontal Centers
Distribute Left Edges

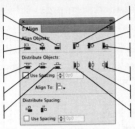

Align To Options

You can use the Align To menu to determine how objects will align.

Using the (default) Align To Selection option, selected objects align to one another based on the outermost edge of the entire selection. In other words, aligning the top edges moves all objects to the same Y position as the highest object in the selection.

By default, the Align Objects options apply based on the outermost edge of the active selection. (Dashed lines indicate the original top edges of the three selected objects.)

If you use the Key Object option, you can click any object in the selection to designate it as the key. (The key object shows a heavier border than other objects in the selection.)

Using the Align To Key Object option, the Align options apply to the edges of the defined key object.

Because you can align objects relative to the document, the align buttons are also available when only one object is selected, allowing you to align any single object to a precise location on the page or spread.

Distribution Options

The Distribute Objects options enable you to control the positions of multiple objects relative to each other. By default, objects are equally distributed within the dimensions of the overall selection; you can check the Use Spacing option to space edges or centers by a specific amount.

By default, the Distribute Objects options equally space the selected objects within the outermost dimensions of the selection.

The Distribute Spacing options place equal space between the overall selected objects. You can also check the Use Spacing option to add a specific amount of space between the selected objects.

Use Spacing places a specific amount of space between the edges (or centers) of selected objects.

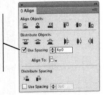

The Distribute Spacing options place a specific amount of space between selected objects.

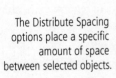

Many of the options from the Align panel are also available in the Control panel; the Align options are also available in all of the built-in workspaces. If you are using the Essentials workspace, the Distribute options are not available in the Control panel; you can turn them on by customizing the panel or by choosing the Advanced workspace option.

15. **Open the Align panel (Window>Object & Layout>Align).**

16. **With all of the rounded rectangles selected, click the Distribute Horizontal Centers button in the Align panel.**

    This button places an equal amount of space between the center points of each selected object. The two outer shapes in the selection act as the anchors; all other objects between the outer objects are repositioned.

Distribute Horizontal Centers

17. **Click any of the selected shapes, press Option/Alt-Shift, and drag down. Position the cloned row near the bottom of the black rectangle, leaving the same amount of space as above the rounded rectangles.**

    By pressing Shift, you constrain the drag/cloning action to 45° angles. In this case, you clone the row of shapes to be automatically aligned below the top row.

18. **Save the file and continue to the next exercise.**

 ## CREATE A COMPOUND PATH

Many shapes are composed of more than one path. The letter "O," for example, requires two separate paths — the outside shape and an inner shape to remove the area inside of the letter; without either path, the shape would be incomplete — just a circle instead of a recognizable letter. In this project, you will combine all of the existing shapes so the filmstrip is treated as a single object rather than 101 separate shapes.

1. **With crowe.indd open, deselect all objects on the page and then click to select only the black rectangle.**

2. **In the Control panel, click the Drop Shadow button.**

    This button applies a drop shadow to the selected object using the default effect settings. As you can see, the shadow is not visible through the sprocket holes because you filled them with the Paper color — which knocks out all underlying color (including the applied shadow). To make the graphic work properly, you have to remove the areas of the rounded rectangles from the black rectangle.

    Note:

    You will learn how to change these effect settings in Project 8: Festival Poster.

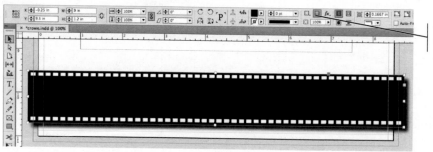

Drop Shadow button

3. **Using the Selection tool, click and drag a marquee that touches all objects that make up the filmstrip graphic.**

Using the Selection tool, any object that is at least partially surrounded by the selection marquee will be included in the resulting selection.

The gray line identifies the selection area.

Objects even partially selected by the marquee are selected.

The Pathfinder Panel in Depth

You can apply a number of transformations to objects using the Pathfinder panel. (The options in the Pathfinder panel are the same as those in the Object>Paths, Object>Pathfinder, Object>Convert Shape, and Object>Convert Point submenus.)

Join Path	Add	Rectangle	Plain Point
Open Path	Subtract	Rounded Rectangle	Corner Point
Close Path	Intersect	Beveled Rectangle	Smooth Point
Reverse Path	Exclude Overlap	Inverse Rounded Rectangle	Symmetrical Point
	Minus Back	Ellipse	
		Triangle	
		Polygon	
		Line	
		Horizontal/Vertical Line	

Path options break (open) a closed path, connect (close) the endpoints of an open path, or reverse a path's direction (start becomes end and vice versa, which is relevant if you use stylized end treatments).

Pathfinder options create complex objects by combining multiple existing objects. When you use the Pathfinder options (other than Subtract), the attributes of the front object are applied to the resulting shape; the Subtract function maintains the attributes of the back object.

- **Add** results in the combined shapes of all selected objects.
- **Subtract** returns the shape of the back object minus any overlapping area of the front object.
- **Intersect** results in the shape of only the overlapping areas of selected objects.
- **Exclude Overlap** results in the shape of all selected objects minus any overlapping areas.
- **Minus Back** results in the shape of the front object minus any area where it overlaps other selected objects.

Convert Shape options change the overall appearance of an object using one of the six defined basic shapes, or using the default polygon settings; you can also convert any existing shape to a basic line or an orthogonal (horizontal or vertical) line.

Convert Point options affect the position of direction handles when a specific anchor point is selected.

- **Plain** creates a point with no direction handles.
- **Corner** creates a point that produces a sharp corner; changing the direction handle on one side of the point does not affect the position or length of the handle on the other side of the point.
- **Smooth** creates a point with opposing direction handles that are exactly 180° from one another; the two handles can have different lengths.
- **Symmetrical** creates a smooth point with equal-length opposing direction handles; changing the length or position of one handle applies the same change to the opposing handle.

4. **Open the Pathfinder panel (Window>Object & Layout>Pathfinder).**

5. **Click the Subtract button in the Pathfinder panel.**

   This button removes the area of front objects from the area of the backmost object. The result is a **compound path**, which is a single shape that is made up of multiple paths; interior paths are removed from the background shape, allowing underlying elements to show through.

   It might take a while for the process to complete because InDesign has a lot of information to process to create the compound shape.

Subtract

The drop shadow is now visible through the holes.

6. **Click away from the active shape to deselect everything.**

7. **Save the file and continue to the next exercise.**

CREATE AND TRANSFORM MULTIPLE FRAMES

Many layouts have defined space requirements for various elements. This letterhead layout, for example, requires eight thumbnail images across the filmstrip graphic, evenly spaced and equally sized — just as you would see on a traditional piece of photographic film. Rather than simply placing the images and resizing the resulting frames for all eight images, you can speed up the process by first creating empty graphics frames that will contain the images when you place them.

1. **With crowe.indd open, arrange your document window and view percentage so you can see the entire filmstrip at the bottom of the page.**

2. **Choose the Rectangle Frame tool in the Tools panel.**

   The frame tools work the same as the basic shape tools; the only difference is that the resulting shape automatically becomes a container for imported graphics or images.

3. **Click the left edge of the filmstrip graphic just below the top row of holes, then drag down and right until cursor feedback shows W: 9 in, H: 0.8 in. Do not release the mouse button.**

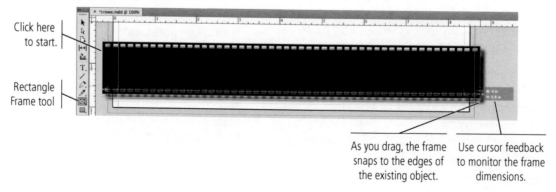

Click here to start.

Rectangle Frame tool

As you drag, the frame snaps to the edges of the existing object.

Use cursor feedback to monitor the frame dimensions.

4. While still holding down the mouse button, press the Right Arrow key.

If you press the arrow keys while creating a frame, you can create a grid of frames within the area that you drag.

- Press the Right Arrow key to add columns.
- Press the Left Arrow key to remove columns.
- Press the Up Arrow key to add rows.
- Press the Down Arrow key to remove rows.

Note:

*This method of creating multiple frames, called **gridified tools**, works with any of the frame or basic shape tools.*

Pressing the Right Arrow key splits the area you draw into two equal-sized frames.

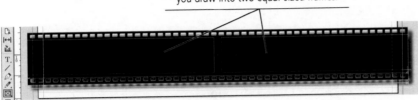

5. Press the Right Arrow key six more times to create a total of eight frames, then release the mouse button.

The resulting frames are equal in size, and have the same amount of space between each.

Crossed diagonal lines indicate that these are empty graphics frames.

6. With the eight resulting frames selected, choose the Selection tool.

As we stated previously, the Selection tool is used to access and manipulate entire objects. Using the Selection tool, you can:

- Click and drag a handle to resize selected objects.
- Shift-click and drag to resize objects proportionally.
- Command/Control-click and drag to scale selected objects.
- Command/Control-Shift-click and drag to scale selected objects proportionally.
- Press Option/Alt with any of these to apply the transformation around the selection's center point.

Note:

In InDesign CC, you can resize, rotate, or scale multiple objects at once without first grouping them.

7. Click the right-center bounding box handle of the active selection. Press and hold the Spacebar, then drag left. When the cursor feedback shows W: 8.625 in, release the mouse button.

As you drag, the space between the selected objects changes; the size of the actual objects is not affected. This method is called **live distribution**; to work properly, you must click the handle before pressing the Spacebar.

Note:

You might need to zoom in to get an accurate three-decimal value in the cursor feedback.

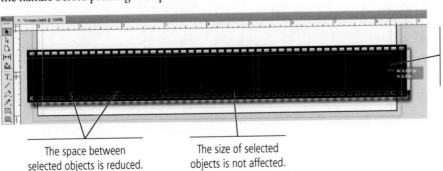

Click the center handle, then press the Spacebar and drag left.

The space between selected objects is reduced.

The size of selected objects is not affected.

8. **Click the right-center handle again. Without pressing the Spacebar, drag right until the handle snaps to the right edge of the filmstrip.**

Simply dragging the handle resizes the entire selection; the spacing and position of various selected objects relative to one another is not affected.

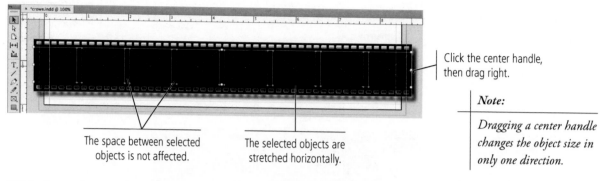

The space between selected objects is not affected.

The selected objects are stretched horizontally.

Click the center handle, then drag right.

9. **With the eight empty frames selected, choose Object>Group.**

Grouping multiple objects means you can treat them as a single unit. This is necessary when you want to use the align options to position the group of frames relative to other objects without affecting the positioning of the placeholder frames relative to one another.

After grouping, a single bounding box outlines the entire group.

10. **Press Shift, and click the filmstrip graphic to add it to the active selection.**

11. **Using the Align panel or the Control panel, click the Align Horizontal Centers and Align Vertical Centers buttons.**

Depending on how precisely you created and transformed the frames, this might have a very noticeable effect; it ensures that the frames are centered to the filmstrip graphic.

12. **In the Control panel, choose the center reference point.**

13. **Place the Selection tool cursor just outside any corner handle of the selection. When you see the Rotate cursor, click and drag up until the cursor feedback shows 3°.**

Place the Selection tool cursor just outside a corner handle to rotate the selection.

The rotation is applied around the selected reference point.

Rotation Angle field

The orange lines show the angle compared to the horizontal plane.

Cursor feedback shows the degree of rotation.

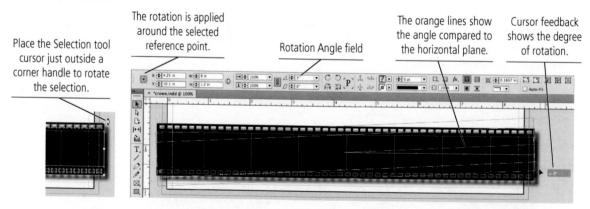

14. **Using the Selection tool, click away from the shapes that make up the filmstrip graphic to deselect the objects.**

15. **Save the file and continue to the next exercise.**

CREATE A SIMPLE LINE

InDesign includes two tools for creating lines: the Line tool for creating straight lines and the Pen tool for creating curved lines called **Bézier curves** (although you can also create straight lines with the Pen tool). In this exercise, you create the most basic element possible: a straight line. You then add anchor points to the line to create a multi-segment path.

Every line is composed of anchor points and line segments that connect those points. Even a simple straight line has two points, one at each end. More sophisticated shapes can be created by adding anchor points, and manipulating the direction handles of those points to control the shape of segments that connect the different points.

This concept is the heart of Bézier curves and vector-based drawing, and can be one of the most challenging skills for new designers to master. The Pen tool (and its variations) is extremely powerful, but also very confusing for new users. The best way to understand this tool is simply to practice. As you gain experience, you will become more comfortable with manipulating anchor points, handles, and line segments.

Note:

Bézier curves can be difficult to master without a relatively deep understanding of geometry or trigonometry. The best training is to practice until you can recognize and predict how moving a point or handle will affect the connected segments.

1. **With crowe.indd open, choose the Line tool in the Tools panel.**

2. **Click the Default Fill and Stroke button at the bottom of the Tools panel.**

   The default options for the Line tool are a 1-pt black stroke with no fill.

3. **At the top of the page, click at the left bleed guide and drag to the right bleed guide. Press Shift, and then release the mouse button.**

   As you drag, the cursor feedback shows the length of the line you are drawing. The blue line previews what will appear when you release the mouse button. Pressing Shift as you draw forces or constrains the line to exact 45° angles — including exactly horizontal.

Note:

When drawing lines, cursor feedback shows the length of the segment you are drawing.

Default values define a
1-pt black stroke.　　　Stroke Weight　Stroke Style

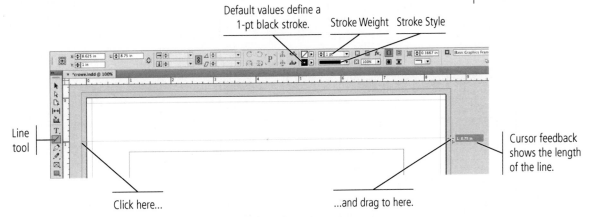

Line tool

Cursor feedback shows the length of the line.

Click here...　　　...and drag to here.

4. **In the Control panel, open the Stroke Weight menu and choose 2 pt.**

   You can choose one of the stroke weight presets from this menu, or simply type any value in the field.

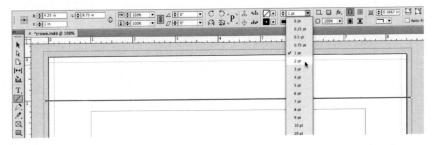

5. At the left end of the Control panel, change the Y field to 1″ and press Return/Enter to apply the change.

Because you constrained this line, changing the Y field moves the entire line.

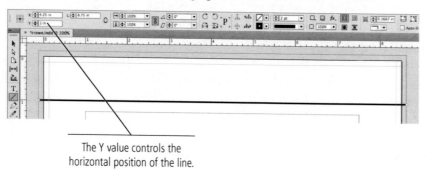

Note:

Remember, you do not need to type the units if you are entering a measurement in the default unit of measurement. We include the units in our steps for the sake of clarity.

The Y value controls the horizontal position of the line.

6. Choose the Pen tool in the Tools panel.

7. Move the cursor over the line you just created.

When the Pen tool is over an existing selected line, it automatically switches to the Add Anchor Point tool cursor; clicking adds a new point to the selected line.

If the Pen tool is over a specific point on a selected line, it automatically switches to the Delete Anchor Point tool cursor; clicking removes that point from the line.

8. When the cursor is at the 3.625″ mark of the horizontal page ruler, click to add a point to the line.

The visible center point of the selected line is a bit deceptive. This simply marks the center of the shape (a line, in this case); it is not an actual point on the line.

When over an existing selected line, the Pen tool cursor changes to the Add Anchor Point tool cursor.

This gray mark shows the position of the cursor.

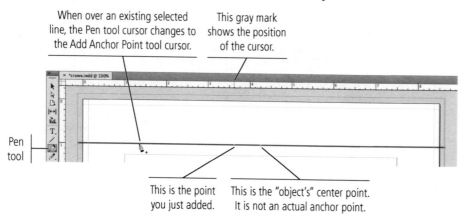

Pen tool

This is the point you just added.

This is the "object's" center point. It is not an actual anchor point.

9. Move the cursor right to the 4.375″ mark and click to add another point.

All vector objects are composed of anchor points and connecting line segments, even if you don't create each point manually. The original line had two regular points, one at each end, and a straight connecting segment. You added two new points, for a total of four points and three connecting segments.

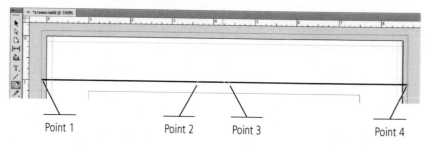

Point 1   Point 2   Point 3   Point 4

10. **Choose the Direct Selection tool in the Tools panel, and click away from the line to deselect it.**

The Direct Selection tool is used to select individual pieces of objects, such as a specific point on a line, or a specific line segment between two points. However, you have to first deselect the entire line before you can select only part of it.

11. **Move the cursor over the left part of the line.**

When the Direct Selection tool cursor shows a small line in the icon, clicking will select the specific segment under the cursor.

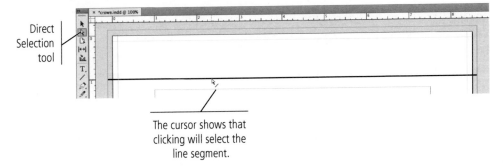

Direct Selection tool

The cursor shows that clicking will select the line segment.

12. **Click anywhere between the first and second points on the line. Press Shift, and drag up until the cursor feedback shows the Y position of 0.2 in.**

The segment you selected moves, and the segment between points 2 and 3 adjusts as necessary to remain connected. The segment between points 3 and 4 is not affected.

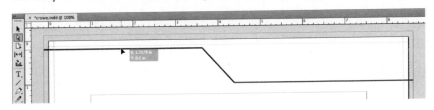

Note:

You might need to zoom in to achieve the correct position for the segment you are dragging.

13. **Using the Direct Selection tool, click the second point from the left (Point 2).**

When the Direct Selection tool cursor shows a small circle in the icon, clicking will select the specific point under the cursor.

14. **In the Control panel, change the X position of the selected point to 3.625 in.**

As you can see, you can control the precise position of every point in a shape.

You can define the exact position of the selected point.

The cursor shows that clicking will select the point.

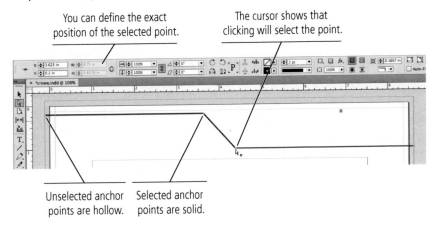

Unselected anchor points are hollow.

Selected anchor points are solid.

15. **Save the file and continue to the next exercise.**

CREATE BÉZIER CURVES

In this exercise you will make very simple manipulations to the straight line you just created. We also encourage you to practice as much as possible using the Pen tool until you are more proficient; for example, try copying the outlines of various shapes in photographs.

1. **With** `crowe.indd` **open, make sure the line at the top of the page is selected.**

2. **Choose the Convert Direction Point tool nested under the Pen tool.**

   The Convert Direction Point tool changes a corner point to a smooth point. **Smooth points** have handles that control the size and shape of curves connected to that point. You can use the Direct Selection tool to drag handles for a selected anchor point.

3. **Click the second point on the line, press Shift, and drag right until the ruler shows that the cursor is at 4.125".**

   When you click a point with the Convert Direction Point tool and immediately drag, you add direction handles to the point. Those direction handles define the shape of the line segments that are connected to the point. As you drag farther away from the point, the affected segment's curve increases.

   Pressing Shift constrains the new direction handles to 45° angles — in this case, exactly horizontal. If you look closely, you can see that the direction handle on the left side of the point is exactly on top of the line.

   By default, clicking and dragging creates a smooth, symmetrical point in which equal-length handles are added to each side of the point directly opposite each other. As long as a point is symmetrical, changing the angle of one handle also affects the handle on the other side of the point.

Note:

Using the Convert Direction Point tool, you can click an existing point and drag to add handles to the point, converting the point to a smooth point.

Note:

If you add points to a curved line segment, the new points automatically adopt the necessary direction handles to maintain the original curve shapes.

Click the point and drag right to add handles.   Press Shift while you drag to constrain the handle to the horizontal.

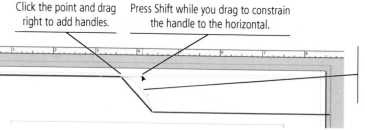

The connected line bends in the direction in which you pull the handle.

4. **Click the third point, press Shift, and drag right until the ruler shows that the cursor is at 4.875".**

   As we just explained, the affected curve gets larger as you drag farther away from the point. Because you're dragging exactly horizontally, the horizontal segment on the right is not curving.

   On the left side of the point, however, you can see the effect of converting Point 3 to a symmetrical point. Dragging to the right side of the point adds direction handles on *both sides* of the point; the length and position of the left handle defines the shape of the curve on the left side of the point — which is the one you want to affect in this step.

Note:

The lines that connect anchor points based on the angle and length of the control handles are called Bézier curves.

Note:

When you drag direction handles, the blue lines preview the effects of your changes.

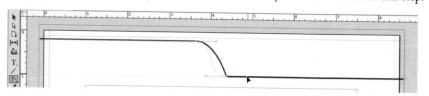

5. **Choose the Pen tool in the Tools panel. (It is now nested under the Convert Direction Point tool.)**

    When you choose a nested tool variation, the nested tool becomes the default option in that position on the Tools panel.

Note:

If you move an anchor point that has direction handles, the handles don't change angle or length. The related curves change shape based on the new position of the point.

6. **Move the cursor over the left endpoint of the line. When you see a diagonal line in the cursor icon, click to connect to the existing endpoint.**

    This icon indicates that clicking will connect to the open endpoint.

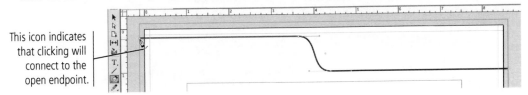

7. **Press Shift, then click at the top-left bleed guide.**

    Shift-click to create a vertical line between the previous point and the point where you click.

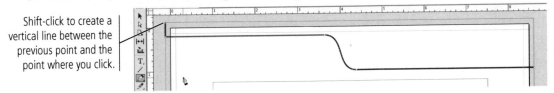

8. **Press Shift, then click the top-right bleed guide.**

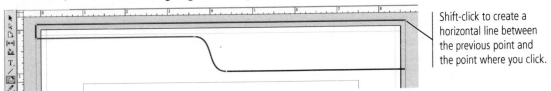

    Shift-click to create a horizontal line between the previous point and the point where you click.

9. **Move the cursor over the open endpoint at the right end of the original line. When you see a small circle in the cursor icon, click to close the shape.**

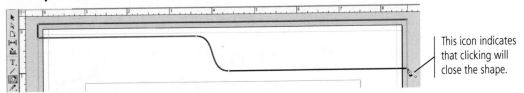

    This icon indicates that clicking will close the shape.

    You could have created this shape as a regular rectangle and then modified the bottom line with the Pen tool. However, our goal was to teach you how to create a basic line, and then how to perform some basic tasks with the Pen tool and its nested variations.

    It's important to realize that there is almost always more than one way to accomplish a specific goal in InDesign. As you gain experience, you will develop personal preferences for the most effective and efficient methods of doing what you need to do.

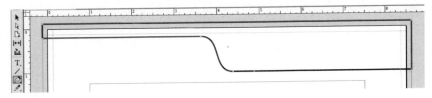

10. **Save the file and continue to the next exercise.**

CHANGE COLOR VALUES

Although there are several default color choices built into the Swatches panel of every InDesign file, you are not limited to these few options. You can define virtually any color based on specific values of component colors. (Keep in mind that when you are building a page to be printed, you should use CMYK colors.)

1. **With crowe.indd open, use the Selection tool to make sure the shape at the top of the page is selected.**

2. **At the bottom of the Tools panel, click the Swap Fill and Stroke button.**

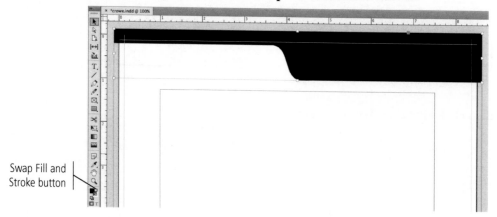

Swap Fill and Stroke button

3. **Open the Color panel (Window>Color>Color).**

4. **Click the Fill swatch to bring it to the front (if it isn't already).**

   When you apply color from any of the Swatches panels (including the ones in the Control panel), the Color panel shows a swatch of that color as a single slider. You can use this slider to easily apply a percentage of the selected swatch.

5. **Click the Options button in the top-right corner of the panel and choose CMYK from the Options menu.**

   This option converts the single swatch slider to the four process-color sliders. You can change any ink percentage to change the object's fill color.

Note:

Remember, all panels can be accessed in the Window menu. Because workspace arrangement is a matter of personal preference, we won't tell you where to place or keep panels.

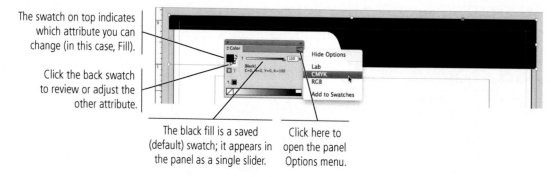

The swatch on top indicates which attribute you can change (in this case, Fill).

Click the back swatch to review or adjust the other attribute.

The black fill is a saved (default) swatch; it appears in the panel as a single slider.

Click here to open the panel Options menu.

6. Click the M slider and drag until the field shows 40%.

This color, 100% black with some percentage of another ink, is called a **rich black** or **super black**. By itself, plain black ink often lacks density. Rich blacks are commonly used to add density or "temperature" to flat black; adding magenta results in "warmer" blacks, and adding cyan results in "cooler" blacks.

Note:

You can change the color by typing a specific value or by dragging the slider.

Click and drag the slider to change the ink percentage.

7. Save the file and continue to the next stage of the project.

Stage 3 Placing External Images

As you saw in the first stage of this project, InDesign incorporates a number of tools for building graphics directly in a layout. Of course, most page-layout projects will include files from other sources — logos created in Adobe Illustrator, raster-based images created in Adobe Photoshop, digital photographs, stock images, and many other types of files can be incorporated into a larger project.

PLACE AN ADOBE ILLUSTRATOR FILE

Every image in a layout exists in a frame. You can either create the frame first and place a file into it, or you can simply place an image and create the containing frame at the same time. In this exercise, you are going to place the client's logo and transform the file to fit into the space to the left of the curved line at the top of the layout.

1. With crowe.indd open, make sure nothing is selected in the layout.

2. Choose File>Place. Navigate to the WIP>Letterhead folder and select crowe.ai. At the bottom of the dialog box, check the box to Show Import Options.

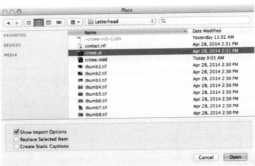

Note:

Artwork in an Illustrator file must be entirely within the bounds of the artboard (page) edge. Anything outside the artboard edge will not be included when you place the file into InDesign.

3. Click Open.

When Show Import Options is checked, the Place [Format] dialog box opens with the options for the relevant file format. Every file format has different available options.

4. **In the General tab, choose Art in the Crop To menu.**

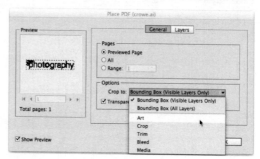

The Crop To menu determines what part of the file will import:

- **Bounding Box** places the file based on the minimum area that encloses the objects on the page. (You can also choose whether to include all layers or only visible layers in the bounding box calculation.)

- **Art** places the file based on the outermost dimensions of artwork in the file.

- **Crop** places the file based on the crop area defined in the file. If no crop area is defined, the file is placed based on the defined artboard dimensions.

- **Trim** places the file based on trim marks defined in the placed file. If no trim marks are defined, the file is placed based on the defined artboard size.

- **Bleed** places the file based on the defined bleed area. If no bleed area is defined, the file is placed based on the defined artboard size.

- **Media** places the file based on the physical paper size on which the PDF file was created. This option is not relevant for native Illustrator files.

Note:

In the General tab, you can also define the specific PDF page or Illustrator artboard of the file to place.

When the Transparent Background option is checked, background objects in the layout show through empty areas of the placed file. If this option is not checked, empty areas of the placed file knock out underlying objects.

5. **Click the Layers tab to display those options.**

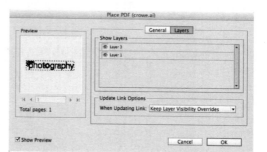

PDF and native Illustrator files can include multiple layers. You can determine which layers to display in the placed file by toggling the eye icons on or off in the Show Layers list. In the Update Link Options menu, you can determine what happens when/if you update the link to the placed file.

- **Keep Layer Visibility Overrides** maintains your choices regarding which layers are visible in the InDesign layout.

- **Use PDF's Layer Visibility** restores the layer status as saved in the placed file.

6. **Click OK to load the cursor with the placed file.**

By default, the loaded Place cursor shows a small thumbnail of the file you're placing. You can turn off the thumbnail preview feature by unchecking the Show Thumbnails on Place option in the Interface pane of the Preferences dialog box.

7. **Click near the top-left corner of the page to place the image.**

Every image in an InDesign layout exists in a frame. When you click an empty area of the page to place an image, the containing frame is automatically created for you.

When the frame is selected, the Control panel defines the frame parameters.

The blue handles show the edge of the graphics frame that contains the logo.

8. **Open the Interface pane of the Preferences dialog box. Choose Immediate in the Live Screen Drawing menu, then click OK.**

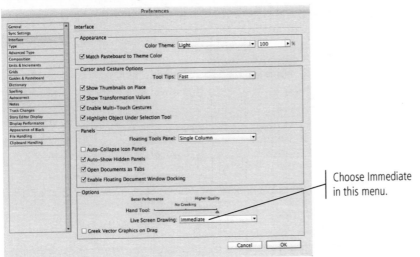

Choose Immediate in this menu.

Note:

Remember, preferences are accessed in the InDesign menu on Macintosh and in the Edit menu on Windows.

Live Screen Drawing controls the appearance of an image when you move or resize it. The default behavior, Delayed, means the image does not appear inside the frame while you change the frame parameters (position, etc.).

Using the Immediate live-screen drawing option, the image inside the frame always appears inside the frame when you move or resize the frame. If Delayed is selected, you can click and hold down the mouse button for a couple of seconds to temporarily access the Immediate preview behavior.

9. **With the placed image selected, check the Auto-Fit option in the Control panel.**

10. **Click the bottom-right corner of the frame, then drag left to make the frame smaller. When cursor feedback shows the frame is 3.6 in wide, release the mouse button.**

By default, the image contained within the frame remains unaffected when you edit the dimensions of a graphics frame. When the Auto-Fit option is checked, however, resizing the frame automatically resizes the contained image to fit the new frame size; the image remains centered inside the frame. Areas of the resized image outside the resized frame remain visible while you hold down the mouse button.

Note:

Unlike raster images, vector graphics can be resized without losing quality.

Note:

When the Auto-Fit option is not selected, you can press the Command key while resizing a frame to scale the content at the same time.

Because the Immediate live-screen drawing option is active, you can immediately see the result of resizing the frame.

When Auto-Fit is checked, resizing the frame also affects the graphic inside the frame.

11. **Uncheck the Auto-Fit option in the Control panel.**

If you don't turn off this option, you will not be able to manually apply other frame fitting commands in the next steps.

Note:

Press Shift while dragging a corner to maintain the original height-to-width aspect ratio in the resized frame.

12. Control/right-click the selected image and choose Fitting>Fit Content Proportionally from the contextual menu.

The fitting options can resize the image relative to its frame, or resize the frame relative to its content.

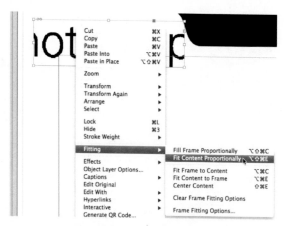

In this case, you defined the available frame width; you are using the fitting options to force the content proportionally into that available space.

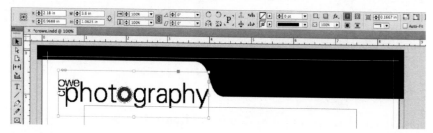

13. With the Selection tool active, move the cursor inside the resized frame.

This reveals the Content Grabber, which you can use to access and manipulate the frame's content without the need to switch tools.

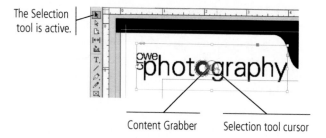

The Selection tool is active.

Content Grabber   Selection tool cursor

14. Click the Content Grabber in the logo frame.

When the frame's content is selected, options in the Control panel relate to the placed object and not the containing frame. The X+ and Y+ fields define the position of the image *within the frame*. The Scale X and Scale Y fields show the file's current size as a percentage of the original.

The Selection tool is active.

The Control panel now shows the parameters of the content in the frame.

The red frame indicates that you are now editing the frame's content instead of the containing frame.

15. With the frame content selected, select the top-left reference point in the Control panel and change the Y+ field to **0**.

16. Control/right-click the frame and choose Fitting>Fit Frame to Content in the contextual menu.

17. Press Esc to return to the frame of the selected object.

The graphics frame is again selected, and the Selection tool is still active.

18. Using the Control panel, choose the top-left reference point and then change the frame's position to X: **0.25 in**, Y: **0.35 in**.

19. Save the file and continue to the next exercise.

PLACE IMAGES INTO EXISTING FRAMES

In many cases, you will need to place an image or graphic into an existing frame and then manipulate the placed file to suit the available space. In the previous stage of this project, you created eight empty graphics frames across the filmstrip graphic; in this exercise, you will place the client's thumbnail photos into those frames.

1. **With crowe.indd open, make the filmstrip graphic at the bottom of the page visible in your document window.**

2. **Using the Selection tool, click one of the empty graphics frames.**

   When objects are grouped, the Selection tool selects the entire group.

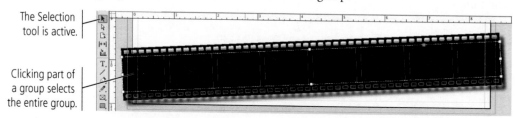

The Selection tool is active.

Clicking part of a group selects the entire group.

3. **Open the Layers panel (Window>Layers), then click the arrow to the left of Layer 1 to expand the layer.**

   Every file has a default layer named "Layer 1," where any objects that you create exist automatically. (You will use multiple layers in a later project to create multiple versions of a document.)

   The Layers panel also serves another purpose. Every object on a layer is listed in the panel, nested under the appropriate layer name. Groups, which you created in an earlier exercise, can be expanded so you can access and manage the individual components of the group.

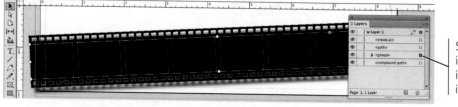

Solid-color squares in this column indicate which items are selected.

4. **Click the arrow to the left of the <group> item to expand the group.**

5. **Click the Select Item button for the first <rectangle> item in the group.**

   This method makes it easy to work with individual items in a group without first breaking apart the group.

Click the arrows to expand or collapse a layer or group.

The smaller square indicates that one or more objects in the group are selected.

Click this icon to select a specific item within the group.

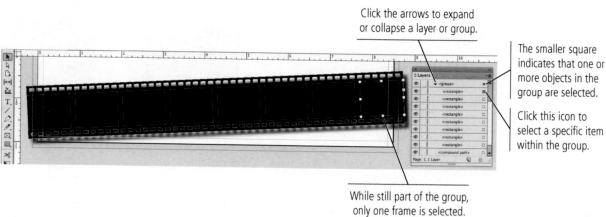

While still part of the group, only one frame is selected.

6. **Using the Selection tool, Control/right-click the selected graphics frame and choose Fitting>Frame Fitting Options in the contextual menu.**

In this case, you know how much space is available, but you don't yet know the size of the images that are intended to fill the space. You can use the Frame Fitting options to determine what will happen when you place any image into the existing frames.

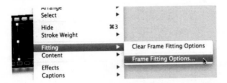

Note:

You can also use the Direct Selection tool to select individual objects within a group.

7. **In the Frame Fitting Options dialog box, activate the Auto-Fit option. Choose Fill Frame Proportionally in the Fitting menu, choose the center point in the Align From proxy, and click OK.**

When an image is placed into this frame, it will fill the entire frame and the aspect ratio of the image will be maintained.

Use these reference points to control the position of placed content relative to the frame.

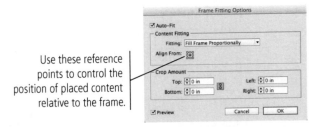

8. **With the Selection tool still active, click the seventh frame to select it.**

When you are already "inside" a group, you can use the Selection tool to select another individual object within the same group.

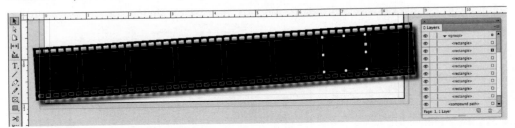

9. **Click the Auto-Fit option in the Control panel.**

Because the center registration point is the default Content Fitting option, you do not need to open the Frame Fitting Options dialog box for each frame in this filmstrip.

10. **Repeat Steps 8–9 for the remaining six placeholder frames.**

11. **Choose File>Place. If necessary, navigate to the WIP>Letterhead folder. Uncheck all options at the bottom of the Place dialog box.**

If you leave Show Import Options checked, you would see the TIFF Options dialog box for each of the selected images. In this case you simply want to place the images, so you don't need to review the file options.

12. Click thumb1.tif to select it. Press Shift and click thumb8.tif to select it and all in-between files.

In many cases, you will need to place more than one image from the same location into an InDesign layout. You can streamline the process by loading multiple images into the cursor at once and then clicking to place each image in the correct location.

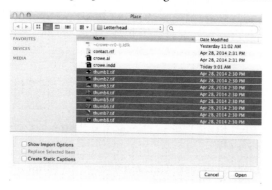

Note:

Press Shift to select multiple contiguous files in a dialog box.

Press Command/Control to select multiple non-contiguous files.

13. Click Open to load the selected files into the Place cursor.

When you select multiple files in the Place dialog box, the cursor is loaded with all of the selected pictures; a number in the cursor shows the number of files that are loaded.

Eight images are currently loaded in the Place cursor.

This thumbnail shows the content of the first file in the cursor.

You can use the Left Arrow and Right Arrow keys to navigate through the loaded images, watching the cursor thumbnails to find the one you want to place.

Note:

When more than one file is loaded in the Place cursor, the Links panel shows "LP" for the item that is active in the Place cursor.

14. Click inside the left placeholder frame to place the first image.

As soon as you place the first file, the next loaded image appears as the cursor thumbnail.

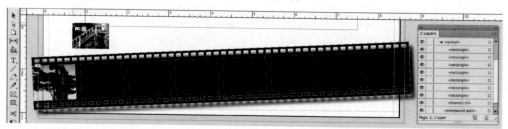

15. Click inside each empty frame to place the remaining loaded images.

16. **Choose the Direct Selection tool, and then click the fifth image thumbnail.**

As already mentioned, the Direct Selection tool can be used to access and manipulate the contents inside a frame. This tool does not require ungrouping. (You could also double-click a grouped item with the Selection tool to access only one item in a group, and then use the Content Indicator icon to access the frame content.)

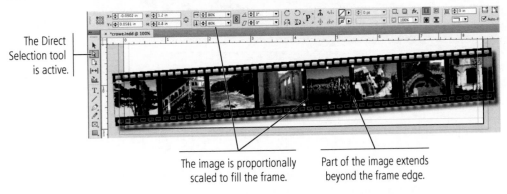

The Direct Selection tool is active.

The image is proportionally scaled to fill the frame.

Part of the image extends beyond the frame edge.

17. **In the Control panel, make sure the link icon for the scaling fields is active (unbroken links). Type 100 in the Scale X field and press Return/Enter to apply the change.**

Because you used the Auto-Fit option, these thumbnail images have all been placed at (approximately) 80% proportionally. The images are already small, and reducing the percentage makes the detail in the fifth image *too* small. You can always change the image scaling after it has been scaled by the Auto-Fit option.

18. **Click inside the frame area and drag until the right edge of the image is approximately aligned to the right edge of the frame.**

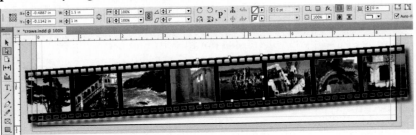

19. **Using the Direct Selection tool, select the seventh image in the filmstrip.**

Remember, the default reference point for the Auto-Fit option centers the image inside the frame. In this image, the horse's head is cut off.

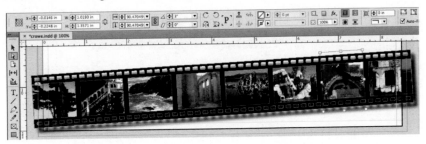

20. Drag the image down inside the frame until the horse's head is visible.

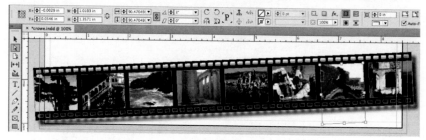

21. Save the file and continue to the next stage of the project.

Stage 4 Creating and Formatting Basic Text

InDesign is ultimately a page-layout application, not an illustration program. **Page layout** means combining text and graphic elements in a meaningful way to convey a message. Text can be a single word (as in the logo used in this project) or thousands of pages of consecutive copy (as in a dictionary). Virtually every project you build in InDesign will involve text in one way or another; this letterhead is no exception.

CREATE A SIMPLE TEXT FRAME

Adding text to a page is a relatively simple process: draw a frame, and then type. In this exercise, you'll create a new text frame and add the client's tag line, then apply some basic formatting options to style the text.

Keep in mind that this project is an introduction to creating elements on a layout page; there is far more to professional typesetting than the few options you use here. InDesign provides extremely precise control over virtually every aspect of every letter and word on the page. In the following projects, you will learn about the vast number of options that are available for setting and controlling type, from formatting a single paragraph to an entire multi-page booklet.

Note:

Remember from the Getting Started section at the beginning of this book: to complete the projects in this book, you should install and activate the ATC fonts that are provided with the book resource files.

1. With **crowe.indd** open, select the Type tool in the Tools panel.

2. Click in the empty space below the placed logo and drag to create a frame.

To type text into a layout, you must first create a frame with the Type tool; when you release the mouse button, you see a flashing bar (called the **insertion point**) where you first clicked to create the text frame.

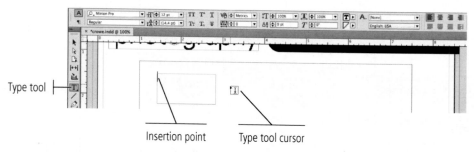

Type tool

Insertion point Type tool cursor

The tag line for the letterhead is supposed to appear in the black area to the right of the logo. However, if you click inside that area with the Type tool, it will convert the existing shape to a type area. In this case you want a simple rectangular text frame, so you are creating it in an empty area, and then moving it into place.

3. Review the character formatting options in the Control panel.

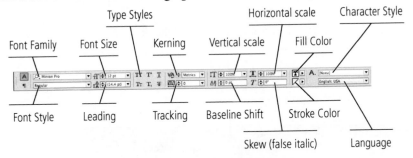

Type Styles — Horizontal scale — Character Style — Font Family — Font Size — Kerning — Vertical scale — Fill Color — Font Style — Leading — Tracking — Baseline Shift — Stroke Color — Skew (false italic) — Language

4. Type urban architecture & natural landscapes.

The text appears, beginning at the flashing insertion point. Depending on the size of your frame, the text might automatically wrap to a second line within the frame.

New text in InDesign is automatically set in black 12-pt Minion Pro. This font is installed along with the application, so it should be available on your computer unless someone has modified your system fonts. Don't worry if your type appears in some other font; you will change it shortly.

Note:

Type defaults to a 100% black fill with no stroke. (You can apply a stroke to type, but you should be very careful when you do to avoid destroying the letter shapes.)

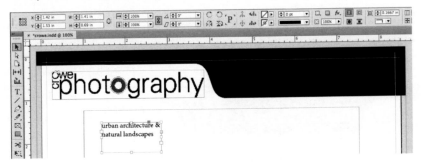

5. Choose the Selection tool in the Tools panel.

You must use the Selection tool to change the position and size of a text frame. You can either drag the handles to manually change the frame, or use the Control panel options to define specific parameters.

6. In the Control panel, choose the bottom-right reference point and then change the frame's dimensions to:

> X: 8.25 in   W: 4.1 in
>
> Y: 0.8 in   H: 0.25 in

Some attributes of a type frame are no different than a graphics frame. You can change the position and size (based on the selected reference point) using the fields on the left end of the Control panel.

Most Control panel options for a type frame are the same as for any other frame.

When the frame is selected, these options define the color attributes of the frame.

Because type is black by default, it is not visible over the black shape.

The Selection tool is active.

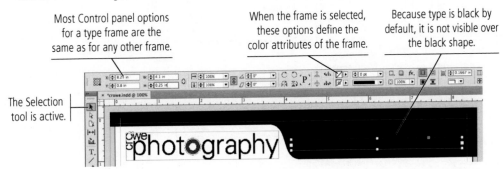

Project 7: Letterhead Design   423

7. **Choose the Type tool, and click inside the repositioned text frame to place the insertion point.**

Because the default type format is black, you can't see the characters on the black background. Because you know they are there, you can still select them.

The insertion point is placed even though you can't see the black text.

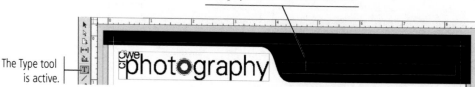

The Type tool is active.

8. **Choose Edit>Select All to select all of the text in the frame.**

Character formatting such as the font, style, and size apply only to selected characters.

9. **In the Control panel, open the Fill swatch panel and click the Paper color.**

The white-filled text now appears over the black background. (It is still highlighted, so it currently appears in reverse.)

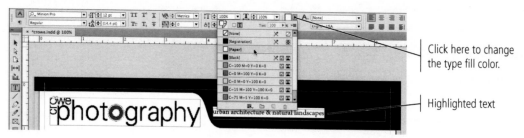

Click here to change the type fill color.

Highlighted text

10. **With the text still selected, click in the Font Family field to highlight the current font name.**

11. **With the font name highlighted, type ATC.**

When you type in the Font Family field, the application automatically presents a menu of all fonts that include the letters you type.

By default, the application presents any font that includes the search characters *anywhere in the font name*; a search for "gar" would find both Garamond and Devangari. This kind of search returns all matching fonts in the pop-up menu.

If you click the magnifying glass icon, you can also choose to Search First Word Only. In this case, typing "gar" would automatically change the Font Family field to the first font that begins with those characters; no menu is presented.

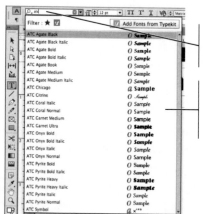

Use this field to search for fonts with specific names.

The resulting menu shows all fonts that include the characters you type.

12. Choose ATC Onyx Italic in the font-search menu.

After choosing the font you want, you should notice that the Control panel shows ATC Onyx in the Font Family menu and Italic in the Font Style menu.

The applied font appears in the Font Family menu.

The specific style appears in the Font Style menu.

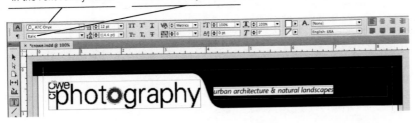

13. Click the Up-Arrow button for the Font Size field until you see a red icon on the right edge of the frame.

Each time you click, you increase the type size by one point. The red X is the **overset text icon**; it indicates that more text exists than will fit into the frame.

Click these buttons to change the type size by 1 point.

Overset text icon

When you see an overset text icon, you can:

- Edit the text to fit the space, which is usually not allowable for a graphic designer.

- Make the frame larger to fit the text, which is not always possible.

- Add more frames to the story and thread the text into the extra frames, which is also not always possible.

- Reduce the type size or adjust other formatting options to make the type fit into the available space, which can make text unreadable (depending on how small you have to make it).

Selecting Text

INDESIGN FOUNDATIONS

You have a number of options for selecting type characters in a frame.

- Select specific characters by clicking with the Type tool and dragging.
- Double-click a word to select the entire word.
- Triple-click a word to select the entire line that contains the word.
- Quadruple-click a word to select the entire paragraph that contains the word.
- Place the insertion point and press Shift-Right Arrow or Shift-Left Arrow to select the character to the immediate right or left of the insertion point, respectively.

- Place the insertion point and press Shift-Up Arrow or Shift-Down Arrow to select all characters up to the same position as the insertion point in the previous or next line, respectively.
- Place the insertion point and press Command/Control-Shift-Right Arrow or Command/Control-Shift-Left Arrow to select the entire word immediately to the right or left of the insertion point, respectively.
- Place the insertion point and press Command/Control-Shift-Up Arrow or Command/Control-Shift-Down Arrow to select the rest of paragraph immediately before or after the insertion point, respectively.

If you click the arrow to the right of the Font Family menu, you will see a menu that lists every font that is available to InDesign.

The top section of the menu lists the ten most **recent fonts**. By default, these appear in the order they were used (the most recently used appears at the top of the menu). In the Type pane of the Preferences dialog box, you can change the number of displayed fonts; you can also choose to list them alphabetically instead of in the order they were used.

The second section of the menu lists **document fonts** (if any). These are fonts that exist in a "Document Fonts" folder that resides in the same folder as the active InDesign file. Document Fonts are available for the active file even if they are not installed on your operating system. (See Project 9: Aerospace Newsletter for more about creating a job package).

Clear the Font Family field — Open the Font menu

Click here to change the search behavior when you type in the Font Family field.

Click a hollow star to add a font to your "favorites" list.

Click a solid star to remove a font from your "favorites" list.

Click an arrow to show all styles available in a specific font family.

Recently used fonts appear at the top of the menu.

Document fonts appear in the second section of the menu.

Available fonts appear in the lower part of the menu.

OpenType font

Typekit font

PostScript font

TrueType font

The top of the Font menu includes options for filtering fonts to show only fonts that are marked as favorites, or fonts that are synced through Typekit. (You can also click the Add Fonts from Typekit button to navigate to the Adobe Typekit Web site, where you can browse and select fonts to sync in your Adobe Creative Cloud account.)

Toggle these buttons to show only favorite fonts or only Typekit fonts.

Each font listed in the Font menu includes a number of elements:

- You can use the star icons on the left side of the font menu to define "favorite" fonts. You can then use the button at the top of the menu to show only those fonts that you have marked as favorites.

- The font family names in each section appear in alphabetical order.

  An arrow to the left of a font name indicates that a specific font family includes more than one style. You can click the arrow to show all possible styles.

  If you apply a font that includes more than one style, the style you choose appears in the Font Style menu below the Font Family field. You can open the Font Style menu to change the style without changing the font family.

Use the Font Style menu to choose a specific style that is available in the selected font family.

- An icon identifies the type of each font.

  PostScript (Type 1) fonts have two file components (outline and printer) that are required for output.

  TrueType fonts have a single file, but (until recently) were primarily used on the Windows platform.

  OpenType fonts are contained in a single file that can include more than 60,000 glyphs (characters) in a single font. OpenType fonts are cross-platform; the same font can be used on both Macintosh and Windows systems.

  Typekit fonts are those that have been activated from the Adobe Typekit Web site through your Creative Cloud account.

  There are other types of fonts, including PS Type 3 and Multiple Master, but these should generally be avoided.

- A WYSIWYG sample of each font appears at the right side of the menu. You can change the size of the sample in the Type pane of the Preferences dialog box.

14. Click the Down-Arrow button once to reduce the type size by 1 point.

This allows all the type to fit in the frame.

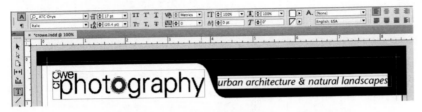

15. Click anywhere in the selected text to place the insertion point.

This removes the highlight, indicating that the characters are now deselected.

16. In the Control panel, click the [Paragraph] Align Right option.

Paragraph formatting — including alignment — applies to the entire paragraph where the insertion point is placed. You don't have to first select the entire paragraph.

Insertion point

Click here to apply right paragraph alignment.

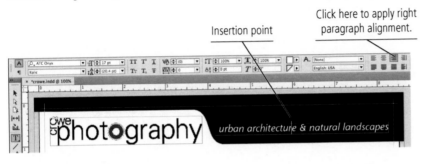

If you don't see the paragraph alignment options in your Control panel, click here to show the paragraph formatting options.

17. Save the file and continue to the next exercise.

☞ PLACE AN EXTERNAL TEXT FILE

You just learned how to create a text frame and create new text. You can also import text that was created in an external word-processing application, which is a common situation when creating page-layout jobs (more common, perhaps, than manually typing text in a frame). In this exercise, you import text that was saved in a rich-text format (RTF) file, which can store type-formatting options as well as the actual text.

1. With crowe.indd open, make sure nothing is selected in the layout and then choose File>Place.

Remember, you can choose Edit>Deselect All, or simply click in an empty area of the workspace to deselect any selected objects.

2. Navigate to **contact.rtf** in the WIP>Letterhead folder. Make sure none of the options are checked at the bottom of the dialog box and click Open.

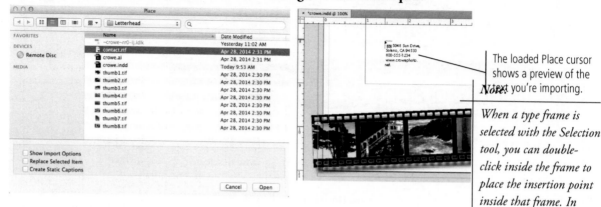

The loaded Place cursor shows a preview of the text you're importing.

3. Click the loaded Place cursor near the bottom of the page, above the filmstrip graphic but within the margin guides.

The resulting text frame is automatically created as wide as the defined margin guides, and extending down to the bottom margin guide on the page.

Placing text from a file automatically creates a text frame to contain the text.

4. Choose the Selection tool. With the text frame selected, click the Fit Frame to Content button in the Control panel.

If you don't see this button, you can Control/right-click the text frame and choose Fitting>Fit Frame to Content.

When working with a text frame, this option reduces the frame to the smallest possible size that can contain the existing text.

Fit Frame to Content button

5. Click the bottom-right bounding box handle of the frame. While still holding down the mouse button, press Command/Control-Shift, and then drag to the right. When the Scale X and Scale Y fields in the Control panel show approximately 125%, release the mouse button.

As you drag the frame handle, pressing Command/Control allows you to resize the type along with the frame. Pressing Shift constrains the scaling to maintain the original height-to-width ratio.

The Scale X and Scale Y fields in the Control panel shows the percentage to which the frame and its content are being scaled.

6. **Move the cursor outside the top-right corner handle until you see the rotation cursor. Click and drag up until you have rotated the frame by 3°.**

This is the same angle that you used for the filmstrip graphic.

Note:

You can also use the Free Transform tool to rotate an object, but changing tools is not necessary since the same rotation functionality can be accessed with the Selection tool.

7. **Using the Selection tool, move the rotated text frame into place just above the filmstrip, with the right edge at 8.25".**

Use the following image as a guide for placing the frame.

8. **Click away from the text frame to deselect all objects, then choose View>Extras>Hide Frame Edges.**

This command turns off the blue borders that surround every frame. Frame edges can be very valuable when you're working with some objects, but they can be distracting in other cases. Always remember that you can toggle the frame edges on and off in the View>Extras submenu.

Note:

If a menu command is not visible, choose Show All Menu Items at the bottom of the menu.

When frame edges are hidden, moving the Selection tool cursor over a frame reveals its edges. This frame highlighting can make it easier to find exactly the object you want, especially when working in an area with a number of overlapping or nearby objects.

9. **Save the file and continue to the final stage of the project.**

Copying and Pasting

The standard Cut, Copy, and Paste options are available in InDesign, just as they are in most applications. Whatever you have selected will be copied or cut to the Clipboard, and whatever is in the Clipboard will be pasted. InDesign has a number of special pasting options in the Edit menu:

Paste. If you are pasting an object (frame, etc.), the object will be pasted in the center of the document window. If you are pasting text, it will be pasted at the location of the current insertion point; if the insertion point is not currently placed, the text is placed in a new basic text frame in the middle of the document window.

Paste without Formatting. This command is available when text is in the Clipboard; the text is pasted using the default type formatting options (12-pt black Minion Pro, if it hasn't been changed on your system).

Paste Into. This command is available when an object is in the Clipboard and another object is selected. The pasted object becomes the contents of the object that is selected when you choose this command.

Paste in Place. This command pastes an object at the exact position as the original. If you paste on the same page as the original, you create a second object exactly on top of the first. You can also use this command to place a copy in the exact position as the original, but on a different page in the layout.

Managing Stacking Order

The top-to-bottom order of objects is called **stacking order**; each object you create is stacked on top of existing objects. When you have multiple stacked objects — especially ones that are closely spaced — it can be difficult to select exactly what you want. Fortunately, the application provides a number of options to make it easier.

When you move the Selection tool cursor over an object, the edges of the object are highlighted. This lets you know what will be selected if you click.

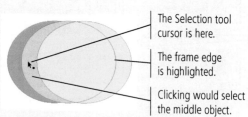

The Selection tool cursor is here.

The frame edge is highlighted.

Clicking would select the middle object.

When an object is already selected, InDesign favors the already selected object. This prevents you from accidentally selecting an object higher in the stacking order (for example, if you want to drag only the middle object), but this also means you have to be careful if you do want to select a different object.

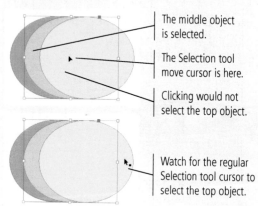

The middle object is selected.

The Selection tool move cursor is here.

Clicking would not select the top object.

Watch for the regular Selection tool cursor to select the top object.

You can use the Object>Select submenu commands (or their related keyboard shortcuts) to access objects relative to their order in the stack.

You can use the Object>Arrange submenu commands (or their related keyboard shortcuts) to change the stacking-order position of objects.

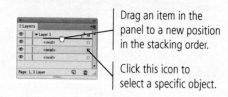

Finally, you can use the individual item listings in the Layers panel to select exactly the object you want, or to rearrange objects in the layer stack.

Drag an item in the panel to a new position in the stacking order.

Click this icon to select a specific object.

Stage 5 Printing InDesign Files

Although the PDF format is the *de facto* standard for submitting files to a commercial printer, you will still need to output printed proofs at some point in your career — whether to show hard copy to a client or to simply review a document's content away from a monitor. Creating those proofs requires a basic understanding of how the software and hardware translate what you see on the screen to ink on paper.

For a printer to output high-quality pages from Adobe InDesign, some method of defining the page and its elements is required. These definitions are provided by Page Description Languages (PDLs), the most widely used of which is Adobe PostScript 3.

When a file is output to a PostScript-enabled device, the raster image processor (RIP) creates a file that includes mathematical descriptions detailing the construction and placement of the various page elements; the print file precisely maps the location of each pixel on the page. In the printer, the RIP then interprets the description of each element into a matrix of ones (black) and zeros (white). The output device uses this matrix to reconstruct the element as a series of individual dots or spots that form a high-resolution bitmap image on film or paper.

Not every printer on the market is capable of interpreting PostScript information. Low-cost, consumer-level inkjet printers, common in the modern graphic design market, are generally not PostScript compatible. (Some desktop printers can handle PostScript, at least with an additional purchase; consult the technical documentation that came with your printer to make certain it can print PostScript information.) If your printer is non-PostScript compatible, some features in the InDesign Print dialog box will be unavailable and some page elements (particularly EPS files) might not output as expected.

If you do not have a PostScript output device, you can work around the problem by first exporting your InDesign files to PDF (see Project 8: Festival Poster) and then opening the PDFs in Acrobat to print a proof. This is a common workflow solution in the current graphic design industry.

PRINT A SAMPLE PROOF

Not too long ago, every job sent to a commercial printer required a hardcopy proof to accompany the disk as an example of the layout content. As digital file submission continues to gain ground, however, physical printer proofs are becoming less common.

In general, every job you create will be printed at some point in the workflow — whether for your own review, as a client comp, or as a final proof that accompanies a file to the commercial printer. So, whether you need a basic proof or a final job proof, you should still understand what is possible in the InDesign Print dialog box.

Composite proofs print all colors on the same sheet, which allows you to judge page geometry and the overall positioning of elements. Final composite proofs that are provided to the printer should include **registration marks** (special printer's marks used to check the alignment of individual inks when the job is printed), and they should always be output at 100% size.

> **Note:**
>
> *It is also important to realize that desktop inkjet and laser printers typically do not accurately represent color.*

1. **With crowe.indd open, choose File>Print.**

   The Print dialog box includes dozens of options in eight different categories.

   The most important options you'll select are the Printer and PPD (PostScript printer description) at the top of the dialog box. InDesign reads the information in the PPD to determine which of the specific print options are available for the current output.

2. **Choose the printer you want to use in the Printer menu, and choose the PPD for that printer in the PPD menu (if possible).**

3. Review the options in the General pane.

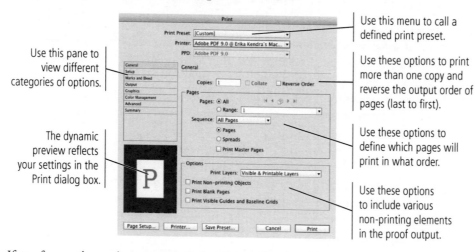

Use this pane to view different categories of options.

Use this menu to call a defined print preset.

Use these options to print more than one copy and reverse the output order of pages (last to first).

The dynamic preview reflects your settings in the Print dialog box.

Use these options to define which pages will print in what order.

Use these options to include various non-printing elements in the proof output.

If you frequently use the same options for printing proofs, simply click the Save Preset button at the bottom of the dialog box after defining those settings. You can then call all of those same settings by choosing the saved preset in the Print Preset menu.

4. Click the Setup option in the list of categories.

These options determine the paper size that will be used for the output (not to be confused with the page size), the paper orientation, and page scaling and positioning options relative to the paper size.

5. If your printer can print to tabloid-size paper, choose Tabloid in the Paper Size menu.

If you can only print to letter-size paper, choose the landscape paper orientation option, and then activate the Tile check box.

To output a letter-size page at 100% on letter-size paper, you have to tile to multiple sheets of paper; using the landscape paper orientation allows you to tile to two sheets instead of four (as shown in the preview area).

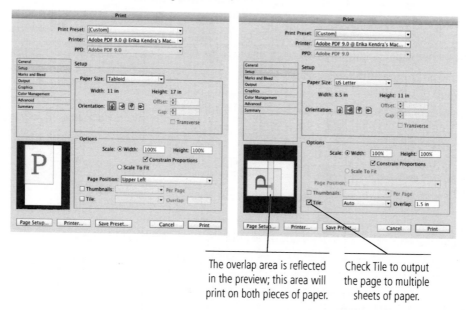

The overlap area is reflected in the preview; this area will print on both pieces of paper.

Check Tile to output the page to multiple sheets of paper.

The Offset and Gap fields should only be used when a job is output to an imagesetter or high-end proofing device. They define page placement on a piece of oversized film or on a printing plate.

6. **Click the Marks and Bleed option in the list of categories. Activate the All Printer's Marks option and change the Offset field to 0.125 in. Make sure the Use Document Bleed Settings option is checked.**

You can specify individual printer's marks, or simply print them all. For proofing purposes, the crop and bleed marks are the most important options to include.

The Offset value determines how far from the page edge printer's marks will be placed; some printers require printer's marks to stay outside the bleed area, which means the offset should be at least the same as the defined bleed area.

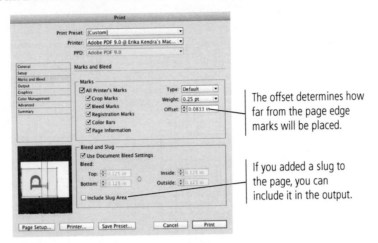

The offset determines how far from the page edge marks will be placed.

If you added a slug to the page, you can include it in the output.

7. **Click the Output option in the list of categories. If you can print color, choose Composite CMYK or Composite RGB in the Color menu; otherwise, choose Composite Gray.**

In the Color menu, you can choose the color model you want to use. (If you only have a black-and-white printer, this menu will default to Composite Gray.) The composite options output all colors to a single page, which is appropriate for a desktop proof. If you choose either Separations option in the menu, the Inks list shows which inks (separations) will be included in the output.

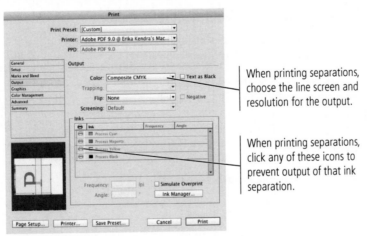

When printing separations, choose the line screen and resolution for the output.

When printing separations, click any of these icons to prevent output of that ink separation.

The Trapping, Flip, Negative, Screening, Frequency, and Angle options should only be used by the output service provider; these options relate to the way separations are imaged on a printing plate for commercial print output.

8. **Click Graphics in the list of categories.**

9. **Choose Optimized Subsampling in the Images Send Data menu.**

   This menu determines how much data is sent to the output device for placed images.

   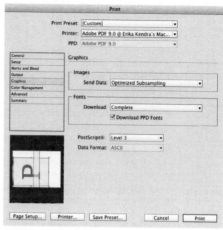

   - All, the default option, sends full-resolution image data.

   - Optimized Subsampling sends only the necessary data to output the best possible resolution on the printer you are using.

   - Proxy outputs low-resolution screen previews, which reduces the time required for output.

   - None outputs all placed images as gray frames with crossed diagonal lines. This is useful for reviewing overall placement when developing an initial layout comp.

10. **Choose Subset in the Fonts Download menu.**

    This menu determines how much font data is downloaded to the printer. (Font data is required by the output device to print the job correctly.)

    - None sends no font information to the printer. (This can cause output problems, especially if you use TrueType fonts.)

    - Complete sends the entire font file for every font that is used in the document.

    - Subset sends font information only for the characters that are used in the document.

11. **Check the Download PPD Fonts option.**

    Professional-quality output devices include a number of resident fonts, from just a few to the entire Adobe type library. If this option is checked, InDesign sends data for all fonts in the document, even if those fonts are installed on the output device. (This can be important because different fonts of the same name might have different font metrics, which can cause text to reflow and appear different in the print than in the file that you created.)

12. **Leave the PostScript and Data Format menus at their default values.**

    The PostScript menu defines which level of PostScript to use. Some older devices cannot process PostScript 3. You should generally leave this menu at the default value.

    The Data Format menu defines how image data is transferred. ASCII is compatible with older devices, and is useful for cross-platform applications. Binary is smaller than ASCII, but might not work on all platforms.

13. **Click Print to output the page.**

14. **When the document comes back into focus, save and close it.**

Note:

We're intentionally skipping the Color Management and Advanced panes in the Print dialog box. We explain them in later projects when they are relevant to the project content.

fill in the blank

1. _____ is the area of an object that extends past the edge of a page to compensate for variations in the output process.

2. The term _____ refers to an object's top-to-bottom position relative to other objects on the page.

3. The _____ defines the outermost dimensions of an object; it is always a rectangle, regardless of the object's specific shape.

4. _____ are based on the concept of anchor points and their defining control handles.

5. _____ is a color swatch that is made up of 100% black and some percentage of another primary ink (typically magenta or cyan).

6. The _____ tool is used to select entire frames or other objects.

7. The _____ tool can be used to select the image contained within a specific frame when the frame is part of a group.

8. The _____ panel can be used to create complex shapes by combining multiple objects.

9. The _____ can be used to access a frame's content when the Selection tool is active.

10. The _____ is context sensitive, reflecting different options depending on what is selected in the document.

short answer

1. Briefly explain how resolution affects a page laid out in InDesign.

2. Briefly explain two ways to select an individual object that is part of a group.

3. Briefly explain the difference between the Selection and the Direct Selection tools.

Use what you learned in this project to complete the following freeform exercise.
Carefully read the art director and client comments, then create your own design to meet the needs of the project.
Use the space below to sketch ideas; when finished, write a brief explanation of your reasoning behind your final design.

art director comments

The owner of your agency is pleased with your work on behalf of your client. She has decided to create more formal branding for your design agency and wants you to create a new logo and the accompanying collateral pieces with the new logo.

To complete this project, you should:

❏ Develop a compelling logo that suggests the agency's purpose (graphic design). Incorporate the agency's name — Creative Concepts — in the logo.

❏ Build a letterhead using the same specifications that you used to design the Crowe letterhead.

❏ Build a business card that is 3.5″ wide by 2″ high, with 1/8″ bleeds.

❏ Build an envelope layout for #10 business-size envelopes (9.5″ × 4.125″).

client comments

For the logo, I want something that really says 'graphic design' — how can we convince clients that we can design their logos if we don't have a good design for our own? Find or create some kind of imagery that people will immediately recognize as graphics- or art-related.

The letterhead should have the company's mailing address, phone number, and Web site. The business card needs to include a name, title, mailing address, email, and phone number. The envelope should only have the mailing address and the Web site. Use your own contact information as placeholder text for everything.

For the envelope, we're going to print pre-folded envelopes so you can't use bleeds. In fact, you need to keep objects at least 0.25″ from the edges.

Keep in mind that you're building a complete identity package, so all pieces should have a consistent look. Whatever you do on the letterhead, you should use similar visual elements on all three pieces.

project justification

_____

_____

_____

_____

_____

_____

_____

_____

_____

_____

_____

_____

_____

We designed this project to introduce you to the basics of page layout with InDesign; you will expand on these skills throughout this book. Creating a new document to meet specific project needs — including page size, margins, and the printer's stated bleed requirements — is one of the most important tasks you will complete in InDesign.

After the page structure is created, InDesign has many tools for creating objects — basic shapes, lines and Bézier curves, placeholder frames, and text frames. The built-in drawing tools can create sophisticated artwork directly on the page, such as the filmstrip in this letterhead layout (although InDesign should not be considered an alternative to Adobe Illustrator for creating all vector artwork). You can also place external image and text files, and then transform those files to meet the specific needs of a given project.

There are many different methods for managing objects and their content. The Selection and Direct Selection tools, the Content Indicator icon, frame edge highlighting, and the Layers panel all provide ways to access only — and exactly — what you want to edit.

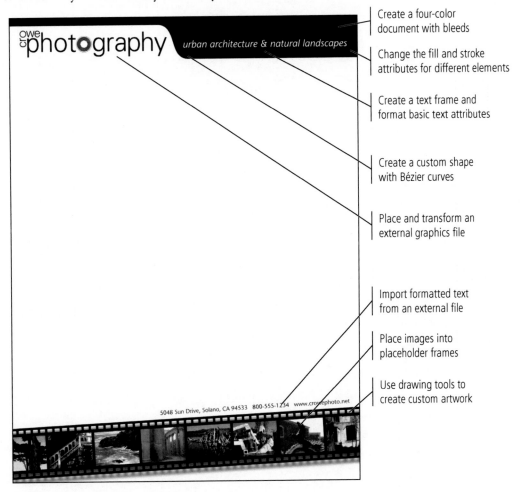

Create a four-color document with bleeds

Change the fill and stroke attributes for different elements

Create a text frame and format basic text attributes

Create a custom shape with Bézier curves

Place and transform an external graphics file

Import formatted text from an external file

Place images into placeholder frames

Use drawing tools to create custom artwork

Festival Poster

Your client is the marketing director for the city of Santa Barbara. She wants to create a poster to advertise the annual Surfrider Festival. She wants to create posters that will be plastered all over the city, from local restaurants and clubs to bus stops and construction sites that don't say "Post No Bills." This type of poster should use very little text set in a large, easy-to-read font, and it needs to be eye-catching from a distance, with large, vivid graphics.

This project incorporates the following skills:

❏ Creating a file with the appropriate settings for a five-color, commercially printed poster

❏ Using gradients, graphics, and image effects to attract the viewer's attention

❏ Adding text elements and applying formatting as appropriate for a poster

❏ Threading a single text story across multiple text frames

❏ Understanding the various options for formatting characters and paragraphs

❏ Using inline graphics to highlight important text elements

❏ Creating a PDF file that meets the printer's requirements

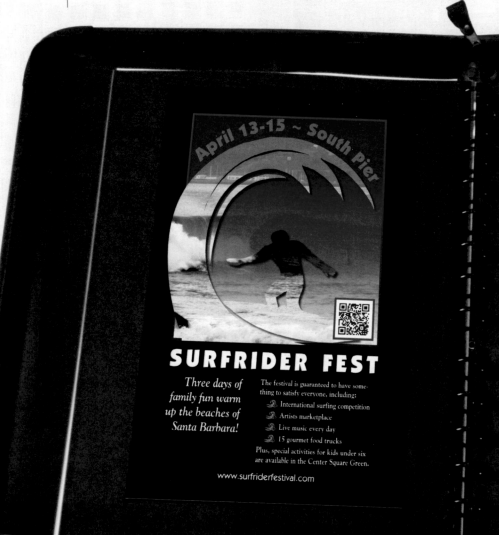

client comments

The poster to promote this festival is basically the "play bill," and we will plaster it all over the city. We want the poster to be very attractive, colorful, and vivid, so the main focus — and most of the poster real estate — should be on the graphics. But the text also has to be readable; I emailed the text I want you to place at the bottom of the poster this morning. Our posters for past years' festivals have always been 11 × 17", and we want to stick with that size.

art director comments

The client has provided all the pieces you need, so you can get started composing the layout. Most of this job is going to involve compositing multiple images and formatting text, but I want you to go beyond basic image placement. InDesign includes many tools for manipulating images; use some of those to make sure this poster consists of more than just plain pictures.

Finally, I want you to use a special metallic ink for the date and location. That should give the poster just a bit more visual impact than regular flat colors. I think the gold 8005 in Pantone's metallic collection will work well with the other visual elements.

You already know the page size, and according to the printer the poster needs a 1/4" bleed allowance just to be safe. The final posters should be saved as PDF using the printer's specs, which I'll email to you.

project objectives

To complete this project, you will:

- ❏ Convert the content type of frames
- ❏ Create a custom gradient to add visual impact
- ❏ Create a custom frame using an image clipping path
- ❏ Apply visual effects to unify various graphic elements
- ❏ Create a QR code
- ❏ Thread the flow of text through multiple text frames
- ❏ Format text characters and paragraphs to effectively convey a message
- ❏ Place inline graphics to highlight important textual elements
- ❏ Place text on a path
- ❏ Apply a spot color
- ❏ Create PDF files for commercial output

Building Graphic Interest

Graphics and text are contained in frames, and that objects (including graphics frames) can have stroke and fill attributes. You can use those foundational skills to build virtually any InDesign layout.

InDesign also includes a number of options for extending your artistic options beyond simply compositing text and graphics that were finalized in other applications. The first stage of this project incorporates a number of these creative tools to accomplish your client's stated goal of grabbing the viewer's attention with vivid, attractive graphics.

SET UP THE WORKSPACE

1. **Download Surfing_Print14_RF.zip from the Student Files Web page.**

2. **Expand the ZIP archive in your WIP folder (Macintosh) or copy the archive contents into your WIP folder (Windows).**

   This results in a folder named **Surfing**, which contains the files you need for this project. You should also use this folder to save the files you create in this project.

3. **With no file open in InDesign, open the Units & Increments pane of the Preferences dialog box (in the InDesign menu on Macintosh or the Edit menu on Windows).**

4. **Change both Ruler Units menus to Inches and click OK.**

   By changing the preferences with no file open, you're changing the application default preferences; the settings that you define will be applied in any new file you create, but not to already-existing files.

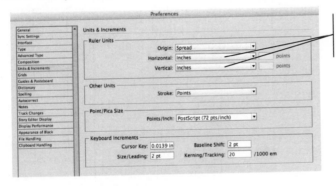

With no file open, change both of these menus to Inches.

Note:

Unless otherwise stated, the remaining projects in this book use inches as the default unit of measurement.

5. **Choose File>New>Document.**

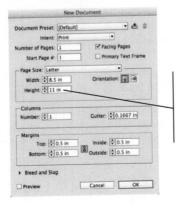

By changing the default units to inches, the measurements in all dialog boxes (including this one) are now shown in inches.

6. Create a new one-page print document that is 11″ wide by 17″ high (Tabloid-size) with 1″ margins and 0.25″ bleeds on all four sides. Create the file with no primary text frame and without facing pages.

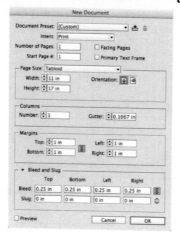

Note:

Industry standards typically call for a 0.125″ bleed, but in this case the printer specifically requested 0.25″ bleed allowance.

7. Save the file as `poster.indd` in your WIP>Surfing folder and then continue to the next exercise.

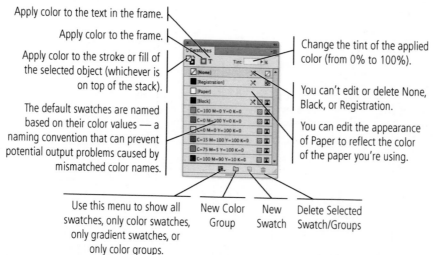

DEFINE COLOR SWATCHES

The Swatches panel is used to apply predefined colors to any element in a layout. Six CMYK color swatches are included in the default set for print documents, as well as three special colors (Paper, Black, and Registration) and a None swatch that removes color from the selected attribute.

Apply color to the text in the frame.

Apply color to the frame.

Apply color to the stroke or fill of the selected object (whichever is on top of the stack).

The default swatches are named based on their color values — a naming convention that can prevent potential output problems caused by mismatched color names.

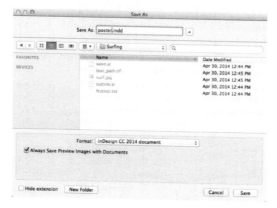

Change the tint of the applied color (from 0% to 100%).

You can't edit or delete None, Black, or Registration.

You can edit the appearance of Paper to reflect the color of the paper you're using.

Use this menu to show all swatches, only color swatches, only gradient swatches, or only color groups.

New Color Group

New Swatch

Delete Selected Swatch/Groups

Note:

Using the Fill and Stroke swatches at the top of the Swatches panel, you can apply different colors to the fill and stroke of selected text.

Note:

Editing the appearance of the Paper swatch only affects the on-screen preview. It does not appear in the print output.

You can define colors based on one of three color models (CMYK, RGB, or LAB), or you can call spot colors from built-in libraries of special inks. Each different mode and type of color has an identifying icon in the Swatches panel.

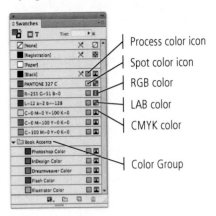

Process color icon
Spot color icon
RGB color
LAB color
CMYK color

Color Group

1. **With poster.indd open, open the Swatches panel (Window>Color>Swatches).**

2. **Open the Swatches panel Options menu.**

   This menu has options for creating four types of color swatches: Color, Tint, Gradient, and Mixed Ink.

   - **Color** swatches store specific colors based on defined percentages of each component ink.

   - **Gradient** swatches store specific transitions from one color to another.

   - A **Tint** swatch is a specific stored percentage of another swatch, which is useful if you frequently use (for example) a 30% tint of C=100 M=42 Y=0 K=73. You can apply that tint with a single click instead of applying the color and then changing the tint of the applied color. Every click you save is a boost in productivity, especially if you're building layouts with multiple elements.

   - **Mixed Ink** swatches allow you to combine percentages of spot and process colors, or of multiple spot colors; this option is only available when at least one spot color exists in the file. The **Mixed Ink Group** option allows you to build multiple swatches at once, based on specific incremental percentages of inks. Be very careful if you use mixed ink swatches; they can be a source of unpredictable color reproduction and potential output problems.

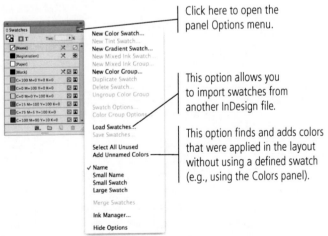

Click here to open the panel Options menu.

This option allows you to import swatches from another InDesign file.

This option finds and adds colors that were applied in the layout without using a defined swatch (e.g., using the Colors panel).

3. **Choose New Color Swatch in the panel Options menu.**

4. **Leave the Name with Color Value option checked. Make sure the Color Type is set to Process and the Color Mode is set to CMYK.**

There is no industry standard for naming colors, but InDesign comes close with the Name with Color Value option. This type of naming convention — basing names on the color components — serves several purposes:

- You know exactly what components the color contains, so you can easily see if you are duplicating colors.

- You can immediately tell that the color should be a process build rather than a special ink or spot color.

- You avoid mismatched color names and duplicated spot colors, which are potential disasters in the commercial printing production process.

Mismatched color names occur when a defined color name has two different values — one defined in the page layout and one defined in an image file that you placed into your layout. When the files are output, the output device might be confused by different definitions for the same color name; the imported value might replace the project's value for that particular color name (or vice versa). The change could be subtle, or it could be drastic.

A similar problem occurs when the same spot color is assigned different names in different applications. For example, you might define a spot color in InDesign as "Border Color"; another designer might define the same spot color in Illustrator as "Spec Blue." When the illustration is placed into the InDesign layout, two different spot-color separations exist even though the different color names have the same values.

Color by Numbers

INDESIGN FOUNDATIONS

If you base your color choices solely on what you see on your monitor, what appears to be a perfect blue sky will probably not look quite right when it's printed with process-color inks. Even if you have calibrated your monitor, no monitor is 100% effective at simulating printed color. As long as monitors display color in RGB, there will always be some discrepancies.

Every designer should have some sort of process-color chart, available from commercial publishers (some printers might provide the charts produced by the exact press on which your job will be printed). These charts contain small squares of process ink builds so you can see, for example, what a process build of C=10 M=70 Y=30 K=20 will look like when printed. These guides usually show samples in steps of 5% or 10%, printed on both coated and uncoated paper (because the type of paper or substrate can dramatically affect the final result).

When you define process colors in an InDesign project, you should enter specific numbers in the CMYK fields to designate your color choices rather than relying on your screen preview. As you gain experience defining colors, you will become better able to predict the outcome for a given process-ink build. Rely on what you know to be true rather than what you hope will be true.

The same concept also applies when using special ink libraries. You should have — and use — swatch books that show printed samples of the special inks. You cannot rely on the monitor preview to choose a special ink color. Rather, you should find the color in a printed swatch book, and then enter the appropriate number in the Pantone field (for example) below the color swatches.

Total Area Coverage

When defining the ink values of a process-color build, you must usually limit your **total area coverage** (TAC, also called **total ink coverage** or **total ink density**), or the amount of ink used in a given color.

This might sound complex, but it can be easily calculated by adding the percentages of each ink used to create the color. If a color is defined as C=45 M=60 Y=90 K=0, the total area coverage is 195% (45 + 60 + 90 + 0).

Maximum TAC limits are between 240% and 320% for offset lithography, depending on the paper being used. If you exceed the TAC limits for a given paper-ink-press combination, your printed job might end up with excess ink bleed, smearing, smudging, show-through, or a number of other printing errors because the paper cannot absorb all of the ink.

5. **Define the swatch with 100% Cyan, 0% Magenta, 100% Yellow, and 25% Black, and then click Add.**

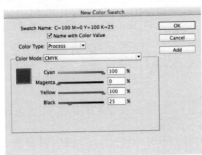

Note:

By clicking the Add button, you can add more color swatches without having to reopen the New Color Swatch dialog box.

Note:

Don't confuse color swatches with ink colors. Because you are using the Process color type, each of these swatches will be printed with the four process inks (CMYK).

6. **Create two more process-color swatches using the following ink values.**

> **Color 1: C=100 M=100 Y=25 K=0**
>
> **Color 2: C=40 M=0 Y=0 K=100**

The third swatch — 100% black and some percent of another color — is called **rich black** or **super black**. Remember, when the inks are printed, adding another ink to solid black enhances the richness of the solid black. Adding cyan typically creates a cooler black, while adding magenta typically creates a warmer black.

7. **In the New Color Swatch dialog box, choose Spot in the Color Type menu.**

8. **Choose Pantone+ Metallic Coated in the Color Mode menu.**

Spot colors are created with special premixed inks to produce a certain color with one ink layer; they are not built from the standard process inks used in CMYK printing. When you output a job with spot colors, each spot color appears on its own separation.

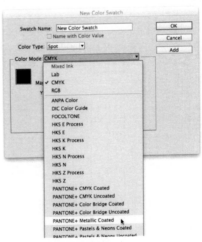

Spot-color inks are commonly used when a special color, such as a corporate color, is required. InDesign includes a number of built-in color libraries, including spot-color systems such as Pantone, Toyo, and DIC. In the United States, the most popular collections of spot colors are the Pantone Matching System (PMS) libraries. TruMatch and Focoltone are also used in the United States; Toyo and DICColor (Dainippon Ink & Chemicals) are used primarily in Japan.

Even though you can choose a color directly from the library on your screen, you should look at a swatch book to verify that you're using the color you intend. Special inks exist because many of the colors cannot be reproduced with process inks, nor can they be accurately represented on a computer monitor. If you specify special colors and then convert them to process colors later, your job probably won't look exactly as you expect.

9. Place the insertion point in the Pantone field and type 8005.

You can also scroll through the list and simply click a color to select it.

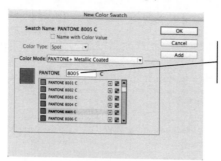

Type a specific color number in this field.

Note:

Spot colors are safely chosen from a swatch book — a book of colors printed with different inks, similar to the paint chip cards used in home decorating.

When choosing spot colors, ask your printer which ink system it supports. If you designate TruMatch, but they use Pantone inks, you won't get the colors you expect.

10. Click Add, then click Done to return to the document window.

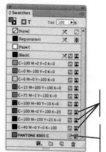

Your three process swatches all use the CMYK model.

This icon identifies the Pantone swatch as a spot color.

11. Save the file and continue to the next exercise.

Working with Color Groups

INDESIGN FOUNDATIONS

Color groups are a convenient way to manage swatches, much as you might organize files in folders on your desktop.

When you click the New Color Group button at the bottom of the Swatches panel, a new group is added to the panel with the default name "Color Group X," where X is simply a sequential number.

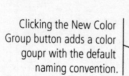

Clicking the New Color Group button adds a color goupr with the default naming convention.

You can double-click the color group name to open the Edit Color Group dialog box, where you can define a specific name for the group.

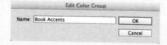

Choosing New Color Group in the panel Options menu automatically opens the Edit Color Group dialog box, where you can name the new group art the time it is created.

If one or more swatches are selected in the panel when you create a new color group, the selected swatches are automatically moved to the new group.

After a group is created, you can drag existing swatches in the group using the following steps:

1a. Click to select a single swatch;
 b. Shift-click to select multiple consecutive swatches, or
 c. Command/Control-click to select multiple nonconsecutive swatches.

2. Release the mouse button.

3. Click one of the selected swatches, away from the swatch name.

4. While holding down the mouse button, drag the selected swatches until a heavy line appears immediately below the color group name.

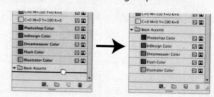

If an existing group, or a swatch inside an existing group, is selected when you create a new swatch, the new swatch is automatically added to the selected group.

CREATE THE POSTER BACKGROUND

The background of this poster is going to be a solid fill of the rich black swatch you defined in the previous exercise. However, an object filling the entire page can cause certain problems. For example, if you try to create a text frame inside the area, you end up converting the frame to a text frame. In this exercise, you use the Layers panel to prevent problems that could be caused by the background shape.

1. **With poster.indd open, choose the Rectangle tool in the Tools panel.**

2. **In the Swatches panel, make sure the Fill swatch is on top and click the C=40 M=0 Y=0 K=100 swatch.**

Click the Fill icon to bring it to the top of the stack (make it active).

Because both are black, it can be hard to tell which attribute is on top.

The Rectangle tool is active.

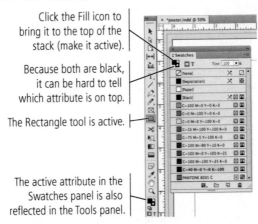

Note:

Remember, all panels (whether docked or not) can be accessed from the Window menu. If you don't see a specific menu command, choose Edit>Show All Menu Items.

The active attribute in the Swatches panel is also reflected in the Tools panel.

3. **Click the Stroke icon at the top of the panel to activate that attribute, then click the None swatch.**

By changing the fill and stroke attributes when no object is selected, you define those attributes for the next object you create.

4. **Using the Rectangle tool, create a rectangle that covers the entire page and extends to the defined bleed guides.**

You can single-click to define the rectangle size, and then drag it into position with the Selection tool. Alternatively, you can simply click and drag with the Rectangle tool, using the Bleed guides to snap the edges of the shape.

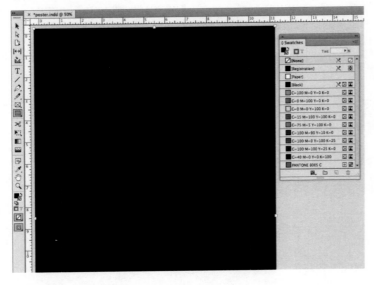

5. **In the Layers panel (Window>Layers), click the arrow to expand Layer 1.**

6. **Click the empty space to the right of the eye icon for the <rectangle> item.**

   The second column in the Layers panel can be used to lock individual items or entire layers. (If you lock a whole layer, all items on that layer are automatically locked.)

   You can click an existing lock icon in the Layers panel to unlock an object or layer.

Note:

You can also click a lock icon on the page to unlock a specific object.

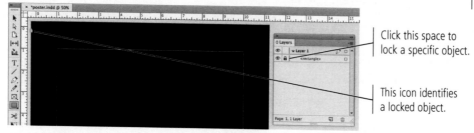

Click this space to lock a specific object.

This icon identifies a locked object.

7. **With the Rectangle tool still selected, change the stroke color to the custom green swatch. Using the Control panel, change the stroke weight to 6 pt.**

   When you locked the rectangle in Step 6, it was automatically deselected. This means that changing the stroke and fill attributes does not affect the existing object.

8. **Click and drag to draw a rectangle that fills the area within the defined margin guides.**

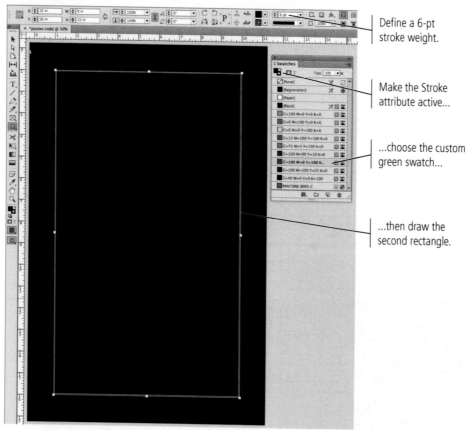

Define a 6-pt stroke weight.

Make the Stroke attribute active...

...choose the custom green swatch...

...then draw the second rectangle.

9. **In the Layers panel, click the eye icon to the left of the locked <rectangle>.**

The visible rectangle has the same fill color as the background shape (which is now hidden). To make it easier to see and work with only specific objects, you can use the Layers panel to toggle the visibility of individual objects or entire layers. (If you hide an entire layer, all objects on that layer are hidden.)

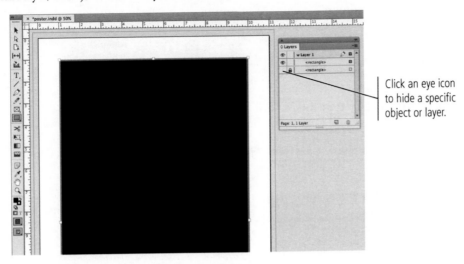

Click an eye icon to hide a specific object or layer.

10. **Save the file and continue to the next exercise.**

DEFINE AND APPLY A GRADIENT

A **gradient**, also called a **blend**, can be used to create a smooth transition from one color to another. You can apply a gradient to any object using the Gradient panel, or you can save a gradient swatch if you plan to use it more than once.

The Gradient panel controls the type and position of applied gradients. You can apply either linear or radial gradients, change the angle of linear gradients, and change the color and location for individual stops along the gradient ramp.

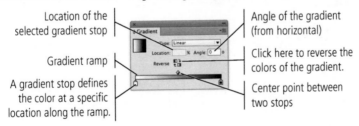

Location of the selected gradient stop

Gradient ramp

A gradient stop defines the color at a specific location along the ramp.

Angle of the gradient (from horizontal)

Click here to reverse the colors of the gradient.

Center point between two stops

1. **With poster.indd open, choose the Selection tool. Click outside the area of the visible rectangle to deselect it.**

2. **Choose New Gradient Swatch from the Swatches panel Options menu.**

3. **Click the gradient stop on the left end of the gradient ramp to select it.**

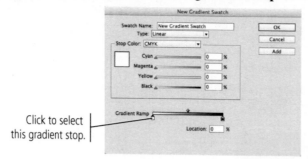

Click to select
this gradient stop.

4. **Make sure Linear is selected in the Type menu, and then choose Swatches in the Stop Color menu.**

You can define gradients using LAB values, CMYK percentages, RGB values, or existing color swatches.

5. **With the first stop selected, click the custom green CMYK swatch.**

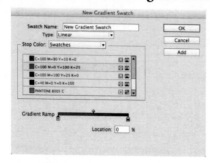

6. **Select the second gradient stop (on the right end of the ramp), and then click the custom blue swatch.**

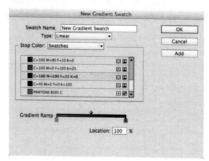

7. **Type Green to Blue in the Swatch Name field and then click OK.**

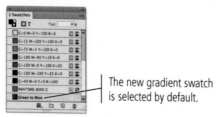

The new gradient swatch
is selected by default.

8. **Using the Selection tool, click the visible rectangle on the page to select it.**

9. **Make the Fill icon active in the Swatches panel, and then click the Green to Blue gradient swatch.**

It is important to remember but easy to forget: make sure the correct attribute (fill or stroke) is active when you change a color.

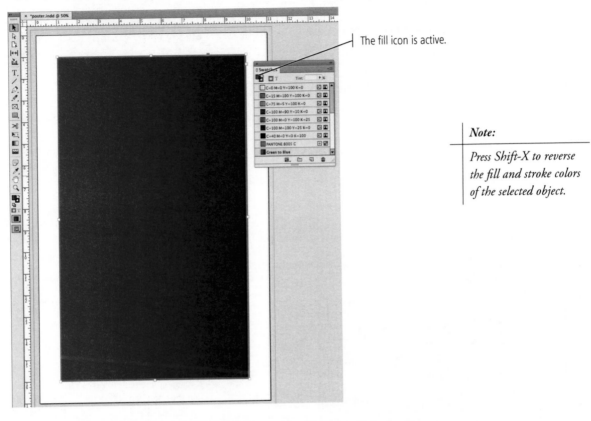

The fill icon is active.

Note:

Press Shift-X to reverse the fill and stroke colors of the selected object.

10. **Make the Stroke icon active in the Swatches panel, and then click the Green to Blue gradient swatch.**

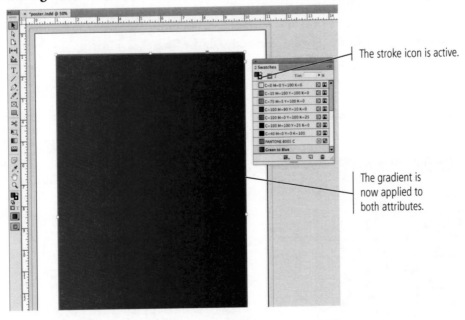

The stroke icon is active.

The gradient is now applied to both attributes.

11. **Save the file and continue to the next exercise.**

As you just saw, it is fairly easy to create and apply a gradient. Once the gradient is in place, you can also modify the specific attributes of a gradient, including its angle and the positioning of specific color stops along its length.

1. **With poster.indd open, make sure the gradient-filled rectangle is selected.**

2. **Using either the Tools or Swatches panel, click to activate the Fill icon.**

3. **Using the Gradient panel (Window>Color>Gradient), change the Angle field to 90° to rotate the gradient.**

Note:

Remember, all panels can be accessed in the Window menu.

4. **Using the Control panel, change the object height to 10 in based on the top-center reference point.**

   When you change the shape dimensions, the applied gradients are adjusted so the end stops still align to the edges of the object.

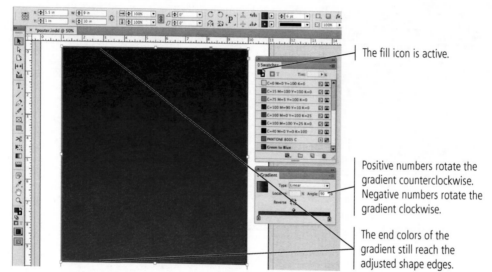

The fill icon is active.

Positive numbers rotate the gradient counterclockwise. Negative numbers rotate the gradient clockwise.

The end colors of the gradient still reach the adjusted shape edges.

5. **With the object still selected, make the Stroke icon active in the Swatches panel.**

   Remember that the attribute on top of the stack is the one you are currently changing. If the wrong attribute is on top of the stack, you will not get the results you are hoping for.

Note:

You can drag a swatch from the Swatches panel to the gradient ramp in the Gradient panel to add a new color stop or to change the color of an existing stop.

6. **In the Gradient panel, change the gradient angle to -90° so the stroke goes from green at the top to blue at the bottom (the reverse of the fill).**

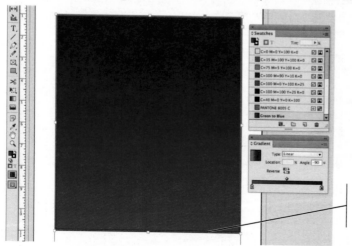

The stroke gradient now has blue on the bottom and green on the top.

7. **Click away from the rectangle to deselect it.**

8. **Use the Screen Mode button on the Tools panel or the Application/Menu bar to display the layout in Preview mode.**

   This option hides all guides and frame edges, which makes it easier to see the subtle effect created by the opposing gradients.

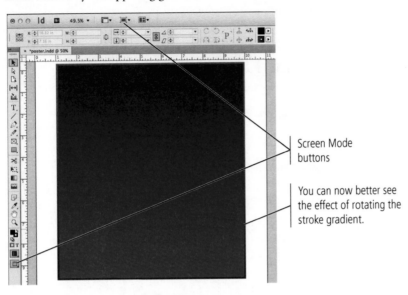

Screen Mode buttons

You can now better see the effect of rotating the stroke gradient.

9. **Restore the document view to the Normal mode in the Screen Mode menu.**

10. **Save the file and continue to the next exercise.**

Using the Gradient Tools

Clicking a gradient swatch adds a gradient to the selected object, beginning at the left edge and ending at the right edge (for linear gradients), or beginning at the object's center and ending at the object's outermost edge (for radial gradients). When you drag with the Gradient tool, you define the length of the gradient without regard to the object you're filling.

Gradient tool

We started dragging here...

...and ended here.

This box is filled with a gradient that has green at the left end and blue at the right end.

The start and end colors appear where we first clicked and where we stopped dragging.

The Gradient Feather tool has a similar function but produces different results. Rather than creating a specific-colored gradient, the Gradient Feather tool applies a transparency gradient, blending the object from solid to transparent.

Gradient Feather tool

We clicked and dragged from here to define the starting point of the feather effect (the area that will be entirely solid).

Dragging to here defines the end point of the gradient feather (the area that will be entirely transparent).

We placed this image over an orange-filled shape.

The resulting effect blends the image from solid to transparent, allowing the background to show.

CREATE AN IRREGULAR GRAPHICS FRAME

You can create basic graphics frames using the Rectangle, Ellipse, and Polygon Frame tools. You can also create a Bézier shape with the Pen tool, and then convert the shape to a graphics frame — which means you can create a frame in virtually any shape. However, it requires a lot of work to trace complex graphics with the Pen tool; fortunately, you can use other options to create complex frames from objects in placed graphics.

1. **In the open poster.indd file, select the gradient-filled rectangle in the layout.**

2. **Choose File>Place. Navigate to outline.ai in the WIP>Surfing folder. Check the Show Import Options and Replace Selected Item options, then click Open.**

This frame should be selected.

Make sure both options are checked.

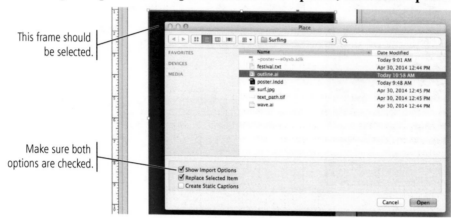

3. **In the resulting dialog box, choose Art in the Crop To menu, then click OK.**

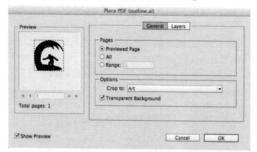

Because the existing rectangle was selected and the Replace Selected Item option was checked, the new image automatically appears in the selected frame. If another image had already been placed in the frame, the surfing image would replace the existing image (hence the name of the command).

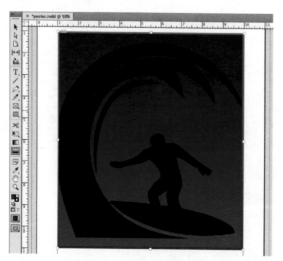

Note:

Refer back to Project 7: Letterhead Design for an explanation of the Crop To options.

Note:

If Replace Selected Item was not checked in the Place dialog box, the image would be loaded into the cursor.

4. Choose Edit>Undo Replace.

If you accidentally replace a selected item, undoing the placement loads the last-placed image into the cursor.

This is an easy fix if you accidentally replace an image — simply choose Edit>Undo Replace, and then click to place the loaded image in the correct location.

Note:

The Undo command undoes the single last action. In this case, placing the image into the frame — even though it happened automatically — was the last single action.

5. Click in the white area near the top-right corner to place the loaded image.

Do not click inside the gradient-filled rectangle; if you do, the loaded image would be placed back into that frame instead of in a new frame.

6. Using the Control panel, select the top-left reference point and then change the new image frame's position to X: 0.5 in, Y: 2 in.

Use the top-left reference point to position the graphics frame.

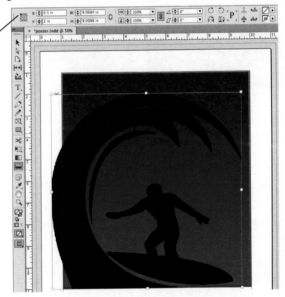

7. With the same frame selected, choose Object>Clipping Path>Options.

A **clipping path** is a hard-edged outline that masks an image. Areas inside the path are visible; areas outside the path are hidden.

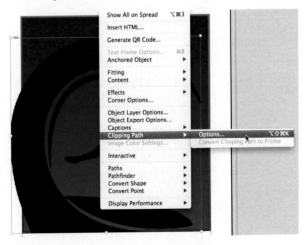

8. **In the resulting dialog box, choose Detect Edges in the Type menu.**

InDesign can access Alpha channels and clipping paths that are saved in an image, or you can create a clipping path based on the image content. Because this graphic is a vector graphic with well-defined edges filled with a solid color, InDesign can create a very precise clipping path based on the information in the file.

9. **Check the Include Inside Edges option.**

When this option is not checked, InDesign generates a clipping path based only on the outside edges of the image. The Include Inside Edges option generates a compound clipping path that removes holes in the middle of the outside path.

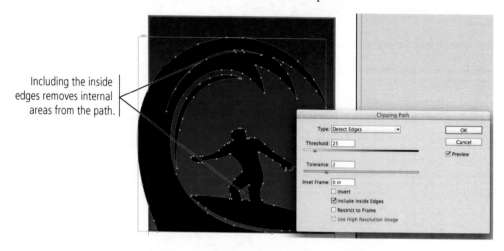

Including the inside edges removes internal areas from the path.

10. **Click OK to close the dialog box and create the clipping path.**

11. **Choose Object>Clipping Path>Convert Clipping Path to Frame.**

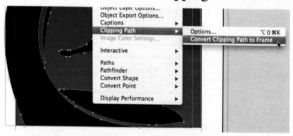

Clipping Path Options

Threshold specifies the darkest pixel value that will define the resulting clipping path. In this exercise, the placed image is filled with solid black, so you can set a very high Threshold value to define the clipping path. In images with greater tone variation (such as a photograph), increasing the Threshold value removes lighter areas from the clipped area.

Tolerance specifies how similar a pixel must be to the Threshold value before it is hidden by the clipping path. Increasing the Tolerance value results in fewer points along the clipping path, generating a smoother path. Lowering the Tolerance value results in more anchor points and a potentially rougher path.

Inset Frame shrinks the clipping path by a specific number of pixels. You can also enter a negative value to enlarge the clipping path.

Invert reverses the clipping path, making hidden areas visible and vice versa.

Include Inside Edges creates a compound clipping path, removing inner areas of the object if they are within the Threshold and Tolerance ranges.

Restrict to Frame creates a clipping path that stops at the visible edge of the graphic. You can include the entire object — including areas beyond the frame edges — by unchecking this option.

Use High Resolution Image generates the clipping path based on the actual file data instead of the preview image.

12. Using the Direct Selection tool, select the image inside the irregular frame.

13. With the frame content selected, press Delete/Backspace to delete the placed file but leave the frame you created.

Deleting the original image leaves the frame you created, based on the InDesign-generated clipping path.

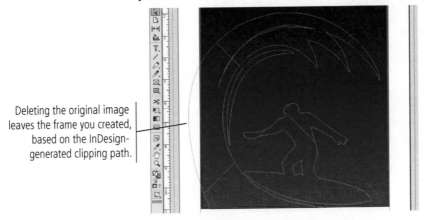

14. Using the Selection tool, click the irregular graphics frame to select it.

15. Choose File>Place and navigate to **surf.jpg** in the WIP>Surfing folder. Uncheck all options at the bottom of the dialog box and click Open.

This frame should be selected.

This option should not be checked.

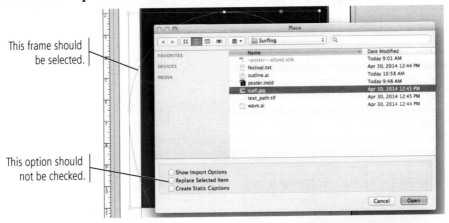

Although the existing frame was selected when you opened the Place dialog box, the new image is loaded into the cursor because you unchecked the Replace Selected Item option.

16. Click inside the empty frame with the loaded cursor to place the image inside the frame.

17. **Move the Selection tool cursor over the image frame to reveal the Content Grabber.**

The Selection tool is active.

The frame is selected.

Content Grabber

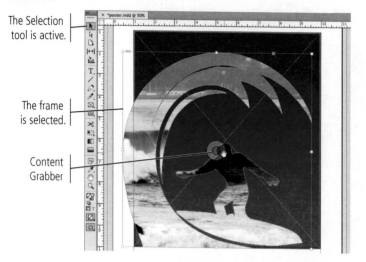

Note:

You can turn off the Content Grabber by choosing View>Extras> Hide Content Grabber.

18. **Click the Content Grabber to access the image in the frame.**

Remember: When you select an image within a frame (using either the Content Grabber or the Direct Selection tool), the Control panel fields define the position of the graphic *relative to* its containing frame. Negative numbers move the graphic up and to the left from the frame edge; positive numbers move the graphic down and to the right.

19. **Using the Control panel, change the image's position inside the frame to X: 0 in, Y: 0 in (based on the top-left reference point).**

By default, placed graphics are centered inside their containing frames. You are adjusting the position of this image so that the top-left image corner aligns to the top-left corner of the frame's bounding box.

The Selection tool is still active.

The image in the frame is selected.

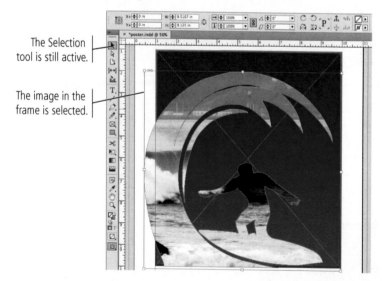

20. **Save the file and continue to the next exercise.**

CREATE VISUAL IMPACT WITH TRANSPARENCY

The image effects and transparency controls in InDesign provide options for adding dimension and depth, allowing unprecedented creative control directly in the page layout. You can change the transparency of any object (or individual object attributes), apply different blending modes so objects blend smoothly into underlying objects, and apply creative effects such as drop shadows and beveling.

Transparency and effects are controlled in the Effects panel. You can change these options for an entire object (fill and stroke), only the stroke, only the fill, the text (if you're working with a text frame), the graphic (if you're working with a graphics frame), or all objects in a group.

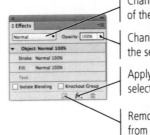

Change the blending mode of the selected attribute.

Change the transparency of the selected attribute.

Apply an effect to the selected attribute.

Remove transparency and effects from the selected attribute.

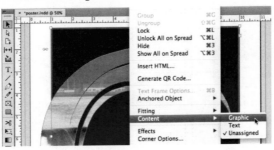

Note:

The Graphic option is only available when a placed graphic (within a frame) is selected. Group replaces Object in the list only when a group is selected with the Selection tool.

Technical Issues of Transparency

Because all of these features and options are related in some way to transparency, you should understand what transparency is and how it affects your output. **Transparency** is the degree to which light passes through an object so that objects in the background are visible. In terms of page layout, transparency means being able to "see through" objects in the front of the stacking order to objects lower in the stacking order.

Because of the way printing works, applying transparency in print graphic design is a bit of a contradiction. Commercial printing is, by definition, accomplished by overlapping a mixture of (usually) four semi-transparent inks in different percentages to reproduce a range of colors (the printable gamut). In that sense, all print graphic design requires transparency.

But *design* transparency refers to the objects on the page. The trouble is, when a halftone dot is printed, it's either there or it's not. There is no "50% opaque" setting on a printing press. This means that a transformation needs to take place behind the scenes, translating what we create on screen into what a printing press produces.

When transparent objects are output, overlapping areas of transparent elements are actually broken into individual elements (where necessary) to produce the best possible results. Ink values in the overlap areas are calculated by the application, based on the capabilities of the mechanical printing process; the software converts what we create on screen into the elements that are necessary to print.

When you get to the final stage of this project, you'll learn how to preview and control the output process for transparent objects.

Note:

Effects applied to text apply to all text in the frame; you can't apply effects to individual characters.

Note:

Transparency is essentially the inverse of opacity. If an object is 20% transparent, it is also 80% opaque.

1. **In the open poster.indd file, use the Selection tool to select the gradient-filled rectangle.**

2. **Choose Object>Content>Graphic.**

Note:

You can also Control/ right-click an object and change its content type in the contextual menu.

When you create a frame with one of the basic shape tools, it is considered "unassigned" because it is neither a text frame nor a graphics frame. You can convert any type of frame (graphics, text, or unassigned) to another type using this menu.

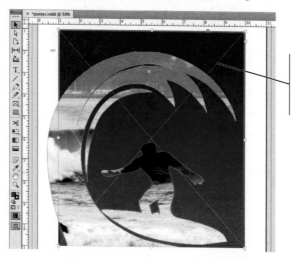

When frame edges are showing, an empty graphics frame shows crossed diagonal lines.

3. **With the gradient-filled rectangle still selected on the page, choose File>Place. Navigate to the WIP>Surfing folder and choose surf.jpg. At the bottom of the dialog box, check the Replace Selected Item option.**

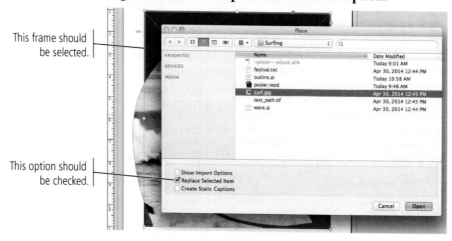

This frame should be selected.

This option should be checked.

4. **Click Open to place the selected file.**

This is the same file you placed into the irregular graphics frame. You are going to use transparency and effects to differentiate the two images.

Because Replace Selected Item was checked, the image is placed directly into the frame.

5. **Move the Selection tool cursor over the image frame to reveal the Content Grabber, then click the Content Grabber to access the image in the frame.**

6. **Using the Control panel, change the image's position inside the frame to X: -0.5 in, Y: 1 in (based on the top-left reference point).**

   This position aligns the image with the irregular-frame image, giving the impression of a single image in both frames (the background rectangle and the irregular surfer-shaped frame).

The Selection tool is still active.

The image in the frame is selected.

7. **Press ESC to restore the frame (not the frame content) as the active selection.**

8. **Open the Effects panel (Window>Effects).**

   When a frame is selected, you can apply various effects to the entire object, or to the object fill only, the object stroke only, or any text within the object.

The image frame is selected.

The Effects panel has options for various attributes of the frame.

9. **Using the Direct Selection tool or Content Grabber, select the image inside the frame.**

When the content inside a graphics frame is selected, you can apply effects to the image itself, independent of the frame.

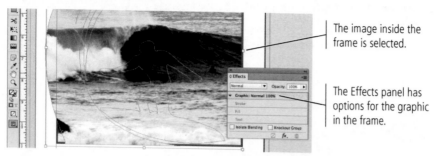

The image inside the frame is selected.

The Effects panel has options for the graphic in the frame.

10. **With the Graphic option selected in the Effects panel, choose the Screen option in the Blending Mode menu.**

The image now blends into the gradient background, but there is still a hard line marking the bottom edge of the placed image.

The Screen blending mode merges the image colors into the object's gradient fill.

Note:

Blending modes in InDesign have the same function as layer blending modes in Photoshop (see Page 318).

11. **Click the *fx* button at the bottom of the Effects panel, and choose Gradient Feather.**

The Effects dialog box opens to show the Gradient Feather options.

Transparency...
Drop Shadow...
Inner Shadow...
Outer Glow...
Inner Glow...
Bevel and Emboss...
Satin...
Basic Feather...
Directional Feather...
Gradient Feather...

Note:

If you use the Gradient Feather tool, the Gradient Feather effect is automatically applied.

12. **In the Effects dialog box, click the Preview check box so you can preview your results before accepting/applying them.**

The Gradient Feather effect creates a transparency gradient so an object blends into underlying objects instead of leaving a hard edge. The effect is created using a gradient that shifts from 100% opacity to 0% opacity. The levels of opacity in the gradient determine the opacity of the object to which the feather effect is applied.

13. To the right of the gradient ramp sample, click the button to reverse the gradient.

14. Click in the Angle circle and drag until the field shows –90° (the line should point straight down).

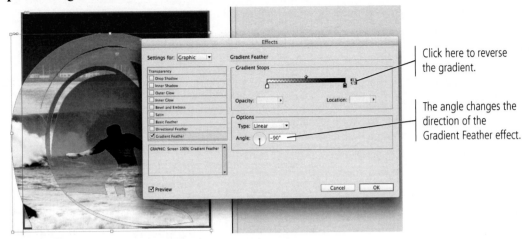

Click here to reverse the gradient.

The angle changes the direction of the Gradient Feather effect.

15. Drag the left gradient stop until the Location field shows 20%.

By extending the solid black part of the gradient to the 75% location, the top three-quarters of the affected image remain entirely visible; only the bottom quarter of the image blends into the background.

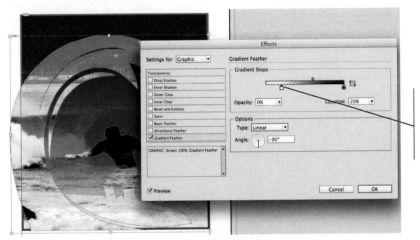

Moving the first stop extends the transparent area of the gradient, which shortens the part of the image that is entirely opaque.

16. Click OK to close the Effects dialog box and apply your choices.

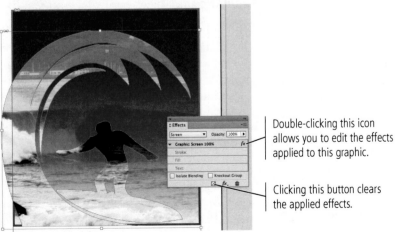

Double-clicking this icon allows you to edit the effects applied to this graphic.

Clicking this button clears the applied effects.

Note:

Effects in InDesign are non-destructive, which means they have no effect on the physical file data.

17. Click away from the active image to deselect it (and its containing frame).

Nine different InDesign effects can be applied by clicking the *fx* button at the bottom of the Effects panel, by clicking the *fx* button in the Control panel, or by choosing from the Object>Effects menu.

Drop Shadow and Inner Shadow

Drop Shadow adds a shadow behind the object. **Inner Shadow** adds a shadow inside the edges of the object. For both types, you can define the blending mode, color, opacity, angle, distance, offset, and size of the shadow.

- **Distance** is how far away the shadow will be from the original object. The Offset fields allow you to define different horizontal and vertical distances.

- **Size** is the blur amount applied to the shadow.

- **Spread** (for Drop Shadows) is the percentage that the shadow expands beyond the original object.

- **Choke** (for Inner Shadows) is the percentage that the shadow shrinks into the original object.

- **Noise** controls the amount of random pixels added to the effect.

When the **Object Knocks Out Shadow** option is checked, areas of the shadow under the object are knocked out or removed. This option is particularly important if the original object is semi-transparent above its shadow.

The **Use Global Light** check box is available for the Drop Shadow, Inner Shadow, and Bevel and Emboss effects. When this option is checked, the style is linked to the "master" light source angle for the entire file. Changing the global light setting affects any linked effect applied to any object in the entire file. (You can also change the Global Light settings by choosing Object>Effects>Global Light.)

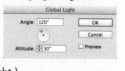

Outer Glow and Inner Glow

Outer Glow and **Inner Glow** add glow effects to the outside and inside edges (respectively) of the original object. For either kind of glow, you can define the blending mode, opacity, noise, and size values.

- For either Outer or Inner glows, you can define the **Technique** as Precise or Softer. **Precise** creates a glow at a specific distance; **Softer** creates a blurred glow and does not preserve detail as well as Precise.

- For Inner Glows, you can also define the **Source** of the glow (Center or Edge). **Center** applies a glow starting from the center of the object; **Edge** applies the glow starting from the inside edges of the object.

- The **Spread** and **Choke** sliders affect the percentages of the glow effects.

Satin

Satin applies interior shading to create a satiny appearance. You can change the blending mode, color, and opacity of the effect, as well as the angle, distance, and size.

Bevel and Emboss

This effect has four variations or styles:

- **Inner Bevel** creates a bevel on the inside edges of the object.

- **Outer Bevel** creates a bevel on the outside edges of the object.

- **Emboss** creates the effect of embossing the object against the underlying layers.

- **Pillow Emboss** creates the effect of stamping the edges of the object into the underlying layers.

Any of these styles can be applied as **Smooth** (blurs the edges of the effect), **Chisel Hard** (creates a distinct edge to the effect), or **Chisel Soft** (creates a distinct, but slightly blurred edge to the effect).

You can change the **Direction** of the bevel effect. **Up** creates the appearance of the layer coming out of the image; **Down** creates the appearance of something stamped into the image. The **Size** field makes the effect smaller or larger, and the **Soften** option blurs the edges of the effect. **Depth** increases or decreases the three-dimensional effect of the bevel.

In the **Shading** area, you can control the light source's **Angle** and **Altitude** (think of how shadows differ as the sun moves across the sky). Finally, you can change the blending mode, opacity, and color of both highlights and shadows created with the Bevel or Emboss effect.

Basic Feather, Directional Feather, Gradient Feather

Basic Feather equally fades all edges of the selection by a specific width. The **Choke** option determines how much of the softened edge is opaque (higher settings increase opacity). **Corners** can be **Sharp** (following the outer edge of the shape), **Rounded** (according to the Feather Width), or **Diffused** (fading from opaque to transparent). **Noise** adds random pixels to the softened area.

Directional Feather allows you to apply different feather widths to individual edges of an object. The **Shape** option defines the object's original shape (First Edge Only, Leading Edges, or All Edges). The **Angle** field allows you to rotate the feathering effect.

Gradient Feather creates a transparency gradient that blends from solid to transparent. This effect underlies the Gradient Feather tool. You can move the start and end stops to different locations along the ramp, or add stops to define specific transparencies at specific locations. You can also choose from a Linear or Radial Gradient Feather effect, and change the angle of a Linear Gradient Feather effect.

18. **Using the Selection tool, select the irregular image frame.**

19. **In the Control panel, click the Drop Shadow button.**

    Clicking this button automatically applies the Drop Shadow effect using the default settings.

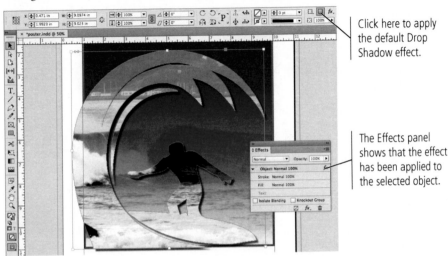

Click here to apply the default Drop Shadow effect.

The Effects panel shows that the effect has been applied to the selected object.

20. **Save the file and continue to the next exercise.**

 CREATE A QR CODE

A **QR code** (short for quick response code) is a type of bar code that provides easy access — using a special QR code reader app on a smartphone or tablet — to additional information that is programmed into the code. InDesign CC includes a built-in option for creating QR codes directly in a layout, which makes it simple to incorporate this kind of marketing tool into any layout.

Note:

The actual behavior of QR codes depends on the specific device and app being used to scan them.

1. **With poster.indd open, create a new rectangle frame in the bottom-right corner of the image area. Define the frame parameters (based on the top-left reference point) as:**

    X: 8 in   W: 1.75 in
    Y: 9 in   H: 1.75 in

2. **If necessary, change the frame's stroke weight to 6 pt. Change the frame's fill color to Paper and stroke color to C=100 M=0 Y=100 K=25.**

3. **With the new frame selected, choose Object>Generate QR Code.**

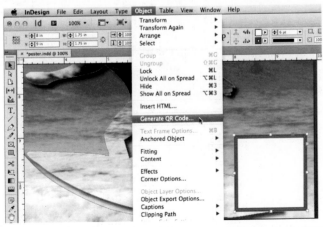

4. **In the resulting dialog box, choose Web Hyperlink in the Type menu and type www.surfriderfestival.com in the URL field.**

You can use the Type menu to define what the QR code does:

- **Web Hyperlink.** If you choose this option, you can define the specific URL that appears when a user scans the code.

- **Plain Text.** If you choose this option, you can define a plain-text message that appears when a user scans the code.

- **Text Message.** If you choose this option, you can define the phone number and message content that will be sent.

- **Email.** If you choose this option, you can define the email address, subject, and email body that will be included in the resulting email.

- **Business Card.** If you choose this option, you can define the specific fields that are common in digital contact applications (name, company, address, etc.).

5. **Click the Color tab at the top of the dialog box. Choose C=100 M=100 Y=25 K=0, then click OK.**

The color you define here determines the color of the actual QR code object. Keep in mind that high contrast between the QR code object and the frame background color helps to make sure the code will work on all devices and apps.

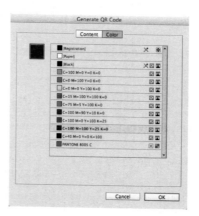

InDesign automatically generates the QR code inside the frame. The resulting graphic is centered in the frame, and scaled to leave a 10-pixel inset from the nearest frame edges.

The QR code is actually created as an embedded EPS graphic (although it does not appear in the file's Links panel). If you select the graphic inside the frame, you can scale it as you would any other placed graphic. Keep in mind, however, that distorting the code graphic might cause it to not work.

The frame containing the QR code is still a graphics frame; the frame's fill color appears behind the QR code.

Note:

You can edit the properties of a QR code by choosing Object>Edit QR code (or by Control/ right-clicking a QR code in the layout and choosing Edit QR Code in the object's contextual menu.)

6. **Save the file and continue to the next stage of the project.**

Stage 2 Importing and Formatting Text

Placing text is one of the most critical functions of page-layout software, whether you create the text directly within InDesign or import it from an external file. InDesign provides all the tools you need to format text, from choosing a font to automatically creating hanging punctuation.

CONTROL TEXT THREADING

Some layouts require only a few bits of text, while others include numerous pages. Depending on how much text you have to work with, you might place all the layout text in a single frame, or you might cut and paste different pieces of a single story into separate text frames. In other cases, you might thread text across multiple frames — maintaining the text as a single story but allowing flexibility in frame size and position.

1. With **poster.indd** open, zoom into the empty area below the placed images.

2. Use the Type tool to create a text frame that is 9″ wide and 1″ high (filling the width between the margin guides).

3. Select the frame with the Selection tool, and then use the Control panel to make sure the top edge of the text frame is positioned at Y: 11.25 in.

When the Selection tool is active, you can use the Control panel to change the position and dimensions of a text frame.

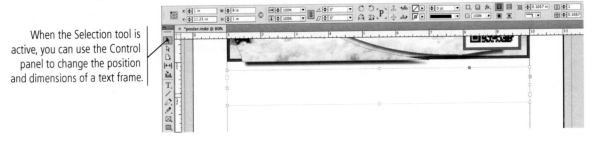

4. Create three more text frames using the following parameters:

   Frame 2   X: 1 in   W: 3.2 in
             Y: 12.45 in H: 3.55 in

   Frame 3   X: 5 in   W: 5 in
             Y: 12.45 in H: 3.55 in

   Frame 4   X: 1 in   W: 9 in
             Y: 16.1 in   H: 0.5 in

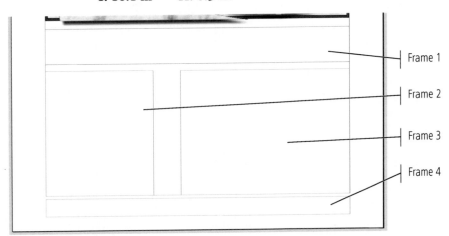

Frame 1

Frame 2

Frame 3

Frame 4

5. Choose the Type tool, and click inside the first text frame to place the insertion point.

When you click in a text frame with the Type tool, you see a flashing insertion point where you click (or in the top-left corner if there is no text in the frame). This insertion point marks the location where text will appear when you type, paste, or import it into the document.

6. Choose File>Place. Navigate to the file named festival.txt in the WIP>Surfing folder.

7. Make sure the Replace Selected Item option is checked and then click Open.

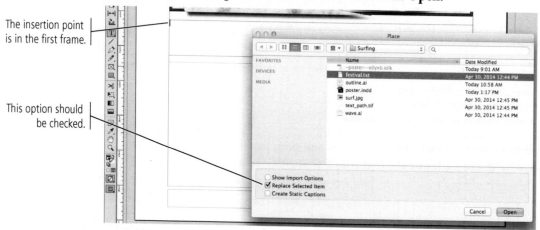

The insertion point is in the first frame.

This option should be checked.

When Replace Selected Item is checked, the text file is automatically imported at the location of the insertion point. (If this option is not checked, the text is imported into the cursor.)

8. Choose the Selection tool in the Tools panel.

When a text frame is selected, you can see the In and Out ports that allow you to link one text frame to another. In this case, the Out port shows the **overset text icon**, indicating that the placed file has more text than can fit within the frame.

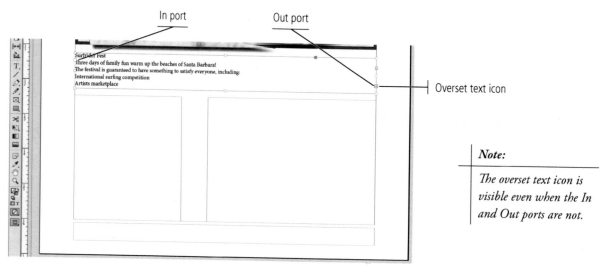

In port

Out port

Overset text icon

Note:

The overset text icon is visible even when the In and Out ports are not.

9. **Click the Out port of the first text frame.**

   Clicking the Out port loads the cursor with the rest of the text in the story. When the loaded cursor is over an existing frame, you can click to place the next part of the story in that frame. When the cursor is not over a frame, you can click and drag to create a frame that will contain the next part of the story. You can do this with the Selection tool (as you just did) or the Direct Selection tool.

   When you load the cursor with overset text, the loaded cursor shows the text from the beginning of the story — even though the beginning is already placed. This is a quirk of the software; when you click with the loaded cursor, the text will flow into the new frame at the proper place in the story.

Note:

You can also press Command/Control while the Type tool is active to click a text frame Out port and thread the frames.

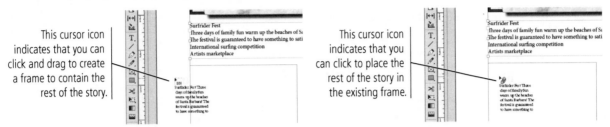

This cursor icon indicates that you can click and drag to create a frame to contain the rest of the story.

This cursor icon indicates that you can click to place the rest of the story in the existing frame.

10. **Click inside the second frame to link it to the first frame.**

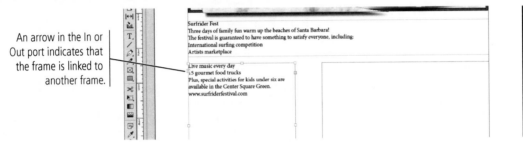

An arrow in the In or Out port indicates that the frame is linked to another frame.

11. **Repeat this process to link from the second frame to the third, and then from the third frame to the fourth.**

    You can define the thread of text frames even when there is no text to fill those frames. Simply use the Selection or Direct Selection tool to click the Out port of one frame, and then click anywhere within the next frame you want to add to the thread.

12. **Choose View>Extras>Show Text Threads.**

    When this option is toggled on (and you are in Normal viewing mode), you can see all of the threading arrows whenever any of the text frames in the thread is selected.

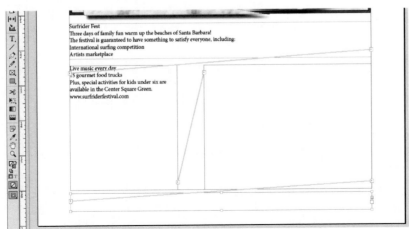

Note:

*Text that appears as a series of gray bars is called **greeked text**. By default, text smaller than 7 pt (at 100%) is greeked to improve screen redraw time. You can change the greeking threshold in the Display Performance pane of the Preferences dialog box.*

View percentage is part of the determination for greeking text; in other words, if your view percentage is 50%, 12-pt text appears as 6-pt text on screen, so it would be greeked using the default preferences.

13. **Save the file and continue to the next exercise.**

DEFINE MANUAL FRAME BREAKS

When you thread text from one frame to another (or to multiple columns in the same frame), you often need to control exactly where a story breaks from frame to frame. InDesign includes a number of commands for breaking text in precise locations.

Note:

You can also toggle the visibility of hidden characters using the View Options button in the Application/Menu bar.

1. **In the open poster.indd file, use the Type tool to click at the end of the first line (after "Surfrider Fest") to place the insertion point.**

   As you complete the following exercises, feel free to zoom in as you think necessary to work with specific areas of your layout.

2. **Choose Type>Insert Break Character>Frame Break.**

   InDesign provides several special break characters that allow you to control the flow of text from line to line, from column to column, and from frame to frame. The Frame Break character forces all following text into the next frame in the thread.

The insertion point is at the end of the first paragraph.

3. **Choose Type>Show Hidden Characters.**

   Each paragraph is separated by a paragraph return character (¶). A paragraph can consist of only one or two words or multiple lines. The important thing is to realize that a paragraph is technically any copy between two paragraph returns (or other break characters).

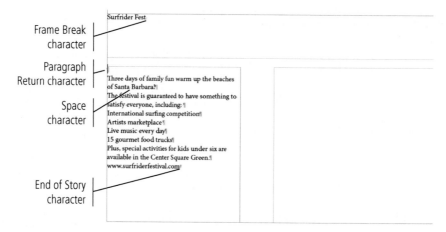

Frame Break character

Paragraph Return character

Space character

End of Story character

   When you placed the Frame Break character in Step 2, everything following the insertion point was pushed to the next frame — including the paragraph return character that had been at the end of the first line. This created an "empty" paragraph that should be deleted.

4. **With the insertion point flashing at the beginning of the second frame, press Forward Delete to remove the extra paragraph return.**

   The Forward Delete key is the one directly below the Help key on most standard keyboards. If you don't have a Forward Delete key (if, for example, you're working on a laptop), move the insertion point to the beginning of the next line ("Three days of family...") and press Delete/Backspace.

5. **With hidden characters visible, highlight the paragraph return character at the end of the first sentence in the second frame.**

6. **Choose Type>Insert Break Character>Frame Break to replace the highlighted paragraph return with a frame break character.**

   When text is highlighted — including hidden formatting characters — anything you type, paste, or enter using a menu command replaces the highlighted text.

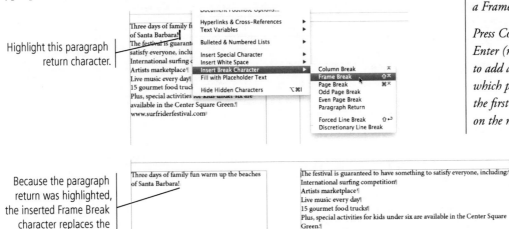

Highlight this paragraph return character.

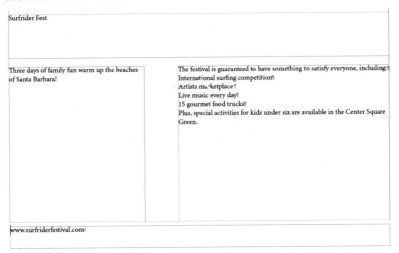

Because the paragraph return was highlighted, the inserted Frame Break character replaces the paragraph return.

7. **Use the same technique to move only the last paragraph (the Web address) into the fourth text frame.**

8. **Save the file and continue to the next exercise.**

Note:

Press Enter (numeric keypad) to add a Column Break.

Press Shift-Enter (numeric keypad) to add a Frame Break.

Press Command/Control-Enter (numeric keypad) to add a Page Break, which pushes all text to the first threaded frame on the next page.

Designing with Placeholder Text

It's always a good idea to begin a project as soon as possible after getting the assignment. When working with clients, however, you will often find that the idea for a project comes before the actual content — sometimes long before the client has finalized the text.

Rather than waiting until the client's content is ready — which is sometimes the day before a project is due — you can design a layout using placeholders to mark the location of pictures and text frames, and even experiment with the appearance of different elements of the text.

With the insertion point placed in a text frame, choosing Type>Fill with Placeholder Text fills the active text frame with **lorem text** (supposedly from a Latin treatise on ethics written by Cicero more than 2000 years ago) using the default text-format settings. If a text frame is linked to other text frames, the placeholder text fills the entire series of linked text frames.

Lorem placeholder text is valuable for experimenting with the appearance of paragraph text, giving you a better idea of what blocks of copy will look like when real content is placed in the layout.

All four threaded text frames are filled with Roman placeholder text.

If you press Command/Control while choosing the Fill with Placeholder Text command, you can define a different language to use for the placeholder text. These options are useful if you want to experiment with a design for a layout in which the text does not use the Roman alphabet — again, the placeholder more accurately represents what the final copy will look like..

All four threaded text frames are filled with Cyrillic placeholder text.

All four threaded text frames are filled with Japanese placeholder text.

APPLY CHARACTER FORMATTING

Once text is in a frame, you can use character formatting attributes to determine the appearance of individual letters, such as the font and type size. These attributes can be controlled in the Character panel (Window>Type & Tables> Character) or the Control panel (depending on which options are visible in the Control panel).

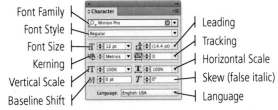

- A **font** contains all of the characters (**glyphs**) that make up a typeface, including upper- and lowercase letters, numbers, special characters, etc. (Fonts must be installed and activated on your computer to be accessible in InDesign.) The **font style** is a specific variation of the selected font, such as bold or condensed.

- **Size** is the height of a typeface measured in points.

- **Leading** is the distance from one baseline to the next. InDesign treats leading as a character attribute, even though leading controls the space between lines of an individual paragraph. (Space between paragraphs is controlled using the Space Before/After options in the Paragraph panel.) To change leading for an entire paragraph, you must first select the entire paragraph. This approach means you can change the leading for a single line of a paragraph by selecting any character(s) in that line; however, changing the leading for any character in a line applies the same change to the entire line that contains those characters. (You can change this behavior by checking the Apply Leading to Entire Paragraph option in the Type pane of the Preferences dialog box.)

  Note:

  You can use the Up and Down Arrow keys to nudge paragraph and character style values when the insertion point is in a panel field.

- **Vertical Scale** and **Horizontal Scale** artificially stretch or contract the selected characters. This type of scaling is a quick way of achieving condensed or expanded type if those variations of a font don't exist. Type that has been artificially scaled in this fashion tends to look bad because the scaling destroys the type's metrics; if possible, you should always use a condensed or expanded version of a typeface before resorting to horizontal or vertical scaling.

- **Kerning** increases or decreases the space between pairs of letters. Kerning is used in cases where particular letters in specific fonts need to be manually adjusted to eliminate a too-tight or too-spread-out appearance; manual kerning is usually necessary in headlines or other large type. (Many commercial fonts have built-in kerning pairs, so you won't need to apply too much hands-on intervention with kerning.)

  Note:

  *Tracking and kerning are applied in thousandths of an **em** (an em is technically defined as width that equals the type size).*

- **Tracking**, also known as "range kerning," refers to the overall space between a range of characters.

- **Baseline Shift** moves the selected type above or below the baseline by a specific number of points. Positive numbers move the characters up; negative values move the text down.

- **Skew** artificially slants the selected text, creating a false italic appearance. This option distorts the look of the type and should be used sparingly (if ever).

In addition to the options in the basic Character panel, several styling options are also available in the panel Options menu.

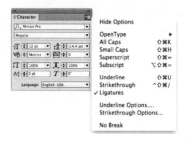

- **All Caps** changes all the characters to capital letters. This option only changes the appearance of the characters; they are not permanently converted to capital letters. To change the case of selected characters to all capital letters — the same as typing with Caps Lock turned on — use the Type>Change Case menu options.

- **Small Caps** changes lowercase letters to smaller versions of the uppercase letters. If the font is an Open Type font that contains true small caps, InDesign uses the true small caps.

- **Superscript** and **Subscript** artificially reduce the selected character(s) to a specific percentage of the point size; these options raise (for superscript) or lower (for subscript) the character from the baseline to a position that is a certain percentage of the leading. (The size and position of Superscript, Subscript, and Small Caps are controlled in the Advanced Type Preferences dialog box.)

- **Underline** places a line below the selected characters.

- **Strikethrough** places a line through the middle of selected characters.

- **Ligatures** are substitutes for certain pairs of letters, most commonly fi, fl, ff, ffi, and ffl. (Other pairs such as ct and st are common for historical typesetting, and ae and oe are used in some non-English-language typesetting.)

1. **With poster.indd open, choose the Type tool in the Tools panel. Triple-click the first line of text in the story to select it.**

   Character formatting options apply only to selected characters.

2. **In the Character panel (Window>Type & Tables>Character), highlight the existing font name and type atc g. Click ATC Garnet Ultra in the resulting menu to apply the new font.**

   The characters you type in the Font Family field result in a menu with all fonts that include the letters you type. After you select the font in the menu, ATC Garnet appears in the Font Family menu and Ultra appears in the Font Style menu.

3. Open the Font Size menu and choose 72.

You can choose one of the built-in font sizes, type a specific value in the field, or click the arrow buttons to change the font size by 1 point.

Note:

Leave the Leading value at the automatic setting. By default, InDesign automatically applies leading as 120% of the type size.

4. Open the Character panel Options menu and choose the All Caps option.

5. In the Character panel, type 130 in the Tracking field and press Return/Enter.

6. Click four times on the text in the second frame to select the entire paragraph.

Clicking twice selects an entire *word*, clicking three times selects an entire *line*, and clicking four times selects the entire *paragraph*.

7. Change the selected text to 35-pt ATC Pyrite Bold Italic and change the Horizontal Scale field to 90%.

Horizontal and vertical scaling are useful for artificially stretching or contracting fonts that do not have a condensed or extended version. Be careful using these options, though, because the artificial scaling alters the character shapes and can make some fonts very difficult to read (especially at smaller sizes).

8. Click three times to select the first line in the third frame, hold down the mouse button, and then drag down to select the other lines in the same frame.

When you triple-click to select an entire line, dragging up or down selects entire lines above or below the one you first clicked.

9. **With all of the text in the third frame selected, apply 22-pt ATC Pyrite Bold with 90% horizontal scaling.**

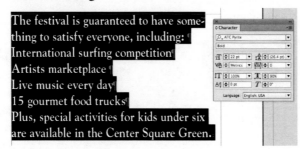

10. **Change the Web address in the fourth text frame to 26-pt ATC Garnet Medium.**

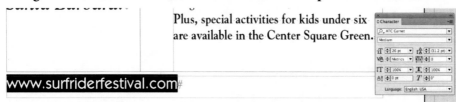

11. **Save the file and continue to the next exercise.**

 ## APPLY PARAGRAPH FORMATTING

Character formatting includes any option that affects the appearance of selected characters, such as font, size, horizontal scale, and a host of others. Paragraph formatting options, on the other hand, affect an entire paragraph (everything between two paragraph return characters). Paragraph formatting can control everything from indents to the space between paragraphs to lines above and below paragraphs.

Paragraph formatting can be controlled in the Paragraph panel (Window>Type & Tables>Paragraph) or the Control panel (depending on which options are available).

Note:

In InDesign, a paragraph is defined as all text between two paragraph return characters (¶), even if the paragraph exists on a single line.

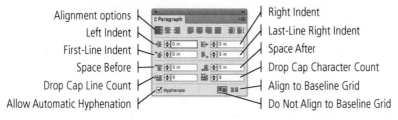

Alignment options	Right Indent
Left Indent	Last-Line Right Indent
First-Line Indent	Space After
Space Before	Drop Cap Character Count
Drop Cap Line Count	Align to Baseline Grid
Allow Automatic Hyphenation	Do Not Align to Baseline Grid

1. **In the open `poster.indd` file, place the cursor anywhere in the paragraph in the first frame.**

2. **In the Paragraph panel, click the Justify All Lines button.**

   Paragraph formatting applies to the entire paragraph where the insertion point is placed, or to any paragraph that is entirely or partially selected. A paragraph does not have to be entirely selected to change its paragraph formatting attributes.

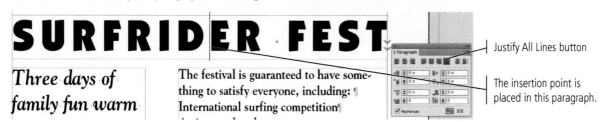

Justify All Lines button

The insertion point is placed in this paragraph.

3. Place the cursor anywhere in the paragraph in the second frame, then apply right paragraph alignment.

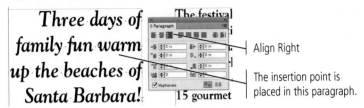

Align Right

The insertion point is placed in this paragraph.

4. Place the insertion point anywhere in the fourth frame (with the Web address) and apply centered paragraph alignment.

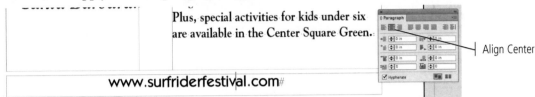

Align Center

5. In the third frame, select any part of the first through fifth paragraphs.

6. In the Paragraph panel, change the Space Before field to 0.1 in.

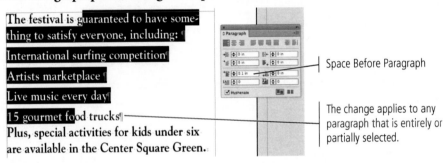

Space Before Paragraph

The change applies to any paragraph that is entirely or partially selected.

Note:

If you want to apply the same formatting to more than one consecutive paragraph, you can drag to select any part of the target paragraphs. Any paragraph that's even partially selected will be affected.

7. Select any part of the second through fifth paragraphs in the same frame and change the Left Indent field to 0.25 in.

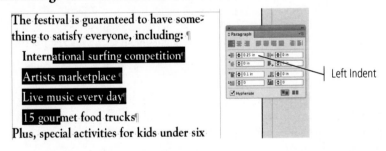

Left Indent

Note:

Remember: A paragraph is all text between two ¶ symbols — even if it occupies a single line.

8. Place the insertion point at the beginning of the sixth paragraph (before the word "Plus") and press Delete/Backspace.

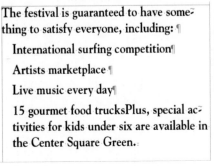

Note:

The arrow buttons for paragraph formatting options step through values in increments of 0.0625 in.

9. Press Return/Enter to separate the two paragraphs again.

When you break an existing paragraph into a new paragraph, the attributes of the original paragraph are applied to the new paragraph.

This is an easy way to copy paragraph formatting from one paragraph to the next. When you re-separate the two paragraphs, the "Plus" paragraph adopts the paragraph formatting attributes of the "15 gourmet food trucks" paragraph.

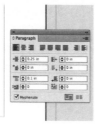

10. With the insertion point at the beginning of the sixth paragraph, change the Left Indent back to 0.

11. Press Command-Option-I/Control-Alt-I to toggle off the hidden characters.

Many designers frequently toggle the visibility of hidden characters while working on any given layout. You should become familiar with the keyboard shortcut for this command.

Copying Type Attributes with the Eyedropper Tool

You can use the Eyedropper tool to copy character and paragraph attributes (including text color), and then apply those attributes to other sections of text.

To copy formatting from one piece of text to another, click with the Eyedropper tool on the formatting you want to copy. If any text is selected when you click the Eyedropper tool, the selected text is automatically re-formatted. If nothing is selected, the Eyedropper tool "loads" with the formatting attributes — the tool icon reverses directions and shows a small i-beam icon in the cursor.

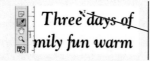

The Eyedropper tool cursor when it is "loaded" with text formatting attributes

You can click the loaded Eyedropper tool on any text to change its formatting, or you can click and drag to format multiple paragraphs at once. As long as the Eyedropper tool remains selected, you can continue to select text to apply

the same formatting. You can also change the formatting in the Eyedropper tool by pressing Option/Alt and clicking text with the new formatting attributes you want to copy.

By default, the Eyedropper tool copies all formatting attributes. You can change that behavior by double-clicking the tool in the Tools panel to access the Eyedropper Options dialog box. Simply uncheck the options you don't want to copy (including individual options in each category), and then click OK.

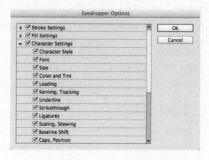

---

12. In the Layers panel, click the empty space to the left of the <rectangle> item to make that object visible again.

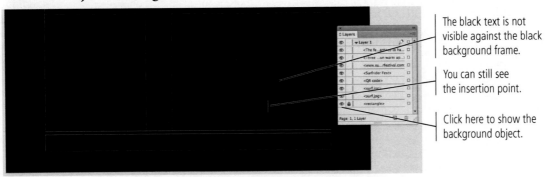

The black text is not visible against the black background frame.

You can still see the insertion point.

Click here to show the background object.

13. With the insertion point still flashing in the now-obscured text, choose Edit>Select All to select all text in the series of linked frames.

The Select All command selects all text in the story, whether that story exists in a single frame or threads across multiple frames. This command also selects overset text that doesn't fit into the current frame (or thread of frames).

14. In the Swatches panel, make sure the Text icon is selected at the top of the panel, and then click the Paper swatch.

In four-color (process) printing, there is no white ink. To achieve white, you have to remove the colors where you want white areas, which is called a **knockout**. By removing or knocking out underlying colors, the paper shows through — regardless of whether it is white or some other color (e.g., if you print on yellow paper, knockout areas will show the yellow color; this is why InDesign refers to this swatch as "Paper" instead of "White").

This "T" icon means you are changing the text color instead of the object color.

15. Click away from the text to deselect it and review the results.

16. Save the file and continue to the next stage of the project.

Applying Optical Margin Alignment

At times, specific arrangements of text can cause a paragraph to appear out of alignment, even though it's technically aligned properly. Punctuation at the beginning or end of a line — such as quotation marks at the beginning of a line or commas at the end of a line — often cause this kind of optical problem. InDesign includes a feature called **optical margin alignment** to fix this type of problem.

Optical margin alignment is applied in the Story panel (Window>Type and Tables>Story).

When this option is turned on, punctuation marks move outside the text margins — either to the left for left-aligned text or right for right-aligned text. (Moving punctuation outside the margins is often referred to as **hanging punctuation**.)

The field in the Story panel tells InDesign what size type needs to be adjusted. The best effect is usually created by defining the size of the type that needs adjustment.

Optical margin alignment option applies to an entire story (including all text frames in the same thread), not just the selected paragraph. If necessary, you can toggle the Ignore Optical Margin option (in the Paragraph panel Options menu) on for individual paragraphs so that the selected paragraph is not affected by optical margin alignment that is applied to the overall story.

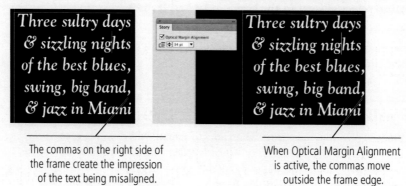

The commas on the right side of the frame create the impression of the text being misaligned.

When Optical Margin Alignment is active, the commas move outside the frame edge.

Stage 3 Graphics as Text and Text as Graphics

Now that you're familiar with the basic options for formatting characters and paragraphs, you can begin to add style to a layout using two techniques — flowing text along a path, and placing graphics inline with text. (You will, of course, learn much more about working with text as you complete the rest of the projects in this book.)

 PLACE INLINE GRAPHICS

Any graphics frame that you create on a page floats over the other elements in the layout. You can position graphics frames over other objects to hide underlying elements, or you can apply a **runaround** so that text will wrap around a picture box.

You can also place images as inline graphics, which means they will be anchored to the text in the position in which they are placed. If text reflows, inline objects reflow with the text and maintain their correct positioning.

There are two methods for creating inline objects. For simple applications, such as a graphic bullet, you can simply place the graphic and format it as a text character. (An inline graphic is treated as a single text character in the story; it is affected by many of the paragraph-formatting commands, such as space before and after, tab settings, leading, and baseline position.) For more complex applications, you can use the options in the Object>Anchored Object menu.

1. **With poster.indd open, place the insertion point at the beginning of the second line in the third frame (before the word "International").**

2. **Choose File>Place and navigate to wave.ai in the WIP>Surfing folder.**

The insertion point is at the beginning of this paragraph.

This option should be checked

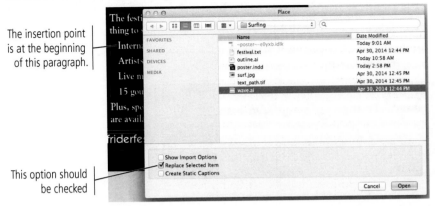

3. **Make sure the Replace Selected Item option is checked, and then click Open.**

   If the insertion point is flashing in a story when you place a graphic using the Replace Selected Item option, the graphic is automatically placed as an inline object.

The line spacing adjusts to fit the placed image.

Note:

You can also select an existing object, cut or copy it, place the insertion point, and then paste the object inline where the insertion point flashes.

4. **Select the inline graphic with the Selection tool, and then scale the graphic and frame to 60% horizontally and vertically.**

   Although inline graphics are anchored to the text, they are still graphics contained in graphics frames. You can apply the same transformations to inline graphics that you could apply to any other placed graphics.

Use these fields to scale the placed graphic and the containing frame.

After you finalize the scaling, the fields show 100% when the frame is selected with the Selection tool.

Note:

When you select the frame with the Selection tool, resizing the frame also resizes the frame content.

5. **Choose Object>Anchored Object>Options. Check the Preview option at the bottom of the dialog box.**

6. **With the Inline option selected, change the Y Offset to −0.05 in. Press the Tab key to show the result in the document.**

   A negative number moves the anchored object down; a positive number moves it up.

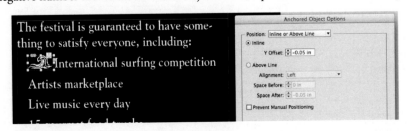

Note:

For the dialog box Preview option to work properly, you have to move the highlight away from the field you changed. Pressing Tab while the dialog box is open allows you to see the results of your changes.

7. **Click OK, and then place the insertion point between the anchored object and the letter "I." Using the Character or Control panel, change the Kerning field to 200.**

Because an anchored graphic is treated like a single character, you can use kerning to add space between the anchored graphic and the following character.

The insertion point is here.

Change the kerning to 200.

8. **Press Shift-Left Arrow to select the anchored object, and then copy the highlighted object/character.**

You can select an inline graphic just as you would any other text character. Copying text in InDesign is the same as copying text in other applications: choose Edit>Copy, or press Command/Control-C.

An anchored graphic can be selected just as you would select any other text character.

Understanding the Baseline Grid

The **baseline grid**, a series of light blue non-printing guides that extend down the page at specific regular intervals, is used for controlling and aligning type. You can show the baseline grid by choosing View>Grids & Guides>Show Baseline Grid.

You can force paragraphs to align to the baseline grid, which overrides the defined leading.

Line spacing is determined by the defined leading.

Click this button when you don't want to align text to the baseline grid.

If the type size or leading is too large to fit each line of text on sequential baselines, the text will skip every other baseline.

Click this button to align a paragraph to the baseline grid.

You can change the overall baseline grid in the Grids pane of the Preferences dialog box. The Start position can be relative to the top of the page (default) or to the top margin. You can also change the increment between lines. The View Threshold value determines the smallest view percentage at which the baseline grid will be visible.

You can also change the baseline grid for a specific frame in the Baseline Options tab of the Text Frame Options dialog box (Object>Text Frame Options).

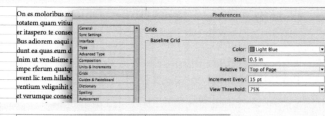

The Anchored Object Options dialog box controls the position of an anchored object relative to the frame in which it is placed. Anchored objects can be aligned inline (such as the wave bullets you created in this project) or above the line.

When an object is anchored using the Above Line option, the object can be anchored to the left, right, or center of the frame. If you're using facing pages, you can also choose Toward Spine or Away from Spine so the anchored object will be placed in the appropriate position relative to the spread center (for example, you might specify that all sidebars have to be on the inside edge, close to the spine).

The Inline option aligns the object with the text baseline, adjusted by the Y Offset value.

The Above Line option moves the object above the line where the object is anchored.

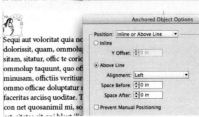

When you use the Above Line option, you can also define the space before and after the anchored object. Space Before defines the position of the object relative to the bottom of the previous line of text. Space After defines the position of the object relative to the first character in the line below the object.

When you work with anchored objects, you can use the Selection tool to drag the object up or down (in other words, change its position relative to the text to which it is anchored). If the Prevent Manual Positioning option is checked, you can't drag the anchored object in the layout.

Custom Anchor Options

For complex applications — such as moving an anchored object outside a text frame — you can choose Custom in the Anchored Object Options Position menu.

The **Relative to Spine** option, which aligns objects based on the center spread line, is only available if your layout has facing pages. When selected, objects on one side of a spread (such as a sidebar in the outside margin) remain on the outside margin even if the text reflows to a facing page.

The **Anchored Object Reference Point** defines the location on the object that you want to align to the location on the page.

The **Anchored Position Reference Point** defines the page location where you want to anchor an object.

The **X Relative To** field defines what you want to use as the basis for horizontal alignment — Anchor Marker, Column Edge, Text Frame, Page Margin, or Page Edge. The **X Offset** setting moves the object left or right.

The anchored object is outside the text frame; it is positioned with custom values.

The **Y Relative To** field specifies how the object aligns vertically — Line (Baseline), Line (Cap Height), Line (Top of Leading), Column Edge, Text Frame, Page Margin, or Page Edge. The **Y Offset** setting moves the object up or down.

When **Keep Within Top/Bottom Column Boundaries** is checked, the anchored object stays inside the text column if reflowing the text would otherwise cause the object to move outside the boundaries (for example, outside the top edge of the frame if the anchoring text is the first line in a column). This option is only available when you select a line option such as Line (Baseline) in the Y Relative To menu.

You can manually reposition a custom-anchored object by simply dragging the anchored object with the Selection tool. You can also review the anchored position by choosing View>Show Text Threads.

When text threads are showing, a dashed blue line indicates the position of anchored objects.

9. **Place the insertion point at the beginning of the next paragraph and paste the copied object.**

As with copying, pasting text — including inline graphics — in InDesign is the same as in other applications: choose Edit>Paste, or press Command/Control-V.

10. **Paste the anchored graphic again at the beginning of the next two paragraphs.**

11. **Save the file and continue to the next exercise.**

Working with Anchored Objects (continued)

Anchored Object Size and Text Position

When an anchored object is larger than the defined leading for the text in which it is placed, it might appear that changing the Y Offset value moves the text instead of the anchored object. In a way, this is true, because the text will move until it reaches the defined leading value; after that, greater changes will move the object and not the text.

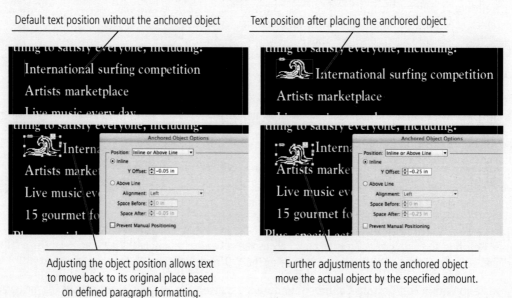

Default text position without the anchored object

Text position after placing the anchored object

Adjusting the object position allows text to move back to its original place based on defined paragraph formatting.

Further adjustments to the anchored object move the actual object by the specified amount.

Creating Anchored Placeholders

If you want to create an anchored object but don't yet have the content, you can use the Object>Anchored Object>Insert option to define the placeholder object. This dialog box allows you to create a frame (unassigned, graphics, or text) of a specific size and even apply object and paragraph styles (if those exist). The Position options are the same as those in the Anchored Object Options dialog box. (You can always resize and reposition the anchored object later.)

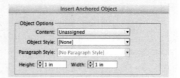

CREATE TYPE ON A PATH

Instead of simply flowing text into a frame, you can also create unique typographic effects by flowing text onto a path. A text path can be any shape that you can create in InDesign, whether using one of the basic shape tools, a complex graphic drawn with the Pen tool, or a path created by converting a clipping path to a frame.

1. **With `poster.indd` open, deselect all objects in the layout.**

   As we explained previously, you can choose Edit>Deselect All, or use the Selection tool to click an empty area of the workspace. If you use the click method, make sure you don't click a white-filled object instead of an empty area.

2. **Choose File>Place. Select `text_path.tif` in the WIP>Surfing folder and click Open. Position the top-left corner of the placed graphic at X: 0 in, Y: 0 in.**

   When this image is loaded into the cursor, click outside the defined bleed area to place the image and not replace the content in one of the existing frames. Then use the Control panel to position the image correctly. (The image that you are placing is simply a guide that you will use to create the shape of the text path for this exercise.)

3. **Click away from the placed graphic to deselect it.**

4. **Choose the Pen tool. Change the stroke value to 2-pt Magenta (C=0 M=100 Y=0 K=0) and change the fill value to None.**

   Because the line in the placed image is black, you're using magenta so you can differentiate your line from the one in the image. The solid white background in the TIF file makes it easy to focus on the line instead of the elements you have already created on the poster.

5. **Using the Pen tool, click once on the left end of the line in the placed image.**

   This first click establishes the first point of the path you're drawing.

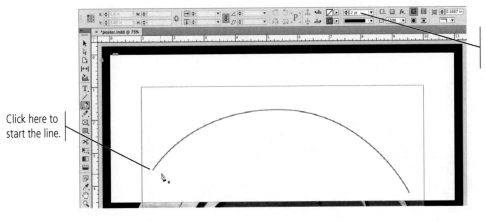

Click here to start the line.

Use these options to define the line attributes.

6. **Click near the top of the arc and drag right to create handles for the second anchor point.**

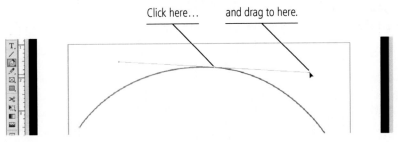

Click here... and drag to here.

7. **Click again at the right end of the line to create the final anchor point.**

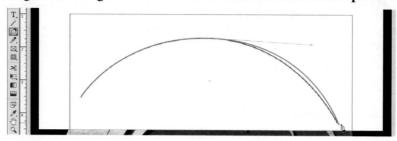

8. **Using the Direct Selection tool, adjust the points and handles until your line closely resembles the one in the placed image.**

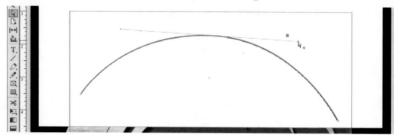

9. **Choose the Type on a Path tool. Move the cursor near the path until the cursor shows a small plus sign in the icon, and then click the path.**

   This action converts the line from a regular path to a type path.

Type on a Path tool

Type on a Path tool cursor

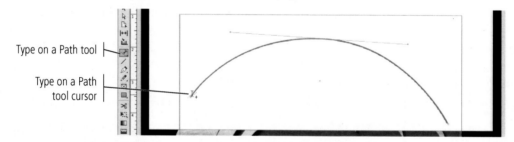

10. **Type April 13–15 ~ South Pier, then format the type as 60-pt ATC Garnet Ultra.**

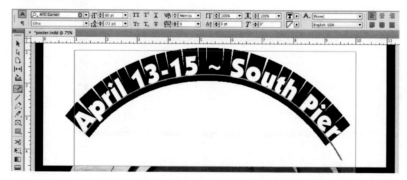

11. **Using the Selection tool, click the text_path.tif image that you used as a guide. Press Delete/Backspace to remove it from the layout.**

12. **Click the text path with the Selection tool to select the actual line.**

13. **Click the bar at the left edge of the text path and drag to the right about 1/4".**

    When you release the mouse button, the left edge of the text moves to the point where you dragged the line. This marks the orientation point of the text on the path.

    Drag this line to move the starting point of the text along the path.

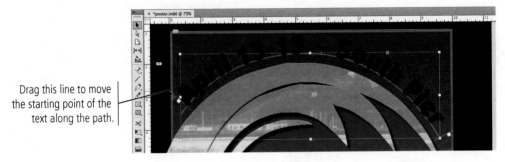

14. **Choose Edit>Undo (Command/Control-Z) to return the orientation point to the left end of the line.**

15. **Place the insertion point in the text path and apply centered paragraph alignment.**

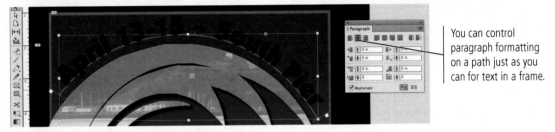

    You can control paragraph formatting on a path just as you can for text in a frame.

16. **With the type-path object still selected, use the Swatches panel to change the object's stroke color to None.**

    A text path can have a fill and stroke value just like any other path. (When a text path has no stroke color, you can still view the path by choosing View>Extras>Show Frame Edges.)

    When the actual path is selected, the Swatches panel defaults to show attributes of the path (not the type).

17. **Click the Text Color button at the top of the Swatches panel, and then click the Pantone 8005 C swatch to change the text color.**

    You don't have to select the actual text on a path to change its color. You can use the buttons in the Swatches panel to change the color attributes of either the path or the text.

    Click here to change the type fill and stroke colors.

18. **Save the file and continue to the next stage of the project.**

You can control the appearance of type on a path by choosing Type>Type on a Path>Options. You can apply one of five effects, change the alignment of the text to the path, flip the text to the other side of the path, and adjust the character spacing around curves (higher Spacing values remove more space around sharp curves).

- The **Rainbow** (default) effect keeps each character's baseline parallel to the path.

- The **Skew** effect maintains the vertical edges of type while skewing horizontal edges around the path.

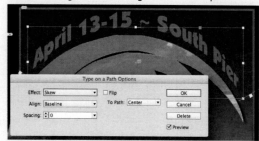

- The **3D Ribbon** effect maintains the horizontal edges of type while rotating the vertical edges to be perpendicular to the path.

- The **Stair Step** effect aligns the left edge of each character's baseline to the path.

- The **Gravity** effect aligns the center of each character's baseline to the path, keeping vertical edges in line with the path's center.

The **Align options** determine which part of the text (Baseline, Ascender, Descender, or Center) aligns to which part of the path (Top, Bottom, or Center).

Stage 4 Outputting the File

If your layout contains transparency or effects, those transparent areas will typically need to be flattened for output. **Flattening** divides transparent artwork into the necessary vector and raster objects. Transparent objects are flattened according to the settings in the selected flattener preset, which you choose in the Advanced options of the Print dialog box (or in the dialog box that appears when you export as PDF, EPS, or another format).

When you work with transparency, InDesign converts affected objects to a common color space (either CMYK or RGB) so transparent objects of different color spaces can blend properly. To avoid color mismatches between different areas of the objects on screen and in print, the blending space is applied for on-screen display and in the flattener. You can define which space to use in the Edit>Transparency Blend Space menu; for print jobs, make sure the CMYK option is selected.

Using the Flattener Preview Panel

You can use the Flattener Preview panel (Window>Output>Flattener Preview) to highlight areas that will be affected by flattening. If you are working on a layout with multiple pages or spreads, you can apply different flattener settings to individual spreads by choosing Spread Flattening in the Pages panel Options menu.

You can highlight different areas and determine which preset to use for each. Clicking Refresh updates the preview based on your choices. You can also choose Auto Refresh Highlight.

- **None** displays the normal layout.

- **Rasterized Complex Regions** highlights areas that will be rasterized based on the Raster/Vector Balance defined in the applied preset.

- **Transparent Objects** highlights objects with opacity of less than 100%, objects with blending modes, objects with transparent effects, and objects with feathering.

- **All Affected Objects** highlights all objects affected by transparency, including the transparent objects and the objects overlapped by transparent objects. All of these objects will be affected by flattening.

- **Affected Graphics** highlights all placed image files affected by transparency.

- **Outlined Strokes** highlights all strokes that will be converted to filled objects when flattened.

- **Outlined Text** highlights all text that will be converted

to outlines when flattened.

- **Raster-Fill Text and Strokes** highlights text and strokes that will have rasterized fills as a result of flattening.

- **All Rasterized Regions** highlights objects (and parts of objects) that will be rasterized when flattened.

Flattener Presets

InDesign includes three default flattener presets:

- **Low Resolution** works for desktop proofs that will be printed on low-end black-and-white printers and for documents that will be published on the Web.

- **Medium Resolution** works for desktop proofs and print-on-demand documents that will be printed on PostScript-compatible color printers.

- **High Resolution** works for commercial output on a printing press and for high-quality color proofs.

You can create your own flattener presets by choosing Edit>Transparency Flattener Presets and clicking New in the dialog box. You can also use the Transparency Flattener Presets dialog box to load presets created on another machine — such as one your service provider created for their specific output device and/or workflow.

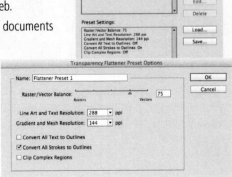

1. **With poster.indd open, choose File>Export.**

2. **Navigate to your WIP>Surfing folder as the target destination and choose Adobe PDF (Print) in the Format/Save As Type menu.**

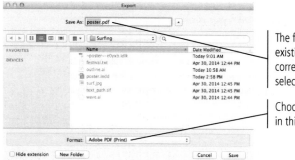

The file name defaults to the existing name, but with the correct extension for the selected format.

Choose Adobe PDF (Print) in this menu.

3. **Click Save.**

   Before the PDF is saved, you have to define the settings that will be used to generate the PDF file.

4. **Choose [High Quality Print] in the Adobe PDF Preset menu.**

   The Adobe PDF Preset menu includes six PDF presets that meet common industry output requirements.

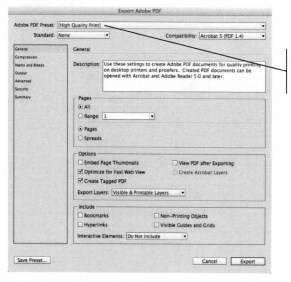

Choose the built-in [High Quality Print] preset in this menu.

Note:

The Export Adobe PDF dialog box defaults to the last-used settings.

Because there are so many ways to create a PDF — and not all of those ways are optimized for the needs of commercial printing — the potential benefits of the file format are often undermined. The PDF/X specification was created to help solve some of the problems associated with bad PDF files entering the prepress workflow. PDF/X is a subset of PDF that is specifically designed to ensure that files have the information necessary for the digital prepress output process. Ask your output provider whether you should apply a PDF/X standard to your files, and if so, which version to use.

5. **Review the options in the General pane, and make sure Visible & Printable Layers is selected in the Export Layers menu.**

- **Pages** options determine which pages to output, and whether to output facing pages on a single page.

- **Embed Page Thumbnails** creates a thumbnail for each page being exported, or one thumbnail for each spread if the Spreads option is selected.

- **Optimize for Fast Web View** optimizes the PDF file for faster viewing in a Web browser by allowing the file to download one page at a time.

- **Create Tagged PDF** automatically tags elements based on a subset of Acrobat tags (including basic formatting, lists, and more).

- **View PDF after Exporting** opens the PDF file after it has been created.

- **Create Acrobat Layers** saves each InDesign layer as an Acrobat layer within the PDF. Printer's marks are exported to a separate "marks and bleeds" layer. Create Acrobat Layers is available only when Compatibility is set to Acrobat 6 (PDF 1.5) or later.

- **Export Layers** determines whether you are outputting All Layers (including hidden and non-printing layers), Visible Layers (including non-printing layers), or Visible & Printable Layers.

- **Include** options can be used to include specific non-printing elements.

6. **Review the Compression options.**

The compression options determine what and how much data will be included in the PDF file. This set of options is one of the most important when creating PDFs, since too-low resolution results in bad-quality printing, and too-high resolution results in extremely long download times.

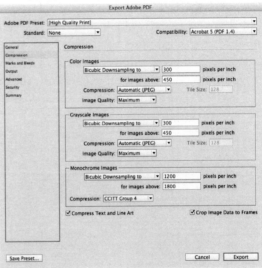

Before you choose compression settings, you need to consider your final goal. If you're creating a file for commercial printing, resolution is more important than file size. If your goal is a PDF that will be posted on the Web, file size is at least equally important as pristine image quality.

You can define a specific compression scheme for color, grayscale, and monochrome images. Different options are available depending on the image type:

- **JPEG compression** options are lossy, which means data is thrown away to create a smaller file. When you use one of the JPEG options, you can also define an Image Quality option (from Low to Maximum).

- **ZIP compression** is lossless, which means all file data is maintained in the compressed file.

- **CCITT compression** was initially developed for fax transmission. Group 3 supports two specific resolution settings (203 × 98 dpi and 203 × 196 dpi). Group 4 supports resolution up to 400 dpi.

- **Run Length Encoding** (RLE) is a lossless compression scheme that abbreviates sequences of adjacent pixels. If four pixels in a row are black, RLE saves that segment as "four black" instead of "black-black-black-black."

Note:

Since you chose the High Quality Print preset, these options default to settings that will produce the best results for most commercial printing applications.

When you resize an image in the layout, you are changing its effective resolution. The **effective resolution** of an image is the resolution calculated after any scaling has been taken into account. This number is actually more important than the original image resolution. The effective resolution can be calculated with a fairly simple equation:

$$\frac{\text{original}}{\text{resolution}} \div \frac{\%\ \text{magnification}}{100} = \frac{\text{effective}}{\text{resolution}}$$

If a 300-ppi image is magnified 150%, the effective resolution is:

300 ppi / 1.5 = 200 ppi

If you reduce the same 300-ppi image to 50%, the effective resolution is:

300 ppi / 0.5 = 600 ppi

In other words, the more you enlarge a raster image, the lower its effective resolution becomes. Reducing an image results in higher effective resolution, which can result in unnecessarily large PDF files.

When you create a PDF file, you also specify the resolution that will be maintained in the resulting PDF file. The Resolution option is useful if you want to throw away excess resolution for print files, or if you want to create low-resolution files for proofing or Web distribution.

- **Do Not Downsample** maintains all the image data from the linked files in the PDF file.

- **Average Downsampling To** reduces the number of pixels in an area by averaging areas of adjacent pixels. Apply this method to achieve user-defined resolution (72 or 96 dpi for Web-based files or 300 dpi for print).

- **Subsampling To** applies the center pixel value to surrounding pixels. If you think of a 3 × 3-block grid, subsampling enlarges the center pixel — and thus, its value — in place of the surrounding eight blocks.

- **Bicubic Downsampling To** creates the most accurate pixel information for continuous-tone images. This option also takes the longest to process, and it produces a softer image. To understand how this option works, think of a 2 × 2-block grid — bicubic downsampling averages the value of all four of those blocks (pixels) to interpolate the new information.

7. **In the Marks and Bleeds options, check the Crop Marks option and change the Offset field to 0.25 in. Check the Use Document Bleed Settings option.**

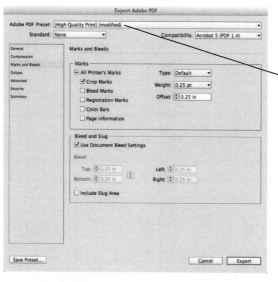

As soon as you choose a setting that is not part of the preset, the preset name shows "(modified)".

8. **In the Compatibility menu, choose Acrobat 4 (PDF 1.3).**

The Compatibility menu determines which version of the PDF format you will create. This is particularly important if your layout uses transparency (as does the one you created in this project). PDF 1.3 does not support transparency, so the file will require flattening. If you save the file to be compatible with PDF 1.4 or later, transparency information will be maintained in the PDF file.

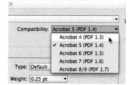

9. **In the Advanced options, choose High Resolution in the Transparency Flattener Preset menu.**

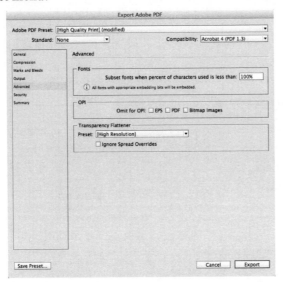

10. **Click Export to create your PDF file. If you see a warning message, click OK.**

   Your PDF file will be flattened, so some features (hyperlinks, bookmarks, etc.) will be unavailable. You didn't use those features in this project, however, so you don't have to worry about this warning.

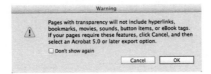

11. **Choose Window>Utilities>Background Tasks.**

   The PDF export process happens in the background, which means you can work on other tasks while the PDF is being created. This panel shows how much of the process has been completed (as a percentage), and will list any errors that occur. When the PDF file is finished, the export process is no longer listed in the panel.

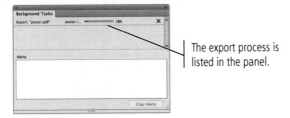

The export process is listed in the panel.

12. **Save the InDesign file and close it.**

Project Review

fill in the blank

1. The _____ tool can be used to draw the direction and position of a gradient within a frame.

2. The _____ menu command reveals characters such as paragraph returns and tabs.

3. _____ is the space between specific pairs of letters. To change this value, you have to place the insertion point between two characters.

4. The _____ is the theoretical line on which the bottoms of letters rest.

5. The _____ indicates that more text exists in the story than will fit into the available frame (or series of linked frames).

6. The _____ can be used to copy type formatting from one type element to another.

7. The _____ panel is used to apply optical margin alignment.

8. _____ are objects that are attached to specific areas of text.

9. True or false: When creating type on a path, the line on which type rests cannot have its own stroke color. _____

10. _____ compression for raster images is lossy, which means data is thrown away to reduce the file size.

short answer

1. Briefly explain how transparency is applied to objects in an InDesign page layout.

2. Briefly define a clipping path; provide at least two examples of how they might be useful.

3. Briefly explain the difference between character formatting and paragraph formatting.

Portfolio Builder Project

Use what you learned in this project to complete the following freeform exercise.
Carefully read the art director and client comments, then create your own design to meet the needs of the project.
Use the space below to sketch ideas; when finished, write a brief explanation of your reasoning behind your final design.

art director comments

Your local community theater is planning a summer production of "Down the Yellow Brick Rabbit Hole," a satirical mash-up of "The Wizard of Oz" meets "Alice in Wonderland." You have been hired to create several pieces to advertise the play in local media and in the community.

To complete this project, you should:

❏ Design a half-page advertisement for the local newspaper (11.5″ × 10.5″ trim size).

❏ Design a full-page advertisement for the community arts and entertainment magazine (8.5″ × 11″ trim size).

❏ Design a poster that can be placed in local storefronts and other public venues (11″ × 17″ trim size).

❏ Find or create artwork that appropriately illustrates the concept of the play.

client comments

As the director and playwright, I was inspired by Gregory Maguire's unique rewrites of classic fairy tales. But then I started to think about what would happen if the characters from different books met somehow... and this play is the result.

I don't want to spoil anything, but some real sparks fly when the Queen of Hearts and the Wizard of Oz get together! And the wicked witch, well, she's got her hands full trying to escape the clutches of an army of talking caterpillars.

This play is one-third mystery, one-third dramedy, and one-third just plain silly! It's got star-crossed lovers, an evil villain, an inept magician, a rather foolish prince, and even a mad flying monkey that wears some very strange hats.

The only text in the ad should be:

Down the Yellow Brick Rabbit Hole
by Stacey Wrightwood
at the Preston Theater this August
800-555-PLAY for ticket information

project justification

This project combined form and function — presenting the client's information in a clear, easy-to-read manner, while using large graphic elements to grab the viewer's attention and reinforce the message of the piece. As the client requested, the main focus is on the graphics in the top two-thirds of the piece while the relevant text is large enough to be visible but isn't the primary visual element.

Completing this poster involved adjusting a number of different text formatting options, including paragraph settings and the flow of text across multiple frames. You should now understand the difference between character and paragraph formatting, and know where to find the different options when you need them.

The graphics options in InDesign give you significant creative control over virtually every element of your layouts. Custom colors and gradients add visual interest to any piece, while more sophisticated tools like non-destructive transparency and other effects allow you to experiment entirely within your page layout until you find exactly the look you want to communicate your intended message.

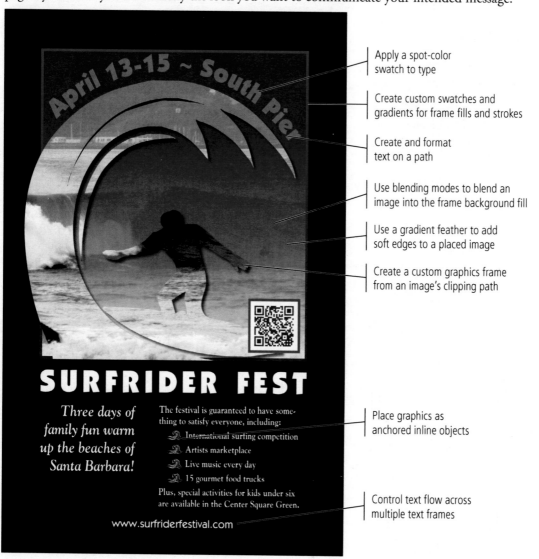

Apply a spot-color swatch to type

Create custom swatches and gradients for frame fills and strokes

Create and format text on a path

Use blending modes to blend an image into the frame background fill

Use a gradient feather to add soft edges to a placed image

Create a custom graphics frame from an image's clipping path

Place graphics as anchored inline objects

Control text flow across multiple text frames

Aerospace Newsletter

Your client is a non-profit foundation that focuses on preserving the history of American innovation in aerospace. It publishes a monthly newsletter for people on various mailing lists, which are purchased from a list-management vendor. The editor wants to change the existing newsletter template, and wants you to take over the layout once the template has been revised.

This project incorporates the following skills:

❏ Opening and modifying an existing layout template

❏ Managing missing font and link requests

❏ Replacing graphics files to meet specific color output needs

❏ Formatting text with template styles

❏ Controlling text-frame inset, alignment, and wrap attributes

❏ Creating a table with data from a Microsoft Excel worksheet

❏ Preflighting the final layout and creating a job package

client comments

In the past our newsletter was printed using two spot colors in our logo. However, the printer just told us that we can save money if we use four-color printing instead.

We also want to go from four columns to three on the front page. Each issue has a highlight image at the top of the front page, which relates to the feature story. The bottom of the front page is a series of photos from one of our affiliates, which are put together by that organization's staff. Half of the back is an ad, and the other half features the same affiliate who provides the photos for the bottom of the front page. If there is room (depending on the content they submit), we can include a table with our ArAA contact information.

We'd like you to make any necessary modifications to the template, and then use the template to create the current issue. We sent you all of the files that will be required to complete July's newsletter — photos, ads, three text files (the main article, a sidebar for the front, and the story for the back), and the Microsoft Excel table with our contact information.

art director comments

Whenever you work with a file that someone else created, there is always the potential for problems. When you first open the template, you'll have to check the fonts and images and make whatever adjustments are necessary. Make sure you save the file as a template again before you build the new issue.

The printer said they prefer to work with native application files instead of PDF, so when you're finished implementing the layout, you'll need to check the various elements, and then create a final job package.

project objectives

To complete this project, you will:

❑ Handle requests for missing fonts and images

❑ Edit master page elements to meet new layout requirements

❑ Save a layout file as a template

❑ Access master page elements on the layout pages

❑ Format imported text using template styles

❑ Build and format a table using data from a Microsoft Excel spreadsheet

❑ Create a final job package for the output provider

Stage 1 Working with Templates

Templates are commonly used whenever you have a basic layout that will be implemented more than once — for example, the structure of a newsletter remains the same, but the content for each issue changes. InDesign templates are special types of files that store the basic structure of a project. Well-planned templates can store layout elements such as nonprinting guides that mark various areas of the job; placeholder frames that will contain different stories or images in each revision; elements that remain the same in every revision, such as the nameplate; and even formatting information that will be applied to different elements so the elements can be consistent from one issue to the next.

 ## INSTALL FONTS FROM ADOBE TYPEKIT

In this project, you are going to use a number of fonts from the you Adobe Typekit library. The process for syncing Typekit fonts through the Typekit Web site is the same, regardless of whether you are using those fonts in Illustrator or InDesign. If necessary, refer to Project 2: Regatta Artwork for detailed instructions on signing in to your Creative Cloud account (Pages 117–118), and installing fonts from the Typekit Web site (Pages 119–123).

1. **In InDesign, open the Help menu and verify that you are signed in to your Creative Cloud account.**

2. **Open the Adobe Creative Cloud application.**

    On Macintosh, this is accessed on the right side of the Menu bar at the top of the screen. On Windows, it is accessed on the right side of the Taskbar at the bottom of the screen.

Macintosh   Windows

3. **Click the Assets tab in the Creative Cloud window, and choose the Fonts option in the secondary list. If you see a Start Syncing button, click that button.**

    Font syncing through Adobe Typekit is part of your Creative Cloud subscription.

    In the next two exercises, you will use both InDesign and the Typekit Web site to sync fonts in your Creative Cloud account.

    However, you have to first enable syncing functionality in your Creative Cloud account for the process to work properly.

4. **Click the Add Fonts from Typekit button.**

5. **Using the Typekit Web site, locate and sync the following font families:**
    - **FF Market (Desktop use, Script)**
    - **Petala Pro (Desktop use, Sans Serif)**

6. **Continue to the next exercise.**

MANAGE MISSING FONTS

When you work with digital page layouts — whether in a template or in a regular layout file — it's important to understand that fonts are external files of data that describe the font for on-screen display and for the output device. The fonts you use in a layout need to be available on any computer that will be used to open the file. InDesign stores a reference to used fonts, but it does not store the actual font data.

1. **Download Newsletter_Print14_RF.zip from the Student Files Web page.**

2. **Expand the ZIP archive in your WIP folder (Macintosh) or copy the archive contents into your WIP folder (Windows).**

   This creates a folder named **Newsletter**, which contains the files you need for this project. You should also use this folder to save the files you create in this project.

3. **Choose File>Open. Select araa-newsletter.indt in the WIP>Newsletter folder, and choose the Open [As] Original option.**

   You have several options when you open an existing template file:

   - If you choose **Open [As] Normal** to open a regular InDesign file (INDD), the selected file appears in a new document window or tab. When you use this option to open a template file (INDT), InDesign creates and opens a new untitled file that is based on the template.

   - When you choose the **Open [As] Original** option, you open the actual InDesign template file so that you can make and save changes to the template.

   - You can use the **Open [As] Copy** option to open a regular InDesign file as if it were a template; the result is a new untitled document based on the file you selected.

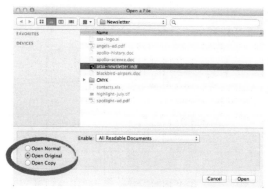

Macintosh   Windows

4. **Click Open, then review the warning message.**

   InDesign stores links to images placed in a layout; the actual image data is not stored in the InDesign file. If placed files are not available in the same location as when they were placed, or if they have been resaved since you placed them, you'll see a warning message when you open the file. You'll correct these problems shortly.

5. Click Don't Update Links, and then review the information in the resulting Missing Fonts dialog box.

Any time you open a file that calls for fonts that are not installed on your computer system, you see this warning.

When you are logged in to your Creative Cloud account, you are synced to the entire Adobe Creative Cloud system. This allows InDesign to access information from a variety of sources, including what fonts area available in the Typekit library. In this case, the Missing Fonts dialog box shows that Enzo OT Light is available to sync from Typekit.

6. Make sure the Sync box is checked for the missing Enzo OT Light font, then click the Sync Fonts button.

This option automatically syncs the selected fonts in your Creative Cloud account, making them available to the applications on your desktop.

As you can see, one font is still missing. You could fix the problem without knowing what will be affected, but we prefer to review problem areas before making changes.

Note:

If you have the ATC fonts from previous editions installed, ATC Colada might not appear in the list of missing fonts.

Note:

Missing fonts are one of the most common problems in the digital graphics output process. This is one of the primary advantages of using PDF files for output — PDF can store actual font data so you don't need to include the separate font files in your job package. (However, PDF can't solve the problem of missing fonts used in a layout template.)

7. Click Close to dismiss the Missing Fonts dialog box.

8. Open the Pages panel (Window>Pages).

The Pages panel makes it very easy to navigate through the pages in a layout, including master pages. You can navigate to any page by simply double-clicking the page's icon, or navigate to a spread by double-clicking the spread page numbers (below the page icons).

The document tab shows you are editing the actual template file (araa-newsletter.indt).

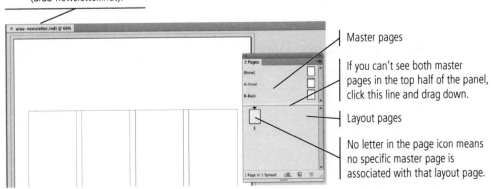

Master pages

If you can't see both master pages in the top half of the panel, click this line and drag down.

Layout pages

No letter in the page icon means no specific master page is associated with that layout page.

Think of master pages as templates for different pages in the layout. This file, for example, has two master pages: Front Page and Back Page. The letters preceding each master page name are automatically added and used to identify which layout pages are associated with which master page. (This will become clear as you continue through this project.)

9. **Double-click the A-Front icon to display that layout.**

The top area of the newsletter (the **nameplate** area) includes the newsletter logotype, as well as the "Published by…" line and the issue date. A pink highlight around the type shows that the font used in this area is not available.

The Missing Font highlighting is only a visual indicator on your screen; it is not included when the job is output. If the nameplate information is not highlighted, open the Composition pane of the Preferences dialog box and make sure the Highlight Substituted Fonts option is checked.

10. **Using the Type tool, click the frame with the missing font to place the insertion point.**

The Control panel shows the missing font name in brackets. Any time you see a font name in brackets, you know you have a potential problem.

Note:

The missing-font highlighting only appears if you are in the Normal viewing mode.

With the insertion point placed, the Control panel shows the name of the missing font.

Highlighting indicates an area where the required font is not available.

The name or number of the active page is highlighted.

The icon of the selected page is highlighted.

11. **Choose Type>Find Font.**

The Find Font dialog box lists every font used in the layout — including missing ones (with a warning icon). You can use this dialog box to replace any font — including missing ones — with another font that is available on your system.

12. **Highlight ATC Colada in the Fonts in Document list. In the Replace With area, choose ATC Onyx in the Font Family menu and choose Normal in the Font Style menu.**

13. **Check the option to Redefine Style When Changing All.**

When this is checked, the font replacement will be applied in paragraph and character style definitions, even if those styles are not currently applied in the layout.

If you don't check the Redefine Style option, you might later introduce another missing-font problem when you apply a style that calls for a missing font.

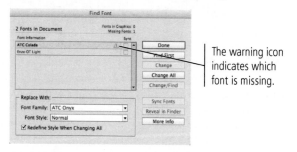

The warning icon indicates which font is missing.

Note:

If you click the More Info button, you can see specific details about the selected font, such as the type of font and where it is used.

14. **Click Change All to replace all instances of ATC Colada.**

    You could also click the Find Next button to review individual instances of a missing font, or click the Change or Change/Find button to replace and review individual instances of the selected font.

    When the Redefine Style option is checked and you use the Change All option, InDesign provides a warning when overrides have been applied to existing styles.

15. **Click OK to dismiss the warning message.**

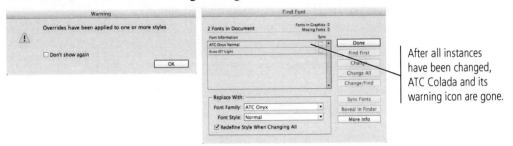

After all instances have been changed, ATC Colada and its warning icon are gone.

16. **Click Done to close the Find Font dialog box.**

    Once you have replaced the missing font, the pink highlighting disappears.

17. **Choose File>Save to save your changes to the template file, and then continue to the next exercise.**

    Because you used the Open Original option, you are editing the actual template file; this means you can simply use the regular Save command to save your changes to the template. If you used the Open Normal option to open and edit a template file, you would have to use the Save As command and save the edited file with the same name and extension as the original template to overwrite the original.

REPLACE MISSING AND MODIFIED GRAPHICS

Placed graphics can cause problems if those files aren't where InDesign thinks they should be. Placed graphics files can be either **missing** (they were moved from the location from which they were originally placed in the layout, or the name of the file was changed) or **modified** (they were resaved after being placed into the layout, changing the linked file's "time stamp" but not its location or file name). In either case, you need to correct these problems before the file can be successfully output.

1. **With araa-newsletter.indt open in InDesign, display the Links panel (Window>Links).**

   The Links panel lists every file that is placed in your layout. Missing images show a red stop-sign icon; modified images show a yellow yield sign.

   Your Links panel might appear different than what you see here, depending on how items are sorted in your version panel. You can click any column heading at the top of the panel to sort items by that criteria; the small arrow icon in one of the headings indicates which category is sorted, and whether items appear in ascending or descending order.

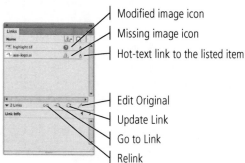

Modified image icon
Missing image icon
Hot-text link to the listed item

Edit Original
Update Link
Go to Link
Relink

2. **Click the modified aaa-logo.ai file in the panel, then click the Go to Link button in the middle of the panel.**

   You can also use the hot-text link to the right of an image name to navigate to a specific placed image. The Pages panel shows that the A-Front master layout is now active because that is where the selected instance exists.

This icon identifies a modified image.

This icon identifies a missing image.

Click the hot-text link or the Go to Link button to navigate to a specific instance.

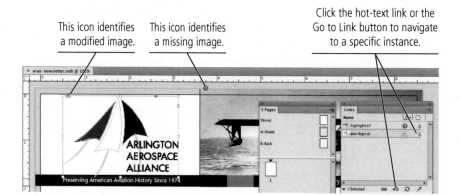

You can easily use the Links panel to navigate to selected images.

- The **Relink** button opens a navigation dialog box where you can locate a missing file or link to a different file.

- The **Go to Link** button selects and centers the file in the document window.

- The **Update Link** button updates modified links. If the selected image is missing, this button opens a navigation dialog box so you can locate the missing file.

- The **Edit Original** button opens the selected file in its native application. When you save the file and return to InDesign, the placed file is automatically updated.

Note:

The issue of missing and modified images is a common problem if you zip a job folder into an archive. When you unzip a job folder and open the InDesign file, you will often see a warning about missing/modified images (especially on Windows).

To avoid this problem in the resource files for this book, we embedded most of the placed images into the layout files.

Note:

If you don't see the Missing and Modified icons in the layout, choose View>Extras>Show Link Badge.

INDESIGN FOUNDATIONS

The Links panel lists all files that have been placed into a layout. By default, the panel shows the item name, the status (missing or modified), and the location of that item in the layout. The lower half of the panel shows important information for the selected link, such as color space and resolution. If you open the Panel Options dialog box (from the Links panel Options menu), you can change which information appears in each section of the panel.

Multiple instances of the same image are grouped together.

Click this bar and drag to expand or contract the Link info area without resizing the panel.

Click the column headings to sort based on specific criteria (e.g., filename, status, or page).

Click the hot-text page number to navigate to an item in the layout.

Click here and drag to resize the panel.

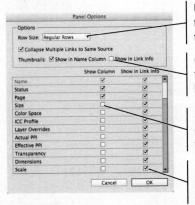

Use this menu to change the size of item thumbnails in the panel.

Check to include item thumbnails in the lower half of the panel.

Use these boxes to change what appears in the top half of the panel.

Use these boxes to change what appears in the lower half of the panel.

Embedding Links

To avoid the problem of missing links, you can embed placed images directly into the layout file by Control/right-clicking an image in the Links panel and choosing Embed Link from the contextual menu.

This icon identifies an embedded link.

When links are embedded, there is no longer any relation to the original source file. This means the source files do not need to be included in the job package, and you will not see a missing-link error if the original source file is moved. It also means, however, that any changes in a source file will not result in a modified link warning.

To edit an image, you have to manually open the original source file in its native application, save it, then manually replace the embedded image with the edited file.

3. **Using the Direct Selection tool, click the placed logo on the page.**

As part of the Adobe Creative Suite, InDesign supports native Adobe Illustrator files (with the ".ai" extension) that have been saved to be compatible with the PDF format. Illustrator files can include both raster and vector information, type and embedded fonts, and objects on multiple layers in a variety of color models (including spot colors, which are added to the InDesign Swatches panel when the AI file is imported).

Note:

Make sure you use the Direct Selection tool, or the Content Grabber, to select the actual placed logo. If you select the frame instead, the Transform panel shows the values for the frame instead of the graphic placed in the frame.

4. **Open the Transform panel (Window>Object & Layout>Transform).**

The options in the Transform panel are the same as those on the left side of the Control panel. As you can see, the selected graphic is placed at approximately 44%.

5. **Click the Modified icon in the top-left corner of the image frame.**

The Missing and Modified icons provide an easy, on-screen method for identifying and correcting image-link problems.

Note:

You can also click the Update Link button in the Links panel to update selected modified files.

6. **Click the updated image with the Direct Selection tool.**

When you update or replace an existing placed image, the new file adopts the necessary scaling percentage to fit into the same space as the original. In this case, the new file is scaled to approximately 54% — the size that is necessary to fit the same dimensions as the original.

This icon identifies a linked image that is up to date.

The link is now up to date.

7. **Click the Missing icon in the top-left corner of the grayscale image.**

Note:

You can also click the Relink button in the Links panel to replace a missing image link.

8. **In the resulting Locate dialog box, navigate to highlight-july.tif in the WIP>Newsletter folder. Click Open to finalize the process.**

   After you identify a new source image, the graphics frame and the Links panel no longer show the Missing warning. The new image preview appears in the same frame.

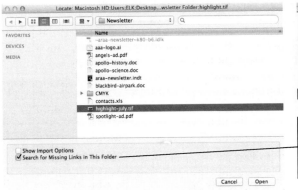

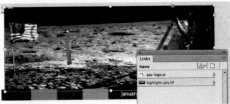

If multiple files are missing, check this box to update all missing links found in the selected folder.

Note:

If the Search for Missing Links option is checked, InDesign will scan the selected folder to find other missing image files.

9. **Save the file and continue to the next exercise.**

Edit Margin and Column Guides

Your client wants to make several changes to the layout, including fewer and wider columns on the front page. These changes will recur from one issue to the next, so you should change the template instead of simply changing the elements in each issue.

Every layout has a default setup, which you define when you create the file. Each master page has its own margin and column settings, which can be different than the default document settings.

1. **With araa-newsletter.indt open, double-click the A-Front icon to show that layout in the document window.**

2. **Choose Layout>Margins and Columns, and make sure the Preview option is checked in the resulting dialog box.**

3. **Change the Left and Right Margins fields to 0.5 in, change the Columns field to 3, and change the Gutter field to 0.2 in.**

   Notice that changing the margin and column guides has no effect on the text frame; you have to change the text frame settings independently.

Note:

Many InDesign dialog boxes have a Preview option, which allows you to see the effects of your changes before finalizing them.

Margin guides are pink.

Column guides are purple.

Frame edges on master pages are dotted.

Frame columns are light blue.

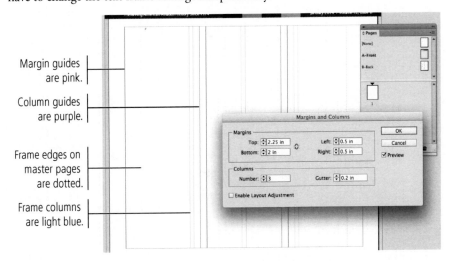

Note:

You can change the default margins and columns for a layout by choosing File>Document Setup.

4. **Click OK to apply the change and close the dialog box.**

5. **Using the Selection tool, click to select the 4-column text frame in the layout.**

6. **Click and drag the outside-center handles to extend the frame edges to match the modified margin guides.**

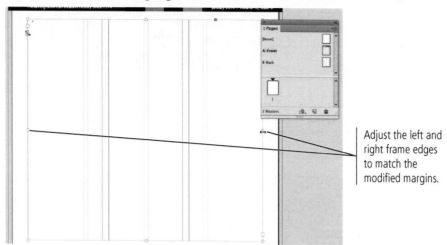

Adjust the left and right frame edges to match the modified margins.

7. **Control/right-click the frame and choose Text Frame Options from the contextual menu.**

Note:

You can also access the Text Frame Options dialog box from the Object menu.

8. **Change the Number of Columns field to 3 and the Gutter field to 0.2″ to match the changes you made to the column guides. Click OK to close the dialog box.**

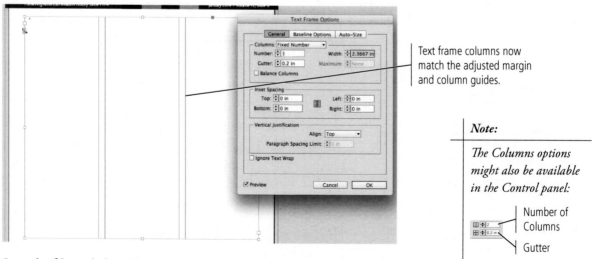

Text frame columns now match the adjusted margin and column guides.

Note:

The Columns options might also be available in the Control panel:

Number of Columns

Gutter

9. **Save the file and close it.**

There are two kinds of pages in InDesign:

- **Layout pages**, which appear in the bottom of the Pages panel, are the pages on which you place content.

- **Master pages**, which appear in the top of the Pages panel, are the pages on which you place recurring information, such as running heads and footers (information at the top and bottom of the page, respectively).

Master pages are one of the most powerful features in page layout software. Think of a master page as a template for individual pages; anything on the master appears on the related layout page(s). Changing something on a master layout applies the same changes to the object on related layout pages (unless you already changed the object on the layout page, or detached the object from the master).

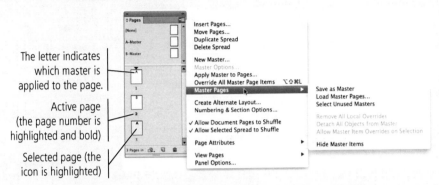

The letter indicates which master is applied to the page.

Active page (the page number is highlighted and bold)

Selected page (the icon is highlighted)

The Pages panel Options menu has a number of indispensable options for working with master pages:

- **New Master** opens a dialog box where you can assign a custom prefix, a meaningful name, whether the master will be based on another master page, and the number of pages (from 1 to 10) to include in the master layout. Because InDesign supports multiple page sizes within a single document, you can also change the size of the master page.

- **Master Options** opens a dialog box with the same options you defined when you created a new master.

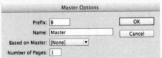

- **Apply Master to Pages** allows you to apply a specific master to selected pages. You can also apply a specific master to a layout by dragging the master icon onto the layout page icon in the lower half of the panel.

- **Override All Master Page Items** allows you to access and change master items on a specific layout page. (It's important to realize that this command functions on a page-by-page basis.) You can also override individual objects by pressing Command/Control-Shift and clicking the object you want to override.

In the Master Pages submenu:

- **Save as Master** is useful if you've built a layout on a layout page and want to convert that layout to a master. Instead of copying and pasting the page contents, you can simply activate the page and choose Save as Master.

- **Load Master Pages** allows you to import entire master pages from one InDesign file to another. Assets such as colors and styles used on the imported masters will also be imported into the current InDesign file.

- **Select Unused Masters** highlights all master pages not associated with at least one layout page (and not used as the basis of another master page). This option can be useful if you want to clean up your layout and remove extraneous elements.

- **Remove All Local Overrides** reapplies the settings from the master items to related items on the layout page. (This option toggles to **Remove Selected Local Overrides** if you have a specific object selected on the layout page.)

- **Detach All Objects from Master** breaks the link between objects on a layout page and objects on the related master; in this case, changing items on the master has no effect on related layout page items. (This selection toggles to **Detach Selection from Master** if you have a specific object selected on the layout page.)

- **Allow Master Item Overrides on Selection**, active by default, allows objects to be overridden on layout pages. You can protect specific objects by selecting them on the master layout and toggling this option off.

- **Hide/Show Master Items** toggles the visibility of master page items on layout pages.

CREATE A NEW FILE BASED ON THE TEMPLATE

Once you have made the client's requested changes in the template, you can easily begin each new issue by simply opening the template. Only a few more things need to be addressed before you're ready to work on the current issue of the newsletter.

Every issue of the newsletter has one front page and one back page. These layouts are already prepared as master pages, but you have to apply those master pages to the layout pages for individual issues. Since this occurs for every issue, it will remove a few more clicks from the process if you set up the layout pages as part of the template.

1. **Choose File>Open and navigate to your WIP>Newsletter folder. Select the `araa-newsletter.indt` template file and choose the Open [As] Normal option at the bottom of the dialog box.**

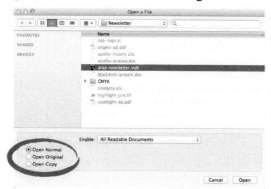

Macintosh   Windows

2. **Click Open to create a new file based on the template.**

Opening a template using the Open [As] Normal option creates a new untitled document that is based on the template.

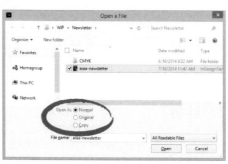

Note:

If you double-click a template file on your desktop, the template opens as if you chose the Open Normal option. To use the Open Original or Open Copy feature, you must choose File>Open from InDesign.

3. **Double-click the Page 1 icon in the Pages panel.**

4. **In the Pages panel, drag the A-Front master icon onto the Page 1 icon in the lower half of the Pages panel.**

   When a master page is applied to a layout page, everything on the master page is placed on the layout page.

Assign a master layout to a specific page by dragging the master icon onto the page icon.

Alternatively, you can choose Apply Master Pages in the Pages panel Options menu. In the resulting dialog box, you can determine which master page to apply to specific layout pages. Some find this easier than dragging master page icons onto individual layout page icons in the panel; it is also useful if you want to apply a specific master layout to more than one page at a time.

5. Click the B-Back icon and drag it into the bottom half of the Pages panel (below the Page 1 icon).

You can add new pages to your layout by dragging any of the master page icons into the lower half of the panel.

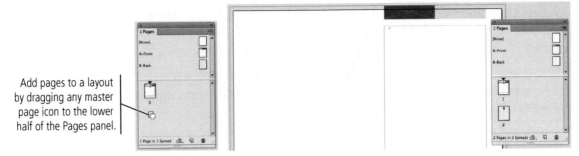

Add pages to a layout by dragging any master page icon to the lower half of the Pages panel.

You can also choose Insert Pages in the Pages panel Options menu. In the resulting dialog box, you can determine how many pages to add, exactly where to add the new pages, and which master page to apply to the new pages. This method makes it easier to add only one page from a master page that includes spreads, or add multiple pages at one time based on the same master.

6. Choose File>Save As. Navigate to your WIP>Newsletter folder as the location for saving the template.

Because you opened the template to create a normal layout file, you have to use the Save As command to overwrite the edited template file.

7. Change the file name to `araa-newsletter`. In the Format/Save As Type menu, choose InDesign CC 2014 Template.

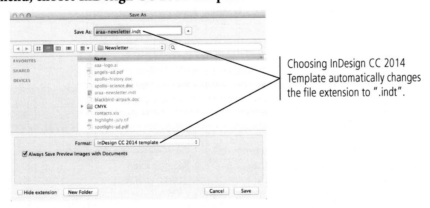

Choosing InDesign CC 2014 Template automatically changes the file extension to ".indt".

8. Click Save, then read the resulting message.

Because you defined the same name as the original template, you have to confirm that you want to overwrite the template file with the new version.

9. Click Replace/Yes. When the save is complete, close the template file.

IMPLEMENT THE NEWSLETTER TEMPLATE

By saving your work as a template, you eliminated a significant amount of repetitive work that would otherwise need to be redone for every issue. There are still some tasks that will need to be done for each issue, such as changing the issue date and adding images to the front and back pages. These elements will change in each issue, so they can't be entirely "templated." But if you review the layout, you'll see that the template includes placeholders for these elements;, so adding these elements is greatly simplified.

1. **Choose File>Open and navigate to your WIP>Newsletter folder. Select the araa-newsletter.indt template file, choose the Open [As] Normal option at the bottom of the dialog box, and click Open.**

   As in the previous exercise, opening the template file creates a new untitled document that is based on the template.

2. **Immediately choose File>Save As and navigate to your WIP>Newsletter folder. Change the file name to newsletter_july.indd and click Save.**

   The Format menu defaults to the InDesign CC 2014 Document option, so you do not have to change this menu to save the new file as a regular InDesign document.

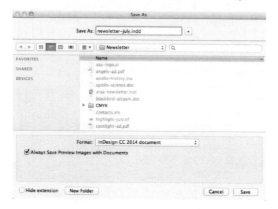

3. **Navigate to Page 1 of the file.**

4. **Using the Selection tool, try to select the text frame that includes the date.**

   This step will have no effect, and nothing will be selected. By default, you can't select master page items on a layout page; changes have to be made on the master page.

   When you change an object on a master page, the same changes reflect on associated layout pages. For example, if you change the red box to blue on A-Front Page, the red box will turn blue on Page 1 as well. Because of this parent-child relationship, it's a good idea to leave objects attached to the master whenever possible.

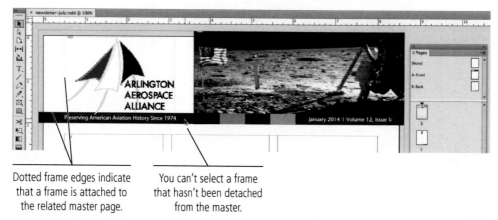

Dotted frame edges indicate that a frame is attached to the related master page.

You can't select a frame that hasn't been detached from the master.

5. **Command/Control-Shift-click the text frame that contains the issue date.**

   This method detaches an individual object from the master page. It is no longer linked to the master page, so changes to the same item on the master will not be reflected on the associated layout page.

6. **Using the Type tool, change the date in the frame to July 2014 and change the issue number to 3.**

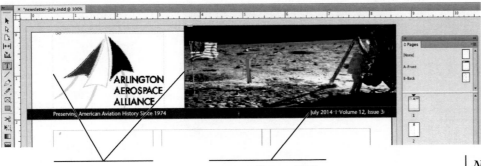

Other frames are still attached to the master.

Command/Control-Shift click to detach a single item from the master page.

You could have accomplished the same basic result by editing the text on the master page. However, we created these steps so you can understand the concept of detaching master page objects.

7. **Save the file and continue to the next exercise.**

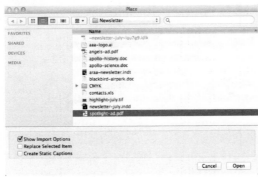

PLACE A PDF FILE

PDF (Portable Document Format) files save layout, graphics, and font information in a single file. The format was created to facilitate cross-platform file-sharing so one file could be transferred to any other computer, and the final layout would print as intended. While originally meant for Internet use, PDF is now the standard in the graphics industry, used for submitting advertisements, artwork, and completed jobs to a service provider.

You can place a PDF file into an InDesign layout, just as you would place any other image. You can determine which page to place (if the file contains more than one page), which layers are visible (if the file has more than one layer), and the specific file dimensions (bounding box) to use when placing the file.

1. **With newsletter_july.indd open, navigate to Page 1 of the newsletter.**

2. **Choose File>Place. In the Place dialog box, select spotlight-ad.pdf (in the WIP>Newsletter folder).**

> **Note:**
>
> *You can detach all items from the master page layout by Control/right-clicking a page icon in the Pages panel and choosing Override All Master Page Items from the contextual menu.*

> **Note:**
>
> *Before placing a PDF file in an InDesign job, make absolutely sure it was created and optimized for commercial printing. Internet-optimized PDF files do not have sufficient resolution to print cleanly on a high-resolution output device; if these are used, they could ruin an otherwise perfect InDesign job.*

3. **Make sure Show Import Options is checked and Replace Selected Item is not checked, and then click Open.**

The options in the Place PDF dialog box are exactly the same as the options you saw when you placed the native Illustrator file. However, the options in the General tab are typically more important for PDF files than for Illustrator files.

PDF files can contain multiple pages; you can review the various pages using the buttons below the preview image. You can place multiple pages at once by choosing the All option, or you can select specific pages using the Range option.

Note:

Import continuous pages by defining a page range, using a hyphen to separate the first page and last pages in the range. Import non-continuous pages by typing each page number, separated by commas.

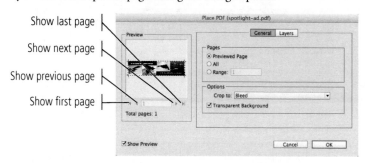

Show last page
Show next page
Show previous page
Show first page

Note:

If you place multiple pages of a PDF file, each page is loaded into the cursor as a separate object.

The Crop To options are also significant when placing PDF files. If the file was created properly, it should include a defined bleed of at least 1/8 inch and trim marks to identify the intended trim size.

4. **Choose Bleed in the Crop To menu and click OK.**

5. **Click the loaded cursor in the empty graphics frame at the bottom of Page 1 to place the loaded file.**

Note:

If you place an Illustrator file that contains multiple artboards, you have the same options for choosing which artboard (page) to place.

6. **Access the placed content by clicking the image with the Direct Selection tool or by clicking the Content Grabber with the Selection tool.**

When you place the image into the frame, it is automatically centered in the frame; if you look carefully, you can see that the text at the bottom of the frame appears very close the bottom page edge.

This file was created with 1/8″ bleeds on all four sides. In this context, however, the top bleed allowance is not necessary; the bleed area on the top causes the image to appear farther down than it should. You need to change the graphic's Y position to eliminate all of the unnecessary bleed at the top of the file.

The Y position shows the graphic's position in relation to the frame edge.

When the content is selected, you can see the image edge beyond the frame edge.

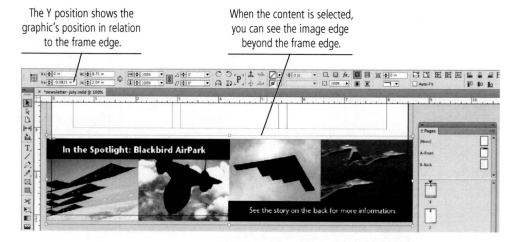

7. **With the placed file still selected, make sure the top-left reference point is selected and then change the picture position (within the frame) to Y+: `-0.125 in`.**

The image bounding box now shows the extra bleed allowance extending beyond the upper edge of the frame.

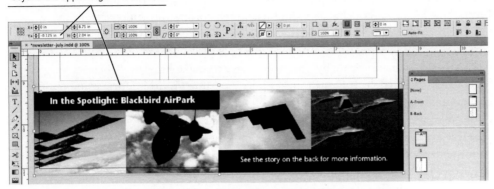

8. **Repeat the process from this exercise to place `angels-ad.pdf` in the empty graphics frame on Page 2 of the newsletter file.**

In this case, the graphics frame includes the required bleed area on the top, left, and bottom edges; the placed image should be positioned at X+: 0, Y+: 0.

9. **Save the file and continue to the next stage of the project.**

Stage 2 Working with Styles

The principles of good design state that headings, subheadings, body copy, and other editorial elements should generally look the same throughout a single job — in other words, editorial elements should be consistent from one page to another, whether the job is two pages or two hundred.

For any bit of text, there are dozens of character- and paragraph-formatting options, from the font and type size to the space above and below paragraphs. Whenever you work with longer blocks of copy, you'll apply the same group of formatting options to multiple pieces of text.

If you were to change each element manually, you would have to make hundreds of clicks to create a two-page newsletter. Fortunately, InDesign makes it easy to store groups of formatting options as **styles**, which can be applied with a single click.

The major advantages of using styles are ease of use and enhanced efficiency. Styles ensure consistency in text formatting throughout a publication; rather than trying to remember how you formatted a sidebar 45 pages ago, for example, you can simply apply a predefined Sidebar style. Changes can be made instantly to all text defined as a particular style (for example, changing the font in the Subhead style from Helvetica to Myriad); when a style definition changes, any text that uses that style automatically changes too.

InDesign supports both character styles and paragraph styles. **Character styles** apply only to selected words; this type of style is useful for setting off a few words in a paragraph without affecting the entire paragraph. **Paragraph styles** apply to the entire body of text between two ¶ symbols; this type of style defines the appearance of the paragraph, combining the character style used in the paragraph with line spacing, indents, tabs, and other paragraph attributes.

In this project, the client's original template included a number of styles for formatting the text in each issue. Because the text frames already exist in the template layout, you only need to import the client's text and apply the existing styles.

Note:

Paragraph styles define character attributes and paragraph attributes; character styles define only the character attributes. In other words, a paragraph style can be used to format text entirely — including font information, line spacing, tabs, and so on.

APPLY TEMPLATE STYLES

Most InDesign jobs incorporate some amount of client-supplied text, which might be sent to you in the body of an email or saved in any number of text file formats. Many text files will be supplied from Microsoft Word, the most popular word-processing application in the U.S. market.

Microsoft Word includes fairly extensive options for formatting text (although not quite as robust or sophisticated as InDesign). Many Microsoft Word users apply **local formatting** (selecting specific text and applying character and/or paragraph attributes); more sophisticated Microsoft Word users build text formatting styles similar to those used in InDesign.

1. **With newsletter_july.indd open, double-click the Page 1 icon in the Pages panel to make that page active in the document window.**

2. **Choose File>Place and navigate to the file apollo-history.doc.**

   All text files for this project are in the WIP>Newsletter folder; we will not continue to repeat the entire path for each file.

3. **Check the Show Import Options box at the bottom of the dialog box and make sure Replace Selected Item is not checked. Click Open.**

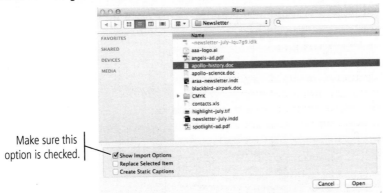

Make sure this option is checked.

4. **In the resulting dialog box, make sure the Preserve Styles and Formatting option is selected and the Import Styles Automatically radio button is selected. Choose Auto Rename in both conflict menus and then click OK.**

When you import a Microsoft Word file into InDesign, you can either preserve or remove formatting saved in the Microsoft Word file (including styles defined in Microsoft Word).

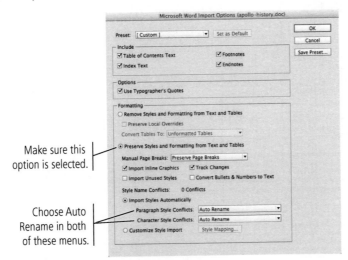

Make sure this option is selected.

Choose Auto Rename in both of these menus.

5. **If you get a Missing Font warning, click OK.**

You're going to replace the Microsoft Word formatting with InDesign styles, which will correct this problem.

6. **Click the loaded cursor in the empty three-column text frame.**

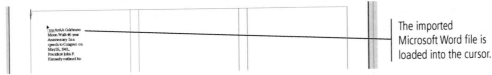

The imported Microsoft Word file is loaded into the cursor.

At this point, the story does not fit into the frame because you haven't yet applied the appropriate styles to the imported text.

Overset text icon

7. **Open the Paragraph Styles panel (Window>Styles>Paragraph Styles).**

8. **Place the insertion point in the first paragraph of the imported story (the main heading) and look at the Paragraph Styles panel.**

The imported text appears to be preformatted, but the Paragraph Styles panel tells a different story. This paragraph is formatted as "Normal+."

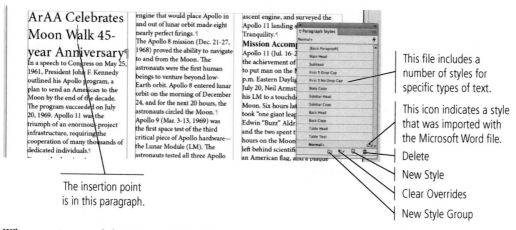

The insertion point is in this paragraph.

This file includes a number of styles for specific types of text.

This icon indicates a style that was imported with the Microsoft Word file.

Delete

New Style

Clear Overrides

New Style Group

When you imported the Microsoft Word file, you preserved the formatting in the file; this is usually a good idea so you can see what the writer intended. Now that the text is imported into your layout, however, you want to apply the template styles to make the text in this issue consistent with other issues.

9. With the insertion point still in place, click the Main Head style in the Paragraph Styles panel.

A number of styles existed in the original newsletter template, so they also exist in any files that are based on that template. You should be able to guess the purpose of these styles from their names; it's always a good idea to use indicative names when you create styles or other user-defined assets.

Using styles, you can change all formatting attributes of selected text with a single click. Because you are working with paragraph styles, the style definition applies to the entire paragraph where the insertion point is placed.

When you apply the style, formatting of the heading changes but the heading now shows a missing-font highlight. When you opened the template file, InDesign warned you about missing fonts. Unfortunately, that warning only includes fonts that are actually used in the existing layout; fonts defined in styles that have not yet been applied are not included in the missing-font warning.

The Main Head style has been applied to this paragraph.

The missing-font highlight indicates that the applied style uses a font that you don't have installed.

Note:

When you import text into InDesign, any number of new styles might appear in the Styles panels; the most common imported style is Normal. Text in a Microsoft Word file is typically formatted with the Normal style — even if you don't realize it; user-applied formatting is commonly local (meaning it is applied directly to selected text instead of with a defined style).

10. Choose Type>Find Font.

You can see that a number of additional fonts are now used in the layout, including two that are used in placed graphics.

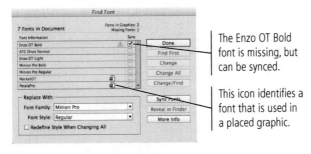

The Enzo OT Bold font is missing, but can be synced.

This icon identifies a font that is used in a placed graphic.

Note:

If you select a font that is used in a placed graphic, you can click the Find Graphic button to navigate to the location of the graphic where the font is used.

11. Make sure the Enzo OT Bold font is checked in the list and click Sync Fonts.

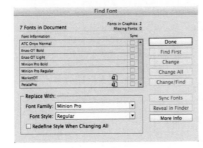

12. Click Close to return to the layout.

13. Place the insertion point in the next paragraph of copy, then click the First ¶ Drop Cap style in the Paragraph Styles panel.

14. Format the next paragraph ("From the beginning...") with the Subhead style.

15. Format the next paragraph with the First ¶ No Drop Cap style.

Microsoft Word files can include a fairly sophisticated level of formatting attributes, from basic text formatting to defined paragraph and character styles to automatically generated tables of contents. When you import a Word file into InDesign, you can determine whether to include these elements in the imported text, as well as how to handle conflicts between imported elements and elements that already exist in your InDesign layout.

If these elements exist in the Microsoft Word file, checking the associated boxes imports those elements into your InDesign file.

Choose this option to convert straight quote marks to typographer's or "curly" quotes.

Choose this option to strip out all formatting applied in the file and import the file as plain text.

Choose this option to import the Microsoft Word file, including formatting.

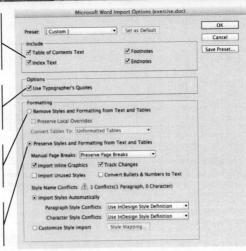

The **Manual Page Breaks** menu determines how page breaks in Word translate to InDesign. You can preserve manual breaks, convert them to column breaks, or ignore them. This option is important because Word users tend to force breaks where appropriate in the file — which rarely translates to a properly formatted InDesign layout. More often than not, you'll end up removing these page breaks, but it might be a good idea to include them in the import and remove them after you've reviewed the imported text.

If graphics have been placed into a Word file, the **Import Inline Graphics** option allows you to include those graphics as anchored objects in the InDesign story. If you choose to include graphics, it is extremely important to understand that the graphics might be embedded into the story instead of linked to the original data file (depending on how the graphic was placed into the Word file).

If you choose **Import Unused Styles**, all styles in the Word file will be imported into the InDesign layout. The most significant issue here is that styles might require fonts that you have not installed.

Word includes a powerful collaboration tool called Track Changes, which allows one person to review another person's changes to a file. (As publishers, we use this feature every day, so editors and authors can review each other's changes before permanently changing the text.) If you check the **Track Changes** option, any tracked changes from the Word file will be included in your InDesign layout. This might cause a lot of items to show up in your text that aren't supposed to be there (typos, errors, or, for example, something the general counsel office removed from the original text for a specific legal reason).

Convert Bullets & Numbers to Text allows you to convert automatically generated numbering and bullet characters into actual text characters. This option is extremely useful if the text includes lists; if you don't check this option, you'll have to manually re-enter the bullets or line numbers into the imported text.

The **Style Name Conflicts** area warns you if styles in the Word file conflict with styles in the InDesign file. (In other words, they have the same style names but different definitions in the two locations). If you are importing styles from the Word file, you have to determine how to resolve these conflicts.

Import Styles Automatically allows you to choose how to handle conflicts in paragraph and character styles. **Use InDesign Style Definition** preserves the style as you defined it; text in the Word file that uses that style will be reformatted with the InDesign definition of the style. **Redefine InDesign Style** replaces the layout definition with the definition from the Word file. **Auto Rename** adds the Word file to the InDesign file with "_wrd_1" at the end of the style name.

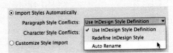

If you choose **Customize Style Import**, the Style Mapping button opens a dialog box where you can review and control specific style conflicts. Click an option in the InDesign Style column to access a menu, where you can choose which InDesign style to use in place of a specific Word style.

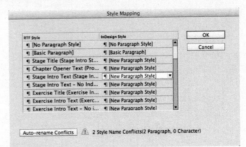

If you always receive Microsoft Word files from the same source, you can save your choices (including Style Mapping options) as a preset, or even click the Set as Default button in the Import Options dialog box.

16. Select any part of the next 4 paragraphs (up to but not including the "Mission Accomplished" paragraph), then click the Body Copy style in the Paragraph Styles panel.

Paragraph styles apply to any paragraph that is partially or entirely selected. You don't have to select an entire paragraph before applying a paragraph style.

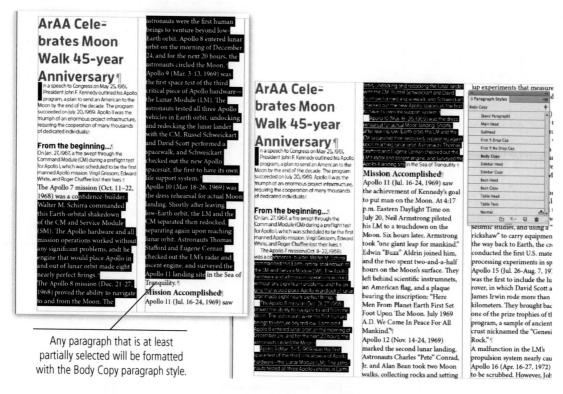

Any paragraph that is at least partially selected will be formatted with the Body Copy paragraph style.

17. Continue applying styles to the remaining copy; use the style names as a guide.

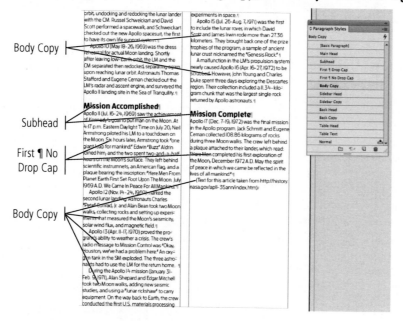

Body Copy

Subhead

First ¶ No Drop Cap

Body Copy

18. Save the file and continue to the next exercise.

EDIT A PARAGRAPH TO SPAN COLUMNS

As a general rule, headlines in newsletters and newspapers extend across the top of the entire related story. In previous versions of the software, this required a separate frame that spanned the width of the multi-column body frame. InDesign includes a paragraph formatting option that makes it easy to span a paragraph across multiple columns *without* the need for a separate frame. This can be applied to individual paragraphs, or defined as part of a paragraph style.

1. With **newsletter_july.indd** open, make sure Page 1 is active.

2. Place the insertion point in the first paragraph of the story (the main head) and then open the Paragraph panel (Window>Type & Tables>Paragraph).

3. With the insertion point still in the same paragraph, open the Paragraph panel Options menu and choose Span Columns.

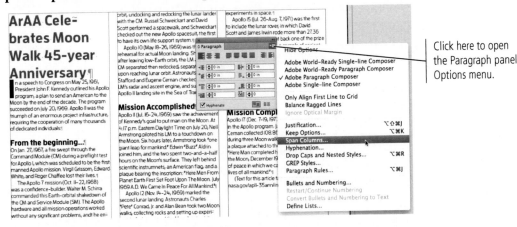

Click here to open the Paragraph panel Options menu.

4. Click the Preview option in the bottom-right corner of the dialog box, then choose Span Columns in the Paragraph Layout menu.

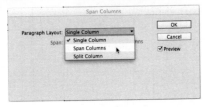

Note:

The Split Column option can be used to divide a specific paragraph into multiple columns within a frame's defined column.

When the Preview option is active, you can see the result of your choices before you finalize them.

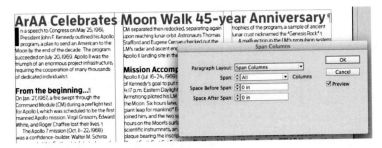

5. Make sure the Span field is set to All.

You can use the Span field to extend a paragraph over only a certain number of columns.

6. Click the Up Arrow button once for the Space After Span field.

The arrow buttons increase or decrease the related values by 0.0625".

The Space Before and Space After fields determine how much space is placed between the span paragraph and the paragraphs above or below. (This is the same concept used in the Space Above and Space Below options for regular paragraph formatting.)

7. Click OK to finalize your changes, then look at the Paragraph Styles panel.

The Main Head style, which you applied to the active paragraph, now shows a + next to the style name. This indicates that formatting other than what is defined in the style has been applied to the selected text (called a **local formatting override**). In this case, the override is intentional.

Local formatting overrides are common, especially when importing text from external sources such as Microsoft Word. This is usually caused by formatting options in the word-processing application that are not supported in InDesign. It is important to realize, however, that if a paragraph includes local formatting, simply clicking a new style name might not work perfectly. You should be aware that you often need to clear overrides in the imported text before the InDesign style is properly applied.

The plus sign indicates that some formatting other than the style definition has been applied.

Clear Overrides in Selection

The **Clear Overrides in Selection** button at the bottom of the Paragraph Styles panel can be used to remove local formatting that is not defined in the applied style. (As the name suggests, it only applies to *selected* text.) You can also clear formatting overrides in selected paragraphs by Option/Alt clicking the applied style name.

8. Save the file and continue to the next exercise.

CONTROL AUTOMATIC TEXT FRAME SIZE

Many page layouts have a primary story, as well as related-but-not-connected stories called **sidebars**. These elements are not always linked to the main story, and they are often placed in their own boxes with some unique formatting to draw attention. Amateur designers often create three separate elements to achieve this effect — an unnecessary degree of complexity when you can change multiple text frame options to create the effect with a single object.

1. On Page 1 of **newsletter_july.indd**, create a new text frame with the following dimensions (based on the top-left reference point):

X: 5″	**W: 3.625″**
Y: 7″	**H: 2″**

2. Fill the text frame with a 20% tint of Pantone 194 C.

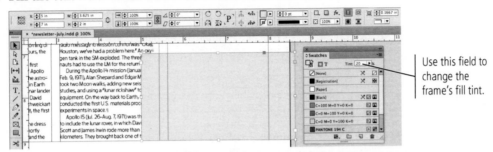

Use this field to change the frame's fill tint.

3. Choose File>Place. Select **apollo-science.doc**, uncheck the Show Import Options box, then click Open. Click OK if you get a Missing Font warning.

Make sure this option is not checked.

4. **Click the loaded cursor inside the tinted frame you just created.**

   Because you turned off the Show Import Options box in the Place dialog box, the file is imported with the last-used import options. In this case, the formatting is maintained, styles are imported, and conflicting styles are automatically renamed — resulting in the new Normal_wrd_1 style, which conflicted with the previously imported Normal style.

Underlying text runs directly beneath the sidebar box.

Placed text runs all the way to the edge of the frame.

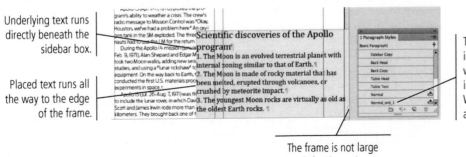

The frame is not large enough for the entire story.

The Normal style in the imported file conflicted with the Normal that was imported with the first Word document, so it was automatically renamed.

5. **Click with the Type tool to place the insertion point in the sidebar box, then press Command/Control-B to open the Text Frame Options dialog box.**

6. **Make sure the Preview option is checked, and click the Auto-Size button at the top of the dialog box to display those options.**

   Auto-size options allow a text frame to expand or shrink as necessary to fit the contained text. You are going to use these options to dynamically change the sidebar box to fit the entire story, regardless of formatting options.

Note:

If the Type tool is active, the Text Frame Options dialog box opens for the frame where the insertion point is placed.

7. **Choose Height Only in the Auto-Sizing menu and choose the bottom-center reference point.**

   The reference points in this dialog box are very similar to the ones in the Control panel; they determine which point will remain fixed when the box changes size.

   In this case, you want the bottom edge to remain in place, so you are choosing the bottom reference point. Because you are only allowing the box's height to change, the left and right reference points are not available.

   You can also use the Constraints options to define a minimum height and width — in other words, the smallest possible size the frame can be. If you allow the frame to change width, you can check the No Line Breaks option to enlarge the frame as much as necessary to fit the entire text on one line.

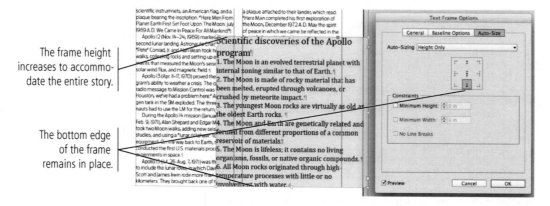

The frame height increases to accommodate the entire story.

The bottom edge of the frame remains in place.

8. **Click OK to apply your changes.**

9. **Format the first line of the sidebar with the Sidebar Head style, and format the rest of the text in this frame using the Sidebar Copy style.**

   The type sizes in the applied styles are considerably smaller, which requires less space for the sidebar. As you can see, the Auto-Size feature shrinks the height of the frame as necessary to exactly fit the contained text.

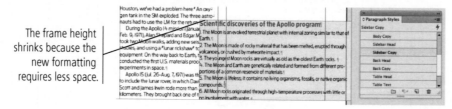

The frame height shrinks because the new formatting requires less space.

10. **Save the file and continue to the next exercise.**

EDIT TEXT INSET AND WRAP SETTINGS

A number of frame attributes can affect the appearance of text both within and around a text frame. In this exercise, you adjust the text inset and text wrap to force text into the proper position.

1. **With newsletter_july.indd open, select the sidebar box with the Selection tool and then and open the Text Frame Options dialog box (Object>Text Frame Options).**

2. **With the Preview option checked, make sure the chain icon for the Inset Spacing fields is active.**

   Like the same chain icon in other dialog boxes, this forces all four inset values to the same value.

3. **Change the Top Inset field to 0.125 in, and then press Tab to move the highlight and apply the new Inset Spacing value to all four fields.**

   Text inset spacing is the distance text is moved from the inside edge of its containing frame. You can define different values for each edge, or you can constrain all four edges to a single value.

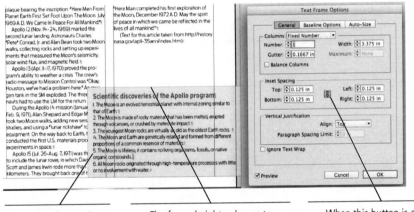

Increasing the text inset moves the text away (in) from the frame edges.

The frame height enlarges to accommodate the new frame options and still contain the entire story.

When this button is active (an unbroken chain), all four inset fields have the same value.

Note:

If you check the Ignore Text Wrap option in the Text Frame Options dialog box, the frame is not affected by wrap attributes of overlapping objects.

4. **Click the Chain icon in the Inset Spacing area to break the link, then change the Right field to 0.625 in.**

   The different right inset value accommodates for the right page margin.

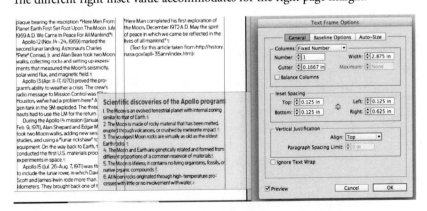

5. **Click OK to close the dialog box and apply your choices.**

6. **With the sidebar frame selected, click the second button from the left in the Text Wrap panel (Window>Text Wrap).**

   Text wrap is the distance around the edge of an object where surrounding text will flow.

7. **Make sure the chain icon is active so all four offset values are the same. Change the Top Offset field to 0.1875 in and then press Tab to apply the value to all four fields.**

   Clicking the up- or down-arrow buttons changes the offset values by 0.0625 in for each click. Because the fields are linked, you could click the up-arrow button for any field to increase all four values by 0.1875 in.

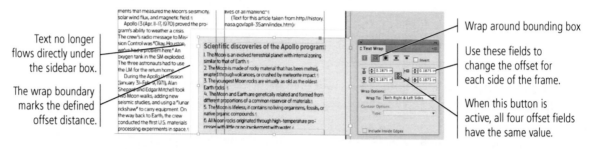

Text no longer flows directly under the sidebar box.

The wrap boundary marks the defined offset distance.

Wrap around bounding box

Use these fields to change the offset for each side of the frame.

When this button is active, all four offset fields have the same value.

8. **Save the file and continue to the next exercise.**

Text Wrap Options

InDesign provides five options for wrapping text around an object; wrap attributes are controlled in the Text Wrap panel.

- **No Text Wrap** allows text to run directly under the object.

- **Wrap Around Bounding Box** creates a straight-edged wrap around all four sides of the object's bounding box.

- **Wrap Around Object Shape** creates a wrap in the shape of the object. In this case, you can also define which contour to use:

  - **Bounding Box** creates the boundary based on the object's bounding box.

  - **Detect Edges** creates the boundary using the same detection options you use to create a clipping path.

  - **Alpha Channel** creates the boundary from an Alpha channel saved in the placed image.

  - **Photoshop Path** creates the boundary from a path saved in the placed image.

  - **Graphic Frame** creates the boundary from the containing frame.

  - **Same as Clipping** creates the boundary from a clipping path saved in the placed image.

  - **User-Modified Path** appears by default if you drag the anchor points of the text wrap boundary.

- **Jump Object** keeps text from appearing to the right or left of the frame.

- **Jump to Next Column** forces surrounding text to the top of the next column or frame.

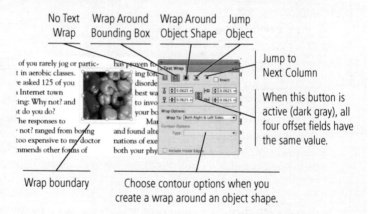

No Text Wrap   Wrap Around Bounding Box   Wrap Around Object Shape   Jump Object

Jump to Next Column

When this button is active (dark gray), all four offset fields have the same value.

Wrap boundary

Choose contour options when you create a wrap around an object shape.

Regardless of which wrap you apply, you can define the offset value (the distance that any surrounding text will remain away from the object). If you use the Object Shape wrap, you can define only a single offset value; for the other types, you can define a different offset for each edge.

If you use the Bounding Box or Object Shape wrap option, you can also define the Wrap To options — whether the wrap is applied to a specific side (right, left, right and left, or the largest side), or toward or away from the spine.

By default, text wrap attributes affect all overlapping objects, regardless of stacking order; you can turn this behavior off by checking the Text Wrap Only Affects Text Beneath option in the Composition pane of the Preferences dialog box.

Many page-layout projects include lists — resources referenced in an article, people involved in planning an event, ingredients in a recipe, steps to take in accomplishing a specific task, to name only a few. InDesign includes the ability to easily format both bulleted and numbered lists. You will use both of these options in this exercise.

1. **With `newsletter-july.indd` open, select all but the first paragraph in the sidebar on Page 1.**

2. **Open the Paragraph panel options menu and choose Bullets and Numbering.**

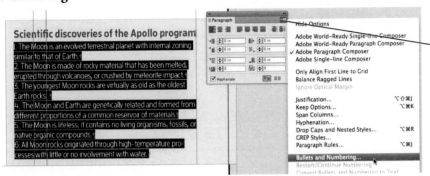

Click here to open the Paragraph panel Options menu.

3. **Make sure the Preview option is checked in the dialog box, then choose Numbers in the List Type menu.**

When you apply a numbered list, sequential numbers are automatically added to the beginning of each selected paragraph. The Numbering Style section of the dialog box defines how the numbers appear:

- **Format** determines what type of numbers are used (Arabic numbers, Roman numerals, upper- or lowercase letters, etc.).

- **Number** defines the format of the paragraph numbers; the default is "number character, period, tab character" (^# and #t are the special character codes for the list number and the tab character, respectively.)

- **Character Style** can be used to apply a character style to all characters in the paragraph number. Other characters in the numbered paragraph are not affected.

- **Mode** determines how a paragraph is numbered — whether it continues from the previous numbered paragraph or begins at a specific defined number.

- If you have more than one level of list items, you can use the **Restart Numbers...** option to reset the numbering each time you begin a new level of list items.

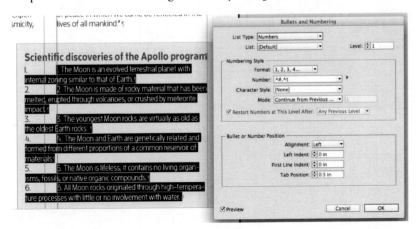

As you can see in the layout, each numbered paragraph now includes a number, a period, and a tab character (the same sequence that is defined in the Number field) before the actual paragraph copy. The added number characters are not selected because they do not technically exist as characters in the text.

Original numbers in the numbered paragraphs are still in place because they are simply characters in the imported text. If you apply actual numbered-list formatting to specific paragraphs, you might have to delete the original numbering characters from the layout.

The text of each numbered paragraph begins 0.5″ from the left frame inset edge, as defined by default in the **Tab Position** field (in the Bullet or Number Position section); the number and period characters still appear at the left edge of the frame or frame inset.

The **Alignment** menu defines how the numbers in a list align to one another (left-aligned, centered, or right-aligned). This is especially useful for aligning the periods in a regular numbered list that includes more than nine items, or in a list using certain numbering formats that have different numbers of characters in each number (such as Roman numerals):

Left	Center	Right	Left	Center	Right
8.	8.	8.	vii	vii	vii
9.	9.	9.	viii	viii	viii
10.	10.	10.	ix	ix	ix
11.	11.	11.	x	x	x

9. **In the Bullet or Number Position section, change the Left Indent to `0.125 in` and change the First Line Indent field to `-0.125 in`.**

A negative first-line indent moves the first line to the left of other lines in the same paragraph; this is sometimes called a **hanging indent**. When applied to a numbered list, the negative first-line indent defines the position of the number character(s) relative to the actual text in each list item.

If you define a negative first-line indents, the Tab Position field is cleared. The left-indent value becomes the default first tab position and the position of text immediately following the number character(s).

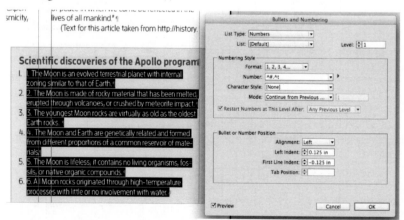

10. **Click OK to finalize the list formatting and return to the layout.**

Note:

You can convert list characters (including bullets or paragraph numbers) by choosing Type>Bullets and Numbering>Convert Bullets and Numbering to Text.

11. **Delete the extra numbers, periods, and spaces from the beginning of each list item.**

12. **Navigate to Page 2 of the layout and make sure nothing is selected.**

13. **Choose File>Place. Select `blackbird-airpark.doc`, uncheck the Show Import Options box, then click Open. Click OK if you get a Missing Font warning.**

14. **Click the loaded cursor within the margin guides on the right side of Page 2.**

15. **Format the first paragraph with the Back Head style, and format the remaining copy with the Back Copy style.**

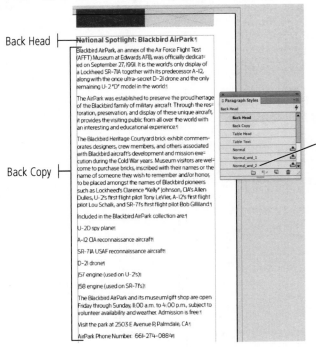

Back Head

Back Copy

The Normal style in the imported file conflicted with the Normal that was imported with the first Word document, so it was automatically renamed.

16. **Select the six paragraphs as shown in the following image. Open the Control panel Options menu and choose Bullets and Numbering.**

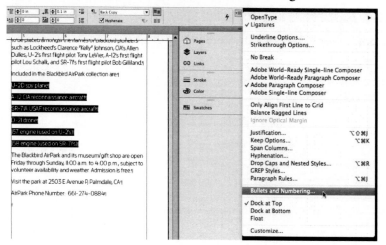

17. **Make sure the Preview option is checked in the resulting dialog box, then choose Bullets in the List Type menu.**

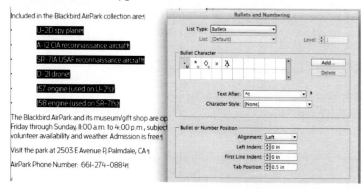

18. **In the Bullet Character section, choose the small star character.**

    Most of the options for bulleted lists are the same as for numbered lists. You can also choose the specific glyph to use as the bullet character. InDesign includes several common bullet characters by default; clicking the Add button allows you to add different bullet characters in any font that is available on your system.

19. **In the Bullet or Number Position section, change the Left Indent to 0.25 in and change the First Line Indent field to -0.125 in.**

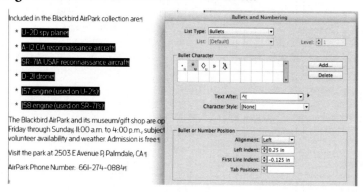

Note:

Macintosh includes two star characters — large and small — in the default character list. Some Windows versions default to include only the small star character.

20. **Click OK to close the dialog box and return to the document window.**

21. **Save the file and continue to the next stage of the project.**

Stage 3 Working with Tables

Many page layouts incorporate tables of information, from basic tables with a few rows and columns to multi-page catalog spreadsheets with thousands of product numbers and prices. InDesign includes a number of options for building tables, each having advantages and disadvantages depending on what you need to accomplish. Regardless of which method you use to create a table, the same options are available for formatting the table, the cells in the table, and the content in the cells.

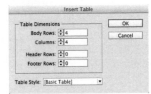

When you place an insertion point in an existing text frame, you can create a new table from scratch by choosing Table>Insert Table. This method allows you to define your own table parameters, including the number of rows and columns, the number of header and footer rows (top and bottom rows that appear in every instance of the table if the table breaks across multiple columns or frames), and even a defined style for the new table (table styles store formatting options such as gridline weight and color, cell inset, and other attributes that will you learn about in this stage of the project).

You can also create a table by selecting a series of tab-delimited text in the layout and choosing Table>Convert Text to Table. (Tab-delimited means that the content of each column is separated by a tab character.) Using this method, the new table becomes an inline object in the text frame that contained the original tabbed text.

Finally, you can create a new table in InDesign by placing a file created in Microsoft Excel, the most common application for creating spreadsheets. You'll use this method to complete this stage of the newsletter project.

PLACE A MICROSOFT EXCEL TABLE

Microsoft Excel spreadsheets can be short tables of text or complex, multi-page spreadsheets of data. In either case, Microsoft Excel users tend to spend hours formatting their spreadsheets for business applications. Those formatting options are typically not appropriate for commercial printing applications, but they give you a better starting point in your InDesign file than working from plain tabbed text.

1. **With newsletter_july.indd open, navigate to Page 2. Click the pasteboard area to make sure nothing is selected.**

2. **Choose File>Place and navigate to the file contacts.xls in the WIP>Newsletter folder.**

3. **Uncheck the Replace Selected Item option, make sure Show Import Options is checked, and click Open.**

Make sure this option is checked.

4. Review the options in the resulting dialog box. Make sure your options match what is shown in the following image, and then click OK.

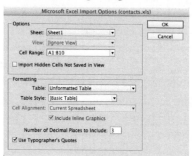

Note:

If you see a warning about missing fonts, click OK; you're going to reformat the table text shortly.

5. With the table loaded into the cursor, click in the pasteboard area to the right of Page 2.

This table will eventually occupy the empty space in the bottom-right corner of the page. Because that space is fairly small, you are going to use the pasteboard as a temporary workspace until you see what you have to work with.

When you place a table into a layout, a text frame is automatically created to contain the table. The new frame matches the width of the defined page margins, regardless of the actual table width. If the page has multiple columns defined, the table's frame matches the defined column width.

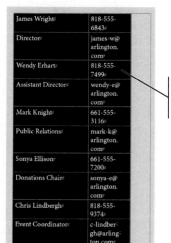

The area outside the actual page, called the pasteboard, is a good workspace for the first part of this exercise.

Imported tables are automatically placed in a text frame.

Obviously this table still needs some significant modification to make it a cohesive part of the newsletter layout. Some placed tables require more work than others, but be prepared to do at least some clean-up work whenever you place a spreadsheet or table.

Note:

If you select the text frame containing a table, you can choose Object>Fitting>Fit Frame to Content to match the text frame dimensions to the table contained in the frame.

6. Select the Type tool and click in the top-left cell of the table.

You have to use the Type tool to select table cells, either individually, or as entire rows/columns.

7. Move the cursor to the top-left corner of the table. When you see a diagonal pointing arrow, click to select the entire table.

The heavy diagonal arrow indicates that clicking will select the entire table.

The insertion point must be placed in the table to access the selection cursors.

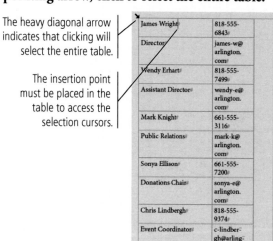

After clicking, all cells in the table are selected.

8. **Click Table Text in the Paragraph Styles panel to format all the text in the selected table cells.**

When you work with tables in InDesign, think of the table cells as a series of text frames. Text in a table cell is no different than text in any other text frame; it can be formatted using the same options you've already learned, including with paragraph and character styles.

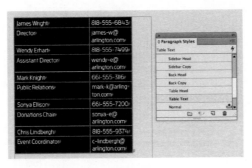

9. **Click any cell to deselect all table cells.**

10. **Save the file and continue to the next exercise.**

FORMAT CELL ATTRIBUTES

As we mentioned in the previous exercise, table cells are very similar to regular text frames. Individual cells can have different attributes such as height and width, text inset, vertical positioning, and text orientation. These options can be controlled in the Table panel, the Control panel, and the Cell Options dialog box.

1. **With newsletter_july.indd open, click in the top-left cell of the table with the Type tool.**

2. **Place the cursor over the top edge of the first column of the table. When you see a down-pointing arrow, click to select the entire column.**

You can also select rows by placing the cursor immediately to the left of a row and clicking when the cursor changes to a right-facing arrow.

The down-pointing arrow means clicking will select the entire column.

3. **Open the Table panel (Window>Type & Tables>Table).**

Use these fields to change the number of rows and columns.

Use these fields to control the height and width of cells.

Use these buttons to change the vertical alignment of text within cells.

Use these buttons to rotate text within the cells.

Use these fields to define inset values for cells.

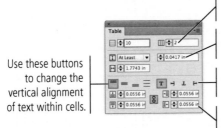

4. **With the left column selected, change the Column Width field to 1.25 in.**

You don't need to select the entire column to change its width. However, in the next step you are going to change the height of each row; you are selecting all cells in the column now, so that they will all be affected by the height change in the next step.

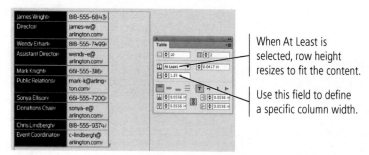

When At Least is selected, row height resizes to fit the content.

Use this field to define a specific column width.

5. **Choose Exactly in the Row Height menu, and then change the field to 0.235 in.**

Table row height uses the At Least method by default, which means they expand or shrink (down to the defined minimum) to accommodate whatever text exists in the cells.

Because you defined a row height using the Exactly method, the row height is now a specific value; the email addresses in the right column no longer fit into the existing cell width, as you can see from the overset text icons in every other cell.

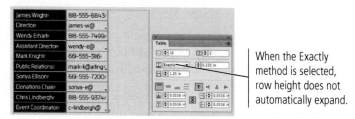

When the Exactly method is selected, row height does not automatically expand.

6. **Click to place the insertion point in any cell in the right column.**

The column does not need to be selected to change its width, either by dragging or using the field in the Table panel.

7. **Place the cursor over the right edge of the first column until the cursor becomes a two-headed arrow.**

When you see this cursor, you can drag the gridline to resize a column or row.

8. **Click and drag right until all of the overset text icons are gone.**

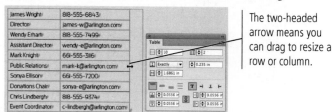

The two-headed arrow means you can drag to resize a row or column.

9. **Place the insertion point in any cell in the left column, then choose Table>Insert>Column.**

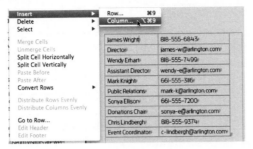

10. **In the resulting dialog box, make sure the Number field is set to 1 and choose the Left option.**

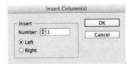

11. **Click OK to return to the table.**

One new column is added to the left of the previous selection.

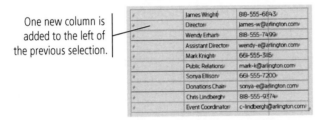

12. **Place the insertion point in the top cell of the new column and type ArAA CONTACTS.**

13. **Click Table Head in the Paragraph Styles panel to format the new text.**

The text, with the Table Head formatting applied, does not fit into the cell.

14. **Select the entire first column in the table, then click the Merge Cells button in the Control panel.**

This function extends the contents of a single cell across multiple cells. You can also choose Table>Merge Cells, or use the same command in the Table panel Options menu.

Merge Cells button

All cells in the active selection are now combined.

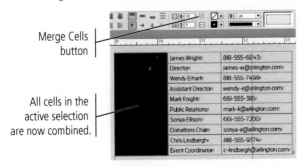

15. **In the Table panel, click the Rotate 270° button.**

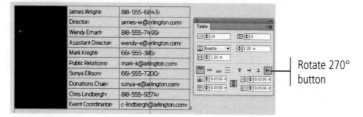

Rotate 270° button

16. **Click the top cell of the second column, hold down the mouse button, and drag down to also select the second cell in that column.**

You can use the click-and-drag method to select any range of consecutive cells, including cells in more than one row or column.

Click here...

...then drag to here.

17. **Click the Merge Cells button in the Control panel.**

When you merge cells, the content in each merged cell is combined into the merged cell. Each cell's content is separated by a paragraph return.

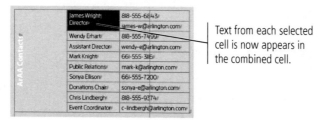

Text from each selected cell is now appears in the combined cell.

18. **Repeat Steps 16–17 for the other name/title cells in the second column.**

19. **Select all cells in the table, then click the Align Center vertical alignment button in the Table panel.**

Because the text in the left column is rotated, this option actually aligns the text between the left and right cell edges. It is important to remember that the vertical align options are based on the orientation of the text.

Align Center button

20. **Save the file and continue to the next exercise.**

As you saw when you originally placed the table into the InDesign file, tables are always contained in a text frame. If you place the table with the loaded Place cursor, a new text frame is automatically created to contain the table. The table itself is an anchored object inside the story, and is treated as a single character in the text frame's story. Rather than creating multiple frames to contain different elements in the newsletter layout, you are going to move the table into the story on Page 2 of the existing layout.

1. **With newsletter_july.indd open, make sure the Type tool is active.**

2. **Click inside the text frame that contains the table; click below the actual table.**

   This places the insertion point in the frame but not in the table.

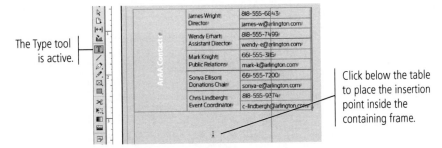

The Type tool is active.

Click below the table to place the insertion point inside the containing frame.

3. **Press Command/Control-A to select everything in the text frame.**

   The table is placed in the frame, but it exists as a single character in that frame (just like anchored graphics).

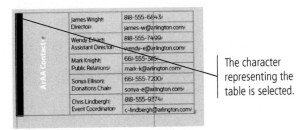

The character representing the table is selected.

4. **Press Command/Control-X to cut the selected element and store it in the clipboard.**

5. **Click with the type tool to place the insertion point in the last paragraph on Page 2 of the newsletter layout.**

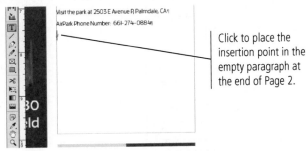

Visit the park at 2503 E Avenue P, Palmdale, CA

AirPark Phone Number: 661-274-0884

Click to place the insertion point in the empty paragraph at the end of Page 2.

6. **Press Command/Control-V to paste the table that you cut in Step 4.**
   If necessary, drag down the bottom-center handle of the containing text frame until the table is visible.

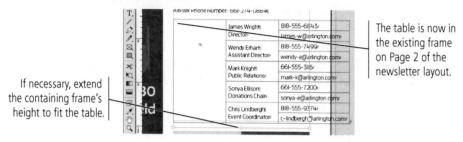

If necessary, extend the containing frame's height to fit the table.

The table is now in the existing frame on Page 2 of the newsletter layout.

7. **Using the Type tool, click to place the insertion point in any cell in the table.**

8. **Place the cursor over the right edge of the left column, then click and drag until the right edge of the table matches the margin guide.**

   It's a good idea to make a table fit into the overall layout. In this case you are adjusting the table to better match the margin guides on the page where it is placed.

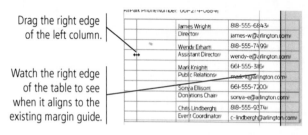

Drag the right edge of the left column.

Watch the right edge of the table to see when it aligns to the existing margin guide.

9. **Place the cursor over the bottom edge of the bottom row, then click and drag until the bottom edge of the table matches the margin guide.**

   When you reduce the height of the final row, two things happen. First, the text in the bottom-right cell no longer fits into the adjusted cell height. Second, the rows are no longer the same height, which looks like an error.

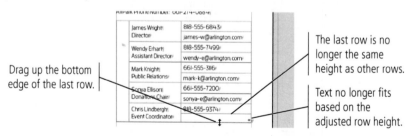

Drag up the bottom edge of the last row.

The last row is no longer the same height as other rows.

Text no longer fits based on the adjusted row height.

10. **Select the entire right column, then choose Table>Distribute Rows Evenly.**

    This command calculates the overall height of the selection, then divides that space evenly over all selected rows; the height of the overall table does not change. All rows in the selection now have the same height, and all text fits into the adjusted row height.

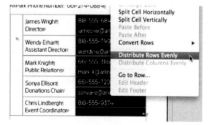

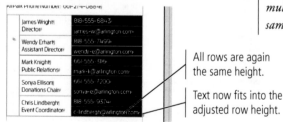

All rows are again the same height.

Text now fits into the adjusted row height.

Note:

If more than one column is selected, you can choose Table>Distribute Columns evenly to make multiple columns the same width.

11. **Using the Selection tool, click the empty frame on the pasteboard to select it, then press Delete/Backspace.**

Although not strictly necessary, it's a good idea to remove unnecessary elements from the file — including the pasteboard around the actual layout pages.

12. **Save the file and continue to the next exercise.**

DEFINE TABLE FILLS AND STROKES

Like text frames, table cells can also have fill and stroke attributes. InDesign includes a number of options for adding color to tables, from changing the stroke and fill of an individual cell to defining patterns that repeat every certain number of rows and/or columns.

1. **With newsletter_july.indd open, place the insertion point anywhere in the table on Page 2. Open the Table panel Options menu and choose Table Options>Table Setup.**

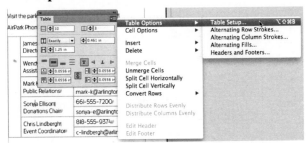

Note:

You can also choose Table>Table Options> Table Setup to access this dialog box.

2. **In the Table Setup tab, apply a 0.5-pt solid border of 100% Pantone 194 C.**

Note:

In the Table Options dialog box, you can use the Row Strokes and Column Strokes tabs to define patterns based on a sequence you choose in the Alternating Pattern menus.

3. **In the Fills tab, choose Custom Row in the Alternating Pattern menu. Set the First field to 2 rows and apply 20% Pantone 194 C. Set the Next field to 2 rows and apply None as the color.**

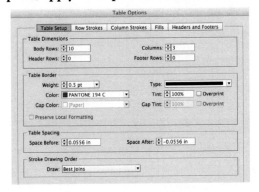
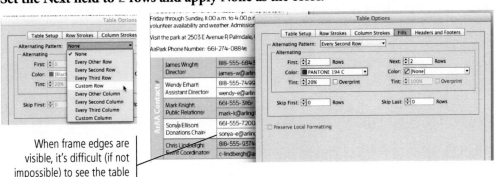

When frame edges are visible, it's difficult (if not impossible) to see the table border and cell strokes.

4. **Click OK to apply your choices.**

5. **Select the left column in the table. Using the Swatches panel, change the cell fill tint to 100% of the Pantone 194 C swatch.**

   Remember, table cells are very similar to individual text frames. You can change the color of cell fills and strokes using the Swatches panel, and you can change the cell stroke attributes using the Stroke panel.

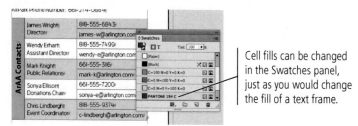

   Cell fills can be changed in the Swatches panel, just as you would change the fill of a text frame.

6. **Select all cells in the table. Open the Table panel Options menu and choose Cell Options>Strokes and Fills.**

7. **In the preview area of the dialog box, click to make sure all lines in the preview area are active.**

   The preview area shows what strokes you are affecting in the dialog box. When a line is blue it is active, which means your changes will affect those lines in the selection. If a line is black it is not active; your changes will not affect those lines.

   You can click any line in the preview to toggle it between active and inactive.

8. **Apply a 0.25-pt, 100% Pantone 194 C stroke value, using the Solid stroke type.**

   These settings change the attributes of all gridlines for all selected cells.

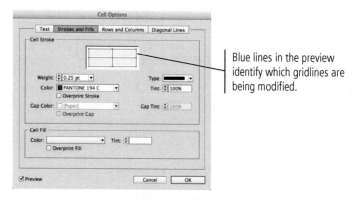

   Blue lines in the preview identify which gridlines are being modified.

9. **Click OK to apply the stroke values to your table.**

10. **Click any cell in the table to deselect the previously selected cells.**

11. At the bottom of the Tools panel, activate the Preview option.

The Preview option hides all non-printing elements, including guides, invisible characters, and frame edges. This makes it easier to get an accurate preview of your table.

ArAA Contacts		
James Wright Director	818-555-6843 james-w@arlington.com	
Wendy Erhart Assistant Director	818-555-7499 wendy-e@arlington.com	
Mark Knight Public Relations	661-555-3116 mark-k@arlington.com	
Sonya Ellison Donations Chair	661-555-7200 sonya-e@arlington.com	
Chris Lindbergh Event Coordinator	818-555-9374 c-lindbergh@arlington.com	

12. Restore the file to the Normal preview mode.

13. Save the file and continue to the next stage of the project.

More about Working with Tables

INDESIGN FOUNDATIONS

Moving Table Rows and Columns

When a table row or column is selected, moving the cursor over any cell in the selection shows a special Move cursor. You can click and drag the selection to reposition the selection somewhere else in the table.

As you drag, a heavy blue line indicates where the moved selection will be placed when you release the mouse button.

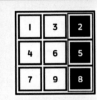

Move the cursor over any cell in a selected row or column.

Drag to the position where you want to move the selection.

Release the mouse button to move the selection.

Managing Table Setup

The Table Setup tab of the Table Options dialog box defines the table dimensions, table border, spacing above and below the table, and how strokes are applied to the table. The **Stroke Drawing Order** option allows you to control behavior where gridlines meet. If Best Joins is selected, styled strokes such as double lines result in joined strokes and gaps.

Best Joins

Row Strokes in Front

Column Strokes in Front

Controlling Cell Attributes

Basic attributes of table cells can be defined in the Text tab of the Cell Options dialog box. Most of these are exactly the same as for regular text frames; the only choice unique to tables is **Clip Contents to Cell**. If you set a fixed row height that is too small for the cell content, an overset text icon appears in the lower-right corner of the cell. (You can't flow text from one table cell to another.) If you check the Clip Contents to Cell option, any content that doesn't fit in the cell will be clipped.

As with any text frame, a table cell can have its own fill and stroke attributes. These attributes can be defined in the Strokes and Fills tab (or using the Swatches and Stroke panels). You can turn individual cell edges (strokes) on or off by clicking specific lines in the preview.

The Rows and Columns tab controls row height and column width. If **At Least** is selected in the Row Height menu, you

can define the minimum and maximum possible row height; rows change height if you add or remove text, or if you change the text formatting in a way that requires more or less space. If **Exactly** is selected, you can define the exact height of the cell.

If you're working with an extremely long table, you can break the table across multiple frames by threading (as you would for any long block of text). The **Keep Options** can be used to keep specific (selected) rows together after a break, and they determine where those rows will go, based on your choice in the Start Row menu.

You can add diagonal lines to specific cells using the Diagonal Lines tab. You can apply lines in either direction (or both) and choose a specific stroke weight, color, style, and tint. The Draw menu determines whether the line is created in front of or behind the cell's contents.

Working with Table Styles

If you've spent any amount of time refining the appearance of a table, and you think you might want to use the same format again, you can save your formatting choices as a style. InDesign supports both table styles and cell styles, which are controlled in the Table Styles panel and Cell Styles panel.

Table and cell styles use the same concept as text-formatting styles. You can apply a cell style by selecting the cells and clicking the style name in the Cell Styles panel. Clicking a style in the Table Styles panel applies the style to the entire selected table.

Table styles store all options that can be defined in the Table Setup dialog box (except the options for header and footer rows). You can also define cell styles (called **nesting styles**) for specific types of rows, as well as the left and right columns in the table.

Cell styles store all options that can be defined in the Cell Options dialog box, including the paragraph style that is applied to cells where

that style is applied.

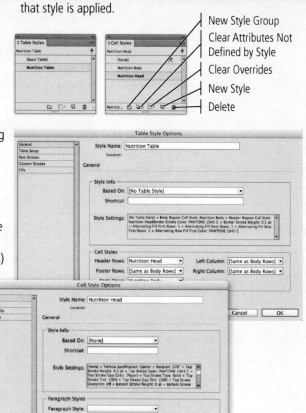

New Style Group
Clear Attributes Not Defined by Style
Clear Overrides
New Style
Delete

Creating Table Headers and Footers

Long tables of data often require more than one text frame (or column, depending on the table). In this case, you can break a table across multiple frames and use repeating headers and footers for information that needs to be part of each instance of the table (for example, column headings). Repeating headers and footers eliminate the need to manually insert the repeating information in each instance of the table.

Repeating header and footer rows are dynamically linked; this means that changing one instance of a header or footer — both content and its formatting — changes all instances of the same header or footer.

Finally, this capability also means the headers and footers remain at the top and bottom of each instance even if other body rows move to a different instance.

You can add new header and footer rows to a table when you create the table, or by changing the options in the Headers and Footers tab of the Table Options dialog box. You can also convert existing rows to headers or footers by selecting one or more rows and choosing Table>Convert Rows>To Header or To Footer. You can also control these elements in the Headers and Footers dialog box.

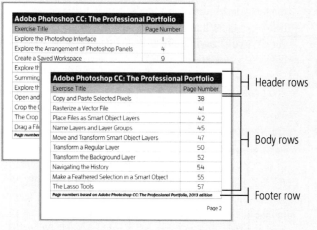

Header rows

Body rows

Footer row

Stage 4 **Preflighting and Packaging the Job**

When you submit an InDesign layout to a commercial output provider, you need to send all of the necessary pieces of the job — the layout file, any placed (linked) graphics or other files, and the fonts used in the layout. Before you copy everything to a disk and send it out, however, you should check your work to make sure the file is ready for commercial printing.

When you opened the original template at the beginning of this project, you replaced missing fonts and graphics — two of the most common problems with digital layout files. However, successful output on a commercial press has a number of other technical requirements that, if you ignore them, can cause a file to output incorrectly or not at all. InDesign includes a preflighting utility that makes it easy to check for potential errors, as well as a packaging utility that gathers all of the necessary bits for the printer.

DEFINE A PREFLIGHT PROFILE

InDesign includes a dynamic, built-in preflighting utility that can check for common errors as you build a file. If you introduce a problem while building a file, the bottom-left corner of the document window shows a red light and the number of potential errors. In the following exercise, you define a profile to check for errors based on the information you have. This is certainly not an exhaustive check for all possible output problems. You should always work closely with your output provider to build responsible files that will cause no problems in the output workflow.

1. **With `newsletter_july.indd` open, look at the bottom-left corner of the document window.**

2. **Click the arrow to the right of the No Errors message and choose Preflight Panel from the menu.**

   The message currently shows no errors, but at this point you don't know exactly what is being checked. The Preflight panel provides an interface for defining preflight profiles, as well as reviewing the specific issues identified as errors.

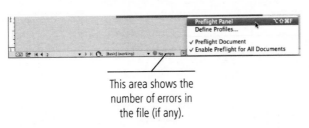

This area shows the number of errors in the file (if any).

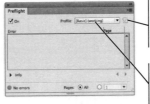

Click this button to embed the current profile into the active document.

The Preflight panel shows which profile is being used to check for errors.

3. **Open the Preflight panel Options menu and choose Define Profiles.**

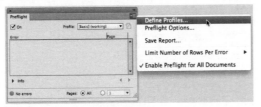

Note:

Ask your output provider if they have defined an InDesign preflight profile that you can load into your application to check for the problems that will interrupt their specific workflows.

4. **In the Preflight Profiles dialog box, click the "+" button in the left side of the dialog box to create a new profile.**

   Rather than relying on generic built-in profiles, you should be aware of and able to control exactly what is (and is not) flagged as an error.

5. **Type ArAA Check in the Profile Name field, then click the empty area below the list of profiles to finalize the new name.**

Click to load external profiles, export profiles for other users, or embed a profile into a document.

Click to delete the selected profile.

Click to create a new profile.

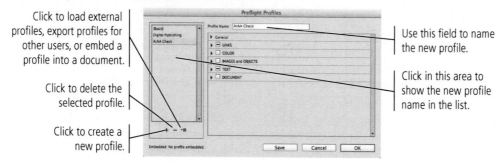

Use this field to name the new profile.

Click in this area to show the new profile name in the list.

6. **With the ArAA Check profile selected on the left side of the dialog box, expand the General category on the right. Highlight the existing text in the Description field, and then type Verify newsletter for 4c press.**

Use these arrows to expand the various categories.

7. **Collapse the General category and expand the Links category. Check the Links Missing or Modified option, and uncheck all other options**.

Image files placed in a layout need to be available when the job is output. By checking this option, you are warned if any placed image has been moved or modified since it was placed into the layout.

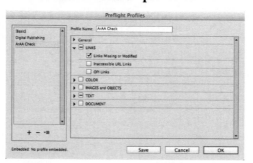

8. **Collapse the Links category and expand the Color category. Check and expand the Color Spaces and Modes Not Allowed option, and then check the RGB and Spot Color options.**

You know this newsletter is going to be output as a 4-color job. Spot colors will create an extra separation, which can be a very costly error. By setting these options, you will receive a warning if you create a spot color in a job that should be output as 4-color.

To achieve the best-quality, predictable output, it's a good idea to check for RGB images and control the conversion process in an image-editing application (i.e., Photoshop).

The Preflight Profiles dialog box includes a number of options for identifying potential errors. If you are going to build responsible files, you should have a basic understanding of what these options mean.

This is by no means an exhaustive list of all potential problems in digital page-layout files; it's a list of the problems Adobe included in the Preflight Profile dialog box. Other problems are beyond the scope of most graphic designers and are better left to prepress professionals to correct, given the specific equipment conditions in their workflows.

It should also be noted that some of these issues are not necessarily errors, but nonetheless should be reviewed before a job is output. For example, blank pages might be intentionally placed into a document to force a chapter opener onto a right-facing page; in this case, the blank page is not an error. In other cases, a blank page might be left over after text is edited; in this case, the blank page would be an error. You can use the Preflight panel to find definite errors, but also use it to verify that what you have is exactly what you want.

Links

- **Links Missing or Modified.** Use this option to receive a warning if a placed file has been moved (missing) or changed (modified) since it was placed into a layout. If a placed file is missing, the output will use only the low-resolution preview that you see on screen. If a placed file has been modified, the output will reflect the most up-to-date version of the placed file — which could be drastically different than the original, potentially destroying your overall layout.

- **Inaccessible URL Links.** Use this option to find hyperlinks that might cause problems if you are creating an interactive PDF document.

- **OPI Links.** OPI is a workflow tool that allows designers to use low-resolution FPO (for placement only) files during the design stage. When the job is processed for output, the high-resolution versions are swapped out in place of the FPO images. Although not terribly common anymore, some larger agencies still use OPI workflows.

Document

- **Page Size and Orientation.** Use this option to cause an error if the document size is not a specific size; you can also cause an error if the current document is oriented other than the defined page size (i.e., portrait instead of landscape or vice versa).

- **Number of Pages Required.** Use this option to define a specific number of pages, the smallest number of pages that can be in the document, or whether the document must have pages in multiples of a specific number (for example, multiples of 16 for 16-page signature output).

- **Blank Pages.** Use this option to find blank pages in the document.

- **Bleed and Slug Setup.** Use this option to verify the document's bleed and slug sizes against values required by a specific output process.

- **All Pages Must Use Same Size and Orientation.** Because InDesign supports multiple page sizes in the same document, you can check this option to verify that all pages in the file have the same size.

Color

- **Transparency Blending Space Required.** Use this option to define whether CMYK or RGB should be used to flatten transparent objects for output.

- **Cyan, Magenta, or Yellow Plates Not Allowed.** Use this option to verify layouts that will be output with only spot colors, or with black and spot colors.

- **Color Spaces and Modes Not Allowed.** Use this option to create errors if the layout uses RGB, CMYK, Spot Color, Gray, or LAB color models. (Different jobs have different defined color spaces. The option to flag CMYK as an error can be useful, for example, if you are building a layout that will be output in black only.)

- **Spot Color Setup.** Use this option to define the number of spot colors a job should include, as well as the specific color model that should be used (LAB or CMYK) when converting unwanted spot colors for process printing.

- **Overprinting Applied in InDesign.** Use this option to create an error if an element is set to overprint instead of trap.

- **Overprinting Applied to White or [Paper] Color.** By definition, White or [Paper] is technically the absence of other inks. Unless you are printing white toner or opaque spot ink, white cannot, by definition, overprint. Use this option to produce an error if White or [Paper] elements are set to overprint.

- **[Registration] Applied.** The [Registration] color swatch is a special swatch used for elements such as crop and registration marks. Any element that uses the [Registration] color will output on all separations in the job. Use this option to find elements that are incorrectly colored with the [Registration] color instead of (probably) black.

INDESIGN FOUNDATIONS

Images and Objects

- **Image Resolution.** Use this option to identify placed files with too little or too much resolution. As you know, commercial output devices typically require 300 ppi to output properly. The maximum resolution options can be used to find objects that, typically through scaling, result in unnecessarily high resolutions that might take considerable time for the output device to process.

- **Non-Proportional Scaling of Placed Object.** Use this option to find placed files that have been scaled with different X and Y percentages.

- **Uses Transparency.** Use this option to find any element affected by transparency. You should carefully preview transparency flattening before outputting the job.

- **Image ICC Profile.** Use this option to find placed images that have embedded ICC profiles. Typically used in color-managed workflows, placed images often store information — in the form of profiles — about the way a particular device captured or created the color in that image. You can cause errors if the image profile results in CMYK conversion, or if the embedded image profile has been overridden in the layout.

- **Layer Visibility Overrides.** Use this option to find layered Photoshop files in which the visibility of specific layers has been changed within InDesign.

- **Minimum Stroke Weight.** There is a limit to the smallest visible line that can be produced by any given output device. Use this option to find objects with a stroke weight smaller than a specific point size.

- **Interactive Elements.** Use this option to find elements with interactive properties.

- **Bleed/Trim Hazard.** Use this option to find elements that fall within a defined distance of the page edge or spine for facing-page layouts (i.e., outside the live area).

- **Hidden Page Items.** Use this option to create an error if any objects on a page are not currently visible.

Text

- **Overset Text.** Use this option to find any frames with overset text.

- **Paragraph Style and Character Style Overrides.** Use this option to find instances where an applied style has been overridden with local formatting.

- **Font Missing.** Use this option to create an error if any required font is not available on the computer.

- **Glyph Missing.** Use this option to identify glyphs that aren't available.

- **Dynamic Spelling Detects Errors.** Use this option to cause an error if InDesign's dynamic spelling utility identifies any errors in the document.

- **Font Types Not Allowed.** Use this option to prohibit specific font types that can cause problems in modern output workflows.

- **Non-Proportional Type Scaling.** Use this option to identify type that has been artificially stretched or compressed in one direction (i.e., where horizontal or vertical scaling has been applied).

- **Minimum Type Size.** Use this option to identify any type set smaller than a defined point size. You can also identify small type that requires more than one ink to reproduce (a potential registration problem on commercial output devices).

- **Cross-References.** Use this option to identify dynamic links from one location in a file to another. You can cause errors if a cross reference is out of date or unresolved.

- **Conditional Text Indicators Will Print.** Use this option to create an error if certain visual indicators will appear in the final output.

- **Unresolved Caption Variable.** Use this option to find dynamic caption variables for which there is no defined metadata.

- **Span Columns Setting Not Honored.** Use this option to find paragraphs with a defined column-span setting that is prevented by other objects on the page.

- **Tracked Change.** Use this option to find instances of text that have been changed but not accepted when Track Changes is enabled.

9. **Collapse the Color category and expand the Images and Objects category. Check and expand the Image Resolution option. Check the three Minimum Resolution options. Change the Color and Grayscale minimums to** `300` **and change the 1-bit option to** `1200`.

Remember, commercial output devices typically require at least 300 ppi to output raster images at good quality. By setting these minimum restrictions, you will receive a warning if your (or your client's) images do not have enough resolution to output at good quality using most commercial printing processes.

Note:

Remember: required resolution is actually two times the line screen (lpi) used for a specific job. If possible, always ask your service provider what resolution to use for your job. If you don't know the lpi (and can't find out in advance), 300 ppi resolution is a safe choice for most printing.

10. **Collapse the Images and Objects category and expand the Text category. Check the Overset Text and Font Missing options.**

Overset text could simply be the result of extra paragraph returns at the end of a story. However, you should always check these issues to be sure that some of the client's text has not been accidentally overset.

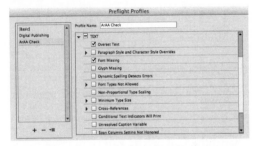

11. **Collapse the Text category and expand the Document category. Check the Number of Pages Required option. Expand that option, choose Exactly in the menu, and type** `2` **in the field.**

You know that every issue of the newsletter should be exactly 2 pages. If your file has fewer or more than 2 pages, you will receive an error message.

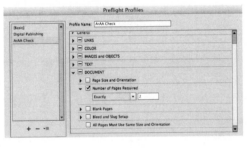

12. **Click OK to save the profile and close the dialog box.**

13. **Continue to the next exercise.**

Now that you have defined the issues that you know are errors, you can check your file for those issues and make the necessary corrections.

1. With **newsletter_july.indd** open, click the Profile menu in the Preflight panel and choose ArAA Check as the profile to use.

2. In the bottom of the panel, make sure the All radio button is checked.

   When the All option is active, the entire document is checked. You can use the other radio button to define a specific page or range of pages to preflight.

   As soon as you call the ArAA Check profile, the panel reports 13 errors.

Note:

Preflight profiles become part of the application, but are not linked to or saved in a specific document unless you intentionally embed the profile.

This pane lists the problem categories that caused the errors.

Use this menu to call a specific profile.

The now-active profile results in 13 errors.

Use this option to check only certain pages.

3. Expand the Info section of the Preflight panel.

   This area offers information about a specific error, and offers suggestions for fixing the problem.

4. Click the arrow to expand the Color list, and then click the arrow to expand the Color Space Not Allowed list.

5. Click the first text frame listing to select it, and then click the hot-text page number for that item.

   The hot-text link on the right side of the Preflight panel changes the document window to show the specific item that caused the error.

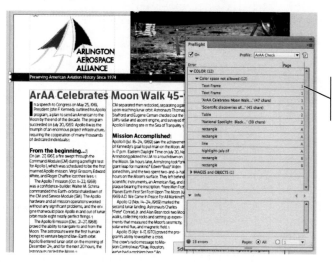

Click the hot text to navigate to a specific instance of the problem.

6. **In the Swatches panel, Control/right-click the Pantone 534 C swatch and choose Swatch Options from the contextual menu.**

Note:

Spot colors are not always errors. Check the project's specifications carefully before you convert spot colors to process. Also, be aware that spot colors are often outside the CMYK gamut; converting a spot color to process can result in drastic color shift.

7. **In the Swatch Options dialog box, choose CMYK in the Color Mode menu and then change the Color Type menu to Process.**

   Because this swatch exists only in the layout file and not any of the placed images, you can change the swatch color mode, type, and name.

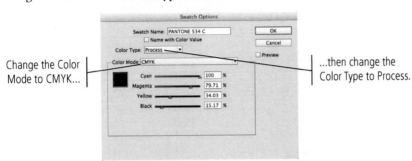

Change the Color Mode to CMYK...

...then change the Color Type to Process.

Note:

If a spot-color swatch was used in a placed file, you would only be able to change the Color Type menu in InDesign.

8. **Click OK to apply the new swatch options.**

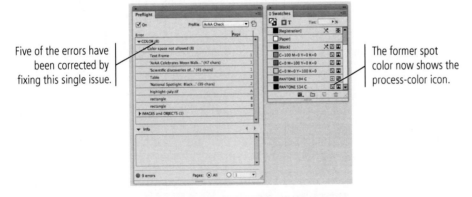

Five of the errors have been corrected by fixing this single issue.

The former spot color now shows the process-color icon.

9. **Repeat Steps 6–8 for the remaining spot color in the InDesign file.**

10. **Select the remaining color problem instance in the Preflight panel and click the hot-text link to show that element in the layout.**

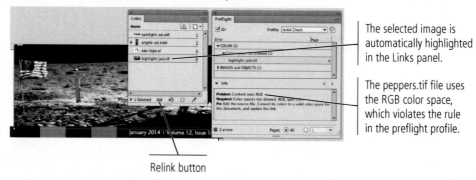

The selected image is automatically highlighted in the Links panel.

The peppers.tif file uses the RGB color space, which violates the rule in the preflight profile.

Relink button

11. **In the Links panel, click the Relink button. Navigate to `highlight-july-cmyk.tif` (in the WIP>Newsletter>CMYK folder) and click Open. If you see the Image Import Options dialog box, click OK to accept the default options.**

   After the image has been relinked, all of the color problems have been corrected. That category no longer appears in the Preflight panel.

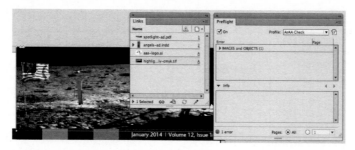

12. **Expand the Images and Objects category, then expand the Image Resolution listing. Click the page link to navigate to the problem file.**

   This image is a placed PDF file, supplied by your client. The Links panel shows that the image is 280 ppi, which is lower than the minimum 300 that you defined for this file.

   In this case, the 280 will probably be enough to satisfy the output process and still produce good quality. But in many instances, supplied-image resolution will be far below what you need for commercial printing. Low resolution is a common problem with client-supplied images. Because the placed image is a PDF file, you can't access the individual components and make changes; you would have to contact the client to resolve the problem.

The placed PDF file does not meet the minimum resolution that you defined in the profile.

13. **Save the file and continue to the next exercise.**

CREATE THE JOB PACKAGE

Now that your file is error-free, you can package it for the output provider. As we have already stated, the images and fonts used in a layout must be available on the computer used to output the job. When you send the layout file to the printer, you must also send the necessary components. InDesign includes a Package utility that makes this process very easy.

1. **With newsletter_july.indd open, choose File>Package.**

2. **Review the information in the Package dialog box and then click Package.**

If you had not preflighted the file before opening the Package dialog box, you would see warning icons identifying problems with image color space or missing fonts. Because you completed the previous exercise, however, potential errors have been fixed, so this dialog box simply shows a summary list of information about the file you are packaging. (You can use the list on the left to review the specifics of individual categories.)

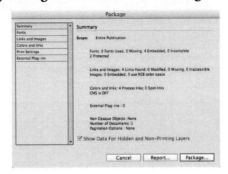

3. **If you see a message asking you to save, click Save.**

4. **In the Printing Instructions dialog box, add your contact information, and then click Continue.**

5. **In the resulting dialog box, navigate to your WIP>Newsletter folder as the target location.**

6. **Change the Folder Name field to Newsletter July Finished.**

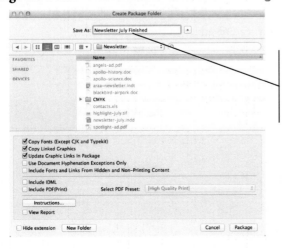

This field defines the name of the folder that will be created. All files for the job will be placed in this folder.

7. **Review the options at the bottom of the dialog box.**

These options determine what will be included in the packaged job folder.

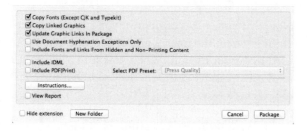

- **Copy Fonts (Except CJK and Typekit).** When checked, this option results in a secondary Document Fonts folder to contain the font files that are used in the InDesign file. If placed graphics require specific fonts, those will also be copied into the job package.

  If you hand off the job package folder to another user (or if someone sends you a job package), the fonts in the collected Document Fonts folder will be available in InDesign when you open the packaged INDD file — even if those fonts are not installed at the computer's system level. These **document-installed fonts** are installed when the related document is opened and uninstalled when you close that file. These fonts supersede any existing font of the same PostScript name within the document. Document-installed fonts are not available to other documents or in other applications.

  As the name of this item suggests, CJK (Chinese/Japanese/Korean) and Typekit fonts are not copied into the job package. If you send a file to other InDesign user, they will have to license the required CJK fonts, or sync the required Typekit fonts using their own Creative Cloud subscriptions.

- **Copy Linked Graphics.** When checked, all linked files are copied into a Links folder in the job package folder. If you have placed InDesign files in your main layout, any graphics used in those files will also be copied into the job package.

- **Update Graphic Links in Package.** When checked, links in the InDesign file are changed to refer to the new copied link files (in the job package Links folder). If this option is not checked, the links still point to the original placed file, which might cause a missing-file warning when you send the job package to another user (or open the file at a later time).

- **Use Document Hyphenation Exceptions Only.** If another user opens your InDesign file, hyphenation exceptions in that user's version of InDesign will automatically apply to the file. If you have defined custom hyphenation exceptions, you can check this option to prevent another users settings from overriding the ones you define in a specific layout.

- **Include Fonts and Links from Hidden and Non-Printing Content.** This option packages elements that is either not visible or has been set to not print (for example, content in hidden conditional text, or on a layer for which the Print option has been disabled).

- **Include IDML.** IDML, which stands InDesign Markup Language, is a special format that allows a file created in the 2014 release of InDesign to be opened in older versions of the software (back to InDesign CS4 and including the original release of InDesign CC). Keep in mind that any features added in later versions will not be available in earlier software, so the document might lose some elements of the design.

- **Include PDF(Print).** You can check this option to automatically create a PDF at the same time you create the job package. When checked, you can also choose the specific PDF Preset containing the export settings you want to use.

8. **Make sure the Copy Fonts, Copy Linked Graphics, and Update Graphic Links options are checked and then click Package.**

   When you create a job package, InDesign automatically creates a new folder for the job.

9. **Read the resulting warning and click OK.**

   As with any software, you purchase a license to use a font — you do not own the actual font. It is illegal to distribute fonts freely, as it is illegal to distribute copies of your software. Most (but not all) font licenses allow you to send your copy of a font to a service provider, as long as the service provider also owns a copy of the font. Always verify that you are not violating font copyright before submitting a job.

   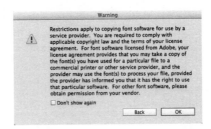

   When the process is complete, the necessary job elements appear in the job folder (in your WIP>Newsletter folder).

10. **Close the InDesign file.**

Photos of the U.S. Blue Angels are copyright Erika Kendra.

Photo of the Moon landing is a NASA photo in the public domain; scanning by NASA Johnson and post-processing by Kipp Teague.

Aircraft images were taken by government employees and as such are in the public domain. Credit for those photos is as follows
B-2: U.S. Navy photo/Jordon R. Beesley   F-117: Bobbi Zapka
F-22: U.S. Air Force photo/Staff Sgt. Samuel Rogers   SR-71: U.S. Air Force photo/Tech. Sgt. Michael Haggerty

1. An image file that has been renamed since it was placed into an InDesign layout shows the status of _____.

2. The _____ is used to monitor the status of images that are placed into a layout.

3. _____ is the distance between the edge of a frame and the text contained within that frame.

4. _____ is the distance between the edge of an object and text in other overlapping frames.

5. _____ apply only to selected text characters; this is useful for setting off a few words in a paragraph without affecting the entire paragraph.

6. _____ apply to the entire body of text between two ¶ symbols.

7. While working in a table, the _____ key has a special function; pressing it does not insert the associated character.

8. When the _____ row height method is selected, table rows change height if you add or remove text from the table cells, or if you change the text formatting in a way that requires more or less space.

9. A(n) _____ is a special kind of table row that repeats at the top of every instance of the same table.

10. _____ is the process of checking a layout for errors before it goes to print.

1. Briefly explain the significance of a Missing Font warning.

2. List three advantages of using templates.

3. Briefly define "styles" in relation to text formatting.

Portfolio Builder Project

Use what you learned in this project to complete the following freeform exercise.
Carefully read the art director and client comments, then create your own design to meet the needs of the project.
Use the space below to sketch ideas; when finished, write a brief explanation of your reasoning behind your final design.

art director comments

Your client is a local food market that sells gourmet and specialty products. To help promote the business, the owners have hired you to create a series of flyers that can be handed out at art festivals and farmers markets.

To complete this project, you should:

❑ Design an 8.5″ × 11″ template that can be reused to feature different sections of the store. The flyer can be printed on both sides of the paper, but should not include bleeds.

❑ Include some type of category identifier that will change for each flyer in the series.

❑ Use the content that has been provided in the **CenterMarket_Print14_PB.zip** archive on the Student Files Web page. You can use some or all of the images that were provided by the client.

client comments

Center Market includes an artisanal cheese market, an old-world bakery that offers hand-crafted breads and desserts, an in-house butcher shop that features a variety of wild game meats, and a large international section with hard-to-find ingredients for just about any type of cuisine.

Our target customers are the home-gourmet "foodie" types, so we want the flyers to speak to that higher-end market. We definitely prefer a classier approach than the "Sale! Sale! Sale!" flyers that you see in regular weekly grocery ads.

We already have text and images for the artisanal cheese, so start with that one. Once we've approved what you come up with, we'll gather up everything you will need for the other pieces.

Other than the text that we already provided you, be sure to include the store name, address, and phone number prominently on the flyer:

4127 West Alton Drive, Los Angeles, CA 90016
800-555-3663

project justification

This project introduced a number of concepts and tools that will be very important as you work on more complex page-layout jobs. Importing text content from other applications — specifically, Microsoft Word and Microsoft Excel — is a foundational skill that you will use in most projects; this newsletter showed you how to control that content on import, and then re-format it as appropriate in the InDesign layout.

Templates, master pages, and styles are all designed to let you do the majority of work once and then apply it as many times as necessary; virtually any InDesign project can benefit from these tools, and you will use them extensively in your career as a graphic designer. This project provided a basic introduction to these productivity tools; you will build on these foundations as you complete the remaining five projects of this book.

- Correct missing and modified graphics
- Replace or locate missing fonts
- Edit master page layouts
- Import formatted text from a Microsoft Word file
- Apply style sheets from the template
- Control text wrap to move surrounding text away from frame edges
- Control text frame inset to move contained text away from frame edges
- Place PDF and INDD files as images
- Format bulleted and numbered lists
- Check for and correct spelling errors
- Import and format a table from Microsoft Excel
- Preflight a file and make corrections based on four-color printing requirements

Combined Brochure

Your client is trying to promote tourism in a newly redeveloped downtown area. As the production artist, your job is to complete the brochure layout, verify that everything is correct, and create the final file for print output.

This project incorporates the following skills:

❑ Managing color in layout files and placed images

❑ Controlling import options for a variety of image file types

❑ Searching and replacing text and special characters

❑ Searching and changing object attributes

❑ Outputting a color-managed PDF file

client comments

We just heard from the printer that we can only use one spot color based on the quote he provided. The logo uses two different spot colors, and those are used throughout the layout as well. We decided to keep the metallic gold, but we need you to change the other one.

Now that it's official, we'd also like to use the actual name "The BLVD" rather than just saying "Downtown Lancaster" in most places.

We have a lot of great pictures from Charlie Essers, a local photographer. We'd like to use as many of those as possible in the layout.

art director comments

The text has already been placed into the template for this brochure, but the original designer had to move on to a different project. As the production artist, your job is to assemble the rest of the pieces and check the text and images for errors or technical problems.

When everything is in place and verified, you will export a color-managed PDF file using high-quality settings for the commercial printer.

project objectives

To complete this project, you will:

❑ Define application color settings

❑ Assign color settings to an existing file

❑ Replace a native Illustrator file

❑ Place a TIFF file with Alpha transparency

❑ Place multiple JPEG images

❑ Place a native InDesign file

❑ Place a native Photoshop file

❑ Preview color separations in a file

❑ Convert spot color in Illustrator

❑ Track changes during the development process

❑ Find and change specific text, with and without formatting attributes

❑ Find and change object formatting attributes

❑ Check document spelling

❑ Export a color-managed PDF file

Stage 1 **Controlling Color for Print**

In Project 6: Menu Image Correction, you worked with color management in Photoshop to correct an image based on a color profile for sheetfed printing. InDesign's color management options allow you to integrate InDesign into a color-managed workflow. This includes managing the color profiles of placed images, as well as previewing potential color problems on screen before the job is output.

DEFINE APPLICATION COLOR SETTINGS

There are two primary purposes for managing color in InDesign: previewing colors based on the intended output device and converting colors to the appropriate space when a file is output (whether to PDF or directly to an output device).

As with Photoshop, the first required step in a color managed workflow is to define the color settings that apply to the file you are building.

1. **With no file open in InDesign, choose Edit>Color Settings.**

   InDesign's color management tools are virtually identical to those in Photoshop. The applications share profiles, which means you can install a profile once and use it throughout the creative process.

   In the Color Settings dialog box the RGB working space defines the default profile for RGB colors and images that do not have embedded profiles. The CMYK working space defines the profile for the device or process that will be used to output the job.

2. **Choose North America Prepress 2 in the Settings menu.**

   Like Photoshop, InDesign includes a number of common option groups, which you can access in the Settings menu. You can also make your own choices and save those settings as a new preset by clicking Save, or you can import settings files created by another user by clicking Load.

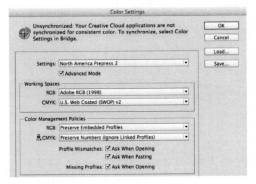

3. **In the Working Spaces RGB menu, choose the profile for your monitor. If you don't see a profile for your specific montior, use Adobe RGB (1998).**

   Remember: a working space is a specific profile that defines color values in the associated mode. Using Adobe RGB (1998), for example, means RGB colors in the InDesign file and imported RGB images without embedded profiles will be described by the values in the Adobe RGB (1998) space.

4. **In the Working Spaces CMYK menu, choose U.S. Sheetfed Coated v2.**

   There are many CMYK profiles; each output device has a gamut unique to that individual device. U.S. Sheetfed Coated v2 is an industry-standard profile for a common type of printing (sheetfed printing on coated paper). In a truly color-managed workflow, you would actually use a profile for the specific press/paper combination being used for the job. (We're using one of the default profiles to show you how the process works.)

5. **In the Color Management Policies, make sure Preserve Embedded Profiles is selected for RGB, and Preserve Numbers (Ignore Linked Profiles) is selected for CMYK.**

   These options tell InDesign what to do when you open existing files or if you copy elements from one file to another.

   - When an option is turned off, color is not managed for objects or files in that color mode.

   - **Preserve Embedded Profiles** maintains the profile information saved in the file; files with no profile use the current working space.

   - If you choose **Convert to Working Space**, files automatically convert to the working space defined at the top of the Color Settings dialog box.

   - For CMYK colors, you can choose **Preserve Numbers (Ignore Linked Profiles)** to maintain raw CMYK numbers (ink percentages) rather than adjusting the colors based on an embedded profile.

6. **Check all three options under the Color Management Policies menus.**

   The check boxes control InDesign's behavior when you open an existing file or paste an element from a document with a profile other than the defined working space (called a profile mismatch), or when you open a file that does not have an embedded profile (called a missing profile).

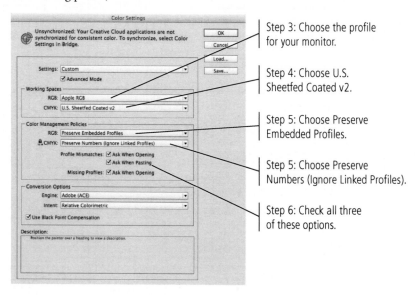

Step 3: Choose the profile for your monitor.

Step 4: Choose U.S. Sheetfed Coated v2.

Step 5: Choose Preserve Embedded Profiles.

Step 5: Choose Preserve Numbers (Ignore Linked Profiles).

Step 6: Check all three of these options.

7. **Click OK to apply your settings, then continue to the next exercise.**

 ASSIGN COLOR SETTINGS TO AN EXISTING FILE

This project requires working on a file that has already been started, so some work has been completed before the file was handed off to you. To manage the process throughout the rest of this project, you need to make sure the existing file has the same color settings that you just defined.

1. **Download Downtown_Print14_RF.zip from the Student Files Web page.**

2. **Expand the ZIP archive in your WIP folder (Macintosh) or copy the archive contents into your WIP folder (Windows).**

   This results in a folder named **Downtown**, which contains the files you need for this project. You should also use this folder to save the files you create in this project.

3. Open the file **boulevard.indd** from the WIP>Downtown folder.

4. **Read the resulting warning message and click Don't Update Links.**

   As you know, InDesign remembers the location of files from when they were placed in the layout file. Those files need to be in the same location as when they were placed for the job to output properly. If a file is not in the same location, or the name has been changed, InDesign warns you when you open the file.

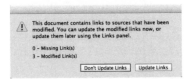

5. **In the Profile or Policy Mismatch dialog box, select the second option (Adjust the document to match current color settings).**

   The existing file has neither a defined RGB nor a CMYK profile. Because you activated the Ask When Opening option in the Color Settings dialog box, InDesign asks how you want to handle RGB color in the file.

   This option assigns the existing RGB color settings (which you defined in the previous exercise) to the existing file.

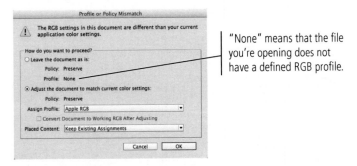

"None" means that the file you're opening does not have a defined RGB profile.

6. **Leave the remaining options at their default values and click OK.**

   Again, your choice in the Color Settings dialog box was to Ask When Opening if a file was missing a CMYK profile. Because the file does not have a defined CMYK profile, you see that warning now.

7. **In the second warning message, choose the second radio button (Adjust the document to match current color settings).**

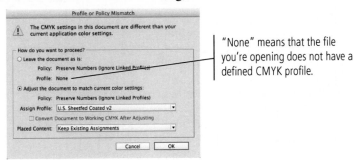

"None" means that the file you're opening does not have a defined CMYK profile.

8. **Click OK to open the file.**

This file contains the layout for a four-page brochure. Some of the content has already been placed; your job is to place the supplied images, complete the layout, and prepare the final PDF file for printing.

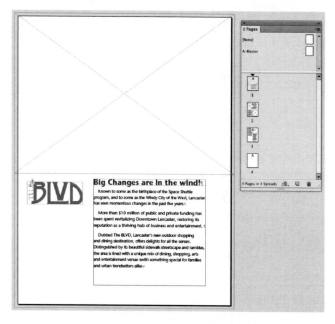

9. **Save the file and continue to the next stage of the project.**

Assigning and Converting Color Profiles

If you need to change the working RGB or CMYK space in a document, you can use either the Assign Profiles (Edit>Assign Profiles) or Convert to Profile (Edit>Convert to Profile) dialog box. Although these two dialog boxes have slightly different appearances, most of the functionality is exactly the same.

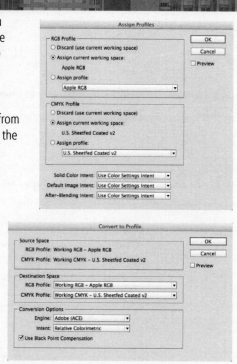

In the Assign Profiles dialog box:

- **Discard (Use Current Working Space)** removes the current profile from the document. This option is useful if you do not want to color manage the document. Colors will be defined by the current working space, but the profile is not embedded in the document.

- **Assign Current Working Space** embeds the working space profile in the document.

- **Assign Profile** allows you to define a specific profile other than the working space profile. However, colors are not converted to the new space, which can dramatically change the appearance of the colors as displayed on your monitor.

You can also define different rendering intents for solid colors, placed raster images, and transparent elements that result from blending modes, effects, or transparency settings. All three Intent menus default to use the intent defined in the Color Settings dialog box, but you can change any or all menus to a specific intent.

In the Convert to Profile dialog box, the menus can be used to change the RGB and CMYK destination spaces. This is basically the same as using the Assign Profile options in the Assign Profiles dialog box. You can also change the color management engine, rendering intent, and black point compensation options.

Stage 2 Working with Linked Files

Adobe InDesign supports a variety of graphics formats. Your ultimate output goal will determine the specific type of graphics used in a particular job. For print applications such as the brochure you're building in this project, you should use high-resolution raster image files or vector-based graphics files.

Depending on what type of file you are importing, you have a number of options when you place a file. This stage of the project explores the most common file formats for print design workflows.

REPLACE A NATIVE ILLUSTRATOR FILE

InDesign supports native Adobe Illustrator files (with the ".ai" extension) that have been saved to be compatible with the PDF format. Illustrator files can include both raster and vector information (including type and embedded fonts), as well as objects on multiple layers in a variety of color modes (including spot colors, which are added to the InDesign Swatches panel when the Illustrator file is imported).

1. **With boulevard.indd open, open the Links panel.**

   The file blvd logo.ai has been placed three times, but the file has been modified since it was placed. Remember from Project 9: Aerospace Newsletter, that placed files need to be present and up to date for the file to output properly.

2. **On Page 1 of the layout, use the Direct Selection tool or the Content Grabber to select the placed graphic with the Modified warning icon.**

   When you select a specific instance of a file that has been placed multiple times, the item expands in the Links panel and the selected instance is highlighted.

Note:

Make sure you select the content inside the frame and not the actual frame.

3. **Open the Transform panel (Window>Object & Layout>Transform).**

   The options in the Transform panel are the same as those on the left side of the Control panel. As you can see, the selected graphic is scaled to approximately 62% proportionally.

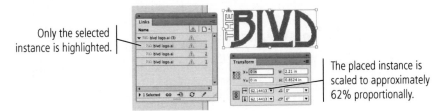

Only the selected instance is highlighted.

The placed instance is scaled to approximately 62% proportionally.

4. **In the Links panel, click the main listing for the blvd logo.ai file and then click the Update Link button.**

   By selecting the main item listing instead of a specific instance, you update all instances of that file at one time. If you want to update individual instances, you can use the Modified warning icons on the page or select only the specific instance in the panel and click the Update Link button.

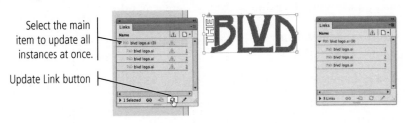

Select the main item to update all instances at once.

Update Link button

5. **On Page 1 of the layout, use the Direct Selection tool or the Content Grabber to select the placed logo graphic.**

The new file is automatically scaled to fit the same dimensions as the original. As you can see, the updated file is now scaled to approximately 82% proportionally.

In this case, the original source file had been proportionally scaled in Illustrator and resaved; the updated link still fits inside the existing frame dimensions. You should be aware, however, that updated links are not always so straightforward. In many cases, updated links include changes that make it necessary to resize the containing frame to show the entire graphic.

Only the selected instance is highlighted.

The updated instance is now scaled to approximately 82%.

6. **Using the hot-text links in the Links panel, navigate to the other two instances of the updated graphic and review the results.**

In this file, each logo instance was cloned from the original placement, so the update caused no problems in any instance. However, it's always a good idea to verify the results when you make this kind of change.

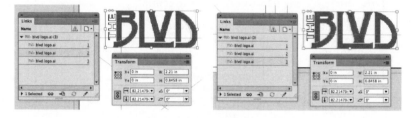

7. **Save the file and continue to the next exercise.**

 ## PLACE A TIFF FILE WITH ALPHA TRANSPARENCY

The TIFF format is used only for raster images such as those from a scanner or digital camera. These files can be one-color (bitmap or monochrome), grayscale, or continuous-tone images.

TIFF files can include layers, although InDesign cannot access the individual layers in the file. If you want to manage image layers inside Photoshop, you should use the native Photoshop format. (You will do so in a later exercise.)

The TIFF format also supports stored clipping paths and Alpha channels. InDesign does provide access to those elements, which can be useful for maintaining transparent image areas when the file is placed into a layout.

1. **With boulevard.indd open, make Page 1 visible in the document window.**

2. **Choose File>Place. Navigate to the file bloom.tif in your WIP>Downtown>Links folder.**

All images for this project are located in the WIP>Downtown>Links folder. We will not repeat the entire path in every exercise.

3. Check the Show Import Options box and uncheck Replace Selected Item, then click Open.

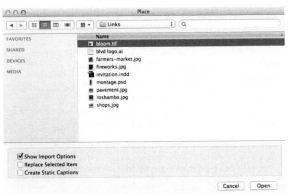

4. In the Image tab of the Image Import Options dialog box, choose outline in the Alpha Channel menu.

Remember from Project 4: Composite Movie Ad, an Alpha channel stores degrees of transparency. These are commonly used to create gradual transitions at the edges of an image — as in this project.

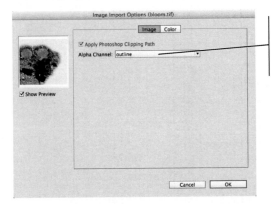

Use this menu to apply a stored Alpha channel in the placed image.

5. Click the Color button at the top of the dialog box.

The Profile menu defaults to the profile embedded in the file. If the file was saved without an embedded profile, the menu defaults to Use Document Default. You can use the Profile menu to change the embedded profile (not recommended) or assign a specific profile if one was not embedded.

When you export the finished layout to PDF, you will use the PDF engine to convert the RGB images to CMYK. This profile tells InDesign how the RGB color is described in the file so it can be properly translated to the destination (CMYK) profile.

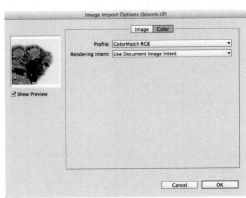

6. **Click OK to load the selected image into the cursor.**

   Because you unchecked the Replace Selected Item option, the image is loaded into the cursor. It doesn't matter if anything was selected in the layout before you opened the Place dialog box.

7. **Click the empty space in the bottom-left corner of the page to place the loaded image.**

8. **Using the Selection tool, move the placed image frame until its bottom-left corner snaps to the bottom-left bleed guides.**

   As you can see (even in the low-resolution screen preview), the edges of the placed image gradually become more transparent until the underlying text is completely visible.

   Because the image is currently obscuring some of the text, you still need to adjust the text wrap settings of the placed image.

9. **With the placed image selected, open the Text Wrap panel (Window>Text Wrap).**

10. **At the top of the panel, click the Wrap Around Object Shape button. In the Contour Options menu, choose Alpha Channel in the Type menu.**

    Rather than wrapping text around the frame, you are using the applied Alpha channel to define a text wrap that allows text to more closely follow the contours in the image.

    When you use an Alpha channel as the basis for a text wrap, the initial result is not always exactly what you expect. In this case, you can see the semi-transparent image pixels are still obscuring some of the text.

    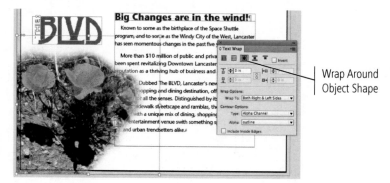

    Wrap Around
    Object Shape

11. Change the Top Offset field to 0.375″, then press Return/Enter to apply the change.

When you use the Wrap Around Object Shape option, you can only define a single offset value that applies to the entire object.

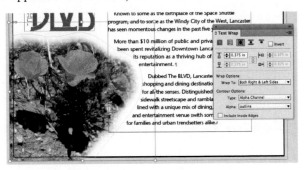

12. Save the file and continue to the next exercise.

 ## PLACE MULTIPLE JPEG IMAGES

The JPEG format is commonly used for raster images, especially images that come from consumer-level digital cameras. Originally used for Web applications only, the JPEG format is now supported by most commercial print-design applications (including InDesign).

The JPEG format can be problematic, especially in print jobs, because it applies a lossy compression scheme to reduce the image file size. If a high-resolution JPEG file was saved with a high level of compression, you might notice blockiness or other artifacts (flaws) in the printed image. If you must use JPEG files in your work, save them with the lowest compression possible.

1. With boulevard.indd open, choose View>Fit Page in Window.

2. Open the Links and Pages panels (if they are not already visible).

3. Choose File>Place. In the Place dialog box, Command/Control click to select the following files:

> **farmers-market.jpg**
>
> **fireworks.jpg**
>
> **pavement.jpg**
>
> **roshambo.jpg**
>
> **shops.jpg**

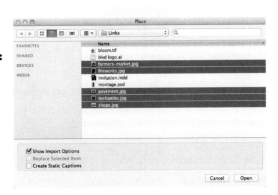

4. Click Open.

In the resulting Image Import Options dialog box, review the Image options.

JPEG files do not support clipping paths or Alpha channels, so the options in this tab are not available for the selected file.

Note:

Remember, pressing Command/Control allows you to select multiple, non-contiguous files in a dialog box.

5. **Click the Color button at the top of the dialog box to show those options.**

JPEG files do support color profiles; when you open a JPEG file, the options in this tab are the same as for TIFF files.

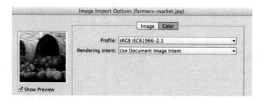

6. **Click OK in each of the remaining dialog boxes to load all five selected images into the cursor.**

When you select multiple files in the Place dialog box and Review Import Options is checked, you will see the Image Import Options dialog box for each selected image.

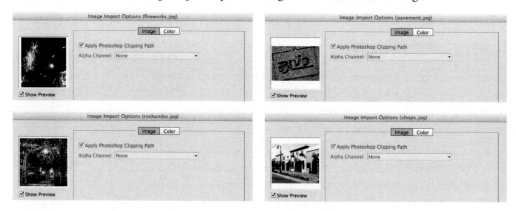

When you load multiple files into the cursor, the cursor icon shows the thumbnail of the active file, and the number of files that are loaded.

In the Links panel, the LP hot text link identifies the file that is active in the cursor.

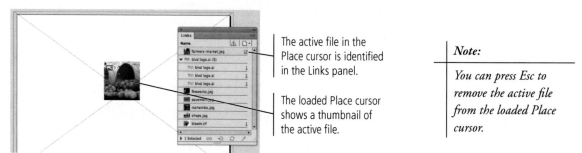

The active file in the Place cursor is identified in the Links panel.

The loaded Place cursor shows a thumbnail of the active file.

Note:

You can press Esc to remove the active file from the loaded Place cursor.

7. **Press the Right Arrow key two times to make the pavement.jpg file active in the Place cursor.**

You can use the arrow keys to change the active file in the loaded cursor.

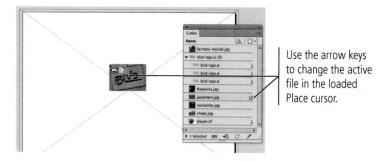

Use the arrow keys to change the active file in the loaded Place cursor.

8. **Click inside the empty frame at the top of Page 1 to place the active image.**

   After you place the image, the next file is automatically loaded into the cursor.

After placing the image, the next file is automatically loaded into the Place cursor.

9. **Double-click the Page 2 thumbnail in the Pages panel to make that page active in the document window.**

   You can still interact with the application interface (panels, menus, etc.) when files are loaded into the Place cursor.

10. **Use the arrow keys to make shops.jpg the active file in the Place cursor.**

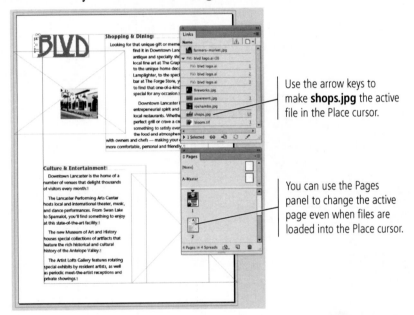

Use the arrow keys to make **shops.jpg** the active file in the Place cursor.

You can use the Pages panel to change the active page even when files are loaded into the Place cursor.

11. **Click inside the empty frame at the top of Page 2 to place the loaded image.**

12. Make `roshambo.jpg` the active file in the Place cursor, then click in the empty frame at the bottom of the page to place the loaded image.

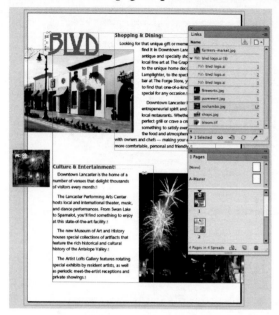

13. Using the same process as in Steps 9–12, place `farmers-market.jpg` in the top frame on Page 3, and place `fireworks.jpg` in the bottom frame on Page 3.

14. Save the file and continue to the next exercise.

PLACE A NATIVE INDESIGN FILE

In addition to the different types of image files, you can also place one InDesign layout directly into another InDesign file. As with PDF files, you can determine which page is placed (if the file contains more than one page), which layers are visible (if the file has more than one layer), and the specific file dimensions (bounding box) to use when the file is placed. Placed InDesign pages are managed as individual objects in the file where they are placed.

1. **With boulevard.indd open, make Page 4 active in the document window.**

2. **Choose File>Place, and select the file invitation.indd.**

3. **Make sure Show Import Options is checked, then click Open.**

4. **In the General tab of the Place InDesign Document dialog box, choose Bleed Bounding Box in the Crop To menu.**

   By default, the first page in the selected file appears as the previewed page that will be loaded into the Place cursor. If you choose to import multiple pages at one time, each page is loaded as a separate file.

   When you place a native InDesign file into another InDesign file, you can use the Crop To menu to place pages based on the defined page, bleed, or slug, as described in the Document Setup dialog box.

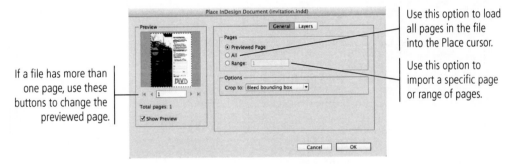

If a file has more than one page, use these buttons to change the previewed page.

Use this option to load all pages in the file into the Place cursor.

Use this option to import a specific page or range of pages.

5. **Click the Layers button at the top of the dialog box.**

   InDesign files can include multiple layers. You can determine which layers to display in the placed file by toggling the eye icons on or off in the Show Layers list.

   In the Update Link Options menu, you can determine what happens when/if you update the link to the placed file.

   - **Keep Layer Visibility Overrides** maintains your choices regarding which layers are visible in the InDesign layout where the file is placed.

   - **Use PDF's Layer Visibility** restores the layer status as saved in the placed file.

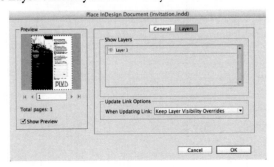

6. **Click OK. Read the resulting warning message and click OK.**

   To output properly, image links need to be present and up to date. Images placed in nested InDesign layouts are still links, so the link requirements apply in those files.

   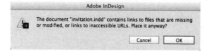

7. **Click to place the loaded file on Page 4 of the active file.**

8. **Using the Selection tool, drag the placed file until the top-left corner snaps to the top and left bleed guides.**

   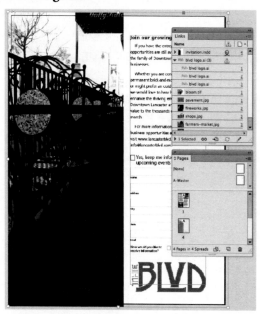

9. **Save the boulevard.indd file.**

10. **In the Links panel, expand the invitation.indd item.**

    Expand the placed InDesign file to review the individual links inside that file.

    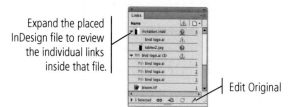

    Edit Original

11. **Select invitation.indd in the Links panel, then click the Edit Original button.**

    The Edit Original function opens the file selected in the Links panel. Because invitation.indd is a placed InDesign file, that document opens in a new document window in front of boulevard.indd.

    When you open any InDesign file, of course, you are first warned if any necessary source file is missing or modified (which you already knew from the Links panel of the boulevard.indd file).

    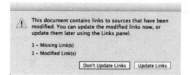

12. **Click Update Links.**

As you saw earlier in this project, the blvd logo file had been modified after it was placed into these layouts. By clicking the Update Links button in this warning message, you update all modified links in the file without reviewing them in the layout.

13. **In the resulting Profile or Policy Mismatch dialog box, choose the Adjust option and click OK.**

This file (invitation.indd) was created without RGB or CMYK profiles. You need to tell InDesign how to manage color in this file, just as you did when you opened the boulevard.indd file.

14. **In the second Profile or Policy Mismatch dialog box, choose the Adjust option and click OK.**

As you have already seen, the software evaluates RGB and CMYK profiles individually, so you have to define the color behavior separately for each mode.

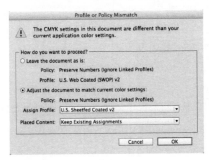

15. **Continue to the next exercise.**

PLACE A NATIVE PHOTOSHOP FILE

You can easily place native Photoshop files (with the extension ".psd") into an InDesign layout. You can control the visibility of Photoshop layers and layer comps, as well as access embedded paths and Alpha channels in the placed file. If a Photoshop file includes spot-color channels, the spot colors are added to the InDesign Swatches panel.

1. **With both InDesign files open and invitation.indd active, click the missing image (tables2.jpg) in the Links panel and click the Relink button.**

   When an image is missing, you can use this option to identify the new location of the selected file. You can also use it to choose a different file, which will replace the existing file with a new one.

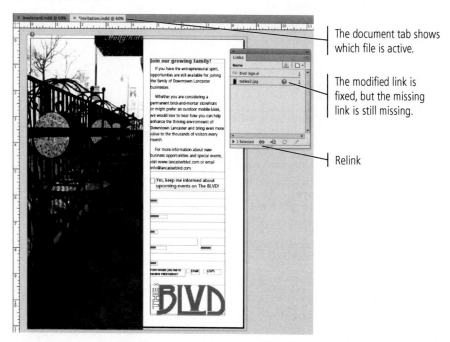

The document tab shows which file is active.

The modified link is fixed, but the missing link is still missing.

Relink

2. **Navigate to montage.psd in the WIP>Downtown>Links folder. Make sure Show Import Options is checked, then click Open.**

   There is no option to Replace the selected item in this dialog box because you used the Relink button — the file you select automatically replaces the selected file.

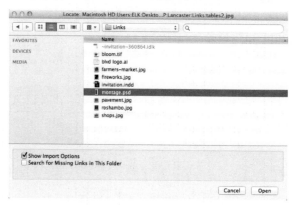

3. **In the resulting Image Import Options dialog box, review the options in the Layers tab.**

Photoshop files can include multiple layers and layer comps (saved versions of specific layer position and visibility). You can turn off specific layers by clicking the eye (visibility) icon for that layer. If the file includes layer comps, you can use the Layer Comp menu to determine which comp to place.

The Update Link Options you see here are the same as those that are available when you place a native InDesign file.

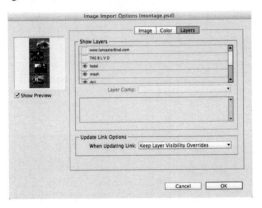

Note:

The options in the Image and Color tabs are the same as those for TIFF files.

Note:

Unless you know what the different layers contain, it is difficult to decide what you want to place based solely on the very small preview image.

4. **Click OK to replace the missing image with the new one.**

5. **Using the Direct Selection tool or Content Grabber, select the image inside the frame on the left side of the page. Review the image scaling in the Control or Transform panel.**

When you replace one link with another, the new file is automatically scaled proportionally to fit the same space as the original image. In this case, the original image was a bit larger than the defined frame size. The montage, however, was created to match the exact space it was supposed to fill. As you can see when the image (not the frame) is selected, the new image is scaled to approximately 113% to fill the same space as the original image.

Note:

After a Photoshop file has been placed, you can change the layer visibility by choosing Object>Object Layer Options.

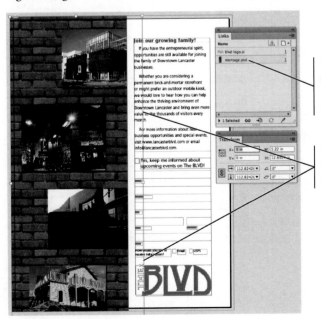

The replaced image is scaled to approximately 113% to fit the same space as the previous image.

The red bounding box shows the edges of the placed image.

Note:

You might want to zoom out to see the entire image bounding box.

6. **In the Control or Transform panel, select the top-left reference point and change the Scale X and Scale Y percentages to 100%.**

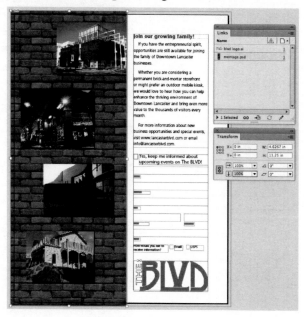

7. **Control/right-click the placed image and choose Edit With>Photoshop CC (Default).**

   As you saw in the previous exercise, the Edit Original button opens a file in its native application. You can also use the Edit With option to open the file in any application that can interpret the file's data. The default option — which would apply if you use the Edit Original option — is identified in the menu.

Note:

If Photoshop is not already running, it might take a while for the file to open. Be patient.

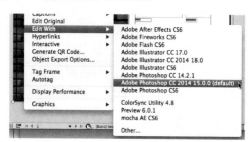

8. **If you see an Embedded Profile Mismatch warning, choose the option to use the embedded profile, then click OK.**

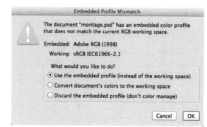

9. When montage.psd opens in Photoshop, review the Layers panel (Window>Layers).

As you saw when you placed the file into InDesign, this image has two hidden layers. You are going to review those layers in Photoshop to make sure you want them to be visible in the final layout.

10. In the Layers panel, click the empty space to the left of the top two layers to make them visible.

These two layers are type layers, identified with a "T" in place of the thumbnail. After making them visible, you can see one is used to add visual interest, while the other presents important information (the client's Web address).

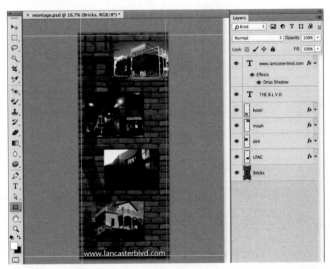

In InDesign, you know that the layout requires 0.125″ bleeds. The image frame correctly extends into the bleed area, and the image was created to match the frame size.

As you can see, the artist who created the file placed guides 0.125″ from each image edge. The Web address at the bottom sits directly on the bottom guide and is centered horizontally on the canvas. However, based on its position in the InDesign layout, the top, bottom, and left edges of the image will be trimmed from the page. This means the position of the Web address is incorrect in the context of the layout where it is placed. You need to move it up and right to appear in the correct location within the *trim area* instead of the overall image area. (This is a common problem in placed image files.)

Note:

Type formatting options in Photoshop are essentially the same as those available in Illustrator. The primary difference, however, is that each type "object" (to relate it to Illustrator's type treatment) in Photoshop is managed on separate, special type layers. In other words, when you click with the Type tool in a Photoshop file, a new type layer is automatically created to contain the type that you enter.

Note:

Photoshop type layers are automatically named based on their content.

11. **Select the web address layer in the Layers panel and make the Move tool active. Turn off the Auto-Select option in the Options bar.**

It can be difficult to actually click the pixels in this thin type, so it is easier to move the layer by manually selecting it and turning off the Auto-Select option.

12. **Click in the canvas area and drag to move the Web address layer content so it snaps to the right guide and there is approximately 1/8″ space between the bottom edge of the type and the bottom guide.**

Note:

You might want to zoom in to make this easier.

Auto-Select is turned off.

The Move tool is active.

The Web address type layer is selected.

Drag to move the layer content up and right.

13. **Save the file, close it, and then return to invitation.indd in InDesign.**

14. **Save the invitation.indd file and close it.**

When you save and close the invitation.indd file, the Links panel for boulevard.indd automatically reflects the new placed file.

15. **Save boulevard.indd and continue to the next exercise.**

To be entirely confident in color output, you should check the separations that will be created when your file is output. InDesign's Separations Preview panel makes this easy to accomplish from directly within the application workspace.

1. **With boulevard.indd open, choose Window>Output>Separations Preview.**

2. **In the View menu of the Separations Preview panel, choose Separations.**

When Separations is selected in the View menu, all separations in the current file are listed in the panel. You can turn individual separations on and off to preview the different ink separations that will be created:

- To view a single separation and hide all others, click the name of the separation you want to view. By default, areas of coverage appear in black; you can preview separations in color by toggling off the Show Single Plates in Black command in the panel Options menu.

- To view more than one separation at the same time, click the empty space to the left of the separation name. When viewing multiple separations, each separation is shown in color.

- To hide a separation, click the eye icon to the left of the separation name.

- To view all process plates at once, click the CMYK option at the top of the panel.

3. **Click Pantone 875 C in the Separations Preview panel to see where that color is used.**

As your client stated, the brochure should use a single spot color — the metallic gold in the main logo.

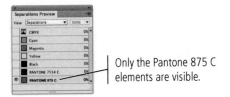

Only the Pantone 875 C elements are visible.

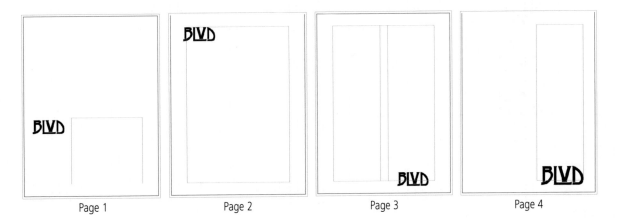

Page 1 Page 2 Page 3 Page 4

4. **Click Pantone 7554 C in the Separations Preview panel to review where that color is used in the layout.**

By reviewing the separation, you can see that the dark brown from the logo is used for all the headings in the text and for the frames on Page 4.

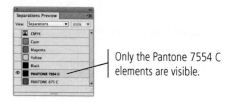

Only the Pantone 7554 C elements are visible.

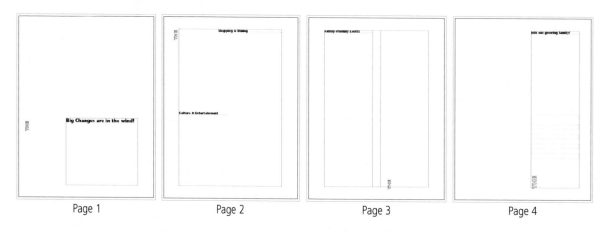

| Page 1 | Page 2 | Page 3 | Page 4 |

5. **Click the empty space left of CMYK in the Separations Preview panel to view the CMYK separations in addition to the Pantone 7554 C separation.**

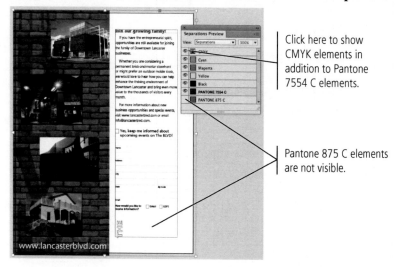

Click here to show CMYK elements in addition to Pantone 7554 C elements.

Pantone 875 C elements are not visible.

6. Choose Off in the View menu at the top of the Separations Preview panel.

When you turn off the separations preview, you again see the frame edges.

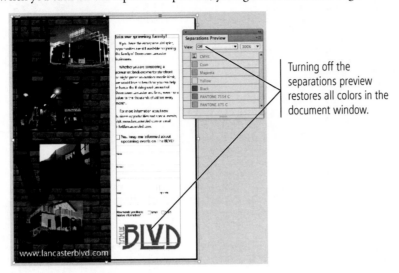

Turning off the
separations preview
restores all colors in the
document window.

7. Continue to the next exercise.

 ## CONVERT SPOT COLOR IN ILLUSTRATOR

You can't simply delete the extra spot color from the InDesign file because it is used in the placed logo file. Instead, you are going to edit the placed file to remove the extra spot color. You will then replace the Pantone 7554 color with Pantone 875 for all InDesign layout elements.

1. With boulevard.indd open, choose blvd logo.ai in the Links panel, then click the Edit Original button.

Remember, this option opens a file in its native application. In this case, the file opens in Illustrator CC. If multiple instances of the file are placed, you don't need to select any specific instance for the Edit Original option to work.

Edit Original

Note:

If Illustrator is not already running when you click the Edit Original button, it might take a while for the file to open. Be patient.

2. In Illustrator, open the Swatches panel.

This file includes two swatches, both of which are spot colors (indicated by the small dot in the corner of the swatch icons).

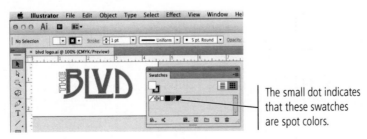

The small dot indicates
that these swatches
are spot colors.

3. **Double-click the Pantone 7554 swatch (the darker one) to open the Swatch Options dialog box.**

4. **Choose CMYK in the Color Mode menu.**

   After you convert the color to the CMYK mode, it is still set to output as a spot color. To avoid an unwanted separation, you also need to change the color to be a process color build.

5. **Choose Process Color in the Color Type menu and leave the Global option checked.**

   When you change a spot color from the Book color mode to process, the software uses the nearest-possible ink values in the converted color.

   In this case, the resulting values are a four-color mix that could be a potential problem in the printing process. To achieve the same overall effect with less potential for problems, you are going to use a rich black to reproduce the word "THE" in the logo.

6. **Change the ink values to C: 0%, M: 50%, Y: 0%, K: 100%.**

   Because the Global option is checked, your changes will automatically be applied to any object where that color is used.

7. **Click OK to redefine the swatch.**

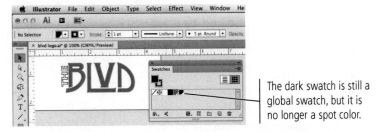

The dark swatch is still a global swatch, but it is no longer a spot color.

8. **Save the Illustrator file and close it, then return to boulevard.indd in InDesign.**

Because you used the Edit Original function to edit the placed logo file, the placed instances are automatically updated when you return to the layout.

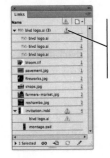

This warning icon is caused by the modified image in the placed InDesign file.

The blvd logo.ai file still shows a warning icon. If you expand that item to show individual instances, you see that all instances in the boulevard layout are now up to date.

The problem is the logo instance in the placed InDesign file — the update process does not trickle down into nested files. You still have to open the placed layout and update the link.

9. **Select invitation.indd in the Links panel and click the Edit Original button.**

10. **In the resulting warning dialog box, click Update Links.**

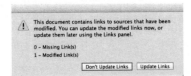

11. **Save the file and close it, then return to the boulevard.indd file.**

All of the modified warnings — in both the main layout and the nested file — are gone.

12. **Save boulevard.indd, then continue to the next stage of the project.**

Stage 3 Fine-tuning Text

Now that all of the images are in place, you can begin the fine-tuning process for the layout text. As your art director informed you during the project meeting, some of the text work had already been completed before the original designer had to move on to a different project. Your assignment in this stage of the project is to verify that all text in the document is correct.

Some text issues have little to do with typography and more to do with "user malfunction" — common errors introduced by the people who created the text (most often, your clients). Regardless of how careful you are, some problems will inevitably creep into the text elements of your layouts. Fortunately, InDesign has the tools you need to correct those issues as well.

ENABLE TRACK CHANGES

In many cases, multiple users collaborate on a single document — designers, editors, content providers, and clients all go back and forth throughout the design process. Each person in the process will request changes, from changing the highlight color in a document to rewriting the copy to fit in a defined space. Because the words in a design are a vital part of communicating the client's message, tracking text changes throughout the process can be useful to make sure that all changes are accurate and approved before the job is finalized.

1. **With boulevard.indd open, navigate to Page 1 and then use the Type tool to place the insertion point in any story.**

2. **Choose Type>Track Changes>Enable Tracking in All Stories.**

   The Track Changes feature can be activated to monitor text editing during development. This allows multiple users to edit the text without permanently altering that text until the changes have been reviewed and approved or rejected. (After you have made all the changes in this stage of the project, you will review and finalize those changes.)

   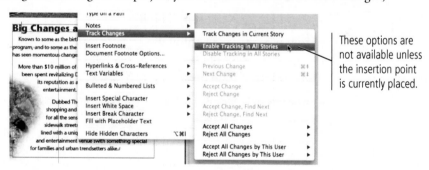

3. **Open the Track Changes pane of the Preferences dialog box.**

4. **Make sure the Include Deleted Text When Spellchecking option is checked at the bottom of the dialog box.**

   It is very easy to make a mistake when spellchecking, so it's a good idea to keep this option checked.

5. **Make sure the Added Text, Deleted Text, and Moved Text options are checked.**

   Remember, preferences are accessed in the InDesign menu on Macintosh or in the Edit menu on Windows.

6. **Choose Underline in the Added Text Marking menu.**

   The Marking options add a visual indicator (strikethrough, underlining, or outlining) so you can more easily identify text that is affected by the Track Changes function.

7. Choose Red in the Deleted Text Background menu.

The Background Color options define the color of highlighting that will identify each type of change. All three options default to the same color; changing the color for Deleted Text will make it easier to identify this type of change when you review the corrections at the end of this stage of the project.

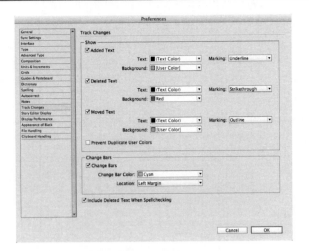

8. Click OK to return to the document, then save the file and continue to the next exercise.

 ## FIND AND CHANGE TEXT

You will often need to search for and replace specific elements in a layout — a word, a phrase, a formatting attribute, or even a specific kind of object. InDesign's Find/Change dialog box allows you to easily locate exactly what you need, whether your layout is two pages or two hundred. For this brochure, you can use the Find/Change dialog box to correct the name of the client's project.

1. With boulevard.indd open, use the Edit Original function to open invitation.indd (the file that is placed on Page 4).

2. Make boulevard.indd the active file, then navigate to Page 1.

3. Using the Type tool, place the insertion point at the beginning of the story on that page.

Both InDesign files should be open.

boulevard.indd should be active.

The insertion point is at the beginning of this story.

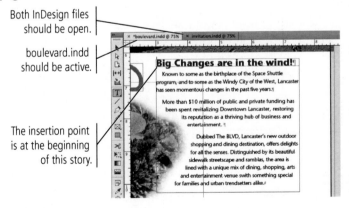

4. Choose Edit>Find/Change.

5. Place the insertion point in the Find What field and type Downtown Lancaster.

6. Press Tab to highlight the Change To field, and type The BLVD.

7. **In the Search menu, choose All Documents.**

   When the insertion point is placed, you can choose to search the entire Document, All [open] Documents, only the active Story, or only text following the insertion point in the selected story (To End of Story).

   Using the Forward Direction option (the default), the search identifies the first instance of the Find What text after the location of the insertion point. If you use the Backward Direction option, the search would identify the first instance preceding the current insertion point.

8. **Click Find Next.**

   The first instance of the Find What text is automatically highlighted in the document.

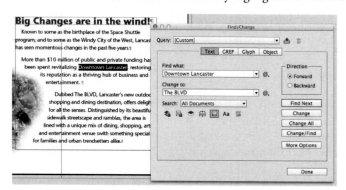

9. **Click the Change/Find button.**

   The next instance of the Find What text is highlighted in the document.

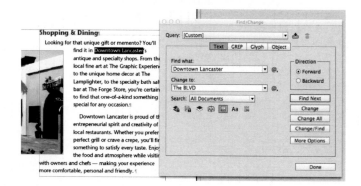

10. **Click Change All.**

11. **When you see the message that 6 replacements were made, click OK.**

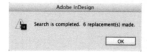

12. **Save both open files, then continue to the next exercise.**

Note:

If the insertion point is not currently placed, you can only choose to search the active Document or All Documents.

Note:

The Find/Change dialog box is one of the few dialog boxes that allow you to interact directly with the document even while the dialog box is still open.

Note:

There is a bug on the Windows version that sometimes causes the Change All function to return a greater number of changes than what actually exists. Don't worry if your results messages show a larger number of changes than what you see in our screen captures.

The Find/Change Dialog Box in Depth

As you have seen, the Text tab allows you to search for and change specific character strings, with or without specific formatting options. The Object tab identifies specific combinations of object formatting attributes, such as fill color or applied object effects. In addition to the tools you use in this project, the Find/Change dialog box has a number of options for narrowing or extending a search beyond the basic options. The buttons below the Search menu are toggles for specific types of searches (from left to right):

- When **Include Locked Layers and Locked Objects** is active, the search locates instances on locked layers or individual objects that have been locked; you can't replace locked objects unless you first unlock them.

- When **Include Locked Stories** is active, the search locates text that is locked; you can't replace locked text unless you first unlock it.

- When **Include Hidden Layers** is active, the search includes frames on layers that are not visible.

- When **Include Master Pages** is active, the search includes frames on master pages.

- When **Include Footnotes** is active, the search identifies instances within footnote text.

- When **Case Sensitive** is active, the search only finds text with the same capitalization as the text in the Find What field. For example, a search for "InDesign" will not identify instances of "Indesign," "indesign," or "INDESIGN."

- When **Whole Word** is active, the search only finds instances where the search text is an entire word (not part of another word). For example, if you search for "old" as a whole word, InDesign will not include the words "gold," "mold," or "embolden."

The GREP tab is used for pattern-based search techniques, such as finding phone numbers in one format (e.g., 800.555.1234) and changing them to the same phone number with a different format (e.g., 800/555-1234). Adobe's video-based help system (www.adobe.com) provides some assistance in setting up an advanced query.

The Glyph tab allows you to search for and change glyphs using Unicode or GID/CID values. This is useful for identifying foreign and pictographic characters, as well as characters from extended sets of OpenType fonts.

You can also save specific searches as queries, and you can call those queries again using the Query menu at the top of the Find/Change dialog box. This option is useful if you commonly make the same modifications, such as changing Multiple Return to Single Return (this particular search and replacement is so common that the query is built into the application).

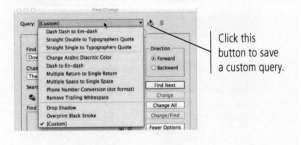

Click this button to save a custom query.

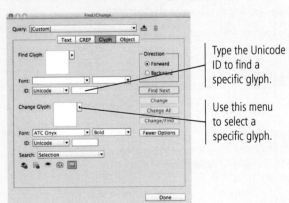

Type the Unicode ID to find a specific glyph.

Use this menu to select a specific glyph.

FIND AND CHANGE TEXT FORMATTING ATTRIBUTES

In addition to finding and replacing specific text or characters, you can also find and replace formatting attributes for both text and objects. For this project, you need to use the gold spot color as the accent, replacing the brown spot color. The Find/Change dialog box makes this kind of replacement a relatively simple process.

1. **With both InDesign files open and boulevard.indd active, choose Edit>Find/Change (if the dialog box is not already open).**

2. **Delete all text from the Find What and Change To fields.**

3. **Choose Wildcards>Any Character in the menu to the right of the Find What field.**

    Wildcards allow you to search for formatting attributes, regardless of the actual text. In addition to searching for Any Character, you can also narrow the search to Any Digit, Any Letter, or Any White Space characters.

    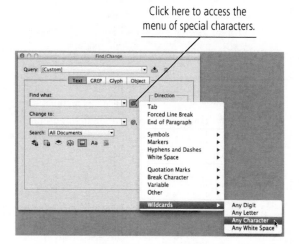
    Click here to access the menu of special characters.

    ^? is the special code for a wildcard character.

4. **Click the More Options button to show the expanded Find/Change dialog box.**

    When more options are visible, you can find and replace specific formatting attributes of the selected text.

    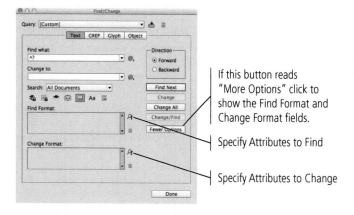
    If this button reads "More Options" click to show the Find Format and Change Format fields.

    Specify Attributes to Find

    Specify Attributes to Change

5. **Click the Specify Attributes to Find button to open the Find Format Settings dialog box.**

    You can search for and replace any character formatting option (or combination of options) that can be applied in the layout.

INDESIGN FOUNDATIONS

You can enter special characters in InDesign dialog boxes using the following special codes, called metacharacters. (Note that these metacharacters are case specific; for example, "^n" and "^N" refer to different special characters.)

Character	Code (Metacharacters)
Symbols	
Bullet (•)	^8
Caret (^)	^^
Copyright (©)	^2
Ellipsis (…)	^e
Paragraph	^7
Registered Trademark (®)	^r
Section (§)	^6
Trademark (™)	^d
Dashes and Hyphens	
Em Dash (—)	^_
En Dash (–)	^=
Discretionary hyphen	^-
Nonbreaking hyphen	^~
White Space Characters	
Em space	^m
En space	^>
Third space	^3
Quarter space	^4
Sixth space	^%
Flush space	^f
Hair space	^| (pipe)
Nonbreaking space	^s
Thin space	^<
Figure space	^/
Punctuation space	^.
Quotation Marks	
Double left quotation mark	^{
Double right quotation mark	^}
Single left quotation mark	^[
Single right quotation mark	^]
Straight double quotation mark	^"
Straight single quotation mark	^'
Page Number Characters	
Any page number character	^#
Current page number character	^N
Next page number character	^X
Previous page number character	^V

Character	Code (Metacharacters)
Break Characters	
Paragraph return	^p
Forced line break (soft return)	^n
Column break	^M
Frame break	^R
Page break	^P
Odd page break	^L
Even page break	^E
Discretionary line break	^j
Formatting Options	
Tab character	^t
Right indent tab character	^y
Indent to here character	^i
End nested style here character	^h
Nonjoiner character	^k
Variables	
Running header (paragraph style)	^Y
Running header (character style)	^Z
Custom text	^u
Last page number	^T
Chapter number	^H
Creation date	^S
Modification date	^o
Output date	^D
File name	^l (lowercase L)
Markers	
Section marker	^x
Anchored object marker	^a
Footnote reference marker	^F
Index marker	^I
Wildcards	
Any digit	^9
Any letter	^$
Any character	^?
White space (any space or tab)	^w
Any variable	^v

6. **Show the Character Color options and click the Pantone 7554 C swatch.**

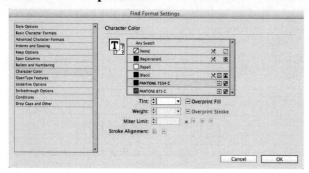

7. **Click OK to return to the Find/Change dialog box.**

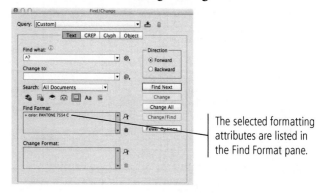

The selected formatting attributes are listed in the Find Format pane.

8. **Click the Specify Attributes to Change button to open the Change Format Settings dialog box.**

9. **Show the Character Color options and click the Pantone 875 C swatch.**

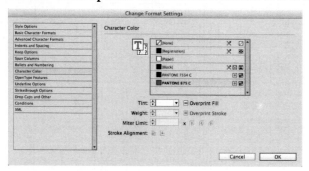

10. **Click OK to return to the Find/Change dialog box.**

11. **Make sure All Documents is selected in the Search menu and click Change All. Click OK to close the message about the number of replacements.**

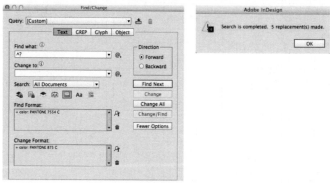

12. In the Find/Change dialog box, delete the wildcard character from the Find What field.

Although clearing the Find What and Change To fields isn't strictly necessary, it is a good habit to develop.

13. Click the Delete buttons to remove the formatting options from the Find Format and Change Format fields.

It can be easy to forget to remove these formatting choices. However, if you leave them in place, your next search will only find the Find What text with the selected formatting. It's a good idea to clear these formatting choices as soon as you're done with them.

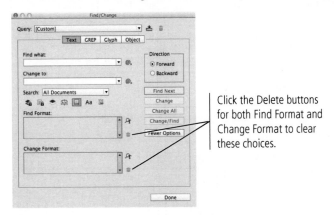

Click the Delete buttons for both Find Format and Change Format to clear these choices.

14. Save both open files and continue to the next exercise.

 ## FIND AND CHANGE OBJECT ATTRIBUTES

In addition to searching for specific text formatting attributes, you can also find and replace specific object formatting attributes. In this exercise you will replace all brown-stroked frames with the gold spot color.

1. With both InDesign files open and **boulevard.indd** active, open the Find/Change dialog box if it is not already open.

2. Click the Object tab in the Find/Change dialog box to display those options.

3. Choose All Documents in the Search menu.

When you search objects, you can search the current document, all documents, or the current selection.

4. In the Type menu, choose All Frames.

You can limit your search to specific kinds of frames, or search all frames.

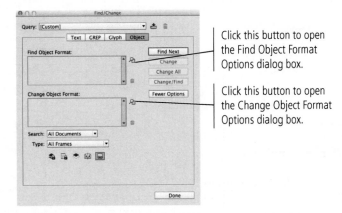

Click this button to open the Find Object Format Options dialog box.

Click this button to open the Change Object Format Options dialog box.

5. **Click the button to open the Find Object Format Options dialog box.**

   You can find and change any formatting attributes that can be applied to a frame.

6. **Display the Stroke options and click the Pantone 7554 C swatch.**

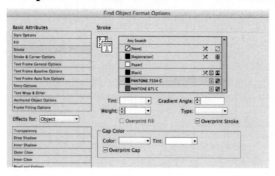

7. **Click OK to return to the Find/Change dialog box.**

8. **Open the Change Object Format Options dialog box and choose the Pantone 875 C swatch in the Stroke options.**

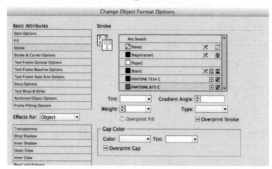

9. **Click OK to return to the Find/Change dialog box.**

10. **Click Change All, then click OK to dismiss the message about the number of changes.**

11. **Click the Delete buttons for both the Find Object Format and Change Object Format options to clear your choices.**

12. **Click Done to close the Find/Change dialog box.**

13. **Save both open files and continue to the next exercise.**

Note:

There is a bug on the Windows version that sometimes causes the Change All function to return a greater number of changes than what actually exists. Don't worry if your results messages show a larger number of changes than what you see in our screen captures.

CHECK DOCUMENT SPELLING

Many designers carefully monitor the technical aspects of a job, but skip another important check — for spelling errors. Misspellings and typos creep into virtually every job despite numerous rounds of content proofs. These errors can ruin an otherwise perfect print job. InDesign's Spell Check utility can be very useful for finding common problems, although some manual decision making and intervention will also be involved.

1. **With boulevard.indd open, open the Dictionary pane of the Preferences dialog box.**

   InDesign checks spelling based on the defined language dictionary — by default, English: USA. You can choose a different language dictionary in the Language menu.

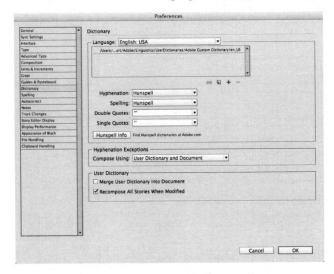

Note:

The application also includes English: USA Legal and English: USA Medical dictionaries that will be of significant benefit to anyone working for either of those industries. If you work with foreign-language publishing, you can choose one of more than 40 different language dictionaries that are installed with InDesign.

2. **Make sure English: USA is selected in the Language menu and click OK.**

3. **Choose Edit>Spelling>User Dictionary.**

   When you check spelling, you are likely to find words that, although spelled correctly, are not in the selected dictionary. Proper names, scientific terms, corporate trademarks, and other custom words are commonly flagged even though they are correct. Rather than flagging these terms every time you recheck spelling, you can add them to a custom user dictionary so that InDesign will recognize them the next time you check spelling.

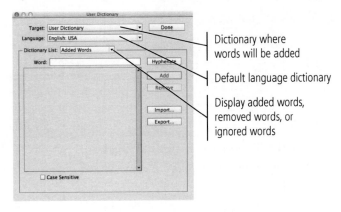

Dictionary where words will be added

Default language dictionary

Display added words, removed words, or ignored words

4. **Make sure User Dictionary is selected in the Target menu.**

   By default, the user dictionary is associated with all documents. You can also define custom words for a specific file by choosing any open file in the Target menu; when you change the user dictionary for a specific file, words you add for that file will still be flagged in other files.

5. **In the Word field, type BLVD.**

   The city's branded name is not a real word. If you know that certain words will be flagged, you can manually add those words to the user dictionary at any time.

6. **Check the Case Sensitive option at the bottom of the dialog box, and then click Add.**

   If Case Sensitive is not checked, InDesign will not distinguish between BLVD (which is correct) and Blvd (which is incorrect).

7. **Click Done to close the User Dictionary dialog box.**

8. **With nothing selected in the layout, choose Edit>Spelling>Check Spelling.**

   As soon as you open the Check Spelling dialog box, the first flagged word is highlighted in the layout. The same word appears in the Not in Dictionary field of the Check Spelling dialog box.

The suspect word is highlighted in the layout.

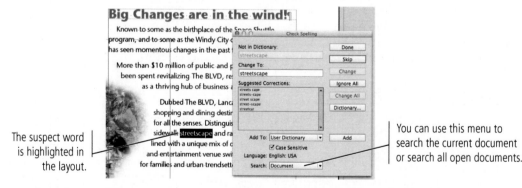

You can use this menu to search the current document or search all open documents.

The flagged word (streetscape) is not misspelled, but it is not recognized in the defined dictionary. Never simply click Change when checking spelling. Review each flagged word carefully and make the correct choices within the context of the layout.

9. **Click the Dictionary button in the Check Spelling dialog box. Choose boulevard.indd in the Target menu, make sure the Case Sensitive option is checked, and click Add.**

If you click the Add button in the Check Spelling dialog box, the words are added to the default user dictionary — which applies to all InDesign files on your computer. When you open the User Dictionary dialog box from the Check Spelling dialog box, you can choose the file-specific dictionary in the Target menu and click Add to add the word to the dictionary for the selected file only.

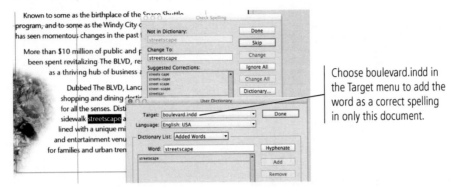

Choose boulevard.indd in the Target menu to add the word as a correct spelling in only this document.

10. **Click Done to close the User Dictionary dialog box and return to the Check Spelling dialog box.**

When you return to the Check Spelling dialog box, streetscape still appears in the Word field. You have to click Skip to find the next suspect word.

11. **Click Skip.**

The next suspect is another word that does not appear in the dictionary. According to your client, however, it is spelled correctly.

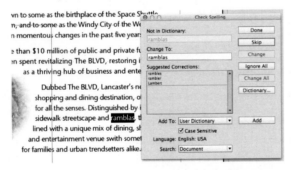

12. **Click the Dictionary button in the Check Spelling dialog box. Choose boulevard.indd in the Target menu, make sure the Case Sensitive option is checked, and click Add.**

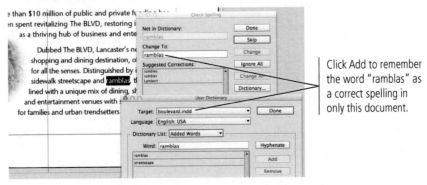

Click Add to remember the word "ramblas" as a correct spelling in only this document.

13. Click Done to close the User Dictionary dialog box and return to the Check Spelling dialog box, then click Skip to show the next suspect word.

14. Review the next error.

This is an example of a very common typo. The word "swith" is identified as an error, but if you look closely, you can see that the previous word is "venue." If you read the entire sentence, you can see that it should read "venues with" rather than "venue swith." The word "venue" is a grammatical error and not a spelling error, so it is not flagged by the Check Spelling process. You have to correct this problem manually.

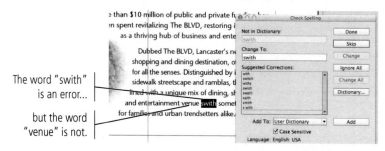

The word "swith" is an error...

but the word "venue" is not.

15. In the layout, place the insertion point before the "s" in "swith", then press the Delete/Backspace key. Add a space after the "s" in "venues."

As soon as you click to place the insertion point in the story, the Check Spelling dialog box reverts to show the Start button. By interacting directly with the document to manually correct an error that the software can't fix, you have to start the spell-check process over again.

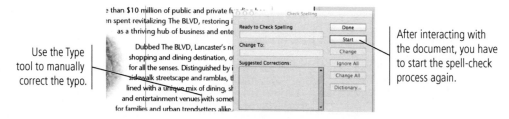

Use the Type tool to manually correct the typo.

After interacting with the document, you have to start the spell-check process again.

16. Click the Start button in the Check Spelling dialog box.

The process continues from the current insertion point to the end of the active story.

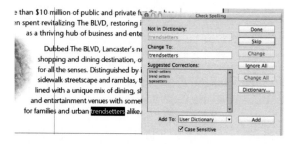

17. With trendsetters highlighted, click Ignore All.

When you click Ignore All, the word is added to a special list in the user dictionary so it will not be flagged again.

The next suspect is automatically highlighted. Although you added BLVD to the user dictionary, the software does not automatically recognize variations (such as this possessive version of the word "BLVD").

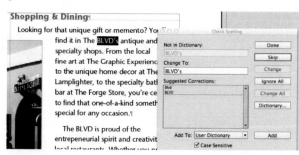

18. Click Skip.

When you use the Skip option, the same suspect will be flagged every time you check spelling in the document.

After clicking skip, the next suspect is automatically highlighted — in this case, an actual misspelled word ("entrepeneurial").

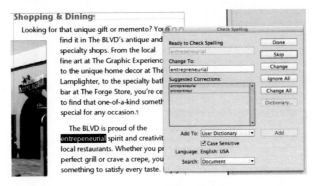

19. Highlight the correct spelling ("entrepreneurial") in the Suggested Corrections list and click Change.

As you can see in the layout, the misspelled word is replaced with the selected alternative; the next suspect word is automatically highlighted in the layout.

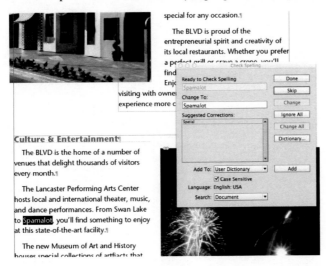

20. Continue checking the spelling in the document. Make the following choices when prompted:

Spamalot	Ignore All
artfiacts	Change to "artifacts"
Prix	Ignore All
BooLVD	Add to the user dictionary for only the active file
Christkindlmarkt	Add to the user dictionary for only the active file

21. **When you see the check mark at the top of the dialog box, click Done to close the Check Spelling dialog box.**

22. **If invitation.indd is not already open, open it using the Edit Original option in the Links panel. Check spelling in the file and correct any errors, then save and close the file.**

The Check Spelling function only interacts with nested files if those files are already open and the All Documents option is selected in the Search menu.

Review the suspects carefully before you decide to make a change. There is one actual spelling error in the file that you should fix ("enviroment").

23. **Save boulevard.indd and then continue to the next exercise.**

Review Tracked Changes

Earlier in this project, you enabled the Track Changes feature for all stories in this document. You might have noticed, however, that there is no visual indication of those changes in the layout. Tracking editorial changes is useful for monitoring changes in the text, but displaying those changes in the layout would make it impossible to fit copy and accurately format the text in a layout. To avoid this confusion, changes are tracked in a special utility called the Story Editor, which more closely resembles a word-processor screen.

1. **With boulevard.indd open, use the Type tool to place the insertion point at the beginning of the text frame on Page 1.**

2. **Choose Edit>Edit in Story Editor.**

   The Story Editor opens in a separate window, showing only the current story. (A **story** in InDesign is the entire body of text in a single frame or string of linked frames.)

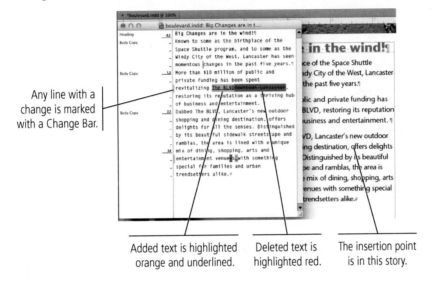

Any line with a change is marked with a Change Bar.

Added text is highlighted orange and underlined.

Deleted text is highlighted red.

The insertion point is in this story.

If your deleted text is not highlighted red, you missed a step in the earlier exercise where you enabled the Track Changes feature (see page 587). You can open the Track Changes pane of the Preferences dialog box and change the highlight options now.

Note:

You can also Option/Alt click the Accept or Reject Change button to apply the change and then automatically highlight (find) the next change.

Note:

This type of decision is usually the client's to make; in this exercise, we are assuming the client would agree.

3. **Open the Track Changes panel (Window>Editorial>Track Changes).**

   When the Story Editor window is active, you can use the Track Changes panel to review the tracked changes.

   A. Enable/Disable Track Changes in Current Story toggles the track changes function on and off.

   B. Show/Hide Changes toggles the visibility of tracked changes in the Story Editor window.

   C. Previous Change highlights the first change before the current location of the insertion point.

   D. Next Change highlights the first change after the current location of the insertion point.

   E. Accept Change makes the highlighted change permanent.

   F. Reject Change restores the original text for deleted text, or removes added text.

   G. Accept All Changes in Story applies the same result as the Accept Change button, but for all tracked changes in the active story; you do not get the opportunity to individually review each change.

   H. Reject All Changes in Story applies the same result as the Reject Change button, but for all tracked changes in the active story; again, you do not get the opportunity to individually review each change.

4. Click the Next Change button in the Track Changes panel.

If you read the text, you can see that this instance refers to the area of Downtown Lancaster. The next paragraph goes on to explain that the area was rebranded as "The BLVD" — so it wouldn't make logical sense to use the term before it is defined.

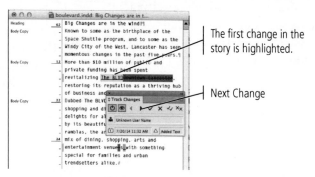

The first change in the story is highlighted.

Next Change

5. Click the Reject Change button, then click the Next Change button.

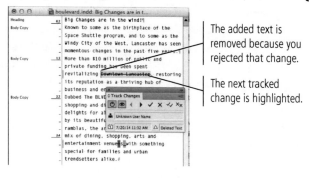

The added text is removed because you rejected that change.

The next tracked change is highlighted.

6. Click the Reject Change button again.

Because you did not keep the replacement text, you need to keep the deleted text.

7. Click the Accept All Changes in Story button at the top of the Track Changes panel.

8. When asked to confirm the change, click OK.

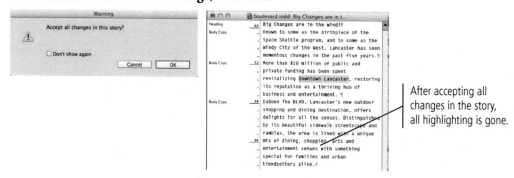

After accepting all changes in the story, all highlighting is gone.

9. **Click the Next Change button.**

Because there were no more changes in the first story, clicking the Next Change button opens the next story where a change is located. Each story appears in a separate Story Editor window.

In Step 8 you only accepted all changes in the active story; the second story in the layout still has tracked changes that should be reviewed. As you can see, the only changes in this story are the replacement of "Downtown Lancaster" with "The BLVD" and the corrected misspellings. Rather than reviewing each instance separately, you can simply accept all changes in the story at one time.

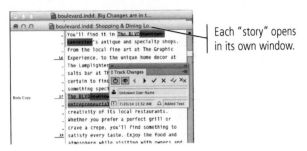

Each "story" opens in its own window.

10. **Open the Track Changes panel Options menu and choose Accept All Changes>In This Document.**

The In This Document option affects all stories in a file, even if they are not currently open in a Story Editor window.

Accepting all changes without reviewing them essentially defeats the purpose of tracking changes. We are telling you that, in this case, it is safe to simply accept all the changes.

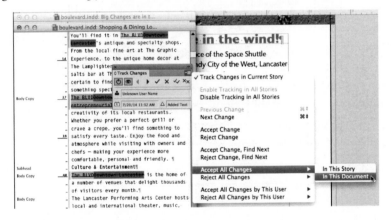

Note:

In a professional environment — and especially if more than one person has been working on the same document — you should be sure to carefully review all tracked changes before finalizing the job.

11. **Click OK to dismiss the Warning dialog box and accept the changes.**

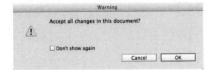

12. **Close both Story Editor windows.**

13. **Save the file and continue to the next exercise.**

EXPORT A COLOR-MANAGED PDF FILE

As you saw when you placed them, the photos in this layout use the RGB model. InDesign allows you to convert the image data to the defined output profile when you create the PDF file for print, while still maintaining the RGB images for the digitally distributed formats. However, because the RGB model allows a much greater gamut than CMYK, some color shift might occur when you export the PDF file for print. It's a good idea to review the potential color shift before you create the final print PDF.

1. **With boulevard.indd open, navigate to Page 1.**

2. **Choose View>Proof Setup>Working CMYK.**

   Remember from the beginning of this project, the working CMYK profile is what you defined as the color characteristics of the intended output device — in this case, a standardized sheetfed press.

3. **Choose View>Proof Colors.**

   This toggle provides a on-screen preview of what will happen when the image is converted to the CMYK working-space profile, without affecting the actual file data. (This option, called **soft proofing**, is more valuable with an accurately calibrated monitor; even with an uncalibrated monitor, however, you should be able to see any significant trouble areas.)

   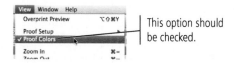

   This option should be checked.

   When Proof Colors is active, the document tab shows the profile being used for soft proofing.

4. **Navigate through the layout and review the differences. Toggle the Proof Colors option on and off for each page to look for significant color shift.**

   In many instances, the color shift will be subtle; most obvious changes will be visible in the brightest colors, such as the blue tarp in the image on the lower half of Page 3.

   We do not include images of the differences here because they do not reproduce well in print. However, you should be able to see the differences on your screen when you toggle the Proof Colors option on and off.

5. **Turn off the Proof Colors option, then choose File>Export.**

6. **Choose Adobe PDF (Print) in the Format/Save as Type menu, then click Save.**

   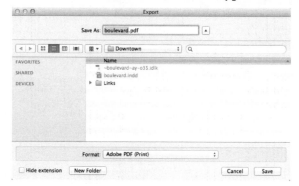

7. **In the Export Adobe PDF dialog box, choose Press Quality in the Adobe PDF Preset menu.**

8. **In the Marks and Bleeds options, check the Crop Marks option and change the Offset value to 0.125 in. In the lower half of the dialog box, check the option to Use Document Bleed Settings.**

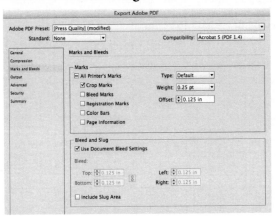

9. **In the Output options, choose Convert to Destination in the Color Conversion menu.**

   You have several options for converting colors when you output a file:

   - **No Color Conversion** maintains all color data (including placed images) in its current space.

   - **Convert to Destination** converts colors to the profile selected in the Destination menu.

   - **Convert to Destination (Preserve Numbers)** converts colors to the destination profile if the applied profile does not match the defined destination profile. Objects without color profiles are not converted.

   The Destination menu defines the gamut for the output device that will be used. (This menu defaults to the active destination working space.) Color information in the file (and placed images) is converted to the selected Destination profile.

10. **Choose Include Destination Profile in the Profile Inclusion Policy menu.**

   The **Profile Inclusion Policy** menu determines whether color profiles are embedded in the resulting PDF file. (Different options are available, depending on what you selected in the Color Conversion menu.)

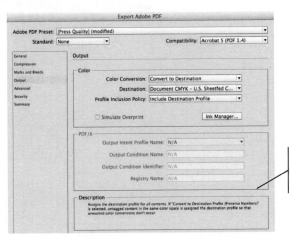

Choose any option in any menu to see a description or explanation of that option.

Note:

Spot-color information is preserved when colors are converted to the destination space.

11. Click the Ink Manager button.

As you already know, this file is only allowed to use one spot color — Pantone 875 C (metallic gold) — when it is printed. Although you converted the elements to the appropriate color in the logo file and in the layout, you did not remove the unwanted spot color swatch (Pantone 7554 C) from the file. This dialog box provides one last checkpoint for unwanted separations before you export the file.

The Ink Manager offers control over specific ink separations at output time. Changes here affect the current output, not how the colors are defined in the document.

All separations in
the file appear in
this window.

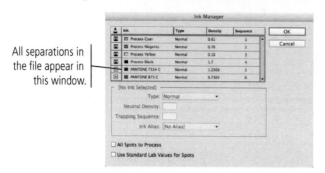

Note:

You can also access this dialog box by clicking the Ink Manager button in the Output pane of the Print dialog box.

12. Click the Spot Color icon to the left of the Pantone 7554 C ink.

This converts the individual ink to a process color for the current output. (Keep in mind that spot colors are often outside the CMYK gamut; there will almost always be color shift in the resulting CMYK build.)

Click this icon to
convert a specific spot
color to a process build.

You can check this
option to convert all spot
colors to process builds.

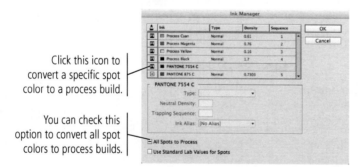

13. Click OK to return to the Export Adobe PDF dialog box, then click Export.

14. If the PDF file opens, close it and then return to InDesign.

15. Save and close any open InDesign files.

Project Review

fill in the blank

1. A(n) _____ describes the color reproduction characteristics of a particular input or output device.

2. The _____ can be used to review the location of specific spot colors in a layout.

3. A(n) _____ can be used to create a smooth transition from solid pixels to transparent pixels in an image.

4. When placing images into a layout, press _____ to select multiple, non-contiguous files in the Place dialog box.

5. When placing a native Photoshop file, you can check the _____ option in the Place dialog box to be able to control layer visibility before the file is placed.

6. When you place an InDesign file as a link, the _____ option in the Place InDesign dialog box determines which area of the file (page, bleed, or slug) is imported.

7. The _____ lists all files that are placed in a layout, including the location and status of each placed file.

8. The _____ can be used to define custom spellings that are not in the main dictionary, such as proper names or trademarked terms.

9. The _____ shows the basic text in a story, without applied formatting; it can be used to review tracked changes.

10. The _____ dialog box can be used to convert specific spot colors to process while the file is being output.

short answer

1. Briefly explain the concept of color management, as it relates to building a layout in InDesign.

2. Briefly explain the concept of color separation.

3. Briefly explain how spot colors relate to print separations.

Portfolio Builder Project

Use what you learned in this project to complete the following freeform exercise.
Carefully read the art director and client comments, then create your own design to meet the needs of the project.
Use the space below to sketch ideas; when finished, write a brief explanation of your reasoning behind your final design.

art director comments

Every professional designer needs a portfolio of their work. If you have completed the projects in this book, you should now have a number of different examples to show off your skills using Illustrator, Photoshop, and InDesign CC.

The projects in this book were specifically designed to include a broad range of *types* of projects; your portfolio should use the same principle.

client comments

Using the following suggestions, gather your best work and create printed and digital versions of your portfolio:

❑ Include as many different types of work as possible, including illustration, photographic manipulation, and page layout.

❑ Print clean copies of each finished piece that you want to include.

❑ For each example in your portfolio, write a brief (one or two paragraph) synopsis of the project. Explain the purpose of the piece, as well as your role in the creative and production process.

❑ Design a personal promotion brochure — create a layout that highlights your technical skills and reflects your personal style.

❑ Create a PDF version of your portfolio so you can send your portfolio via email, post it on job sites, and keep it with you on a flash drive at all times — you never know when you might meet a potential employer.

project justification

_____

_____

_____

_____

_____

_____

_____

_____

_____

_____

_____

_____

_____

As you have seen, placing pictures into an InDesign layout is a relatively easy task, whether you place them one at a time or load multiple images at once and then simply click to place the loaded images into the appropriate spots. InDesign allows you to work with all of the common image formats; you can even place one InDesign layout directly into another. The Links panel is a valuable tool for managing images, from updating file status, to replacing one image with another, to opening an external file in its native application so you can easily make changes in placed files. Fine-tuning a layout requires checking for common errors — both technical and practical, such as spelling errors.

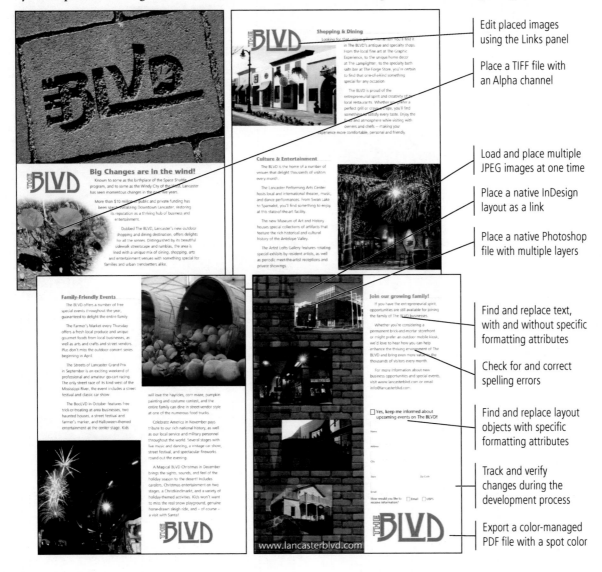

Edit placed images using the Links panel

Place a TIFF file with an Alpha channel

Load and place multiple JPEG images at one time

Place a native InDesign layout as a link

Place a native Photoshop file with multiple layers

Find and replace text, with and without specific formatting attributes

Check for and correct spelling errors

Find and replace layout objects with specific formatting attributes

Track and verify changes during the development process

Export a color-managed PDF file with a spot color

Index

Use our portfolio to build yours.

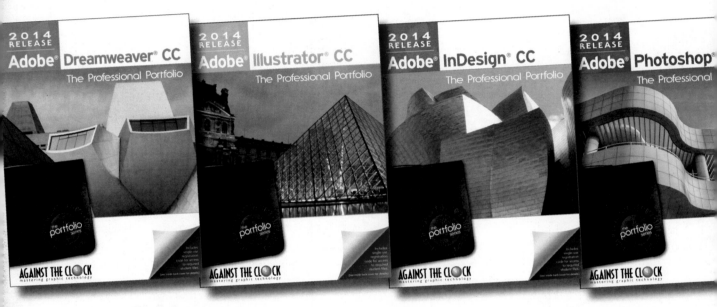

The Against The Clock Professional Portfolio Series walks you step-by-step through the tools and techniques of graphic design professionals.

Order online at www.againsttheclock.com
Use code **PFSE2014** for a 10% discount

Go to **www.againsttheclock.com** to enter our monthly drawing for a free book of your choice.